SOCIAL PROBLEMS

A CRITICAL APPROACH

THIRD EDITION

Kenneth J. Neubeck
Department of Sociology
University of Connecticut

McGRAW-HILL, INC.

New York St. Louis San Francisco Auckland Bogotá
Caracas Hamburg Lisbon London Madrid Mexico Milan Montreal New Delhi
Paris San Juan São Paulo Singapore Sydney Tokyo Toronto

SOCIAL PROBLEMS

A Critical Approach

This book was set in Times Roman by the College Composition Unit
in cooperation with General Graphic Services, Inc.
The editors were Phillip A. Butcher, Sylvia Shepard, and Elaine Rosenberg;
the production supervisor was Louise Karam.
The cover was designed by Fern Logan.
The photo editors were Mira Schachne and Kathy Bendo.
Arcata Graphics/Halliday was printer and binder.

1 2 3 4 5 6 7 8 9 0 HAL HAL 9 5 4 3 2 1 0

ISBN 0-07-557741-0

Library of Congress Cataloging-in-Publication Data

Neubeck, Kenneth J.
Social problems: a critical approach/Kenneth J. Neubeck. —3rd ed.
p. cm.
ISBN 0-07-557741-0
1. Social lproblems. 2. Social history—20th century. 3. United States—Social conditions—1980 I. Title.
HN18.N47 1991
361.1—dc20 90-44438

CHAPTER OPENER PHOTO CREDITS

Introduction: *UPI/Bettmann Newsphotos* **Chapter 1:** *Thomas Hopker/Woodfin Camp & Associates* **Chapter 2:** *Elliot Erwitt/Magnum* **Chapter 3:** *David Strickler/The Image Works* **Chapter 4:** *Barbara Alper/Stock, Boston* **Chapter 5:** *Pamela Price/The Picture Cube* **Chapter 6:** *James Holland/Stock, Boston* **Chapter 7:** *Joel Gordon* **Chapter 8:** *Jerry Howard/Positive Images* **Chapter 9:** *Supreme Court Historical Society and The National Geographic Society* **Chapter 10:** *Elizabeth Crews* **Chapter 11:** *MacDonald Photography/The Picture Cube* **Chapter 12:** *Michael Weisbrot/Stock, Boston* **Chapter 13:** *Jeff Albertson/Stock, Boston* **Chapter 14:** *Jerry Berndt/The Picture Cube* **Chapter 15:** *Bruce Kliewe/Jeroboam* **Chapter 16:** *Alan Carey/The Image Works* **Chapter 17:** *Allen Tannenbaum/Sygma.*

ABOUT THE AUTHOR

KENNETH J. NEUBECK is Associate Professor of Sociology at The University of Connecticut–Storrs. Before receiving his Ph.D. at Washington University—St. Louis, he held research positions in civil rights and education offices at what was then known as the U.S. Department of Health, Education, and Welfare (now known as Health and Human Services).

Professor Neubeck is also the author of *Corporate Response to Urban Crisis.* He has contributed to anthologies on such topics as the impact of racism on welfare policies, income maintenance experimentation and poverty politics, and political and economic factors influencing downtown city development. Additional articles have appeared in such journals as *Social Problems, Social Policy,* and *Teaching Sociology.* He is currently at work on an exploration of data sets dealing with the consumer and investment behaviors of American families and with the relationship between executive compensation and corporate financial success.

To Gig, Michael, Kara, and Christopher Neubeck

CONTENTS IN BRIEF

CONTENTS

PREFACE

Social Problems: A Critical Approach is now in its third edition. Our goal is to encourage students to seriously analyze some of the causes and implications of many of the most pressing social problems confronting people today. The text is intended to provoke spirited thought, discussion, and debate among students, rather than to simply present a series of dry facts. Out of this process should come new views, knowledge and awareness, and for some students the will to act when possible to help attack those social problems of greatest concern to them.

As the table of contents indicates, *Social Problems: A Critical Approach* opens with an introductory chapter that presents traditional approaches to the study of social problems and then describes the approach taken in this book. Our approach involves examining two different types of social problems: problems of societal organization and problems of individuals. We analyze causes and effects and—in many cases—posit possible solutions or steps toward mitigating the problems. These solutions or steps toward mitigation may themselves invite healthy debate.

In the first part of the text, students are introduced to eleven "macro problems"—key organizational features of society that are to us demonstrably harmful to millions of people. In the second part, students are presented with six "micro problems"—individual behaviors that have an adverse impact on other people and/or are self-harmful.

The text is organized to make it possible for instructors to assign the chapters they wish to use in the sequence they prefer. However, it is our feeling that the micro problems involving individual behaviors are most logically handled after—and thus in the context of—macro problems depicting features of societal organization that are harmful to so many people.

As a learning device, a textbook must be comprehensible to students and must engage their interest. Like the first two editions, this text presents information in a straightforward and (I hope) highly readable manner, even when rather complex and abstract ideas are being addressed. Conflicting and contrasting views on problems are clearly delineated. Tables, figures, and photographs are directly linked to the text in order to underscore important ideas. Specialized terms and concepts are defined and illustrated in the text.

Each of the chapters on macro and micro problems contains a boxed reading that addresses—often poignantly—the impact of the problem on human beings. These readings, entitled "Public Problem, Private Pain," are carefully chosen excerpts from published interviews, autobiographies, and journalistic accounts. This special feature increases student interest by grounding sometimes abstract problems in more concrete human experiences with which students may identify. For example, in the reading in Chapter 1, The Global Context, a newspaper correspondent frankly discusses his experiences and feelings during a visit to a famine-stricken area of Ethiopia. Some of the other Public Problem, Private Pain readings present the views of a woman whose family is homeless, the memories and attitudes of a disabled Vietnam veteran, and the thoughts of a young woman who experienced sexual abuse.

Another feature of this text that will promote student involvement in discussing the subject matter is the series of provocative questions at the end of each chapter. These questions can form the bases of classroom or small-group discussions, or they may be used in conjunction with outside assignments. Many of the questions are designed to encourage debate and to get students to consider different positions or viewpoints on social problems. We have used the discussion questions with great success, and highly recommend class assignments and/or panels around them.

Many instructors will want to know how this third edition differs from the second. We begin by saying that very little was removed from the second edition (basically outdated events and data). The extremely favorable reception accorded the second edition led instead to our expansion of what we were—according to users and reviewers—already doing right. The principal addition is a new chapter on health care. A number of original chapters have new sections to cover topics of increasing significance. For example, there are new sections on the "greenhouse effect," hunger, homelessness, illiteracy, gun control, capital punishment, and AIDS and drug abuse. A section on research methods was added to the Introduction. And care has been taken to bring citations, data, and treatment of all social problems covered as up to date as is possible. *Social Problems* is accompanied by an instructor's manual, which includes a test bank.

Many people have selflessly contributed to the successful completion of the third edition. My appreciation goes to the staff of McGraw-Hill, especially to Phil Butcher, Sylvia Shepard, and Elaine Rosenberg. I am also grateful to colleagues at the University of Connecticut and at many other institutions who took time to make suggestions about the second edition.

I am greatly indebted to Dennis Breslin for his research assistance. His initiative, good judgment, and sense of humor helped me immeasurably. Thanks, Dennis.

I wish also to thank undergraduate students. Their reactions—both in and outside the classroom—helped guide the direction and development of this edition. Students' enthusiasm has made my labor so worthwhile.

McGraw-Hill and I would like to thank the following reviewers for their helpful comments and suggestions: William Cockerham, University of Illinois, Urbana Champaign; Keith Crew, University of Northern Iowa; Arlene Kaplan Daniels, Northwestern University; David Ellison, Rensselaer Polytechnic Institute; William Feigelman, Nassau Community College; Erich Goode, SUNY–Stony Brook; and Ira Wasserman, Eastern Michigan University.

Finally, I again thank Gig, Michael, Kara, and Christopher Neubeck for their love and support. Bet you thought I'd never get this edition done.

Kenneth J. Neubeck

SOCIAL PROBLEMS

A CRITICAL APPROACH

HOMELESS
AND
POOR
WALK
TO

Introduction

As we look back at the twentieth century, now rapidly drawing to an end, there is much to be struck by. From technological breakthroughs to movements for freedom and liberation, the one constant feature of this century has been change.

In the United States we have passed many historical milestones and displayed achievements that are said to have made this country great. And yet equally striking are the many serious social problems that continue to plague us. These problems, far from being resolved, provide a bothersome contrast to the many positive tendencies and accomplishments that characterize U.S. society.

Social Problems: A Critical Approach analyzes the most serious of today's social problems, ranging from the concentration of political and economic power in the hands of a few to drug abuse. The book looks at the causes and effects of these problems and considers solutions to many of them. None of the social problems analyzed in this text has a simple solution, and all pose challenges to our collective wisdom and ingenuity.

We begin this introduction with a review of the various approaches sociologists have traditionally taken toward the study of social problems. Next, the approach taken in this book—a *critical approach* to social problems—is set forth. We then discuss some reasons for change in the level of societal concern with particular problems over a period of time. Finally, we comment on sociological methods of research that help to shed light on many social problems.

TRADITIONAL APPROACHES TO THE STUDY OF SOCIAL PROBLEMS

Sociologists around the world have long been interested in the problematic aspects of social life. In fact, the nineteenth-century scholars who pioneered in the development of sociology within the United States did so out of deep concern over social conditions, particularly the problems in the nation's rapidly expanding cities. During the 1800s this society experienced the almost simultaneous impact of industrialization, urbanization, and the arrival of millions of immigrants from abroad. Property crime, violence, alcoholism, and mental troubles seemed to be on the increase. The early sociologists hoped that a better understanding of America's problems might provide clues on how to improve conditions. The new discipline of sociology was not simply an academic exercise; rather, its proponents saw sociology as a means to an end—the reduction of suffering, strife, and destructive behavior.

Historically, there have been two major approaches to the study of social problems.[1] The first, the *social pathology approach,* was popular primarily during the nineteenth and early twentieth centuries. Social pathologists were largely concerned with individuals whose behavior they thought deviant. They assumed that this deviant behavior was to a large degree due to biological or psychological deficiencies. After World War I, the social pathology approach gave way to a second orientation toward the study of social problems—the *social disorganization approach.* This approach also focused on the deviant behavior of individuals. But somewhat more attention was given to the influence of the social environment in explaining deviance.

It is important to stress that these two approaches reflect a fundamental division in social science thinking that in one or another form continues even today; that is, to some the only social problems of true importance are those revolving around the behavior of individuals. Both the problems and their causes are reducible to the individual level. In contrast, those who would take a more "structural" approach tend to view the organization and operation of society itself (or particular institutions within society) as problematic. The system poses problems for those who live within it. The social pathology approach tends toward the first, whereas the social disorganization approach is somewhat more concerned with matters of societal structure.

The Social Pathology Approach

The approach to the identification of social problems taken by the scholar–reformers of the nineteenth and early twentieth centuries has earned them the title of *social pathologists.* Borrowing ideas from the biological sciences, these sociologists preferred to conceive of American society as an organism. Like living organisms, said the social pathologists, society is subject to the dangers of disease and illness—in this case, such undesirable behavior as criminality and mental disorders. Social pathologists defined as social problems those behaviors which, in their judgment, ran contrary to the maintenance of a healthy society—a society that harbored little or no deviance.

The social pathologists typically cast the blame for such behaviors onto the individuals involved. They explained phenomena like crim-

[1] Our treatment of these approaches is based on Earl Rubington and Martin S. Weinberg, eds., *The Study of Social Problems,* 4th ed. (New York: Oxford University Press, 1989); and Ritchie P. Lowry, *Social Problems* (Lexington, Mass.: D. C. Heath & Company, 1974).

inality largely in terms of such presumed personal weaknesses as character deficiency and psychological inadequacy. Many suggested or implied that criminals and other "undesirable" individuals were genetically or biologically inferior to "normal" people. While social pathologists were aware of the unsettling changes under way in America, they were less concerned with the effect of these changes on individuals than they were with the effect of "defective" people on society. As social pathologist Samuel Smith suggested, "defective" people created more "defective" people:

> In social pathology the interrelation of the abnormal classes is one of the most impressive facts. Paupers often beget criminals; the offspring of criminals become insane; and to such an extent is the kinship of the defective, dependent, and delinquent classes exhibited, that some have gone so far as to hold that under all the various forms of social pathology there is a common ground in the nervous morbid condition of individuals.[2]

Although Smith and other social pathologists were concerned with what they called "bad environment," they believed that social problems primarily involved "weakness of the individual mind or will, the lack of development and the lack of self-control" among certain groups of people in society.[3]

Carefully selected family histories were often used by social pathologists to support their views. One such history, which was to become widely cited, concerned the Jukes family.[4] Max Jukes, a backwoodsman born in 1720, was described as an extremely ignorant man who married an equally ignorant woman. Allegedly, most of their descendants between 1740 and 1874 turned out to be criminals, paupers, and mentally troubled individuals.

Another family history concerned the Kallikaks.[5] Martin Kallikak, a soldier in the revolutionary war, married a young girl who was said to be feebleminded. Of their 480 descendants, all but 46 were criminals, prostitutes, illegitimate children, or other types of "deviates." In his second marriage, Kallikak took a wife who was said to come from "good stock." This marriage produced 496 descendants, almost all of whom were doctors, lawyers, and other well-regarded members of their communities. Such family histories were regarded as proof that "defective" people produced offspring whose behavior constituted the social problems of the day.

Modern-day scholars have harshly criticized such family studies as scientifically worthless.[6] For example, the studies are said to have reflected bias in the choice of families investigated and in the categorization of various family members as defective. The most common criticism is that social pathologists failed to address the impact of social and cultural influences on those whose behavior was singled out for scrutiny.

Nonetheless, social pathologists used their findings as the basis of their proposals for solutions to social problems. According to these scholars, individuals whose behavior interfered with societal health had to be dealt with. Depending on the illness, the cure might entail education, counseling and moral guidance, disciplinary punishment and forced labor, or even involuntary confinement. Since the social pathologists blamed many social problems on the growing immigrant population, they frequently suggested denying various "defective" ethnic groups entry into the country. In fact, this idea influenced federal legislation; the Immigration

---

[2] Samuel Smith, *Social Pathology* (New York: The Macmillan Company, 1911), pp. 8–9; reprinted in part as "The Organic Analogy," in Rubington and Weinberg, *The Study of Social Problems*, p. 22.

[3] Ibid., p. 23.

[4] Richard L. Dugdale, *The Jukes* (New York: G. P. Putnam's Sons, 1877).

[5] Henry H. Goddard, *The Kallikak Family* (New York: The Macmillan Company, 1914).

[6] See Allan Chase, *The Legacy of Malthus* (New York: Alfred A. Knopf, 1977), pp. 138–75.

Act of 1924 drastically reduced the legal quotas of Jews, Italians, Russians, Poles, Hungarians, Spaniards, Greeks, and other eastern and southern Europeans, who, along with nonwhites, were considered "racial defectives."[7]

These early analysts of American society clearly were making moral and political judgments about who and what were to be considered social problems. These judgments seem to have been based on social class biases and rigid personal moral codes that viewed anything other than native-born white, Protestant, middle-class attitudes and behavior as "bad." What we would today call *racism*, directed against southern and eastern Europeans and nonwhites, also appeared to guide their judgments. The social pathology approach was consistent with widespread public beliefs in *social Darwinism*.[8] This body of ideas was based on the belief that people's social-class position was linked to their biological quality. Those living at the bottom levels of the socioeconomic scale were thought to be less fit for survival than the more affluent.

The approach taken by the social pathologists also implicitly embodied a belief that the United States—a rapidly growing, industrial, capitalist society—was basically benign and wholesome, as social orders go. Certainly, no major overhaul or transformation of American institutions was thought to be needed. Instead, certain defective individuals were seen as the real social problems of the day. Though there were "bad environments," these were localized conditions of an exceptional nature, and they could easily be eradicated. The major reform efforts, then, were to focus on the troublesome populations. Thus, social pathologists defined social problems in such a way as to make them solvable within the boundaries of the prevailing social order.

The social pathology approach still lingers on, although only among a minority of social thinkers. Edward Banfield's work on the urban poor is perhaps the best example. In *The Unheavenly City* Banfield—a former White House adviser on urban affairs—explained the plight of America's slum-dwellers in terms of their alleged personal deficiencies:

> The lower class individual lives in the slum and sees little reason to complain. He does not care how dirty and dilapidated his housing is, either inside or out, nor does he mind the inadequacy of such public facilities as schools, parks and libraries; indeed, where such things exist he destroys them by acts of vandalism. Features that make the slum repellant to others actually please him.[9]

Banfield, with such incorrect and misleading "facts," both promotes and panders to existing ignorance about the poor. His ideas are embarrassing in their naivety and reflect no contact with low-income people. Yet Banfield's proposed solutions to urban poverty are consistent with the social pathology approach. He suggested the involuntary sterilization of poor people and the removal of newly born infants from their parents for placement in more "normal" middle-class surroundings. Such solutions are virtually identical to those proposed to handle so-called defective European immigrant groups in the not-so-distant past. Unlike his predecessors, though, Banfield did not expect his ideas to be carried out, since they would not be seen as politically feasible in today's society.

---

[7] Ibid., pp. 289–91.

[8] Richard Hofstadter, *Social Darwinism in American Thought*, rev. ed. (Boston: Beacon Press, 1965).

[9] Edward C. Banfield, *The Unheavenly City* (Boston: Little, Brown & Company, 1970), p. 62. See also his *The Unheavenly City Revisited* (Boston: Little, Brown & Company, 1974).

The Social Disorganization Approach

After World War I a number of sociologists had grown dissatisfied with the biological analogy that social pathologists used to discuss the workings of American society. They also began to feel that the deviant behaviors identified as social problems by the social pathologists were not totally the fault of those involved. Seeking an alternative way to explain such behaviors, sociologists moved toward a new approach involving the concept of *social disorganization.* As we shall see, this concept enabled scholars to pay more attention to the immediate environments within which problematic behaviors were found. As they focused on such environments, they discovered that "deviant" behavior was likely to be expressed only under certain kinds of societal conditions.

This shift in scholarly focus was not only an advance toward a better understanding of deviance; it was also a step forward in the intellectual sophistication of the new discipline of sociology. During the post–World War I period, sociologists were increasingly concerned with establishing credibility as *scientists.* In order to obtain greater scholarly recognition and respect within the academic world, they needed to separate the study of social problems from reformist moralizing. A more objective approach was deemed desirable—one in which sociologists might consciously stand back and examine problems within the context of basic social laws and processes, just as other scientists objectively study physical phenomena. The concept of social disorganization was thought to provide a scientifically neutral and value-free approach to social phenomena. In focusing on the workings of society, rather than on presumed psychological or biological traits of individuals, the new approach was also more distinctly *sociological.* This fit well with the desire of sociological practitioners to clarify the boundaries of their new academic field.

Normlessness and Social Disorganization. Those who emphasized the social disorganization approach rejected the social pathologists' biological conception of society. Rather, they saw society as a complex organizational unit—a *social system*—whose parts were all interrelated and interdependent. The organization of society was made possible by sets of *norms,* or rules for appropriate behavior. Norms were dictated by and flowed from American culture. If all members of society accepted and adjusted their behavior to these norms, that is, if they fulfilled their appropriate *social roles,* the social system would function smoothly. In this case, the social system would be in a state of equilibrium and would grow and progress by means of natural evolutionary tendencies.

Against this theoretical background, sociologists still had to explain why all was not well in America. Why did such phenomena as violence, property crime, and alcoholism exist, and why did America's growing urban centers particularly seem to be the scenes of these problems? Their answer was that certain sectors of the population were overwhelmed by the very difficult demands associated with change. Deviant behaviors were due to the existence of social disorganization within parts of the social system.

For example, the progressive movement of people from rural areas to crowded cities that accompanied industrialization meant that many migrants had to make great life adjustments. The norms that regulated interpersonal relationships and life-styles in a small town were often inapplicable to fast-paced city living, much to the surprise of new migrants. Urban life often meant daily contact with strangers, new and stressful living conditions, and subservience to the impersonal demands of officialdom at work and in the realm of law. Past experiences provided little support and few guidelines for a quick adjustment to the city, it was suggested. In the absence of clearly defined norms, or with the failure of migrants to internalize existing norms readily, deviant behavior was likely to occur. Deviance was thus viewed as an indication of *normlessness,* a response to the confusion and disorientation associated with being caught up in change.

As a result of such ideas, sociologists began to examine America's urban scene and tried to relate its features to nonconforming behavior. A famous series of studies was carried out in Chicago.[10] Urban sociologists noted that Chicago consisted of several ecological zones, each of which differed in terms of economic status, neighborhood stability, and the degree to which relations among residents were closely knit. They found that such phenomena as mental disorders and juvenile delinquency appeared most frequently in unstable areas of the city—neighborhoods that were in a constant state of flux because most of the inhabitants were new arrivals and transients. They concluded that neighborhood instability caused social disorganization—the absence of norms to guide people's behavior—and that, as a result, deviant behavior abounded.

Similar difficulties were said to confront new immigrants from abroad. Many foreigners entering the United States came from rural backgrounds and followed others of their national origins into ethnic enclaves in the nation's cities. Also, sociologists suggested, the native cultures of many of these people were at variance with the dominant culture of native-born white Anglo-Saxon Protestant America. The demands of "Americanization" meant that many immigrants had to shed their traditional and taken-for-granted ways of living. Often they were caught between wanting to learn and adapt to the American way and wanting to cling to the ethnic identities and ancestral life-styles with which they felt most comfortable. Furthermore, the norms of behavior of the old country seemed out of place in America. Hence, sociologists saw the *culture conflict* arising out of immigration as yet another source of deviant behavior. Culture conflict was also thought to be a result of change processes taking place within this society.

Perhaps the most influential study in this area was *The Polish Peasant in Europe and America,* by William I. Thomas and Florian Znaniecki.[11] Basing their findings primarily on an analysis of letters to and from Polish immigrants, these researchers documented the personal troubles caused by dealing with American culture. This society's emphasis on individualism, competition, and material gain, for example, ran counter to traditional Polish communal values. The stresses associated with adapting to a new culture and its norms frequently led to marital problems and family instability. Conflict between the generations was common, as children came in contact with American cultural values at school. The Polish immigrant was finding it hard to become integrated into American society, and deviant behavior was often the result.

Merton's Anomie Theory. The concept of social disorganization also led some sociologists to look at America's opportunity structure and its role in nurturing deviant behavior. The best example is Robert K. Merton's influential *anomie theory.*[12] American culture, Merton observed, places a great deal of emphasis on getting ahead and attaining material success. Yet the means for pursuing these cultural goals are not equally distributed within the population. People do not

---

[10] See, for example, Robert E. L. Faris and H. Warren Dunham, *Mental Disorders in Urban Areas* (Chicago: University of Chicago Press, 1939); and Clifford Shaw and Henry McKay, *Juvenile Delinquency and Urban Areas* (Chicago: University of Chicago Press, 1942).

[11] William I. Thomas and Florian Znaniecki, *The Polish Peasant in Europe and America* (New York: Alfred A. Knopf, 1927), 2 vols.

[12] Robert K. Merton, "Social Structure and Anomie," *American Sociological Review,* 3 (October 1938): 672–82. The concept of anomie was introduced into sociology by Emile Durkheim, *The Division of Labor in Society* (New York: The Free Press, 1965).

have the same family resources, access to educational opportunities, and important connections. Some people are discriminated against because of their racial or ethnic backgrounds. Moreover, aside from race and class membership, not everyone has internalized the approved norms governing the pursuit of material success equally.

If an individual has the means to pursue cultural goals and has internalized the socially approved norms for doing so, deviance is unlikely. In Merton's terms, such a person will be a *conformist*. Otherwise, an individual may experience *anomie* (normlessness) and act in accordance with other norms of behavior.

Anomic individuals may respond to their situations in any one of four ways, according to Merton. (1) In *innovation*, a person pursues cultural success goals by socially disapproved means. This category encompasses, among others, those who commit crimes against property—from purse-snatching to white-collar offenses by government and corporate executives. (2) *Ritualism* takes place when an individual slackens the pursuit of material success by lowering aspirations and rejecting the pressures to compete and get ahead but still accepts the societal means. The low-level bureaucrat who has little hope for upward mobility and simply plods along year after year, enforcing the bureaucratic rules, exemplifies the ritualist. (3) In *retreatism* a person rejects and abandons both the goals and the means of pursuing them, simply withdrawing from the "game." The seriously mentally troubled, the chronic alcoholic, the drug addict, and the Skid Row vagrant are examples. (4) Finally, *rebellion* involves the attempt to change both the cultural goals and the means by which they are pursued. This category includes individuals who have committed themselves to radical revolutionary change in the values and structure of social life.[13]

In sum, Merton and other social disorganization theorists blamed social problems on the uneven workings of the societal opportunity structure, industrialization, urbanization, and immigration, which, they said, carried disruptive consequences for some segments of the American population. Changes taking place in society often rendered norms unclear, difficult to learn and adjust to, and even of questionable utility. Persons caught up in situations of social disorganization were problems. But the explanation for deviant behavior went beyond questions of individual character and personality deficiency. Instead, the major problem was social disorganization itself, which meant that parts of the social system were out of kilter and in need of some minor adjustment.

Social Disorganization and the Ideal Society. Like the social pathologists, those sociologists who turned to the social disorganization approach made certain moral and political judgments about the nature of social problems in American society. Despite claims to the contrary, their approach was not totally scientific and objective. Rather, it reflected a set of assumptions about the ideal state of society. These sociologists believed that society *should* be a well-organized social system characterized by relative homogeneity in cultural beliefs, individual conformity to the norms of the dominant culture, and the absence of behavior that deviated from accepted norms.

As we have seen, the way in which a social problem is defined has a great deal to do with possible solutions. For theorists of social disorganization, the solutions seemed to require a twofold strategy. First, the norms of the dominant culture had to be clarified and efforts had to be made to bring deviants in line with these norms. Second, means had to be found to slow down change or, at least, to reduce the harmful effects of change and to take some of the kinks out of the opportunity structure. In practical

[13] From Robert K. Merton, *Social Theory and Social Structure*, rev. ed. (New York: The Free Press, 1964), pp. 140–57.

terms, the first strategy was probably easier. It was also consistent with the solutions to social problems that had already been advanced by the social pathologists.

Thus, the focus of those employing the social disorganization approach was largely on deviant individuals, although there was sympathetic consideration of the difficulties imposed by their immediate environments. Consequently, solutions to social problems were essentially viewed as matters of administration. Deviant behaviors could be taken care of by proper intervention, without reorganizing or transforming the entire social system. Some minor adjustments to some parts of the system were perhaps necessary, but for all practical purposes it would be much easier if the deviants were to do most of the adjusting.

The social disorganization approach continues to have a following among sociologists. During the 1960s, for example, Daniel Moynihan wrote a federal report that attempted to explain why black Americans continue to be overrepresented among the poor.[14] Moynihan argued that the era of slavery created a tradition of family instability and disorganization among blacks. The black family, he alleged, was still in a state of breakdown; illegitimacy, crime, delinquency, unemployment, and welfare dependency were among the results of this breakdown. Only if the black family were strengthened and stabilized would equality with whites be achieved.

Critics have pointed out that Moynihan was talking about a minority of black families and that he was ignoring the continuing existence of white racism as a hindrance to black advancement. Instead, Moynihan was subtly blaming blacks for their historical and current position of social, economic, and political subordination. Consistent with the social disorganization approach, Moynihan's solution was for blacks to become better adjusted to society and model their families after an ideal that many whites have failed to achieve.

Both the social pathologists and the social disorganization theorists have tended to view various forms of deviant behavior as the principal focus for the study of social problems. Proponents of both approaches have, to one degree or another, failed to see the organization and operation of society itself as problematic. In reaction to this, an increasing number of sociologists have moved away from the more traditional approaches.[15] These sociologists contend that scholars should not simply accept the prevailing order as a given, but that they should instead treat it as worthy of examination and critical review. Few would deny that the troublesome and troubled behavior of individuals continues to merit serious attention. But certain key features of society are at least as problematic as individual deviance.

In the next section we shall set forth the critical approach to social problems that is followed in the remaining chapters of this book. This approach focuses not only on problems associated with the behavior of individuals, but also on societal features that are harming millions of people.

A CRITICAL APPROACH TO SOCIAL PROBLEMS

In identifying social problems, a sociologist's own values are inevitably brought into play. In particular, it is impossible to state that a specific phenomenon is a social problem without making implicit reference to an assumed ideal

---

[14] See Lee Rainwater and William L. Yancey, *The Moynihan Report and the Politics of Controversy* (Cambridge, Mass.: The M.I.T. Press, 1967).

[15] Excellent examples are provided by D. Stanley Eitzen, *Social Problems*, 3rd ed. (Boston: Allyn and Bacon, 1986), and Elliott Currie and Jerome H. Skolnick, *America's Problems*, 2nd ed. (Glenview, Ill.: Scott, Foresman & Company, 1988).

societal state. The social pathologists valued a "healthy" society, one in which the illness of socially undesirable behavior was absent. Proponents of social disorganization theory valued a smooth-working, culturally homogeneous social system in which people adapted their behavior to accepted norms.[16] All these theorists possessed a vision of the ways in which a society should work. It was against this vision that they determined who and what were to be identified as social problems.

Is it possible not to have a vision of the ideal society somewhere in your mind whenever you say X, Y, or Z is a social problem? No. In fact, all authors of social problems textbooks possess such a vision, even if they do not directly acknowledge the values leading them to choose certain problems for inclusion in their books.[17]

The *critical approach* taken in this book is likewise based on a vision or ideal against which the status quo is judged. This vision has informed and guided the identification of social problems that are addressed in the chapters that follow. By placing this vision in full view, we are making it possible for readers to determine whether the critical approach furthers understanding of the realities of contemporary life.

Our vision or ideal possesses the following characteristics:

1. Our relationship with poor, underdeveloped nations is nonexploitative and supportive of movements to secure basic human rights.
2. Members of society are able to participate actively in or influence directly those political and economic decisions that affect them.
3. Our government provides international leadership and sets a strong example for other nations in its approach to nuclear disarmament and the cooperative, nonviolent settlement of differences.
4. Resources are devoted to the preservation and conservation of the natural environment, and technological decisions take into account the well-being of future generations.
5. Work is freely available to all. It is organized cooperatively, with special attention to providing meaning, dignity, and satisfaction.
6. Gross differences in personal wealth and income are greatly reduced, so that the life chances of all Americans are relatively equal and so that all share more equitably in the goods and services being produced.
7. Each individual has ready and continuing access to the education and training needed to develop his or her interests and capabilities to the fullest extent.
8. There is no personal and institutionalized discrimination against individuals on the basis of group membership (e.g., race, ethnicity, sex, and age).
9. Adequate health care is understood to be a human right and thus is made accessible and affordable to all.
10. Special attention and support are freely given to troubled families and their members, including single-parent households. Moreover, the bases for violence and abuse within families of all types are absent.
11. Members of American society are at peace with themselves and with one another. The vicarious rewards associated with such activities as crime, violence, and drug abuse have no attraction, and the social factors that provoke mental troubles and suicide are absent.

We might view our list of features as constituting something similar to what German so-

[16] C. Wright Mills, "The Professional Ideology of Social Pathologists," *American Journal of Sociology*, 49 (September 1943): 165–80.

[17] Such acknowledgments are rare and are usually expressed only in passing, almost furtively. An exception is a text its authors state is guided by the Universal Declaration of Human Rights, adopted by the United Nations in 1948. See Michael S. Bassis, Richard J. Gelles, and Ann Levine, *Social Problems* (Orlando, Fla.: Harcourt Brace Jovanovich, 1982), pp. 15–19.

ciologist Max Weber called an "ideal type."[18] To Weber an ideal type is simply an abstract description of some form of social organization that is put together by a sociologist on the basis of examining examples of it. No particular case fits the description exactly, but the description contains the essential features that are to be found in reality. Although we have no examples of societies that in reality fit our vision or ideal, by considering our list of features as adding up to an "ideal type" we are in a position to see how closely U.S. society (or any other society for that matter) approximates it.

After having said this much, it should be obvious that the approach to be taken in this text to social problems is necessarily "critical." Given the gap between our vision and the stark realities, we are forced to find fault with and judge severely the very structure and operation of American society as a whole, as well as its relationships with poorer, weaker societies. We do not take our society as a given; we instead see it as problematic in and of itself. At the same time, we find ourselves looking with understanding—though not always with approval—at the variety of troubled and troublesome behaviors of individuals who find themselves cast as deviants within the prevailing order.

Our vision of the ideal society is, obviously, rather utopian. No society in the world today comes close to matching its features, though we expect that some society will someday manage to do so. Our vision of the ideal society is simply a tool, a measuring rod that provides a set of criteria by which to assess the real-life status quo.

In line with the critical approach, we examine two major types of problems in this book. The first type, *macro problems*, encompasses key features of society that are problematic. The second type, *micro problems*, includes forms of individual behavior that may be harmful to others and/or to the person.

[18] See Max Weber, *Economy and Society*, Ephraim Fischoff et al., trans. (New York: Bedminster Press, 1968).

Macro Problems

Certain very fundamental organizational features of society stand in the way of our individual and collective development as human beings. That is, certain economic, political, social, and technological arrangements that have come to prevail are problematic because these arrangements harm millions of people. In Part I we emphasize these problematic organizational or structural features of society. We shall be looking at ongoing processes and patterned group relationships that are empirically observable over time.

Part I of this text begins with a chapter on the global context within which the United States functions, with attention to world population and poverty. Then Chapter 2 examines the unequal distribution of political and economic power as an integral feature of American society that has a vast impact on the life chances of millions. This and other structural features of U.S. society—economic inequality and poverty; unequal opportunities for education and for health care; the subordination of people on the basis of race, sex, or age; militarism; environmental abuse; and work—are matters with which Americans are confronted daily. We refer to such large-scale, systemic features as *macro problems* to underscore their scope and pervasiveness.

Because macro problems are rooted in societal organization, their reduction or elimination may well require an eventual transformation of the prevailing order. Macro problems will not yield to minor technical or administrative reforms. They can be dealt with only if men and women work consciously and collectively to bring about change. To do so, people must analyze, plan, and seek to reorganize society with a vision in mind. The kind of transformation our own vision suggests cannot come about by wishful thinking. Nor is it likely to happen if we simply back away and trustingly leave our future in the hands of societal elites and their

Micro problems—or problems involving individual behaviors—touch a wide range of people. Drug abuse, for example, has been of particular concern because of its effects, and law enforcement efforts against sellers have been increased. Here, dealers of "crack" cocaine are being arrested. (*Allan Tannenbaum/Sygma*)

appointed "experts." We must all be involved in the solution of macro problems.

Micro Problems

Although our critical approach emphasizes the harmful effects of key features of society, we cannot ignore the troublesome and troubled behavior of individual societal members. Millions of Americans are engaging in behavior that adversely affects other people and/or is at times self-destructive. Though theories on the causation of such behavior abound, we have a great deal to learn about family violence and abuse, criminality, mental illness, suicide, alcoholism, and drug abuse.

We shall refer to such forms of behavior, which are analyzed in Part II, as *micro problems*. The term *micro* is not used to belittle the significance of this behavior. Rather, it simply underscores the difference between problems largely involving the macro order—the structure of society—and those arising from the actions of individuals, or the micro order.

In the traditional approaches to social problems, the behaviors we consider micro problems were seen as forms of *deviant behavior*. We wish to avoid this term, for it carries unnecessarily negative connotations. Those whose behavior is troubled or troublesome can in many instances be considered to be acting normally, given the life situations with which they may be faced.

Moreover, the concept of deviance implies that people are being judged unacceptable and that they should be made to adjust to society and its norms. Yet the behavior in question could be viewed in quite a different manner. In ways we are still seeking to fully understand, some forms of deviance may be caused by the organization of society. It is senseless to ask people to adjust or conform to societal conditions that may be harming them. The more logical solution is to alter these conditions.

Analysis of the relationship between features of society at the macro level and people's behavior at the micro level has come to be viewed as a central challenge facing sociologists.[19] Our ability to fathom many micro problems may well await progress on this front by contemporary theorists of society.

THE LIFE CYCLE OF SOCIAL PROBLEMS

For decades sociologists have claimed that social problems have a natural history or *life cycle*. As early as the 1940s, attempts were made to specify the general stages through which problems were believed to go. One such early attempt, which still influences contemporary thinking on the matter, was developed by Richard Fuller and Richard Myers.[20] According to this approach, the cycle begins when people become aware of some objective situation which, in their estimation, is problematic. They are not quite sure what to do about it, and they begin to communicate their concern to others. What often follows is public debate over the problem, with conflicting ideas put forth as to why the situation exists and what is to be done. In the course of public debate, the various groups whose interests are affected by the problem and/or its solution make their positions known. Finally, we come to the stage of reforms. Official policies for dealing with the problem, which were hammered out through debate and influenced by the jockeying of various interest groups, are finally implemented.

Not too long ago two sociologists—Robert Ross and Graham Staines—attempted to update and extend earlier efforts to specify problem life cycles. Many of their ideas are supportive of our critical approach. According to these sociologists, the following process takes place during the career of a social problem:

> Private or interest group recognition of the social problem; political recognition of the problem as an appropriate issue for public discussion; public debate and social conflict about the causes of the problem; a set of political outcomes of this sequence.[21]

Defining a Social Problem

Ross and Staines note that an individual or group defines a given phenomenon as problematic in terms of their *ideology* or sense of what the ideal state of affairs should be. (This is much like what we have been calling a vision against which objective reality can be compared.) They suggest that social problems are defined largely in terms of an individual's or group's perceived self-interest. Thus, the initial definition of a social problem can be a highly political event, particularly when opposing interests get involved.

Take, for example, the denial of voting rights

[19] George Ritzer, *Sociological Theory*, 2nd ed. (New York: Alfred A. Knopf, 1988), p. 198.

[20] Richard C. Fuller and Richard R. Myers, "The Natural History of a Social Problem," *American Sociological Review*, 6 (June 1941): 320–28.

[21] This section is based on Robert Ross and Graham L. Staines, "The Politics of Analyzing Social Problems," *Social Problems*, 20 (Summer 1972): 18–40; quotation from p. 18.

that until quite recently confronted many black citizens in the southern and border states. Unrealistic qualifications were often set up to prevent blacks from voting, and persons who pushed too hard to exercise the franchise were frequently threatened or harmed. The civil rights movement of the 1950s and 1960s denounced the discrepancy between black voter participation and the rights granted to all citizens under the Constitution. As the civil rights movement saw it, blacks should be voting and electing political representatives who would respond to their interests. Many whites, on the other hand, viewed black involvement in politics as an erosion of their monopoly over political affairs. Opposing interests were thus involved in the definition of racism in politics as a social problem.

Transformation into a Public Issue

The next stage in the sequence involves the transformation of a problem into what Ross and Staines call a *public issue.* In their opinion, this transformation will take place only if the privately recognized problem is seen as publicly important and legitimate for public consideration. A number of different "social actors" are typically involved as a problem becomes an issue. Coverage by the mass media is critical in terms of making a problem visible and in determining its importance and legitimacy.

The changes demanded by the civil rights movement required that racism in politics be seen as a public issue. Hence, large-scale demonstrations were organized in the early 1960s—demonstrations that drew thousands of blacks, members of other minority groups, and sympathetic whites. The demonstrations were covered in the national news media, and they were considered even more newsworthy because of the violent responses they frequently met. Television viewers saw peaceful sign-carrying marchers being beaten with police batons, shocked by cattle prods, battered by the spray from high-pressure hoses, and trampled by horses. Other violent events during the early 1960s, including the murders of black and white civil rights workers and deaths resulting from the bombing of black churches, simply underscored the issue of racism in politics.

Ross and Staines see the reaction (or even nonreaction) of public officials as an element in the equation. Sometimes there is conflict between media representatives and public officials over whether a given problem deserves the status of public issue. Again, this may be a matter of perceived self-interest, as officials can attempt to downplay the importance of problems and provide their own interpretation of events. For example, many southern politicians, who had been elected with white votes, saw civil rights as nothing to get excited about. In their view, a handful of "outside agitators," racemongers, and riffraff who did not understand or appreciate the "southern way" were stirring up trouble. While the media brought racism in politics and white resistance to change into the limelight, many southern officials tried to deny there was any issue deserving such concern.

Debating Causes and Solutions

Once a privately recognized social problem becomes a public issue, according to Ross and Staines, debate about its causes begins. This stage is extremely important, for perceived causes have a definite relationship to the types of solutions that are considered. Ross and Staines distinguish between two different causal interpretations commonly brought to bear on social problems. On the one hand, a problem may be given a *systemic attribution:* the system itself is problematic and/or generates difficulties for individuals. Our critical approach leans toward this category. On the other hand, a problem may simply be blamed on the people involved; it is their deficiency, their faults, that "causes" the social problem. This second causal interpretation is termed *personal attribution*. Earlier we saw how the social pathology approach and, to a lesser extent, the social disorganization approach tend to lead in such a direction.

For participants in and supporters of the civil rights movement, the lack of black participation in elections was a result of a well-organized system of racist exclusion and denial of voting opportunities. The outcome was black political powerlessness and the election of white candidates who served only white interests. Engaging in systemic attribution, the civil rights movement demanded that this system be changed and that black efforts to exercise the franchise be protected. Many southern officials, on the other hand, claimed that blacks could vote if they were "qualified," but that most were not really interested in doing so. If the "outside agitators" and "liberal media" had not come in to stir up trouble, there would be no problem. Here the causal interpretation of personal attribution was being employed; those demonstrating and demanding change were the *real* problem, not the "southern way."

Different groups find either systemic or personal attribution in line with their perceived self-interest. Ross and Staines observe that public officials often prefer to blame the people facing problems for their troubles, rather than to encourage a belief that the prevailing order is itself somehow problematic and deserving of transformation. It seems likely that all dominant groups will tend to favor personal attribution, for they manage, control, and profit from the system that could be called into question.

After the opposing groups make public their interpretation of the causes, serious debate begins. As Ross and Staines put it: "Since causal diagnoses of social problems are reached by different people in different political situations, conflict between alternative patterns of attribution becomes inevitable."[22] The result is a complex bargaining process between authorities and the "partisans" of the social problem that eventually results in a compromise between the groups. The political outcome is often in the form of legislation or administrative changes through which the problem, as it has come to be defined, is addressed.

In the case of the demands of the civil rights movement, the compromise was debated and reached at the national level. The Voting Rights Act of 1965 outlawed the formal procedures used by many southern states to block black voter participation, and the federal government provided observers at polling places to check on overt efforts to intimidate black voters. Though the law could not address the more informal means by which whites attempted to discourage blacks from voting, it did put the force of national policy behind those who wanted to enter the polling booth. Whites still dominate the political scene in the southern and border states, except in communities in which blacks predominate. And Congress found sufficient reason to extend the protections provided by the Voting Rights Act in 1970, 1975, and 1982. Nonetheless, the civil rights movement won something—even if it was only a slow acquiescence to the presence of blacks in the voting booth. Southern political leaders have to take black votes into account and to curry black support by avoiding the racial issues that were long a major theme in southern politics.

The Role of Power

The message implicit in Ross and Staines' discussion is that *power* determines how problems are ultimately defined and, thus, what solutions are likely to be considered and implemented. By *power* sociologists usually mean the probability that individuals or groups can implement their desires even though they may be resisted. Groups have different self-interests to advance or protect, and those that cannot mobilize power (even if only to disrupt the status quo) are likely to lose out to those whose dominance is well established.

---

[22] Ibid., p. 32.

People or groups who possess power are in the best position to:

1. Determine whether a privately recognized problem will be permitted to become a public issue;
2. Advance their self-interested version of the sources or causes of a problem;
3. Control the ways in which a given problem will come to be defined; and
4. Determine what, if anything, will be done to solve the problem.

The power of the civil rights movement lay in its ability to mobilize public opinion against racism in politics, thus pressuring government officials to take steps against denial of blacks' constitutional rights.

The life cycle of social problems and, especially, the role of power have direct implications for the critical approach. The macro problems discussed in this book can be reduced or eliminated. But attempts to do so are a threat to the perceived self-interests of those who benefit from the ways in which American society is now organized. Thus, those who derive power and special privilege from maintaining the status quo will prefer to keep macro problems from becoming public issues. If the problems do become issues, dominant groups will actively push for solutions that are consistent with their self-interests. To the degree to which they are successful either nothing will change or those changes that are made will be easily incorporated into the prevailing order.

Take, for example, economic inequality. According to U.S. census data, almost a fifth of the U.S. population is poor or near-poor, while a small minority lives in almost unimaginable affluence. During the 1980s the gap between America's affluent and its poor noticeably grew.

The civil rights movement inspired other groups in the United States, especially women, to assert their rights. As sexism has come to be perceived as a problem, many women—including those physically abused by their lovers and husbands—have looked to other women for help. In this photograph, caseworkers chat with clients in a shelter for battered women. (*Mark Antman/The Image Works*)

Homelessness among poor families visibly increased. The sharp reduction of economic inequality would require a drastic shift in the ways in which income and wealth are distributed, with the more affluent giving up much of their wealth. Certainly the affluent are not about to bring the fact of economic inequality before the public, nor are they likely to champion a movement for redistribution. Such a position would not be in their self-interest. But when the poor and their supporters do cry out, when economic inequality does come to public awareness, affluent groups will take an active interest. They will sanction solutions that do not make serious inroads on their economic privilege.

This occurred during the 1960s, when poverty became a public issue. At that time, the solutions came from Congress and the president (offices of the affluent) and focused almost entirely on changing the poor. These solutions included family planning, support for self-help organizations, extensions of free legal aid, and some minimal training for the hard-core unemployed. Such solutions to the macro problem of poverty were easily incorporated into the prevailing order, satisfying dominant economic groups. Yet neither poverty nor affluence were measurably reduced by these programs, and the "war on poverty" was ended by the Nixon administration (1968–74). Since then, public awareness and concern over poverty have been permitted to dissipate. In the 1980s, as the poverty rate rose back to 1960s levels, federal aid actually was cut back.[23]

On the other hand, it *is* in the interests of dominant groups to permit micro problems to enter public awareness and to be seen as the *real* problems of the day. Micro problems are easily blamed on the traits of individuals rather than on the character of the system—in other words, they lend themselves to personal attribution. Each year more resources are earmarked for handling micro problems as economic, political, and social elites throw their support behind enlarged police and penal systems, campaigns against drug and alcohol abuse, and expanded mental health services, among other programs. The point is that these social problems are widely considered amenable to administrative and technical adjustments—more research, more tax money, more experimental programs, and more surveillance and control of people. Since none of these strategies threatens the existing order from which dominant groups draw benefits, such groups obviously see it as better for the public to focus on "deviance" when they reflect on problems of this society. In this way public attention is diverted from the societal arrangements that are harmful and that may even contribute to the generation of the "deviant" behavior.

METHODS OF RESEARCH

In order to learn more about social problems—their nature, extent, effects, and causes—social scientists conduct research using different methods. Unlike those people who lay claim to knowledge of conditions or groups with which they have had little or no contact, sociologists and other social scientists doggedly go after facts. Such researchers develop a healthy skepticism toward everyday taken-for-granted ideas about society and its members. They prefer to base statements on the best available evidence gained through systematic, objective inquiry. In sharing descriptions of their work with others, including the general public, social scientists open both their methods and findings to critical scrutiny. Much of this text revolves around information elicited by sociologists and other social scientists, used in this case to shed as much light as possible on serious social problems.

Three methods of research are of interest.

[23] Michael Harrington, *The New American Poverty* (New York: Holt, Rinehart & Winston, 1984), and Ruth Sidel, *Women and Children Last* (New York: Penguin Books, 1986).

First, there is *survey research,* wherein a carefully selected sample of individuals is asked to respond to a set of questions. Second, there is *field research,* which involves direct contact with and observation of people whose behavior and thinking are the subject of study. Third, there is *experimental research,* wherein a comparison is made between the behavior of two (or perhaps more) groups, each of which is subjected to different conditions.

In this section we use examples to illustrate each of these methods. The examples are from research on the topic of poverty, a topic taken up in more detail in Chapter 6.

Survey Research

The survey research method can be used to gather descriptive information about people's characteristics, including their attitudes and behaviors. Public opinion polls are a case in point. But survey research can be undertaken for reasons that go beyond a desire for description. Sociologists and other social scientists often conduct surveys to gain information that would shed light on the adequacy of a particular theory or to help develop new theories. In either case survey research commonly requires that the researcher choose a representative sample of the population about which he or she wishes to generalize.

Typically a survey is a "one-time" exercise. That is, those included in the sample are asked to respond to a set of questions on a one-time basis. If a researcher is particularly interested in changes taking place among people over a period of time, it may be preferable to conduct a type of survey known as a "panel study." Here the people in the original representative sample are questioned more than once, that is, at periodic time intervals. Panel studies are more difficult to administer and more expensive to conduct than one-time surveys, but they can provide very useful information. Our example of survey research is a panel study.

In 1968 researchers at the University of Michigan Survey Research Center began the Panel Study of Income Dynamics. Each year 5,000 American families, chosen to serve as a representative sample, provide information about their employment and economic circumstances as well as other events in their lives. Even as family members leave the household (e.g., divorced spouses or grown children) they remain on the panel of people surveyed. Hence it has been possible to document important changes in America's families in recent years.

In his book *Years of Poverty, Years of Plenty* researcher Greg Duncan reported on a selection of findings for the decade 1969–78.[24] In this case Duncan was interested in those families that experienced poverty. Many people believe that "the poor" are a homogeneous and stable group whose membership is pretty much the same from year to year. It is also common to find people believing that most poor people live in poverty generation after generation. Using the survey research method, and employing a panel study for its advantages in studying change in people's lives, Duncan proved the common wisdom was wrong.

His work revealed that there is a very high degree of turnover—people moving in or out of poverty—from year to year. Most poverty-stricken people are what Duncan calls the "temporarily poor." Two-thirds of those living in families with incomes under the government-defined poverty line in any given year were still poor the following year, meaning a full one-third were not.[25]

Duncan defined as "persistently poor" individuals who were poor for at least eight of the ten years for which he was examining data. Only one-third of the poor fell into this category, or some 3 percent of the U.S. population.

---

[24] Greg J. Duncan, *Years of Poverty, Years of Plenty* (Ann Arbor: University of Michigan, Institute for Social Research, 1984).

[25] Ibid., p. 60.

Researchers have used various methods to understand some of the factors responsible for widespread poverty in the United States. Surveys have found that one of the most common reasons families fall into poverty is job loss by the principal wage earner, a situation that befell the family pictured here. (*J. P. Laffont/Sygma*)

Clearly, relatively few people experience generations of poverty.[26]

Moreover, the research revealed that far more Americans have experience with poverty than anyone previously had realized. Annual statistics from the U.S. Census portrayed poverty rates in the 1969–78 period typically in the 11–12 percent range. But Duncan found that fully a quarter of the American population lived in poor families in one or more years over that time period. The census data had simply masked the true extent to which Americans must deal with economic deprivation.

Nor was Duncan able to find any particular characteristic that distinguished the vast majority of poor, who have relatively brief contact with poverty, from everyone else. In his words,

> Few people are immune to such events as personal illness, adverse local or national economic conditions, or the death or departure of a spouse; and for a substantial proportion, these events can precipitate a year or two of severe hardship.[27]

This opening up of new facts about poverty, through the survey research method, obviously provides badly needed guidance to policy mak-

[26] Ibid.

[27] Ibid., p. 61.

ers concerned with attending to the needs of both the temporarily and persistently poor.

Field Research

There are times when the direct observation of people is the best (and perhaps the only) route to obtaining information about their thinking and behavior. Field research may vary in the degree to which one must actually get involved with those being studied. At one extreme, the researcher may play the role of a nonparticipant observer, simply recording what is going on and attempting to make sense of it. At another extreme, the researcher may play the role of participant observer, being directly immersed in the activities of those whose thinking and behavior is to be understood. In some cases it may be possible and desirable for someone to participate without his or her role as a researcher being known, so as to avoid that having an impact on the behavior observed. But often people do not mind knowing they are of interest to researchers and can be of great assistance in understanding the unfamiliar.

One of the most important decisions a field researcher must make is the choice of research site. Whereas survey researchers can choose individuals to serve as research subjects based on certain statistical procedures and assumptions about their representing a larger population, often field researchers face much more limited degrees of freedom. Generalizability of research findings may be an issue, at least until other researchers (perhaps even using other research methods) come up with confirming data.

On the other hand, the field research may be aimed at obtaining information about a group or organization that is for some reason unique. This situation raises an issue that is common to most field research. Would a different researcher have been likely to come up with the same or similar findings? This issue arises because of the amount of judgment left in the hands of field researchers in determining what will be considered data and how data will be interpreted.

Field research, like survey research, may be a way of gaining a set of descriptive information about people. It may also be oriented toward assessing an existing theory or producing a new one. In the example of field research we consider here, what began as an exploratory effort with descriptive goals produced findings with important theoretical implications. When this occurs, no doubt the researchers find the tremendous amount of labor and personal sacrifice that can go into spending time "in the field" to have been very worthwhile.

Over an eighteen-month period in 1962 and 1963, researcher Elliot Liebow conducted participant observation among some two dozen black men. His findings were reported in a book that is considered a classic in field research even today, *Tally's Corner.*[28] The men Liebow studied hung out on and near a particular neighborhood street corner in a ghetto area of Washington, D.C. One of the men with whom Liebow developed a close relationship was called Tally, hence the name of the book.

The purpose of Liebow's field research was to record and interpret the everyday lives of low-income black men, a group about which social scientists felt they knew very little. Liebow's research was to be exploratory; he did not start out with the goal of assessing some theory about these men. Rather he wanted to try to understand their lives in their terms, from their point of view.

Elliot Liebow had grown up in Washington, D.C., the son of a white grocer whose family lived in and ran a succession of stores in predominantly black neighborhoods. He was well acquainted with black people, including low-income blacks, while growing up. Thus, when a research team with which he was working

---

[28] Elliot Liebow, *Tally's Corner* (Boston: Little, Brown & Company, 1967).

asked him to supplement data it was gathering on low-income child-rearing practices with field research on adult black males, Liebow welcomed the opportunity. The head of the research team directed him to a particular neighborhood and urged him to immerse himself in the day-to-day routines of ordinary people.

Liebow began hanging out in a local carry-out shop across from a street corner popular with neighborhood men. His race alone marked him as an outsider and people were curious (and some very suspicious) as to who he was and why he was there. When asked, Liebow simply explained he was "working on a study of family life in the city."[29] For most that was a sufficient explanation and little more was ever asked.

As weeks and months went by, Liebow worked to meet people. Slowly he made friends and built close personal relationships. Liebow came to move freely from the street corner and carry-out shop, to popular bars and alley hangouts, and to the homes of the men he befriended. His relationships extended not only to these men but to their families and other members of their networks.

All along Liebow knew, and certainly those whom he studied knew, that he was an outsider. This was obvious in terms of his race, occupation, residence, and speech. Despite this, Liebow states,

> I was also a participant in the full sense of the word. The people I was observing knew that I was observing them, yet they allowed me to participate in their activities and take part in their lives to a degree that continues to surprise me.[30]

Around the time that Liebow was conducting his field research, a number of social scientists were introducing a theory about poor people. The so-called culture of poverty theory argued that low-income people had a unique set of cultural values that set them apart from middle-class people and that in effect kept them poor. For example, it was suggested that low-income people have different values pertaining to work and that this gets in the way of economic success.

While he did not start out with the intention of doing so, Liebow's in-depth, day-in-and-day-out contacts with a group of low-income black men produced unique and invaluable data bearing on the culture of poverty theory. Unlike the theorists, Liebow had firsthand knowledge of how work is viewed and the values surrounding it.

Briefly, he found that many of the men were employed; they were unskilled laborers of different types, menial workers in retailing or other service areas. Others were unemployed; some, because of mental or physical disability, were unemployable. All, in one form or another, shared the values of the larger society pertaining to work. They saw work as important, both as a source of economic gain and security and as a source of self-identity and self-respect. The problem was the type of work available to them offered very little in these areas. In taking any jobs they were able to find, they perceived their work experience as demeaning and exploitative. At the same time, the men secretly suspected and feared that this was what they deserved, thus undermining any further aspirations.

Liebow's subjects clearly revealed they did not possess a unique set of cultural values with regard to work that kept them poor. Indeed, their sensitivity to mainstream values was underscored by Liebow's findings:

> The man sees middle-class occupations as a primary source of prestige, pride and self-respect; his own job affords him none of these. To think about his job is to see himself as others see him, to remind him of just where he stands in this society. And because society's criteria for placement are generally the same as his own, to talk about

[29] Ibid., p. 238.
[30] Ibid., p. 253.

> his job can trigger a flush of shame and a deep, almost physical ache to change places with someone, almost anyone else.[31]

Experiencing themselves as "losers," the men sought sanctuary on the street corner. There, among others of like situation, painful topics could be avoided and at least temporarily forgotten. The fun-loving, freewheeling public face became a "fiction" at which none of the men wished to look too closely.

While Liebow's work, like many other pieces of field research, produced findings about which one must be cautious in making wide generalizations, these findings illustrate the pain often accompanying poverty. This could be readily missed or simply assumed not to exist were our knowledge of poor people to be informed by less intensive methods of research.

Experimental Research

Sociologists and other social scientists at times have used experimental studies, similar in principle to experiments in the natural sciences, to study human beings. Such research has most commonly been conducted in laboratory settings and involved a limited number of individuals or small groups of people as subjects. Less common, though of interest to us here, are experiments conducted in "natural" (that is, nonlaboratory) settings.

Experimental research involves, in its simplest form, the creation of two groups of subjects. The first group, known as the "experimental group," is treated to carefully controlled conditions designed by the researcher. He or she is interested in the impact of these conditions on the thinking and/or behavior of members of the experimental group.

The second group, known as the "control group," is purposely *not* exposed to the researcher-designed conditions, which are commonly called the "experimental treatment." Nonetheless, the control group's members' thinking and/or behavior are also monitored. This is because the researcher wants to be sure what happens in the experimental group is due to the conditions he or she introduced and probably would not have occurred otherwise. The control group is thus very important to making that determination.

In short, those doing experimental research seek to ensure that the conditions introduced, and not some other factor or "variable," account for what is observed in the experimental group. Hence it is very important that characteristics of the members of both experimental and control groups not differ in any important way. By randomly assigning subjects to one or the other group, it is hoped that such differences will be minimized.

Typically experimental research is conducted with some kind of theory in mind; this guides researchers' choice of the conditions to impose on the experimental group. This is the case whether the research is taking place in the laboratory or in a natural setting. Exploratory goals are possible but generally are limited by the theory of interest to the researcher.

Laboratory experiments are most frequently employed by researchers who need to maximize their hold over the conditions to which both experimental and control groups are exposed. Precision may thus be attained, but observations made in a laboratory setting, involving a relatively small number of people, may be open to questions about the "real-life" applicability of the findings. This is somewhat similar to the issue of generalizability often faced by those conducting field research.

On the other hand, conducting experimental research in nonlaboratory or natural settings may sacrifice the quest for precision laboratory researchers enjoy. Moreover, there may be practical, administrative, financial, or ethical reasons why research in a natural setting cannot be done. For such reasons, this type of research is

[31] Ibid., p. 60.

less common than that conducted in the laboratory.

Probably the most common type of experimental research in a natural setting involves the attempt to assess the impact or effectiveness of government programs. In the example presented here, data were gathered to help policymakers project the possible effects of introducing a guaranteed minimum income for people finding themselves living in poverty. Both the findings and their interpretation have proven to be quite controversial, as different groups have jockeyed to use this research to pursue their own self-interests.

As mentioned earlier in this chapter, in the 1960s federal government officials declared a "war on poverty." It was hoped that by providing more services to low-income people—from job-training programs to legal aid—poverty could be defeated. This "service approach" was questioned by critics who saw poverty as a straightforwardly economic matter. They favored an "income approach" that would put more money, not simply services, in the hands of the poor. They argued that all families should be guaranteed a minimum income that would help them avoid poverty.

At that time little was known about the possible effects of an income approach, particularly its effects on the incentive of people to work and on marital stability. To investigate such matters the federal government began sponsorship of a series of experiments in the late 1960s. The largest, known as the Seattle–Denver Income Maintenance Experiment (SIME/DIME), began in 1970 and continued for almost a decade.[32]

Like the other experiments in the series, SIME/DIME involved a particular form of guaranteed income: the negative income tax, or NIT. The NIT has two important features. First is the "maximum benefit"—the annual amount of money a family is guaranteed if it has no other source of income. Second is the "benefit reduction rate," or tax rate at which the maximum benefit is reduced in response to a family's employment earnings. At a certain point, when the employment earnings become high enough, the tax rate reduces the cash benefit from the program to zero.

SIME/DIME involved almost 5,000 low-income families residing in Denver and Seattle. These families were randomly assigned to experimental and control groups. In the experimental group families were exposed to one or another of eleven maximum benefit and tax rates, as the researchers were interested in comparing the impacts of different versions of an NIT. The control group was not subject to NIT treatment but simply received income from any employment opportunities and/or government programs to which its members had access. Families in both experimental and control groups were periodically interviewed on a wide variety of matters it was thought could be affected by an NIT. These interviews took place during and immediately after the experiment.

A principal focus of the researchers was on work effort. It was theorized that a guaranteed income would be likely to reduce work effort, but there was only speculation as to how much. The results of the experiment did reveal some reduction, varying by subjects' role in the family, type of NIT benefit/tax rate, and other factors. For example, husbands in families receiving NIT treatment worked fewer hours annually than husbands in the control group. Yet controversy has arisen over how to interpret this statistical finding. It would seem that few persons who were employed left their jobs in response to the experimental treatment. Rather, experimental group husbands who became unemployed (defined as out of work but looking for a job) took more time to find work than did

---

[32] U.S. Department of Health and Human Services, *Overview of The Seattle–Denver Income Maintenance Final Report* (Washington, D.C.: U.S. Government Printing Office, 1983).

control group husbands. While some read this as a sign of lower incentive to work, others argued it was rational behavior given the very negative job experiences persons forced to take low-wage positions routinely face.

A second focus of the researchers was on marital stability. Critics of welfare in the United States have long argued that its bureaucratic regulations help to break up intact families. Half of all states refuse welfare benefits to homes with children in which both parents are present. Critics suggest this often forces desperate fathers to abandon their wives and children in return for their getting welfare assistance. Because the NIT experiment made income available to intact low-income families as well as single-parent families, researchers anticipated it would be a stabilizing force for families.

Did the NIT treatment help to keep families from breaking up? The answer is no. Marriages ended more frequently for couples in the experimental group than in the control group. Again, there was variation depending on the NIT plan to which the subjects were exposed and other factors. Still, controversy arose over these findings. Did families break up that never should have? Does an income guarantee provide women with economic security that allows escape from an unhappy marriage? Is marital dissolution for many a positive event as opposed to, by definition, a negative one?

The researchers made their findings public, subjecting both the findings and the research methods that led to them to critical scrutiny. They were scrupulous in underscoring the fact that the SIME/DIME sample is nationally unrepresentative and that their findings, although suggestive, cannot simply be extrapolated to a permanent national NIT program. The researchers also acknowledged the difficulty of interpreting findings such as those we have looked at here. In stark contrast, politicians and others with relatively little sympathy for the plight of poor people have been uninterested in the researchers' wise cautions.[33] To them the message of the findings was that an NIT broke up families and fostered indolence. The cautions and ambiguity surrounding the findings were thus put to political use to derail further consideration of an "income approach" to reduce the economic distress of poor people. But the uses to which findings from this particular research were put notwithstanding, experiments in natural settings offer another method for studying how people deal with their environment and its problems.

SUMMARY

In this introduction we have looked at various approaches to the study of social problems and have set forth the approach that will be followed in this text. We began with an overview of the two approaches that have dominated the field. The *social pathology approach* saw deviant behavior as the major social problem and blamed this behavior on biological and psychological deficiencies of the people involved. The *social disorganization approach*, on the other hand, focused on disruptions in social life as the cause of social problems. Like the social pathology approach, this approach tends to focus on deviant behavior of individuals.

The *critical approach* to social problems looks mainly at problems in the structure and organization of society. Like the two older approaches, the critical approach identifies social problems on the basis of moral and political judgments. Such judgments are inevitable when deeming something to be a "problem." The judgments behind our critical approach are set forth within the context of our vision of or hope for society.

Macro problems are organizational features of

---

[33] See Kenneth J. Neubeck and Jack L. Roach, "Income Maintenance Experiments, Politics and the Perpetuation of Poverty," *Social Problems*, 28 (February 1981): 308–20.

society that do harm to millions of people, while *micro problems* involve individuals whose behavior is self-harmful or has an adverse impact on others. The reduction or elimination of macro problems may well require an eventual transformation of the ways in which society is organized.

The *life cycle* or career of a social problem is a political process in which power plays a decisive role. As problems enter public awareness, those who benefit from the maintenance of the status quo have a stake in ensuring that the accepted causes and solutions do not infringe upon their perceived self-interest. In practical terms, this means that macro problems—even when they somehow are brought into public awareness—may fail to be "solved." Since preferred solutions tend to be those that do not disrupt the prevailing order, macro problems tend to remain with us.

The degree to which a solution to a macro problem can be incorporated into the prevailing order will affect what is done about it. At the same time, dominant groups have no real reason to discourage public awareness and concern with micro problems, since attacks on these can more easily be accommodated without appreciably altering the status quo.

Sociologists and other social scientists, in seeking to learn more about social problems, conduct research using different methods. Surveys, field research, and experiments in natural settings provide means for objective, systematic inquiry. The findings may be of theoretical importance and at times become politically controversial.

DISCUSSION QUESTIONS

1. What is the most serious social problem facing us today? Discuss the criteria you used to choose this problem.
2. Are people who are poor, or mentally troubled, or involved in heavy drug use "normal"? What assumptions or set of values does your answer to this question reflect?
3. Edward Banfield blames the plight of America's urban slum-dwellers on their attitudes and behavior—a case of personal attribution. What factors would one look to if trying to explain the slum-dwellers' plight in terms of systemic attribution?
4. Look at the front page of today's newspaper. What "social problems" are reported? Take one problem and discuss alternative solutions to it, considering the individual or group self-interests the various solutions would affect.
5. The mass media, according to Ross and Staines, play a major role in rendering problems into public issues. What does this suggest about the significance of the attitudes and values of those who own or work for the mass media?
6. It is not necessary that you share the same vision of the ideal society that the author sets forth. Where do you disagree? What elements or characteristics of the ideal society would you eliminate or add? Why?

SUGGESTED READINGS

Finsterbusch, Kurt. *Taking Sides: Clashing Views on Controversial Social Issues*, 6th ed. (Guilford, Conn.: Dushkin Publishing Group, 1990).
Dissenting opinions on a wide range of issues, from population growth to crime in the streets.

Horton, John. "Order and Conflict Theories of Social Problems," *American Journal of Sociology*, 71 (May 1966): 701–13.
Classic statement on the assumptions underlying opposing views of who and what are social problems.

Lewontin, R. C., Steven Rose, and Leon J. Kamin. *Not in Our Genes* (New York: Pantheon Books, 1984).
Comprehensive critique of theories that reduce explanations for complex human behaviors down to biological factors.

Nock, Steven L., and Paul W. Kingston. *The Sociology of Public Issues* (Belmont, Calif.: Wadsworth Publishing Company, 1990).
Uses sociology to critically evaluate public issues as presented in the mass media.

Rubington, Earl, and Martin S. Weinberg, eds. *The Study of Social Problems,* 4th ed. (New York: Oxford University Press, 1989).
Examination of several alternative perspectives on social problems, with illustrative readings.

Ryan, William. *Blaming the Victim,* rev. ed. (New York: Vintage Books, 1976).
Explores examples of the tendency to blame individuals for the social problems in which they are caught up (e.g., blaming poor people for poverty).

PART I

Macro Problems

1. The Global Context: Population and Underdevelopment
2. Concentration of Political and Economic Power
3. Militarism and War
4. Environmental Abuse
5. Work
6. Economic Inequality and Poverty
7. Schooling and Unequal Educational Opportunity
8. Racism
9. Sexism
10. Ageism
11. Health Care

The study of social problems is demanding. It is also important, for it is through such study that we may begin to understand and to seek ways to alter conditions that may be harming millions of people. As we saw in the Introduction, when harmful conditions become public issues there is hope of significant change and improvement.

In the first part of this book we address eleven *macro problems*—societal features that stand in the way of members' individual and collective development. Macro problems are not mere intellectual constructs; they are very real conditions that are part of people's everyday lives.

We begin this book with an overview of conditions affecting most of humanity. Today when we look outside the United States, we see a world afflicted by very high rates of population growth, often accompanied by conditions of chronic malnutrition and poor health. Chapter 1 explores some of the societal features that contribute to these conditions and suggests that the instability arising from such conditions in poor nations ultimately will affect us as well.

Within our own society our ability to adapt to demands from the global context within which we must operate, as well as domestic demands, makes the topic of power relevant. The slang expression "money talks" reflects the fact that at the national level government seems to be conducted largely by affluent people and their appointees (Chapter 2). Moreover, important constraints on national political decision making may exist because of the demands of our corporate capitalist economic system. Profits may thus come before the needs of the victims of social problems.

Our economy depends greatly on defense and preparation for war. This defense spending is fed by federal tax dollars at rates unprecedented in peacetime (Chapter 3). Moreover, the use of these funds by the military precludes their use to improve the overall quality of life. Such proliferation of weaponry, both at home and abroad (through export sales), increases the probability of war, including war that might involve nuclear weapons.

To some degree America's economic development has been pursued at the cost of environmental safety (Chapter 4). By gobbling up natural resources, some of which are irreplaceable, by manufacturing ecologically questionable products, and by spewing harmful wastes into the air, water, and earth, our economic institutions have been destroying the natural environment. Unless this process stops, future generations will be threatened.

Our economic system influences everyone's life through the medium of work (Chapter 5). Yet the U.S. economy is not organized to provide work for all those who want and need it. The structure and content of many jobs create stress and dissatisfaction even for many who are employed. Recognition of the centrality of work in people's lives must be forthcoming and work force participation must be made a more positive and meaningful experience.

Partly because of the ways in which the means of production are owned and work opportunities are distributed, distribution of income and wealth is seriously uneven in the United States. A small number of people enjoy almost unimaginable luxury while millions of others subsist at the poverty level (Chapter 6). In recent years the situation has been growing worse. Until we create mechanisms to reduce the vast gap between rich and poor, the life chances of many Americans will be extremely limited.

Economic inequality is directly reflected in the amount and quality of formal education we have available (Chapter 7). Bright children from poor families are far less likely to go to college and to finish there than are similar children from more affluent families. Since educational credentials influence where one will enter the occupational hierarchy, unequal educational opportunities result in wasted talent.

In terms of income, wealth, and occupational achievement, minority groups are grossly disadvantaged in comparison with the majority white population (Chapter 8). While formal practices of discrimination and exploitation have been banned by legislative and judicial actions, subtle practices of racism continue. Consequently, interracial tension, periodic conflict, and suppression of talent that could be used for the benefit of all continue.

Sexism, again often subtle, works to place women at a disadvantage in comparison with men (Chapter 9). Males hold a monopoly over America's opportunity structure—in education, employment, and politics—and frequently thwart the potential contributions of women.

All of us, of whatever group, grow older. The treatment of older Americans is often based on stereotypical thinking and is fraught with subtle forms of discrimination (Chapter 10). Ageism, whether engaged in by individuals or institutions, creates problems for the older members of U.S. society. Since most of us will join this particular "minority group," we have a vested interest in combating maltreatment of its members.

Millions of Americans lack access to quality, affordable health care (Chapter 11). Our collective health status falls short of that achieved in other Western industrialized societies. Our inadequate health care system now faces new demands from the AIDS epidemic and the chronic health needs of our growing population of elders. We all depend on health care and must play a role in its improvement.

Problems, such as the macro problems to be discussed, invite solutions. Some of us are more or less hopeful than others that such solutions are likely to be forthcoming in our own lifetimes. Making a real effort to understand macro problems is an important first step, without which discussion of solutions does not make sense. We hope the first eleven chapters help you toward this understanding and that they stimulate you to become part of the solution process.

CHAPTER 1

The Global Context: Population and Underdevelopment

Our relationship with poor, underdeveloped nations should be nonexploitative and supportive of movements to secure basic human rights.

INTRODUCTION

If you have been fortunate enough to travel abroad and happened to be exposed to the mass media in nations you visited, you may have seen substantial news space devoted to the United States. The reverse is less often the case: U.S. media tell us comparatively little about what is going on in the countries you may have visited. Citizens elsewhere often are very interested in and surprisingly aware of U.S. affairs. They are also often very sensitive to the political and economic relationships between their own nations and others, including our own. In contrast, we seem myopic.

Ignorance and lack of awareness are dangerous. Catch phrases such as the "global village" and "spaceship earth," popular in recent years, underscore an important fact: Humanity's 5.25 billion members occupy a relatively small planet with finite resources. The fate of any one segment of that population is tied to that of every other segment. In effect, a society's fortunes are determined to a large degree by the global context within which it operates. The United States is not an exception.

Ignorance of the global context within which U.S. society functions is at times accompanied by a rather distorted view of our role in the world at large. In its extreme this view may hold that the United States has produced the best society that has ever existed, that no other way of life even approaches ours, that all other nations should emulate us, and that our superiority as a people gives us the right (and responsibility) to police the rest of the world, using force when necessary to protect our vested interests. This is more than patriotism, which involves love of and loyalty to one's country, and it goes beyond nationalism, which emphasizes devotion to the interests of one's nation. Rather, it is a type of *ethnocentrism,* which is the inability to understand other societies except in terms of one's own. In ethnocentric terms, the "American Way" becomes the revered standard against which other nations are measured and by definition fall short. In this way indifference toward, and even maltreatment of, other nations can be justified. As Ian Robertson points out,

> [Ethnocentrism] can encourage racism, it can cause hostility and conflict between groups, and it can make a people unwilling to recognize the need for changes in their own culture.[1]

The global context in which our society functions is not always apparent to us, but it involves problems that are reaching crisis proportions and that are inflicting incredible suffering on hundreds of millions of our fellow human beings. Ethnocentrism poses obstacles to the rational discussion of these problems and gets in the way of the pursuit of solutions. Yet the handling of such problems now may well determine the human prospect for generations to come.[2]

Our first concern in this chapter is world population growth, with primary attention paid to underdeveloped nations (often referred to as the "Third World"), where most of humanity lives. Then we focus on the life chances presently available to citizens of such nations. Their life chances are severely limited by hunger, malnutrition, and starvation; by ill health and susceptibility to preventable disease; and by extremely high rates of infant mortality and low life expectancy.

Many would argue that high rates of population growth, and thus overpopulation, cause life chances to be limited in underdeveloped nations. However, we approach these topics from a different angle. High population growth rates and severely limited life chances among citizens of underdeveloped nations will be understood largely as *outcomes* of a fact that too often is ignored: The gross economic inequality in these nations and the widespread poverty resulting from the policies and fact of a small ruling political elite.

Yet underdeveloped nations exist in a world context. Thus, in the final pages of this chapter we discuss some of the relationships between underdeveloped nations and developed nations such as our own. Does the United States contribute in any way to the underdevelopment of other nations? Does the United States benefit from world poverty? What is our position toward movements seeking fundamental change—political, economic, and social—in underdeveloped nations? This chapter closes with comments on the instabilities inherent in the relationships between developed nations and their poverty-stricken counterparts.

---

[1] Ian Robertson, *Sociology,* 2nd ed. (New York: Worth Publishers, 1981), p. 67.

[2] For a provocative set of speculations about the future, see Robert L. Heilbroner, *An Inquiry into the Human Prospect,* rev. ed. (New York: W. W. Norton & Company, 1980).

WORLD POPULATION GROWTH

The earth's population is growing relentlessly,[3] currently at an estimated rate of 1.6 percent annually, which means that each year there are 84 million or more human beings than there were the year before. (These statistics are estimates because of the unreliability of census figures.) This fact has caused some to fear that humanity is beginning to tax the resources of the planet and has raised the specter of widespread struggles between have and have-not nations.

The 5.25 billion people who now occupy this planet could easily grow to over 6 billion by the end of this century and to over 8 billion by the year 2025. To understand what is going on we must explore briefly some of the dynamics of world population growth. It is particularly important to see where this growth is most rapid. As we shall see, "technological" solutions, such as increased use of birth-control devices, are likely to have only limited impact on overall growth rates.

The phrase *population explosion* is an apt description of the real situation. Indeed, it was not until the 1960s that world population growth even became a serious international issue. The rapidity and abruptness with which the population increase burst on the world have been underscored by Erik Eckholm:

> Two thousand years ago humans scarcely numbered 250 million; only in the early 1800s did the figure reach one billion. A second billion was added in one hundred years, a third in thirty years, and a fourth in just the fifteen years from 1960 to 1975.[4]

To get from that 4 billion in 1975 to over 8 billion people in the year 2025 involves a doubling of the earth's population in a mere 50 years!

The statistics denoting population growth are based on two factors that deserve attention: (1) birth rate (expressed as the number of births per 1,000 members of the population in a given year) and (2) death rate (the number of deaths in a given year per 1,000 members of the population). When one subtracts the number of deaths from the number of births, the result is usually expressed as an annual percentage called the *growth rate.* As mentioned earlier, the world population growth rate is now 1.6 percent annually. (This is down from a high of 2 percent in 1970.)

An annual growth rate of 1.6 percent may seem modest, but the growth is exponential (i.e., each year's growth rate is applied to the size the population grew to the previous year), so that the so-called doubling time of a population is relatively short. For example, at a 1 percent rate of growth a population doubles in 70 years; at 2 percent only 35 years is required.

GROWTH IN DEVELOPED VS. UNDERDEVELOPED NATIONS

It is important to emphasize the differences in rates of population change among nations. The developed nations—the most affluent, heavily industrialized, consumer-oriented societies—are located primarily in the Northern Hemisphere and tend to have low growth rates. For example, the U.S. growth rate is 0.7 percent, and in Europe there are about a dozen nations where the annual births and deaths are roughly equal, resulting in nearly zero population growth. Overall, the average annual growth rate for developed nations is 0.6 percent.

In contrast, the "underdeveloped" nations tend to have much higher population growth rates. (See Figure 1.1.) These are generally poor nations with very limited industrial activity and low levels of consumption and are located mostly in the Southern Hemisphere. Most hu-

---

[3] Discussion on population draws heavily on Erik P. Eckholm, *Down to Earth: Environment and Human Needs* (New York: W. W. Norton & Company, 1982), pp. 37–48, and Lester R. Brown, "Analyzing the Demographic Trap," in Worldwatch Institute, *State of the World 1987* (New York: W. W. Norton & Company, 1987), pp. 20–37.

[4] Eckholm, *Down to Earth,* p. 37.

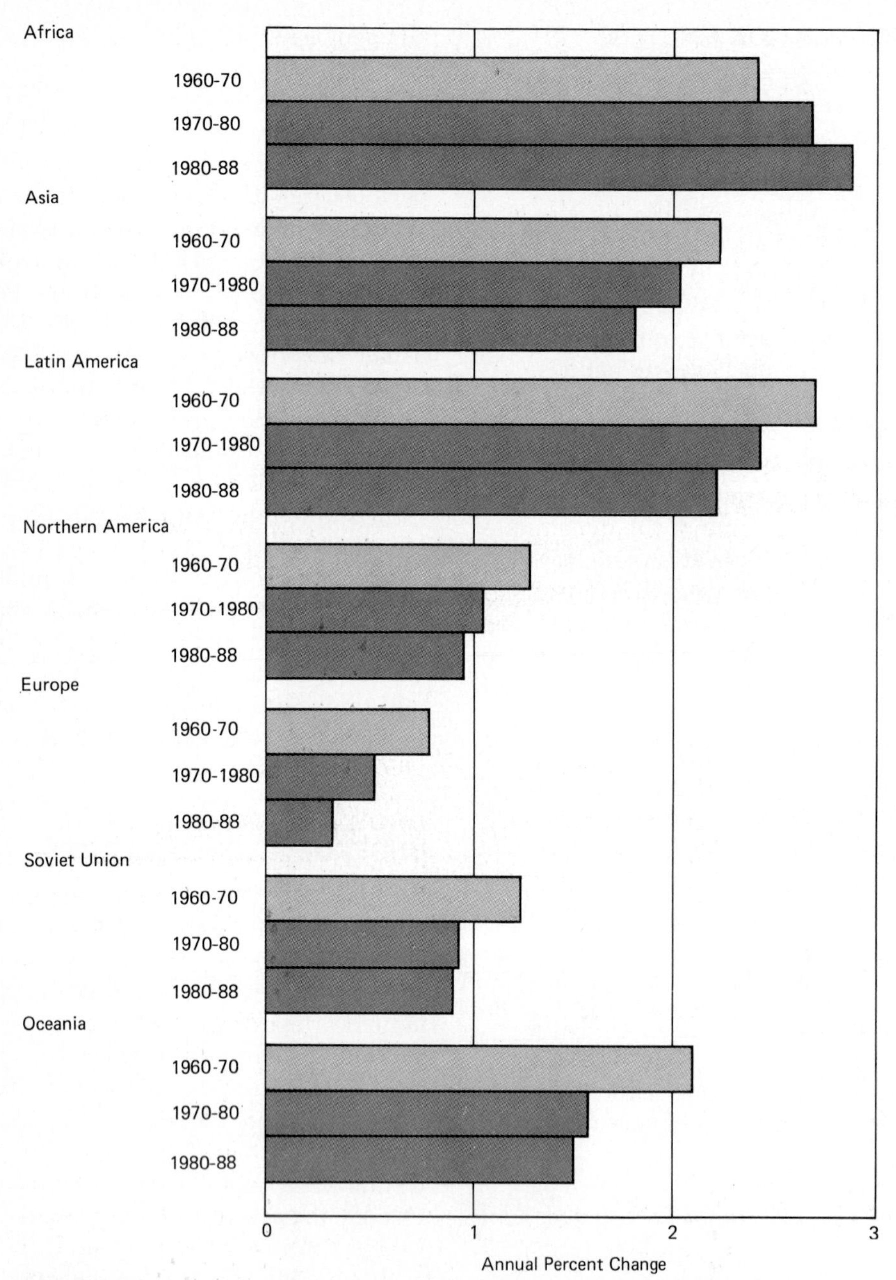

FIGURE 1.1 World Population—Annual Growth Rate, by Continent: 1960–88
Source: U.S. Department of Commerce, Bureau of the Census, *Statistical Abstract of the United States, 1989* (Washington, D.C.: U.S. Government Printing Office, 1989), p. 808.

man beings—*some 75 percent*—live in underdeveloped nations! The population growth rate for such nations now averages over 2 percent annually. If present trends continue, an even higher percentage of the world's population will live in the underdeveloped nations. If, as has been projected, the present world population grows to over 8 billion in 2025, almost 7 billion persons will then be living outside the nations of affluence. (See Table 1.1.) Many will be our near neighbors in Latin America.

Some differences in population growth rates do exist among underdeveloped nations. For instance, the People's Republic of China, a nation of over 1 billion people, has a growth rate of 1 percent annually. However, India, with a quarter fewer people than China, has a much higher growth rate (2.3 percent). At the present rates of growth India will surpass China as the world's largest single nation by the year 2010.

Latin America has an overall growth rate of 2.3 percent, a figure that clearly is very high. But the highest rates today (and for the foreseeable future) are found on the African continent. Population there is growing, on the average, at 2.8 percent per year. In nations such as Nigeria, with a 3 percent population growth rate, the term *population explosion* becomes most apt. Nigeria, a nation of 52 million people in 1960, could have 532 million people by the middle of the twenty-first century, almost as many people as were alive in all of Africa in the mid-1980s.[5]

We shall turn shortly to some of the reasons for high population growth rates. But first let us focus on the life chances presently available to many people in those nations where population is growing most rapidly.

[5] Brown "Analyzing the Demographic Trap," p. 23.

LIFE CHANCES AND UNDERDEVELOPMENT

We have seen that the bulk of humanity lives in the underdeveloped nations of the world, where population growth rates are typically quite high. In this section we discuss two interrelated factors that limit life chances for hundreds of millions of people: chronic malnutrition or "undernutrition" and poor health.

Hunger may afflict people for different reasons. Historically, periods of famine have been relatively common. Famine may occur as a result of a natural catastrophe (e.g., severe flooding or prolonged drought) or of human actions (as when people are involuntarily displaced from their homes and lands during war). Famines occur for these reasons today, although with modern communication and transportation it is at times possible to limit their devastating effects somewhat by timely relief efforts.

In late 1984 United Nations disaster relief officials and officials of the International Red Cross drew attention to severe drought-related famines in 27 African nations (while noting that food shortages exist in all areas of Africa). Seventeen of these were said to be especially hard hit, with over 35 million people desperately hungry. In Ethiopia alone 6 million to 7 million human beings were facing starvation and death. Television news programs showed the dead and dying in living color during Americans' evening dinner hour, prompting outcries to the U.S. government. Private relief agencies increased their efforts. The citizens of other developed nations were similarly moved by the horrors in Ethiopia and sent aid. Yet aid experts indicated that even with relief on the way, the death toll across Africa would be extremely high. The weakest—infants and children—would die first and in large numbers.

But hunger is not always a matter of emergent conditions that create temporary food scarcity. Hundreds of millions of human beings live

TABLE 1.1 World Population and Vital Statistics, by Continent and Region, 1970–88, and Projections, 1990 and 2000 (in millions)

Continent and region	Midyear Population (millions)					Annual rate of growth* (%)			Crude birth rate		Crude death rate		Total fertility rate (number)		Life expectancy (years)	
	1970	1980	1988	1990	2000	1970–1980	1980–1990	1990–2000	1988	2000	1988	2000	1988	2000	1988	2000
World total	**3,721**	**4,476**	**5,143**	**5,320**	**6,241**	**1.8**	**1.7**	**1.6**	**26.8**	**23.2**	**9.7**	**8.4**	**3.49**	**3.04**	**61.3**	**65.0**
More developed regions	1,049	1,137	1,196	1,211	1,269	.8	.6	.5	14.9	13.3	9.7	9.7	1.95	1.91	73.3	75.6
Less developed regions	2,672	3,339	3,945	4,109	4,971	2.2	2.1	1.9	30.4	25.8	9.7	8.1	3.96	3.33	59.5	63.6
Percent of world	72	75	77	77	80	(x)	(x)	(x)	(x)	(x)	(x)	(x)	(x)	(x)	(x)	(x)
Africa†	376	493	622	660	887	2.7	2.9	3.0	43.9	39.4	14.1	10.7	6.26	5.48	52.7	57.7
Asia	2,111	2,594	3,004	3,111	3,655	2.1	1.8	1.6	27.1	22.3	9.1	7.8	3.44	2.81	61.0	65.3
More developed regions	104	117	123	124	129	1.1	.6	.4	11.9	12.6	7.1	9.0	1.79	1.78	77.8	78.5
Less developed regions	2,007	2,477	2,882	2,988	3,526	2.1	1.9	1.7	27.7	22.7	9.2	7.7	3.51	2.85	60.7	65.0
East Asia	991	1,181	1,304	1,334	1,481	1.8	1.2	1.0	18.9	15.2	6.7	6.7	2.20	1.79	69.4	73.1
South Asia	1,120	1,412	1,700	1,777	2,174	2.3	2.3	2.0	33.4	27.2	10.9	8.5	4.39	3.51	57.3	62.4
Latin America†	286	365	436	455	551	2.4	2.2	1.9	29.1	23.9	7.1	6.1	3.62	2.92	66.8	70.4
Middle America†	70	93	112	116	141	2.9	2.2	2.0	29.8	24.3	6.3	5.3	3.65	2.75	67.8	71.4
Caribbean†	25	29	33	34	39	1.6	1.4	1.4	25.3	21.1	8.2	7.2	2.98	2.60	65.8	69.0
South America†	191	242	291	304	370	2.4	2.3	2.0	29.3	24.0	7.2	6.2	3.68	3.02	66.5	70.2
Northern America‡	226	252	272	277	296	1.1	.9	.7	15.2	12.5	8.6	8.9	1.84	1.84	75.5	76.9
Europe‡	460	484	497	499	510	.5	.3	.2	13.2	12.1	10.6	10.6	1.76	1.76	74.3	75.9
Soviet Union‡	243	266	286	291	312	.9	.9	.7	18.8	16.2	10.6	9.4	2.45	2.27	68.9	73.2
Oceania	19	23	26	26	30	1.6	1.5	1.3	19.8	17.7	8.1	8.3	2.58	2.37	69.2	71.2
Australia and New Zealand‡	15	18	20	20	22	1.4	1.2	1.0	15.6	14.0	7.7	8.3	1.92	1.92	75.9	76.9
Less developed regions	4	5	6	6	8	2.5	2.4	2.2	34.0	29.4	9.5	8.2	4.81	3.79	59.0	62.6

[Crude birth rate, number of births during 1 year per 1,000 persons (based on midyear population). Crude death rate, number of deaths during 1 year per 1,000 persons (based on midyear population). Total fertility rate, average number of children that would be born per woman if all women lived to the end of their childbearing years and, at each year of age, they experienced the birth rates occurring in the specified year.]

Key: X, not applicable.

*Computed by the exponential method.

†Less developed regions.

‡More developed region.

Source: U.S. Department of Commerce, Bureau of the Census, *Statistical Abstract of the United States, 1989* (Washington, D.C.: U.S. Government Printing Office, 1989), p. 812.

Hunger and malnutrition are widespread in most underdeveloped nations. Famine situations have become commonplace across the African continent. In this photo a mother and child who have fled famine and civil war in Ethiopia await food in a rescue clinic in the neighboring nation of Sudan. (*Sarah Putnam/The Picture Cube*)

routine daily lives in which they are in no danger of outright starvation. Yet they are in a state of chronic malnutrition or "undernutrition." For such persons food scarcity is a never-ending way of life.

We who live in developed nations are often worried about being overweight. For many in the underdeveloped world, however, the average person consumes two-thirds of our calorie intake and one-half of our protein consumption. The average American takes in a hefty 3,000 or more calories per day; hundreds of millions of people elsewhere must function with far less.

It is difficult for experts to determine the extent of chronic malnutrition. One difficulty lies in objectively defining malnutrition. How many calories are needed for people to function up to their physical and mental potential? How much protein must a diet have to be adequate? Nutritional experts disagree over the answers to such questions, but the numbers of people considered to be in dietary need depend on these answers.

In the 1960s the United Nations Food and Agriculture Organization (FAO) estimated that some 1.5 billion people were malnourished—at that time nearly half of the world's population. Later, in the mid-1970s, the figure was reduced to less than 0.5 billion people. Was chronic malnutrition miraculously reduced? Hardly. The FAO simply revised downward its definition of the amount of calories and protein needed in an adequate diet. Still, the lower figure encompassed a quarter of the population of underdeveloped nations.[6]

Chronic malnutrition may not be as visible as famine-related hunger, but its effects are severe. One such effect is a much greater susceptibility to disease. Those who are particularly at risk include women attempting to breast feed, infants, and small children. In biologist William W. Murdoch's words,

> Malnutrition probably is the biggest single contributor to the high childhood mortality in the developing countries.... In Latin America malnutrition is a primary or contributory factor in over half of the deaths of children under five.... The FAO reports that more than 300 million children [in underdeveloped nations] have grossly retarded physical growth as a result of poor diets. Perhaps most serious, mental health may be irreversibly damaged, since the brain completes most of its growth and development in the first two years.[7]

The life chances of the poorest world citizens are reduced by poor health. Lost battles with illness and disease are reflected in statistics on life expectancy. (See Table 1.2.) In developed nations average life expectancy is in the seventies. Yet there are many countries in Africa and Asia where on average people die in their forties and fifties. Our middle age is old age to others. Moreover, the very young die at astonishing rates. Consider the following:[8]

> In many developed nations the death rate among infants in their first year of life is less than 1 in 100; in some African and Asian nations it is 1 in 5.
>
> In developed nations deaths during childhood are infrequent (1 per 1,000 persons in the population annually), and most are due to accidents. Children under five account for half of *all* deaths in underdeveloped nations, with most dying from disease.
>
> Fourteen million infants and children under five die each year in underdeveloped nations; if these nations' health care resources were equivalent to those in northern Europe, most of these deaths would be prevented.

A simple doctor's prescription written not for medicine but for *food* is often the first requirement for the prevention of disease. Malnourished children do not fight disease well; moreover, some diseases reduce the body's ability to assimilate food.

What are some of the other conditions that affect the health of people in underdeveloped nations? Such conditions often include:

> Extreme shortages of uncontaminated water, so necessary for personal hygiene, drinking, cooking, and the cleansing of eating and cooking utensils and clothing.
>
> Nonexistent or inadequate means of disposing of human and animal excrement and other wastes that are linked to disease.
>
> Daily exposure to numerous infectious parasites that thrive in water and in soil, including hookworm and roundworm.

As a result of such conditions, diarrheal and other intestinal illnesses are rampant in the underdeveloped world, resulting in tens of millions of deaths annually. Once again the impact on children is greatest: "Known to the well-off as an occasional nuisance, diarrhea is one of the world's major killers, taking at least five million children's lives a year."[9] Diarrhea often leads to severe dehydration, inability to assimilate nutrients, and loss of strength to fight off new disease. Debilitated people are vulnerable to diseases that most of us will never experi-

---

[6] William W. Murdoch, *The Poverty of Nations* (Baltimore: The Johns Hopkins University Press, 1980), pp. 95–97.

[7] Ibid., pp. 99 and 101.

[8] See Erik P. Eckholm, *Down to Earth,* Chapter 4, and his *The Picture of Health* (New York: W. W. Norton & Company, 1977). Recent trends are assessed in United Nations Children's Fund, *The State of the World's Children, 1988* (New York: Oxford University Press, 1988).

[9] Eckholm, *Down to Earth,* p. 54.

TABLE 1.2 Key Differences Between a Selected Group of the Poorest and Richest Nations

	GNP per Capita Dollars 1986	Life expectancy at birth (years) 1986	Births attended by health staff (%) 1984	Maternal mortality (per 100,000 live births) 1980	Infant mortality (per 1,000 live births) 1986
		Poorest Nations			
Low-income economies	270	61	—	329	69
China and India	300	64	—	237	56
Other low-income	200	52	52	607	106
Ethiopia	120	46	58	2,000	155
Bhutan	150	45	3	—	139
Burkina Faso	150	47	—	—	140
Nepal	150	47	10	850	130
Bangladesh	160	50	—	600	121
Malawi	160	45	59	250	153
Zaire	160	52	—	800	100
Mali	180	47	—	—	144
Myanmar	200	59	97	135	64
Mozambique	210	48	28	479	120
Madagascar	230	53	62	300	130
Uganda	230	48	—	300	105
Burundi	240	48	12	—	114
Tanzania	250	53	74	370	108
Togo	250	53	—	476	96
Niger	260	44	47	581	135
Benin	270	50	34	1,680	117
Somalia	280	47	2	1,100	134
Central African Republic	290	50	—	600	134
India	290	57	33	500	86
Rwanda	290	48	—	210	116
China	300	69	—	44	34
Kenya	300	57	—	510	74
Zambia	300	53	—	140	82
Sierra Leone	310	41	25	450	154
		Richest Nations			
Spain	4,860	76	96	11	11
Ireland	5,070	74	—	7	9
New Zealand	7,460	74	99	14	11
Italy	8,550	77	—	13	10
United Kingdom	8,870	75	98	—	9
Belgium	9,230	75	100	10	10
Austria	9,990	74	—	11	10
Netherlands	10,020	77	—	5	8
France	10,720	77	—	13	8
Australia	11,920	78	99	11	10
Germany, West	12,080	75	—	11	9
Finland	12,160	75	—	5	6
Denmark	12,600	75	—	4	8
Japan	12,840	78	100	15	6
Sweden	13,160	77	100	4	6
Canada	14,120	76	99	2	8
Norway	15,400	77	100	4	9
United States	17,480	75	100	9	10
Switzerland	17,680	77	—	5	7

Source: The World Bank, *World Development Report, 1988* (New York: Oxford University Press, 1988). Data on the poorest nations adapted from pp. 222 and 286; data on the richest nations adapted from pp. 223 and 287.

PUBLIC PROBLEM, PRIVATE PAIN

Exposing the Hunger of the World's Poor ...

Blaine Harden is in Africa as a correspondent for The Washington Post. *In this capacity he has visited Ethiopia, one of many African nations where people face famine, disease, and premature death. Here he describes not only what he saw, but the emotions he experienced as a visitor and newcomer to the Third World.*

"Mister Blaine, a woman, her baby died. You want to interview her?"

The questioner was my "minder," an employee of the Ethiopian Ministry of Information and National Guidance, an impresario of countless press tours of the feeding camps where starving Ethiopians are available to reporters.

We were at Korem, a camp of 45,000, inside the hospital, a long shed of corrugated tin, with a dirt floor and stone beds.

The air was sour with the smell of excrement. There was little noise but for coughing and the clink of bedpans. The mother whose baby had just died was waiting for me outside.

I went to Ethiopia late last year to get the particulars on the great famine, to put in words what millions were seeing on television at suppertime every night.

A grieving mother with a newly dead child was precisely what I was after. So I followed my minder (and my translator) out of the shed.

We found the mother, Sakarto, a girl of about 19, standing stiffly, tears running down her cheeks, beside a hospital worker who was holding a tiny body. The baby was wrapped in a gray blanket.

For 15 minutes, as Sakarto wept and the hospital worker stood by with the baby in his arms, I interviewed her.

How long had she walked to get to Korem? One and a half days.

Where was her husband? Gone, resettled by the government 1,000 miles to the southwest.

Did she expect to join him? No.

Would she let me take her picture? Yes.

I was out of film and asked Sakarto to wait while I walked back to a Jeep, about a quarter of a mile away, to reload my camera.

I returned to find the mother standing unmoved in the equatorial highland sun. She waited, as if fearing punishment from me: a white foreigner whose face was hidden behind dark sunglasses, a baseball cap and a zoom lens.

When I finished taking pictures and asking more questions, I turned away. I felt ashamed, and I cried for a few minutes.

The point of telling this story is not to expiate my guilt for having been a ghoul, although there may be something to that, but rather to get at the jumble of confused emotions an American and newcomer to the Third World feels as a temporary voyeur amid tens of thousands of dispossessed human beings.

Most notably, there was emptiness. The distance between Sakarto and me, in language and culture, made our interview a charade. I believe she thought I was a doctor. I came no closer to her than if I had seen her on television.

My feeling for Sakarto had less to do with her and her country's poverty than with me and my country's wealth.

At Korem, as at other large feeding (and dying) camps across Ethiopia, nearly everyone was visibly ill.

Heads were shaved to get rid of lice. Arms were painted a shocking violet, with antiseptic dye, to kill scabies. Tuberculosis and leprosy, dysentery and gastroenteritis, eye infections and skin diseases were epidemic. Sakarto's fingertips were falling off.... .

In places like Korem, all I managed to do was look at starving people. Interviews with them elicited responses that, after being processed by my government-paid translator, were bleached of any emotion.

Unless they cried in front of me, I didn't have any idea what these curiously passive people were thinking or feeling, what they were afraid of, what sense of panic or shame the famine had forced upon them.

In this vacuum I wrote about what famine looks like: two-dimensional surface descriptions that painted victims, not human beings.

Only when children crowded around us during our guided tours did I, or most of the other Western famine-watchers, have a chance to actually touch anyone in the feeding camps.

The children had amazing recuperative power. With regular meals of rice porridge and a high-energy goop made of milk, butter oil and sugar, they metamorphosed in a couple of weeks from immobile skeletons to giggling kids.

At the feeding camps these kids ran to be near foreigners. They wanted to hold hands. Sometimes four or five of them would try to touch one of my hands, each attempting to claim a finger. When they had a finger, they would throw their heads back, look up at me and smile.

Back in my hotel we had discussed this hand-holding at some length. The children don't use toilet paper, we had said. Their cute little hands carry all kinds of diseases.

One representative of the U.S. Information Service said at lunch at the Addis Ababa Hilton that his wife thought anyone who feared touching the children was a jerk.

In the feeding camps, with children bobbing around my knees, begging to touch my hands, sometimes I would let them hold my fingers. Sometimes I would not.

Source: Blaine Harden, "Exposing the Hunger of the World's Poor," *Hartford Courant* (April 16, 1985): B9.

ence. In tropical climates these include malaria and schistosomiasis (a disease caused by parasites in the blood vessels and involving disorders of the liver, bladder, lungs, or central nervous system). A million children under five die of malaria each year. But people who are so weakened by diarrheal and other intestinal diseases even die of illnesses we take in stride, such as measles, which kills almost 2 million children under five each year.

A major goal of the World Health Organization is "Health for All by the Year 2000." Conditions such as those just mentioned—coupled with a severe, if not complete, lack of modern health care—make this praiseworthy goal seem hopelessly far-fetched.

RELATIONSHIP BETWEEN POVERTY AND POPULATION GROWTH

How is one to make sense of spiraling population growth? What is its relationship to the poverty-stricken conditions in which so many suffer in underdeveloped nations? Does population growth result in poverty, or does poverty lead to population? The answers will dictate the appropriate strategies for bringing growth rates under control.

The conventional wisdom holds that population growth produces poverty. It is argued that too many people are engaging in sexual relations without effective birth control, resulting in high birth rates. The problem is exacerbated by the preponderance of young people, capable of procreation, in underdeveloped nations.

This view goes on to suggest that the numbers of people to be fed overwhelm food-producing resources, creating food scarcity and subsequent health problems. The solution that follows from this conventional wisdom is to emphasize family planning. Ignorance, superstition, and any other source of resistance to family planning must be overcome.

Few would argue that population growth is irrelevant to a nation's economic circumstances. It seems obvious that any effort to overcome underdevelopment in a poverty-stricken nation might well include close attention to family planning as a positive measure. But is population growth really the cause of world poverty? Some would say no, that such logic is simplistic and naive.

Many have challenged the conventional wisdom. Among its severest critics are Frances Moore Lappé and Joseph Collins, best known for their research on food and hunger.[10] They believe that the conventional wisdom is based on a number of myths. Consequently, the solutions put forth, which largely blame the poor, will not work. Here we consider three of these myths, along with the gist of Lappé and Collins' rebuttals. While their primary focus is on hunger, their analysis does provide some significant insights into the relationship between population growth and poverty in underdeveloped nations.

Myth 1: "People are hungry because of scarcity"

The concept of scarcity deserves to be questioned as it is currently applied. Enough food to nourish all people on earth adequately is being produced now. We must carefully examine how this food is currently distributed and consumed. Inequitable distribution and consumption *among* nations is definitely part of the problem. But inequitable distribution *within* nations can be an important factor underlying what, on the surface, looks like absolute scarcity.

In most underdeveloped nations a small, elite class is overfed at the same time that many others go hungry. Scarcity may be maintained, at least to some degree, by a political power structure which assumes it is within its right to determine who will consume and under what conditions. (Even in the United States there are millions of people who suffer from hunger.[11] No one would try to explain this in terms of a scarcity of food in the nation.) Thus, it is possible for "scarcity" to exist in a nation when it could be eliminated if food were shared.

Myth 2: "Hunger results from overpopulation"

The relation between population size and the availability of food is not simple. Lappé and Collins offer China as a dramatic example. It has more people than any other country in the world, yet it has managed to bring hunger under control in a couple of decades, despite a population that continues to grow at a rate that is much higher than the average for developed nations. China has sought to maximize the utilization of existing food resources while developing systems of distribution that try to provide all groups within the society with adequate nutrition. Large population size alone cannot explain hunger.

In addition to the artificial scarcity created by the ways in which food is distributed, many nations appear nowhere near to full utilization of existing cultivable land.[12] Perhaps less than half of the world's cultivable land is now being used for crops. Moreover, crop yields from the land that is being utilized are often well below their full potential, particularly in underdeveloped nations. Why are resources underutilized in underdeveloped nations? To begin to answer this question, one must examine patterns of land ownership.

Myth 3: "To solve the problem of hunger we must grow more food"

Lappé and Collins cite evidence that per capita food production in a nation can increase simultaneously with an increase in the number of persons who are hungry! How can such a contradiction exist?

---

[10] See Frances Moore Lappé and Joseph Collins, *Food First; Beyond the Myth of Scarcity*, rev. ed. (New York: Ballantine Books, 1979), and their *World Hunger: Ten Myths*, 4th ed. (San Francisco: Institute for Food and Development Policy, 1982).

[11] See Physician Taskforce on Hunger in America, *Hunger in America: The Growing Epidemic* (Cambridge, Mass.: School of Public Health, Harvard University, 1985).

[12] Lappé and Collins, *World Hunger*, p. 10.

In those underdeveloped nations where governments have made sure people receive a just share of income and wealth, population growth rates drop and health conditions improve. This Chinese couple and their child experience far greater economic well-being and security than their counterparts in most other poor nations. (*Bruce Rosenblum/The Picture Cube*)

First, it must be understood that land ownership in underdeveloped countries is concentrated typically in the hands of a small but wealthy propertied class. Landholdings are retained within families through inheritance and gifts and within the class itself through intermarriage and the merging of business interests. Much of the land available for cultivation, and usually the best land, is monopolized by this class.

Second, land ownership carries with it the prerogative of deciding if the land will be planted and if so, with what; the decision of what technology to use in the growing process is also the owner's. These kinds of decisions tend to be made with profit in mind. The impact of such decisions, however, is felt by the majority of the population, for in underdeveloped nations agricultural activities are generally the core of the economy.

Landowners' policies often contribute to poverty, malnutrition, and ill health. For example, chemicals and machines bought from developed nations are used to increase production while reducing labor costs. Agricultural laborers, on the other hand, are left to suffer from overexposure to pesticides and from unemployment resulting from the new technology, which is replacing traditional methods of agriculture, transforming cultivable lands into corporate food factories.

Production of specialized goods for export, usually to developed nations, often means using the best lands to grow luxury commodities (e.g., cocoa, tea, coffee). Meanwhile locally needed foodstuffs are underproduced. For example, grain may be grown and then used to fatten cattle for beef export to developed nations; this grain is then unavailable for local consumption. Indeed, many countries, because of landowners' production priorities, have become *importers* of grain and other foodstuffs they have produced or could produce.

Landowners' profits from such practices are frequently used to increase landholdings, thereby limiting even further the ability of families to engage in production for local markets or for their own subsistence. The plight of small growers has been exacerbated in recent years as rising petroleum prices have driven up the costs of fuel and fertilizer. Many small producers have been forced to sell out to the heavily capitalized large landowners. The desperation of rural families, increasingly finding themselves landless and without opportunities for employment, drives many to the city. There they attempt to subsist in massive overcrowded, unsanitary slums, often claiming squatters' rights to a few square feet of city property in order to erect a bare shack. In fact, the largest population growth rates, now and in the foreseeable future, are in urban areas of the underdeveloped world.

Lack of *control* over food-producing resources by those who most need food helps to explain why food production and hunger can increase simultaneously. These types of considerations help us to put the issue of population growth in underdeveloped nations in some kind of context. To Lappé and Collins, high birth rates are symptoms of the "insecurity and poverty of the majority resulting from the monopolizing of productive assets by a few."[13]

If you live in an agricultural society but do not own land and have no employment security, children may be one of your only assets. Whether in rural settings or in the urban shantytown, children provide extra hands to help make survival possible. They may perform household tasks (including care of younger siblings) that free adults to work, or they may earn enough to help those who cannot find work.

Underdeveloped nations are not "welfare states," with social security and retirement plans. Children must be around to help parents and other family members, particularly as they face infirmity from illness and aging. Given the high probability that many of those born will die quite young, high birth rates are a must. These needs obviously place tremendous demands on females in underdeveloped nations. Poverty forces women into high-risk childbearing and traditional family roles. They have no other options.

ECONOMIC SECURITY AND REDUCTION OF FAMILY SIZE

The solution to poverty—and the hunger and ill health typically accompanying it—is not simply birth control, as the conventional wisdom has it. Efforts in that direction can have only limited impact on birth rates, given the quite rational incentives that move poor people to have many children. However, population growth rates can be changed by combining family planning programs with fundamental political, economic, and social changes. Fertility falls as people experience improved economic welfare. (See Figure 1.2.) Steps must be taken in underdeveloped nations both to increase and to spread the benefits of production more equitably so as to minimize poverty.[14]

Earlier in this chapter we mentioned the case of China. While China now contains over 1 billion people, its present population growth rate is lower than most other underdeveloped nations. While the latter average over 2 percent growth annually (where China was in the early 1970s), the Chinese are making serious efforts to bring the growth rate eventually to zero.

Prior to 1949 China's situation resembled that of many underdeveloped nations today: Land was held by a few, food was inequitably dis-

[13] Ibid., p. 11.

[14] Murdoch, *The Poverty of Nations*, pp. 307–10.

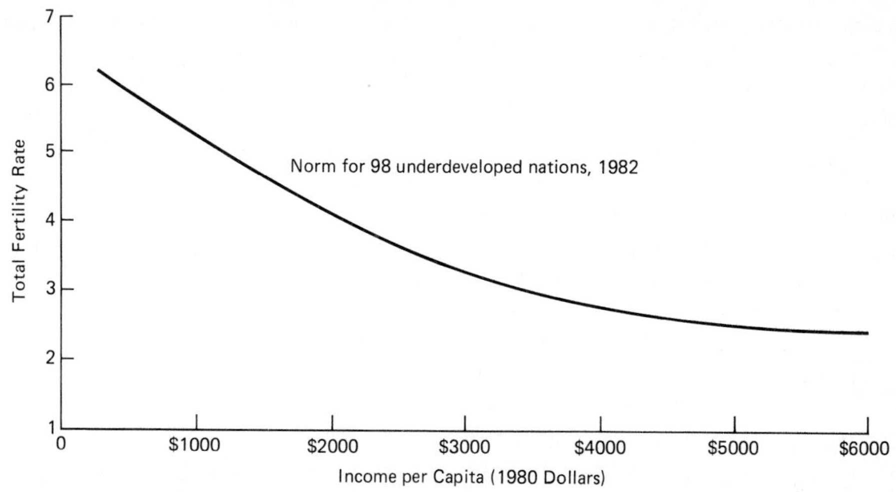

FIGURE 1.2 Fertility in Relation to Income in Underdeveloped Nations, 1982
Source: The World Bank, *World Development Report, 1984* (New York: Oxford University Press, 1984), p. 70.

tributed, and poverty was extremely widespread. These problems were centuries old and were periodically exacerbated by natural catastrophes and armed conflicts which produced massive famine-related deaths. In 1949 China began a series of fundamental political, economic, and social changes within a socialist framework. Particular attention was given to a more equitable distribution of wealth and income and to land reform, in which control over production was given to the landless.

It was not until these changes were well under way that the Chinese leadership felt confident in promoting family planning in a serious way. That is, successful steps toward the creation of economic security preceded efforts to reduce family size. Once this poverty-stricken population knew it could count on having food, clothing, shelter, health care, and old-age assistance, the incentive for large numbers of children was greatly undermined. It was further undermined as the Chinese leadership moved to broaden the rights of women. Family economic security was coupled with increased female control over the reproductive process through easy access to birth control.

In the early 1970s China began to push for two-child families, and in 1979 a campaign was begun to reduce the number of children per family to one. The goal has been zero population growth rate by the year 2000, to be achieved by mobilizing a variety of economic incentives for couples, neighborhood and work group peer pressure, and improved contraceptive measures. The implementation of such stringent birth policies has been most successful in urban areas. In the countryside it has been less so. Nonetheless, in seeking to dramatically reduce family size, China has undertaken an unprecedented and controversial experiment but one that is necessary if the standard of living of its people is to increase.

Elsewhere the picture is much more bleak. Erik P. Eckholm observes:

> As a rule, birth rates have fallen most rapidly in countries where the benefits of development have been most widely shared and have reached the poor majority on the bottom.[15]

---

[15] Eckholm, *Down to Earth*, p. 41.

Similarly, Lappé and Collins note,

> In countries where the decline in birth rate has been significant, the causal factors do not appear to be direct birth control programs so much as a shift in resources toward the poorest groups.[16]

However, in most of the underdeveloped world resources are *not* shifting toward the poorest groups, nor are birth rates in significant decline. We mentioned earlier that in a number of developed European nations there is virtually no population growth. In contrast, there are thirty-four underdeveloped nations whose populations are expanding at a rate of 3 percent or more annually, meaning they could experience a 1,922 percent increase in the next 100 years![17]

Who or what stands in the way of the steps necessary for fundamental change in underdeveloped nations? Naturally, the wealthy, propertied classes in these nations resist such change, for they benefit from the status quo. But ironically, rich, developed nations—including the United States—stand in the way of any change that could threaten their own interests. It is to this topic that we now turn.

DEVELOPMENT, UNDERDEVELOPMENT, AND THE COLONIAL LEGACY

The economic gap between affluent developed nations such as the United States and poor underdeveloped nations is on the steady increase. In the mid-1980s the per capita income for persons in the United States was $14,461. In contrast, the per capita income of our nearest underdeveloped neighbor, Mexico, was $2,240. In India per capita income was $240. In famine-stricken Ethiopia per capita income was $110. As rich nations hold their population growth rates down at the same time that so many poor nations cannot, the gap in per capita income widens progressively.

But population growth rates alone do not fully explain the disparities that exist. One must also have some sense of history to account for the present. Until quite recently, most peoples of the underdeveloped world were subjected to colonialism and other forms of outside domination. A group of what were to become some of today's developed nations implemented and enforced this domination through the exercise of greater military, political, and economic power. As recently as World War I most of the earth's inhabitants were subject to colonial rule and many nations gained independence only in the last five decades. (See Table 1.3.) The external rulers were joined by coopted (and thus cooperative) native elites *within* underdeveloped societies. The purposes of colonization—in Africa, Asia, Latin America, and elsewhere—included the exploitation of cheap labor, the extraction of raw materials and agricultural products, and the creation of new markets.

It is important to understand that these colonized and otherwise dominated societies were coerced into adopting forms of economic and political organization that would best serve the interests of those who ruled. The cultural traditions and ways of life that had enabled these societies to live self-sufficiently were progressively destroyed. To those who ruled, the needs of the colonized were secondary. In effect, the ability of these nations to develop, except as dictated from afar, was blocked. Poverty, hunger, ill health, and limited life chances were manufactured, while local discontent was typically put down by military force.

In the present century sweeping changes have occurred. In all areas of the world colonial relations have been severed, often after long-lasting warfare and rebellion against the colonial powers and their native representatives. In most instances, however, the end of formal colonization left underdeveloped nations in extremely poor condition. Although independent

---

[16] Lappé and Collins, *Food First*, p. 34.

[17] Lester R. Brown, "Stabilizing Population," in Worldwatch Institute, *State of the World 1984* (New York: W. W. Norton & Company, 1984), pp. 20 and 21.

TABLE 1.3 Chronological List of 98 Newly Independent Nations (since 1943)

Year	Date	Country
1943	Nov. 22	Lebanon
1944	Jan. 1	Syria
	June 17	Iceland
1946	Mar. 22	Jordan
	July 4	Philippines
1947	Aug. 14	Pakistan
	Aug. 15	India
1948	Jan. 4	Myanmar
	Feb. 4	Sri Lanka
	May 15	Israel
	Aug. 15	Korea
1949	Mar. 8	Vietnam
	July 19	Laos
	Nov. 8	Cambodia
	Dec. 28	Indonesia
1951	Dec. 24	Libya
1956	Jan. 1	Sudan
	Mar. 2	Morocco
	Mar. 20	Tunisia
1957	Mar. 6	Ghana
	Aug. 31	Malaysia
1958	Oct. 2	Guinea
1960	Jan. 1	Cameroon
	Apr. 27	Togo
	June 27	Madagascar
	June 30	Zaire
	July 1	Somalia
	Aug. 1	Benin
	Aug. 3	Niger
	Aug. 5	Burkina Faso
	Aug. 7	Ivory Coast
	Aug. 11	Chad
	Aug. 13	Central African Republic
	Aug. 15	Congo
	Aug. 16	Cyprus
	Aug. 17	Gabon
	Aug. 20	Senegal
	Sept. 22	Mali
	Oct. 1	Nigeria
	Nov. 28	Mauritania
1961	Apr. 27	Sierra Leone
	June 19	Kuwait
	Dec. 9	Tanzania
1962	Jan. 1	Western Samoa
	July 1	Burundi
	July 1	Rwanda
	July 5	Algeria
	Aug. 6	Jamaica
	Aug. 31	Trinidad and Tobago
	Oct. 9	Uganda
1963	Dec. 12	Kenya
1964	July 6	Malawi
	Sept. 21	Malta
	Oct. 24	Zambia
1965	Feb. 18	Gambia, The
	July 26	Maldives
	Aug. 9	Singapore
1966	May 26	Guyana
	Sept. 30	Botswana
	Oct. 4	Lesotho
	Nov. 30	Barbados
1967	Nov. 30	Yemen (South)
1968	Jan. 31	Nauru
	Mar. 12	Mauritius
	Sept. 6	Swazlland
	Oct. 12	Equatorial Guinea
1970	June 4	Tonga
	Oct. 10	Fiji
1971	Aug. 14	Bahrain
	Sept. 3	Qatar
	Dec. 2	United Arab Emirates
1972	Apr. 4	Bangladesh
1973	July 10	Bahamas, The
1974	Feb. 7	Grenada
	Sept. 10	Guinea-Bissau
1975	June 25	Mozambique
	July 5	Cape Verde
	July 12	São Tomé and Principe
	Sept. 16	Papua New Guinea
	Nov. 11	Angola
	Nov. 25	Suriname
	Dec. 31	Comoros, The
1976	June 28	Seychelles
1977	June 27	Djibouti
1978	July 7	Solomon Islands
	Oct. 1	Tuvalu
	Nov. 3	Dominica
1979	Feb. 22	Saint Lucia
	July 12	Kiribati
	Oct. 27	Saint Vincent and the Grenadines
1980	Apr. 18	Zimbabwe
	July 30	Vanuatu
1981	Sept. 21	Belize
	Nov. 1	Antigua and Barbuda
1983	Sept. 19	Saint Kitts and Nevis
1984	Jan. 1	Brunei
1986	Oct. 21	Marshall Islands
	Nov. 3	Micronesia, Federated States of

Source: U.S. Department of State, Bureau of Intelligence and Research, *Geographic Notes,* No. 10 (Washington, D.C.: Department of State, September 1989). Special issue devoted to "Status of the World's Nations."

politically they had been so ravaged by the colonial experience that economic self-sufficiency was difficult. For many such nations it would be an elusive goal.

In recent decades we have seen new tactics from many developed nations, including the United States. Such nations have at times taken advantage of the vulnerability of underdeveloped nations, subtly re-creating relations of dominance and exploitation. What might be called *neocolonialism* has emerged, in many cases promoting the continuing poverty and suffering to which attention was drawn earlier in this chapter. The United States has been a participant in this process.

THE UNITED STATES AND THE UNDERDEVELOPED WORLD

As other chapters in this text note, the economic system of the United States has become increasingly global. It is a central part (if not *the* central part) of what some describe as a world capitalist system. This system dominates economic activity and influences political policy in most of the developed and underdeveloped nations of the world.[18]

The United States has developed widespread economic vested interests outside its political boundaries but within the world capitalist system. One indicator of these interests is direct investments made by U.S. firms abroad. In 1987 the value of these investments was $309 billion, a figure that represents substantial growth since the years after World War II. Some three-quarters of this $309 billion have been invested in nations in the developed world, largely in Europe and Canada. While investments worth $71 billion have been made in underdeveloped nations, their dollar value does not indicate their full significance to U.S. firms. This is because the rate of return from investments in underdeveloped nations is usually quite a bit higher than returns from, say, Europe and Canada. On the other hand, the investment risks are often also higher.

While investments by U.S. firms (so-called multinational corporations) span the globe, when it comes to underdeveloped nations these investments are relatively concentrated. Over half, in 1987, were in Latin America,[19] where the United States has acted as a self-appointed overseer (even if not a colonial power) for many generations. Here is Thomas Jefferson writing to James Monroe in 1801:

> However our present interests may restrain us within our limits, it is impossible not to look forward to distant times when our rapid multiplication will expand itself beyond those limits, and cover the whole northern, if not the southern continent, with a people speaking the same language, governed in similar form, and by similar laws.[20]

Since Jefferson's time the U.S. government has viewed Latin America as within its "sphere of influence." The United States has not hesitated to intervene politically, and even militarily, in Latin American nations to influence developments thought to bear on our national interest.

Today the large-scale investments that have been made in Latin America are an important component of this national interest. (See Table 1.4.) U.S. multinational business firms have developed a strong dependency on profits from this area of the underdeveloped world. The average rate of return from dollars invested in Latin America is about 20 percent, whereas the international average is barely a third of that.[21]

The needs of today's multinational firms are quite similar to those of the traditional colonial

---

[18] See, e.g., Immanuel Wallerstein, *The Capitalist World-Economy* (Cambridge: Cambridge University Press, 1979).

[19] Figures from the U.S. Department of Commerce.

[20] Quoted in James Chace, *Endless War* (New York: Vintage Books, 1984), p. 11.

[21] For updates see U.S. Department of Commerce, *Survey of Business*, a periodical.

powers: cheap labor, inexpensive raw materials and agricultural goods, and markets for manufactured goods. Production can be quite cheap in underdeveloped nations, where unemployment is rife, unions virtually nonexistent, and people so desperate for wages that health, safety, and environmental practices outlawed in the United States are common. The profits find their way back to the developed world.

To date, investment by U.S. firms in underdeveloped nations has neither assisted in their overall economic development nor spread meaningful benefits to the low-income sectors in such nations. For the most part those who prosper are those native elites chosen by U.S. firms to participate in management and supervisory positions. The local population derives nowhere near the benefits that accrue to the investing firms.

In many cases the impact of investment may actually contribute to further underdevelopment. Raw materials extracted from the ground are ordinarily irreplaceable. In the long run this is a form of material impoverishment (a fact that helped to motivate the dramatic price increases of oil-producing nations in the 1970s). Agricultural production devoted solely to the most technologically efficient production of items for export can, as we have seen, adversely affect local employment opportunities and food supplies. Indifference to health and safety needs of workers and abuse of air, water, and land with dangerous pollutants that affect the general population create further serious problems in living. The movement of the rural poor to urban areas in the remote hope of finding work contributes to congestion, housing shortages, public health problems, and further cycles of birth and impoverishment.

Economic foreign aid provided to many underdeveloped nations through the U.S. government in cooperation with banking institutions has generally been in the form of loans. Underdeveloped nations, desperate for resources, take these loans, but economic circumstances are such that new loans must be negotiated simply to pay the interest rates on old ones. Now caught up in heavy, inescapable debt, underdeveloped nations become captives of a world economic system in which they possess practically no influence. Their dependence on outside loans and investments means that the developed world, including the United States, can dictate internal economic, and thus political, policies.

Underdeveloped nations, with very few exceptions (e.g., China), are entrapped; their economic development is systematically stymied. Much as in colonial days, there are classes within underdeveloped nations that are willing to cooperate with the neocolonial powers in return for privileges and life-styles that most of their fellow citizens cannot enjoy. Thus, a minority within most underdeveloped nations sees itself as benefiting from the status quo, as do the investing multinational firms, for the status quo is profitable.

The profitability of multinationals' investments contributes to their prosperity and to the prosperity of their home nations. Thus, the profitability of U.S. multinationals operating in the underdeveloped world contributes to the prosperity of the United States, which interferes with change in our relations with poor countries. Daniel Chirot, author of *Social Change in the Twentieth Century*, put it this way:

> Rich societies have not been, and are not presently, interested in turning poorer societies into independent and prosperous ones. Rather they are interested in keeping the poorer areas dependent, and overspecialized in the production of certain cheap goods. Balanced development in any poor society, therefore, is likely to meet the active resistance of the rich societies.[22]

Thus, movements for broad change that ep-

---

[22] Daniel Chirot, *Social Change in the Twentieth Century* (Orlando, Fla.: Harcourt Brace Jovanovich, 1977), p. 9.

TABLE 1.4 U.S. Investment Position Abroad, by Country, 1987 (in millions of dollars)

Country	Total*	Manufacturing	Petroleum	Finance†
All countries	**308,793**	**126,640**	**66,381**	**49,097**
Developed countries	233,315	104,759	43,762	35,946
Canada	56,879	25,800	11,931	8,851
Europe‡	148,954	67,475	25,785	24,525
Austria	387	109	117	23
Belgium	7,078	3,486	547	708
Denmark	1,114	253	170	53
France	11,478	8,374	531	244
Greece	215	94	132	(D)
Ireland	5,484	4,111	−23	1,389
Italy	8,449	6,084	252	446
Luxembourg	723	193	(D)	288
Netherlands	14,164	5,318	3,078	2,432
Norway	4,142	91	3,552	(D)
Portugal	381	193	(D)	(D)
Spain	4,037	2,567	124	21
Sweden	1,188	617	(D)	127
Switzerland	19,973	1,720	(D)	7,136
Turkey	241	52	88	—
United Kingdom	44,673	18,268	11,011	9,571
West Germany	24,450	15,974	3,319	1,674
Japan	14,270	7,073	2,561	945
Australia, New Zealand, and South Africa	13,212	4,411	3,484	1,624
Australia	10,988	3,493	2,943	1,478
New Zealand	635	211	(D)	72
South Africa	1,590	707	(D)	74
Developing countries	71,174	21,881	19,009	13,150
Latin America	42,337	15,902	5,771	10,496
South America‡	19,312	11,084	3,020	1,707
Argentina	2,854	1,616	398	158
Brazil	9,955	7,730	273	1,183
Chile	224	−221	59	78
Colombia	2,037	585	1,013	96
Ecuador	497	157	237	(D)
Peru	1,102	63	367	(D)
Venezuela	2,124	1,061	534	174

(continued)

isodically flow from the poorer population segments within underdeveloped nations are commonly interpreted by U.S. government officials as dangerous to our national interest. In reality, such movements represent aspects of those societies that are dangerous simply because they are not under our control. U.S. officials (to the degree to which they express concern about it) discuss world poverty in terms of the need for more effective birth control. They tend not to discuss it in terms of unjust systems of political and economic inequality that must be transformed.

Movements for change within underdeveloped nations often have been officially interpreted as part of a communist threat—perhaps

TABLE 1.4 U.S. Investment Position Abroad, by Country, 1987 (in millions of dollars) *(continued)*

Country	Total*	Manufacturing	Petroleum	Finance†
Central America	10,430	4,553	841	2,597
Mexico	4,997	3,959	65	198
Panama	4,780	278	648	2,380
Other‡	654	316	129	19
Costa Rica	141	(NA)	(NA)	(NA)
El Salvador	51	(NA)	(NA)	(NA)
Guatemala	159	(NA)	(NA)	(NA)
Honduras	203	(NA)	(NA)	(NA)
Other Western Hemisphere‡	12,594	264	1,910	6,192
Bahamas, The	2,566	26	792	505
Bermuda	18,229	—	530	17,230
Dominican Republic	(NA)	(NA)	(NA)	(NA)
Jamaica	90	106	(D)	(D)
Netherlands Antilles	−13,208	21	(D)	−13,500
Trinidad and Tobago	356	7	311	3
Other Africa‡	5,085	308	4,237	57
Egypt	1,663	41	1,400	(Z)
Libya	252	—	246	—
Nigeria	1,267	40	1,120	—
Middle East‡	4,762	408	2,812	234
Israel	793	201	(D)	156
Saudi Arabia	2,385	163	1,079	−17
United Arab Emirates	762	20	595	(D)
Bahrain	95	(NA)	(NA)	(NA)
Other Asia and Pacific	18,991	5,264	6,188	2,364
China: Taiwan	1,312	983	−14	20
Hong Kong	5,453	563	462	1,849
India	466	416	−14	(D)
Indonesia	3,929	234	3,251	195
Malaysia	1,111	329	704	11
Philippines	1,211	602	101	1
Singapore	2,521	1,493	579	72
South Korea	1,018	339	7	180
Thailand	1,282	256	857	9
Other	687	48	254	(D)
People's Rep. of China	325	(NA)	(NA)	(NA)
OPEC§	11,498	1,677	7,334	479

[Direct investments represent private enterprises in one country owned or controlled by investors in another country or in the management of which foreign investors have an important role. Negative position occurs when U.S. parent company's liabilities to the foreign affiliate are greater than its equity in, and loans to the foreign affiliate.]

Key: D, suppressed to avoid disclosure of data of individual companies. NA, not available. Z, less than $500,000.

*Includes industries not shown separately.

†Includes insurance.

‡Includes countries not shown separately.

§OPEC = Organization of Petroleum Exporting Countries. Includes Algeria, Ecuador, Gabon, Indonesia, Iran, Iraq, Kuwait, Libya, Nigeria, Qatar, Saudi Arabia, United Arab Emirates, and Venezuela.

Source: U.S. Department of Commerce, Bureau of the Census, *Statistical Abstract of the United States, 1989* (Washington, D.C.: U.S. Government Printing Office, 1989), p. 779.

Many products that could be made in the United States are produced and sometimes sold in underdeveloped nations by branches of U.S. multinational corporations. These firms obtain low-wage labor from persons in need of work and direct the profits from their operations back to U.S. headquarters. (*Owen/Franken/Sygma*)

the product of outside agitation by agents of Soviet intrigue. That suffering peoples may have just reasons for seeking fundamental reordering of their own societies becomes irrelevant. Since it is against the self-interest of developed nations such as the United States to help the poor overturn systems from which the developed nations profit, it should not be surprising that those trying to effect change at times accept aid from sympathetic socialist nations. We leave them little choice.

In recent years a new development—the demand for illegal drugs—has helped to fashion relationships between the United States and a number of underdeveloped nations. The U.S. Drug Enforcement Agency estimates that people in the United States spend tens of billions of dollars for such drug imports as cocaine, marijuana, and heroin. Latin America is a major exporter and pipeline for these drugs, only a fraction of which are seized while being smuggled into the United States. Other exporters of illegal drugs are located in the Near and Middle East and in Asia.

A great deal of public attention has come to focus on cocaine use in the United States and its connection to underdeveloped countries in Latin America. We in this country spend an estimated $15 billion to $20 billion a year on cocaine, most of which comes from Colombia, Peru, and Bolivia. Our demand has helped to exacerbate the economic and political difficulties faced by such countries. They have begun to suffer tragic costs as a direct consequence of large-scale involvement in the drug trade.[23]

The cultivation of coca (the raw material of

[23] See Ethan A. Nadelmann, "U.S. Drug Policy: A Bad Export," *Foreign Policy*, 70 (Spring 1988): 83–108.

cocaine) and its transformation into a marketable product have provided economic benefits to some segments of the exporting countries. The illegality of cocaine in the United States helps to keep its price high. Hence, many farmers in Colombia, Bolivia, and Peru find they can earn more money by growing coca for the drug trade than they can by cultivating other crops. In addition, employment opportunities are provided by virtue of the need to process, transport, and provide security for the product. But most of these people benefit only indirectly. The bulk of the profit goes to the key actors in a small number of well-organized crime cartels (known as narcotraficantes), who monopolize the trafficking of cocaine to the United States and take advantage of the highly inflated prices it brings. Commenting on the situation in Colombia, a writer from that country points to the economic affluence of one group of narcotraficantes operating out of the city of Medellín:

> In 1986 the nation's total export to world markets from industries as powerful as coffee and oil, and representing the combined efforts of several million workers, was $5 billion. Just a few men in Medellín, however, export an estimated $3 billion to $6 billion a year in cocaine. These drug lords are richer and more powerful than the country.[24]

Thus far we have spoken only of the economic benefits cocaine brings to certain segments of the underdeveloped nations involved. These benefits are being dwarfed by a number of tragic costs.[25] These include increased cocaine use by youth in Colombia, Bolivia, and Peru; traffickers' corruption of officials—from police officers to cabinet ministers—who either ignore the drug industry or actively assist in it; and the shift of political power to enormously wealthy criminal groups whose willingness to use extortion and violence has rendered them makers of their own laws. The power these groups have begun to accrue has a chilling effect on those who would seek to combat the drug trade through governmental action. Key law enforcement officials (supreme court judges, attorneys general, police chiefs) have been subject to death threats and murdered with impunity.

The appetite for illegal drugs in the United States is enormous: "There are today an estimated 1.2 million addicts in the U.S. and 23 million recreational users, spending more on drugs annually than a company like GM [General Motors] earns."[26] The users are interested in the vicarious pleasures of the drug experience, in this case the "cocaine high." Ironically, users' drug purchases help to promote widespread corruption, violence, and lawlessness in nations already burdened with wrenching poverty, hunger, malnutrition, and ill health. While drug users in the affluent United States take their pleasures, it is at the cost of some of the most vulnerable of the world's peoples.

WHERE IS IT ALL GOING?

The situation described in this chapter seems overwhelming. We prefer to be optimistic about problems, believing that they can somehow be solved, and grow very frustrated when ready (even easy) solutions do not offer themselves. The experts make it difficult to be optimistic about the future. For example, here is economist Robert Heilbroner:

> We are entering a period in which rapid population growth, the presence of obliterative weapons, and dwindling resources will bring international tensions to dangerous levels for an extended period. Indeed, there seems no reason for these levels of danger to subside unless population equilibrium is achieved, and some rough measure of

[24] Oscar Calle, "The Families of Medellin," *Newsweek* (March 14, 1988): 6.

[25] Nadelmann, op cit., p. 86.

[26] "The Demand-side Drug Fix," *U.S. News and World Report* (March 14, 1988): 20.

> equity reached in the distribution of wealth among nations. . . . Whether such an equitable arrangement can be reached—at least within the next several generations—is open to serious doubt.[27]

In Ethiopia, where millions have faced starvation, the per capita income is $110 annually. In the United States, many house pets, such as dogs and cats, have higher per capita incomes, based on what is spent on their food and care for one year. People in such underdeveloped lands, if history is our guide, may increasingly welcome death resulting from the struggle for change to the passive death to which they have been condemned. We are likely to see more and more movements for change develop, with an escalation of violence and terrorism. This is part of the global context in which we operate.

The current approach of the United States to the instabilities inherent in the relationships that have evolved between developed and underdeveloped countries can be expressed with a metaphor:

> If the world were a global village of 100 residents 6 of them would be Americans. These 6 would have half of the village's income; and the other 94 would exist on the other half.
>
> How would the wealthy 6 live "in peace" with their neighbors? Surely they would be driven to arm themselves against the other 94 . . . perhaps even to spend, as we do, more per person on military defense than the total per person income of the others.[28]

Is this the way we want to live? Is this the only way we are capable of relating to the desperate conditions of most of the rest of the world? The answers to these questions must be no.

As the problems worsen and tensions grow, as crisis follows crisis, human survival ultimately will call for that which we are currently successfully avoiding: cooperation among nation-states, rich and poor.[29] Neither weaponry nor intrigue will ensure the survival of humanity. Cooperation will. What it will take for this realization to penetrate the thinking and practice of developed nations such as the United States is one of the most profound questions of our day.

SUMMARY

The global context within which the United States functions is not always readily apparent. Yet it contains problems that are reaching crisis proportions and inflicting suffering on hundreds of millions of people. Two phenomena are of particular importance: the dynamics of world population growth and the impact of underdevelopment on most of the world's peoples.

The size of the earth's population is growing relentlessly. The most rapid population growth is taking place in underdeveloped nations—poor societies in which 75 percent of all human beings live. Population growth rates are high in much of Asia, Latin America, and Africa. In contrast, growth rates in the more affluent developed nations, such as the United States and nations in Europe, are quite low.

Life chances are very limited for many residents of the underdeveloped world. Hundreds of millions of people suffer routinely from hunger and chronic malnutrition, while others periodically fall victim to famine-related starvation. Malnutrition contributes to people's vulnerability to illness and disease and ultimately to lower life expectancy. Underdeveloped nations experience particularly high death rates among women, infants, and children.

Conventional wisdom has it that high rates of population growth cause world poverty and the malnutrition and poor health that accom-

---

[27] Heilbroner, *An Inquiry into the Human Prospect*, p. 149.

[28] A passage from the February 1974 *Fellowship* magazine (of the Fellowship of Reconciliation) as quoted in Richard J. Barnet and Ronald E. Müller, *Global Reach* (New York: Simon & Schuster, 1974), p. 122.

[29] See Richard J. Barnet, *The Lean Years* (New York: Simon & Schuster, 1981), Chapter 11.

pany it. According to this view, if we reduce population growth rates by birth control, the situation will improve. Critics view this logic as simplistic and naive; they point out that food and other resources are adequate to serve the world's growing population. The problem lies with how these resources are utilized and distributed, both among nations and within them. By and large, most members of underdeveloped nations lack control over such resources. Their children become assets, providing extra hands to help make family survival possible. For the critics, poverty produces population growth.

Thus, the solution to world poverty—and the hunger and poor health which typically accompany it—is not simply more effective birth control. In most underdeveloped nations political, economic, and social changes must occur. Production must be rechanneled and its fruits more equitably spread among low-income groups. With economic security, families will have less reason to produce many children.

Obstacles to such changes abound. Underdevelopment has meant vulnerability and dependency, so that developed nations have been able to exploit formerly colonized peoples. Neocolonialism has been the result, as developed nations such as the United States have come to look to poor nations for cheap labor, inexpensive raw materials and agricultural products, and markets. For example, American multinational corporations have invested billions of dollars for such purposes in underdeveloped Latin American nations. Consequently, movements for change in such nations are commonly viewed as dangerous to our national interest.

Conditions in underdeveloped nations, if left unaltered, are likely to produce more and more movements for change. Violence and terrorism will escalate within these nations. The relationships between the underdeveloped world and developed nations such as the United States will become extremely unstable. Human survival ultimately will call for cooperation among nation-states, rich and poor. The conditions under which the need for cooperation will be realized is one of the most profound questions of our day.

DISCUSSION QUESTIONS

1. Think about how underdeveloped, or Third World, nations are portrayed typically in the mass media. What stereotypes might the portrayals help to create or to reinforce? What aspects of life are not communicated?
2. In battlefield jargon, *triage* involves separating incoming casualties into three groups: those whose wounds are not serious, those with quite serious wounds, and those who are almost certain to die even with treatment. When medical resources are limited, primary attention goes to the middle group, not to those who are most in danger of death. Some would argue that triage should be the approach taken to aiding other nations that are in distress. Take a position on this and defend it.
3. Choose an underdeveloped nation and do research into the quality of life of its people before, during, and in the wake of colonization. What conclusions are suggested by your research?
4. Economist Robert L. Heilbroner, in *Inquiry into the Human Prospect*, suggests it is unlikely that we would willingly make sacrifices in order to improve the well-being of people around the world who presently live in abject poverty. Do you agree with Heilbroner? Why or why not?
5. Many colleges and universities have foreign student or international centers where students from outside the United States often congregate. Visit such a center and talk with students about the differences they see between their own societies and the United States. Report your findings to members of the class.

SUGGESTED READINGS

Benjamin, Medea, and Andrew Freedman. *Bridging the Global Gap* (Cabin John, Md.: Seven Locks Press, 1989).
Handbook describing ways in which people of the United States can assist people in underdeveloped nations.

Lappé, Frances Moore, and Joseph Collins. *World Hunger: Twelve Myths* (New York: Grove Press, 1986).
Mobilization of data in support of the position that world hunger is not inevitable or necessary.

Murdoch, William W. *The Poverty of Nations* (Baltimore, Md.: The Johns Hopkins University Press, 1980).
Shows how improvements in underdeveloped nations' economic conditions relate to drop in birth rates.

Seitz, John L. *The Politics of Development* (New York: Basil Blackwell, 1988).
Overview of global issues with consideration of possible alternative futures.

United Nations Children's Fund. *The State of the World's Children 1989* (New York: Oxford University Press, 1989).
Annual publication on the health and well-being of children, with special focus on problems in underdeveloped nations.

Worldwatch Institute. *State of the World 1989* (New York: W. W. Norton & Company, 1989).
Annual review of worldwide environmental and population developments, underscoring emergent trends.

CHAPTER 2

Concentration of Political and Economic Power

Members of society should be able to actively participate in or directly influence those political and economic decisions that affect them.

It is common to refer to the United States as a democracy. From kindergarten on, children are taught about the democratic character of the American political system. Ours, it is often said, is a government "of, by, and for the people." Students are encouraged to study the U.S. Constitution and to learn about the various branches of government. Frequently, the American political system is favorably contrasted with others that are called totalitarian or dictatorial. In short, the schools act as agencies of political socialization; they function to provide future adult citizens with a belief in the noble origins and operation of the American political system and to urge faith in its democratic workings.[1]

Unfortunately, the schools too often fail to distinguish between democratic ideals and political realities. Everyday observations and practical experiences have led many Americans to doubt the democratic character of the American political system. Many contend that political power has become concentrated in the

[1] See discussion of "political socialization" in Chapter 7.

hands of a select few and that, to the degree such concentration exists, we do not have a government of, by, and for the people. Instead, decisions affecting all Americans are made by persons primarily concerned with the pursuit of their own self-defined interests.

This chapter begins by examining the conventional pluralist perspective on the distribution of political power. This perspective holds that power is equitably distributed and that America is a democratic society in which no one group is politically dominant. Although this conventional view is widely held, we point to indications of doubt and disagreement that have emerged in recent years among the public. Next we set forth three alternative perspectives on the distribution and use of power.[2] The power elite perspective sees power as having become concentrated among those holding top positions in America's bureaucratic organizations. The instrumentalist perspective emphasizes the power-wielding capabilities of the wealthy and their representatives. The structuralist perspective reminds us that needs of our economic system may constrain political decision making. Finally, we consider some of the consequences of the concentration of power for political participation and suggest some steps that might move America's political system closer to the democratic ideal.

POWER IN AMERICA: WHO RULES?

Is the United States a democratic society? Those holding the *pluralist perspective* would say that it is. In this section we present the views of David Riesman, whose book *The Lonely Crowd* cogently expresses the pluralist position.[3] We then look at survey results that indicate that many Americans entertain doubts about the validity of this perspective.

The Pluralist Perspective

In *The Lonely Crowd* sociologist David Riesman commented on American politics while making a large-scale assessment of our nation's culture and personality. Riesman argued that great changes have taken place in the American political system during the twentieth century. At various times during the nineteenth century, Riesman noted, wealthy businessmen and industrialists exercised an inordinate amount of power over the federal government and its policies. It almost appeared that an economic upper class ruled America. Riesman contended that upper-class domination over government has disintegrated in the present century and that our society has become pluralistic in its national politics. That is, there are now many other groups capable of countering the political powers historically held by men of great wealth and high incomes. Riesman used the term *veto groups* in referring to those organized bodies strong enough to make a direct impact on key national policy decisions. In his view, farm groups, labor and professional organizations, and ethnic and regional groups, among others, have all developed the political strength to veto policies that might adversely affect their interests. To a somewhat lesser extent, such groups can also initiate actions and mobilize pressures to gain the adoption of policies they want.

The pluralist perspective, as espoused by Riesman, essentially contends that political power is dispersed and distributed among a

---

[2] Contending perspectives on the true nature of the American political system might be considered a struggle among conflicting intellectual "paradigms." See Thomas S. Kuhn, *The Structure of Scientific Revolutions*, 2nd ed. (Chicago: University of Chicago Press, 1970).

[3] David Riesman, *The Lonely Crowd*, abridged ed. (New Haven, Conn.: Yale University Press, 1961), Chapter X. Pluralist literature is reviewed in Martin N. Marger, *Elites and Masses*, 2nd ed. (Belmont, Calif.: Wadsworth, 1987), Chapter 5.

multitude of competing and contending interest groups. No group is capable of dominating at all times, nor is any group even interested in all questions of national policy. The distribution of power in America is a constantly shifting and rather amorphous phenomenon. Occasionally, political alliances form among different interest groups, only to be dissolved when new issues revive conflicting interests. The federal government is assumed to be a neutral body—an arbitrator, a compromiser—which soothes conflict and works out matters in the best interests of all. It is responsive to all groups and dominated by none.

Thus, from the pluralist perspective, the United States is a democratic society. All persons are free to join or otherwise support organized groups that promise to represent their interests in the national political arena. The leaders of such groups, in order to gain strength and make themselves felt at the national level, must appeal to the citizenry for support. Organizations representing great business interests, according to the pluralist perspective, are just like any other group in this respect.

Not coincidentally, *The Lonely Crowd* dismissed the idea that there are continuing, large-scale economic inequalities in American society. In fact, according to Riesman, "America is a middle-class country." He asked rhetorically "whether one would not find, over a long period of time, that decisions in America favored one group or class... over others." He answered that this was not the case. "Does not wealth exert its pull in the long run? In the past this has been so; for the future, I doubt it."[4] The rise of a multitude of veto groups has neutralized the historical power of wealth, according to Riesman. The wealthy are just like any other group: They must compete and struggle to be heard.

We are thus presented with an orthodox picture of the national political scene, one that coincides with the content of many American social studies textbooks. Riesman in his own way expressed the dominant belief about the distribution of power in the United States. But is political power really so completely dispersed throughout American society? Is the federal government just a neutral body that responds to the best interests of the American people? Is political decision making at the national level divorced from the interests of wealth and ownership? Is the upper economic class just one among many groups constantly scrambling for power? Does one group or class really run things in this society? Let us look at recent public beliefs about these issues.

[4] Riesman, *The Lonely Crowd*, p. 222.

American Beliefs About Political Power

Over the years, there have been several major surveys of American beliefs about political and economic power. These surveys, which have been conducted on both the local and national levels, have found that a significant proportion of Americans do not believe in the pluralist position. Instead, the results indicate that many Americans feel that they are powerless and that the United States is run by a small group of powerful people.

The Muskegon Studies. During the 1960s William Form and Joan Rytina conducted a survey on beliefs about the way power is distributed in the United States. They carried out a series of interviews with a sample of persons residing in the city of Muskegon, Michigan. The researchers selected participants from three economic groups—the rich, the middle class, and the poor.[5]

[5] William H. Form and Joan Rytina, "Ideological Beliefs on the Distribution of Power in the United States," *American Sociological Review*, 34 (February 1969): 19–31. See also Joan Huber and William Form, *Income and Ideology* (New York: The Free Press, 1973).

During the course of interviews, participants were asked to decide which of the following three statements best described the national distribution of power:

A. "No one group really runs the government in this country. Instead, important decisions about national policy are made by a lot of different groups such as labor, business, and religious and educational groups. These groups influence both political parties, but no single group can dictate to the others, and each group is strong enough to protect its own interests."

B. "A small group of men at the top really run the government in this country. These are the heads of the biggest business corporations, the highest officers in the Army, Navy and Air Force, and a few important senators, congressmen, and federal officials in Washington. These men dominate both the Republican and Democratic parties."

C. "Big businessmen really run the government in this country. The heads of the large corporations dominate both the Republican and Democratic parties. This means that things in Washington go pretty much the way big businessmen want them to."[6]

Three-fifths of those interviewed selected statement A, which is a summary of the pluralist perspective. But there was not an overwhelming consensus. Roughly one-fifth selected statement B and the remaining fifth chose statement C. An intriguing finding emerged when the researchers matched the economic level of the participants with the statements they chose. The higher their family income, the more likely persons were to state that pluralism best described our national system of power. Lower income persons and members of minority groups in the poor and middle classes were far more likely to select the alternative statements.

[6] Form and Rytina, "Ideological Beliefs," p. 22.

Form and Rytina concluded that persons in different economic positions see the structure of power from different vantage points and in terms of their own perceived interests. Those at higher income levels, finding that the political system generally works for them and in their class interests, are likely to voice the conventional view that this is a democratic society. On the other hand, the poor and members of minority groups have not found the political system so responsive to their needs and perceived interests; they have experienced domination and thus feel the absence of a pluralist democracy. Statements B and C, which suggest dominance, fit quite well with the everyday reality of their lives.

A decade after the study by researchers Form and Rytina, sociologist Steven Stack focused once again on Muskegon.[7] Stack wanted to see if views on the distribution of political power had changed. Although his research method differed quite a bit from that of the original study, Stack's findings—along with other work to be discussed shortly—indicate an incredibly widespread *rejection* of the pluralist perspective as time has passed.

In the Form and Rytina study three-fifths of those surveyed saw pluralism as an accurate depiction of the distribution of power in America; in Stack's study this was not the case. Indeed, three-quarters of his respondents agreed with the following statement (similar to statement B in the earlier study): "Big business executives, top governmental officials, and the military brass hold the real power in the U.S."[8] Once again low-income people were most likely to agree with this view, but clearly it had spread dramatically upward to other classes in the decade since the Form and Rytina study. More recent surveys, conducted nationally, under-

[7] Steven Stack, "Ideological Beliefs on the American Distribution of Opportunity, Power, and Rewards," *Sociological Focus*, 11 (August 1978): 221–33.

[8] Ibid., p. 227.

score the powerlessness many Americans have come to feel. These national surveys reveal that such feelings extend well beyond the poor and members of minority groups.

Polls on Attitudes Toward Government. Since the mid-1960s national surveys of public attitudes toward government officials and institutions have revealed an extraordinary degree of dissatisfaction.[9] Americans have decried secrecy and corruption in government and claimed that their interests were being sacrificed in favor of powerful special interest groups. Many Americans have described themselves as alienated and disenchanted, unable to influence the actions of their government. Sixty-six percent of those polled in 1988 agree with the statement that "most public officials are not really interested in the problems of the average man."[10] Such expressions of alienation have generally been on a steady increase at least since 1966.

In addition to political alienation and loss of respect for and trust in those who run governmental institutions, Americans have less confidence in the government. As of 1988 only 16 percent of Americans polled were able to state that they had a "great deal of confidence" in the executive branch of the federal government. Congress fared worse: Only about 15 percent of the American people had a great deal of confidence in Congress. Doing slightly better, but nonetheless poorly, were the Supreme Court (at 32 percent) and the military (at 33 percent).[11]

But various polls also have indicated that Americans continue to believe that their government *could* be made to work effectively and to meet their needs. They are not ready to toss the political system out the window.[12] In a report distributed by the U.S. Senate,[13] specially commissioned polls revealed that people saw a need for "an increased diffusion of power—both inside the structure of government and through greater scrutiny of its workings and leadership. The mandate is for participation, not direction. ...And the message is...that people want to be included and informed, not managed and ignored." The Senate report went on to note that "the people are opting strongly for a restoration of open, democratic government, where the people are trusted and consulted." This seems to indicate that, while the American people may feel managed and dominated from above and are dissatisfied over their plight, they are not willing to continue with such a situation. On an ominous note, the Senate report concluded that "if the preconditions for open government are not met, then frustration, alienation, and polarization are likely to proceed apace. And the distrust of the governed for those who govern is a dangerous development indeed."

A society in which the people feel that they cannot influence their governmental leaders, one in which so few have great confidence in those who run government, does not seem to be a *democratic* society. Instead, it appears to be a society marked by the erosion of political democracy and the concentration of power in the hands of a few.

Polls on Attitudes Toward Business. One of the other key participants in the exercise of power over the American people—the corporate world—has also undergone a crisis of faith

[9] Seymour Martin Lipset and William Schneider, *The Confidence Gap: Business, Labor, and Government in the Public Mind* (New York: The Free Press, 1983), pp. 14–29.

[10] General Social Survey for 1988, National Opinion Research Center, University of Chicago.

[11] *Harris Survey*, April 1988, by Louis Harris and Associates.

[12] See Lipset and Schneider, *The Confidence Gap*, pp. 375–412.

[13] Data and direct quotations from U.S. Senate, Committee on Government Operations, Subcommittee on Intergovernmental Relations, *Confidence and Concern: Citizens View American Government*, Part 1 (Washington. D.C.: U.S. Government Printing Office, December 3, 1973).

PUBLIC PROBLEM, PRIVATE PAIN

"Shallow" Candidates Running on "Blue Smoke and Mirrors"

Over the last decade or so, millions of Americans have chosen not to step into voting booths—not even to help select the president of the United States. In this selection Walter Dean Burnham, a widely respected political scientist at the Massachusetts Institute of Technology, comments on the current political climate as experienced by voters and nonvoters alike.

Q Professor Burnham, the American political system seems to be in a period of significant change. What's happening?

A Several things. The most important is the rise of the individually packaged campaign operation for the Presidency—the candidate, his media staff, his pollsters, his operatives and such—that the modern, primary-oriented nominating rules have done a lot to promote. Campaigns also are getting longer, due largely to the impact of the mass media, the erosion of parties and the trend of campaigners to organize what is called the permanent campaign that now starts more than a year before Election Day....

Q Is there any evidence that today's candidates are less qualified than their predecessors?

A A lot of folks have said that but we still don't have enough of a track record to know the answer. We've had long sweeps of history where the quality of candidates was not too high.... But, basically, it's true that candidates now tend to be pretty shallow on both sides. They often are unaware of what's really going on and, therefore, subject to being swayed by their own inarticulate prejudices and by smart advisers who feed them what they want to hear. On the whole, the modern political system tends to stimulate the candidacy of people who are photogenic, who go down smoothly on the TV tube and who are hyperactive. They have to be constantly banging around all over the place, and that's not exactly the kind of milieu in which careful, meditative kinds of people are likely to be happy.

Q Have these changes affected the discussion of issues?

A People typically romanticize about the attention paid to issues in politics once upon a time—say the Lincoln–Douglas debates of 1858. But there's no question that issues, however you want to think of them, used to be vastly more important relative to personalities than they are now.

Nowadays, candidates have issues and agendas, and they put them into place once they get elected, as Reagan and his friends did in 1981. But the election itself is really very much a blue-smoke-and-mirrors kind of thing.

Q Are you saying that what you see is not necessarily what you get in a political candidate these days?

A Put it this way: The candidate may even tell you what you're going to get, but it's not clear that, in a media-dominated election, the total package gives voters much incentive to really pay attention to that side of it, as compared to the personal, *People*-magazine sort of stuff....

Q On another topic, why do so few Americans vote, compared with other Western democracies?

A The underlying answer is that there is a very large number of Americans for whom the political system offers nothing, or nothing they can relate to effectively. If you don't think you're going to get anywhere by doing something, you rarely do it. Our personal-registration requirements and inadequately administered electoral machinery also make it difficult for people to vote, even if they want to. We collect taxes efficiently, and we certainly know how to process draftees efficiently. But when it comes to voting, it's catch as catch can. You've only got to hope that the local election board is up to administering a halfway-complex election.

Q How do our voter-registration laws compare?

A Our laws are uniquely American. In Canada, Australia and New Zealand, not to mention Europe, the assumption has always been that it is the job of the state to compile and maintain electoral registers—and not the job of the individual to go through a complex bureaucratic process to prove that he or she is entitled to exercise franchise. We have a turnout rate in presidential elections that is typically 25 to 30 percent lower than in most of the rest of the West. It can be demonstrated quite precisely that at least 9 percentage points of the differential can be attributed directly to personal-registration statutes.

Q Is the average voter today well enough informed?

A It is always a question as to whether anybody, even Ph.D.'s in political science, knows enough to cast intelligent votes on certain kinds of questions. The problem, in part, is that the information flow is largely controlled by the mass media and by candidates who manipulate the media. Any effective candidate knows how to do this. That means that an awful lot of what the media report—by no means all of it—is sort of artificially created. A great deal of the rest is packaged in short segments on TV, which doesn't really provide a whole lot of depth or breadth of coverage. Frequently, a voter has to look to somebody he trusts, whose expertise and commitments will help to shape his understanding....

Source: Interview, "'Shallow' Candidates Running on 'Blue Smoke and Mirrors,'" *U.S. News & World Report* (October 8, 1984): 89–90.

in recent years.[14] Most Americans continue to believe in the basic principles of the capitalist economic system—for example, that business and industry belong under private control and ownership. Survey reports indicate that Americans oppose the notion of nationalization, or federal takeover, of industries (by a government they distrust). But most believe that the national government should be "tougher" on big business. The fact that relatively few believe that corporate power will actually be curbed demonstrates the public's sense of impotence in the face of both their national government and the power now believed to be wielded by the corporate world.

Between 1966 and 1988 the percentage of the American people expressing a "great deal of confidence" in major companies dropped from 55 to 19 percent.[15] Public confidence in the quality of goods and services being sold also dropped markedly, and people expressed an ever stronger belief that they were paying out more and receiving less for their money. There were more complaints about the failure of the corporate world to provide enough steady jobs for people. Fewer Americans thought business offered young people a chance to get ahead or that it allowed people to utilize their full creative talents. Survey results show that few of the American people agree that business really cares about the individual. There is a feeling that the corporate world is not making an adequate contribution in such areas as pollution control and the support of educational, cultural, health, and charitable activities.

At the same time, the majority of the American people believe that business could and should be doing more to improve the public welfare. Americans expect business to use its money and power to help eliminate racial discrimination, wipe out poverty, rebuild the cities, control crime, and raise moral standards. Despite public expectations the corporate world has failed to respond.

As a result, public respect for the corporate world has markedly declined. While the public has in past years looked to business and industry to fill the vacuum created by government ineffectiveness, the corporate world has chosen to concentrate on the pursuit of narrow economic goals. From the perspective of the American people, the corporate world is unresponsive to their needs and too far outside the realm of popular control through governmental restraint. In 1988, some 71 percent of adults agreed that "large corporations have too much power for the good of the country."[16]

[14] See Lipset and Schneider, *The Confidence Gap*, pp. 163–98.

[15] *Harris Survey*, April 1988.

[16] Survey by ABC News/Washington Post, July 1988.

Americans continue to hold negative attitudes toward government and business, with a majority feeling themselves powerless in the face of corporate and governmental interests. It seems clear that the pluralist perspective does not coincide with the views and experiences of millions of Americans. In the view of a significant proportion of citizens and of many scholars, the United States is not working as a democracy of, by, and for the people. Power, like wealth, is not distributed equally.

THE POWER ELITE PERSPECTIVE

Shortly after the publication of David Riesman's *The Lonely Crowd*, another sociologist, C. Wright Mills, directly challenged the pluralist perspective, offering a different version of the way power is distributed in American society.[17] His work, *The Power Elite*, set off a debate that has not yet ceased. Mills' study has caused many sociologists to take a new and more critical look at the national political system.

The Attack on Pluralism

In *The Power Elite*, C. Wright Mills attacked the pluralist perspective as a form of romanticism. The position taken by scholars like Riesman, Mills felt, reflected what we might *like* American society to be rather than what it is. The United States is not a democratic society, despite whatever vestiges of pluralism might be said to exist. Rather, in Mills' eyes, it is a society dominated by a set of *elites*—the men (and in rare instances, women) who hold the very highest offices in the large-scale bureaucratic hierarchies that have come to prevail in the United States.

Mills did not deny the existence of farm groups, labor and professional organizations, and other interest groups. Such groups clearly exist, but Mills felt they exist at a secondary level of power. The power to make decisions of national and international significance is on another level altogether, a level above and beyond the reach of the multitude of veto or interest groups deemed so significant by Riesman. It is the *power elite* alone that makes the decisions that shape the nature and course of the society in which we live. To Mills, Congress is not part of this power elite. It too exists on the secondary level of power. The decisions made by Congress—often under the buffeting pressures of one or another set of interest groups—are ordinarily made within an overarching political and economic framework determined and promoted by the power elite.

Identifying the Power Elite

Who are the members of the power elite? Mills answered this question by tracing the historical ascendancy of three major components of American society. The first component is *big business and the corporate rich*. Unlike Riesman, Mills denied that the political significance of economic elites has undergone a decline in the twentieth century. To Mills, the persons who sit at the very highest levels in America's giant corporations and other financial institutions retain enormous political strength. Whether through direct participation in national government, campaign contributions to political candidates, or other forms of political activity, economic elites work to ensure that their particular interests are met.

Second, Mills identified the *military* as a bureaucratic entity whose top officials possess membership in the power elite. Mills traced the historical ascendancy of the American military

[17] C. Wright Mills, *The Power Elite* (New York: Oxford University Press, 1956). Mills' influence is readily detectable in other works; see, for example, Ralph Miliband, *The State in Capitalist Society* (New York: Basic Books, 1969). Critiques of Mills' work can be found in William Domhoff and Hoyt B. Ballard, eds., *C. Wright Mills and the Power Elite* (Boston: Beacon Press, 1968).

from a marginal arm of civilian government, important only in times of war, to a vast hierarchical institution that has become an integral part of the American scene. Reaching preeminence during World War II, it has since grown in size and in political and economic importance. As do members of the nation's economic elite, the highest officers in the military establishment have particular interests to pursue and protect. Their positions at the very top provide them with the means to do so.

Third, Mills focused on the *executive branch* of the federal government. Top officials of this branch, including the president, have come to reign over an immense bureaucratic network. The office of the president and the cabinet agencies under this office have progressively expanded in size and importance. In Mills' view, the executive branch overwhelms Congress in terms of power, and Congress largely responds to initiatives and decisions that flow from the executive branch. The two governmental bodies are not coequal, in Mills' estimation, and those persons in the top positions of the executive branch are prominent members of the power elite.

Thus, Mills presented a complex of elites in which there is a three-way sharing of power, a triumvirate that sits in judgment over major national and international decisions of the day. No segment of the elite—economic, political, or military—dominates, though a close reading of Mills' study can easily lead one to conclude that he saw economic elites as first among equals. Nevertheless, each segment of the power elite has definite interests it wishes to pursue. These interests can be met only by close cooperation with the others:

Among the ways in which the affluent influence political policies is by contributing to political campaigns. Their participation in such affairs as fund-raising dinners earns the gratitude of candidates and assures contributors that their interests are unlikely to go ignored if their candidates win. (*Owen Franken/Stock, Boston*)

> The power to make decisions of national and international importance is . . . seated in the political, military, and economic institutions. As each has assumed its modern shape, its effects on the other two have become greater and the traffic between the three has increased. As each of these domains has coincided with the others, as decisions have become broader, the leading men of each . . . have tended to come together to form the power elite of America.[18]

The persons who participate in this powerful triumvirate, in Mills' judgment, form a self-contained, cohesive social group. In his study, Mills attempted to show the bases of their group cohesion. The members of the power elite, he argued, come from similar social origins. Close personal and family ties exist among those whose bureaucratic positions provide elite status. And there is a frequent interchange of personnel between the hierarchies commanded by the elite. Top corporate executives are tapped for key appointments in the executive branch, and persons of wealth are routinely invited to take on ambassadorial posts around the world. Such persons move in and out of government with ease. High-ranking executive branch officials and retiring military officers frequently enter key offices in business and industry. The ease of movement, to Mills, is a visible indication of the close ties among those at the top, as well as an indication that elites tend to think alike. To Mills, members of the power elite are of a similar social type, thereby contributing to the unity of the power elite as a group.

The Erosion of Public Involvement

As we have seen, Riesman argued that Americans exert political influence through the medium of organized veto or interest groups. Mills did not have so optimistic a view of the role of the public. According to Mills, dominance by the power elite produced the *massification* of the American people. By this he meant that the public, in succumbing to manipulation by the powerful, had become increasingly unable to define and act on its own political interests. In Mills' terms, the American majority had turned into a *mass society* and existed on the third or lowest level of power.

The power elite manipulates the American public through careful orchestration of the mass media, the major means by which people find out what is going on. By selective censorship of information, by limiting the realm of national debate, by emphasizing entertainment over messages that inform, the mass media minimize serious political discussion and controversy. This is to be expected, since the national media are owned, controlled, and financed (by advertising) by the economic component of the power elite. The American public is not properly informed and thus cannot participate in deciding the issues that affect all people. Thus, Mills argued, members of the mass society are progressively less capable of understanding issues and comprehending decisions that are allegedly made in their interest by those at the top.

As a result of manipulation from above and their powerlessness over important national decisions, citizens of the mass society have become less and less interested in politics. Political democracy becomes less possible, and the majority of Americans find themselves at the mercy of forces they can neither understand nor control. Slowly but perceptibly, the members of the power elite have become more inaccessible and less accountable to those affected by their high-level decisions.

Inaccessibility and lack of accountability open the way for abuses of power. Such abuses no doubt often go undetected and unreported, thus remaining uninvestigated. But many fail to remain hidden. In his book *The Criminal Elite,* James William Coleman surveys many such abuses both in government and in the business world. If we restrict our attention to events in-

---

[18] Mills, *The Power Elite,* p. 9.

volving political officials at the national level, examples examined by Coleman include:[19]

Acceptance of illegal campaign contributions in return for political favors;

Illegal surveillance and harassment of civil rights and other protest organizations;

Burglary of political opponents' offices and the illegal tampering with the U.S. mail;

Maintenance of secret lists of "potentially dangerous" subversives who would be picked up and imprisoned in times of "national emergency";

Spreading harmful "disinformation" (false information) to discredit and defame political opponents or to create divisiveness and discord among them;

The use of agents provocateurs to incite others to commit crimes or to provoke others to violence so as to secure arrests; and

Involvement in an encouragement of assassination attempts on foreign leaders with whose policies there was disagreement.

These are not the kinds of behaviors common sense tells us we should expect from public figures in a democratic society.

THE INSTRUMENTALIST PERSPECTIVE

C. Wright Mills' concept of the power elite—wherein leaders of corporations, the executive branch of government, and the military were seen as coequal wielders of power—sidesteps one central issue, that of the relationship between *class inequality* in America and the distribution of political power. By focusing on bureaucratic elites and their self-interests in maintaining their institutional positions, Mills seemed to overlook the possibility that government actually functions in the interests of a particular social class. Is government, while purporting to represent the interests of *all* the people in America, really a servant of the upper class? Is it an *instrument* of that class, catering to its interests even at the expense of others? Some would say yes. This "instrumentalist" perspective, as it has been called,[20] is revealed in the works of G. William Domhoff. His first major study in this area appeared in the late 1960s under the title of *Who Rules America?* and has become part of an ongoing debate over the true nature of governance in nominally democratic societies.[21]

America's Social and Economic Upper Class

Domhoff began by trying to establish the existence of a social upper class of national dimensions—that is, an exclusive social grouping that reigns supreme in terms of status and prestige. As evidence of the existence of such a class, Domhoff pointed to the social registers that have long been maintained in a score of major American cities. The individuals and families listed in these registers are there by virtue of family pedigree and economic circumstance. They are members of "high society."

Domhoff also identified a set of institutions and events that cater to the exclusive tastes and interests of upper-class individuals. These include private schools, elite universities and colleges, clubs and resorts, and parties and balls. Domhoff argued that they provide a basis for cohesiveness among members of the upper class, for it is at such institutions and events

[19] James William Coleman, *The Criminal Elite*, 2nd ed. (New York: St. Martin's Press, 1989), pp. 51–55 and 58–72.

[20] See David A. Gold, Clarence Y. H. Lo, and Erik Olin Wright, "Recent Developments in Marxist Theories of the Capitalist State," *Monthly Review*, 27 (October 1975): 29–43.

[21] G. William Domhoff, *Who Rules America?* (Englewood Cliffs, N.J.: Prentice-Hall, 1967). Domhoff pulls together accumulating evidence in support of his perspective in *Who Rules America Now?* (New York: Simon & Schuster, 1983).

that these people mingle with one another.[22] The outcomes are the formulation of friendships, the establishment of business and social contacts, and the exposure of youth to potential marriage partners of the "right kind." Adults and children of this social upper class readily sense their high status and are easily able to differentiate themselves from others who do not "belong."

Having established to his satisfaction that such an upper class exists, Domhoff turned to another question. Is this *social* upper class also an *economic* upper class? He found a great overlap between those with the greatest wealth and highest incomes and those who are considered at the top in social terms. Members of the social upper class are, for the most part, wealthy businessmen and their families or descendants of such men. They comprise that component of society Mills called the economic elite.

America's Governing Class

Domhoff was particularly interested in discovering whether this national social and economic upper class is also a ruling or *governing class* in a political sense. Domhoff defined a governing class as "a social upper class which owns a disproportionate amount of a country's wealth, receives a disproportionate amount of a country's yearly income, and contributes a disproportionate number of its members to the controlling institutions and key decision-making groups of the country."[23] Thus, Domhoff looked at the ways in which members of the social and economic upper class participate in the nation's major institutions.

One place major decisions are made is in the dominant economic institutions that, by virtue of their overall size, sales, and assets, are the foundation of the American economy. Decisions made at the top levels of these institutions often have an impact on the economic well-being of the entire nation. The largest corporations and financial institutions, according to Domhoff, are under the control of the upper class. Upper-class individuals either play the roles of directors and managers of such institutions themselves or handpick persons from non–upper-class backgrounds for such key decision-making roles.

Obviously, high-ranking officials in the federal government also hold a great deal of power. In Domhoff's words, "Members of the American upper class and their employees control the Executive Branch."[24] To support this assertion, he examined the ways in which presidential nominees are controlled. The key here is money. Financing a national political campaign has become an increasingly expensive proposition. Candidates are generally unable to support most of the costs themselves, and contributions by the public are generally insufficient. Thus, private benefactors must be sought out. Upper-class individuals and corporate contributors are most likely to support candidates who best articulate upper-class goals and values and who are unlikely to threaten upper-class economic interests. Donations or loans implicitly mean favors in return, and the debts of successful presidential candidates to wealthy benefactors are reflected, in Domhoff's view, in key policy decisions.

Furthermore, the president appoints individuals to key posts in the federal bureaucracy and the judiciary. Appointees to such positions of importance, according to Domhoff, tend to come from the social and economic upper class in far greater frequency than one would expect, given its small size. Those individuals who lack upper-class backgrounds, Domhoff suggests, are appointed on the basis of their past demonstrated

[22] See, e.g., Peter Cookson and Caroline Persell, *Preparing for Power: America's Elite Boarding Schools* (New York: Harper & Row Publishers, 1985).

[23] Domhoff, *Who Rules America*, p. 9.

[24] Ibid., p. 84

performance in understanding and serving upper-class interests. Through this and through data on financial contributions, Domhoff was able to support his argument that the upper class is, in reality, a governing or ruling class.

Pluralism Below

Congress is heavily influenced but not controlled outright by the upper class, in Domhoff's view. Members of Congress are often dependent on upper-class contributions for their election campaigns. (Table 2.1 provides an overview of individual and corporate campaign financing.) They are also directly subject to influence by the powerful, well-financed lobbies that represent upper-class economic interests. Many legislators are themselves from upper-class backgrounds. However, Congress is also subject to pressures from many groups that do not represent upper-class interests. Thus, senators and representatives are very much subject to influence but are not under absolute upper-class control.

It is with regard to Congress and on the local and state levels of government that Domhoff feels the pluralists may have a point. While decisions and policies made in the executive branch of the federal government and in the corporate world may be under the control of upper-class individuals or their representatives, more political diversity exists below. Domhoff saw no incompatibility between top-level control by the upper class and pluralism at another level. Here he seems to be siding with Mills, who also conceptualized a secondary level of power operating within a framework of domination imposed from above.

But Domhoff departed from Mills by insisting that, despite the existence of a governing class, the United States is still democratic. He argued that the governing class is not monolithic and that there are splits and divisions within it. Not all members of the upper class agree on just what policies and decisions will best coincide with their short-term and long-term interests. Domhoff suggested that competing factions within the upper class may find themselves forced to indirectly seek support from non–upper-class groups in order to meet their self-defined needs. Thus, members of the upper class may be divided over whether to throw their weight behind Democratic or Republican candidates for national office. It is a question of which party and candidate promises to best protect those aspects of the societal status quo the upper class wishes to preserve. Domhoff suggests that American democracy is based primarily on cleavages within the governing class itself, at the same time that this class effectively shapes the nature and course of American life.

THE STRUCTURALIST PERSPECTIVE

Since the power elite and the instrumentalist perspectives have been put forth, yet another view has surfaced to raise important issues about the use of power by those in whose hands it may be concentrated. The so-called structuralist perspective does not deny that political power is concentrated in the hands of a few. The perspective acknowledges Domhoff's findings that in the United States the "few" are by and large members of the social and economic upper class or their helpers. What the structuralist perspective does suggest is that the wielders of political power are constantly constrained by the need to attend to the demands of our corporate capitalist economy.[25] Such constraints have implications for decision making, no matter what group manages to ascend to elected or appointed political office.

Let us look briefly at the nature of America's capitalist economic system and then at the structuralist perspective as it relates politics to eco-

[25] See Gold, Lo, and Wright, "Recent Developments in Marxist Theories of the Capitalist State."

TABLE 2.1 Congressional Campaign Finances—Receipts and Disbursements, 1981–86

	House of representatives						Senate					
	Amount (mil. dol.)			Percent distribution			Amount (mil. dol.)			Percent distribution		
Item	1981–82	1983–84	1985–86	1981–82	1983–84	1985–86	1981–82	1983–84	1985–86	1981–82	1983–84	1985–86
Total receipts*	**213.2**	**222.5**	**257.7**	**100.0**	**100.0**	**100.0**	**141.5**	**174.7**	**214.4**	**100.0**	**100.0**	**100.0**
Contributions												
$500 and over	34.0	37.5	50.4	15.9	16.8	19.6	36.6	44.0	68.6	25.9	25.2	32.0
Party committee	6.1	5.5	3.6	2.8	2.5	1.0	1.2	1.1	1.4	0.8	0.6	0.6
Non-party committee	61.1	75.7	87.4	28.6	34.0	33.9	22.6	29.7	45.3	15.9	17.0	21.1
Democrats	108.8	121.4	139.9	51.1	54.6	54.3	69.0	84.2	91.8	48.8	48.2	42.8
Republicans	104.1	100.5	117.7	48.8	45.2	45.7	72.1	90.3	122.5	51.0	51.7	57.1
Others	0.3	0.5	0.1	0.1	0.2	(z)	0.4	0.2	0.1	0.3	0.1	(z)
Incumbents	110.6	132.4	149.7	51.9	59.5	58.1	55.1	74.8	90.3	38.9	42.8	42.1
Challengers	53.7	55.5	49.2	25.2	25.0	19.1	48.0	38.9	67.2	33.9	22.3	31.3
Open seats†	48.9	34.6	58.8	22.9	15.5	22.8	38.4	61.0	56.9	27.1	34.9	26.5
Total disbursements	204.0	203.6	239.3	100.0	100.0	100.0	138.4	170.5	211.6	100.0	100.0	100.0
Democrats	103.1	111.0	128.7	50.5	54.5	53.8	66.9	82.0	89.0	48.3	48.1	42.0
Republicans	100.6	91.8	110.5	49.3	45.1	46.2	71.1	88.3	122.6	51.4	51.8	57.9
Others	0.3	0.7	0.1	0.2	0.3	(z)	0.4	0.2	(z)	0.3	0.1	(z)
Incumbents	102.6	114.9	132.5	50.3	56.5	55.4	52.9	72.1	89.3	38.2	42.3	42.2
Challengers	53.1	54.7	48.8	26.1	26.9	20.4	47.6	38.3	66.2	34.4	22.5	31.3
Open seats†	48.2	33.9	58.0	23.6	16.7	24.2	37.9	60.1	56.1	27.4	35.3	26.5

[Covers all campaign finance activity during two-year calendar period indicated for primary, general, runoff, and special elections. For 1981–82 relates to 1,957 House of Representatives candidates and to 283 Senate candidates; for 1983–84, to 1,782 House of Representatives candidates and 254 Senate candidates; for 1985–86, to 1,611 House of Representatives candidates and 262 Senate candidates. Data have been adjusted to eliminate transfers between all committees within a campaign.]

Key: Z, less than $50,000 or 0.05 percent

*Includes other types of receipts, not shown separately.

†Elections in which an incumbent did not seek reelection.

Source: U.S. Department of Commerce, Bureau of the Census, *Statistical Abstract of the United States, 1989* (Washington, D.C.: U.S. Government Printing Office, 1989), p. 263.

According to the instrumentalist perspective, it is at the state and local levels that the people are most likely to have a voice in political policies and decisions. In this photograph a legislator meets with a group of citizens lobbying for her support on issues of concern to them. (*Joel Gordon*)

nomics. As we shall see, governmental elites, no matter what their class background now or in the future, may have problems *not* serving the upper class over and above all other Americans.

From Free Enterprise to "Corporate Capitalism"

The United States has a capitalist economy.[26] For the most part its "productive apparatus" (i.e., its means of producing goods and services for sale in the marketplace) is privately owned. Moreover, production is undertaken first and foremost for the purpose of making profits. Private owners are prone to reinvest much of their profits so as to make even more profits in the future. This general picture of what capitalism looks like could fit the U.S. economy at almost any point in its history.

Until the mid-nineteenth century the U.S. economy consisted largely of numerous individual productive units, small and often organized around the extended family. Each unit provided goods and services for sale in localized markets and for self-consumption. The majority of American workers were self-employed, primarily in agriculture but also in various crafts, trades, professions, and sales activities. This was the system of "free-enterprise" capitalism—small entrepreneurs, often engaged in competition with one another—that was glowingly de-

---

[26] An informative overview of American capitalism is found in Richard C. Edwards, Michael Reich, and Thomas E. Weisskopf, eds., *The Capitalist System*, 2nd ed. (Englewood Cliffs, N.J.: Prentice-Hall, 1978).

scribed by Adam Smith in his 1776 classic, *The Wealth of Nations*.

Large-scale changes in the nature of economic organization began to take place after the Civil War and have continued until this day. Industrialization reduced self-employment and diminished the number of competing entrepreneurs. Only the most successful survived and grew; most others fell by the wayside. The modern large corporation was born as the wealthy combined their resources to purchase the new machine technology that would make regional and national markets possible. Such firms drove the less well-endowed competitors out of business. Free-enterprise capitalism thus slowly gave way to "corporate capitalism"—a capitalist economy in which a few large firms came to dominate most product and service areas.

Michael Parenti underscored the degree to which our economy has become concentrated:

> In just about every industry a few giant companies do from 80 to 98 percent of the business. Some 200 companies account for 80 percent of all resources used in manufacturing.[27]

Likewise, Thomas Dye points out how few people today are in a position to make decisions that affect the economic affairs and well-being of tens of millions of Americans:

> About 4,500 individuals—two one-thousandths of one percent of the population—exercise formal authority over half of the nation's industrial assets, over half of all banking assets, over half of all assets in communications, transportation and utilities, and over two thirds of all insurance assets.... The reason for this concentration of power in the hands of so few people is found in the concentration of industrial and financial assets in a small number of gigantic corporations.[28]

[27] Michael Parenti, *Democracy for the Few*, 4th ed. (New York: St. Martin's Press, 1983), pp. 11–12.

[28] Thomas R. Dye, *Who's Running America?* 3rd ed. (Englewood Cliffs, N.J.: Prentice-Hall, 1983), p. 20.

Corporate Capitalism and Politics

From the instrumentalist perspective, government at the national level largely serves as an instrument of the upper class (a class primarily made up of rich businessmen, their families, and their descendants, according to G. William Domhoff). This implies that if only non–upper-class groups could obtain high-level government positions, they too could make government an instrument. Interests other than those of the upper class could be served.

However, those holding to a structuralist perspective would take issue with such possibilities. For government may be seen as somewhat of a captive of the ongoing needs of corporate capitalism. The maintenance of a healthy economic order—on which not only large corporations and the rich, but everyone else depends—must take precedence in policymaking, no matter who runs the government.

Martin N. Marger succinctly summarizes the structuralist position:

> Since the viability of the state is dependent upon a healthy economy... state leaders *must* promote the interests of big business (that is, the corporations) regardless of who they are or what their views may be. If the economy declines, tax revenues dry up, imperiling government programs and weakening public support for elected officials and other government leaders. The general interests of the capitalist class are thus naturally served. Indeed, state leaders may be more aware of the general need for maintaining a stable social order (that is, a capitalist system) than profit-oriented capitalists.[29]

Since the needs of capitalism (e.g., a lower tax burden on corporations to enhance profits) are often at odds with the needs of the population at large (e.g., a higher tax burden on individuals to offset corporate tax reductions) tradeoffs

[29] Marger, *Elites and Masses*, p. 43.

must be made.[30] The structuralist perspective is suggesting that no matter who is in charge of our governmental institutions, the needs of capitalism by necessity overwhelm all others. To the degree to which this is true in practice, and it is clear from survey data that the public senses that this is what goes on, it is small wonder that so many persons are disillusioned with and alienated from this deformed version of political democracy.

The structuralist perspective provides a context within which we can interpret federal policymakers' actions in recent years. For example, during the Reagan administration (1981–88) numerous actions were undertaken to serve the interests of large corporations and the wealthy upper class. Income tax rates were lowered in ways that disproportionately favored the rich, while firms were allowed new tax reductions, deductions, and writeoffs to increase their economic health.[31] Huge sums were spent to buttress the well-being of the aerospace–defense industry, a central component of America's "permanent war economy" (see Chapter 3) on which many private fortunes depend. In these and other ways federal policymakers sought to enhance even further the economic advantage of those among whom America's economic assets have become highly concentrated. In this way, the policymakers believed, investment in economic activity and growth would be encouraged and ultimately the benefits would "trickle down" to the general population.

As the U.S. government acted to meet the needs of our capitalist economy in the foregoing ways, it balanced these actions with various cost-cutting initiatives. In particular, it decided that the costs associated with encouraging economic growth would be borne by cutting back spending on programs for the nonwealthy. Unfortunately, this all was taking place during a period when large numbers of Americans were in greater need of such programs than ever.[32] More people, especially women and children, were experiencing economic dislocation and poverty. For the first time since the 1960s widespread hunger began to be reported. Homeless people began to appear on the nation's streets. But federal policymakers cut back spending on low-income housing. They moved to reduce expenditures on government food programs and income assistance to poor individuals and families. Eligibility requirements were tightened to discourage participation in programs ranging from social security for the disabled to medical care for low-income children. Federal policymakers resisted efforts to increase the minimum wage and dismissed proposals for government subsidization of day care, which would allow more mothers to work outside the home.

Nor has the middle class been spared a share of the burden from federal policymakers' fixation with the need to promote the welfare of those at the top. Besides being asked to shoulder a larger part of the tax burden (since the rich and corporations are shouldering less), those in the middle have seen their real incomes fall in the face of rising costs of living with which wages and salaries fail to keep pace. While the costs of higher education have zoomed, federal policymakers tightened eligibility for student financial aid and substituted loan programs for those providing outright grants. Meanwhile, escalating rents and prices of houses have forced members of the middle class (and those less affluent) to spend an ever higher percentage of income on shelter. While the wealthy deduct the interest paid on their home loans from their income tax, these interest rates remain so high and purchase prices so inflated that increasing

[30] See James O'Connor, *The Fiscal Crisis of the State* (New York: St. Martin's Press, 1973).

[31] Steve Brouwer, *Sharing the Pie* (Carlisle, Pa.: Big Picture Books, 1988), p. 6.

[32] Ibid., p. 4. See also Center for Popular Economics, *A Field Guide to the U.S. Economy* (New York: Pantheon Books, 1987).

numbers of young adults cannot afford to own homes.

U.S. capitalism as a system may be working, as government policies provide economic incentives and rewards to its key operatives and owners. As the system benefits, so by definition does the upper class. This, in the 1980s, was made possible only by escalating the level of sacrifice, deferred dreams, and outright suffering among the majority. As our political apparatus makes such tradeoffs, which at times it *must* from the structuralist perspective, estrangement from this apparatus can only be reinforced.

POLITICAL NONPARTICIPATION

As we have seen, many Americans are asking whether our political system is truly democratic and whose interests political representatives are serving. Feeling that their voices are not being heard, a significant proportion of citizens have become alienated and have withdrawn from participation in national politics.

Unofficially, the United States maintains a two-party system. The Democratic and Republican parties dominate elections for national office. In the past three or four decades, an ever-increasing percentage of the voting population has been unwilling to identify with either major party. According to Gallup poll data, a substantial bloc of people are choosing to call themselves independents.[33] The growth of this bloc reflects numerous factors, among which is the substantial dissatisfaction that has developed over the conduct of national politics.

Even more serious a reflection of political alienation is the apathy of eligible voters. Over one-third of the U.S. citizens who are eligible are not registered to vote. And participation of eligible voters in elections has been low for a long time.[34] In the 1980, 1984, and 1988 elections barely more than half of all eligible voters participated in the choice of the new president. (See Table 2.2.) Ronald Reagan's 1980 "landslide," as the media called it, was provided by the little more than one-quarter of the eligible voters who wanted him elected. The number of voters choosing him in 1984 was somewhat higher but still comprised a minority of those eligible to vote. George Bush was likewise elected by a minority in 1988. An even greater level of indifference is discernible with regard to the election of persons to the U.S. Congress.

Low voter turnout could simply be due to satisfaction (or dissatisfaction) with all competing candidates. But given the other indices of political alienation we have mentioned, it seems more likely that declining turnouts represent cynicism and disgust over the workings of the political system in general.[35]

The term *democracy* refers to a political system through which it is possible—and in which members of society want—to have some input into those decisions that affect them. In such a system, the people themselves play an informed and active role in determining the nature and course of their society. Power rests in the hands of the people, and government expresses their will. It seems clear that the American political system is not meeting these criteria.

The concentration of power in the hands of a few—be it a power elite or a governing class—means that many of the crucial issues of our times are decided for us, if they are even raised at all. The consequences are felt in terms of how, for example, questions such as the following get answered: Shall we have a more equitable system of taxation, one that minimizes economic inequalities? Shall we set up mechanisms to redistribute wealth and income in the interests of eliminating poverty? Shall we reorganize this

[33] Data on political party identification appear periodically in *Gallup Opinion Index*.

[34] See Frances Fox Piven and Richard A. Cloward, *Why Americans Don't Vote* (New York: Pantheon Books, 1988).

[35] See Marger, *Elites and Masses*, pp. 239–41.

TABLE 2.2 Participation in Elections for President and U.S. Representatives, 1980–88

Year	Resident population (incl. aliens) of voting age* (1,000)	Votes cast: For president (1,000)	Votes cast: Percent of voting age population	Votes cast: For U.S. representatives (1,000)	Votes cast: Percent of voting age population	Year	Resident population (incl. aliens) of voting age* (1,000)	Votes cast: For president (1,000)	Votes cast: Percent of voting age population	Votes cast: For U.S. representatives (1,000)	Votes cast: Percent of voting age population
1960	109,672	68,838	62.8	64,133	58.5	1974	146,338	(x)	(x)	52,495	35.9
1962	112,952	(x)	(x)	51,267	45.4	1976	152,308	81,556	53.5	74,422	48.9
1964	114,090	70,645	61.9	65,895	57.8	1978	158,369	(x)	(x)	55,332	34.9
1966	116,638	(x)	(x)	52,908	45.4	1980	164,595	86,515	52.6	77,995	47.4
1968	120,285	73,212	60.9	66,288	55.1	1982	169,939	(x)	(x)	64,514	38.0
1970	124,498	(x)	(x)	54,173	43.5	1984	174,447	92,653	53.1	83,231	47.7
1972	140,777	77,719	55.2	71,430	50.7	1986	178,335	(x)	(x)	59,619	33.4
						1988	182,628	91,610†	50.2	(NA)	(NA)

[As of **November.** Estimated resident population twenty-one years old and over, 1960–70, except as noted, and eighteen years old and over thereafter; includes Armed Forces. District of Columbia is included in votes cast for president beginning 1964 and in votes cast for representative beginning 1972]

Key: NA, not available. X, not applicable.

*Population eighteen and over in Georgia and Kentucky, nineteen and over in Alaska, and twenty and over in Hawaii, 1960–70.

†Source: Committee for the Study of the American Electorate, Washington, D.C., *Non-Voter Study, '88–'89,* forthcoming.

Source: U.S. Department of Commerce, Bureau of the Census, *Statistical Abstract of the United States, 1989* (Washington, D.C.: U.S. Government Printing Office, 1989), p. 258.

society's productive apparatus so as to eliminate unemployment and fully utilize our productive capabilities? Are there particular elements of business and industry that should be taken out of private hands and placed under public ownership and control? Shall we limit defense expenditures in favor of improving the quality of life? Would the resources devoted to space exploration be better used for more earthly needs? Shall we require corporations to bear the full costs of ending their pollution and environmental destruction, instead of passing the costs on to the consumer and taxpayer? To what degree are we to share our wealth and technology with underdeveloped nations around the world?

In a democratic society these issues should be debated and decided by the people. In the United States they are decided by a minority of men, many of whom have more than a passing interest in protecting the status quo. With power concentrated in the hands of a few, the majority of society's members cannot help but feel powerless and alienated from their rulers. People become objects rather than actors, victims of history rather than makers of it.

TOWARD THE DEMOCRATIC IDEAL

The concentration of political and economic power can be arrested and reversed. Persons must inject themselves into the political arena and make their concerns heard and felt. Staying silent is equivalent to sanctioning the status quo. Americans must take greater advantage of the lessons of the 1960s, when the collective political activities of people committed to change had a significant impact on national policies.

In the early 1960s, centuries of American tradition were overturned by the efforts of an active and aggressive grassroots civil rights movement. Segments of the racial minority and white populations entered into the political arena, stirring up a major shift in race relations in this country. Governmental elites, as indifferent to racism as their predecessors, were pressured into providing federal legislation to protect and enhance opportunities for racial minorities. If those who dared to launch and join that civil rights movement had written off change as hopeless, governmental indifference would have continued.

By the late 1960s, a series of presidential decisions, made secretly and without reference to the public, had embroiled the United States in a war in Southeast Asia. As American involvement escalated and as the costs of the war became clear, tens of millions of people voiced their outrage in the national political arena. Governmental elites were forced to alter their stance on the war and withdraw from involvement in it, in response to the popular pressures placed upon them. If those who attacked America's presence in Southeast Asia had not done so, the wartime carnage might still be going on.

It is not correct to assume that participation in political activity will make no difference. In fact, as the preceding examples indicate, the fabric of national politics is much more delicate and vulnerable to change from below than we often recognize. Much can be done when people cease being spectators to decisions of national consequence and seek ways to help shape such decisions.

College students are in an excellent position to analyze and reflect on major political issues. Indeed, students played key roles in the initiation and conduct of the civil rights movement of the 1960s and antiwar movements of the 1960s and early 1970s. By joining or creating organizations that are outspokenly dedicated to progressive societal change, students can help generate the public discussion necessary for such change to be realized. Such discussion and the pressures for change to which it is likely to give rise are unlikely to be generated from other than grassroots directions. Certainly those whose political and economic power depends on maintaining the status quo are unlikely to stimulate discussion of change.

During the late 1960s and early 1970s, increasing numbers of Americans participated in demonstrations and voiced their outrage over the war in Southeast Asia. In this photo a Vietnam veteran adds his voice to the anti-war effort. With similar commitment, Americans could help shape national policy on the many crucial issues that concern us today. (*Walter S. Silver/The Picture Cube*)

Along with grassroots movements for change must come major alterations in the conduct of government. In the mid-1970s, in the aftermath of Watergate, Congress passed campaign financing laws to limit direct private contributions to presidential candidates and to collect public funds for use in campaigns. These laws should be progressively strengthened and loopholes should be eliminated. For example, wealthy candidates can still use their own personal funds to outspend less affluent ones in political campaigns, and congressional campaigns are not subject to the financing laws. So-called PACs (political action committees), allowable under the law, permit powerful interest groups to make campaign contributions of such a magnitude that incumbents' favoritism is easily bought. (See Table 2.3.) This must cease.

All candidates for national political office and all elected and appointed officials and their staffs should be required by law to make regular full disclosure of their economic interests. Members of Congress, for example, should not be permitted to sit on committees or vote for bills that are directly connected to their economic holdings. The tie between economic self-interest and political behavior must be completely broken if the concerns of the American public are to be addressed effectively.

It is also important to facilitate greater public involvement in national politics. The federal government should be working to encourage all citizens to register to vote. It should be subsidizing regular television coverage of significant congressional debates and committee hearings. Election procedures should be simplified so that anyone can run for public office without going through a great deal of red tape. Presidential primaries and elections should be conducted on a national basis, rather than state by state. All such changes would bring more people into politics and increase the probability that democracy will become more than a symbolic ideal in this society.

SUMMARY

There are four major perspectives on the workings of American's political system. The conventional view is that America is democratic and pluralistic and that no one group or class dominates politics at the national level. Yet many Americans feel dominated and see themselves as powerless to affect decisions that affect them.

Two alternative perspectives suggest that political power has become concentrated in the hands of a few. The power elite perspective emphasizes the important role played by those in top positions in the corporate world, the military, and the executive branch of government. The instrumentalist perspective emphasizes the power-wielding capabilities of the rich as they participate in or otherwise influence government decisions. While differing in their emphases, these two perspectives seem closer to the reality experienced by many Americans than does the pluralist view. Meanwhile, the structuralist perspective calls our attention to the constraints on governmental leaders—even were they to be from non–upper-class origins—stemming from the needs of corporate capitalism.

To the degree to which political power is concentrated in the hands of a few, abuses of power can be expected. With such concentration and abuses comes political alienation. Americans must overcome this sense of alienation and challenge concentrated power, seeking changes and reforms that will bring the political system closer to the democratic ideal.

DISCUSSION QUESTIONS

1. How were you taught to view the workings of the American political system in elementary school? In high school? How much of what you were taught seems to fit with reality?
2. How important is it for people to vote in elections? Do you feel that voting or not voting makes a difference? In what way?
3. How do your family and friends view politics and politicians at the national level? To what degree and in what ways do you share their views?
4. While the 1960s and early 1970s were years of widespread protest, especially by college students, very little of this kind of activity is going on now. Why do you think this is the case?
5. Are you optimistic or pessimistic about whether America's political system can be moved closer to the democratic ideal? On what do you base your optimism or pessimism?

TABLE 2.3 **Contributions to Congressional Campaigns by Political Action Committees (PACs) by Type of Committee, 1970–86 (in millions of dollars)**

	House of Representatives						Senate					
Type of committee	Total	Demo-crats	Republi-cans	Incum-bents	Chal-lengers	Open seats*	Total	Demo-crats	Republi-cans	Incum-bents	Chal-lengers	Open seats*
1979–80, total†	**37.9**	**20.5**	**17.2**	**24.9**	**7.9**	**5.1**	**17.3**	**8.4**	**9.0**	**8.6**	**6.6**	**2.1**
Corporate	12.2	4.8	7.5	8.1	2.6	1.5	6.9	2.1	4.8	2.7	3.3	0.9
Trade association‡	11.7	5.1	6.6	8.0	2.2	1.5	4.1	1.9	2.2	2.2	1.4	0.5
Labor	9.4	8.9	0.4	6.6	1.5	1.2	3.8	3.4	0.4	2.7	0.7	0.4
Nonconnected§	3.1	0.9	2.1	1.0	1.4	0.7	1.9	0.5	1.4	0.5	1.1	0.3
1981–82, total†	**61.1**	**34.2**	**26.8**	**40.8**	**10.9**	**9.4**	**22.6**	**11.2**	**11.4**	**14.3**	**5.2**	**3.0**
Corporate	18.9	7.0	12.0	14.4	2.0	2.6	8.6	2.4	6.2	5.5	1.7	1.4
Trade association‡	16.8	7.2	9.7	12.4	2.1	2.3	5.0	2.2	2.8	3.7	0.8	0.5
Labor	15.4	14.7	0.7	8.5	4.3	2.6	4.9	4.5	0.4	3.0	1.3	0.5
Nonconnected§	7.4	3.9	3.5	3.4	2.5	1.6	3.3	1.6	1.7	1.5	1.3	0.5
1983–84, total†	**75.7**	**46.3**	**29.3**	**57.2**	**11.3**	**7.2**	**29.7**	**14.0**	**15.6**	**17.9**	**6.3**	**5.4**
Corporate	23.4	10.4	13.1	18.8	2.6	2.0	12.0	3.2	8.8	8.8	1.1	2.2
Trade association†	20.4	10.5	9.9	16.5	2.1	1.7	6.3	2.7	3.7	4.5	0.9	1.0
Labor	19.8	18.8	1.0	14.3	3.5	2.0	5.0	4.7	0.3	1.6	2.3	1.2
Nonconnected§	9.1	4.7	4.4	4.9	2.9	1.3	5.4	3.0	2.4	2.4	2.0	1.0
1985–86, total	**87.4**	**54.7**	**32.6**	**65.9**	**9.1**	**12.4**	**45.3**	**20.2**	**25.1**	**23.7**	**10.2**	**11.4**
Corporate	26.9	12.9	14.0	22.9	1.0	3.0	19.2	4.8	14.4	11.7	2.7	4.9
Trade association‡	23.4	12.3	11.2	19.3	1.3	2.8	9.5	3.8	5.7	5.7	1.6	2.1
Labor	22.6	21.1	1.6	14.7	4.3	3.6	7.2	6.6	0.6	2.2	3.2	1.9
Nonconnected§	11.1	6.6	4.5	6.1	2.4	2.6	7.7	4.2	3.4	3.1	2.4	2.2
Cooperative	1.9	1.1	0.8	1.7	(z)	0.2	0.6	0.3	0.3	0.4	0.1	0.1
Corporation without stock	1.4	0.8	0.6	1.2	0.1	0.2	1.0	0.4	0.6	0.6	0.2	0.2

[Covers amounts given to candidates in primary, general, runoff, and special elections during the two-year calendar period indicated]
Key: Z, less than $50,000.
*Elections in which an incumbent did not seek reelection.
†Includes other types of political action committees not shown separately.
‡Includes membership organizations and health organizations.
§Represents "ideological" groups as well as other issue groups not necessarily ideological in nature.
Source: U.S. Department of Commerce, Bureau of the Census, *Statistical Abstract of the United States, 1989* (Washington, D.C.: U.S. Government Printing Office, 1989), p. 263.

SUGGESTED READINGS

Domhoff, G. William. *Who Rules America Now?* (New York: Simon & Schuster, 1983).
Mobilization of evidence that the United States is ruled by and in the interests of the economic upper class.

Donner, Frank. *The Age of Surveillance* (New York: Vintage Books, 1981).
How the U.S. government has spied on its own citizens and the dangers of such abuses of political power for a democracy.

Dye, Thomas R. *Who's Running America?* 5th ed. (Englewood Cliffs, N.J.: Prentice-Hall, 1990).
Descriptive study of the members of America's elites in the corporate, government, and public interest sectors.

Ermann, M. David, and Richard J. Lundman. *Corporate and Governmental Deviance,* 3rd ed. (New York: Oxford University Press, 1987).
Case studies of unethical and illegal behavior by those in top decision-making positions in large organizations.

Piven, Frances Fox, and Richard A. Cloward. *Why Americans Don't Vote* (New York: Pantheon Books, 1988).
Reasons why so many Americans—in contrast to citizens in other industrial democracies—fail to exercise their voting rights.

Simon, David R., and D. Stanley Eitzen. *Elite Deviance,* 3rd ed. (Boston: Allyn and Bacon, 1990).
Overview of crime and corruption at the highest levels of the public and private sectors.

CHAPTER 3

Militarism and War

To an irrational degree America's resources are devoted to military aggression and violence against other peoples of the world. Instead, our nation and others must move toward disarmament and the peaceful settlement of differences.

In the spring of 1975 the American military officially withdrew from South Vietnam, a small peasant society located 8,000 miles away in Southeast Asia. Vietnam was reunited under a revolutionary government that the United States had failed to defeat in a decade of military action that left over 58,000 Americans dead and hundreds of thousands more maimed and disabled. Still others are "missing in action."

Even today many survivors of the Vietnam experience suffer greatly. Mental troubles among Vietnam veterans have been both common and similar enough to have been termed *posttraumatic stress syndrome.* Still other veterans are trying to deal with the long-term aftereffects of exposure to Agent Orange, a herbicide used to kill foliage and thus minimize enemy hiding places in Vietnam. One of the aftereffects of exposure to this chemical is cancer.

The war in Vietnam also caused years of unprecedented domestic political unrest. It cost American taxpayers an estimated $150 billion and created a cycle of inflation and recession in our overall economy. The devastating impact of the war on the Vietnamese people and on members of other nations involved in the conflict will probably never be calculated in full.

Even after the United States retreated from South Vietnam, the domestic institutional forces that had sustained our military involvement remained intact. The United States government warned the world that the setback in Southeast Asia was not to be interpreted as a sign of weakness. The United States, proclaimed President Gerald Ford, would not hesitate to unleash her military power again. Ford almost immediately proved the truth of this statement by sending military forces to free the merchant ship *Mayagüez* from temporary Cambodian capture.

Since Ford's actions, other presidents have employed the military for a variety of purposes. In 1980 President Carter sent troops and helicopters in a failed attempt to rescue sixty Americans held hostage by the government of Iran. In 1983 President Reagan sent naval warships and marines to Lebanon, partly in an effort to shape the outcome of a long-term civil war in that country. In the same year, U.S. troops were ordered to the small Caribbean island of Grenada, where they ended that nation's short-lived experiment with socialism. In 1986 U.S. planes were sent to bomb the living quarters of Col. Muammar el-Qaddifi, head of socialist Libya, based on allegations of Libyan involvement in European terrorist incidents. Meanwhile, President Reagan also had uniformed military advisers in El Salvador to guide that country's army in a civil war involving peasant revolutionaries and was openly using mercenaries trained by the U.S. Central Intelligence Agency in an effort to overthrow the government of Nicaragua. In 1989 President Bush employed 12,000 troops in a U.S. invasion of Panama. And in 1990, he used military force in response to the threat of disruption in supplies of Middle Eastern oil.

In the period since U.S. withdrawal from Vietnam, the military developed a "Rapid Deployment Force" of 290,000 persons that could be sped to intervene anywhere in the world. Government officials talked of the possibility of engaging in "limited" and "winnable" nuclear warfare with such nations as the Soviet Union. The government moved toward developing technology that would give the U.S. military advantage in (if not control over) outer space, while simultaneously selling tens of billions of dollars' worth of weaponry to other countries.

According to contemporary critics, the United States is a "weapons culture" and a "warfare state."[1] Retired Marine Colonel James A. Donovan has written, "America has become a militaristic and aggressive nation embodied in a vast, expensive, and burgeoning military–industrial–scientific–political combine which dominates the country and affects much of our daily life, our economy, our international status, and our foreign policies."[2] The "combine" to which Colonel Donovan refers is more popularly called America's *military–industrial complex*.[3] It is an ongoing human creation that contributes to this society's predisposition to police the world and to saturate it with the technology of violence. With the rapid proliferation of conventional and nuclear arms here and abroad (see Figure 3.1), the possibility of warfare increases daily. But the military-industrial complex that produces such weaponry continues to grind on.

Why has such a dangerous situation come about? What are the domestic institutional forces that provide the momentum for American militarism? What are the critical "national interests" that must be served, protected, or extended—even in the face of contributing to the possible destruction of the human species? We address these questions in the sections that follow.

---

[1] Richard E. Lapp, *The Weapons Culture* (New York: W. W. Norton & Company, 1968), and Fred J. Cook, *The Warfare State* (New York: The Macmillan Company, 1962).

[2] James A. Donovan, *Militarism, U.S.A.* (New York: Charles Scribner's Sons, 1970), p. 1.

[3] This term was made popular by President Dwight D. Eisenhower in his farewell address in 1961.

In December 1989 President George Bush ordered United States troops to invade Panama in order to oust General Manuel Antonio Noriega from political office and to bring him to the U.S. to face drug-related charges. Many Americans have questioned the legality and wisdom of this and other examples of U.S. military and paramilitary intervention in Latin American nations' internal affairs. (*Reuters/Bettmann Newsphotos*)

THE MILITARY–INDUSTRIAL COMPLEX

As the Vietnam war began to escalate in 1965, Marc Pilisuk and Thomas Hayden wrote an article that asked, "Is there a military–industrial complex which prevents peace?" Their conclusion—still relevant almost three decades later—was that "American society *is* a military–industrial complex."[4] The complex is usually said to have emerged at the time of World War II.[5] It consists of several components—the uniformed military, the aerospace–defense industry, the civilian national security managers, and the U.S. Congress.

Each component of the military–industrial complex promotes and protects its own interests while reinforcing the interests of the other components:

> Each institutional component of the military–industrial complex has plausible reasons for continuing to exist and expand. Each promotes and protects its own interests and in doing so reinforces the interests of every other. That is what a "complex" is—a set of integrated institutions that act to maximize their collective power.[6]

The uniformed military jockeys for the resources required to sustain, if not to expand, America's war-making capabilities. The aerospace–defense

[4] Marc Pilisuk and Thomas Hayden, "Is There a Military–Industrial Complex Which Prevents Peace? Consensus and Countervailing Power in Pluralistic Society," *Journal of Social Issues*, 21 (July 1965): 67–117.

[5] The roots of the military–industrial complex actually go back much further than World War II. See Carroll W. Pursell, Jr., ed., *The Military–Industrial Complex* (New York: Harper & Row Publishers 1972), Introduction.

[6] Richard J. Barnet, *The Economy of Death* (New York: Atheneum Publishers, 1969), p. 59. Our analysis of the components and operation of the military–industrial complex is based largely on Barnet. See also Gordon Adams, *The Iron Triangle: The Politics of Defense Contracting* (New Brunswick, N.J.: Transaction Books, 1982).

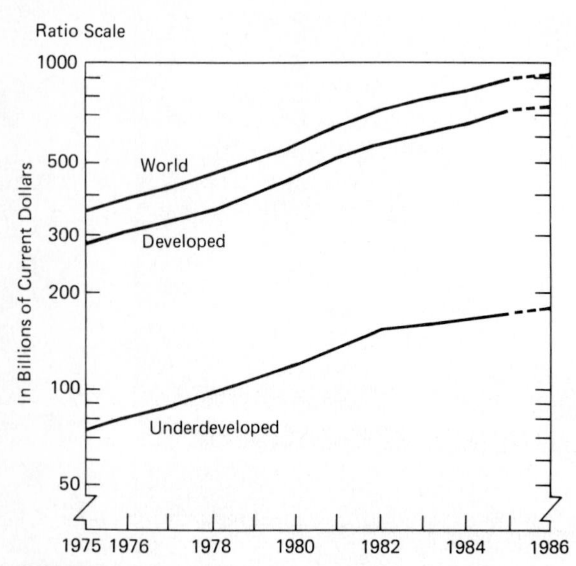

FIGURE 3.1 World Military Expenditures, 1975–86
Source: U.S Arms Control and Disarmament Agency, *World Military Expenditures and Arms Transfers, 1987* (Washington, D.C.: U.S. Government Printing Office, 1988), p. 1.

industry presses for a continuing flow of procurement contracts, under which it can pursue profits at low risk. The civilian national security managers champion the large military expenditures central to their definition of national security and the formulation of foreign policy. And members of Congress provide the tax dollars that keep the military–industrial complex humming, enjoying credit for the impact of this money on the economic life of their states and districts.

The Rise of the Military–Industrial Complex

Before World War II the United States did not routinely maintain large numbers of men and women in uniform, nor did it devote much in the way of national resources to the maintenance of massive war-making capabilities. During World War I, for example, people and matériel (equipment and supplies) were mobilized as needed. When the war had been won, the military establishment was virtually dismantled, and war industries were converted back to peacetime operations. With World War II this pattern of mobilization and postwar demilitarization was to change.

During World War II the United States became a highly efficient war machine. The American economy, which had been unable to break out of years of peacetime depression in the 1930s, boomed as a consequence of wartime production demands. Depression-level unemployment—wherein 13 million people, or over 25 percent of the labor force, were out of work—ceased to be a problem, given the labor requirements of industry and the uniformed military services. A sense of national purpose and unity grew in response to the challenge of achieving victory overseas. By the war's end, the United States had demonstrated a level of military power unequaled in history. It had developed and shown a willingness to use nuclear arms. And it had escaped the war intact and (unlike many of its European and other allies) virtually unscathed because of its geographic isolation from military action.

At the end of World War II, the war machine was not wholly dismantled. High-ranking military officers, having gained great public honor from the victory and enjoying command over an unprecedentedly huge military establishment, campaigned to keep their powers and responsibilities intact. Governmental and corporate elites feared that a full-scale military demobilization and industrial conversion would lead the United States back into an economic depression. Moreover, corporate chieftains had learned that a lot of money could be made from government contracts for military weapons, equipment, and supplies.

A further justification for maintaining a permanent war economy was simultaneously provided by the outbreak of the cold war with the Soviet Union—a war in which both nations have jockeyed for world dominance without actually using their enormous military arsenals directly against one another. After World War II, American elites saw the Soviet Union as constituting a political and military threat. They pointed to the spread of Soviet domination within Eastern Europe as evidence of that threat. Further, they warned that Soviet socialism posed a real danger to all governments committed to maintaining capitalist economies. When the Soviet Union demonstrated its potential as a nuclear power in the 1940s, and when mainland China moved toward building a socialist society in 1949, it seemed clear to elites that socialism could be held in check only by the threat or use of military power.

For well over forty years now this society's military–industrial complex has continued to ride on the fears of expanding socialism. During these four decades we have witnessed American military and paramilitary (e.g., CIA) interventions across the globe and a spiraling nuclear arms race with the Soviet Union. At the same time, more and more nations, particularly those in the economically underdeveloped areas of the world, have moved toward varying types of socialist economic systems.

There are signs that the United States' relations with the Soviet Union may be undergoing fundamental change, and that our government's attitudes toward some socialist nations are becoming more enlightened. Yet suspicion and fear are still used to justify our large-scale military expenditures. (See Table 3.1.)

The Uniformed Military

Among the institutional components central to the military–industrial complex is the uniformed military. The United States Air Force, Army, Navy, and Marine Corps are all under the authority of a civilian-headed umbrella organization—the Department of Defense (DOD). Since World War II the military services have developed into vast bureaucracies commanded by professional career officers who make up an *officer class*. The services receive many tens of billions of dollars annually from the federal government in order to carry out their domestic and foreign operations. They control property and weapons systems valued in the hundreds of billions of dollars, including networks of military bases and installations around the world. At a signal from the president, who is the commander in chief of the military, the civilian head of DOD can call any or all of the 2.1 million active-duty uniformed military into immediate action—to move people and equipment or even to obliterate whole segments of the earth's population. The duty of the uniformed military is to follow orders.

Since World War II, each of the military services has carved out its own roles or *missions* in defense and active warfare. Each service is constantly competing with the others for new responsibilities and resources and the "honor" of being used first in military action. Large annual budgets, new weapons systems, and increased personnel are the prizes that the officer class of each service tries to win as they all justify the strategic importance of their activities and plans. In a word, each of the services is continually striving to *sell* the notion of its flexible capabilities and indispensability.

Selling has meant working to persuade governmental civilians and the public that there are serious military dangers for which this society must be prepared.[7] Top-ranking officers pressure their civilian Department of Defense overseers and the White House to prepare budgets that will enlarge the authority and prestige of their respective services. Military personnel join DOD and White House officials in briefing Congress, which provides funds for these budgets. Interservice rivalries revolve around identifying new dangers to be guarded against, whether

[7] See J. William Fulbright, *The Pentagon Propaganda Machine* (New York: Liveright, 1970).

TABLE 3.1 Defense Expenditures as a Share of Gross National Product for Selected Countries

	Percentage					
Country	**1965**	**1970**	**1975**	**1980**	**1985**	**1987**
Australia	4.4	3.3	2.6	2.2	2.5	2.5
Austria	1.2	1.1	1.1	1.1	1.3	1.2
Belgium	3.1	2.9	3.0	3.4	3.1	3.0
Canada	3.0	2.4	1.9	1.8	2.2	2.2
Denmark	2.8	2.3	2.5	2.5	2.3	2.2
Finland	1.7	1.5	1.4	1.6	1.6	NA
France	5.2	4.2	3.8	4.0	4.0	4.0
Greece	3.5	4.7	6.6	5.5	7.0	6.2
Ireland	1.4	1.1	1.8	1.7	1.8	NA
Italy	3.3	2.5	2.5	2.1	2.3	2.5
Japan	1.0	0.8	0.9	0.9	1.0	1.0
Luxembourg	1.4	0.8	0.8	0.9	0.8	0.8
Netherlands	4.0	3.4	3.2	3.1	3.1	3.1
New Zealand	2.1	2.0	1.7	2.0	2.0	2.2
Norway	3.8	3.5	3.3	3.0	3.1	3.4
Portugal	6.0	6.5	5.3	3.6	3.3	3.2
Spain	2.7	3.1	2.7	2.3	2.5	2.4
Sweden	3.9	3.6	3.3	3.1	3.0	2.9
Switzerland	2.6	2.1	1.9	2.4	2.4	2.1
Turkey	5.0	4.2	5.8	4.0	4.6	4.4
United Kingdom	5.9	4.7	4.9	5.0	5.2	4.7
United States	7.2	7.6	5.7	5.3	6.6	6.5
West Germany	4.3	3.3	3.6	3.3	3.2	3.0
Less developed countries	NA	5.8	6.9	6.2	6.3	5.1

[Military expenditures are for current and capital expenditures to meet the needs of the armed forces, including expenditures of national defense agencies for military programs; expenditures for the military components of such mixed activities as atomic energy, space, and research and development; military assistance to foreign countries; and expenditures on paramilitary forces where they contribute substantially to a country's military capabilities.]

Key: NA, not available.

Source: U.S. Central Intelligence Agency, *Handbook of Economic Statistics, 1989* (Washington, D.C.: CIA, 1989), p. 38.

immediate or potential, to back up fund requests.

As a tribute to the military sales effort, Congress presently allocates billions in tax funds each year for guns, tanks, planes, bombs, missiles, ships, submarines, and communications devices for undersea and outer-space use. Additional funds go for research, development, and production of new weapons systems to enlarge America's military arsenal and to replace the obsolete. Since military threats and weapons technology alter with time, obsolescence is often under way before the new tools of warfare are finished and in place. More than 29 percent of total annual federal expenditures ($291 billion in 1988; an estimated $299 in 1989) go toward defense (see Figures 3.2 and 3.3).[8] While recent thaws in U.S. relations with the Soviet Union are producing reductions in defense spending, the reductions are thus far minor given the massive size of the annual budget.

Since most Americans take this use of their

[8] Robert Pear, "'89 Reagan Budget, Reflecting Unity, Goes to Congress," *New York Times* (February 19, 1988): A1.

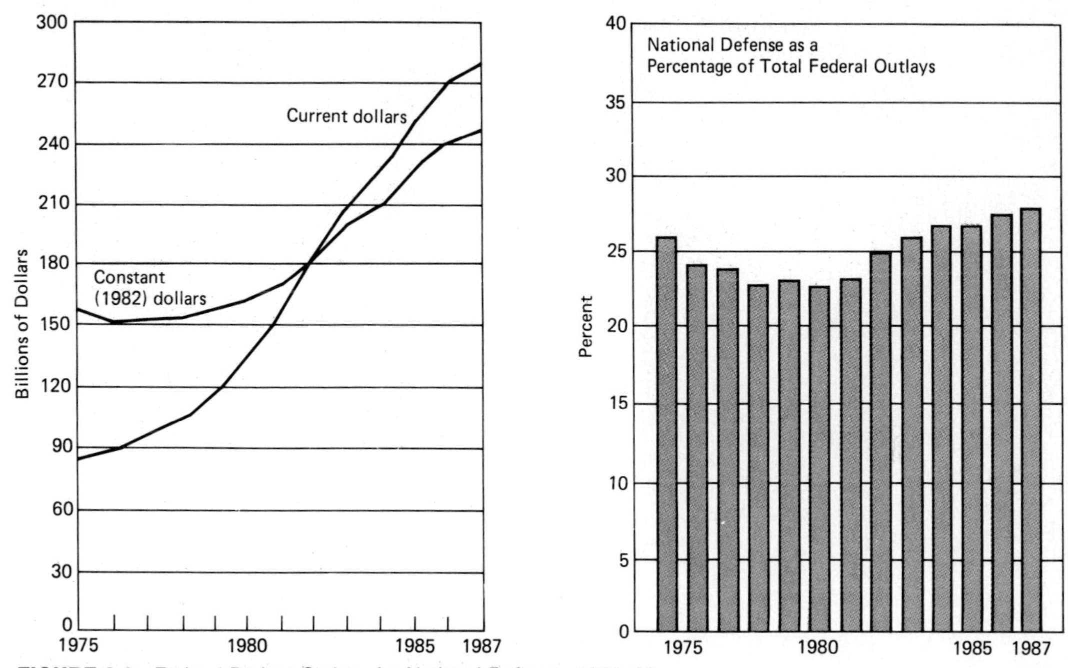

FIGURE 3.2 Federal Budget Outlays for National Defense, 1975–87
Source: U.S. Department of Commerce, Bureau of the Census, *Statistical Abstract of the United States, 1989* (Washington, D.C.: U.S. Government Printing Office, 1989), p. 324.

tax dollars for granted, the uniformed military services are in a position to exploit their institutional self-interests. How many of us are expert enough to judge the importance of missions and the consequent military claims on the federal budget? How many of us can assess accurately the validity and seriousness of military dangers alleged to exist around the world? Even if we were experts, we would find it hard to get the facts, for the uniformed military and its civilian overseers in the DOD and White House attempt to maintain a ring of secrecy around such matters. Even Congress finds this secrecy hard to counter.

The massive resources provided to the uniformed military allow them to wage substantial public relations campaigns. The services remind the American public of their patriotism, demonstrate some of their war-making capabilities, and allude to the nightmares that presumably make American military power deserving of support. Military speakers and seminars are made available to interested citizens' groups around the country. Community leaders are invited to tour military facilities, where they receive VIP (Very Important Person) treatment. Armed Forces Day is celebrated at military bases and installations each year, usually with displays of military hardware for the public to enjoy. Mobile informational displays on military missions and weaponry are installed in shopping centers. Tapes and films dealing with military matters are mass-produced for use by schools and citizens' organizations. Local newspapers regularly receive news releases from military press units. Civilian advertising agencies are hired to promote the virtues of military service. And DOD has cooperated with Hollywood

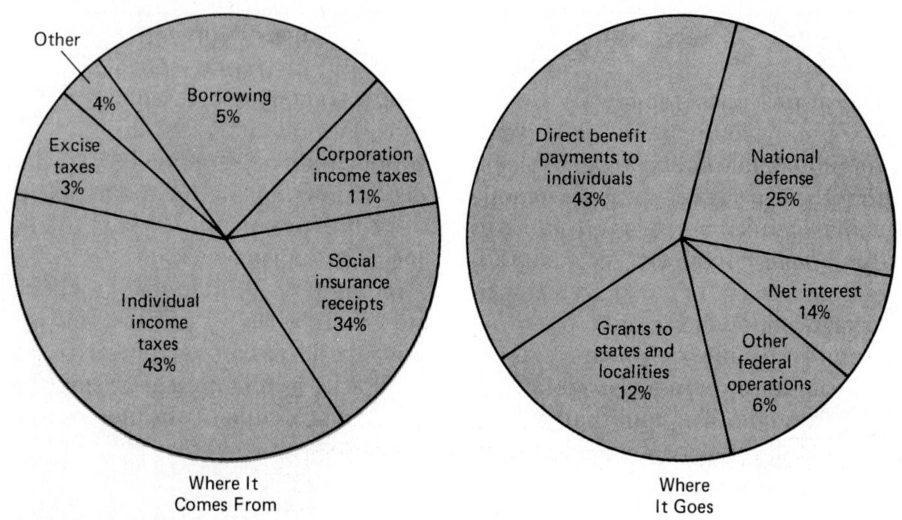

FIGURE 3.3 Federal Budget Income and Expenditures
Source: "The Federal Budget," *The Hartford Courant* (January 30, 1990), p. A1.

to produce war extravaganzas that reflect well on American military prowess. In sum, millions of tax dollars are used each year to promote the uniformed military and legitimate its activities.

Some observers have claimed that the military is the key element in the military–industrial complex, which they see as a conspiracy orchestrated by a handful of top-ranking "warlords."[9] We do not agree. Though the officers of the respective services do have personal and institutional self-interests to pursue, the uniformed military is under firm civilian control. The influence of the military within the military–industrial complex is strong, but it appears to be fed by—and feeds—other institutional components, which also have a major stake in keeping the complex going.

The Aerospace–Defense Industry

American militarism is big business.[10] The billions upon billions in tax dollars spent annually by the military establishment have been the mainstay of the permanent war economy since the 1940s. Handsome stockholder revenues for members of America's ownership class (see Chapter 6) are one result of such expenditures. In addition, the livelihood of millions of American workers has come to depend on the permanent war economy.

Each year the Department of Defense enters into contracts for the purchase and procurement of weapons, ammunition, equipment, supplies, and services. The recipients of these contracts include 25,000 to 30,000 principal firms classi-

[9] See Charles C. Moskos, Jr., "The Concept of the Military–Industrial Complex: Radical Critique or Liberal Bogey?," *Social Problems,* 21 (April 1974): 498–512.

[10] See Richard F. Kaufman, *The War Profiteers* (Garden City, N.Y.: Anchor Books, 1972), and Jacques S. Gansler, *The Defense Industry* (Cambridge, Mass.: The M.I.T. Press, 1980). The world arms trade is analyzed in Anthony Sampson, *The Arms Bazaar* (New York: Viking Press, 1977) and Michael T. Klare, *American Arms Supermarket* (Austin: University of Texas Press, 1984).

PUBLIC PROBLEM, PRIVATE PAIN

Wounded in Battle

Ron Kovic was born on July 4, 1946, to a highly religious and patriotic family. Throughout his childhood, Kovic and his friends played "war" and dreamed of being combat heroes. An all-around high-school athlete, he had an opportunity to try out for the New York Yankees upon graduation. But consistent with his boyhood dreams, he chose to enlist in the Marine Corps where, according to the recruiters, he would become a man and get to serve his country. In this excerpt from his autobiography, Kovic describes his last battle, which began when the Viet Cong fired at his outfit as they walked toward a South Vietnamese village. Kovic, who will spend the rest of his life in a wheelchair, became an antiwar activist shortly after returning to the United States for medical treatment and physical therapy.

I had started walking toward the village when the first bullet hit me. There was a sound like firecrackers going off all around my feet. Then a real loud crack and my leg went numb below the knee. I looked down at my foot and there was blood at the back of it. The bullet had come through the front and blew out nearly the whole of my heel.

I had been shot. The war had finally caught up with my body. I felt good inside. Finally the war was with me and I had been shot by the enemy. I was getting out of the war and I was going to be a hero. I kept firing my rifle into the tree line and boldly, with my new wound, moved closer to the village, daring them to hit me again. For a moment I felt like running back to the rear with my new million-dollar wound but I decided to keep fighting out in the open. A great surge of strength went through me as I yelled for the other men to come out from the trees and join me. I was limping now and the foot was beginning to hurt so much, I finally lay down in almost a kneeling position, still firing into the village, still unable to see anyone. I seemed to be the only one left firing a rifle. Someone came up from behind me, took off my boot and began to bandage my foot. The whole thing was incredibly stupid, we were sitting ducks, but he bandaged my foot and then he took off back into the tree line.

For a few seconds it was silent. I lay down prone and waited for the next bullet to hit me. It was only a matter of time, I thought. I wasn't retreating, I wasn't going back, I was lying right there and blasting everything I had into the pagoda. The rifle was full of sand and it was jamming. I had to pull the bolt back now each time trying to get a round into the chamber. It was impossible and I started to get up and a loud crack went off next to my right ear as a thirty-caliber slug tore through my right shoulder, blasted through my lung, and smashed my spinal cord to pieces.

I felt that everything from my chest down was completely gone. I waited to die. I threw my hands back and felt my legs still there. I couldn't feel them but they were still there. I was still alive. And for some reason I started believing, I started believing I might not die. I might make it out of there and live and feel and go back home again. I could hardly breathe and was taking short little sucks with the one lung I had left. The blood was rolling off my flak jacket from the hole in my shoulder and I couldn't feel the pain in my foot anymore, I couldn't even feel my body. I was frightened to death. I didn't think about praying, all I could feel was cheated.

All I could feel was the worthlessness of dying right here in this place at this moment for nothing.

Source: Ron Kovic, *Born on the Fourth of July* (New York: Pocket Books, 1977), pp. 220–22.

fied as "primary contractors" and 50,000 subcontractors. In recent years, however, over two-thirds of the DOD procurement budget has gone to a mere 100 large corporations.

The top defense contractors are General Dynamics, McDonnell Douglas, United Technologies, Boeing, General Electric, Lockheed, Hughes Aircraft, Grumman, Northrup, Raytheon, Rockwell, and Tenneco. Between 1970 and 1980 eight of these firms received a quarter of the business done with DOD and over a third of the business done with the National Aeronautics and Space Administration. For most of these firms the DOD is their largest customer by far.[11] The aerospace–defense industry has, understandably, developed an outlook on military spending comparable to that of the uniformed services.

Pentagon Capitalism. The relationship between the aerospace–defense industry and the Department of Defense has been characterized as *Pentagon capitalism.*[12] Among other things, this term denotes the rather special relationship between the department and its contractors. Doing business with the department is quite different from operating in the civilian marketplace and selling consumer goods to the public.

Corporations that produce goods and services for the civilian marketplace often must compete for customers' attention and dollars. They must adjust their production to actual and anticipated public demand. There is a degree of risk involved in dealing with the public—there will be no profits if goods and services cannot be sold. Errors in production may prove quite costly. Such risks are taken for granted by firms that service the public, though efforts are constantly made to minimize them.

Under Pentagon capitalism, on the other hand, most procurement contracts are issued to principal contractors without requiring competition among them. Aerospace–defense firms frequently develop their products and services in close cooperation with their military customers. The amounts to be produced are specified in advance, and the demand is guaranteed. In contrast to doing business in the civilian marketplace, production for the military establishment involves few risks and assured profits. Even if the goods and services turn out to cost more than originally anticipated (*cost overruns*), the aerospace–defense contractor can request and usually get supplemental funds. If errors in production occur, or if the time schedule for delivering goods and services cannot be observed, DOD cooperates, waits, and often shoulders any extra costs involved.[13]

The highly dependable and lucrative nature of DOD procurement contracts—under which cost overruns, errors, waste, and assured profits are taken for granted—has made aerospace–defense firms strong backers of American militarism. The aerospace–defense industry serves its own interests by responding to the perceived needs and plans of the officer class, supporting their constant pursuit of new missions, responsibilities, and budgetary resources. On its own initiative, the industry develops products and services that might encourage the military to push for new missions not yet in existence. Under the drive for profits, the industry has engineered a community of interest with the military establishment within which each embellishes the momentum of the other.

The Community of Interest. The community of interest between industry and the military has been cemented through the circulation of personnel. Executives from the aerospace–defense industry have, with startling frequency, moved into important civilian positions in DOD. Top-ranking military officers, as well as lesser members of the officer class, have retired and moved into positions in the industry. In the latter case, contractors have been able to exploit the specialized knowledge and skills of former

[11] Sheila Tobias et al., *What Kinds of Guns Are They Buying for Your Butter?* (New York: William Morrow & Company, 1982), pp. 245–47.

[12] The term is Seymour Melman's in *Pentagon Capitalism* (New York: McGraw-Hill Book Company, 1970). The Pentagon is, of course, the Washington, D.C., headquarters of the Department of Defense.

[13] Tobias, *What Kinds of Guns,* p. 249. See also Seymour Melman, *Profits Without Production* (New York: Alfred A. Knopf, 1983).

officers as well as their familiarity with people and procedures involved in procurement contracting at DOD. The circulation of military personnel to aerospace–defense corporations raises the concern that some military officers may be tempted to bestow favors on particular firms in order to ensure themselves employment upon retirement from active duty. The same potential conflict of interest exists for persons holding key civilian positions in DOD.

In 1975 the Council on Economic Priorities found that between 1969 and 1973 the 100 largest defense contractors had hired 14,000 former Department of Defense employees. In yet another study done for the council it was discovered that between 1970 and 1979 almost 1,700 former members of the military, along with former civilian employees of DOD and NASA, were hired by the eight top defense contractors. Moreover, 270 employees from these eight firms moved to DOD or NASA.[14]

In a 1969 speech, Senator William Proxmire pointed out some of the issues involved in the "community of interest" that has evolved between industry and the military establishment:

> When the bulk of the budget goes for military purposes; when 100 companies get 67 percent of the defense contract dollars; when cost overruns are routine and prime military weapon system contracts normally exceed their estimates by 100 to 200 percent; when these contracts are let by negotiation and not by competitive bidding; and when the top contractors have over 2000 retired high-ranking military officers on their payrolls; there are very real questions as to how critically these matters are reviewed and how well the public interest is served.[15]

Over two decades later the same very real questions remain.

In June 1988 the news media publicized a massive scandal involving federal defense expenditures. Investigators charged that defense contractors, acting through middlemen, bribed top Department of Defense staff members to steer defense contracts their way. Offices searched for evidence by the Federal Bureau of Investigation included the headquarters of some of the nation's largest defense contractors. Those calling for criminal prosecution claimed that the case could involve tens of billions of dollars. Thus the "community of interest" between industry and the military establishment may easily lead to corruption, given the huge amounts of money at stake.

The National Security Managers

As we have seen, the military services are under civilian control within the Department of Defense. The ultimate responsibility for safeguarding national security and for formulating foreign policy outside the White House is held by executives in DOD and civilian representatives from such other agencies as the Department of State and the Central Intelligence Agency.

Who are the people who have determined that militarism is in the interest of national security? Richard J. Barnet has attempted to identify the backgrounds and hint at the world view of America's civilian *national security managers*, the top-level civilian executives of the federal agencies mentioned above. When Barnet examined the backgrounds of ninety-one individuals who held key executive posts between 1940 and 1967, he found that seventy "were from the ranks of big business or high finance."[16] Barnet took this to mean that military policy was formulated largely on the basis of business interests:

---

[14] Adams, *The Iron Triangle*, p. 78.

[15] From a congressional speech by Senator William Proxmire, March 24, 1969. Reprinted in Pursell, *The Military–Industrial Complex*, p. 258. Senator Proxmire has been one of the few long-term critics of the waste of taxpayers' money.

[16] Barnet, *The Economy of Death*, p. 88.

> Defining the national interest and protecting national security are the proper province of business. . . . For a National Security Manager recruited from the world of business, there are no other important constituencies to which he feels a need to respond.[17]

But despite the fact that the national security managers to this day tend to come from the business elite,[18] care must be taken in drawing conclusions about the role of business interests in the process of formulating policy. Nevertheless, at the very least, the fact that the national security managers are usually drawn from business constitutes another case of conflict of interest. Since massive military expenditures are the mainstay of America's permanent war economy, the national security managers recruited from big business and high finance are unlikely to tamper with the status quo. This is particularly so in that national security managers often move in and out of governmental service, using it as a means of enhancing their career chances in the business world. The potential of conflict of interest is highest in the case of executives recruited from the aerospace–defense industry, an industry to which they are likely to return.

As we saw in Chapter 1, America's business community has progressively taken on multinational dimensions. Many of the economy's largest corporations have increasingly come to depend on profits generated by investments and sales abroad. A global military posture can readily be rationalized as a means of protecting American corporate interests around the world. National security managers who come from big business and high finance can be expected to be sensitive to such matters, insofar as the national interest can be equated with the well-being of the American economy.

The Militarized Congress

The uniformed military, the aerospace–defense industry, and the national security managers are the main institutional components of the military–industrial complex. But for this complex to exist, billions of tax dollars must be given it every year. The national security managers and the uniformed military prepare annual budget requests and justifications for proposed expenditures. These are then presented to Congress, which alone has the authority to appropriate the funds requested. As the controller of the purse strings that must be loosened for American militarism to continue unhampered, Congress has virtually become an institutional component of the complex.

In past years the United States Senate and House of Representatives have, almost without exception, responded favorably to requests for funds to support the military establishment and its procurement contracts. Periodic investigations by congressional committees and individual senators and representatives have resulted in harsh criticism of the costs of military procurement and errors and waste on the part of contractors. But when it comes time to vote on military budgets, most members of Congress support the high spending levels. (See Figure 3.3.) An annual ritual in Congress involves hearings on the military budget. During these hearings a few legislators pose some sharp questions, pare some money off the requests, and end up approving most of the funds requested.

There are several reasons for congressional support of the permanent war economy. Many members of Congress are themselves veterans and retired or reserve officers, so they identify favorably with the military as an institution. Despite their positions of responsibility, many are as uninformed as most citizens when it comes to judging national security needs, the relevance

[17] Ibid., pp. 89 and 100.

[18] Others come from elite academic backgrounds. See Fred Kaplan, *Wizards of Armageddon* (New York: Simon & Schuster, 1982), and Noam Chomsky, *Towards a New Cold War* (New York: Pantheon Books, 1982).

of missions, the necessity for weapons systems, and the dangers against which military power must be poised. There is thus a tendency to accept the authoritative judgments of the national security managers and top-ranking military officers.

Many members of Congress are affluent, which means that they are likely to own stock in American corporations, including aerospace–defense firms. And even if they do not, certainly many of those who provide contributions for their campaign expenses do. Hence, their stand on military budget requests may make the difference between being reelected or finding a new job, especially since DOD money is channeled into the states or districts of most members of Congress. There is obviously little political incentive to vote down military expenditures if this means the loss of bases, procurement contracts, and employment for constituents. Rather, there is even more reason to approve such expenditures.

Thus, Sidney Lens, author of *The Military–Industrial Complex,* has posed this rhetorical question:

> Who can tell in this game of *quid pro quo* how many legislators vote for a weapons system they don't think is necessary in order to get a contract for their own business community, and how much pork is put into the budget by the Pentagon to lure a congressional vote?[19]

In response to the "pork" (extra proposed expenditures), to lobbying efforts by the various institutional components of the military–industrial complex, and to pressures from such special interest groups as organized labor and veterans' associations, Congress goes along with the game. But when public outrage becomes intense, as in the later stages of the Vietnam War, we have seen Congress adjust its stance on American militarism.

[19] Sidney Lens, *The Military–Industrial Complex* (Philadelphia: Pilgrim Press, 1970), p. 45.

PROTECTING AMERICAN ECONOMIC INTERESTS ABROAD

America's economic system has often been labeled *corporate capitalism* in recognition of the key role that large corporations have come to play within it. According to U.S. government income tax data, there were 16 million business enterprises in 1984. But most of the nation's business is done by a very tiny percentage of these enterprises. In 1984 only 3.7 percent of these firms had receipts of $1 million or more. Yet this tiny percentage of firms accounted for 86.5 percent of all business receipts that year.[20]

Another way to underscore the significance of large corporations to our economy is to look at industrial firms. In 1980 there were 200,000 industrial corporations in the United States, with total assets of $1.2 trillion. The largest 100 firms controlled 55 percent of these immense assets. A mere five firms controlled 13 percent. Such concentration of economic activity is also found in such areas as transportation, communications, utilities, insurance, and banking.[21] The economic well-being of these large corporations is crucial to American society. To the degree they are successful in meeting their objectives of profit and growth, this society's capitalist economy avoids stagnation.

In order to grow and profit, American corporations have found it necessary to extend their activities well beyond the political boundaries of the nation. In the years since World War II, we have witnessed the growth (both in size and numbers) of multinational firms, businesses

[20] U.S. Bureau of the Census, *Statistical Abstract of the United States: 1988* (Washington, D.C.: U.S. Government Printing Office, 1987), p. 495.

[21] Thomas R. Dye, *Who's Running America?*, 3rd ed. (Englewood Cliffs, N.J.: Prentice-Hall, 1983), pp. 20 and 26.

with plants and offices around the world.[22] Between 1960 and 1976, direct corporate investments in foreign nations grew from $31.9 billion to $137 billion. The value of such investments was $309 billion in 1987. Most of this money has been channeled into the developed economies of Canada and Western Europe, where American-owned enterprises cater to markets for manufactured goods. The rest has gone to Middle East petroleum suppliers and to a number of economically underdeveloped nations in the Third World (Latin America, Africa, and Asia). For the most part, investments in the Middle East and elsewhere in the Third World have been for the purpose of obtaining natural resources to be used in production in the United States and other developed economies. Even though corporate investment dollars have gone primarily into Canada and Western Europe, the rates of return on Third World investments have proven to be higher.

Earnings from foreign operations comprise an increasing percentage of the annual net incomes of many of America's largest firms. It seems fair to conclude that the economic health of the United States has come to depend, to a significant degree, on the multinationals' ability to penetrate the economies of other nations. In doing so, the multinationals gain access to and control over valuable raw materials, including many materials utilized by such key industries as aerospace–defense. Many of these raw materials are in short supply or would be more expensive to extract in the United States. In addition, multinational corporations are able to cultivate new markets for products manufactured in this country and in their plants abroad. Particularly in the Third World, such firms are able to take advantage of large pools of cheap labor, thus cutting costs. The profits from such operations flow back to corporate headquarters in the United States, where they can be used to reward stockholders and/or provide a basis for further investments.

[22] Richard J. Barnet and Ronald Müller, *Global Reach* (New York: Simon & Schuster, 1974).

The Corporate–Governmental Partnership

The spread of American economic interests across the globe has been greatly facilitated by the federal government—or, more specifically, by the national security managers.[23] Given their background in business and finance, it is not surprising that these managers have tailored foreign policy to protect corporate operations abroad.

For example, after World War II the government financed what came to be called the Marshall Plan, a program of aid designed to help rebuild the war-torn nations of Western Europe. The Marshall Plan was initiated during the emergence of the cold war, at a time when Soviet socialism was perceived as a growing danger to Western European capitalist nations. At a cost of $13 billion, the aid program succeeded in revitalizing these nations' economies within a capitalist framework. This revitalization provided immense investment and market opportunities for American corporations, thus helping stimulate their increased involvement abroad.

At the same time, America's national security managers entered into a military pact with these and other friendly nations, a pact calling for mutual cooperation in the event of outside aggression (e.g., by the Soviet Union). This involved the creation of the North Atlantic Treaty Organization (NATO) in 1949. Through NATO, the United States has maintained permanent

[23] See Michael Tanzer, *The Sick Society* (New York: Holt, Rinehart & Winston, 1971), pp. 63–93. America's corporate–governmental partnership abroad is placed in historical context in Harry Magdoff, *Imperialism: From the Colonial Age to the Present* (New York: Monthly Review Press, 1978), and William Appleman Williams, *Empire as a Way of Life* (New York: Oxford University Press, 1980).

military capabilities in Europe and elsewhere. This society's involvement in NATO has also served to protect American economic interests and has enabled our military–industrial complex to benefit from overseas demands for troops and weapons systems.

The national security managers have also provided foreign economic and military aid to many underdeveloped countries of the Third World. Economic aid has often taken the form of loans that require the recipients to purchase goods and services from American corporations. Such aid has also been used to encourage Third World nations to allow multinational corporations access to raw materials and low-wage labor.

Since the Third World has been prone to political upheaval and often to revolutionary change, corporate investments have also required protection. American military aid has enabled the governments of Third World nations to purchase military equipment produced by America's military–industrial complex. The export of American arms and weapons systems (including those to developed nations) was $9.4 billion, or 32.5 percent of the world export market, in 1985. In the five-year period 1981–85 the United States exported $49.3 billion worth of arms to other nations, making it the world's leading arms supplier.[24] Military aid directed into Third World nations has often been designed to help governments contain internal movements for change—e.g., toward socialism. (See Table 3.2.)

Defending the World Against Socialism

As many of the examples we have discussed indicate, American militarism has often been seen as a means of protecting the world from socialism. Michael Tanzer, in *The Sick Society*, argues that the threat posed by socialism is not wholly, or even necessarily, a military one:

> Once granted that economic interests play the major role in foreign policy, then it makes a great deal of difference whether a country is . . . socialist or capitalist, even if the country is totally incapable of threatening us militarily. Each country that shifts from the capitalist world to the socialist world is a country where the United States loses valuable existing investments as well as potential outlets for profitable future investments (and possibly trade).[25]

After all, the United States has the power to destroy any nation that poses a military threat.

Moreover, socialism is not a threat to democratic freedoms and civil liberties in some of the nonsocialist societies the United States is allied with. The American government has often provided economic and military aid to harsh dictatorships, so long as they in turn have been friendly to U.S. corporate interests. In recent years such regimes included Argentina, Brazil, Chile, Colombia, the Dominican Republic, El Salvador, Ethiopia, Greece, Guatemala, Haiti, Indonesia, Iran, Laos, Morocco, Nicaragua, Pakistan, Paraguay, Peru, the Philippines, Portugal, Saudi Arabia, South Korea, South Vietnam, Spain, Tunisia, Turkey, and Uruguay.[26]

What, then, is the threat of socialism to America? It would seem that it is largely economic. American militarism is one means by which corporate economic interests—so often subtly equated with national interests—can be served, protected, and extended.

Several different military strategies have been developed in the battle against socialism.[27] In the post-World War II period, when the cold war was expected to include military aggression by the Soviet Union, the military–industrial

[24] U.S. Bureau of the Census, *Statistical Abstract of the United States: 1988*, p. 319.

[25] Tanzer, *The Sick Society*, p. 66.

[26] Joshua Cohen and Joel Rogers, *On Democracy* (New York: Penguin Books, 1983), p. 37. Cohen and Rogers state the United States supplied these nations with "military aid, advisers, or torture equipment."

[27] See Micheal T. Klare, *War Without End* (New York: Vintage Books, 1972), and *Beyond the "Vietnam Syndrome"* (Washington, D.C.: Institute for Policy Studies, 1981).

TABLE 3.2 U.S. Military Deliveries to the Less Developed Countries (in millions of dollars)

Country	1975–88	1980	1982	1983	1984	1985	1986	1987	1988
Total	**106,400**	**5,973**	**8,579**	**10,715**	**7,778**	**7,156**	**8,135**	**10,953**	**7,892**
North Africa and the Middle East	**76,453**	**4,324**	**6,500**	**8,685**	**5,612**	**4,879**	**5,474**	**7,396**	**4,157**
Egypt	6,248	209	1,066	1,037	348	669	692	1,152	605
Iran	10,182	7	0	0	0	2	0	0	0
Israel	13,270	853	1,122	459	495	717	487	1,890	1,598
Jordan	2,164	277	193	344	100	151	89	114	89
Kuwait	1,099	79	92	78	66	48	85	69	58
Lebanon	605	17	39	191	221	53	14	15	13
Morocco	953	69	64	67	77	55	43	50	81
North Yemen	339	72	40	17	10	12	4	7	7
Oman	121	8	34	26	8	5	5	6	5
Saudi Arabia	39,259	2,640	3,782	6,092	3,681	2,992	3,893	3,614	1,562
Tunisia	566	11	16	26	140	161	48	50	32
Other	1,647	82	52	348	466	14	114	429	107
Sub-Saharan Africa	**1,318**	**53**	**160**	**96**	**122**	**83**	**166**	**108**	**121**
Cameroon	50	3	3	4	12	—*	8	3	4
Kenya	187	4	25	21	6	8	13	16	9
Liberia	50	1	1	10	7	10	11	2	4
Nigeria	156	11	13	7	10	3	39	4	5
Somalia	122	0	14	21	23	21	13	14	16
Sudan	375	22	94	14	44	22	58	28	30
Zaire	110	10	7	8	5	11	10	11	8
Other	268	2	3	11	15	8	14	30	45
Latin America	**3,905**	**139**	**239**	**233**	**331**	**493**	**434**	**619**	**495**
Argentina	180	12	10	7	4	5	9	15	12
Brazil	413	15	14	29	21	15	44	36	46
Chile	151	10	0	0	0	1	1	2	1
Colombia	160	5	21	12	14	9	18	6	39
Ecuador	179	11	13	31	10	5	12	30	8
El Salvador	610	2	59	47	85	117	111	79	95
Mexico	434	4	76	31	4	10	28	220	42
Peru	190	15	11	9	4	4	6	18	7
Venezuela	868	20	30	43	146	257	91	89	39
Other	720	45	5	24	43	70	114	124	206
Asia	**20,843**	**1,329**	**1,390**	**1,525**	**1,540**	**1,464**	**1,745**	**1,994**	**2,283**
India	189	9	6	6	19	11	28	45	15
Indonesia	598	117	29	41	26	44	30	43	46
Malaysia	504	24	29	51	40	25	45	29	20
Pakistan	2,122	57	151	261	518	379	203	134	140
Philippines	617	56	53	32	22	30	43	56	75
Singapore	1,098	29	44	105	49	45	224	144	221
South Korea	5,627	497	404	331	314	303	546	551	430
Taiwan	5,302	269	467	510	356	476	477	586	732
Thailand	2,342	248	171	183	190	144	132	257	360
Other	2,444	23	36	5	6	7	17	149	244
Europe	**3,881**	**128**	**290**	**176**	**173**	**237**	**316**	**836**	**836**
Portugal	528	20	88	33	70	111	42	39	57
Spain	3,353	108	202	143	103	126	274	797	779

[Fiscal years. Including deliveries under the following programs: (1) military assistance program grants under the various Mutual Security Acts; (2) foreign military sales, which consist of U.S.-financed arms, U.S.-guaranteed private arms credits, and U.S.-approved commercial sales; and (3) military assistance excess stocks, which involved surplus equipment that has been valued at 33 percent of the original acquisition value.]

*Negligible.

Source: U.S. Central Intelligence Agency, *Handbook of Economic Statistics, 1989* (Washington, D.C.: CIA, 1989), pp. 182–83.

complex came up with the means of "massive retaliation." The idea was that American nuclear arms, visibly poised for use, would act as a deterrent against Soviet military adventure. When it became known, shortly after World War II, that the Soviet Union was also developing a nuclear capability, the United States began to strengthen its military arsenal to make possible a "first strike." The idea here was that the Soviet Union would be deterred from using its weapons, since the United States could put the nuclear arms to use first. The nuclear arms race has been going on ever since; and the United States and the Soviet Union have progressively escalated their respective destructive capabilities to the point where neither could survive a full-scale nuclear war.

In the meantime a score of other nations, both capitalist and socialist, have proceeded to join the "nuclear club," thereby increasing the likelihood of a future holocaust. By the 1980s this nuclear club included the United States, the Soviet Union, the United Kingdom, France, China, and India. These nations are known to possess nuclear weaponry. Nations on the brink of nuclear capacity, able or actively seeking to produce weapons, include Pakistan, South Africa, Israel, Iran, Brazil, Argentina, Egypt, Taiwan, West Germany, and Japan, among others (perhaps as many as thirty in all).

A second type of military strategy has been "limited warfare," the direct use of military power involving conventional, rather than nuclear, arms. American involvements in Korea in the 1950s and later in Southeast Asia were defined as limited wars against the encroachment of socialism. In both the costs were extremely high in terms of lives lost; but both were considered the only acceptable alternative to the use of nuclear force.

A third type of military strategy is "counterinsurgency warfare," utilizing the resources of such paramilitary agencies as the CIA.[28] Here the approach has been to combat the threats posed by socialism through secret, disruptive tactics. In 1953 the CIA organized the overthrow of the government of Iran, where American oil interests had been threatened. The following year the CIA was involved in altering the government of Guatemala, which was encroaching on American investments and hampering explorations for oil. Oil interests were also at stake in the CIA's participation in overthrowing the government of Indonesia in 1958. In the 1960s, before becoming a major participant in the war in Southeast Asia, the CIA participated in organizing the abortive Cuban Bay of Pigs invasion and has since been implicated in attempts to assassinate Cuban socialist leader Fidel Castro. The government of Cuba had appropriated a billion dollars worth of American corporate investments shortly after its succession to power in 1959. In 1974 the elected government of Chile, whose socialist program effected a takeover of American-owned copper production, was "destabilized" with the assistance of the CIA. In the 1980s Nicaragua received similar CIA attention. Since the activities of the CIA are supposed to be secret, it is impossible to know when and where other efforts at destabilization have been attempted.

It is not always the absolute dollar value of American economic interests abroad that provokes militaristic responses to socialism. Certainly the United States had no corporate investments in South Vietnam even remotely worth the $150 billion spent on fighting socialism there. Rather, the national security managers have often feared that movements toward socialism in a given country can set an example for others. The so-called domino theory of foreign affairs—still embraced in national security circles—interprets the successful move toward socialism in one part of the world as inviting experimentation elsewhere. Socialism in South Vietnam was viewed as unacceptable, not be-

[28] Victor Marchetti and John Marks, *The CIA and the Cult of Intelligence* (New York: Alfred A. Knopf, 1974).

Though the war in Vietnam was officially defined as a "limited war" or "police action," it cost Americans approximately $150 billion, took 58,000 American lives, and left hundreds of thousands disabled. Ironically, even at this enormous cost, the American military was unable to achieve its goal of keeping South Vietnam free of socialism. (*Larry Burrows* Life *Magazine © Time Inc.)*

cause that country was a military threat to America or because of corporate investments there, but because of what that could mean in terms of the future of Southeast Asia as a whole. Socialism in Cuba, Chile, and Nicaragua promised similar developments in the rest of the underdeveloped nations of Latin America.

Hence, from the perspective of America's national security managers, dominoes must not be allowed to fall, because if they do, we might be economically isolated and forced to deal with other nations on less advantageous terms. Counterinsurgency, limited warfare, and the threat of all-out nuclear annihilation—all made possible by a well-financed military–industrial complex—are used to make the world "safe" for America to do business. The irony behind using war to create peaceful business conditions is rarely questioned within American society, despite the dangers to which it gives rise.

THE EFFECTS OF MILITARISM

American militarism affects more than the nature of our relations with socialist and nonsocialist nations. It has negative influences on the civilian economy of the United States and the quality of life of citizens. It also poses the threat of bringing an end to civilization as we know it.

Military Expenditures and the Civilian Economy

Since World War II, American military, political, and economic elites have claimed that large military expenditures benefit the United States in many ways. Often such expenditures are portrayed as a positive force in promoting domestic economic health—even apart from their relationship to the protection of American corporate interests abroad. In the words of Seymour Melman, "the belief that war brings prosperity has served as a powerful organizing idea for generating and cementing a cross-society political consensus for active or tacit support of big military spending."[29] This belief is just as influential in keeping the military–industrial complex going as are external threats of socialism. But as Melman and others have come to argue, there are a number of rarely considered negative consequences associated with big military spending. No society can maintain a permanent war economy without some adverse internal effects.[30]

It is frequently estimated that 10 percent of the American work force is, in one way or another, directly dependent on military expenditures. But the goods and services produced through these expenditures do not really serve basic needs of the American population. We cannot consume aircraft carriers, supersonic fighters, or munitions. The funds spent on maintaining and equipping people in uniform do not enhance the quality of everyday life. The vast productive apparatus that military expenditures support—plants, equipment, tools—is isolated from civilian-oriented use. Thus a significant segment of the American economy, from people to matériel, is nonproductive in terms of public well-being.

Another effect of the permanent war economy has been the creation of firms that have little knowledge of business other than their ability to exist on tax funds. As we have seen, many aerospace–defense firms depend on continued military expenditures for their economic survival. They cannot operate successfully in the civilian marketplace but have instead geared their products and talents toward the security provided by Pentagon capitalism. Their managerial and professional personnel have had no need to gain experience in advertising, marketing, and product planning to meet the needs of civilian consumers. Many aerospace–defense firms would find it exceedingly difficult to convert to non–military-related business.

Related to this has been the "brain drain" of technically educated workers, wherein people have been siphoned away from civilian industry into nonproductive aerospace–defense jobs. This brain drain has been encouraged by massive military expenditures that have opened up lucrative employment opportunities in the military–industrial complex. Scientific and engineering talent that could have been put to use in other settings has been usurped. According to Richard J. Barnet, "more than half the scientists and engineers in the country work directly or indirectly for the Pentagon."[31] More-

[29] Seymour Melman, *The Permanent War Economy* (New York: Simon & Schuster, 1974), p. 18.

[30] Ibid. See also Melman's *Pentagon Capitalism* and his *Our Depleted Society* (New York: Holt, Rinehart & Winston, 1965); also Paul Blumberg, *Inequality in an Age of Decline* (New York: Oxford University Press, 1980), Chapters 3 and 4.

[31] Barnet, *The Economy of Death*, p. 50.

over, the skills and technical knowledge possessed by many such persons are not easily transferred elsewhere. Even the nation's universities are affected, as federal research and development funds—important sources of income for many institutions—have largely gone to meet military-related requirements.

Seymour Melman has argued that, despite the apparent prosperity of the American economy, non–war-related industries have become progressively underdeveloped—both in terms of their productive potential and in comparison with industries in other nations (e.g., in Western Europe and Japan) that spend relatively little on militarism.[32] With so much of our labor force and productive apparatus engaged in remaining the world's number one military power, our production of peacetime goods and services has begun to suffer. Important sectors of the civilian economy are afflicted with low levels of productivity, inefficiency and the need for modernization, inability to maintain quality, and unnecessarily high production costs that inflate prices. Inflated prices then stimulate worker demands for higher wages, thereby increasing the cost of living.

One result is that the United States is finding it increasingly difficult to compete successfully with other nations in world trade. Many American-made products cannot find foreign buyers, and the United States has begun to import finished goods that formerly had been produced domestically. The United States has become more and more dependent on selling its agricultural products abroad. And it has, as we have seen, become involved in selling billions of dollars worth of military weapons systems and equipment—also to help balance off the value of imported goods.[33] The value of United States arms exports was almost a third of the world total in 1985 (Figure 3.4).

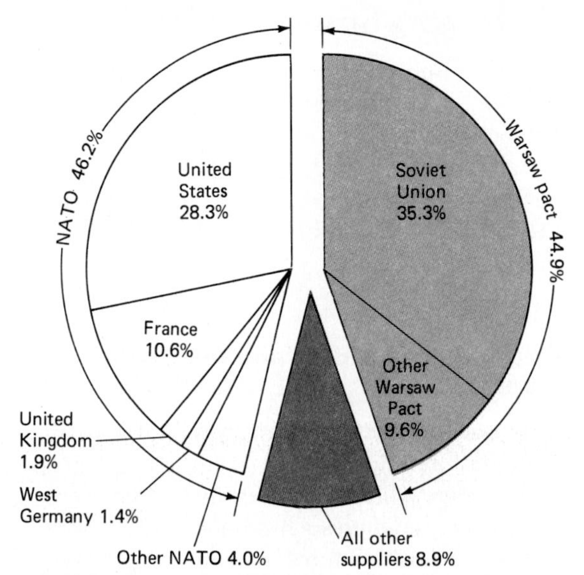

FIGURE 3.4 Shares of World Arms Exports, 1985
Source: U.S. Arms Control and Disarmament Agency, *World Military Expenditures and Arms Transfers, 1987* (Washington, D.C.: U.S. Government Printing Office, 1988), p. 10.

The deteriorating state of domestic civilian industry has made it necessary for American corporations to invest outside this country in order to keep profits high.[34] By opening up plants elsewhere, corporations can cut transportation and labor costs so as to render their products more competitive with those of other nations. This strategy exacerbates domestic economic problems. Corporate investments abroad mean that these dollars are not being utilized to update and improve deteriorating stateside industries. Moreover, such investments often function to ship jobs abroad, putting more Americans out of work. Finding it

[32] Melman, *The Permanent War Economy*, pp. 74–104. See also his *Profits Without Production*.

[33] Blumberg, *Inequality in an Age of Decline*, Chapters 3 and 4.

[34] Barry Bluestone and Bennett Harrison, *The Deindustrialization of America* (New York: Basic Books, 1982).

difficult to afford higher priced, domestically made goods, unemployed people, and many who are employed, turn to cheaper imported products. This then throws more Americans out of work.

One need not be an economic genius to understand that the foreign investments of the last thirty years have been developing a cumulative effect that is just beginning to be felt. By allocating massive societal resources to militarism, other activities that are important to our daily lives have been allowed to go into decline. Military expenditures, in Seymour Melman's judgment, have "become a major source of corrosion of the productive competence of the American economy as a whole."[35]

The Quality of Life

High military expenditures have also created underdevelopment in the area of social welfare. The money allocated toward military expenditures could be used to improve the quality of life for millions.

Political scientists Joshua Cohen and Joel Rogers offer an example of the losses our high rates of military spending entail. They point out that the cost overruns for five new weapons—the XM-1 tank, the F-18 and F-16 fighter planes, the UH-60A helicopter, and the Trident missile submarine—totaled $77 billion by 1981. This amount of money would have wiped out poverty in America completely for four years.[36]

It is not hard to think of other examples. The areas of environmental pollution control and cleanup, education, medical and health care, housing, public transportation, recreation, assistance to the aged, and child care, among others, are all underdeveloped, while talent and resources are skewed toward maintaining the permanent war economy.

Militarism affects the quality of life in more than just economic ways. It also interferes with our democratic rights and civil liberties. It is not surprising that a militarized government committed to a warlike posture toward external enemies should attempt to repress imagined threats from within. President Dwight D. Eisenhower warned of this possibility in his farewell address on January 17, 1961:

> In the councils of government we must guard against the acquisition of unwarranted influence, whether sought or unsought, by the military–industrial complex....
>
> We must never let the weight of this combination endanger our liberties or democratic processes. We should take nothing for granted. Only an alert and knowledgeable citizenry can compel the proper meshing of the huge industrial and military machinery of defense with our peaceful methods and goals so that security and liberty can prosper together.[37]

Since the early 1960s, America's military and paramilitary apparatus has been used at times against lawful activities by citizens. Many of the internal "enemies" were individuals and groups who actively protested military expenditures, the uses to which they have been put (particularly in Southeast Asia), and the adverse effects of all this for American society. Among the activities carried out under the rationale of protecting internal security were wiretapping and spying; organized disruption of dissident groups; the employment of agents provocateurs; burglary and violation of the mails; infiltration of campuses and classrooms; maintenance of

[35] Melman, *The Permanent War Economy,* p. 260.

[36] Cohen and Rogers, *On Democracy,* p. 36. See also Seymour Melman, "Looting the Means of Production," *New York Times* (July 26, 1981): E21.

[37] U.S. Department of State, *Bulletin,* Vol. 44. February 6, 1961.

secret dossiers on thousands of innocent people; and legal harassment and intimidation.[38]

After public exposure and widespread condemnation of these abuses in the 1970s, it was hoped that such treatment of citizens would not occur again. Yet it appears that not only was the machinery for the violation of democratic rights and civil liberties not dismantled by the federal government—it was used again in the 1980s. In early 1988 it was revealed that the FBI had conducted a lengthy and aggressive surveillance effort against persons opposed to the Reagan administration's policies in Central America. Over 100 church, civil rights, union, education, and political organizations were encompassed in the surveillance, which began in 1983. Like earlier government violations of U.S. citizens' rights, it included the use of secret informants and undercover agents.

The Nuclear Threat

All macro problems cause harm to and limit the life chances of millions of people. But as tragic and wasteful of human potential as they are, none of these problems can create anywhere near the carnage that would result from the use of nuclear arms.[39] It is amazing that we can go about our daily lives either ignorant of or apathetic to the dangers to which American militarism contributes. (Our nuclear forces are described in Table 3.3.)

A simple miscalculation of other nations' military intentions or a bravado show of brinksmanship can plunge the American military establishment into an exercise in unprecedented destruction. Over 116,000 Americans died in World War I, and more than 407,000 were killed in World War II. These figures are nothing in comparison to the likely outcome of a nuclear war. One study conservatively estimates that from 35 to 45 percent of the U.S. population—currently some 80 million to 100 million people—would be killed or badly injured in a full-scale nuclear attack on major urban areas. Within the urban areas themselves casualties would approach 80 percent.[40] Even a more limited attack on military installations would produce millions of deaths and injuries.

Yet not every expert agrees that there would be survivors in the event of nuclear war. Fear has been expressed over the possible impact of exploded weaponry on the earth's atmosphere, climate, and weather. The earth could well be rendered unfit for any form of life.[41]

In recent years some scientists have been using the concept of "nuclear winter" to describe the probable outcome of the extensive utilization of nuclear weaponry. Such warfare would result in the creation of massive clouds of radioactive dust and debris, according to the scientists. A climatic catastrophe would engulf the whole planet, as the sun's rays were blocked, temperatures on the earth fell, crops failed, and human and animal life slowly flickered out in the frigid darkness. The worst-case scenario raises the possibility of human extinction, while even those who are more optimistic suggest that the impact of a nuclear winter would be incredible.[42]

But even if there were survivors here in America, what kind of land might they inherit?

---

[38] See Alan Wolfe, *The Seamy Side of Democracy* (New York: David McKay Co., 1973); Paul Cowan et al., *State Secrets* (New York: Holt, Rinehart & Winston, 1974); David Wise, *The American Police State* (New York: Random House, 1976); and Frank Donner, *The Age of Surveillance* (New York: Alfred A. Knopf, 1980).

[39] See Arthur M. Katz, *Life After Nuclear War* (Cambridge, Mass.: Ballinger Publishing Company, 1982). Also see Michael Riordan, ed., *The Day After Midnight* (Palo Alto, Calif.: Cheshire Books, 1982), and Eric Chivian et al., eds., *Last Aid: The Medical Dimension of Nuclear War* (San Francisco: W. H. Freeman and Company, 1982).

[40] Katz, *Life After Nuclear War*, pp. 100 and 120.

[41] See Jonathan Schell, *The Fate of the Earth* (New York: Alfred A. Knopf, 1982).

[42] Owen Greene, Ian Percival, and Irene Ridge, *Nuclear Winter: The Evidence and the Risks* (Cambridge, Mass.: Polity Press, 1985).

TABLE 3.3 Intercontinental Ballistic Missiles (ICBMs), Submarines, and Bombers—U.S.–U.S.S.R. Balance, 1980–87

Weapons system	1980	1981	1982	1983	1984	1985	1986	1987	Net change 1980–87
ICBMs									
United States*	1,052	1,052	1,049	1,040	1,030	1,017	999	996	−56
Minuteman II	450	450	450	450	450	450	450	450	--
Minuteman III	550	550	550	550	550	550	534	514	−36
Peacekeeper (MX)	—	—	—	—	—	—	10	32	32
Soviet Union	1,398	1,398	1,398	1,398	1,398	1,398	1,418	1,389	−9
SS-11	640	580	550	520	520	448	440	420	−220
SS-13	60	60	60	60	60	60	60	60	--
SS-17	150	150	150	150	150	150	150	145	−5
SS-18	308	308	308	308	308	308	308	308	—
SS-19	240	300	330	360	360	360	360	350	110
Warheads									
United States	2,152	2,152	2,149	2,140	2,130	2,117	2,157	2,312	160
Soviet Union	5,002	5,302	5,862	6,420	6,420	6,420	6,440	6,400	1,398
Submarine systems									
SLBMs:†									
United States*	576	512	520	568	592	600	640	640	64
Trident I	80	112	200	264	288	312	384	384	304
Poseidon	416	384	320	304	304	288	256	256	−160
Soviet Union*	985	985	969	961	946	931	967	969	−16
SS-N-6	464	416	384	368	336	304	272	256	−208
SS-N-8	292	292	292	292	292	292	292	286	−6
SS-N-17	12	12	12	12	12	12	12	12	—
SS-N-18	160	206	224	224	224	224	224	224	64
Warheads									
United States	4,880	4,752	4,800	5,152	5,344	5,376	5,632	5,632	752
Soviet Union	1,625	1,817	1,865	1,957	2,122	2,307	2,695	2,941	1,316
Bombers									
United States*	376	376	355	297	297	297	312	363	−13
B-1B	—	—	—	—	--	--	26	81	81
B-52G	151	151	151	151	151	151	150	150	−1
B-52H	90	90	90	90	90	90	84	84	−6
FB-111	60	60	56	56	56	56	52	48	−12
Soviet Union*	220	235	245	260	300	325	325	326	106
Tu-95 BEAR	100	100	100	100	100	100	100	100	—
Tu-95 BEAR-H	—	—	—	—	25	50	50	60	60
Tu-22M Backfire	75	90	100	115	130	145	160	165	90

Key: X, not applicable.
*Includes weapons not shown separately.
†Submarine-launched ballistic missile.
Source: U.S. Department of Commerce, Bureau of the Census, *Statistical Abstract of the United States, 1989* (Washington, D.C.: U.S. Government Printing Office, 1989), p. 334.

Some have said such survivors would come to envy the dead. Institutions we now take for granted would be largely crippled, if not destroyed: national and regional communications systems as well as means of transportation; means of producing and distributing goods such as food, medicine, and fuel; and law enforcement. Sources of water would very likely be contaminated, if not destroyed. The injured would need medical treatment, but those who could provide it would themselves be among the dead and injured. Many "survivors" of blast effects would die quickly from the effects of radiation poisoning, with dehydration resulting from uncontrollable vomiting and diarrhea. Other "survivors" would, if they last long enough, die from cancer. Reflecting on such possibilities, students at Brown University have asked that cyanide be held at the campus infirmary for use in the event of a nuclear war.

Nuclear weaponry proliferates around the world, and, despite arms limitation talks, the end to America's arms race with the Soviet Union is not in sight. In the absence of adequate safeguards, a deranged political leader could touch off a World War III that will leave no historians to debate its origins. The technical knowledge and even the materials required to construct a nuclear weapon are now relatively accessible; not only other nations but also domestic and foreign bandit groups may gain access to such means of total destruction. At-

Nagasaki and Hiroshima are reminders of the monumental horrors that would be associated with any further nuclear warfare. The United States is the only nation ever to use nuclear weapons, the effects of which are seen in this photograph of a residential neighborhood in Hiroshima in 1945. (*AP/Wide World Photos*)

tempts at nuclear blackmail may not be limited to the pseudoreality of nighttime television thrillers.[43]

Despite massive military expenditures, there is no real way this society can be protected from nuclear annihilation. And yet America's national security managers gamble daily with the possibility of a nuclear Armageddon. A strongly sanitized jargon obscures the destructive potential of our buildup of submarines, missiles, bombers, tanks, and artillery pieces equipped with thermonuclear capabilities. What, after all, does Congressional funding of MIRV mean to the average citizen? Stripped of its alphabetical neutrality, MIRV stands for an advance in destructive capability that allows the United States to launch multiple nuclear warheads at different targets from the same single shot. While MIRV enhances America's ability to wipe out every single living thing on the planet a dozen times over, the billions spent on it do not provide a whit of additional security for this society.

The effects of exploded nuclear weaponry are expected by some to be so obscenely destructive as to make recent efforts to promote "civil defense" a cruel hoax.[44] The Federal Emergency Management Agency has been in the process of developing evacuation plans wherein citizens would be encouraged to flee from probable blast areas to outlying communities. While preparing these plans, the agency has also been coordinating the stockpiling of materials that might be needed in the aftermath of nuclear warfare—including 130,000 pounds of opium for pain. Meanwhile, the U.S. Postal Service reportedly is ready to distribute emergency change of address cards for survivors separated from their home mailing addresses. The U.S. Department of Agriculture has developed plans for food rationing, and the U.S. Department of the Treasury supposedly has plans to impose a national sales tax to temporarily replace anticipated disruptions in the receipt of income taxes caused by nuclear holocaust. Tax expenditures on these activities have been justified with the argument that the Soviet Union is drawing ahead in the "civil defense race." Yet far more tax dollars and plans are going to creating the conditions for war to take place.[45]

In March 1983 President Ronald Reagan announced his plan for a space-age system that would protect the mainland United States from incoming ballistic missiles by shooting them down before they could strike their targets. The Strategic Defense Initiative (SDI, dubbed "Star Wars" by the media) was projected to cost over $1 trillion. The project has understandably been welcomed by components of the military–industrial complex. Critics suggest that the types of scientific and technological discoveries required to build such a system are many years away, and that even if such a system could be built there would be no way to know if it would work short of a full-scale nuclear attack. Others charge that the Strategic Defense Initiative project will further heat up the U.S.–U.S.S.R. arms race, as the Soviet Union seeks out new weaponry and strategies to outwit SDI.[46] To many, Star Wars would seem to offer about as little security from nuclear annihilation as civil defense officials' planning to relocate citizens to "safe" areas upon notice of impending nuclear attack.

---

[43] See Robert L. Heilbroner, *An Inquiry into the Human Prospect*, rev. ed. (New York: W. W. Norton & Company, 1980).

[44] The U.S. government plans for nuclear war survival are detailed in Edward Zuckerman, *The Day After World War III* (New York: Viking Press, 1984).

[45] See Robert Scheer, *With Enough Shovels* (New York: Vintage Books, 1983); Peter Pringle and William Arkin, *S.I.O.P.: The Secret U.S. Plan for Nuclear War* (New York: W. W. Norton & Company, 1983); and Robert C. Aldridge, *First Strike: The Pentagon's Strategy for Nuclear War* (Boston: South End Press, 1983).

[46] See Jonathon Green, *The A–Z of Nuclear Jargon* (New York: Routledge & Kegan Paul, 1986).

CHOOSING HUMAN SURVIVAL

The institutional forces promoting militarism are indeed formidable. But we must seek ways to offset them so that the human species can survive.

People around the world are growing increasingly fearful over the dangers involved in the U.S.–U.S.S.R. arms race and the continued proliferation of nuclear weaponry.[47] In many nations, the United States included, one response has been outcries of "enough is enough." There has been a multiplicity of groups and organizations taking a principled stand in opposition to militarism in general and the arms race in particular. For example, during the 1980s in the United States there appeared a grassroots citizens' movement aimed at achieving a "nuclear freeze," that is, an end to further development, building, and deployment of nuclear arms. A similar movement appeared in the late 1970s and swept European nations at the same time. Although unsuccessful to date in realizing its goals, the nuclear freeze movement has put unprecedented pressure on American and Soviet elites to address issues of arms control.

Because the choice may very well be between militarism and the existence of the human species, it seems obvious that multilateral disarmament is imperative. War is no longer a viable solution for the problems facing this or any other society, since it may well mean the end of the human species. While we do not know what it will take to achieve disarmament elsewhere, at home it will mean combating institutional forces whose self-interests are tied up in an economy of death.

In the 1980s the U.S. government was dominated by the heavily promilitaristic policymakers of the Reagan–Bush administration. The Soviet Union, on the other hand, underwent sweeping leadership changes and its government expanded the range of issues conceivably open to negotiation. Political scientist Michael Parenti notes that, besides other initiatives,

> the Soviets unilaterally stopped underground nuclear tests and asked Washington to do the same; proposed a 50-percent cut in long range nuclear missiles and the eventual elimination of all nuclear weapons by the year 2000; signed a no first-strike pledge regarding nuclear weapons; supported a ban on all weapons in outer space; called for mutual cuts in conventional forces in Europe; and endorsed a bilateral, verifiable nuclear freeze. In each instance, [the U.S. government] either did not respond or denounced the proposals and actions as "propaganda ploys."[48]

Clearly it is desirable for U.S. elites to radically alter their posture and embrace opportunities that would enhance the probability of human survival. Grassroots pressures in that direction are likely to continue, both in this nation and abroad.

While the superpowers jockey for position in the shadow of a potential nuclear holocaust, the worldwide costs of militarism and war escalate. Many peoples' survival is in question even without nuclear warfare, simply as a function of misplaced priorities. Annual military expenditures by the United States and other nations total well over $1 trillion. If such sums were channeled to peace-oriented activities, the well-being of everyone on this planet would be greatly enhanced. Investments in such areas as food production, housing, clean water, and disease control would easily be possible.

In the United States alone the federal budget for "defense" of our citizens' security is now over $300 billion per year. Such a priority allows, as we shall see in a later chapter, some 20 million Americans to be living with hunger and

[47] See Peter Beckman et al., *The Nuclear Predicament* (Englewood Cliffs, N.J.: Prentice-Hall, 1989), for a thorough overview of the dangers.

[48] Michael Parenti, *Democracy for the Few*, 5th ed. (New York: St. Martin's Press, 1988), p. 86.

2 million to 3 million to be without homes. Such a priority means that twenty-one other nations have lower rates of infant mortality than we do. Casualties, including deaths, occur without a shot being fired. They will continue to occur until citizens successfully offset the institutional forces favoring militarism.

The term "arms control" implies agreement to stabilize or to reduce the rate of production and deployment of weapons. This is not the same as disarmament, which refers to the outright elimination of weapons by dismantling and/or destroying them. If human survival is the goal, then disarmament will play an important role in meeting it. But the first step is to reduce the availability of weaponry. The United States must stop making the world into an unstable armed camp through its sale and export of arms and military-related technology to other nations. An argument for continuing such sales is that if America does not do so, other nations will. But the behavior of other nations cannot diminish our responsibility for the carnage our own contributions help foster. Others argue such sales help to buttress the U.S. economy. Surely there are other products we can successfully market to other nations instead, products whose function is not the delivery of death.

As we begin to roll back our commitment to militarism and use our influence to press other nations in joining a movement toward disarmament, funds will be freed for use on any of a number of projects. We can choose to upgrade and modernize underdeveloped areas in the civilian economy and to retrain and place workers displaced by reduced spending on the military–industrial complex. In the 1940s the United States quickly mobilized its productive resources for war; a conversion back to peace—an end to the "permanent war economy"—is possible with careful planning. America need suffer few disruptions should "peace break out."

In the conduct of our daily lives we usually seek to avoid unnecessary conflict and certainly we try to keep out of situations whose outcomes may involve violence. It is possible for nations to conduct themselves in much the same way. This and other societies must perfect nonviolent means of resolving conflicts—for example, diplomacy, adjudication of differences by neutral international bodies, techniques of passive resistance designed to make a point and influence world opinion. Nations will always disagree, but there is no reason why such disagreement must be resolved by the continued threat or use of armed force. On campuses around the United States students may take courses or even major in "peace education" or "peace studies." The focus is on conflict and how to avoid or resolve it. The appearance of peace studies as a legitimate component of higher education is yet a further expression of the fear and concern militarism and war arouse.

A more peaceful world will also require that we and other nations cease meddling in others' affairs. There is no good reason to use covert paramilitary forces (e.g., the CIA and its equivalents) to solve problems. The involvement of American intelligence forces in other nations' domestic affairs—as has been the case with regard to U.S. intervention in Nicaragua—has been internationally condemned and must cease.

Some of these ideas may sound utopian. Perhaps they are. But each day that passes makes it that much more difficult for America and the rest of the world to avoid war deaths—and possibly a grotesque end to life as we know it.[49] That is why local community groups, churches, student organizations, to name a few, have begun to reiterate "enough is enough."

SUMMARY

America maintains a large-scale military–industrial complex whose impact is felt in areas

---

[49] See Helen Caldicott, *Missile Envy* (New York: William Morrow & Company, 1984).

ranging from foreign policy to the quality of domestic life. The components of this complex include the uniformed military, the aerospace–defense industry, the civilian national security managers, and the U.S. Congress. Each component of the military–industrial complex, which has existed since World War II, has its own interests to pursue and protect. In doing so, each serves the interests of every other component.

Following the end of World War II, a number of factors contributed to the continued existence of the military–industrial complex. The uniformed military campaigned to keep the powers and responsibilities of the military establishment intact. Governmental and corporate elites, fearful of a return to prewar depression conditions, were reluctant to end the war economy. Corporate elites had found military spending highly profitable. The outbreak of the cold war with the Soviet Union provided a further justification for maintaining a permanent war economy. American elites viewed socialism, and the threat of its spread, as requiring a military response. Fears of expanding socialism have been important to the maintenance of the military–industrial complex for over forty years.

Each component of the military–industrial complex plays a role in its operation. The uniformed military services have carved out missions in defense and active warfare and work to sell the importance of their role to governmental civilians and the public. The aerospace–defense industry, the second component of the complex, profits from large-scale tax expenditures on militarism. The industry's relation to the U.S. Department of Defense has been characterized as Pentagon capitalism. Military-related products and services are provided by aerospace–defense firms under conditions involving far less competition and risk, and more assured profits, than is the case in production for the consumer public.

The third component of the military–industrial complex consists of the national security managers, governmental civilians who are responsible for safeguarding national security and formulating foreign policy. They are usually drawn from the world of big business and high finance and are thus likely to be sensitive to the economic implications of military spending. Such spending has an impact on the domestic economy, for millions of jobs depend on it. As American corporations have become increasingly involved in doing business in other countries, our military capabilities provide a means of protecting our economic interests abroad.

The U.S. Congress, the final component of the military–industrial complex, provides the tax funds that keep the complex going. Congress typically appropriates most of the money requested by the national security managers and the uniformed military each year. One major reason is that military expenditures have an important economic impact on the home states or districts of senators and representatives.

American corporate investments overseas have grown enormously since World War II, as have the number and size of multinational firms. An increasing percentage of the net incomes of many of America's largest corporations comes from foreign operations. Operating overseas, multinational firms are able to gain access to valuable raw materials, cultivate new markets for their goods and services, and take advantage of low labor costs. The spread of American economic interests abroad has been facilitated by government foreign and military policies. These policies have included efforts to combat the spread of socialism, which elites see as a danger to capitalist economic activities.

Several military strategies have been employed to fight against socialism. These include the threatened use of nuclear arms, conventional nonnuclear warfare, and counterinsurgency warfare involving such paramilitary agencies as the CIA. In addition, America sells over $19 billion in arms each year to friendly governments that allow American corporate involvement in their economies. These strategies—all made possible by a well-financed military–industrial complex—are used to make the world safe for American business.

Critics have pointed to negative effects of militarism on the American civilian economy. That sector of the economy that produces military-related goods and services is said to be nonproductive, in that it does not serve basic needs of the civilian population. Many firms that have grown dependent on producing for the Department of Defense would find it exceedingly difficult to convert to production for civilian consumption. Many technically educated persons have been siphoned away from civilian industry into aerospace–defense jobs, creating a "brain drain" or loss of talent that could have been used in other settings. Finally, investment in militarism is said to have caused the underdevelopment of sectors of the civilian economy, leading to inefficiency and higher production costs. The productive competency of the American civilian economy has become corroded, and this has begun to interfere with our ability to complete in the world market.

Militarism also has negative effects on the quality of life in the United States. Tax funds going to support the military–industrial complex could be used for other purposes—cleaning the environment, ending poverty and hunger, rebuilding the nation's cities, and so on. The maintenance of a militaristic posture also affects domestic civil liberties. A government oriented toward the use of force against external enemies is prone to repress imagined threats from within. Since the early 1960s, America's military and paramilitary apparatus has at times been used against citizens engaged in lawful activity—for example, persons and groups protesting militarism.

One final negative effect of militarism is the constant possibility of nuclear warfare. Nuclear weaponry has been proliferating around the world. As more nations join the "nuclear club," the likelihood of nuclear holocaust increases. Should nuclear warfare occur, the carnage would be immense. There is no way of telling what kind of world the survivors—if any—would inherit. Despite our massive military expenditures, there is no real way this society can be protected from nuclear annihilation.

In the interests of human survival, efforts to bring about worldwide multilateral disarmament must take place, and expenditures on militarism must be directed into peace-oriented activities. The United States must cease selling weaponry to other nations. Ultimately, this and other societies must perfect nonviolent means of resolving conflicts.

DISCUSSION QUESTIONS

1. What arguments can be made for and against resolving disagreements through violence? Are there circumstances under which the ends justify violent means?
2. In all past wars, at least some Americans have refused to be inducted into military service. Should people have the right to decide whether they will follow the demands of a government that engages the nation in warfare?
3. In what ways and to what degree is your community or state dependent on military expenditures? Discuss what would happen if these expenditures were to suddenly cease.
4. Who ultimately benefits the most from the maintenance of a permanent war economy in the United States? In what ways?
5. How often have you thought about the possibility of this society's involvement in nuclear warfare? What are your feelings about that possibility?
6. Is the propensity to engage in warfare a part of human nature? Or is it the outcome of socioeconomic and political forces? Give evidence in support of your answer.

SUGGESTED READINGS

Adams, Gordon. *The Iron Triangle: The Politics of Defense Contracting* (New Brunswick, N.J.: Transaction Books, 1982).
Analysis of the politics of defense spending and the corporate beneficiaries.

Evan, William M., and Stephen Hilgartner, eds. *The Arms Race and Nuclear War* (Englewood Cliffs, N.J.: Prentice-Hall, 1987).
Readings exploring the nuclear arms race, its dynamics, and strategies to prevent nuclear holocaust.

Klare, Michael T., and Peter Kornbluh. *Low Intensity Warfare* (New York: Pantheon Books, 1988).
Involvement of the United States in undeclared warfare in politically volatile areas of the underdeveloped world.

Kovic, Ron. *Born on the Fourth of July* (New York: Pocket Books, 1977).
Recently a successful motion picture, the story of how a young man came to reject war as a solution to problems.

Melman, Seymour. *Profits Without Production* (New York: Alfred A. Knopf, 1983).
Long-time critic of massive defense budgets relates these budgets to the deterioration of the quality of everyday life.

Union of Concerned Scientists. *The Fallacy of Star Wars* (New York: Vintage Books, 1984).
Critiques of the rationale for and probable ineffectiveness of federal plans to engage nuclear enemies in space warfare.

M.E
SCRA

CHAPTER 4

Environmental Abuse

Resources should be devoted to the preservation and conservation of the natural environment, and technological decisions must take into account the well-being of future generations.

Americans have long been abusing their environment. We routinely pour gaseous and solid wastes into the air and water, poison and otherwise misuse the land, and use up irreplaceable commodities. We are all aware of environmental abuse—and we all contribute to it. When we drive our cars, discard trash, do the laundry with phosphate detergents, or set thermostats high in winter and low in summer, we are helping abuse the environment. Billboards blocking the view, airplanes roaring overhead, and trucks crowding our highways are some of the kinds of environmental abuse we take for granted.

The term *ecology* is used to refer to "the intricate web of relationships between living organisms and their living and nonliving surroundings."[1] Every action we take within our

---

[1] Council on Environmental Quality, *First Annual Report, August 1970* (Washington, D.C.: U.S. Government Printing Office, 1970), p. 6.

environment—indeed our very presence—has some impact on the earth. Our environment is not "out there" and apart from humanity. We and our societal institutions are a part of it, whether we think in such terms or not.

The nature of the relationship between human beings and the environment is brought out in the following basic principles of ecology:

1. Living organisms (including people) and their surroundings are mutually interdependent. The earth is one big *ecosystem* in which each part—including human institutions—serves functions that have a bearing on the system as a whole. In turn, the well-being of the whole has implications for the various parts.
2. Every living organism is part of this global ecosystem. All life is, however indirectly and distantly, interconnected.
3. Each species of life carries out its activities in its own environmental niche. Some species have proven to be much more adaptable to changes in their surroundings than others. Adaptability contributes to ecosystem stability.
4. The more species there are, the more stable the ecosystem is likely to be. This is because of the increased probability that some species will take over an important system function if another cannot.
5. Species tend to be dependent on one another and to be interconnected through chains or cycles. For example, we live by inhaling oxygen from the air and exhaling carbon dioxide. Plants, in effect, do the reverse. Thus, people and plants need one another. Likewise, just about every species of life uses another as food and in turn serves as nourishment for an additional species.
6. It is impossible to throw anything away in the global ecosystem. Everything must go somewhere. When something is disposed of, there is an impact on the part of the system from which it is removed and on the part into which it is discarded.
7. No part of the ecosystem is "free." Whenever we use or deplete some part of the system, this affects the functioning of the ecosystem as a whole.
8. People and the institutions people create are only one part of the global ecosystem, and perhaps not even the most important part. We are far more dependent on other living species than they are on us. The ecosystem could probably easily survive without humanity.[2]

These principles make it clear that polluting the air, land, and water; spreading radioactivity into the atmosphere; generating increasing levels of noise; creating numerous wastes; and consuming irreplaceable resources change or otherwise affect the global ecosystem. Since human beings are part of the ecosystem, we too are affected by these activities. The term *ecocatastrophe* is an apt description of the overall effect such harmful human activities seem to be having. While obviously not all human activities are ecologically harmful, those cited appear to be undoing millions of years of nature's complex work.

In some cases the damage being done to the air, water, land, and the life they sustain poses a threat to human survival. Since all people are participants in the global ecosystem, this threat goes beyond the political boundaries of the United States. Many other nations are engaged in environmental abuse. But the United States stands out in terms of its massive contribution to environmental ills. For example, no other nation consumes so much of the world's unrenewable natural resources each year.

In this chapter we look at the macro problem of environmental abuse. We distinguish among

[2] These ecological principles are adapted from Alan Bock. *The Ecology Action Guide* (New York: Pyramid Books, 1972), pp. 21–25.

a number of types of environmental abuse, indicating their extent and their implications for the future. Finally, we examine the causes of and possible solutions to this basic and far-reaching problem, discussing the institutional and individual obstacles that we must work to overcome.

NATURE AND EXTENT OF ENVIRONMENTAL ABUSE

The term *environmental abuse* refers to several varied types of human activities, from dirtying the atmosphere to depleting irreplaceable resources. In this section we look at major types of environmental abuse. We estimate the extent of each type and look at the possible effects on human survival.

Air Pollution

Most of us take the life-sustaining activity of breathing for granted. But threats to this activity have been emerging all around us, most noticeably since the 1960s. Prior to that time, most people saw "dirty air" as a localized phenomenon, not as the national and international threat it is.

The earth's atmosphere contains a finite amount of air—5 to 6 quadrillion tons of it. Under ordinary circumstances, this air is constantly being recycled and cleansed of contaminants through a complex process involving wind, rain, and changes in temperature. Air pollution occurs when so many contaminants are released into the atmosphere that the recycling and cleansing functions begin to break down.

An estimated 141 million metric tons of pollutants are released into the air each year in the United States (see Table 4.1). While this tonnage may seem insignificant in relation to the amount of air in the earth's atmosphere, it is not really the weight of pollutants that counts. More important is the fact that pollution is concentrated in particular geographical areas—most notably in large cities and their suburbs. Since most Americans live in and around cities, air pollution directly affects most Americans. Of course, pollutants from cities migrate into rural areas.

There are several common classes of air pollutants, according to studies by the federal government.[3] *Carbon monoxide* is a colorless, odorless, poisonous gas that constitutes 53 percent of air pollution tonnage. Over two-thirds of this gas comes from internal combustion engines. *Particulate matter*—that is, solid and liquid substances that may or may not be visible to the naked eye—makes up 5 percent of pollution tonnage. Particulates are emitted during industrial operations and the combustion of fuels in stationary sources (e.g., electric power plants). *Sulfur oxides* enter the air as a by-product of the use of sulfur-containing fuels (coal and oil). Industry and generators of electric power are the biggest users. The oxides are released in the form of poisonous, corrosive gases and comprise 15 percent of our annual pollution output. *Nitrogen oxides* represent 14 percent of our pollution tonnage. They are a major component of what is commonly called *smog*. The major contributors are power plants and transportation vehicles. *Hydrocarbons* also play a role in smog formation. Hydrocarbons, which make up 13 percent of pollution tonnage, are primarily emitted by automobiles. In the formation of smog, hydrocarbons and nitrogen oxides react in sunlight to form ozone (smog's principal constituent).

Researchers do not agree about the effects of particular pollutants on the human body, but it is certain that some or all of them do have negative effects. For example, medical researchers

[3] See annual reports of the President's Council on Environmental Quality, published since 1970 by the U.S. Government Printing Office in Washington, D.C. A good overview of the problem is found in Lewis Regenstein, *America the Poisoned* (Washington, D.C.: Acropolis Books, 1982), Chapter 5.

TABLE 4.1 Air Pollutant Emissions, by Pollutant and Source, 1970–86 (in millions of metric tons)*

Year and pollutant	Total emissions	Controllable emissions						Misc. uncontrollable	Percent of total		
		Transportation		Fuel Combustion†		Industrial processes	Solid waste disposal		Transportation	Fuel combustion	Industrial
		Total	Road vehicles	Total	Electric utilities						
1970											
Carbon monoxide	98.7	71.8	62.7	4.4	.2	9.0	6.4	7.2	72.7	4.5	9.1
Sulfur oxides	28.4	0.6	0.3	21.3	15.8	6.4	—	0.1	2.1	75.0	22.5
Volatile organic compounds	27.5	12.4	11.1	1.1	—	8.9	1.8	3.3	45.1	4.0	32.4
Particulates	18.5	1.2	0.9	4.6	2.3	10.5	1.1	1.1	6.5	24.9	56.8
Nitrogen oxides	18.1	7.6	6.0	9.1	4.4	0.7	0.4	0.3	42.0	50.3	3.9
Lead‡	203.8	163.6	156.0	9.6	0.3	23.9	6.7	—	80.3	4.7	11.7
1980											
Carbon monoxide	76.1	52.6	45.3	7.3	0.3	6.3	2.2	7.6	69.1	9.6	8.3
Sulfur oxides	23.9	0.9	0.4	19.3	16.1	3.8	—	—	3.8	80.8	15.9
Volatile organic compounds	23.0	8.2	6.9	2.2	—	9.2	0.6	2.9	35.7	9.6	0.4
Particulates	8.5	1.3	1.1	2.4	0.8	3.3	0.4	1.1	15.3	28.2	38.8
Nitrogen oxides	20.3	9.2	7.2	10.1	6.4	0.7	0.1	0.2	45.3	49.8	3.4
Lead‡	70.6	59.4	56.4	3.9	0.1	3.6	3.7	—	84.1	5.5	5.1
1986											
Carbon monoxide	60.9	42.6	35.4	7.2	0.3	4.5	1.7	5.0	70.0	11.8	7.4
Sulfur oxides	21.2	0.9	0.5	17.2	14.3	3.1	—	—	4.2	81.1	14.6
Volatile organic compounds	19.5	6.5	5.3	2.3	—	7.9	0.6	2.2	33.3	11.8	40.5
Particulates	6.8	1.4	1.1	1.8	0.4	2.5	0.3	0.8	20.6	26.5	36.8
Nitrogen oxides	19.3	8.5	6.6	10.0	6.6	0.6	0.1	0.1	44.0	51.8	3.1
Lead‡	8.6	3.5	3.3	0.5	0.1	1.9	2.7	—	40.7	5.8	22.1

*Metric ton = 1.1023 short tons.
†Stationary.
‡In thousands of metric tons.
Source: U.S. Department of Commerce, Bureau of the Census, *Statistical Abstract of the United States, 1989* (Washington, D.C.: U.S. Government Printing Office, 1989), p. 200.

have found a correspondence between air pollution and coughing, colds, and other respiratory diseases, lung cancer, cardiovascular diseases, infant mortality rates, death rates among the elderly, and the speed of recovery from illness.[4]

One federal study addressed the special risks air pollution poses for persons living in or near urban centers. Its conclusions are sobering:

> Of all urban dwellers, one in five—more than 35 million people—are at special risk from such illnesses as emphysema and bronchitis as a result of exposure to air pollution.... In general, industrialized, densely populated metropolitan areas have higher cancer mortality rates than rural areas, especially for lung cancer.[5]

Efforts have been made to estimate the financial benefits to be gained by reducing and preventing common classes of air pollutants. While such estimates are crude at best, it is thought that such pollution costs Americans over $20 billion per year. These costs stem from treatment of unnecessary health problems, damage to residential property, extra cleaning expenses, and harm to vegetation and materials (e.g., steel, rubber, marble).[6] No real dollar value can be assigned to the ways air pollution hastens the death of living things—including people.

The "Greenhouse Effect"

For some years now, scientists have been warning that air pollution could create a "greenhouse effect" that would produce increased temperatures all over the world. While many scientists remain cautious in their statements about this, some argue that the greenhouse effect is now upon us, and that it will have a tremendous impact in the not-too-distant future.[7]

We can start with the fact that the earth and its surrounding atmosphere function naturally much as a greenhouse. Sunlight, on which we depend and which we generally enjoy, strikes the earth. The earth then radiates heat in the form of infrared rays. Some of these warming rays escape through the earth's atmosphere and into space, yet the carbon dioxide (CO_2) in this atmosphere captures some of the warmth. Without this natural process the planet would be afflicted with subfreezing temperatures.

Human activities, scientists have warned, were likely to undo the delicate balance of sun, earth, and atmosphere. In 1988 some claimed that the loss of balance was under way. The first five months of 1988 were said to be the warmest in 100 years of record-keeping. The 1980s contained four of the warmest years in the last century. This, together with new data on pollutants residing in the earth's atmosphere, has led to urgent warnings about the implications for the future.

What actually is happening? The level of concentration of CO_2, which traps heat and thus warms the earth, has been increasing in the atmosphere. Scientists blame this on the increased burning of fossil fuels, such as oil and coal. Systematic measurements begun in 1958 indicate the CO_2 level in the atmosphere has gone up 25 percent since that time. It is thought that the United States and the Soviet Union are responsible for half of the CO_2 emissions.

But other factors are responsible for the CO_2 buildup as well. In many underdeveloped nations large landholders have been cutting down tropical forests at an unprecedented rate, both

[4] See Council on Environmental Quality, *Toxic Chemicals and Public Protection* (Washington, D.C.: U.S. Government Printing Office, May 1980).

[5] Ibid., pp. 121–22.

[6] A. Myrick Freeman III, *Benefits of Air and Water Pollution Controls* (Washington, D.C.: Council on Environmental Quality, 1980).

[7] This section draws from Lester R. Brown and Christopher Flavin, "The Earth's Vital Signs," in Worldwatch Institute, *State of the World 1988* (New York: W. W. Norton & Company, 1988), pp. 3–21; and "The Endless Summer?," *Newsweek* (July 11, 1988): 18–20.

Scientists suspect that the increase in carbon dioxide in the atmosphere is prompting changes in the earth's temperatures and climatic patterns. Widespread destruction of forests, such as is pictured here in Brazil, are believed to be contributing to the problem. *(H. Collart Odinetz/ Sygma)*

for the wood and to expand open land for agriculture. Some 27.2 million acres of forest are permanently destroyed each year. Nations like Brazil are leaders in this regard, as tropical forests give way to massive cattle ranches intended to produce beef products for export to rich developed nations (see Chapter 1). But the trees cut down are no longer available to naturally absorb CO_2 from the air, and new CO_2 is released from the cut-down trees and the earth disturbed by the cutting process. Deforestation, as this process of forest elimination is called, makes a direct contribution to the greenhouse effect.

Scientists estimate that the CO_2 buildup accounts for about half of the warming associated with the greenhouse effect. Other pollutants help produce the rest. Methane is one such pollutant, resulting from wood burning, the raising of farm animals such as cattle, and similar activities. Nitrous oxide, a common component of power plant and motor vehicle emissions, is another pollutant. Finally, there are chlorofluorocarbons (CFCs), chemicals that are commonly used as refrigeration and air conditioner coolants as well as in foam products (e.g., the food packaging used by many fast-food restaurants). CFCs are also believed to be largely responsible for the growing destruction of the earth's ozone layer, to be discussed in the next section.

As the pollutants—from CO_2 to CFCs—concentrate in the earth's atmosphere, more and more heat is trapped and the earth's temperature rises. Scientists speculate that the temperature could rise on average anywhere from three to eight degrees Fahrenheit by the years 2030 to 2050. The increases are unlikely to be spread evenly around the earth: Temperature increases near the equator could be small, whereas the upper latitudes could have increases that are twice the global average.

Such a warming trend will affect climates, although no one is sure precisely how. Here is one projection:

> A warming is likely to change rainfall patterns, prevailing winds, and ocean currents, which might lead to more severe storms as the temperature differential between the equatorial region and the higher latitudes widens. Higher temperatures in some areas would also bring an overall increase in evaporation and rainfall, but the changes would not be evenly distributed. Some regions would become wetter; others drier.[8]

Such climatic transformations have enormous implications for agricultural activity. Farming goes on where it does, and takes on the form that it does, in response to a history of relatively constant climatic conditions. Change these conditions and world food production could be seriously affected. Nations' entire economies could be placed under disruptive stresses.

But there is more. Due to the greenhouse effect the level of the world's oceans is expected to rise dramatically in coming decades—a process scientists say is now under way. As temperatures increase, water warms and expands. Beyond this, warming reduces the water now held within polar ice caps and glaciers; a melting process adds to the oceans' waters. Predictions are that the oceans may rise as much as seven feet by the year 2100. (Since 1900 the oceans have risen four inches.)

Areas of the world where a great deal of food production takes place in low-lying flood plains and river deltas—such as Asia with its rice crops—could be decimated. Populations living in cities and towns along coastal areas around the world may have to abandon their places of work and residence. In the United States, for example, more than half the population resides near the Atlantic or Pacific Ocean, the Gulf of Mexico, or the Great Lakes. The costs and dislocations associated with coastal flooding would be without precedent. All continents would be affected.

Biological species other than humans would also face many new demands as a result of the greenhouse effect. Many species of plants and animals which had adapted to past climatic features may not be able to survive the new temperatures and seasons, particularly given the rapidity with which these changes could occur. The biological diversity of and natural balance among species will change in ways that cannot be predicted.

A former chairman of the President's Council on Environmental Quality, Gus Speth, provided this warning to the U.S. Senate back in 1980:

> The insidious nature of the CO_2 problem is that if a response is postponed until significant and harmful climate changes are actually observed or until scientific uncertainties are largely resolved, it may be too late to avoid even more severe climate changes.[9]

Today, as more becomes known and warnings arrive from more quarters, scientific discussions are under way in many different nations on what can and should be done. But the most concerned scientists suspect that the actions yet to be taken will do little more than slow the impact of the greenhouse effect, thus affording us more time to prepare for the inevitable.

Ideas as to what to do next abound. Slow down fossil fuel consumption and look to alternative energy sources such as solar or even nuclear power. Eliminate totally the use of such chemicals as CFCs, introducing environmentally acceptable substitutes. Develop new crops that can adapt to heat and drought and resist predatory insects. Encourage economic growth and population settlement away from endangered

---

[8] F. Brown and Flavin, "The Earth's Vital Signs," p. 16.

[9] Quoted in Regenstein, *America the Poisoned*, p. 203.

coastal areas, and build protective sea walls where possible for areas at risk of flooding. Be ready to undertake massive investments in irrigation and drainage projects in geographic areas that become favorable to agricultural production. Although such ideas are being introduced in many nations, the sense of urgency necessary for worldwide action is lacking, at least right now.

Ozone Layer Depletion

In the previous section we alluded in passing to yet another case of major environmental damage for which humans can take responsibility: destruction of the ozone layer that is in the earth's upper atmosphere. Like the greenhouse effect, the implications of this ozone depletion are far-reaching.[10]

About fifteen miles above the earth's surface there is a paper-thin layer of ozone (a modified form of oxygen). This ozone layer serves important protective functions for all forms of life. While scientists have been theorizing about this since the early 1970s, it was not until 1985 that firm evidence of ozone depletion became available. A few scientists found a way to actually measure ozone levels and discovered that atmospheric ozone over Antarctica was in decline. Further inquiries revealed that the process of ozone depletion had been going on for some time and increasing steadily each year. In 1987 there was literally a hole in the earth's ozone layer as big as the continental United States!

Why is the hole there? In 1930 researchers discovered a new group of chemical compounds—chlorofluorocarbons, or CFCs. As mentioned in the previous section of this chapter, CFCs are widely used in refrigeration and air-conditioning units. They are used in foam products, such as building insulation and fast-food containers. They have been used in aerosol spray cans. The sales of CFCs in the United States amount to $750 million each year, and they are used in products that have sales of many billions more. Although CFCs are useful, some of their properties present dangers we must now confront. Products in which they are used release the CFCs into the air, whereupon they float up into the upper atmosphere. Under complex conditions that scientists are trying to understand, the CFCs eat away at the ozone. As more CFCs are introduced into the environment, the process of ozone depletion continues.

The ozone layer is critical to maintain, for it shields life on earth from the damaging effects of ultraviolet radiation from the sun. This radiation, unless blocked, can do many things. It can disrupt the oceans' food chains, upon which many forms of life (including human) depend. As the ozone layer is depleted, the ultraviolet radiation will increase the incidence of skin cancers and cataracts of the eye. This radiation can damage our immune systems, leaving us helpless to fight off a variety of infectious diseases. Construction materials, particularly plastics, will more quickly deteriorate. And damage to crops could be monumental.

In 1987 U.S. Secretary of the Interior Donald Hodel urged White House policymakers to adopt his preferred solution to the ozone depletion problem. It was his belief that individuals should undertake "personal protection" measures. This, he felt, was preferable to possible government interference in the economy (i.e., restrictions on production and sales of CFCs). Secretary Hodel suggested the White House wage a public relations campaign to encourage people to wear hats, sunglasses, and sunscreens. One critic noted "you cannot protect crops or the marine environment by personal protection. It's very hard to get fish to wear sunscreen".[11]

---

[10] See Brown and Flavin, "The Earth's Vital Signs," pp. 19–20; "A Gaping Hole in the Sky," *Newsweek* (July 11, 1988): 21–22; and "Lethal Leaks in the Roof of the World," *U.S. News & World Report* (March 28, 1988): 10.

[11] *Washington Post* (May 29, 1987): Al.

Fortunately, wiser heads in government prevailed. In 1987 the United States joined with many other nations in working out an international accord designed to restrict CFC use and substantially cut production by 1999. The largest reductions will have to be by industrial nations such as the United States, which produce and use most of the CFCs and thus make the largest contribution to the problem. This international accord is a milestone in environmental cooperation among nations, and it may provide a model for dealing with other environmental problems that do not recognize national boundaries.

Despite this significant progress, however, the damage continues. For example, as we discard unwanted refrigeration units, air conditioners, etc., the CFCs within will join those already in the atmosphere. And the depletion process cannot easily be reversed. In the words of one scientist, "The only way to return things to the way they were is to stop using chlorofluorocarbons completely and then wait a couple of centuries."[12]

Acid Rain

In recent years a new airborne pollutant has come to be recognized as a serious problem in a number of nations in the Northern Hemisphere, including the United States.[13] We refer here to acid rain, perhaps more properly referred to as acid precipitation, also an outcome of burning fossil fuels (particularly coal and, to a much lesser degree, oil and natural gas). Coal-burning power plants and industrial processors are the heaviest contributors to acid rain.

The sulfur dioxide and nitrogen oxides that are produced by burning coal, for example, rise up into the air, where they combine with water to form acid droplets. Eventually acidic precipitation comes back down to earth in the form of rain, snow, sleet, and hail or attached to particles of dust. In effect, the land and water are being sprinkled with dilute forms of nitric and sulfuric acids—the dangers of which are familiar to anyone who has been exposed to a chemistry course.

Acid rain has come to be seen by some as a serious problem for different reasons. It enters lakes and streams and kills aquatic life. It endangers the safe use of reservoirs that are major public water supplies. Acid rain is a menace to crops as well as to forests, and it eats away at buildings and historical monuments. Moreover, it is thought to contribute to respiratory and cardiovascular disease as well as to cancer. Its destructive potential is enormous if it goes unchecked. Acid rain has been called the "single most important environmental threat to the United States and Canada."[14]

At present the United States emission of sulfur into the atmosphere is over 20 million metric tons a year. Emission of nitrogen is also about 20 million metric tons. Much of this flows out of smokestacks in the industrial Midwest, coming down as acid rain hundreds, even thousands of miles away. It is possible that three-fourths of the acid rain that falls in Canada originates with U.S.-based emissions. Environmental officials have estimated that 50,000 lakes in the United States and Canada could die (i.e., have no aquatic life) by 1995.[15] While Canada has begun to take steps to reduce seriously its own contribution to the acid rain problem, similar measures have until recently lagged in the United States. Federal air pollution legislation enacted in 1990—once fully implemented—will help.

[12] "Lethal Leaks in the Roof of the World," p. 10.

[13] See Robert H. Boyle and R. Alexander Boyle, *Acid Rain* (New York: Schocken Books, 1983), and Robert Ostmann Jr., *Acid Rain* (Minneapolis: Dillon Press, 1982). For a very readable technical treatment, see Allan Wellburn, *Air Pollution and Acid Rain: The Biological Impact* (New York: John Wiley & Sons, 1988), Chapter 4.

[14] Boyle and Boyle, *Acid Rain,* p. 12.

[15] Congressional Quarterly, *Environmental Issues: Prospects and Problems* (Washington, D.C.: Congressional Quarterly, 1982), p. 64. This volume is a collection of Editorial Research Reports.

As the United States has sought to reduce its consumption of imported oil, increased coal burning has become economically attractive. While technology is available that allows coal to be burned without such harmful emissions, it is expensive. The question of who is to pay for this remains unanswered. The threat of acid rain therefore continues to mount.

Water Pollution

Travelers to foreign countries are often warned against drinking anything but sterilized liquids sealed in bottles. Contaminated water is a major problem in the United States as well. Over the years, we have managed to pollute virtually every major body of water in the nation. Rivers, streams, and lakes have been fouled with organic and inorganic chemical wastes. Public water supplies and even private wells have been found to contain substances linked with cancer. Water, like air, is a prerequisite of life. We drink it, bathe in it, use it for recreational purposes, eat many of the creatures that live in it, and rely on it for use in agriculture and industry. Water pollution constitutes a threat that is just as serious as the abuse of the earth's air. There is a distinct possibility that we could run out of usable water, not only because of pollution but also because of the increasing demand for fresh water. In addition, according to biologist Barry Commoner, pollution of our surface waters "may expose human beings to a host of new and unaccustomed diseases for which immunity may be lacking."[16]

Many pollutants have been found in our water, and there is good reason to believe that many others have not yet been discovered. How these pollutants affect one another is unknown.

One of the major contaminants is *industrial waste*. Overall, industry accounts for 60 percent of this society's water pollution. Over 300,000 factories discharge water containing wastes, many of which are known to be toxic. Over half the wastes come from the paper, organic chemicals, steel, and petroleum industries.

Thermal pollution is also one of the most serious types of water pollution, and the waste heat problem is expected to grow much worse in the future. The main source of thermal pollution is the electric power industry, which uses great amounts of water for coolant purposes. The used water is then poured back into rivers, streams, and lakes, raising their temperature and adversely affecting aquatic life.

Municipal wastes make up about 25 percent of all water pollution. The treatment of wastes generated in homes, commercial establishments, and industry remains at a primitive level in most urban areas. Only about half of the nation's population is served by safe means of sewage disposal.

Agricultural wastes include animal and chemical wastes. Each year animals produce the same amount of organic wastes as do 2 billion people. Increasingly, agricultural animals have been reared in centralized feedlots, where their wastes become highly concentrated and are impervious to natural decomposition. Elements of these wastes then seep into underground water channels and surface waters. A similar process occurs as a consequence of the heavy use of chemical fertilizers and pesticides in farm areas.

Our waters are also being widely contaminated by land erosion and sediments. Oil and other hazardous substances are frequently spilled—by accident or on purpose—in waterways. And mine drainage (particularly from strip mining) fills streams and rivers with toxic metals and acids.[17]

---

[16] Barry Commoner, *The Closing Circle* (New York: Bantam Books, 1974), p. 220.

[17] See William Ashworth, *Nor Any Drop to Drink* (New York: Summit Books, 1982), and Regenstein, *America the Poisoned*, Chapter 4.

Environmental catastrophe occurred in Alaska on March 24, 1989, when the tanker Exxon-Valdez ran aground and spilled millions of gallons of oil into the sea. In this photo an oil-coated sea otter, fortunate to have been rescued for treatment, looks up as if perplexed by the human actions that contribute to the destruction of the ecosystem. *(Bill Nation/Sygma)*

Noticeable changes are also taking place in the oceans. For years it was assumed that the oceans could readily dilute and absorb whatever we decided to dump into them. The results of this assault are finally being felt.[18] Since toxic wastes are absorbed by fish and other forms of sea life, the chemicals dumped in the oceans often appear on our dinner plates. In many areas, beaches have been spoiled and recreational activities disrupted.[19] Oil and other substances dumped are thought to have implications for our climate. Solid wastes, sludge from sewage, industrial and hospital wastes, explosives, radioactive wastes, and dredge spoils (e.g., from harbor construction) threaten to turn the oceans into huge cesspools.

[18] Edward D. Goldberg, *The Health of the Oceans* (Paris: UNESCO Press, 1976), and R. Johnston, ed., *Marine Pollution* (Orlando, Fla.: Academic Press, 1977).

[19] See "Don't Go Near the Water," *Newsweek* (August 1, 1988): 43–47.

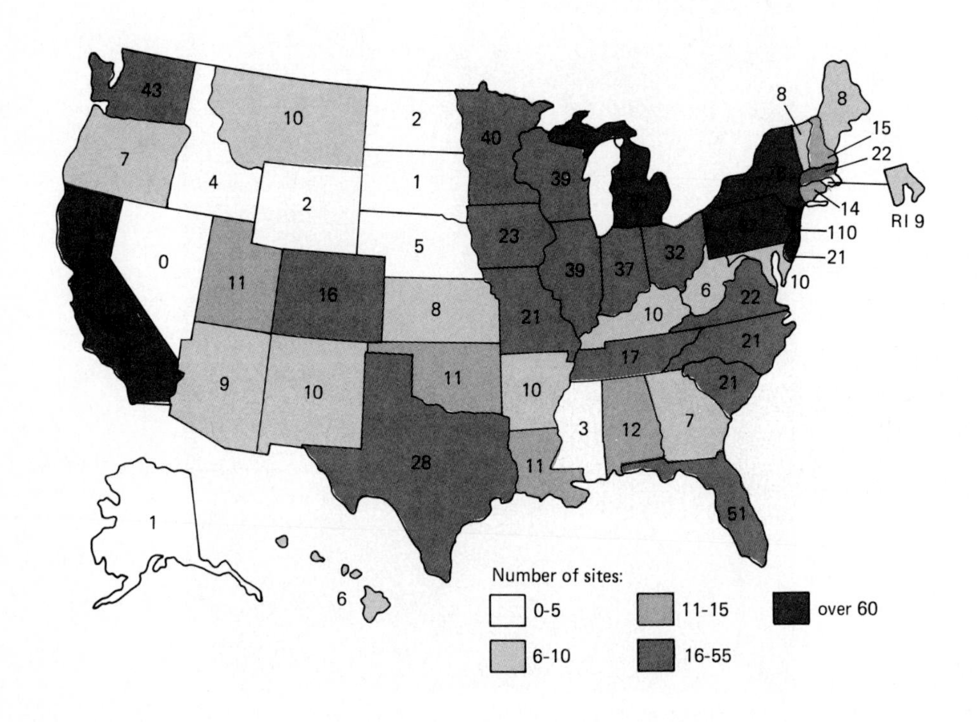

FIGURE 4.1 Hazardous Waste Sites (Final and Proposed)—Number of Sites on National Priority List, June 1988
Note: Total sites in U.S. 1, 177, including nine in Puerto Rico and one in Guam.
Source: U.S. Department of Commerce, Bureau of the Census, *Statistical Abstract of the United States, 1989* (Washington, D.C.: U.S. Government Printing Office, 1989), p. 202.

Toxic Substances

Only in the last decade or so have we begun to understand the full implications of the unsafe disposal of man-made toxic substances. The U.S. Environmental Protection Agency estimates that there are anywhere from 32,000 to 50,000 sites in America where hazardous wastes have been disposed. Anywhere from 1,200 to 2,000 pose highly significant health risks to people and other living things. Figure 4.1 indicates states with the most hazardous known sites. As recently as 1980 some 200 new chemical waste sites were being discovered each month.[20]

[20] Regenstein, *America the Poisoned*, p. 137.

Dramatic incidents, such as Love Canal (to be discussed), are really only manifestations of a much larger problem: How are we to prevent many of the 70,000 chemicals manufactured each year from being used and/or disposed of in such a way that they endanger health and lives? Why are we not looking at the health dangers that may accompany the 500–1,000 new chemical compounds that manufacturers introduce into the environment annually? Only now are we starting to feel the full danger of the mindless poisoning of our land and water with highly toxic substances.[21]

The story of Love Canal, a small suburb of Niagara Falls, New York, was and is terrifying.[22] In 1978, 240 families were forced to evacuate their homes in Love Canal. These families, ordered from their homes by the state government, all lived within two blocks of an abandoned canal that was used as a landfill. Substances known to be toxic, and in some cases known to cause cancer, were discovered in the soil, groundwater, and air around these homes. Later, in 1980, an additional 710 families were forced to evacuate. To this day no one is sure just how dangerous Love Canal is, what the potential health damages ultimately may be for those who were living there, or how close one may safely reside now without being at risk.

The story is not a pretty one. Investigations revealed that dozens of chemicals, including such known carcinogens as benzene and toluene, had seeped into the soil and contaminated water underground. Since 1942 the Hooker Chemical Company had been dumping millions of pounds of waste chemicals, including some of the most dangerous known to modern science. Several hundred pounds of one chemical were found, of which less than three ounces are sufficient to lethally poison millions of people.

In 1953 Hooker Chemical, knowing what it had deposited on the site of Love Canal, nonetheless agreed to sell the land and surrounding property to the school board and the city of Niagara Falls. The corporation's price was $1.00, and the property was sold with the understanding that Hooker Chemical would henceforth not be liable for any injuries or damages resulting from the property's contents. With the dangers of what lay beneath the surface left unrevealed, the city built an elementary school on the site. New homes were erected.

Love Canal residents now appear to be victimized by much higher than expected rates of diseases such as cancer as well as miscarriages and birth defects. The human and dollar costs associated with this toxic time bomb are incalculable.

In newspapers across the nation, news stories daily depict new discoveries of situations that parallel the Love Canal poisoning. The U.S. Environmental Protection Agency (EPA) has issued statements that imply our entire society is becoming a big Love Canal. For example, the EPA has estimated that 440 million pounds of PCBs (polychlorinated biphenyls)—among the most toxic substances ever synthesized—are present in the environment. An EPA study released in 1978 showed that nearly one-third of 1,038 breast milk samples from nursing mothers were contaminated with toxicologically significant levels of PCBs.[23] (See Table 4.2.)

Such developments led a former EPA administrator, Douglas Costle, to state:

> We look back on the Middle Ages and we say "No wonder they had bubonic plague—they used to throw their garbage in the streets." Now I just hope that in the year 2025 my grandchildren don't look back on this generation and say, "No won-

[21] See Samuel S. Epstein, Lester O. Brown, and Carl Pope, *Hazardous Waste in America* (San Francisco: Sierra Club Books, 1982), and Michael Brown, *Laying Waste: The Poisoning of America by Toxic Chemicals* (New York: Pantheon Books, 1980).

[22] Brown, *Laying Waste,* Chapters 1–4.

[23] Regenstein, *America the Poisoned,* pp. 296–98.

PUBLIC PROBLEM, PRIVATE PAIN

Laying Waste: The Poisoning of America by Toxic Chemicals

Abuse of our environment is often discussed as if it were largely a technological problem, and a complex one at that. Yet people stand at the center of environmental abuse. While some people make the decisions that help bring the abuse about, still others must suffer the consequences of these decisions. In this selection we sense the slow, creeping effect of Love Canal on a family exposed unknowingly to its toxic dangers.

A major proportion of those who live in the city of Niagara Falls work in chemical plants, the largest owned by the Hooker Chemical Company. Timothy Schroeder did not. He was a cement technician by trade, dealing with the factories only if they needed a pathway poured or a small foundation set. Tim and his wife, Karen, lived on 99th Street in a ranch-style home with a brick and wood exterior. They had saved all they could to redecorate the inside and to make additions, such as a cement patio covered with an extended roof. One of the Schroeders' most cherished possessions was a fiberglass pool, built into the ground and enclosed by a redwood fence. Though it had taxed their resources, the yard complemented a house that was among the most elegant in a residential zone where most of the homes were small frame buildings, prefabricated and slapped together *en masse.* It was a quiet area, once almost rural in character, and located in the city's extreme southeast corner. The Schroeders had lived in the house only since 1970, but Karen was a lifelong resident of the general neighborhood. Her parents lived three doors down from them, six miles from the row of factories that stood shoulder to shoulder along the Upper Niagara.

Karen Schroeder looked out from a back window one October morning in 1974 and noted with distress that the pool had suddenly risen two feet above the ground. She called Tim to tell him about it. Karen then had no way of knowing that the problem far exceeded a simple property loss—that in fact it was the first sign of a great tragedy.

Accurately enough, Mrs. Schroeder figured that the cause of the uplift was the unusual groundwater flow of the area. Twenty-one years before, an abandoned hydroelectric canal directly behind their house had been back-filled with industrial rubble. The underground breaches created by this disturbance, aided by the marshy nature of the region's surficial layer, had collected large volumes of rainfall, and this water had undermined the backyard. The Schroeders allowed the pool to remain in its precarious position until the next summer and then pulled it from the ground, intending to replace it with a cement one. Immediately, the gaping hole filled with what Karen called "chemical water," rancid liquids of yellow and orchid and blue. These same chemicals, mixed with the groundwater, had flooded the entire yard: they attacked the redwood posts with such a caustic bite that one day the fence simply collapsed. When the groundwater receded in dry weather, it left the gardens and shrubs withered and scorched, as if by a brush fire....

Karen's parents had been the first to experience problems with seepage from the canal. In 1959, her mother, Aileen Voorhees, noticed a strange black sludge bleeding through the basement walls. For the next twenty years, she and her husband, Edwin, tried various methods of halting the irritating intrusion, coating the cinder-block walls with sealants and even constructing a gutter along them to intercept the inflow. Nothing could stop a smell like that of a chemical plant from permeating the entire household, and neighborhood calls to the city for help were unavailing. One day, when Edwin punched a hole in the wall to see what was happening, quantities of black liquid poured out. The cinder blocks were full of the stuff.

Although later it was to be determined that they were in imminent danger, the Voorhees treated the problem at first as a mere nuisance. That it involved chemicals, industrial chemicals, was not particularly significant to them. All their life, all of everyone's life in the city, malodorous fumes had been a normal ingredient of the surrounding air.

More ominous than the Voorhees' basement seepage was an event that occurred in the Schroeder family at 11:12 P.M. on November 21,

1968. Karen gave birth to her third child, a seven-pound girl named Sheri. But no sense of elation filled the delivery room, for the baby was born with a heart that beat irregularly and had a hole in it, bone blockages of the nose and partial deafness, deformed external ears, and a cleft palate. By the age of two, it became obvious that the child was mentally retarded. When her teeth came in, there was a double row of them at the bottom. She also developed an enlarged liver.

The Schroeders looked upon these health problems, as well as certain illnesses among their other children, as acts of capricious genes, a vicious quirk of nature. Like Aileen and Edwin Voorhees, they were mainly aware that the chemicals were devaluing their property. The crab-apple tree and evergreens in the back were dead, and even the oak in the front of the house was sick: one year, the leaves fell off on Father's Day....

Source: Michael H. Brown, *Laying Waste: Love Canal & The Poisoning of America*, pp. 4–7.

der they had problems—look at all the chemicals just carelessly introduced into the environment, uncontrolled."[24]

Nor should we be sanguine about the possibility of large-scale accidents in which literally thousands of men, women, and children become victims of exposure to toxic substances. Consider, for example, the enormous tragedy in Bhopal, India. On December 3, 1984, a toxic gas used in the production of pesticides—methyl isocyanate—leaked from a plant owned by Union Carbide, a U.S. firm. The result was the largest number of casualties from an industrial accident in history. Some 2,500 people died. Another 150,000 were injured, many of them permanently disabled with everything from breathing difficulties to impaired vision.[25] The possibility of a Bhopal in the United States—a nightmare to even consider—is real.

Nuclear Radiation

Almost fifty years ago, a group of American scientists and technicians participated in the secret, federally sponsored Manhattan Project. This wartime effort resulted in the first atomic bombs, which were used in the war against Japan. The explosion of atomic bombs in Hiroshima and Nagasaki in 1945 produced death, injury, and property destruction on a scale never before seen. Scientists throughout the world began working with nuclear power, not only for military uses but also for peacetime needs, particularly to meet growing energy demands.

It was not until the 1950s that some serious dangers of nuclear power began to be discerned.[26] The United States, Great Britain, and the Soviet Union were detonating atomic explosions in remote areas for test purposes. Suddenly, scientists found that the tests were producing radioactive debris that was literally showering down on the earth far away from the test sites. Radioactivity was appearing everywhere—in water, soil, plants, animals. One component of the *nuclear fallout*—strontium 90—was a possible cancer-causing agent. Other radioactive elements were associated with genetic defects. For the first time, atomic radiation be-

[24] Quoted in *Newsweek* (August 21, 1978): 28.

[25] "Disabling and Incurable Ailments Still Afflict Thousands," *New York Times* (March 31, 1985): 1.

[26] The story of how these dangers were discovered is told in Commoner, *The Closing Circle*, pp. 45–62. See also Harvey Wasserman and Norman Solomon, *Killing Our Own: The Disaster of America's Experience with Atomic Radiation* (New York: Dell, 1982).

TABLE 4.2 Public's Ranking of Environmental Risks (and Percentage Rating Risks "Very Serious")

Rank	Risk factor	Percentage
1	Active hazardous waste sites	62%
2	Abandoned hazardous waste sites	61%
3	Workers exposed to toxic chemicals	60%
4	Industrial water pollution	58%
5	Nuclear accident radiation	58%
5	Radioactive waste	58%
7	Underground storage tank leakage	55%
8	Pesticide harm to farmers	54%
9	Pesticide residues harming consumers	52%
10	Industrial accident pollution	51%
11	Farm runoff pollution	50%
12	Contaminated tap water	49%
13	Industrial air pollution	48%
14	Ozone layer destruction	47%
14	Contamination of oceans and coastal waters	47%
16	Water pollution from sewage	45%
17	Vehicle exhaust air pollution	38%
17	Oil spills	38%
19	Acid rain	36%
20	Water pollution from runoff on city streets	35%
20	Contaminated and destroyed wetlands	35%
20	Release of genetically altered materials	35%
23	Nonhazardous waste sites	33%
23	The greenhouse effect	33%
25	Indoor air pollution from cleaners, smoke etc.	26%
26	X-ray radiation	22%
27	Indoor radon gas pollution	21%
28	Microwave oven radiation	14%

Source: Adam Clymer, "Polls Show Contrasts in How Public and E.P.A. View Environment," *New York Times* (May 22, 1989): B7.

gan to be seriously appreciated for what it is—a major threat to life. While such atmospheric testing has since been sharply curtailed, radioactivity from the original tests is still around and will be for many years. Persons living in the United States during the 1950s and 1960s may not know it, but they are members of an "atomic generation."

Even the peacetime uses of atomic energy have become a major source of concern in recent years. The United States joined other nations in the 1960s and early 1970s in an expanding program of nuclear power plant construction. However, by the late 1970s and early 1980s the nuclear power industry began to unravel through a combination of factors.[27] Costs of construction were beginning to be exorbitant, well outpacing original estimates, and members of the public began to awake to some of the real and potential dangers associated with nuclear power.

[27] See Daniel Deudney and Christopher Flavin, *Renewable Energy* (New York: W. W. Norton & Company, 1983), pp. 24–30.

As a consequence, construction has been curtailed. More than 140 of the 170 new plants expected to be in operation by the year 2000 have been canceled or deferred.[28] Still, by 1983 some 80 nuclear power plants were operating in the United States, representing some 12.6 percent of the nation's total electrical capacity.

There are several dangers inherent in the production of nuclear power.[29] Nuclear power plants require enormous amounts of water and produce far more heat pollution than do conventional power generators. They emit radioactive effluents as well, such as krypton 85 and tritium. Although only small amounts are involved, a progressive buildup of these elements in the atmosphere could create a serious health hazard.

Nuclear power plants also produce extremely dangerous radioactive wastes that must be handled carefully. These wastes must be isolated from humanity for many, many years. High-level radioactive wastes are classified as either nuclear fission products or by-products. Strontium 90 and cesium 137, the most abundant fission products, have half-lives of 300 years. (A half-life is the time it takes for half of the radioactive atoms to disintegrate.) Thus, these fission products will remain dangerously radioactive for 600 to 1,000 years. Plutonium 239, a fission by-product, has a 240,000-year half-life; it must be kept away from humanity for almost 500,000 years.

Presently, wastes from nuclear power plants are primarily stored on the site of the plants. This can only be a temporary measure. On-site storage facilities are filling up rapidly, but there is *no* method of permanent storage yet devised that scientists agree is safe. Even worse, very few ideas exist on how to deal with plants that wear out and/or permanently break down.

There is also the constant danger of radiation leakage from power plants. On March 28, 1979, water pumps broke down at the Three Mile Island nuclear power plant near Harrisburg, Pennsylvania. When the plant's cooling system failed, the plant overheated and began a core meltdown, leaking radiation into the surrounding environment. State authorities asked for the evacuation of all children and pregnant women living within five miles of the plant.

By the time matters were under control, the partial meltdown of the core of the reactor had destroyed it. The damaged reactor remains shut down, and the estimated costs of cleaning up the radioactive wastes that remain in the reactor building are over $1 billion. What was the primary cause of all this? Human error.[30]

A more recent incident in the Soviet Union has reinforced concern over nuclear power plant safety. On April 26, 1986, a nuclear reactor at the Chernobyl Nuclear Power Station in the Ukraine accidentally overheated and subsequently released the largest amount of radioactivity into the atmosphere that has ever been recorded. The radioactivity released "was equivalent to the fallout from several dozen Hiroshima bombs."[31] Once in the atmosphere, it traveled throughout the Northern Hemisphere, although its principal impact was on the western Soviet Union and parts of Europe.

The Chernobyl accident, said to be the result of nuclear reactor design flaws and errors by plant managers, killed 31 people and caused many cases of acute radiation sickness. Approximately 115,000 people had to be evacuated from Chernobyl and its surrounding area. The community was turned into a ghost town. Even today many have been unable to return to their homes and places of work in the area. Still others remain dependent on food being transported

[28] Congressional Quarterly, *Environment and Health* (Washington, D.C.: Congressional Quarterly, 1981), p. 58.

[29] See Anna Gyorgy, *No Nukes* (Boston: South End Press, 1979).

[30] Congressional Quarterly, Inc., *Environment and Health*, pp. 57–65.

[31] Christopher Hohenemser and Ortwin Renn, "Chenobyl's Other Legacy," *Environment*, 30 (April 1988): 5.

in from outside the Chernobyl region, since land around Chernobyl is considered too radioactively contaminated to produce crops safe to eat.

All told, almost 3 billion people in the Northern Hemisphere received some radiation from the Chernobyl accident; 26 percent of these, or about 800 million, received enough to be statistically at risk to a greater degree from cancer.[32] The increased risk is small, particularly for those residing outside the general area in which the nuclear plant is located, and deaths are expected to be statistically indistinguishable from cancer deaths occurring from other causes. Nonetheless, Chernobyl-like incidents understandably are feared and condemned as intolerable. While as of this writing no nuclear accident of this magnitude has occurred in the United States, it is within the realm of possibility.

Nuclear power plants are also susceptible to sabotage and military attack—even a war with conventional weapons could unleash radiation. Unforeseeable accidents or such natural disasters as earthquakes could lead to similar results. Finally, with the increased use, production, and transport of radioactive materials around the country, the possibility of theft increases. It may be possible for an individual or group to use stolen materials to construct a nuclear weapon.

Presently, all of us are subject to some degree of exposure to radiation. Natural radiation regularly enters the atmosphere from outer space. Radioactive elements can be found in water and mineral deposits. We are often exposed to radiation from X rays, luminous watch dials, color television sets, microwave ovens, and radar. Some workers are routinely bombarded at their place of employment. Scientists seem to agree that *all* radiation is harmful, but there is little consensus on the amount we can safely tolerate. Nuclear warfare (even the use of such weapons in a limited war) and/or the long-term effects of nuclear power plant proliferation could provide a tragic answer to the question of tolerance.

Radon: An Indoor Threat

The various environmental hazards described in this chapter may make people yearn to remain in the safety and security of their homes. The discovery of a deadly indoor pollutant—radon gas—makes one wonder whether homes are necessarily sanctuaries.[33]

The formation of earth some 4.5 billion years ago left us with deposits of uranium, a highly radioactive element. Left alone, uranium undergoes a natural process of decay and becomes harmless. Perhaps half of the earth's uranium has undergone this decay process. Out of this process comes various by-products, including radioactive radon gas. The gas is invisible and cannot be detected by taste or smell. Wherever uranium deposits are found, radon gas silently seeps out of rock deposits, sediments, and soil. It may enter the air we breathe.

Scientists have known for over thirty years that radon gas may be life-threatening, noting that rates of lung cancer are extremely high among those who work in uranium mines. But it was not until 1984 that evidence revealed radon gas was to be found in dangerous concentrations in people's homes.

Radon gas typically enters homes through cracks and holes in basement floors or foundation walls. Then, attached to particles in the air, it is carried throughout the house. After years of breathing this radioactive indoor pollution, people are likely to succumb to lung cancer. Officials at the federal Environmental Protection Agency believe that anywhere from 5,000 to

[32] Lynn R. Anspaugh, Robert J. Catlin, and Marvin Goldman, "The Global Impact of the Chernobyl Reactor Accident," *Science*, 242 (December 16, 1988): 1513.

[33] See "Indoor Radon: The Deadliest Pollutant," *Science*, 240 (April 29, 1988): 606–8, and "The Risk from Radon," *Newsweek* (September 26, 1988): 69.

20,000 deaths per year are attributable to radon gas. As one scientist has put it,

> Hundreds of thousands of Americans living in homes that have high radon levels receive as large an exposure of radiation yearly as those people living in the vicinity of the Chernobyl nuclear power plant did in 1986.[34]

Consequently, people are as likely to die from long-term exposure to radon gas as they are from at-home falls or fires.

No one knows for sure the extent of the threat. While more definitive research results are being sought, a survey by the EPA suggests that growing public concern is well placed. After surveying 11,000 homes in seven states, the EPA estimated that some 8 million households across the country may have radon concentrations at a level high enough to suggest occupants take actions to protect their health and safety. In actuality, there is no "safe" radon level: Its presence in any amount may carry potential health risks.

The threat posed by radon gas is natural rather than humanly constructed, which sets it apart from many other environmental hazards we are discussing. Yet steps can be taken to minimize the threat. Since there seems to be a synergistic effect between smoking and exposure to radon gas—that is, lung cancer is much more likely to occur when both are present—cessation of smoking must be a major part of any solution. In addition, radon gas levels may be substantially reduced where it is possible to use pipes and vents to route the gas from beneath foundations into the outside air.

In 1988 the EPA and the Office of the Surgeon General advised that every home and every apartment up to a building's second floor be tested for radon gas. Inexpensive test kits for "do-it-yourselfers" are widely available and there are signs that many Americans are taking this environmental threat seriously. Significantly, it is not unusual for potential home buyers to request radon test results. Pressures may grow on builders to adopt new construction standards to combat what some are now calling the deadliest air pollutant.

Solid Wastes

A key indicator of America's material affluence is its volume of junk, garbage, and other forms of solid waste. Most of it is in the form of agricultural, mineral, and industrial waste.[35]

Agricultural and mineral waste generally go unnoticed, for they are concentrated in nonurban settings. Industrial waste is far more noticeable, since it often contributes to the waste disposal problems facing highly populated areas. Fly ash from electric utility companies, scrap metals, rags, and bales and drums of industrial by-products must all be thrown away somewhere.

Our output of junk is almost mind-boggling (see Table 4.3). According to environmental investigator Michael Brown,

> Americans are consuming 50 percent of the earth's industrial raw materials although their country has only 7 percent of the planet's population. In an average year, Americans discard 60 million tons of paper, 38 billion bottles and jars, 76 billion cans, and $5 billion worth of metals.[36]

In 1960 municipalities accumulated 87.5 million metric tons of waste from residential, commercial, and institutional disposers. This figure rose to 157.7 million metric tons by 1986. (See Table 4.3.)

Where does it all go? The solid waste collected in most municipalities is simply hauled away to open dumps. Only a small percentage gets buried in sanitary landfills or burned in incin-

[34] "Indoor Radon: The Deadliest Pollutant," p. 607.

[35] Brown, *Laying Waste*, pp. 266–74.

[36] Ibid., p. 272.

TABLE 4.3 Municipal Solid Waste Generation, Recovery, and Disposal, 1960–86 (in millions of tons, except as indicated)

Item and material	1960	1965	1970	1975	1980	1981	1982	1983	1984	1985	1986
Gross waste generated	87.5	102.3	120.5	125.3	142.6	144.8	142.0	148.3	153.6	152.5	157.7
Per person per day (lb.)	2.65	2.88	3.22	3.18	3.43	3.45	3.35	3.47	3.56	3.49	3.58
Materials recovered	5.8	6.2	8.0	9.1	13.4	13.2	12.9	13.9	15.3	15.3	16.9
Per person per day (lb.)	0.18	0.17	0.21	0.23	0.32	0.31	0.30	0.32	0.35	0.35	0.39
Processed for energy recovery	(NA)	0.2	0.4	0.7	2.7	2.3	3.5	5.0	6.5	7.6	9.6
Per person per day (lb)	(NA)	0.01	0.01	0.02	0.06	0.05	0.08	0.12	0.15	0.17	0.22
Net waste disposed of	81.7	95.9	112.1	115.5	126.5	129.3	125.6	129.5	131.8	129.7	131.2
Per person per day (lb.)	2.48	2.70	3.00	2.93	3.04	3.08	2.96	3.03	3.05	2.97	2.96
Percent distribution of net discards*											
Paper and paperboard	30.0	33.5	32.4	29.6	32.5	33.1	32.1	34.1	35.7	35.5	35.6
Glass	7.8	8.8	11.1	11.4	11.0	10.9	10.7	9.9	9.3	8.9	8.4
Metals	12.8	11.1	12.0	11.5	10.1	9.8	9.7	9.6	9.3	9.0	8.9
Plastics	0.5	1.5	2.7	3.8	5.9	5.9	6.5	6.8	6.9	7.1	7.3
Rubber and leather	2.1	2.3	2.7	3.2	3.2	3.1	2.9	2.5	2.4	2.5	2.8
Textiles	2.1	2.0	1.8	1.9	2.0	2.6	2.2	2.1	2.0	2.0	2.0
Wood	3.7	3.6	3.6	3.8	3.8	3.3	3.9	3.9	3.7	3.9	4.1
Food wastes	14.9	12.9	11.4	11.5	9.2	9.2	9.3	8.9	8.8	9.0	8.9
Yard wastes	24.5	22.5	20.6	21.7	20.5	20.3	20.9	20.4	20.1	20.4	20.1
Other wastes	1.6	1.7	1.6	1.7	1.7	1.7	1.8	1.8	1.7	1.8	1.8

[Covers postconsumer residential and commercial solid wastes, which comprise the major portion of typical municipal collections. Excludes mining, agricultural and industrial processing, demolition and construction wastes, sewage sludge, and junked autos and obsolete equipment wastes. Based on material-flows estimating procedure and wet weight as generated]

Key: NA Not available.

*Net discards after materials recovery and before energy recovery.

Source: U.S. Department of Commerce, Bureau of the Census, *Statistical Abstract of the United States, 1989* (Washington, D.C.: U.S. Government Printing Office, 1989), p. 202.

erators. Dumping exhausts land space that could be more fruitfully used; it also poses possible health hazards. Incineration (along with fires due to spontaneous combustion in open dumps) contributes to pollution of the air.

To underscore the problems involved, let us look at some examples. By weight, paper and paper products are a major type of refuse. In recent years paper consumption has increased to the point that the average American now uses several hundred pounds annually. Much of this is associated with the use of heavily packaged products. Very little paper is recycled in the United States—80 percent is simply dumped or burned. While paper and paper products are bulky and take up space, fortunately they do eventually decompose. When burned, however, they contribute to air pollution.

Plastics are a different matter. The production and use of plastics have grown enormously in recent years. Modern plastics are substances with high durability and resistance to biological decomposition. Plastics thus are being used in the place of wood, metals, and cloth for many

Part of the millions of tons of solid wastes Americans dispose of simply ends up littering our cities. Junk and garbage create health and safety hazards and also make an area look unpleasant and unlivable. *(Staff)*

products. It is their very properties that render plastics an ecological problem. Since they do not decompose, they simply pile up permanently. If burned, plastics are likely to melt and foul up incinerator operations, while emitting gaseous pollutants that are often poisonous. It has been claimed that plastics pollute the air even in garbage dumps, because of solar heat and the heat processes that lead to spontaneous combustion.

Metal cans and glass bottles are another solid waste problem. Cans decompose too slowly to disappear before even more cans are dumped. Glass is rather invulnerable to natural decomposition. Bottles, along with some metals used in cans, can be reclaimed for use. But too little is being done along such lines. Corporate producers could help reduce waste volume. Instead they sell throwaways, which often end up littering our roadways and recreational areas. The throwaway trend may be convenient for consumers, but it is not a sign of ecological sanity. Though a number of states have begun to restrict the use of disposable bottles, the waste problem overall continues to grow.

Automobiles, besides being a major source of air pollution, tend to be a rather conspicuous form of solid waste. There are over 100 million vehicles registered for use in the United States, and 9 million go permanently out of service annually. Of these, almost 1 million are simply abandoned. The rest wind up in our 33,000 auto junkyards. Only a small percentage are recycled for scrap; most, having been cannibalized for usable parts, are left in piles where the metal rusts and the plastic parts remain. Between 2.5 and 4.5 million abandoned autos, of little value to junk firms, lie along city streets, in vacant lots, and in rural settings. The millions of auto tires tossed out each year are bulky and difficult to get rid of. When they are burned, tires pollute the air.

Noise and Visual Pollution

We tend to take the sounds of our surroundings for granted and to consider the noise level as somehow inevitable. The sounds of home appliances, traffic, factory and office machinery, aircraft, boats, lawn mowers, construction projects, and sirens affect Americans daily. Urban dwellers in particular are bombarded by a constant, almost unremitting din.

The effects of noise on people have been found to vary, for not all individuals are equally sensitive to sounds. Nevertheless, there is reason for concern about the dangers to human hearing.[37] According to the U.S. Environmental Protection Agency, some 20 million Americans are victimized by levels of noise that can impair their hearing permanently. Eighteen million already have hearing loss as a consequence of excess noise, often connected with the workplace.[38] Excess levels of noise are known to have a bearing on physiological functioning. In experiments, noise has caused the constriction of arteries, increased pulse and respiration rates, involuntary muscle reactions, and abnormal fatigue. In addition, noise is often simply distracting and annoying. Extremely loud noises, such as the sonic booms created by jet aircraft, fit into this description. (Sonic booms have also been known to cause physical damage to buildings and other structures.)

We rarely think about visual pollution, except when we are confronted with its most extreme manifestations. One type of visual pollution actually prevents people from seeing their surroundings. Photochemical smog, for example, is more than a health hazard. For drivers and pilots it can be a safety hazard as well. It can also be an aesthetic nuisance, blocking out views that are visually pleasing.

There are aspects of our surroundings that many persons, when given a choice, would just as soon not see. This second type of visual pollution is, one might argue, really a matter of taste. Billboards and signs dot the countryside

---

[37] See Lucy Kavaler, *The Dangers of Noise* (New York: Crowell, 1978), and reports of the U.S. Environmental Protection Agency.

[38] Congressional Quarterly, *Environmental Issues*, p. 84.

and proliferate in metropolitan areas. Attention-seeking architecture surrounds us, often in the form of neon-lit commercial "strips." Buildings are often put up with no attention to the views they block. Roads and highways tear up neighborhoods and areas of scenic beauty. Polluted rivers and lakes not only smell bad, but are ugly. Mining operations denude the countryside in many areas, as soil and timber are stripped away to expose coal seams. Public dumps and auto junkyards are not known for their aesthetic appeal. Despite rather expensive efforts to cope with it, litter continues to assault the eyes. In so many ways, human activities continually alter the color, shape, and context of parts of the ecosystem without regard to taste and sensibility.

Land Misuse

Many of the examples of visual pollution relate to the impact of human activities on America's land. But the environmental abuses associated with land use go far beyond aesthetics and taste. According to the President's Council on Environmental Quality, "Misuse of the land is now one of the most serious and difficult challenges to environmental quality, because it is the most out-of-hand, and irreversible.[39]

The casual way this nation's 2.3 billion acres of land have been used is indicative of what Gene Marine calls the "engineering mentality." Marine says that the engineering mentality is displayed when public or private landowners tamper with land resources without regard to the well-being of the ecosystem as a whole. Their focus is limited to the financial costs and technical feasibility of projects intended to meet immediate, narrowly defined objectives.[40] As with other mindless assaults on the ecosystem, the cumulative effects of land misuse are coming back to haunt us. Here we shall consider some major examples.[41]

Americans seem to assume that this nation has an unlimited abundance of land for unhindered development and exploitation. But our supply of open land is finite, and shortages are beginning to appear. Among the reasons are urban development and suburban sprawl; the linking of major cities by strips of densely populated, developed land; airport and highway construction; and the creation of reservoirs and large-scale flood control projects. Each year approximately a million acres of rural land are gobbled up. Farmlands are turned over to other uses. Irreplaceable marshes and wetlands—the environmental niches in which many species breed and survive—disappear permanently. Such land misuse spreads pollution of all types and eliminates areas that previously had recreational value.

The construction of dams, canals, and waterways also alters land-use patterns. Dredging, draining, filling, and changing the natural routes of streams and rivers have all been done without concern for the environmental consequences. As a result, the habitats of fish and animals have been destroyed, land has been taken away from other uses, and water pollution has inadvertently been exacerbated.

In recent years we have become aware of the impact of mining practices on America's land. Surface or strip mining, which has blighted the coal-rich Appalachian region and has spread into a number of western states, involves ripping the natural covering off the land (including hills and mountainsides) in order to get at the mineral seams. This is followed by blasting and gouging so that the seams can be fully exposed for removal. The result is often total destruction of natural land contours. Vegetation and wildlife are uprooted, their niches in the

[39] Council on Environmental Quality, *First Annual Report*, p. 165.
[40] Gene Marine, *America the Raped* (New York: Simon & Schuster, 1969), p. 18.

[41] These examples are drawn from Walter A. Rosenbaum, *The Politics of Environmental Concern* (New York: Praeger Publishers, 1973).

ecosystem destroyed. Drainage from such mining areas, containing acids and sediments, contaminates inland waters to the detriment of aquatic life.

Exploitation of the nation's public and private forest lands is having similar adverse consequences. Commercial operations in timber reserves have increasingly taken the form of *clearcutting*, in which large areas are stripped of all trees, leaving behind nothing but short stumps. Logging roads to remote sections bisect otherwise unblemished wilderness. Clearcutting also negatively alters soil conditions, since removal of forest covering exposes soil to the weather, weakening its nutrient properties. Land erosion increases, and streams become choked with debris and sediments. Again, vegetation and wildlife habitats are despoiled.

A major controversy over the use of public lands arose in the early 1980s. The administration of President Ronald Reagan sought to open millions of acres of federal (i.e., taxpayer-owned) rangeland, forest, and wilderness and much of the ocean-covered Outer Continental Shelf to commercial exploitation. Rights to accelerate development of property previously untouched and kept guarded out of concern for conservation were to be granted to interested large corporations. In other cases property would be sold outright to the highest corporate bidder. In effect, government officials were preparing to abandon conservation in favor of improving the profitability of firms that would be given inexpensive access to important reserves of timber, oil, natural gas, coal, uranium, and other mineable materials. The outcry of concerned members of the public, along with unprecedented political activity on the part of conservation and environmental organizations, slowed the government's efforts.[42]

Resource Depletion

Our discussion has for the most part focused on what American society puts *into* the ecosystem, rather than what we take *from* it. Obviously, these two matters are interrelated, given the basic ecological principle that what we throw away had to be first removed from somewhere. In this section we shall deal with America's need for minerals and other materials. Nothing in the ecosystem is really free for the taking. As we shall see, the costs of resource depletion promise to be extremely high.

The Exhaustion of Irreplaceable Commodities. Not too long ago the society's gross national product—the sum value of all the goods and services produced each year—rose to $5 trillion. The GNP is a rough indicator of a nation's overall economic activity, and that of the United States is the largest in world history. Such unprecedented economic activity is dependent on, among other things, access to mineral supplies, including those that provide energy. This is not a profound observation, but it is one that few Americans have had to think about until the 1970s. The point was most dramatically brought home during the nationwide energy crisis that jarred us in 1973–74, when shortages and increased costs of oil, gasoline, and natural gas forced many people to turn down thermostats, turn off lights, drive less, and pay higher prices for virtually all goods and services. The crisis is not over, and it may never be.

With 7 percent of the world's total population, the United States consumes between 50 and 70 percent of the world's resources. Moreover, we are voracious users of energy. If annual U.S. energy consumption is converted to its coal equivalent (a standard measure), it equaled 2.3 billion tons in 1981. In that same year the entire world consumed the equivalent of 8.5 billion tons.[43]

---

[42] See Friends of the Earth. *Ronald Reagan and the American Environment* (San Francisco: Friends of the Earth Books, 1982), pp. 16–27.

[43] U.S. Department of Commerce, Bureau of the Census, *Statistical Abstract of the United States, 1984* (Washington, D.C.: U.S. Government Printing Office, 1983), p. 875.

Though most of the minerals and other materials we consume are available domestically, the insatiable demands of the American economy are beginning to endanger our supplies. Of eighty-seven commodities currently crucial to our economic well-being, known domestic reserves of forty-seven will fall short of our needs by the year 2000. We are already dependent on imports in a number of crucial areas. From 90 to 100 percent of such commodities as manganese, cobalt, mica, and bauxite must be sought outside the United States. (See Table 4.4.) We import from 50 to 90 percent of our tin, nickel, zinc, chromium, and titanium. Lesser but still significant amounts of iron, lead, copper, and gypsum are also imported. At present, 36 percent of the petroleum we use comes from other nations. Over time the United States has moved from being a resource-rich nation to one that cannot grow economically—or even sustain itself as is—without purchasing key resources from other nations.

This situation, which is expected to grow even worse in coming decades, raises some extremely important issues. The resources necessary for our high GNP—and, indeed, our lifestyles—are finite. All of them are probably subject to depletion at some point.[44] At present, the United States, the consumer society par excellence, is making the greatest single contribution to the exhaustion of irreplaceable commodities. We and other consumer societies then restore these resources to the global ecosystem in the form of wastes and other pollutants.

Resource Depletion and the Underdeveloped Third World. The threat of resource depletion is real. But the timetable is unclear because of a number of unpredictable factors: the possibility of new discoveries, the costs of extraction and processing, changes in technology, and the degree to which more readily available commodities can be substituted for scarcer ones. The depletion issue is also related to the fact that many of the minerals and materials on which our economy is dependent, and which we increasingly must import, are located in poor, underdeveloped nations of the Third World. As we saw in Chapter 3, "Militarism and War," this society's economic dominance rests on its ability to exploit underdeveloped nations' raw materials cheaply.[45] The gap between rich nations and poor nations promises to be the main political challenge confronting our foreign policy–makers in the remaining years of this century.[46] In the area of resources, the stakes are great.

Third World nations cannot develop economically or socially without expanded resource consumption opportunities. In practical terms, the advance of these poor nations—within which three-fourths of the world's population lives—can take place in one of two ways. Resources could be distributed away from the United States and other rich nations and to the nations of the Third World. Or Third World nations could simply join the rich nations on the road to resource exploitation. This would involve more intense exploitation of existing commodity supplies. The United States probably won't be willing to give up economic growth in favor of stagnation and a declining standard of living. Pronouncements from the White House consistently reflect a definite preference for the second scenario. Third World nations—fearing that choice would not close the rich–poor gap—are not so enthusiastic.

Our growing dependence on key imports from the Third World has produced another issue, one revealed through the Third World oil-producing nations' embargo on petroleum shipments and the subsequent price increases. The

[44] See Council on Environmental Quality and Department of State, *The Global 2000 Report to the President*, Vol. 1 (Washington, D.C.: U.S. Government Printing Office, 1980).

[45] See Harry Magdoff, *The Age of Imperialism* (New York: Monthly Review Press, 1969).

[46] This theme runs through Robert L. Heilbroner, *An Inquiry into the Human Prospect*, rev. ed. (New York: W. W. Norton & Company, 1980).

TABLE 4.4 Net U.S. Imports of Selected Minerals and Metals as Percentage of Apparent Consumption, 1970–86, and by Major Foreign Sources, 1982–85

Mineral	1970	1980	1982	1983	1984	1985	1986	Rank of major foreign sources, 1982–85
Columbium	100	100	100	100	100	100	100	Brazil, Canada, Thailand
Mica (sheet)	100	100	100	100	100	100	(NA)	India, Belgium, France
Strontium	100	100	100	100	100	100	(NA)	Mexico, Spain
Manganese	95	98	99	99	98	100	100	**Ore:** Gabon, Brazil, South Africa
Bauxite*	88	94	96	96	96	96	96	**Bauxite:** Guinea, Jamaica, Brazil; **alumina:** Australia, Jamaica, Suriname
Platinum group	78	88	81	89	89	92	92	South Africa, United Kingdom, Soviet Union
Tantalum	96	90	92	97	92	89	91	Thailand, Brazil, Australia
Cobalt	98	93	92	95	95	94	85	Zaire, Zambia, Canada
Potassium	42	65	65	75	74	77	(NA)	Canada, Israel
Chromium	89	91	85	76	80	75	79	South Africa, Turkey, Zimbabwe
Nickel	71	71	76	75	68	72	75	Canada, Australia, Botswana
Tin	81	79	68	73	74	72	74	Thailand, Malaysia, Bolivia, Indonesia
Asbestos	83	78	74	65	75	71	(NA)	Canada, South Africa
Zinc	54	60	58	65	68	70	73	**Ore:** Canada, Mexico, Honduras; **metal:** Canada, Mexico, Peru
Banum	45	44	55	65	69	69	(NA)	Canada, Morocco, Chile
Titanium†	24	32	74	(D)	(D)	(D)	(D)	Australia, Canada, South Africa
Silver	26	7	55	59	58	59	71	Canada, Mexico, United Kingdom
Tungsten	50	53	42	52	70	68	70	Canada, China (Mainland), Bolivia
Antimony	40	48	50	54	58	(D)	(D)	**Metal:** China (Mainland), Mexico, Bolivia; **ore:** Bolivia, Mexico, China
Mercury	41	26	32	30	57	50	(D)	Spain, Algeria, Japan
Cadmium	7	56	73	72	51	57	66	Canada, Australia, Mexico
Selenium	11	59	55	39	47	(D)	(D)	Canada, United Kingdom, Japan
Vanadium	21	35	24	26	54	(D)	(D)	**Minerals:** South Africa, Venezuela; **chemicals:** E.E.C.,‡ Canada, South Africa
Gypsum	39	35	36	40	38	38	(NA)	Canada, Mexico, Spain
Petroleum§	23	39	30	30	32	29	36	Mexico, Canada, Venezuela
Iron ore	30	25	34	37	19	21	33	Canada, Brazil, Venezuela
Copper	([6])	14	1	19	23	28	27	Chile, Canada, Peru
Aluminum	([6])	—#	7	17	7	16	26	Canada, Japan, Ghana
Iron and steel	4	15	20	16	23	22	21	E.E.C,‡ Japan, Canada
Sulfur	—#	14	4	15	16	5	(NA)	Canada, Mexico
Natural gas	4	5	5	5	4	5	4	Canada, Algeria

[Figures based on net imports, which equal the difference between imports and exports plus or minus government stockpile and industry stock changes.]

Key: D, withheld to avoid disclosure. NA, not available.

*includes alumina

†limenite

‡European Economic Community

§includes crude and products

Source: Beginning 1980, Energy Information Administration, *International Energy Annual.*

#Net exports

Source: U.S. Department of Commerce, Bureau of the Census, *Statistical Abstract of the United States, 1989* (Washington, D.C.: U.S. Government Printing Office, 1989), p. 680.

poor but resource-rich countries, by cooperating with one another and forming cartels to control commodity production and prices, may be able to force important concessions from the developed world. Such nations eventually could collectively decide to improve their well-being by forcing a redistribution of consumption opportunities away from the rich nations and to the poor. Should such a stranglehold be placed upon this society (and/or other rich nations in which we hold substantial economic interests), it could well generate a military response. For example, in the aftermath of the Arab oil embargo, as Middle East petroleum prices continued to rise due to cartel action, federal officials and the mass media discussed and/or hinted at the desirability of military action. Given that this society and other developed nations are steadily arming various Third World nations as a means of "befriending" them (and to boost sagging domestic economies through arms exports), military aggression against such countries could exact a horrendous toll.

The world is presently facing a tension-filled dilemma. Irreplaceable resources are being depleted. The United States must bear a large amount of the responsibility for this attack on the global ecosystem. If we try to maintain the status quo, the depletion rate will continue—but so will the misery and political hostility of the poor nations. Cartels and efforts to squeeze greater rewards in return for declining resource supplies will be the order of the day, perhaps calling forth a military solution. If, on the other hand, we attempt to maintain our present growth rates while offering to help poor nations increase theirs, serious conflict may be avoided. But resource depletion rates will escalate, and conflicts are bound to emerge once serious scarcities begin to be felt.

SEARCHING FOR CAUSES

The changes now occurring in the global ecosystem are obviously the consequence of human activities. Our environment is not polluting and depleting itself. But there is little agreement about just what it is about people and their actions that is causing the current ecocatastrophe. A consensus on causes is a crucial first step toward ending environmental abuse. Here we shall highlight some of the different views, indicating which ones make the most sense.

Human Nature

Now and again observers claim that environmental abuse is a result of human nature. People, it is alleged, are basically dirty. Unlike other forms of animal life, we are prone to "fouling our own nests."[47] This being the case, there is really no way to stop the destruction of the environment short of eliminating people from the global ecosystem.

This view is very seductive, perhaps because of its simplicity. But there is no evidence that it is correct. Other animals are "clean" only because they return what they remove from the ecosystem in forms useful to those parts of the system on which they are dependent. They do not violate the chains and cycles on which their survival is based. There is no evidence to suggest that people cannot do the same, even if we cannot match the efficiency of other animal species. Human beings are capable of making conscious, rational choices as to how they wish to relate to the rest of the ecosystem. Over time our choices have been ecologically disastrous. But our awareness of environmental deterioration offers the possibility of our choosing to end it—assuming that we can figure out how, that we are willing to bear the costs, and that it is not too late. If we accept the human nature argument, we can only sit back and wait for the Big Collapse or hasten the collapse through an orgy of environmental abuse.

[47] "Nest fouling" is discussed in Commoner, *The Closing Circle*, pp. 122–23.

Population and Affluence

An alternative view stresses the significance of the growth in population that is taking place in the United States and around the world. Environmental deterioration, it is alleged, is an inevitable outcome of loading the earth with too many people. The more people there are, the greater the impact they make on the ecosystem as a whole. Increased world population means increased demands on finite resources, along with more waste disposal problems, land misuse, pollution, and so on.[48] The solution to environmental abuse, in this view, is to limit or even decrease the world's population—particularly in the many poor countries of the Third World, where a "population explosion" is well under way.

This view is also attractively simple: Increase the effectiveness of birth control and the ecocatastrophe will go away. As we saw in Chapter 1, uncontrolled population expansion is a serious problem primarily in nations where food is scarce and/or the productive resources are held by and benefit a small elite. The major perpetrators of environmental deterioration are *not* these poorer societies. Rather, the economically developed nations, such as the United States, which are not experiencing severe population explosions are contributing most to the ecocatastrophe. They consume most of the world's irreplaceable resources while indiscriminately dumping wastes and harmful contaminants back into the global ecosystem. This is not to say that Third World nations live in harmony with this system or that future developments will not see them playing a more important role in environmental deterioration.[49] But it does mean that we have arrived at the present level of crisis without too much help from their population problems.

Even if we limit ourselves to the United States, it is hard to find a direct correspondence between population expansion and rates of environmental deterioration. Using pollution levels as a main indicator, Barry Commoner has found that our environment is becoming contaminated far more quickly than population growth alone can explain. Between 1946 and 1968, the population of the United States increased 42 percent, while pollution levels rose from between 200 and 2,000 percent (depending on what and how one chooses to measure).[50] Something more than numbers of people is involved here.

All Americans do not pollute equally. As noted in Chapter 6, "Economic Inequality and Poverty," the affluent are more able to consume due to the unequal distribution of wealth and income. Just as rich nations consume and pollute at far higher rates than poorer ones, the affluent minority in this country makes a greater contribution to environmental deterioration than its numbers would indicate.

Obviously, population growth and size have something to do with the demands being made on the ecosystem. But population alone does not explain the problem.

Science and Technology

Many who reject the population argument blame environmental deterioration on modern science and technology. Somehow, it is alleged, modern science and technology have taken on a life of their own. We are now at the mercy of our own cultural ingenuity; the tools that originally were developed to conquer nature have begun to run wild. We have lost control of these tools and are being forced to bow to their im-

---

[48] See, for example, Lester Brown, *By Bread Alone* (New York: Praeger Publishers, 1974). A critique of this position is found in Frances Moore Lappé and Joseph Collins, *Food First*, rev. ed. (New York: Ballantine Books, 1979).

[49] Mexico City provides a striking case. See "A Proud Capital's Distress," *Newsweek*, 124 (August 6, 1984): 26–35.

[50] Commoner, *The Closing Circle*, pp. 122–37.

peratives, and environmental deterioration is the result.[51]

According to this view, we cannot solve the problem with more technology. People must retreat to the "golden years" of the past when small groups of families lived simply, spartanly, and communally in the woods or on the prairies. Life in those days may have been short and brutish, but at least the entire global ecosystem was not threatened by scientific and technological change. You could breathe the air, drink the water, eat plants and animals, admire the untouched scenery, and enjoy quiet.

As with population expansion, it would be erroneous to say that science and technology have nothing to do with environmental deterioration. On the other hand, neither is it true that these areas of human activity have a life of their own or have created a set of imperatives to which we must bow. Science and technology are tools, and tools can be used in many different ways. How or whether we use them is a matter of *choice*. We can use science and technology to help us live in harmony with the rest of the ecosystem or to hasten its collapse.

Economic Organization

When we look at science and technology as causes of the ecocatastrophe, we must also consider the societal contexts in which such tools are employed. This realization has led some analysts to contrast environmental policies in capitalist and socialist societies, the idea being that the political and economic priorities of a society ultimately dictate the uses to which science and technology are put. According to Barry Weisberg, environmental deterioration

> is rooted in the systemic imbalance between the capitalist organization of society and the life-sustaining capacity of this planet. . . . The trillion dollar economy [of the United States] brings with it a structure of commodities which requires the fantastic production of dangerous chemicals, surplus packaging, solid waste, and effluents which are incompatible with the life-sustaining capacities of the planet itself.[52]

In this view, the ecocatastrophe is a result of a system of economic organization that benefits only a tiny percentage of the world's peoples. The benefits—wealth, power, and prestige—may prove to be hollow for the few that enjoy them.

In capitalist societies such as the United States, economic and political priorities often place profits before people. Environmental abuse is an inevitable by-product of the private pursuit of money. Pollution, land misuse, and resource depletion are "costs" that are being passed on to the population in return for an enlarged gross national product. A large GNP means jobs and consumer goods. Eliminate capitalism and its quest for unlimited growth as a way of organizing and operating America's productive system, say proponents of this view, and you undercut the coming ecological collapse.

It does seem to be true that the activities of business and industry frequently run counter to environmental sanity. Go back and think about who, or whose products, are intimately tied to each of the forms of environmental abuse reviewed earlier in this chapter. Then check Chapter 2, "Concentration of Political and Economic Power," for some ideas about why such abuse is only being monitored, regulated, measured, and studied rather than totally eliminated.

Earlier we cited Barry Commoner's observa-

[51] This concern is implicit in Heilbroner, *An Inquiry into the Human Prospect,* wherein "industrialization" is seen as a key cause of environmental deterioration. Heilbroner suggests that we may want to use preindustrial societies as a model for our future life-styles.

[52] Barry Weisberg, *Beyond Repair* (Boston: Beacon Press, 1971), pp. 1 and 75.

tions that the pollution rates well outstripped population growth. Commoner suggests that the current ecocatastrophe began after World War II. Beginning in 1946, American corporations began to draw upon advances in science and technology to produce new products in new ways, with ecologically devastating results. Why? Commoner strongly believes that the answer lies with short-term profit interests.[53] Since 1946 the GNP has grown enormously, while the ecosystem has been assaulted.

A few examples of developments that have taken place only since World War II will make the point. Plastics are cheaper to produce than many of the materials they have displaced, but while the plastics industry has grown so have the plastic products we cannot get rid of. Synthetic fibers require less labor to produce than wool or cotton and are hence very profitable. They are about as impervious to destruction as plastics. Rearing agricultural animals on feedlots, rather than grazing them in pastures, produces a lot of meat quickly and inexpensively. But the animal wastes pose a monumental disposal problem. Cars built in most years of the post–World War II era have been bigger and heavier, with more powerful engines than cars built earlier. They also pollute more and contribute to fuel depletion. They have proven a boon to oil, steel, chromium, plastic, glass, and rubber firms. While fuel supplies have been pressed to keep up with demand, until recently utility companies encouraged electric heating, the use of air conditioners and freezers, plenty of lighting, and more. Even while open land is being depleted, land speculators and developers encourage us to "spread out" without regard to the ecological implications. This, of course, means that we must have more roads and highways—a requirement that does not go unnoticed by automobile and oil concerns.

In recounting such post–1946 changes, in which business and industry leaders have been key decision-makers, Commoner concludes:

> Human beings have broken out of the circle of life, driven not by biological need, but by the social organization which they have devised to "conquer" nature: means of gaining wealth that are governed by requirements conflicting with those which govern nature. The end result is the environmental crisis, a crisis of survival. Once more, to survive, we must close the circle.[54]

Capitalism plus science and technology equals environmental deterioration. In other words, the organization and operation of our society, ecologically speaking, harm living things—including people.

Environmental abuse is of concern in noncapitalist societies like the Soviet Union and the People's Republic of China.[55] While the United States is far ahead of any other nation—capitalist or socialist—in its contribution to environmental deterioration, it is not possible to determine the exact reason. Is it because of our corporate capitalist economy? Or is it a result of our advanced levels of consumption and "dirty" production techniques? The socialist societies to which the United States is usually compared tend to be less advanced in terms of industrialization, to utilize lesser amounts of the earth's resources, and to produce fewer consumer goods on a per capita basis.

On the other hand, socialist societies that are not geared toward satisfying the profit interests of a handful of private owners, but instead try to meet the all-around needs of society as a whole, may find it easier to rationalize the costs of environmentally sane operations. In capitalist societies, where business and industry are

[53] Commoner, *The Closing Circle*, pp. 266–67.

[54] Ibid., pp. 298–99.

[55] Ibid., pp. 277–81. See also Barry Commoner, *The Poverty of Power* (New York: Alfred A. Knopf, 1976); and Weisberg, *Beyond Repair*, pp. 146–84. While Weisberg believes that socialism is well equipped to deal with the environmental crisis, Commoner sees this as an open question.

privately owned, corporate elites do not want to absorb costs that cut into the maximization of profits. They can only pass on some of the costs of pollution control to consumers in the form of higher prices or lower quality goods and to workers in the form of restricted wages. In socialist societies, however, business and industry are typically state-run. The decision to institute environmentally sound economic operations can be made centrally by the government and the costs can be balanced against the well-being of the citizenry.

So at least in theory it would be much easier to make environmentally sound decisions in socialist societies. But such societies presently also place strong emphasis on economic growth, and it remains to be seen whether they will avoid or repeat capitalism's contribution to the eco-catastrophe. It also remains to be seen whether capitalist nations—the United States in particular—will be able to find a "cheap" way out of their current problems.

SEARCHING FOR SOLUTIONS

Why don't we do something about environmental abuse? In this section we will see how our lack of knowledge about the relationship between human beings and the environment has slowed down attempts to correct environmental abuse. We will then look at some of the things we can do to protect the environment.

Problems in Combating Environmental Abuse

It is only in the last two decades that awareness of ecological matters has existed on a nationwide basis. International interest is even more recent. Some observers believe that national concern began in 1970, with the celebration of the first Earth Day. Since that time, agencies of government and private industry have started to curb environmental abuse—frequently in response to public discontent and aggressive legal actions by citizens' organizations.

Ignorance is a serious problem. We must work toward a fuller understanding of the ways in which human activities affect the ecosystem. Until quite recently, scientists were not particularly interested in such practical knowledge.[56] Thus, much environmental damage has been done almost inadvertently. It is growing increasingly true that a process of production or a product thought to be harmless today is suddenly seen as calamitous as its effects become felt.

Nor does there seem to be any consensus about the causes of environmental deterioration. Is there a link between abuse of the environment and human nature? Is such abuse an inevitable outcome of population growth? Is it caused by the excess of capitalism? Or is it a result of lack of foresight in the use of technology, resources, and industrial capabilities? As we have seen, agreement on causes will have a great deal to do with solutions. We must work toward a consensus in this area.

Besides our ignorance about the impact of human activities on the global ecosystem and our disagreements about the causes of environmental deterioration, solutions are being held up by other difficulties. Cultural drives, apathy, economic considerations, and political hurdles seem to work against the total elimination—as opposed to the slowdown—of environmental abuse. The initial sense of crisis of the early 1970s has given way to a process of monitoring and regulating the production and distribution of damage.[57] In other words, now that our efforts to *conquer* our surroundings have failed, we are trying to *manage* the ecosystem. Given the basic ecological principles outlined earlier, this is akin to expecting the tail to wag the dog. We are no longer even asking whether the managerial ap-

---

[56] See Barry Commoner, *Science and Survival* (New York: The Viking Press, 1966).

[57] This observation is offered in Weisberg, *Beyond Repair*, p. 34.

proach (setting "standards" and "tolerance levels," minimizing "impact," balancing "priorities," etc.) is the wisest course to take, given our past track record.

The financial costs and economic dislocations that may ultimately be required to bring human activities into harmony with the rest of the ecosystem are difficult to estimate. The question of who should be made to bear these costs has yet to be seriously addressed. For example, are we willing to shut down dirty production facilities if it means some will lose their jobs? At present we appear to be looking for the cheapest way out of the ecocatastrophe. Ultimately it must be ended no matter what the costs, if we are to provide for the survival of future generations.

At least one writer doubts that we care about the well-being of future waves of humanity. In the words of economist Robert L. Heilbroner:

> When men can generally acquiesce in, even relish, the destruction of their living contemporaries, when they can regard with indifference or irritation the fate of those who live in slums, rot in prison, or starve in lands that have meaning only insofar as they are vacation resorts, why should they be expected to take the painful actions to prevent the destruction of future generations whose faces they will never live to see?[58]

Changing Institutions and Activities

What are you willing to give up? In return for what? How serious are you about this? Really? The answers to such questions will determine whether people will find a niche in the ecosystem to enjoy after you are gone. From chlorofluorocarbons to billboards, from radiation to plastics, from climatic modification to toxic chemicals—this particular macro problem is all around us.

Can we end, not just slow down, America's current contribution to ecosystem collapse? We can, but it will not be easy or occur overnight.

Strict controls must be imposed over what is produced in our economy and how. Presently, political and economic policymakers are much more concerned with increasing the GNP than they are with the environmental impact of the economic activities it represents. We must turn away from a fixation with the dollar value of this society's productive efforts and begin considering the ecological value.

A start in this direction has already been made by the federal government. In recent years, states and localities have been required to assess the environmental impact of proposed projects and programs prior to receiving federal funding. While this procedure is far from perfect, it has helped promote environmental consciousness in the public sector of the economy.

In the private sector, however, business and industry pour out goods and services that require no environmental assessment or are restricted only after extreme damage has been done. The private sector must be made responsible and accountable for its actions, for example, through the federal chartering of firms. Federal chartering means that firms would be required to obtain a license from the federal government in order to operate. To receive this license or charter, the firms would be required to assess and publicly report on the environmental impact of their operations and products. They would also have to agree to be subject to nationwide regulations, tailored to particular types of business and industry, designed to minimize or eliminate negative environmental practices. Any business that failed to abide by the conditions of its charter could either be shut down or placed under public ownership and control—in effect, put under federal receivership—until it met the conditions. Such "infringement" on the freedom of the private sector seems to be unavoidable so long as short-range profit interests continue to override ecological sanity.

---

[58] Heilbroner, *An Inquiry into the Human Prospect*, p. 165.

Furthermore, we must be willing to alter our own life-styles. Basically, this means directing our consumption patterns into ecologically sane pathways. What is needed is a profound cultural shift wherein the "good life" is no longer defined in terms of the possession of things that are of danger to the environment. Our use of energy and energy-using products could easily be cut down. We could demand increased production of goods made of recyclable materials. A change in life-style also seems to be unavoidable if we have any interest in the world we are leaving future generations. As consumers, we must allow the demands of the ecosystem to begin to manage us as individuals as well as the economic institutions to which we look to meet our basic needs.

SUMMARY

Environmental abuse occurs as humans violate basic principles of ecology. Polluting the air and water, spreading radioactivity into the atmosphere, increasing levels of noise, creating numerous wastes, and consuming irreplaceable resources—all affect the global ecosystem. Since human beings are part of the ecosystem, we too are affected by these activities.

There are a number of major types of environmental abuse. Air pollution is known to have harmful effects on health and property and contributes to highly damaging acid precipitation. Pollution of water brings the threat of disease, shortages of clean water, and destruction of plant and aquatic life. Toxic substances pose serious threats to public health. Nuclear power poses dangers of radioactive contamination. Solid wastes, many of which are not biologically decomposable, accumulate. Noise and visual pollution are on the increase, the former affecting health and both harming the appeal of our environment. Land is being lost to misuse, often to the detriment of vegetation and wildlife. Finally, irreplaceable resources (e.g., energy-producing fuels and ores crucial to manufacturing) are facing rapid depletion. Conflict over scarce resources, many of which are located primarily in poor Third World countries, promises to emerge in the future.

There are different views on why environmental abuse is taking place. Some feel it is a result of human nature. Blame has also been placed on population growth, as well as on a loss of control over science and technology. Finally, the profit-seeking and unlimited growth orientation of capitalism has been blamed. There is little consensus on causes.

Many obstacles stand in the way of eliminating environmental abuse. Ignorance is a serious problem. Cultural drives, apathy, economic considerations, and political hurdles seem to work against the elimination—as opposed to the slowdown—of environmental abuse. Possible solutions include imposing strict controls over what is produced in our economy and how. We must alter our life-styles by directing our consumption patterns into ecologically sane pathways.

DISCUSSION QUESTIONS

1. Go into a supermarket and record the ingredients from the labels of commonly used bottled, canned, and boxed products. Discuss what you do and do not know about the ingredients and their effects on your health.
2. Take an inventory of all the things you own. How many of these items are made to be disposable or to have a limited useful life? How many are biologically decomposable? How many are cheaper to repair than to dispose of and replace?
3. List the aspects of your everyday activities and life-style that are directly affected by a concern for the ecosystem. List the aspects that are not. Compare your lists with those of others, and discuss the impact you are having on the environment.
4. Is the American Dream of material affluence and luxurious consumption compatible with

the basic principles of ecology outlined in this chapter? Why? If we must adapt our lifestyles to the demands of the ecosystem, what are the implications for the American Dream?
5. Most people would probably be outraged if someone sprayed them with poisonous air or fed them dangerous chemicals. In effect, this is what industrial polluters and many of their products are doing. Why, then, are people not outraged?
6. You have magically acquired the power to totally eliminate any one type of environmental abuse. Which would you choose and why? What vested interests would your action most adversely affect?

SUGGESTED READINGS

Block, Alan A., and Frank R. Scarpitti. *Poisoning for Profit: The Mafia and Toxic Waste in America* (New York: William Morrow & Company, 1985).
Exploitation of America's waste disposal dilemma by criminal elements is explored.

Council on Environmental Quality and Department of State. *The Global Year 2000 Report to the President*, Vol. 1 (Washington, D.C.: U.S. Government Printing Office, 1980).
The only comprehensive overview of resource and environmental trends commissioned to date by the federal government.

Edelstein, Michael R. *Contaminated Communities* (Boulder, Colo.: Westview Press, 1988).
The impact of exposure to toxic materials on local communities and their residents' responses.

Heilbroner, Robert L. *An Inquiry into the Human Prospect*, rev. ed. (New York: W. W. Norton & Company, 1980).
Provocative essay on the potentially catastrophic consequences of ignoring danger signs from our environment.

Hollender, Jeffrey. *How to Make the World a Better Place* (New York: William Morrow & Company, 1990).
Specific actions people can take to improve the environment and effect positive social change at home and elsewhere.

"Planet of the Year: Endangered Earth," *Time*, 133 (January 2, 1989).
Popular treatment of the frightening environmental developments that cry out for attention in the 1990s.

LEXINGTON

CHAPTER 5

Work

Work must be freely available to all. It should be organized cooperatively, with special attention to providing meaning, dignity, and satisfaction.

Most broadly defined, *work* is an "activity that produces something of value for other people."[1] This definition encompasses a broad range of human behavior. Child care and household tasks are forms of work. Such home labor is socially necessary and economically useful. So is the informal volunteer work performed in American society. Each year tens of millions of people contribute their time and effort to everything from visiting the hospitalized to assisting in political campaigns. While we recognize that the term *work* means more than paid labor, we limit our attention in this chapter primarily to work activity for which people receive wages or salaries.

Sociologists have been studying work for a long time. In the nineteenth century French sociologist Emile Durkheim observed that the division of labor in society made people dependent on one another. Durkheim felt that this interdependence contributed to societal stability and integration, both of which he believed

[1] *Work in America*, Report of a Special Task Force to the Secretary of Health, Education, and Welfare (Washington, D.C.: U.S. Government Printing Office, 1973), p. 2.

to be necessary for human well-being.[2] Another nineteenth-century thinker, Karl Marx, saw labor as the principal means by which the human species sought to fulfill its potential. Marx believed that the industrializing societies of his day were turning work into a degrading, dehumanizing experience for the majority of workers.[3] As we shall see, Marx's concerns are still relevant.

Contemporary social scientists have suggested a number of ways in which work is central to our everyday lives.[4] Work is the means by which we are expected to pursue the American Dream—the acquisition of material goods and services and financial security. The pay we receive for our labor helps determine our standard of living and our life-style. The jobs we hold are also major determinants of our position in the overall class structure. This is true not only in purely economic terms but also with regard to power and prestige. Thus, the nature of our work often tells other people who we are. We may be treated with deference, accepted as an equal, or dismissed as a nonperson depending on our work status.

Social scientists have found that work has a very personal meaning to people. It can serve as an important source of self-esteem. If we are confronted by challenges at work, and if we overcome them, we gain a sense of accomplishment. Work tasks may give us the chance to feel a sense of mastery over our immediate environment and to display particular talents. Our self-esteem may be further enhanced if our work is valued and rated positively by others, both on and off the job. All in all, work serves as a measure of our social worth and a key source of our personal identity.

Unfortunately, millions of people today are unable to find work or face the prospect of unemployment. Many unemployed men and women, while wanting and needing jobs, have become so discouraged that they have given up looking for them. As we shall see in Chapter 6, "Economic Inequality and Poverty," the wages received by the working poor and near-poor are woefully inadequate; and for them, pursuit of the American Dream by means of work is presently impossible. Nor are work status and earnings the only job-related issues that have been troubling millions of Americans. Social scientists have detected a serious degree of dissatisfaction among people—especially among the young, women, and minorities—with regard to the *kind* of work they find themselves doing. Job dissatisfaction appears to exist at all levels of the American occupational system. Before examining some of these topics in more detail, we look at the historical trends that have helped shape today's work world.

THE CHANGING WORLD OF WORK

Unemployment, worker dissatisfaction, and other work-related problems are a result of certain historical trends in the world of work. In particular, three trends have, since the Industrial Revolution of the nineteenth century, helped create the work world we know today. The first trend is the shift from an agricultural society first to an industrial and more recently to a "deindustrialized" society. Related to this is the second trend, the decline of self-employment among workers. Finally, the past century has also seen a dramatic increase in the bureaucratization of the workplace.

The Deindustrialized Society

Social scientists often divide a society's system of work activity into three sectors: *primary* (ag-

[2] Emile Durkheim, *The Division of Labor in Society* (New York: The Free Press, 1965).

[3] T. B. Bottomore and Maximilien Rubel, eds., *Karl Marx: Selected Writings* (New York: McGraw-Hill Book Company, 1964).

[4] See, for example, Lee Braude, *Work and Workers* (New York: Praeger Publishers, 1975).

TABLE 5.1 Distribution of Employment by Major Sector, 1850–1989 (in percent)

Year	Agriculture	Goods-producing	Service-producing
1850	64.5	17.7	17.8
1860	59.9	20.1	20.0
1870	50.8	25.0	24.2
1880	50.6	25.1	24.3
1890	43.1	28.3	28.6
1900	38.0	30.5	31.4
1910	32.1	32.1	35.9
1920	27.6	34.6	37.7
1930	21.8	31.7	46.6
1940	18.3	33.1	48.6
1952	11.3	35.5	53.3
1957	9.8	34.3	56.0
1962	7.8	33.1	59.1
1967	5.3	34.7	60.1
1972	4.4	31.4	64.2
1977	3.7	29.7	66.6
1979	3.6	30.2	66.3
1982	3.6	27.2	69.2
1989 (Oct.)	2.8	22.8	74.4

Source: U.S. Department of Labor, *Monthly Labor Review*, 107 (April 1984): 16, and U.S. Department of Labor, *Employment and Earnings*, 36 (November 1989): 12 and 49.

riculture), *secondary* (manufacturing), and *tertiary* (services). Two hundred years ago most members of the American labor force were engaged in the primary sector. There was little industry, and most of that was in the hands of individual craftsmen and artisans. Then, under the impetus of the Industrial Revolution of the nineteenth century, the proportion of the labor force engaged in agriculture underwent a marked decline. Not only were more people needed to fill the growing numbers of new jobs in manufacturing, but advances in agricultural production meant that fewer workers could provide the American population with food. By the end of the nineteenth century, 30.5 percent of the labor force was involved in the secondary sector of the economy. (See Table 5.1.)

In the present century, particularly since World War II, there has been an explosive expansion of the tertiary, or service, sector. Today over 70 percent of all workers are engaged in providing services in such fields as business, transportation, communications, utilities, education, health, and government. The percentage of the labor force holding manufacturing jobs has actually changed very little since 1900, being now about 23 percent. The major change has been in agriculture, where 3 percent of U.S. workers are now employed.

As we look into the future there is strong reason to believe that America's manufacturing sector will decline dramatically. Many observers feel that the economy is already experiencing the early stages of what has come to be called "deindustrialization."[5] For it has become apparent that our long-heralded productivity in manufacturing currently lags far behind our productivity in agriculture and that we have been losing

[5] See Barry Bluestone and Bennett Harrison, *The Deindustrialization of America* (New York: Basic Books, 1982).

rapidly the ability to compete in the world market with other goods-manufacturing nations.[6] Thirty years ago we supplied 98 percent of our own products. Now we are dependent on foreign imports, unable to find buyers for many of our own products abroad (agricultural products and some high technology, including weaponry, being the main exceptions).[7]

The future of manufacturing in America is uncertain. The changes that may yet take place in this sector will have dramatic effects on the work force as we move toward the end of the twentieth century.

The Decline of Self-employment

Today when we think of joining the labor force, we are likely to think in terms of working *for* someone. This was not always the case. At the time of the American Revolution, 80 percent of the labor force was self-employed. (For the purposes of this discussion, we are leaving aside consideration of the sizable slave population.) Most were engaged in family farming. But whatever their role in the division of labor, working people typically owned their own tools and income-producing property. Government was for the most part neither an active overseer of the domestic economy nor a source of employment.

By 1880 the self-employed made up only a third of the labor force, and today they represent less than 10 percent of it. In the wake of the Industrial Revolution, industry and then agriculture were progressively taken over by large-scale corporate enterprises. With the expansion of productive capability that stemmed from technological advances, the creation of modern transportation and communication networks, and the emergence of regional and national markets for inexpensively produced goods, independent entrepreneurs (business owners) and family farmers could not compete with heavily capitalized firms. More and more people found that they had to depend on jobs offered by others in order to survive. Today we are a nation of employees, forced to compete with one another for employment opportunities. In the words of one observer, most labor force participants

> have virtually no access to income from property or control over the production process. [Their] economic welfare is determined by the vicissitudes of the labor market.[8]

Along with the growth of big business and corporate agriculture has come the expansion of public employment. Today 15 percent of the labor force is employed by government in service jobs. The federal government employed over 2.8 million civilians in 1986, while state and local governments had more than 13 million employees on their payrolls. We have come a long way from the days when government workers were a rarity.

Given that most members of the labor force lack any means of economic subsistence apart from that provided in return for their labor, workers are in a state of dependence and extreme vulnerability. Economic decisions made by affluent executives, both in and out of government, routinely throw out of work people whose faces the decision-makers never see. The loss of self-employment has been also a loss of self-determination, for it has rendered most workers subject to the whims of others over whom they have no control.

---

[6] See Paul Blumberg, *Inequality in an Age of Decline* (New York: Oxford University Press, 1980), Chapter 3; Ira C. Magaziner and Robert B. Reich, *Minding America's Business* (New York: Vintage Books, 1983); and Samuel E. Bowles, David M. Gordon, and Thomas E. Weisskopf, *Beyond the Wasteland* (Garden City, N.Y.: Anchor Books, 1984).

[7] See Editors of *Business Week, The Reindustrialization of America* (New York: McGraw-Hill Book Company, 1984).

[8] Michael Reich, "The Development of the Wage-Labor Force," in *The Capitalist System*, Richard C. Edwards et al., eds., 2nd ed. (Englewood Cliffs, N.J.: Prentice-Hall, 1978), p. 181.

Farming was once seen as an occupation in which individuals could be their own bosses and set their own working conditions. Today, however, most of America's food is produced on huge corporate farms, where agricultural machinery and hired workers perform the tasks once done by farmers and their families. *(Loomis Dean* Life *Magazine© Time Inc.)*

Bureaucratization of the Workplace

Implicit in the decline of self-employment is a third historical trend, the rise of the formal organization, or *bureaucracy,* as a setting for work activity. The term *bureaucracy* is not used loosely by sociologists. It refers to places in which the following features are normally present:

1. A clear-cut division of labor, within which each worker is formally assigned specialized tasks and duties;
2. A hierarchy of authority, in which every individual has a supervisor or boss whose work-related directives must be obeyed;

3. Organizational rules and regulations that govern work performance, delineate the rights and responsibilities of each individual, and dictate proper channels of communication;
4. Demands for rationality and efficiency in the performance of work tasks, requiring individuals to set aside their personal feelings when dealing with others;
5. A ladderlike system of material and symbolic rewards based on technical qualifications and the ability to perform specialized work tasks. The rewards are intended to motivate individuals to compete for movement upward in the bureaucracy and to stimulate loyalty to the work organization.[9]

Bureaucratic organization facilitates employers' control over work and workers in the interest of attaining a particular goal. In the corporate world, the goal is generally to maximize profits, while the goal for government is to provide public services dictated by law (e.g., tax collection, defense, law enforcement, aid to the disadvantaged). Work policies, the rules and regulations developed to attain the goal, are decreed by those who hold command positions in a bureaucracy. Workers are expected to obey, even if they do not agree with the policies or the organizational goals. Compliance, or doing what they are told, is a virtue expected of those who wish to remain employed.

This is not to say that those who labor in bureaucratic settings are mindless robots whose every action is controlled. Sociologists have long used the term *informal organization* to underscore the nonofficial behaviors engaged in by workers and their peers.[10] Workers may help a bureaucracy operate more efficiently when they bypass red tape and official channels. On the other hand, informal organization may also enable workers to sabotage superiors' planned use of their labor. In either case, the existence of informal organization indicates that bureaucratic control is by no means total.[11]

Beginning with the Industrial Revolution, an ever larger proportion of the American labor force has come to be employed in bureaucratic settings. Today 20 percent of our industrial work force is employed by a mere sixteen giant corporations. A firm like American Telephone and Telegraph, before being broken up by court order, monitored a system of subsidiary companies employing over a million people. Earlier we noted that the federal government, as a single employer, carries more than 2.8 million people on its civilian payroll.

Not all persons who work do so in bureaucratic settings. But enough do to have caused a federal task force to conclude:

> The trend is toward large corporations and bureaucracies which typically organize work in such a way as to minimize the independence of the workers and maximize control and predictability for the organization.[12]

Work in America most certainly means entering a competitive labor market and seeking to become someone's employee. With increasing frequency, it means taking a job in the growing service sector, particularly as the specter of "deindustrialization" looms. And, finally, work in America increasingly means becoming part of a bureaucracy and submitting to the authority of persons who command higher organizational rank.

---

[9] H. H. Gerth and C. Wright Mills, eds., *From Max Weber* (New York: Oxford University Press, 1968), Chapter 8.

[10] See Peter M. Blau and Marshall W. Meyer, *Bureaucracy in Modern Society,* 3rd ed. (New York: Random House, 1971), pp. 37–50.

[11] See Richard Edwards, *Contested Terrain* (New York: Basic Books, 1979).

[12] *Work in America,* p. 18.

UNEMPLOYMENT

Though most persons who wish to participate in the world of work are able to do so, millions of Americans have been unable to market their labor. In the early 1980s the United States was in the throes of an economic recession more severe than any since World War II. There was a slowdown in production and hiring, and according to the U.S. Department of Labor, the official rate of unemployment reached 10.8 percent in December 1982—the highest rate since the Great Depression of the 1930s. Out of a total labor force of over 100 million people, 12 million were said to be involuntarily out of work. Most of the unemployed either had been dismissed from their last job or were new entrants to the labor force who could not find work.[13]

During the 1970s and 1980s unemployment was a very serious problem. But it is not only during recessions that millions of people are out of work. In our society, a 4.5 percent unemployment rate is considered "full employment." Over time we have come to tacitly accept a permanent pool of jobless people. There have been relatively few years since World War II in which the rate has dipped below the 4.5 percent level, and we experienced levels well above this throughout the 1970s and 1980s (see Table 5.2). What do such statistics mean? Why does unemployment seem to be a permanent feature of American society, even during nonrecessionary years? What impact does joblessness have on people?

Extent of Unemployment

Government statistics on unemployment have been severely criticized for *underestimating* the extent of joblessness.[14] Much of this criticism is directed at the ways in which the U.S. Department of Labor defines the term *labor force.* The civilian labor force is said to consist of people who are sixteen years of age or older (with the exception of inmates of institutions). To be counted as a member of the labor force, people must either have a full-time or part-time job or have been actively seeking work in the four-week period prior to the Labor Department's monthly unemployment survey. People who do not meet these criteria are not considered members of the labor force and hence are not counted as employed or unemployed.

If the government's definition of *labor force* were not so restricted, say critics, the unemployment rate would be dramatically higher. Many fourteen- and fifteen-year-olds are capable of and interested in holding jobs—at least part-time—but their joblessness is ignored. Many older students would prefer a full-time job to school attendance, but they are not considered in labor force statistics. Housewives, many of whom do not look for work because their pay would not offset extra child-care costs, are also excluded. Then there are the individuals who have become discouraged in the search for employment and have simply given up. They just drop out of existence in terms of official unemployment statistics. Meanwhile, workers who are on strike, on vacation, or ill are counted as part of the employed labor force even if they are not receiving wages.

Thus, a more inclusive definition of the American labor force would probably give us an unemployment rate far greater than that now reported by government. The rate would expand even more if we counted all the part-time workers who need and want full-time jobs.

Government unemployment statistics generally do not depict the changes that take place in the pool of people who are jobless. Over a given

[13] For statistics on unemployment and the labor force, see the *Monthly Labor Review,* published by the U.S. Department of Labor.

[14] See National Commission on Employment and Unemployment Statistics, *Counting the Labor Force* (Washington, D.C.: U.S. Government Printing Office, 1979).

TABLE 5.2 Employment Status of the Civilian Noninstitutional Population Sixteen Years and Over, 1955 to date (in thousands)

Year and month	Civilian noninstitutional population	Civilian labor force: Total	Civilian labor force: Percent of population	Civilian labor force: Employed	Civilian labor force: Unemployed	Unemployment rates: Total	Unemployment rates: Men	Unemployment rates: Women
1955	109,633	65,023	59.3	62,170	2,852	4.4	4.2	4.9
1956	110,954	66,552	60.0	63,799	2,750	4.1	3.8	4.8
1957	112,265	66,929	59.6	64,071	2,859	4.3	4.1	4.7
1958	113,727	67,639	59.5	63,036	4,602	6.8	6.8	6.8
1959	115,329	68,369	59.3	64,630	3,740	5.5	5.2	5.9
1960	117,245	69,628	59.4	65,778	3,852	5.5	5.4	5.9
1961	118,771	70,459	59.3	65,746	4,714	6.7	6.4	7.2
1962	120,153	70,614	58.8	66,702	3,911	5.5	5.2	6.2
1963	122,416	71,833	58.7	67,762	4,070	5.7	5.2	6.5
1964	124,485	73,091	58.7	69,305	3,786	5.2	4.6	6.2
1965	126,513	74,455	58.9	71,088	3,366	4.5	4.0	5.5
1966	128,058	75,770	59.2	72,895	2,875	3.8	3.2	4.8
1967	129,874	77,347	59.6	74,372	2,975	3.8	3.1	5.2
1968	132,028	78,737	59.6	75,920	2,817	3.6	2.9	4.8
1969	134,335	80,734	60.1	77,902	2,832	3.5	2.8	4.7
1970	137,085	82,771	60.4	78,678	4,093	4.9	4.4	5.9
1971	140,216	84,382	60.2	79,367	5,016	5.9	5.3	6.9
1972	144,126	87,034	60.4	82,153	4,882	5.6	5.0	6.6
1973	147,096	89,429	60.8	85,064	4,365	4.9	4.2	6.0
1974	150,120	91,949	61.3	86,794	5,156	5.6	4.9	6.7
1975	153,153	93,775	61.2	85,846	7,929	8.5	7.9	9.3
1976	156,150	96,158	61.6	88,752	7,406	7.7	7.1	8.6
1977	159,033	99,009	62.3	92,017	6,991	7.1	6.3	8.2
1978	161,910	102,251	63.2	96,048	6,202	6.1	5.3	7.2
1979	164,863	104,962	63.7	98,824	6,137	5.8	5.1	6.8
1980	167,745	106,940	63.8	99,303	7,637	7.1	6.9	7.4
1981	170,130	108,670	63.9	100,397	8,273	7.6	7.4	7.9
1982	172,271	110,204	64.0	99,526	10,678	9.7	9.9	9.4
1983	174,215	111,550	64.0	100,834	10,717	9.6	9.9	9.2
1984	176,383	113,544	64.4	105,005	8,539	7.5	7.4	7.6
1985	178,206	115,461	64.8	107,150	8,312	7.2	7.0	7.4
1986	180,587	117,834	65.3	109,597	8,237	7.0	6.9	7.1
1987	182,753	119,865	65.6	112,440	7,425	6.2	6.2	6.2
1988	184,613	121,669	65.9	114,968	6,701	5.5	5.5	5.6
1989 (Oct.)	186,871	124,105	66.4	117,545	6,561	5.3	5.3	5.3

Annual Averages

Source: U.S. Department of Labor, *Employment and Earnings*, 36 (November 1989): 14.

period, *different* people are constantly becoming employed and unemployed. If the federal government were to give more publicity to the numbers of persons who experience unemployment over, say, a year's time, its full impact would be better revealed. The U.S. Department of Labor has investigated this situation. In 1986 the official unemployment rate averaged 7 percent over the course of the year, or an average of 8.2 million people monthly. Yet when researchers inquired into how many different people experienced unemployment at some point during 1986 the results were quite startling. Sixteen percent of the labor force was touched by joblessness—a total of 20.7 million people![15]

The statistics with which the federal government depicts unemployment are chosen for their political neutrality, according to the critics. By making the rate of joblessness seem to be lower than it truly is, the government is able to obscure the extent to which satisfactory work opportunities are absent. As unemployment grows, there has even been discussion of moving the "full employment" rate above 4.5 percent in order to discourage discussion of the fact that there are just not enough employment opportunities to go around.

Causes of Unemployment

What factors underlie America's seeming inability to deliver enough jobs to its people? A quick but erroneous explanation is that millions of people simply do not care to work. There is no evidence that this is the case. (See Table 5.3.) On the contrary, surveys indicate that most persons would choose to work even if their financial situations did not require it.[16] Similarly, experimental income-supplement programs for low-income people have not shown that economic security diminishes the desire to improve one's position in the labor market.[17]

To understand the causes of unemployment we must look beyond the millions of jobless individuals to focus on factors that are largely beyond their control. In a subsequent chapter we shall see that there are forces creating and perpetuating poverty. Likewise, there are forces that the unemployed cannot counter or overcome. Moreover, many of the underlying causes of poverty are the same as those that put and keep people out of work.

Automation and Technological Change. One cause of unemployment is the introduction of computers and other "labor-saving" machines into the workplace. Employers install new machinery in order to increase worker productivity and/or cut labor costs. Automation, computerization, introduction of robotics, and other such technological changes often displace workers from existing jobs and also close certain categories of work opportunities for newcomers to the labor force. There are fewer jobs for telephone operators, coal miners, and farm laborers, among others, because of technological displacement. The steel and auto industries have found that substituting machines for people can help hold down labor costs. While automation and technological change do create new job categories—for example, computer programmer and skilled machine technician—it seems likely that more jobs are lost than are created. Furthermore, technologically displaced workers are likely to find it difficult to qualify for and adjust themselves to the new opportunities that open

[15] Earl F. Mellor and William Parks II, "A Year's Work: Labor Force Activity from a Different Perspective," *Monthly Labor Review,* 111 (September 1988): 17.

[16] Robert P. Quinn and Graham L. Staines, *The 1977 Quality of Employment Survey: Descriptive Statistics with Comparison Data from the 1969–70 and 1972–73 Surveys* (Ann Arbor: University of Michigan, Institute for Social Research, 1979).

[17] See Leonard Goodwin, *Causes and Curses of Welfare* (Lexington, Mass.: Lexington Books, 1983).

TABLE 5.3 Unemployed Persons by Reason for Unemployment, Sex, and Race (in thousands)

Reason for unemployment	Total unemployed		Men, 20 years and over		Women, 20 years and over		Both sexes 16–19 years		White		Black	
	Oct. 1988	Oct. 1989	Oct. 1988	Oct. 1989	Oct. 1988	Oct. 1989	Oct. 1988	Oct. 1989	Oct. 1988	Oct. 1989	Oct. 1988	Oct. 1989
Number of Unemployed												
Total unemployed	**6,182**	**6,222**	**2,618**	**2,606**	**2,430**	**2,494**	**1,134**	**1,122**	**4,572**	**4,489**	**1,434**	**1,516**
Job losers	2,641	2,625	1,632	1,604	830	849	180	171	1,962	1,942	618	615
On layoff	691	620	440	365	217	231	34	25	550	509	127	91
Other job losers	1,950	2,004	1,192	1,239	613	619	146	146	1,412	1,432	491	524
Job leavers	1,059	1,052	421	381	457	459	182	212	851	823	177	187
Reentrants	1,805	1,933	486	522	1,004	1,033	316	378	1,295	1,367	448	482
New entrants	676	613	79	99	140	152	457	362	465	357	191	232
Percent Distribution												
Total unemployed	**100.0**	**100.0**	**100.0**	**100.0**	**100.0**	**100.0**	**100.0**	**100.0**	**100.0**	**100.0**	**100.0**	**100.0**
Job losers	42.7	42.2	62.3	61.6	34.1	34.1	15.9	15.3	42.9	43.3	43.1	40.6
On layoff	11.2	10.0	16.8	14.0	8.9	9.2	3.0	2.2	12.0	11.3	8.9	6.0
Other job losers	31.5	32.2	45.5	47.6	25.2	24.8	12.9	13.0	30.9	31.9	34.2	34.6
Job leavers	17.1	16.9	16.1	14.6	18.8	18.4	16.0	18.9	18.6	18.3	12.4	12.3
Reentrants	29.2	31.1	18.6	20.0	41.3	41.4	27.8	33.7	28.3	30.5	31.2	31.8
New entrants	10.9	9.9	3.0	3.8	5.8	6.1	40.3	32.2	10.2	7.9	13.3	15.3
Unemployed as a Percentage of the Civilian Labor Force												
Job losers	2.2	2.1	2.6	2.5	1.6	1.6	2.3	2.3	1.8	1.8	4.6	4.6
Job leavers	.9	.8	.7	.6	.9	.9	2.4	2.8	.8	.8	1.3	1.4
Reentrants	1.5	1.6	.8	.8	1.9	2.0	4.2	5.0	1.2	1.3	3.4	3.6
New entrants	.6	.5	.1	.2	.3	.3	6.0	4.8	.4	.3	1.4	1.7

Source: U.S. Department of Labor, *Employment and Earnings,* 36 (November 1989): 28.

TABLE 5.4 Fastest Growing Occupations, 1988–2000, Moderate Alternative Projection (in thousands)

Occupation	Employment		Numerical change	Percent change
	1988	2000		
Paralegals	83	145	62	75.3
Medical assistants	149	253	104	70.0
Home health aides	236	397	160	67.9
Radiologic technologists and technicians	132	218	87	66.0
Data processing equipment repairers	71	115	44	61.2
Medical records technicians	47	75	28	59.9
Medical secretaries	207	327	120	58.0
Physical therapists	68	107	39	57.0
Surgical technologists	35	55	20	56.4
Operations research analysis	55	85	30	55.4
Securities and financial services sales workers	200	309	109	54.8
Travel agents	142	219	77	54.1
Computer systems analysts	403	617	214	53.3
Physical and corrective therapy assistants	39	60	21	52.5
Social welfare service aides	91	138	47	51.5
Occupational therapists	33	48	16	48.8
Computer programmers	519	769	250	48.1
Human services workers	118	171	53	44.9
Respiratory therapists	56	79	23	41.3
Correction officers and jailers	186	262	76	40.8

Source: U.S. Department of Labor, *Monthly Labor Review*, 112 (November 1989): 60.

up.[18] Many such opportunities are listed in Table 5.4.

Those hit hardest by technological displacement are unskilled and semiskilled workers, such as clerical employees, laborers, and lower level blue-collar workers. These workers often do not have the educational attainments and training to qualify for jobs requiring more skills. Technical and professional workers and white-collar administrative personnel are more likely to be insulated from technological displacement and are frequently flexible in terms of the work roles they can readily assume.

The precise impact of automation and technological change on unemployment statistics remains a matter of conjecture. But it is clear that, in selected sectors of the economy, people have been put out of work. Observers disagree about the prospects in store for the future.[19] Some downplay the topic of unemployment, suggesting only that changes will be taking place in the nature of work and in the forms of work organization in which people will be employed. Others feel that the growth of new work opportunities will fail to keep up with the natural growth of the labor force and that a steady increase in unemployment will be the result. Still others contend that there will be plenty of work, but that labor force members will have to work fewer

[18] See U.S. General Accounting Office, *Advances in Automation Prompt Concern over Increased U.S. Unemployment* (Washington, D.C.: U.S. Government Printing Office, 1982), and Wassily W. Leontief, "The Distribution of Work and Income," *Scientific American*, 247 (September 1982): 188–90.

[19] Optimists include Richard K. Vedder, *Robotics and the Economy* (Washington, D.C.: U.S. Government Printing Office, 1982).

Modern technology has made it possible for corporations to use robots to replace human labor. In this photograph, a robot nicknamed "Sweet William" by auto workers picks up engine blocks and places them on an assembly line. In the future the use of robots for production and service tasks may have profound effects on the structure of work opportunities. *(Michael Hayman/Stock, Boston)*

hours per week in order to spread job opportunities around. Whatever the future, it is unlikely to be the unemployed who determine its direction. Such decisions are in the hands of public and private employers—those who hold command positions in bureaucratic work settings.

Job Export and Goods Import. Many of the largest American corporations have been opening plants in other countries. Foreign operations have made it possible for such firms to take advantage of cheaper foreign labor and gain better accessibility to foreign markets.[20] According to organized labor, multinational corporations that invest in plants outside this country and/or close down domestic facilities to reopen elsewhere are guilty of exporting jobs.

Corporate leaders typically reject this charge, arguing that a substantial percentage of their increased profits flow back into this country. They claim that foreign investments create new jobs in the United States—for example, through the expansion of operations at company headquarters. However, as in the case of automation and technological change, it is not clear that the numbers of jobs being exported are fully offset by the new ones created. Similarly, workers whose jobs disappear because of factory closings are unlikely to qualify for the new and different work opportunities with which old jobs are replaced. Thus, we see with increasing frequency "downward mobility" among workers (e.g., in the auto and steel industries) whose

[20] See Richard J. Barnet, *The Lean Years* (New York: Touchstone, 1981), Chapter 9; also Bluestone and Harrison, *The Deindustrialization of America,* Chapter 2.

plants have closed and whose jobs have been exported. Formerly able to support their families modestly with factory jobs, many such workers are now eking out a living in low-wage positions—becoming janitors, fast-food workers, hospital orderlies. These are the types of "service sector" jobs that many are forced into in the face of deindustrialization.[21]

Corporate relocation has an effect similar to job export. Corporate relocation occurs when employers move their facilities from one place to another within the country. For example, firms that want low-wage, nonunionized workers have at times found it desirable to relocate in the South or even in Puerto Rico, a commonwealth of the United States in which unemployment is usually extraordinarily high. Many workers cannot uproot themselves and their families in order to follow. They must hunt for other jobs, and they are often found among the unemployed. Workers are also left behind when companies move their headquarters and plants out of central city areas—often to gain tax relief, to obtain inexpensive labor, or to gain additional space in which to conduct operations. Left behind are those who cannot afford to relocate or commute far beyond city limits. Over the last twenty years, the movement of business and industry out of central city areas has contributed to the erosion of the tax bases on which the services of city governments depend. Services mean jobs—from sanitation work to public school teaching. The financial crises of such large cities as New York, in which thousands of public employees have lost their jobs, are linked at least in part to corporate relocation.

Earlier we mentioned that the United States has become a goods-importing nation. This has a direct bearing on unemployment. Although foreign-made goods are often cheaper than their domestically produced equivalents, purchase of such goods, again, is akin to exporting jobs. In a rather short time period production of radios, television sets, stereos, bicycles, automobiles, and ships—to mention a few products—has come largely under the control of foreign manufacturers. Semiconductors, solar cells, and videotape recorders were invented in the United States but are now among our imports from elsewhere. Our historic dominance in the manufacture of aircraft, plastics, and drugs is slowly ebbing away. The import of steel from Japan and other nations has helped to undermine employment in an industry that has long been central to our economy. In sum, manufacturing jobs are being lost. (See Table 5.5.)

Government Spending and Taxation. Since the depression of the 1930s, the federal government has played an ever more active role in determining the overall course of the economy. In two areas—spending and taxation—federal policies directly affect unemployment rates.

Each year the federal treasury is the recipient of billions of dollars that it turns back into the economy. In fiscal year 1988 for example, government revenues were roughly $900 billion. This money came from personal and corporate income taxes, social security taxes, excise taxes, and loans from private financial institutions. That year, the government spent some $1050 billion (or $150 billion more than its revenues) on the defense establishment, grants to states and localities, payments to individuals, loan debts, and general federal operations.

There are legal limitations on how the federal government may use the money in its treasury. For example, each year billions of dollars must go to social security recipients and federal retirees. However, some flexibility is often permitted within the law, and new legislation is always being passed and old restrictions modified. Given the huge amounts of money involved, spending priorities directly affect the existing structure and growth of work oppor-

[21] Bruce Steinberg, "The Mass Market Is Splitting Apart," *Fortune* (November 28, 1983): 76–82.

TABLE 5.5 Unemployed Persons by Occupation and Sex

	Thousands of persons		Unemployment rates (percent of total)					
	Total		Total		Men		Women	
Occupation	1988	1989	1988	1989	1988	1989	1988	1989
Total, 16 years and over	**6,182**	**6,222**	**5.0**	**5.0**	**4.9**	**4.8**	**5.3**	**5.3**
Managerial and professional specialty	583	593	1.9	1.9	1.5	1.6	2.5	2.2
Executive, administrative, and managerial	291	337	2.0	2.2	1.5	1.9	2.8	2.6
Professional specialty	292	256	1.9	1.6	1.4	1.3	2.3	1.8
Technical, sales, and administrative support	1,455	1,541	3.9	4.1	3.7	3.3	4.0	4.5
Technicians and related support	94	99	2.5	2.7	2.8	3.3	2.2	2.2
Sales occupations	672	664	4.6	4.5	3.4	3.0	5.8	6.1
Administrative support, including clerical	689	777	3.6	4.0	4.6	4.0	3.4	4.1
Service occupations	1,130	1,032	6.8	6.3	6.3	6.2	7.1	6.3
Private household	53	41	5.5	4.9	—*	—*	4.9	4.8
Protective service	97	62	4.7	3.2	4.2	2.7	7.2	5.7
Service, except private household and protective	980	928	7.3	6.8	7.1	7.4	7.4	6.5
Precision production, craft, and repair	712	652	5.0	4.5	4.9	4.4	5.1	5.4
Mechanics and repairers	176	147	3.9	3.2	3.8	3.1	7.3	5.0
Construction trades	345	348	6.3	6.1	6.2	6.0	10.5	9.6
Other precision production, craft, and repair	190	156	4.3	3.7	4.4	3.3	4.1	4.9
Operators, fabricators, and laborers	1,368	1,438	7.0	7.3	6.6	6.9	8.1	8.7
Machine operators, assemblers, and inspectors	616	632	6.9	7.2	6.0	6.0	8.2	8.8
Transportation and material moving occupations	210	267	4.1	5.0	4.1	4.9	3.8	5.5
Handlers, equipment cleaners, helpers, and laborers	542	538	9.8	9.9	9.8	10.0	9.8	9.8
Construction laborers	141	104	13.5	12.4	13.2	12.6	—*	—*
Other handlers, equipment cleaners, helpers, and laborers	401	435	9.0	9.5	8.8	9.4	9.5	9.8
Farming, forestry, and fishing	238	233	6.3	6.3	6.2	6.2	6.7	6.8
No previous work experience	678	695	—	—	—	—	—	—
16–19 years	458	415	—	—	—	—	—	—
20–24 years	120	132	—	—	—	—	—	—
25 years and over	100	148	—	—	—	—	—	—

*Data not shown where base is less than 75,000

Source: U.S. Department of Labor, *Employment and Earnings,* 36 (November 1989): 26.

tunities. For example, during the 1980s the federal government began to escalate its rate of spending on research, development, and production of weapons systems to be made available to the nation's military forces. A five-year plan was instituted in which total defense expenditures, including spending in the areas mentioned previously, would total some $1.6 trillion. Those states and communities fortunate enough to be major recipients of defense dollars were able to maintain some semblance of economic stability even as unemployment rates elsewhere reached double-digit figures (e.g., in late 1982).

At times, as in the 1980s, the federal government has tried to restrict annual spending on nondefense programs, both by eliminating them outright and by reducing their funding. This strategy, which is considered a way of fighting inflation, also increases unemployment across the country. Federal policymakers at times tell us that higher unemployment rates are a cost this society must be willing to bear in order to slow down inflation and the rising costs of living. The idea is that people will then have more money to spend on consumer goods and services, and ultimately the unemployed (or at least some of them) will be called back to work. Unfortunately, many are not called back. They remain unemployed, or they drop in earning ability by desperately taking almost any work to survive.

Taxation policy also has an impact on unemployment. Of each dollar flowing into the federal treasury, 43.3 cents comes from individual income taxes and 11.6 cents from corporate income taxes. When individual income tax rates are lowered, consumers have more money to spend on goods and services. Assuming that they choose to spend this money, sales will increase, creating more jobs in business and industry. When corporate taxes are cut, firms may choose to invest in new equipment, expanded operations, or higher wages for employees—all of which help create jobs. On the other hand, lower personal and/or corporate income taxes also may mean less revenue for the federal treasury and pressure to slow down government spending. The negative effect of the latter on unemployment somehow must be balanced against anticipated job growth in the private sector of the economy—a very tricky balancing act indeed.

Discrimination. Discrimination may not directly cause unemployment per se, as much as it determines who will be without a job. Institutional discrimination directly affects the employment opportunities open to minorities and women. Minority unemployment rates are ordinarily quite high. Blacks, for example, are twice as likely as whites to be out of work and are usually jobless for longer periods of time. The unemployment rates for women are normally higher than those for men. Considering the defects of government unemployment statistics, the true rates of joblessness among minorities and women are no doubt considerably understated.

Discrimination on the basis of age is pervasive in the world of work. Young persons between the ages of sixteen and nineteen—especially minority teenagers—have extraordinarily high joblessness rates. Since they are likely to possess few skills and little work experience, it is difficult for them to get a decent start in the labor market. Old age, on the other hand, may mean that education and skills are out of date. Even where this is not the case, employers whose main concern is to cut labor costs often find it desirable to replace older employees with persons who will work for less.

There has been a steady decline in the labor force participation of persons over sixty-five. A good deal of this decline is attributable to the existence of social security and pension plans. In 1900 two-thirds of the men aged sixty-five and over were in the labor force; today the figure is around 20 percent and is declining. While most elderly people look forward to retirement from work, others do not. Retirees often face financial problems (one person in eight who is sixty-five or older lives in poverty) and/or difficulties adjusting to the loss of a work role and job-related friendships. Forced retirement of workers in their sixties, despite its often negative impact, has been common.

During the 1970s America's "senior citizens" (whose presence is increasingly noticeable because of changes in the age composition of the population) became politically active. Their grassroots organizing has been felt at the national level on such issues as mandatory retirement. In 1978 Congress passed legislation that removed the mandatory retirement age from most federal jobs and placed it at seventy years of age for most jobs in the private sector. This action was intended to provide some protection for those who otherwise would automatically be pushed out of work in their early or mid-sixties.

The Impact of Unemployment

Individuals who find themselves involuntarily unemployed often discover that their lives and the lives of their families have changed for the worse. For example, Michael Aiken and his associates conducted a study of automobile workers who lost their jobs when their plant was permanently shut down.[22] As their financial resources became depleted, many of the unemployed workers withdrew from contact with friends and relatives because they could not afford to return social favors and obligations. Thus, the unemployed avoided the very persons whose contacts might have been useful in finding new work. Beyond this, the unemployed workers were unhappy over the loss of on-the-job friendships that had helped give meaning to their everyday lives. Not only did they feel a sense of social isolation, but the loss of a work role made them doubt whether they were useful to society. Work was no longer providing personal identity and a sense of social worth. The unemployed had to depend on other family members to bear wage-earning responsibilities, frequently resulting in serious tensions in the home. The economic deprivation stemming from unemployment led many of the persons studied to agree that:

> You sometimes can't help wondering whether life is worth living anymore.
>
> These days I get a feeling that I'm just not a part of things.
>
> No one is going to care much about what happens to you when you get right down to it.[23]

In *Rusted Dreams,* David Bensman and Roberta Lynch explore some of the human dilemmas and tragedies attributed to the decline of the steel industry.[24] This is one of several industries in which large numbers of jobs have simply vanished in the deindustrialization process. Bensman and Lynch show how the unemployment statistics mask these kinds of realities:

> Skilled workers no one will hire even for unskilled positions because they are thought to be overqualified, too old (even if in their fifties), or judged likely to leave for other jobs;
>
> People whose health insurance was in effect only so long as they were employed, now pleading with or even lying about their insurance status to doctors and hospitals in order to receive medical treatment;
>
> Workers who have no source of income to support their families and whose unemployment compensation has run out, now finding they are ineligible for welfare or food stamps because they own a car or a home;
>
> The offspring and spouses of the unemployed who find themselves victimized by

[22] Michael Aiken et al., *Economic Failure, Alienation, and Extremism* (Ann Arbor: The University of Michigan Press, 1968).

[23] Ibid., p. 67

[24] David Bensman and Roberta Lynch, *Rusted Dreams* (New York: McGraw-Hill Book Company, 1987), Chapter 4.

violence and abuse in the home, as the worker vents his or her frustration and anger (often exacerbated by alcohol and other drugs);

The children of workers without jobs who engage in juvenile crime out of a sense of aimlessness and hopelessness generated by a deteriorating family situation;

The women whose job loss sends their families into economic spirals and those whose husbands are out of work, can no longer deal with marriage, and opt for divorce or simply abandonment of their families;

The workers who give up all hope: "I used to work with the kid. After the mill closed he was about to lose his home. He took a gun to his head and blew his brains out."[25]

The stress, anxiety, tension, and depression found among the jobless testify to the central role work plays for people in this society.[26]

Nor are the distresses associated with unemployment found only among blue-collar workers. A study of white-collar professionals—including engineers, scientists, and technicians—produced similar findings.[27] The unemployed professionals tended to go through several stages, according to researchers Douglas H. Powell and Paul F. Driscoll. Most of the professionals had been anticipating being laid off as they followed the problems being faced by their employers. So their first feeling was relief when the expected occurred. Given their educational credentials and long employment experience in responsible positions, the professionals were confident about finding new work. They tended to put off looking for a position right away; they wanted to enjoy their newly discovered freedom for a while. Family life, in this initial stage, remained normal.

In the second stage the unemployed professionals began to tire of full-time leisure and to get concerned about not having a job. At this point, they launched highly organized efforts to find work. Economic deprivation had not yet been a problem, as most had savings and other resources to carry them along. Family and friends offered encouragement, and the confidence level of the unemployed was high.

For those whose job-seeking efforts yielded no concrete results, the third stage was characterized by doubt and depression. Their psychological moods interfered with the job search, and relationships with friends and family began to fall apart. The jobless professionals, like their blue-collar counterparts, began to doubt their worth. Confronting feelings of obsolescence, they became alternately frustrated, furious, and filled with despair. Family relations were at their lowest ebb. It was in this stage that suicides were most likely to occur.

In the fourth and final stage, malaise and cynicism set in among the jobless. Job-seeking efforts slowed down to a cursory level, and anxieties decreased as the professionals settled unhappily into their assigned roles. Family relations improved with the recognition of an extremely difficult situation. In the words of researchers Powell and Driscoll:

> The image of competent and energetic men reduced to listless discouragement highlights the personal tragedy and the loss of valuable resources when there is substantial unemployment.... Perhaps more significantly, the situation of these middle-class unemployed further dramatizes the plight of the larger numbers of unemployed nonskilled workers whose fate is to deal with unemployment often during their lifetime.[28]

---

[25] Ibid., p. 98.

[26] See also Terry F. Buss and F. Stevens Redburn, *Shutdown at Youngstown* (Albany: State University of New York Press, 1983), Chapter 3.

[27] Douglas H. Powell and Paul F. Driscoll, "Middle Class Professionals Face Unemployment," *Society*, 10 (January/February 1973): 18–26.

[28] Ibid., p. 26.

For workers who fall into the unskilled category, unemployment simply makes the already difficult challenge of supporting a family that much more difficult. Unskilled workers feel worthless and doubt themselves even when they are employed. In his classic study, *Tally's Corner*, social anthropologist Elliot Liebow examined the lives of a group of men who lived in a poor neighborhood in Washington, D.C. The men were either unemployed or were construction workers, day laborers, and menial workers in retail and service establishments. Given their position in the occupational structure, all these men had experienced and/or could realistically look forward to bouts with joblessness. Marriages regularly broke down, and some men were reluctant to embark on permanent marital relationships because of their precarious economic situations. According to Liebow: "The way in which the man makes a living and the kind of living he makes have important consequences for how the man sees himself and is seen by others."[29] In their search for some source of pride and self-esteem—since neither work nor home provided these—the men turned to one another, hung around on street corners, and tried to forget their economic, social, and personal sense of failure.

Researcher M. Harvey Brenner is among those who have examined the relationship between rising unemployment rates and various social costs.[30] Brenner's work indicates that as unemployment rises, there are sharp increases in a variety of problem areas. Summarizing some of Brenner's conclusions, Barry Bluestone and Benjamin Harrison note:

> [A] one percent increase in the aggregate unemployment rate sustained over a period of six years has been associated with approximately:
> —37,000 total deaths (including 20,000 cardiovascular deaths)
> —920 suicides
> —650 homicides
> —500 deaths from cirrhosis of the liver
> —4,000 state mental hospital admissions
> —3,300 state prison admissions[31]

As research bearing on unemployment has proceeded, the focus has come to include family members of the unemployed, who are also victims. The stresses that are borne by spouses, children, and other members of the household are often extremely serious. Psychological and physical abuse may accompany more general family discord, leading to family breakup.[32] By and large, social service providers, unions, and companies are ill prepared to be of help as these kinds of difficulties arise in so many households.

JOB SATISFACTION

If asked, each of us could probably come up with a list of attributes to be found in the ideal job. What kinds of things are most important to working people today? The most comprehensive attempt to answer this question is a series of University of Michigan studies conducted since 1969.[33] As a part of their research, the investigators conducted lengthy interviews with a carefully selected sample of employed persons. Those interviewed said that the following things were important in a job: work that is

---

[29] Elliot Liebow, *Tally's Corner* (Boston: Little, Brown & Company, 1967), p. 210.

[30] See M. Harvey Brenner, *Mental Illness and the Economy* (Cambridge, Mass.: Harvard University Press, 1973); *Estimating the Social Costs of National Economic Policy*, Report Prepared for the Joint Economic Committee of Congress (Washington, D.C.: U.S. Government Printing Office, 1976); and "Personal Stability and Economic Security," *Social Policy*, 8 (May/June 1977): 2–4.

[31] Bluestone and Harrison, *The Deindustrialization of America*, p. 65.

[32] For a selected overview of research, see Ramsey Liem and Paula Rayman. "Health and Social Costs of Unemployment," *American Psychologist*, 37 (October 1982): 1116–23.

[33] See Graham L. Staines and Robert P. Quinn, "American Workers Evaluate the Quality of Their Jobs," *Monthly Labor Review*, 102 (January 1979); 3–12. Also see Robert P. Quinn and Graham L. Staines, *The 1977 Quality of Employment Survey* (Ann Arbor: University of Michigan, Institute for Social Research, 1979).

interesting; enough help, equipment, information, and authority to get the job done: an opportunity to develop one's special abilities; the opportunity to see the results of one's work; good pay; and job security. In other words, the content of the job, the resources to do it well, and a chance to realize one's talents were of as much importance as the pay.

If these are the things working people consider important, how satisfied are members of the work force with the jobs they hold? The concept of *job satisfaction* is extremely difficult to measure. Most experts agree that efforts to measure satisfaction and dissatisfaction have been primitive. Thus we must consider any findings as indicative, rather than final and firm.

In some studies workers have simply been asked if their work is satisfying. Over the years, public polling firms such as Gallup have asked this question, and anywhere from 80 to 90 percent of those responding have expressed satisfaction. It is difficult to discern any trends. Critics of such polls assert that this approach does not probe deeply enough into worker attitudes. There is a possibility that most workers answer positively because they have become resigned to their fate. Such criticisms have been lent credence by the University of Michigan's Quality of Employment Surveys. When the Michigan researchers have probed, many of the respondents who claimed to be satisfied admitted to definite complaints about particular aspects of their jobs—for example, their inability to influence supervisors' decisions and to get responses to suggestions on how their work might be better performed.[34]

Another way of measuring job satisfaction has been to ask questions about workers' desire to change jobs. In the Michigan surveys, employees interviewed were asked, "Taking everything into account, how likely is it that you will make a genuine effort to find a new job with another employer within the next year?" In response, a *third* of those asked said that it was likely.[35]

In a slightly different approach, workers have been asked about job choice. In one such study, 93 percent of urban university professors and 83 percent of lawyers said they would choose similar jobs again. Among nonprofessional white-collar workers, the proportion was only 43 percent, indicating a sharp difference in job satisfaction within the white-collar category. Among blue-collar workers, the overall percentage of those who would choose similar work again dropped down to a mere 24 percent.[36] When half to three-quarters of the persons holding a particular type of job express such opinions, it seems fair to say they are dissatisfied.

In general, the data on job satisfaction indicate that the higher the social status of a job, the more satisfied are those who hold it. The status continuum of occupations and professions tends to be correlated with the monetary rewards associated with different categories of work. But just as important, the ranking of jobs in terms of satisfaction appears to fit with the probable presence or absence of those things workers feel are important about a job. The jobs of nonprofessional white-collar workers and blue-collar workers, unlike those of many professionals, are unlikely to be intrinsically interesting or to allow for the development of talents. Other items that workers see as important—from enough resources to get the job done well to job security—are also likely to be associated with the higher status, better paying professional positions.

Survey findings also suggest that racial minorities and women are extremely dissatisfied with their work situations. This is to be ex-

[34] Staines and Quinn, "American Workers Evaluate the Quality of Their Jobs," p. 7.

[35] Ibid.

[36] Robert L. Kahn, "The Work Module," in *Work and the Quality of Life*, James O'Toole, ed. (Cambridge, Mass.: The M.I.T. Press, 1974), pp. 203–4.

pected, given the overrepresentation of such groups in nonprofessional white-collar and blue-collar jobs and the barriers they face in advancement. And, finally, young workers seem to be dissatisfied with much greater frequency than their elders. There is "a significant gap between the expectations or values of young workers and what they actually experience on the job."[37] Since about a quarter of the labor force is under thirty years of age, the failure of work to live up to the expectations of youthful workers is by no means a minor problem.

According to a federal task force report, job dissatisfaction reveals itself in a number of ways. The productivity of many workers is lower than it should be. In many sectors of the economy, worker absenteeism rates are extremely high, as is annual turnover of employees. Periodically, groups of workers stage wildcat strikes, simply walking off the job on the spur of the moment. Sabotage occurs, with the production of poor-quality products as one result. The task force detected "a reluctance by workers to commit themselves to their work tasks" and suggested that job dissatisfaction is on the increase in the United States.[38] Although the limitations of existing empirical data make it impossible to know whether dissatisfaction is increasing, it is clear that work today is not meeting the economic, social, and personal needs of a substantial proportion of the labor force.

The Blue-Collar Worker

If we were to distinguish between "brain jobs" and "brawn jobs," blue-collar workers would be found performing most of the latter.[39] Blue-collar jobs, held by fewer than 30 million workers, encompass a wide variety of skills and skill levels. The unskilled worker is usually employed in a job for which the training requirements are negligible. The required work tasks are so repetitive and routine that they can be learned in a very short time. By contrast, skilled blue-collar work often demands extensive training, ordinarily carried out during a period of apprenticeship. Obviously, the difference between the skill requirements for assembly-line work and cabinet-making is extreme.

In the last fifty years, employment opportunities for the unskilled have steadily diminished. Today only 10 percent of the blue-collar work force is unskilled. Most blue-collar workers hold either skilled or semiskilled jobs, with about 45 percent falling into each of these categories. Such semiskilled jobs as truck driver, machine tender, and short-order cook require relatively commonplace talents but more mental effort than unskilled labor.

Unskilled workers, as we have already noted, are most vulnerable to unemployment and low, often poverty-level, wages. The semiskilled tend to be slightly better off in terms of income, but they still have little job security. The persons who perform semiskilled work are easily interchangeable. Skilled workers are best off economically. However, they are concerned with protecting the rewards that flow from holding a monopoly over a given trade. In times of economic recession, as in the 1970s and 1980s, even skilled workers confront the issue of job security. The fact that skilled workers are more likely to hold union membership than the other two groups is no guarantee against periodic layoffs.

Despite the differences noted, virtually all

---

[37] *Work in America*, p. 37.

[38] Ibid., p. xi. The University of Michigan Surveys confirm this. But see the critique of this position in Anthony F. Chelte, James Wright, and Curt Tausky, "Did Job Satisfaction Really Drop During the 1970's?," *Monthly Labor Review*, 105 (November 1982): 33–36.

[39] The "brain" versus "brawn" distinction is made in Andrew Levison, *The Working-Class Majority* (New York: Coward, McCann & Geoghegan, 1974). Levison feels that many nonprofessional white-collar and service jobs are essentially of the "brawn" variety. He argues that most members of the labor force—not just blue-collar workers—work primarily with their hands, not their heads.

blue-collar workers suffer from low social status. This is reflected in, and no doubt reinforced by, the treatment accorded blue-collar workers in the mass media. Their activities are rarely considered worthy of news reporters' attention, except when there are strikes, layoffs, or serious accidents. With a few ethnic and regional exceptions, blue-collar workers are not commonly the subject of popular music. Television programs have tended to mock "brawn" workers, portraying them as stupid, closed minded, bigoted, chauvinistic, and politically conservative—erroneous stereotypes rarely applied to white-collar workers. Federal task force interviews with blue-collar workers have

> revealed an almost overwhelming sense of inferiority: the worker cannot talk proudly to his children about his job, and many workers feel they must apologize for their status. Thus the working-class home may be permeated with an atmosphere of failure—even of depressing self-degradation.[40]

Blue-collar work is also physically punitive and often dangerous.[41] Each year almost as many persons die in industrial accidents as were being killed at the height of the Vietnam conflict. In 1986, for example, a U.S. Department of Labor study covering the health status of private sector workers revealed 3,600 work-related fatalities occurred that year. Another 5.6 million workers suffered occupational injuries and illnesses in 1986. The rate of injury and illness was 10.6 per 100 full-time workers in manufacturing, compared to 7.9 per 100 for the total private sector.[42]

Whereas the war in Vietnam called forth protest against human carnage, the daily toll among blue-collar workers generates no such concern. "Brawn" workers are constantly exposed to the possibility of permanent physical impairment and temporary total disability through on-the-job injuries. Occupational diseases—involving everything from respiratory problems to cancer—plague members of the blue-collar sector. We have already noted that blue-collar workers have the highest rates of job dissatisfaction; evidence has begun to accumulate linking this to longevity—the physical and mental stresses at work actually reduce life expectancy.[43]

In recent years, politicians have characterized blue-collar workers as the "silent majority" and the "forgotten Americans." Research indicates a definite relationship between blue-collar status and political alienation. The sense of inferiority, social isolation, and economic insecurity of many blue-collar workers makes them ripe for exploitation by political demagogues who know how to channel the frustrations of blue-collar life into the voting booth, while leaving the objective sources of their discontent intact.[44]

The White-Collar Worker

At the turn of the century, the superior wages, social status, and working conditions accorded white-collar workers clearly distinguished them from manual workers. At that time, only 18 percent of the labor force could be counted as white-collar workers. Today the figure is closer to 54 percent. With this growth in the proportion of workers wearing white collars, the sharpness of the distinction between white- and blue-collar work has faded. Particularly affected have been sales and clerical workers. Today there are about

---

[40] *Work in America*, p. 29. See also Richard Sennett and Jonathan Cobb, *The Hidden Injuries of Class* (New York: Vintage Books, 1972).

[41] See, for example, Paul Brodeur, *Expendable Americans* (New York: Viking Press, 1974), and Daniel Berman, *Death on the Job* (New York: Monthly Review Press, 1978).

[42] Martin E. Personick and Katharine Taylor-Shirley, "Profiles in Safety and Health," *Monthly Labor Review*, 112 (January 1989): 3.

[43] *Work in America*, p. 62.

[44] Aiken et al., *Economic Failure, Alienation, and Extremism*. See also Harold L. Sheppard and Neal Herrick, *Where Have All the Robots Gone?* (New York: The Free Press, 1972).

PUBLIC PROBLEM, PRIVATE PAIN

Working

Author Studs Terkel has been widely hailed for his many interviews with "average" people. In this excerpt from his classic book Working, *a woman describes her dissatisfaction with the position she holds, that of technical writer. Her words remind us that even people holding "high-level" jobs today have difficulty drawing meaning from them.*

Jobs are not big enough for people. It's not just the assembly line worker whose job is too small for his spirit, you know? A job like mine, if you really put your spirit into it, you would sabotage immediately. You don't dare. So you absent your spirit from it. My mind has been so divorced from my job, except as a source of income, it's really absurd.

As I work in the business world, I am more and more shocked. You throw yourself into things because you feel that important questions—self-discipline, goals, a meaning of your life—are carried out in your *work*. You invest a job with a lot of values that the society doesn't allow you to put into a job. You find yourself like a pacemaker that's gone crazy or something. You want it to be a million things that it's not and you want to give it a million parts of yourself that nobody else wants there. So you end up wrecking the curve or else settling down and conforming. I'm really in a funny place right now. I'm so calm about what I'm doing and what's coming...

I paper the walls of my office with posters and bring in flowers, bring in an FM radio, bring down my favorite ceramic lamp. I'm the only person in the whole damn building with a desk facing the window instead of the door. I just turn myself around from all that I can. I ration my time so that I'll spend two hours working for the Institution and the rest of the time I'll browse. (Laughs.)

I function better if they leave me alone more. My boss will come in and say, "I know you're overloaded, but would you mind getting this done, it's urgent. I need it in three weeks." I can do it in two hours. So I put it on the back burner and produce it on time. When I first went there, I came in early and stayed late. I read everything I could on the subject at hand. I would work a project to the wall and get it really done right, and then ask for more. I found out I was wrecking the curve, I was out of line.

The people, just as capable as I and just as ready to produce, had realized it was pointless, and had cut back. Everyone, consciously or unconsciously, was rationing his time. Playing cards at lunch time for three hours, going sun bathing, or less obvious ways of blowing it. I realized: Okay, the road to ruin is doing a good job. The amazing, absurd thing was that once I decided to stop doing a good job, people recognized a kind of authority in me. Now I'm just moving ahead like blazes.

I have my own office. I have a secretary. If I want a book case, I get a book case. If I want a file, I get a file. If I want to stay home, I stay home. If I want to go shopping, I go shopping. This is the first comfortable job I've ever had in my life and it is absolutely despicable.

I've been a waitress and done secretarial work. I knew, in those cases, I wasn't going to work at near capacity. It's one thing to work to your limits as a waitress because you end up with a bad back. It's another thing to work to your limits doing writing and editing because you end up with a sharper mind. It's a joy. Here, of all places, where I had expected to put the energy and enthusiasm and the gifts that I may have to work—it isn't happening. They expect less than you can offer. Token labor. What writing you do is writing to order. When I go for a job interview—I must leave this place!—I say, "Sure, I can bring you samples, but the ones I'm proud of are the ones the Institution never published."

It's so demeaning to be there and not be challenged. It's humiliation, because I feel I'm being forced into doing something I would never do of my own free will—which is simply waste itself. It's really not a Puritan hang-up. It's not that I want to be persecuted. It's simply that I know I'm vegetating and being paid to do exactly that. It's possible for me to sit here and read my books. But then you walk out with no sense of satisfaction, with no sense of legitimacy! I'm being had. Somebody has bought the right to you for eight hours a day. The manner in which they use you is completely at their discretion. You know what I mean?

I feel like I'm being pimped for and it's not my style. The level of bitterness in this department is stunning. They take days off quite a bit. They don't show up. They don't even call in. They've adjusted a lot better than I have. They see the Institution as a free ride as long as it lasts. I don't want to be party to it, so I've gone my own way. It's like being on welfare. Not that that's a shameful thing. It's the surprise of this enforced idleness. It makes you feel not at home with yourself. I'm furious. It's a feeling that I will not be humiliated. I will not be dis-used.

For all that was bad about my father's vocation, he showed me it was possible to fuse your life to your work. His home was also his work. A parish is no different from an office, because it's the whole countryside. There's nothing I would enjoy more than a job that was so meaningful to me that I brought it home....

I'm coming to a less moralistic attitude toward work. I know very few people who feel secure with their right just to be—or comfortable. Just you being you and me being me with my mini-talents may be enough. Maybe just making a career of being and finding out what that's about is enough. I don't think I have a calling—at this moment—except to be me. But nobody pays you for being you, so I'm at the Institution—for the moment....

Source: From Studs Terkel, *Working: People Talk About What They Do All Day and How They Feel About What They Do*, pp. 521–524.

as many nonprofessional white-collar workers as there are professional, technical, and managerial personnel. White-collar nonprofessionals confront some, if not most, of the work-related difficulties under which blue-collar workers tend to suffer.[45]

Like the industrial workplace, large retail establishments and offices are typically highly bureaucratic. In offices, small armies of clerks, typists, secretaries, receptionists, and office assistants perform segmented work tasks under the constant supervision of higher ranking authorities. The same type of bureaucratic environment typically prevails in retail establishments. The social status attached to many nonprofessional jobs is low, and in some cases the wages are less than those accorded semiskilled blue-collar workers. It is for such reasons that job dissatisfaction is high among nonprofessionals, as indicated by the fact that less than half of those surveyed say they would choose similar work again.[46] In the last two decades, nonprofessionals have begun to make up an increasing percentage of the nation's union membership. (Only about 17 percent of all workers in America are union members, a figure well below that in most modern, industrialized societies. See Table 5.6.) Faced with low pay and factorylike working conditions, they are turning to the promises of relief and protection unions have long extended to blue-collar workers.

Nor is the world of work consistently rosy even for white-collar professionals, despite their generally high performance on measures of job satisfaction and their relatively high income and status and good working conditions. In libraries, public school systems, hospitals, colleges and universities, and social welfare agencies, as well as in law, architecture, and engineering firms, professionals are fighting to maintain

---

[45] The changing nature of white-collar work was observed by C. Wright Mills in *White Collar* (New York: Oxford University Press, 1951). See also Harry Braverman, *Labor and Monopoly Capital* (New York: Monthly Review Press, 1974), pp. 293–373.

[46] Kahn, "The Work Module," pp. 203–4.

In offices across the nation computerized word-processing has become commonplace. Supervisors are able to monitor the pace of workers' output through computerized reports, much like the foremen who keep disciplined watch over workers on a manufacturing assembly line. Workers who do not rise to supervisors' output quotas may be disciplined or fired. *(Ellis Herwig/The Picture Cube)*

their prerogatives and autonomy in the face of control by administrative authorities. Pay and the availability of resources have also become major issues. The institutions just mentioned are all client-oriented. Any increase in the number of clients without an attendant increase in professional staff and supportive services is akin to the assembly-line speedup industrial workers are continually battling. Slowly, members of the professional sector are beginning to suffer many of the same work-related problems as lower level workers. Groups of professionals—for example, teachers—have affiliated with organized labor and engaged in strikes in response.

Another white-collar group facing work difficulties is middle management, bureaucratic authorities who report to the top executives and oversee professional and technical employees as well as lower level supervisors. Middle managers now represent some 5 percent of the labor force, and the pressures and problems they confront are inevitably felt by those millions who labor below them. Members of this group have complaints about salaries, job insecurity, forced early retirement, limits to upward mobility, and heavy responsibilities that are combined with constraints on their authority from above.[47]

Sociologists have often restricted the term *working class* to refer only to blue-collar workers. Some sociologists have suggested that a "new working class" is in the making.[48] The erosion of white-collar privilege, the bureaucratization of virtually all white-collar work, job-related complaints that sound like those factory workers often voice, movements toward white-collar unionization—all suggest that virtually no part of the labor force is immune to job dissatisfaction.

Job Dissatisfaction and the Consumer Society

Members of the American labor force do more than produce something of value for other people in return for monetary rewards. Workers and their families are also consumers, a fact that must not be divorced from a discussion of the significance of work.

According to Paul Baran and Paul Sweezy, corporate advertisers are constantly "waging, on behalf of the producers and sellers of consumer goods, a relentless war against saving and in favor of consumption."[49] Psychologist Erich Fromm contends that they have been immensely successful:

> Modern man, if he dared to be articulate about his concept of heaven, would suggest a vision which would look like the biggest department store in the world. . . . He would wander open-mouthed in this heaven of gadgets and commodities, provided only that there were ever more and newer things to buy, and perhaps that his neighbors were just a little less privileged than he.[50]

Work provides the financial means—at least for most members of the labor force—of entering this visionary heaven here on earth.

One can speculate that spending money on consumer goods is one way dissatisfied workers can temporarily blot out and separate themselves from the lack of fulfillment provided by their jobs. For most members of the labor force, work is strictly segmented from leisure pursuits. A boring workday can be offset by the hours spent at home tinkering with tools, guns, and cars. In the after-work pursuit of crafts and hobbies, employees who are told what to do all day on the job are transformed into their own bosses. Here they can make up for the lack of opportunities to develop their special abilities, and here they can see the results of their own work. Status denied workers within a bureaucratic setting can be gained by the conspicuous consumption of commodities—from color televisions to camping trailers—that will be noticed and admired by others. Ironically, play, recreation, and leisure have themselves become commodities as corporate advertisers pitch their advertising campaigns to unfulfilled interests and needs.

The wages and salaries of millions of workers are not high enough to enable them to buy all the commodities they are encouraged to crave. Nevertheless, the producers and sellers

[47] Emanuel Kay, "Middle Management," in O'Toole, ed., *Work and the Quality of Life,* pp. 106–26.

[48] See Bertram Silverman and Murray Yanowitch, eds., *The Worker in "Post-Industrial" Capitalism* (New York: The Free Press, 1974), Chapter 4.

[49] Paul A. Baran and Paul M. Sweezy, *Monopoly Capital* (New York: Monthly Review Press, 1969), p. 128.

[50] Erich Fromm, *The Sane Society* (Greenwich, Conn.: Fawcett Publications, 1955), p. 123. See also Stuart Ewen, *Captains of Consciousness* (New York: McGraw-Hill Book Company, 1976), and Stuart Ewen and Elizabeth Ewen, *Channels of Desire* (New York: McGraw-Hill Book Company, 1982).

TABLE 5.6 Union Members, by Selected Characteristics: 1987 (in thousands)

Characteristic	Employed wage and salary workers					Median usual weekly earnings‡ (dollars)			
	Total	Union members*	Represented by unions†	Percent union members	Percent represented by union	Total	Union members*	Represented by unions†	Not represented by unions
Total	**99,303**	**16,913**	**19,051**	**17.0**	**19.2**	**373**	**465**	**459**	**342**
16–24 years	19,553	1,299	1,538	6.6	7.9	242	318	312	235
25–34 years	30,197	4,752	5,436	15.7	18.0	373	436	430	354
35–44 years	23,443	5,080	5,664	21.7	24.2	435	493	490	409
45–54 years	14,718	3,442	3,821	23.4	26.0	429	492	492	400
55–64 years	9,349	2,142	2,367	22.9	25.3	405	462	463	381
65 years and over	2,042	198	224	9.7	11.0	310	404	406	283
Men	52,938	11,071	12,144	20.9	22.9	433	494	493	406
Women	46,365	5,842	6,907	12.6	14.9	303	388	385	288
White	85,525	13,972	15,712	16.3	18.4	383	477	474	355
Men	46,079	9,407	10,288	20.4	22.3	450	501	500	419
Women	39,446	4,565	5,424	11.6	13.8	307	394	392	293
Black	10,838	2,445	2,769	22.6	25.5	301	399	395	268
Men	5,329	1,381	1,531	25.9	28.7	326	423	420	288
Women	5,509	1,065	1,238	19.3	22.5	275	357	355	251
Hispanic§	7,215	1,234	1,371	17.1	19.0	284	395	392	261
Men	4,315	859	938	19.9	21.7	306	418	417	276
Women	2,900	374	434	12.9	15.0	251	311	311	239
Full-time workers	80,836	15,670	17,567	19.4	21.7	373	465	459	342
Part-time workers	18,467	1,243	1,484	6.7	8.0	(x)	(x)	(x)	(x)
Managerial and professional specialty	23,378	3,512	4,286	15.0	18.3	522	521	519	523
Technical, sales, and administrative support	31,801	3,265	3,868	10.3	12.2	332	413	407	319

TABLE 5.6 Union Members, by Selected Characteristics: 1987 (in thousands) *(Continued)*

Characteristic	Employed wage and salary workers					Median usual weekly earnings‡ (dollars)			
	Total	Union members*	Represented by unions†	Percent union members	Percent represented by union	Total	Union members*	Represented by unions†	Not represented by unions
Service occupations	13,876	1,953	2,187	14.1	15.8	234	375	370	209
Precision, production, craft, and repair	11,567	3,132	3,364	27.1	29.1	419	521	517	378
Operators, fabricators, and laborers	16,920	4,956	5,234	20.0	30.9	308	420	416	268
Farming, forestry, and fishing	1,763	96	113	5.4	6.4	217	373	369	210
Agricultural wage and salary workers	1,469	33	37	2.2	2.5	219	(B)	(B)	217
Private nonagricultural wage and salary workers	80,993	10,826	11,850	13.4	14.6	362	458	452	339
Mining	782	143	153	18.3	19.5	514	532	528	506
Construction	5,052	1,060	1,123	21.0	22.2	397	594	585	351
Manufacturing	20,235	4,691	5,008	23.2	24.7	389	426	424	370
Transportation and public utilities	5,819	1,947	2,106	33.5	36.2	482	519	516	432
Wholesale and retail trade, total	20,401	1,440	1,572	7.1	7.7	292	397	394	285
Finance, insurance, and real estate	6,738	158	217	2.3	3.2	373	363	369	373
Services	21,965	1,387	1,673	6.3	7.6	327	375	375	322
Government	16,841	6,055	7,164	36.0	42.5	424	475	470	388

[Annual averages of monthly data. Covers employed wage and salary workers sixteen years old and over. Excludes self-employed workers whose businesses are incorporated although they technically qualify as wage and salary workers. Based on Current Population Survey.]

Key: B, data not shown where base is less than 50,000. NA, not available. X, not applicable.

*Members of a labor union or an employee association similar to labor union.

†Members of a labor union or an employee association similar to a union as well as workers who report no union affiliation but whose jobs are covered by a union or an employee association contract.

‡For full-time employed wage and salary workers.

§Hispanic persons may be of any race.

Source: U.S. Department of Commerce, Bureau of the Census, *Statistical Abstract of the United States, 1989* (Washington, D.C.: U.S. Government Printing Office, 1989), p 416.

of consumer products must unload their goods on a regular basis if they are to realize profit goals. Thus, credit has been extended to virtually anyone holding a job. By going into debt—that is, by taking out loans or buying on the installment plan—members of the labor force are able to buy and consume well beyond their immediate means. Producers and sellers prosper. Indeed, easy credit actually means more jobs for workers. But members of the labor force, in order to pay off debts and maintain a credit rating that will allow more debt in the future, must continue to labor. The extension of consumer credit carries with it the subtle effect of forcing workers to the job—even if the job is highly unsatisfying. Workers who would like to quit, to rebel against their bureaucratic superiors, or to take a more satisfying job that pays less must weigh such moves against their debts. Ironically, it would actually harm workers to reject the consumer society, the way the economy is now organized. To reject debt and commodities would not only limit the outlets currently available to the dissatisfied; it would throw millions more people out of work.

CONTROLLING PEOPLE/CONTROLLING WORK

In the realm of paid labor, people today are forced to function somewhat like objects—subject to economic forces, institutional constraints, and the will of bureaucratic superiors. Becoming employed or unemployed more and more happens *to* people; they have little control over it. Pay, rank, and working conditions are set *for* employees, not by them. Job dissatisfaction is a result of events and conditions that impinge *upon* workers and that cannot easily be altered or escaped.

Work and Other Macro Problems

Many of the macro problems we have or will consider simultaneously express themselves in the world of work. With the exception of the very rich, for whom property ownership is the major source of income, the economic well-being of most Americans depends on the marketing of their labor. The income inequalities that prevail in this society and that help determine people's life chances reflect existing employment opportunities.

Political decisions at the national level have a direct impact on unemployment, wages, and prices. To the degree political power is concentrated in the hands of a few, decisions in these areas will be made *for* working people rather than by them. The erosion of political democracy is being replicated at the workplace, where many people perform dissatisfying labor within the confines of bureaucratic control from above.

Institutional racism and sexism, coupled with inequalities in educational opportunity, arbitrarily disqualify millions who are basically capable of filling positions toward the top of the job hierarchy. Since work is linked to one's sense of self-worth, subordination based on race, sex, or performance in class-biased educational systems creates millions of unhappy, unfulfilled people. They are joined by the aged in their sense of human obsolescence.

The notion of work as an activity that produces something of value for other people is perverted by the dependence of many workers on the "economy of death." While billions of dollars are allocated to upgrade the production of military-related goods, dangerous and disease-producing conditions persist in the underdeveloped, civilian economy. In both the civilian and military sectors, products are developed and by-products discarded that pose an immense threat to the surrounding environment and to people.

To improve the world of work, we would want to alter unemployment, job dissatisfaction, the stark relationship between work status and life chances, barriers to the full utilization of human talent, and production that leads to the destruction of life, rather than its enhancement.

In our concern with work, we are simultaneously confronted with the challenge of dealing with all the macro problems considered in this book.

Improving the Nature of Work

There is a critical need to revise the official definition of *unemployment* so that it reflects more accurately the extent to which our economy fails to provide sufficient work opportunities. Approaches to unemployment that focus only on reducing the official defined rate ignore the work needs of millions.

There is a need for centralized coordination and control over the introduction of new technologies that displace workers and eliminate jobs. Such coordination and control might be handled through the federal chartering of business firms (see page 148 for a discussion of federal chartering). Or it might be handled by a board responsible for national industrial policy and planning.

There is also a need for control over the degree to which business and industry are permitted to invest money outside this country or to move productive activities elsewhere. The profit benefits of such activities may well be offset by the human and social welfare costs of domestic unemployment. This tradeoff needs to be investigated.

Given the paucity of work opportunities for all who want and need them, federal and state governments should be willing to serve as "employers of last resort." If government is unable to fully stimulate the private sector into providing sufficient work for people to do, it should find ways to organize and allocate its own resources to pick up the slack. Most Americans support this notion today. Likewise, training and retraining (for mis-skilled and/or displaced workers) fall far short of what might be done. As new jobs are created and old ones disappear, workers must be assisted in making transitions, not left to flounder and forced into downward mobility.

It is time to move beyond the assumption that putting all members of the labor force in a job is sufficient in and of itself. Work conditions themselves are in need of drastic change. There are many possibilities here, including federal incentives for business firms to develop comprehensive programs of worker participation and control. What is needed is increased worker involvement in planning and decision making and decreased hierarchy and bureaucratic control from above. Some firms are taking such steps now.

It is also time to begin breaking up concentrated ownership within the private sector, spreading it more widely among the producers of corporate wealth. Federal chartering of business firms, alluded to earlier, might be used to help workers buy some of the firms to which they contribute their labor. This would be another way of democratizing the workplace.

As we saw in Chapter 2, "Concentration of Political and Economic Power," the interests of elites may run counter to change that is in the general interest. Pressure for change must come from organized labor, the unemployed, and all men and women who want to leave their children a better world in which to labor.

SUMMARY

Work, an activity that produces something of value for other people, is central to our everyday lives. We are encouraged to pursue the American Dream of material affluence through work. Work helps determine our class position and life-style, and the jobs we do may affect how others treat us. Finally, work is an important source of self-esteem and self-identity.

The world of work has been changing as a result of three historical trends. The United States has moved from an agricultural society to one in which manufacturing and, more recently, the provision of services occupy most workers. The "deindustrialization" of America is under way. Most members of the labor force were self-employed 200 years ago; few are today. And workers have increasingly become part of large-scale organizations in which they are subject to bureaucratic authority and control.

Our labor force totals over 100 million people, yet millions are unemployed. Government unemployment statistics, critics charge, underestimate the true extent of joblessness. Various factors underlie unemployment. These include automation and technological changes that displace workers; the movement of corporate plants abroad or out of urban areas in which the need for jobs is great; government taxation and spending policies that affect consumer and corporate activities; and patterns of discrimination that affect who is jobless on the basis of race, sex, and age. The impact of unemployment on many of those affected is highly negative—whether we are talking about white-collar professionals or unskilled, blue-collar workers.

When asked what is important to them in work, people generally mention the content of the job, the resources to do it well, and a chance to realize their talents. These are as important as pay. There are signs that numerous workers are dissatisfied with the jobs they hold (e.g., they would prefer different jobs). Dissatisfaction is greatest among blue-collar workers, followed by white-collar nonprofessionals. White-collar professionals show the least dissatisfaction. The ranking of jobs in terms of satisfaction appears to reflect the presence or absence of those things workers feel are important to them in work. Dissatisfaction is reflected in lowered productivity, high absenteeism and turnover rates, wildcat strikes, and sabotage.

Blue-collar workers perform most of the "brawn jobs," as opposed to the "brain jobs." Wages and job security vary, depending on a worker's skill level. But blue-collar workers in general suffer from low social status. Their work is physically punitive and often dangerous.

White-collar nonprofessionals confront many similar work-related difficulties. They often labor in a setting that is as bureaucratic as the industrial workplace. The social status of many nonprofessional jobs is low, as are wages. White-collar professionals express the most job satisfaction, yet even they face difficulties. In many instances, professionals must fight to maintain their prerogatives and autonomy in the face of control by administrative authorities.

American society emphasizes consumption, and this may be one way that dissatisfied workers can blot out and separate themselves from the lack of fulfillment provided by their jobs. Consumption means that many must go into debt through the use of credit and loans. Such debt carries with it the subtle effect of forcing workers to the job—even if the job is highly unsatisfying.

The world of work is linked to many of the problems considered in this book, and in altering work we are confronted with the challenge of dealing with those problems. Among the steps to be taken to improve the nature of work are revising the official definition of unemployment to make statistics on joblessness more accurate; coordinating and controlling new technologies that displace workers and eliminate jobs; limiting corporate investments overseas that create more domestic unemployment; using federal and state governments as employers of last resort; expanding training and retraining opportunities; expanding worker participation in planning and decision making; and promoting increased worker ownership of the firms to which they contribute their labor.

DISCUSSION QUESTIONS

1. With all the work that needs to be done in this society, how is it that millions of people do not have jobs? Who or what is responsible for their joblessness?

2. Would you rather be self-employed or an employee? Justify your choice. Which are you most likely to be in the future? Why?
3. Think about the work activity for which you most recently received wages or salary. Would you care to perform this work on a permanent basis? Why?
4. If your financial security were guaranteed, would you still want to be a part of the work force? Why?
5. Most of us agree that some positions in the world of work are far less desirable than others. What arguments could be made for and against dramatically increasing the pay and benefits associated with the least desirable jobs?
6. What do you see as the advantages and disadvantages of increased worker participation in planning and decision making in the organizations where they work? Who or what are the obstacles to such increased participation?

SUGGESTED READINGS

Bluestone, Barry, and Bennett Harrison. *The Deindustrialization of America* (New York: Basic Books, 1982).
Classic work that drew attention to the erosion of the U.S. industrial base and its impact on local communities.

Eitzen, D. Stanley, and Maxine Baca Zinn, eds. *The Reshaping of America* (Englewood Cliffs, N.J.: Prentice-Hall, 1989).
Overview of technological and economic changes sweeping the United States and their consequences for work and nonwork life.

Garson, Barbara. *All the Livelong Day* (New York: Penguin Books, 1980).
Case studies and personal statements on the demeaning nature of much routine work.

Hearn, Frank, ed. *The Transformation of Industrial Organization* (Belmont, Calif.: Wadsworth, 1988).
Readings tracing America's industrial origins to present-day changes toward a service economy facing unprecedented world competition.

Laff, Walli F., and Marilyn G. Haft. *Time Without Work* (Boston: South End Press, 1983).
The personal impact of unemployment poignantly portrayed.

Shaiken, Harley. *Work Transformed: Automation and Labor in the Computer Age* (New York: Holt, Rinehart & Winston, 1984).
The extraordinary impact computers and microelectronics are having in the workplace and implications for the future.

CHAPTER 6

Economic Inequality and Poverty

Gross differences in personal wealth and income should be greatly reduced, so that the life chances of all Americans are relatively equal and so that all share more equitably in the goods and services being produced.

In the past decade tens of millions of American men, women, and children have experienced economic insecurity, deprivation, and stress at a level not seen in many years. Largely because of unemployment, changes in the occupational structure, and an increase in female-headed families, rates of poverty have risen to where they were in the 1960s, when the situation was considered very severe. Early in that decade the federal government declared a "War on Poverty." Clearly, the war has not been won. Yet many of us may feel that poverty does not really affect us, and we may find it hard to identify with the people it does affect. At least part of our complacence stems from the knowledge that we are members of one of the most affluent societies in the world. America's material abundance stands in stark contrast to the scarcity experienced by most of the world's peoples. And our sense of national well-being is reinforced

It is estimated that 2 to 3 million Americans lack homes. Not only individuals, but increasingly families are among the homeless. This family found itself living for months in a school bus before being fortunate enough to find a home; for many others the shortage of affordable housing poses an overwhelming obstacle. *(David Wells/The Image Works)*

and supported in many ways. Political leaders periodically conjure up visions of our society's historical progress and international economic leadership. Economic problems are usually portrayed as temporary situations that can be righted. Our gross national product, one measure of our nation's economic vitality and growth, is measured in the trillions of dollars. Stores and shops are filled with an amazing array of items awaiting consumption. Time- and labor-saving devices for the home and workshop abound. Indeed, we cannot flip through a magazine or newspaper without being reminded of the wide diversity of goods and services available for our use and enjoyment.

Yet while our society enjoys tremendous productive capacity, not all share equally in the goods and services produced. The poor and near-poor—nearly one in five Americans in 1988—receive very little at all.[1] While many suffer economic deprivation quietly, virtually invisible to more affluent citizens, the most desperate have grown noticeable in their numbers and needs.

Thus, in the 1980s we began to see more and more persons, including whole families, who had no permanent shelter. Their numbers are estimated at up to 3 million people nationwide.[2] Homeless persons and others of the nation's poverty-stricken population have also become

[1] U.S. Department of Commerce, Bureau of the Census, *Money Income and Poverty Status in the United States: 1988* (Washington, D.C.: U.S. Government Printing Office, 1989).

[2] Gwen Ifill, "Homelessness Takes Hold as National Issue," *Washington Post* (February 5, 1989): A1.

more visible as they desperately search for ways to cope with hunger.[3]

In this chapter we look at evidence of the greatly unequal distribution of wealth and income and the prevalence of poverty and near poverty in our society. As we shall see, gross economic inequality is an integral feature of American life. Such inequality is not in the process of disappearing, and its continuance poses consequences that each of us should be willing to confront.

THE REALITY OF ECONOMIC INEQUALITY

The economic status of an individual or a family is based on the possession of wealth and income. In this section we will examine data indicating that both wealth and income are disproportionately concentrated in the hands of a few. Moreover, we will see that minority group members are particularly disadvantaged in terms of sharing the wealth and income that are available.

Concentration of Wealth and Ownership

Any consideration of economic inequality in the United States must recognize that ours is basically a capitalist economy. The key institutions that comprise the economy—business and industry—are privately owned. Ownership of the largest, most economically significant businesses takes the form of shares of corporate stock. These shares increase or decrease in dollar value in rough accordance with the economic success and profitability of the corporation.

Corporate stock is, and has long been, one of the principal forms of wealth available to members of this society. Income is derived from stock ownership in two ways. First, the directors of the corporation may pay shareholders an annual dividend for each share held—a significant form of income for those who hold many shares. Second, owners of shares may buy and sell holdings in such a way as to realize substantial monetary gains. The distribution of stock ownership can tell us a lot about economic inequality in the United States.

Stock ownership is concentrated in the hands of an extremely small percentage of the population. In 1983 the University of Michigan Survey Research Center conducted a national survey of family wealth holdings for the Federal Reserve System. The findings (see Table 6.1) revealed that 19 percent of American families own shares of stock. But the most affluent 10 percent of families (ranked by income) have 72 percent of all the stock available to be owned. The most affluent 2 percent of America's families own *50 percent* of all family-owned stock! This minuscule *ownership class* of 2 percent of all families has legal possession of much of the American economy. The vast majority of Americans lack the surplus cash to lay out for the purchase of stock and thus own no shares at all. The ownership of a share of stock gives an individual a vote on corporate policy. This franchise is monopolized by a highly privileged few.

The concentration of stock ownership within what amounts to several hundred thousand households is not a new and unique phenomenon. Ownership has been concentrated for many decades. Stock is often passed from one generation to the next through gifts and inheritance. Intermarriage among members of the minuscule ownership class has also contributed to continued concentration of stock holdings by individuals and family groupings.[4]

Among the most significant members of the ownership class are the top managers and di-

[3] J. Larry Brown, "Hunger in the U.S.," *Scientific American,* 256 (February 1987): 37–41.

[4] See Ferdinand Lundberg, *The Rich and the Super-Rich* (New York: Bantam Books, 1969), for a revealing portrait of America's wealthy families and the means by which they enlarge their riches.

TABLE 6.1. Selected Characteristics of Asset Owners and Assets, by Type of Asset, 1983

Type of asset	Percent of all families owning	Median size of asset (dollars)	Median income of owners (dollars)	Median total financial assets of owners (dollars)	Percent held by selected families, ranked by income	
					Top 10 percent	Top 2 percent
Financial assets, total						
Liquid assets	88	2,850	21,600	3,501	51	30
Checking account	79	500	23,000	4,355	41	23
Savings account	62	1,151	23,580	4,839	26	8
Money market account	14	8,000	33,190	27,360	40	15
Certificates of deposit	20	10,000	26,000	26,750	33	15
IRA or Keogh account	17	4,000	38,170	20,961	48	17
Savings bonds	21	325	29,003	8,782	26	12
Other financial assets						
Stocks	19	4,016	33,438	22,626	72	50
Bonds	3	10,000	42,500	71,952	70	39
Nontaxable holdings*	3	14,125	52,575	115,250	86	71
Trust	4	10,000	32,128	25,395	46	34
Other assets						
Property	19	35,000	31,000	12,036	50	20
Business	14	50,000	32,138	11,300	78	33

*Municipal bonds and shares in certain mutual funds.
Source: "Survey of Consumer Finances, 1983," *Federal Reserve Bulletin*, 70 (September 1984): 689.

rectors of business and industry and their heirs. High-level executives not only receive large salaries, annual bonuses, expense accounts, and other benefits of rank, but they are also typically granted options to purchase stock in their own companies at attractive rates. The rationale behind granting stock options is that they provide an added incentive for executives to push for increased profitability, since this enhances the value of their own holdings.

Wealth other than corporate stock is also generally concentrated in the hands of a few—not surprisingly, the same richest 2 percent of families that control half of all family-owned stock. As Table 6.1 indicates, a disproportionate amount of all tax-exempt bonds, cash, trusts, real estate, and other property of major economic value is owned by 2 percent of the population. One consequence is that a small number of wealthy people—among whom are the directors and managers of our largest economic institutions—possess an inordinate degree of economic power. This economic power includes more than the ability to spend and consume; it also includes the ability to influence decisions that bear on the direction in which our society will go. (See Chapter 2.)

Thus far we have concentrated on the holdings of a small ownership class. What about the distribution of wealth within the American population as a whole? The University of Michigan survey, referred to previously, provides valuable insights into the net worth of America's families. Table 6.2 reveals that as family income goes up so does net worth. The 9 percent of families with the lowest incomes (less than $5,000) have a mean net worth of $12,051. In contrast, the 10 percent of families with the highest incomes ($50,000 and more) have a mean net worth of $262,254. As shown in Table 6.2,

TABLE 6.2. **Mean and Median Net Worth, by Selected Family Characteristics, 1983**

Characteristic	Percent of families	Net worth (dollars) Mean	Net worth (dollars) Median
Family income (dollars)			
Less than 5,000	9	12,051	514
5,000–7,499	8	20,146	2,725
7,500–9,999	7	27,832	2,140
10,000–14,999	14	36,277	11,575
15,000–19,999	13	36,816	15,383
20,000–24,999	11	45,564	22,820
25,000–29,999	9	60,513	28,876
30,000–39,999	13	69,083	45,981
40,000–49,999	7	95,658	63,941
50,000 and more	10	262,254	130,851
Age of family head (years)			
Under 25	8	4,218	5
25–34	23	20,391	3,654
35–44	19	51,893	28,721
45–54	16	81,350	43,797
55–64	15	119,714	55,587
65–74	12	125,284	50,181
75 and over	7	72,985	35,939
Education of family head			
Grades 0–8	16	37,419	16,152
Grades 9–11	13	40,791	12,489
High school diploma	32	52,968	23,671
Some college	20	71,754	20,418
College degree	19	122,842	54,805
Occupation of family head			
Professional, technical	14	81,094	40,079
Manager	11	109,147	57,129
Self-employed manager	5	231,773	87,399
Clerical or sales	13	65,321	24,452
Craftsman or foreman	18	48,928	26,402
Operative, labor, or service worker	29	26,574	8,338
Farmer or farm manager	2	121,710	69,735
Miscellaneous	8	52,044	4,027
Housing status			
Own	64	97,239	50,125
Rent or other	36	10,603	15
Race of family head			
Caucasian	82	74,743	31,904
Nonwhite and Hispanic	18	27,605	1,353
Life-cycle stage of family head			
Under 45 years			
Unmarried, no children	12	16,289	1,075
Married, no children	7	24,948	7,540
Married, with children	23	41,371	17,864
45 years and over			
Head in labor force	26	107,124	54,527
Head retired	22	103,041	43,213
All ages			
Unmarried, with children	9	22,765	477
All families	**100**	**66,050**	**24,574**

Source: "Survey of Consumer Finances, 1983," *Federal Reserve Bulletin,* 70 (December 1984): 863.

it is clear that the average American household falls short of any real affluence. One way of comprehending the meaning of the concentration of wealth is to imagine how long the majority of family units could survive on their "wealth" if they had to live on the sale of what they owned, and to contrast this with the highest net worth class, where survival would not be anywhere near a problem.[5]

In order for the nation's total wealth to be more equitably distributed among the American population, property holdings worth hundreds of billions of dollars would have to be removed from the ownership class and reallocated among tens of millions of households. At present this is an unlikely event. There is a definite relationship between the ability to command great economic power and the ability to exercise influence over political questions of national significance, as we saw in Chapter 2.

Unequal Distribution of Income

The members of the ownership class derive most of their annual incomes from their property holdings, not their jobs. Most Americans are not so fortunate. Instead, they are forced to base their economic well-being on the sale of their labor to others (less than 10 percent are independently self-employed). In return for the sale of their labor, members of the work force receive annual salaries or hourly wages, and their earned income rests on their *marketability*—the demand for their labor on the part of public and private employers. Those people who cannot work—because of age, disabilities, or the lack of anyone who wants to buy their labor—must depend on alternative sources of income, such as retirement benefits, pensions, social security payments, veterans' benefits, welfare payments, and unemployment compensation.

Like wealth, income is not distributed equally among members of the American population. In fact, the unequal distribution of income grew worse in the 1980s.[6]

Figure 6.1 shows how imbalanced the distribution of income is in the United States. In this figure, the total number of American families is divided into five equally sized groups, ranked from high to low in order of annual family income. The top fifth, consisting of the 20 percent of families having the highest annual incomes, received 44 percent of the total family income in 1988. The bottom fifth, the 20 percent of families having the lowest annual incomes, received 4.6 percent of the total. If income were equally distributed among families, each group would receive 20 percent of the total—no more and no less.

To carry this a bit further, the top two fifths, or most affluent 40 percent, received 68 percent of total family income, while the bottom three fifths—the majority of American families—had to make do with 32 percent. It seems clear that a minority of family units appropriates the majority of income and consequently possesses unequal access to the goods and services of the affluent society. After the ownership class and other high-income earners take out their share, the remaining economic resources are divided among the many.

The economic well-being of the majority of Americans would be even more tenuous were it not possible for them to charge consumer purchases on credit cards and take out loans for major expenditures. By buying on the promise of future income—in effect, by going into

[5] An alternative source of data on wealth distribution, one that points to the same conclusions, is U.S. Department of Commerce, Bureau of the Census, *Household Wealth and Asset Ownership: 1984* (Washington, D.C.: U.S. Government Printing Office, 1986).

[6] See Lester C. Thurow, "A Surge in Inequality," *Scientific American*, 256 (May 1987): 30–37; Thomas Edsall, "The Return of Inequality," *Atlantic Monthly* (June 1988): 86–94; and Martin Tolchin, "Richest Got Richer and Poorest Poorer in 1979–87," *New York Times* (March 23, 1989): A1.

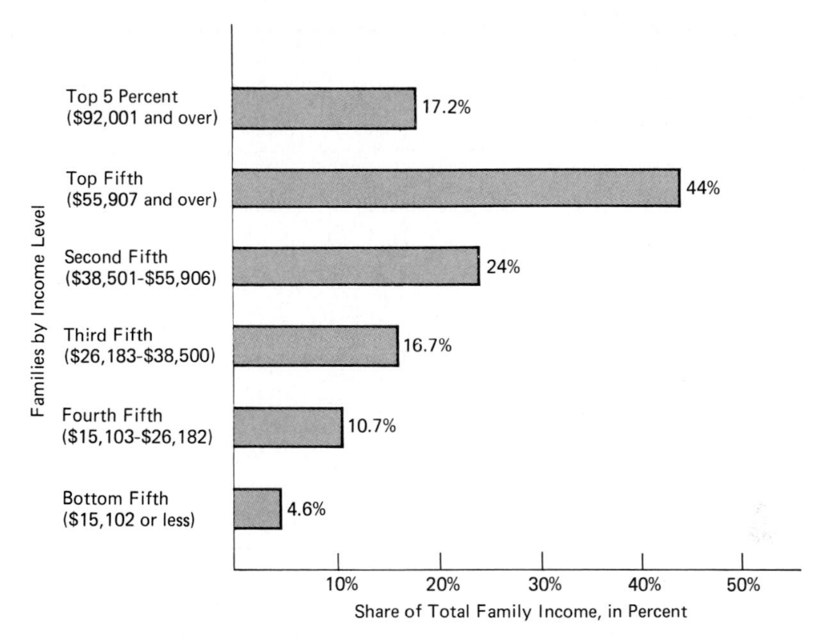

FIGURE 6.1 Distribution of Income Among American Families, 1988
Source: U.S. Department of Commerce, Bureau of the Census, *Money Income and Poverty Status in the United States, 1988* (Washington D.C.: U.S. Government Printing Office, 1989), p. 31.

planned debt—many members of the work force are able to gain an additional share of the goods and services they help produce. It is on this rather shaky basis that the supposed "middle classness" of the American people rests.

With inflation periodically eating away at the purchasing power of the dollar, and with constant increases in the prices of essential goods and services, the income stability of the average American household has been under attack in recent years. Lacking funds to invest as a hedge against inflation—a luxury taken for granted by members of the ownership class and others with surplus income—many members of the labor force find themselves running in place. Income gains are quickly eaten up by the rising costs of living. Old debts must be paid off, and new ones seem to constantly emerge. Increasingly, families can remain in the middle class only by accumulating new debts and/or increasing the number of family members who work outside the home.

Growing Economic Disparities

The data in the previous section illustrate the vast gap in income shares received by families at the very top and at the very bottom of our class structure. But these data cover only a single year and thus mask a trend that has been the subject of a great deal of comment and speculation. The trend involves growing economic disparities between the majority of American families, including those of the middle class, and the families of the affluent minority.

The trend is seen in Table 6.3. This table compares the distribution of after-tax family income in 1977 to the distribution in 1988. If one examines the changes that occurred over this period, some significant facts emerge. First, the

TABLE 6.3 Average After-Tax Family Income (in 1987 dollars)

Income group by deciles	1977 average income	1988 average income	Percent change	Dollar change
First	$ 3,528	$ 3,157	−10.5%	−$371
Second	$ 7,084	$ 6,990	−1.3%	−$94
Third	$ 10,740	$ 10,614	−1.2%	−$126
Fourth	$ 14,323	$ 14,266	−0.4%	−$57
Fifth	$ 18,043	$ 18,076	+0.2%	+$33
Sixth	$ 22,009	$ 22,259	+1.1%	+$250
Seventh	$ 26,240	$ 27,038	+3.0%	+$798
Eighth	$ 31,568	$ 33,282	+5.4%	+$1,714
Ninth	$ 39,236	$ 42,323	+7.9%	+$3,087
Tenth	$ 70,459	$ 89,783	+27.4%	+$19,324
Top 5%	$ 90,756	$124,651	+37.3%	+$33,895
Top 1%	$174,498	$303,900	+74.2%	+$129,402
All groups	**$ 24,184**	**$ 26,494**	**+9.6%**	**+$2,310**

Source: Thomas B. Edsall, "The Return of Inequality," *Atlantic Monthly* (June 1988): 89.

poorest American families were on average worse off in 1988 than in 1977: The poor literally have grown poorer. Second, families at middle-income levels experienced a good deal of income stagnation if not net income loss. Finally, the highest income families—especially the extremely affluent—were far better off in 1988 than they were in 1977. In effect, the trend has been for economic power to slowly seep upward, leaving the poor ravaged and the middle-income strata struggling to hold their own. As we shall see, there is a definite relationship between the worsening of conditions for low-income families and, for example, the spread of homelessness and hunger in America.

As these changes in family income distribution occurred, the implications for the future of America's middle class became the subject of debate.[7] Some argued that the middle class may be in danger of disappearing, turning the United States into a two-tier society, "leaving the country torn, like many third-world societies, between an affluent minority and a horde of the desperately poor."[8] Such a development would reflect "an occupational structure characterized by a polarization between highly paid professional and technical workers on the one hand and poorly paid, unorganized, lower level workers on the other."[9]

Whether or not such prognoses come true in the years ahead, it is clear that middle-income families are feeling some serious economic squeezes. It has, for example, become much more difficult for such families to keep up with the constantly rising costs of children's college attendance, and virtually impossible to send them to expensive private institutions. This situation has been exacerbated by federal cutbacks in student aid that middle-income families had depended upon. And the children themselves—

[7] See Bob Kuttner, "The Declining Middle," *Atlantic Monthly* (July 1983): 60–72; Michael W. Horrigan and Steven E. Haugen, "The Declining Middle-Class Thesis," *Monthly Labor Review*, 111 (May 1988): 3–13; and Robert I. Lerman and Harold Salzman, "Deskilling and Declassing: Whither the Middle Stratum?," *Society* (September/October 1988): 60–66.

[8] Barbara Ehrenreich, "Is the Middle Class Doomed?," *New York Times Magazine* (September 7, 1986): 44

[9] Michael Harrington and Mark Levinson, "The Perils of a Dual Economy," *Dissent* (Fall 1985): 417–26.

even those fortunate to go on to pursue a college education—increasingly find themselves wondering how they will be able to afford to purchase a home and life-style similar to that of their family. Meanwhile, reflecting the top end of the income spectrum and its growing affluence, sales of imported luxury motor vehicles, boats, second and third homes, jewelry, furs, and art objects all continue to boom. At the bottom end of the spectrum are people without any homes at all, without the money to purchase sufficient food.

Minorities and Economic Inequality

Economic well-being depends to a large extent on whether one belongs to a minority group. In 1988 the median family income for white families was $33,920. In that same year, the median family income for black families was $19,330. Or, using the government poverty-level figure of $12,091 for a family of four, we find that in 1988 some 10.1 percent of the white population was poor, while 31.6 percent of blacks fell into this category. Other minorities have not been faring much better. For example, 26.8 percent of Spanish-origin Americans were living in poverty in 1988.[10]

We do not need elaborate tables to realize that minority group members are dramatically underrepresented in the upper income ranges and grossly overrepresented in the lower ranges. Moreover, we may be sure that America's ownership class is almost "lily-white." It is also clear that only a massive reallocation of economic resources can change the distribution of wealth and income between whites and racial or ethnic minorities. These economic resources have to come from somewhere. Thus it becomes easier to understand the uneasiness displayed by many running-in-place white Americans as minorities press for an increased share of the economic pie. In the absence of any reallocation of income and wealth, most whites are forced to compete with minority group members for the relatively small amount left over after the affluent have taken their bite. Intergroup hostilities may be increased under the prevailing competition for scarce resources—in this case job slots at higher income levels.

Despite periodic governmental announcements, the white–minority differential is not in a state of decline. (See Table 6.4.) It is true that the household income of blacks, for example, has risen substantially since World War II. But so has the income of whites, and black income has not risen appreciably *relative* to that of the racial majority. Blacks must make even greater annual percentage gains than whites just to keep the already wide income gap from widening further.

PERPETUATION OF ECONOMIC INEQUALITY

As we have seen, income and wealth are far from equally distributed among individuals and families in the United States. The net worth of most households is minimal, a reflection of what little property people have been able to collect on the basis of the sale of their own labor to employers. Real wealth, on the other hand, is monopolized by a small ownership class. In this section we will look at the reasons why inequality remains such a permanent part of our economic life.

Wealth Begets Wealth

What does the ownership class *do* with all its money?[11] Enormous wealth makes possible a

[10] U.S. Department of Commerce, Bureau of the Census, *Money Income and Poverty Status in the United States, 1988* (Washington, D.C.: U.S. Government Printing Office, 1989), pp. 4 and 5.

[11] For the life-styles of the rich, see G. William Domhoff, *Who Rules America Now?* (Englewood Cliffs, N.J.: Prentice-Hall, 1983), pp. 17–55, and Susan Ostrander, *Women of the Upper Class* (Philadelphia: Temple University Press, 1984).

TABLE 6.4 Money Income of Households—Percent Distribution of Money Income Level in Constant (1988) Dollars, by Race and Hispanic Origin of Householder

Race and Hispanic origin of householder and year	Number (thous-ands)	Percent distribution									Median Income
		Under $5,000	$5,000–9,999	$10,000–14,999	$15,000–24,999	$25,000–34,999	$35,000–49,999	$50,000–74,999	$75,000–99,999	$100,000 and over	Value (dollars)
All Races											
1988	92,830	6.2	10.8	10.3	18.6	16.0	17.3	13.4	4.2	3.2	27,225
1980	82,368	6.3	12.0	11.1	20	17.5	17.5	11.3	2.9	1.6	25426
1975	72,867	5.7	12.2	10.6	20	17.9	18.3	11.1	2.5	1.6	25,947
1970	64,778	7.3	10.4	9.3	20	14.5	18.6	10.8	2.6	1.6	26,630
White											
1988	79,734	5	9.8	9.8	18.6	16.5	18.1	14.2	4.5	3.4	28,781
1980	71,872	5.2	11.1	10.6	20	17.9	18.4	12	3.1	1.8	26,824
1975	64,392	4.9	11.2	10.3	14.9	18.4	19.1	11.8	2.7	1.7	27,134
1970	57,575	6.6	9.6	8.9	19.5	20.1	19.5	11.4	2.7	1.7	27,736
Black											
1988	10,561	15.4	18.4	13.1	19.4	12.5	11.4	7.3	1.6	1	16,407
1980	8,847	15.5	19.3	15	20.1	13.6	10.2	5.3	0.7	0.3	15,454
1975	7,489	12.7	20.9	13.6	21.7	14.4	11.3	4.5	0.7	0.2	16,2889
1970	6,180	13.8	17.8	13.3	24	14.6	10.8	4.7	0.8	0.2	16,882
Hispanic Origin*											
1988	5,910	9.9	13.6	13.7	22.1	15.5	14.3	7.3	2.2	1.3	20,359
1980	3,906	8.7	14.8	15.2	23.5	15.7	13.9	6.3	1.2	0.7	19,598
1975	2,948	8.0	15	15.1	24.9	17.8	12.9	5	0.8	0.5	19,493
1972	2,655	5.2	14.1	14.2	26.1	20.1	13.2	5.4	1.2	0.6	21,727

*Persons of Hispanic origin may be of any race.

Source: U.S. Department of Commerce, Bureau of the Census, *Money Income and Poverty Status in the United States, 1988* (Washington, D.C.: U.S. Government Printing Office, 1989), pp. 23–24.

The financial resources of members of the ownership class enable them to purchase and consume luxurious goods and services without imperiling their financial standing. The very rich can afford the most expensive leisure-time pursuits—vacations in exclusive resorts, opening nights at the opera or ballet, elaborate dinner parties and balls—and still have plenty of money left over for investment. This photograph shows a fox hunt, an expensive sport enjoyed almost exclusively by the wealthy. *(Elliot Erwitt/Magnum Photos)*

great deal of luxurious consumption. Wealth can be used to obtain the best available goods and services. Yet while members of the ownership class are capable of material acquisition far beyond the level of most Americans, such spending can be managed without making much of a dent in their overall holdings.

More important, wealth is used to accumulate more wealth. With professional financial and legal assistance, members of the ownership class are able to keep their wealth active. Their money managers advise them on buying and selling holdings and guide them to investments in profitable income-producing properties that will further enhance or protect their net worth. Through such activities, wealth recreates itself, and the increased wealth recreates itself. The problem facing the very rich is one of deciding how best to increase their affluence in the face of a host of opportunities, not how to hold on to it. As wealth begets wealth, the economic gap between the ownership class and the majority of Americans is maintained over time.

On the other hand, even if the majority of Americans could afford to pay for financial and legal assistance, they would have little money to invest. They certainly would not have assets of the magnitude to get involved in the most profitable large-scale investments open to the ownership class. Thus, one might also say that nonaffluence begets nonaffluence. The economic condition of most Americans is one of relative stagnation and almost total dependence on the sale of their labor and/or various government benefits for continued economic maintenance. If you have wealth, it is easy to parlay it into more; if you have little or none, then that is likely to remain the case.

The Unequal Burden of Taxation

Many people view the various taxes levied at different governmental levels as means of decreasing economic inequality, particularly income inequality. But is the existing tax structure really a progressive force, a mechanism of income leveling and income redistribution, or does it simply support economic inequality? When we examine the tax structure and the ways in which the burden of taxation is distributed, we must conclude that the outcome is to perpetuate economic inequality.[12]

Many Americans believe that more affluent people bear a heavier tax burden than those who are less well off. But the affluent, with the financial and legal talent only they can afford to employ, are able to seek out and take advantage of various tax loopholes that effectively reduce their tax burden to a minimum.

For example, the affluent invest in expensive first and second homes, secure in the knowledge that their mortgage interest is tax deductible. The 17 percent of Americans who earn over $50,000 a year receive 52 percent of these deductions. In effect, the more affluent you are, the more the government rewards you for purchasing shelter. (Meanwhile, as we shall see, federal programs for low-income housing have been cut drastically in recent years.) Federal tax deductions for home mortgage interest work out as a form of welfare for the rich, since they disproportionately reap the benefits.[13]

Similarly, another way the affluent invest surplus cash is by purchasing tax-exempt state or local bonds. (Go back to Table 6.1.) Such bonds are sold to help finance many worthwhile public projects. The interest received from these bonds is tax-free. This is quite unlike the interest the average person receives on a savings account, on which taxes must be paid. In effect, it is another form of welfare, a reward or subsidy for being wealthy enough to buy such bonds.

Certain common taxes affect the average worker more than they do the affluent. We are all familiar with the sales tax, levied by states and localities around the country. Most families must spend a substantial percentage of their annual incomes on essentials; what is left over may go toward some luxury items. This means that a large amount of their income is spent on items subject to the sales tax. The more affluent do not spend most or all of their income in this manner. Instead, they save or invest surplus income, and the returns on these investments offset much of the burden stemming from sales tax on their consumer expenditures. Hence, the burden of sales tax weighs most heavily on the

---

[12] Michael Parenti, *Democracy for the Few*, 5th ed. (New York: St. Martin's Press, 1988), pp. 97–101.

[13] Ann Mariano, "Is It a Mortgage Deduction, or a Housing Subsidy for the Wealthy?," *The Washington Post National Weekly Edition* (October 24–30, 1988), p. 20.

average family, who can neither avoid nor offset the tax. Lower income families, who must spend literally all of their income, feel the burden of this type of tax more than anyone else. Thus, the sales tax, rather than being a progressive form of taxation that decreases economic inequality, is actually a regressive tax that penalizes the nonaffluent.

A similar situation prevails with regard to social security taxation. As this tax is set up, workers pay a certain percentage of their annual wages or salaries to the government up to a specified dollar cutoff point. In 1988, for example workers earning up to $45,000 were taxed at a rate of 7.51 percent. Since the vast majority of workers earn less than this, the average worker's entire income tends to be subject to this form of taxation. In the case of the affluent, however, only a small percentage of annual income may be subject to this tax, since this group makes so much money above the official cutoff point. Moreover, most of their income is from investments, not job earnings subject to this tax. Again this tax hits hardest at the nonaffluent majority, while the economically privileged generally escape its impact.

As these examples indicate, the majority of American working people bear the brunt of taxation out of all proportion to their ability to pay. The tax structure, rather than reducing economic inequality, permits such inequality to continue unabated.

Ideological Supports for Inequality

Thus far we have considered two primary reasons why extreme economic inequality is such an integral feature of American society. Wealth begets wealth in a cumulative process that favors the propertied few. Moreover, the overall tax structure is organized so that economic inequalities go virtually unaffected. A third reason economic inequalities persist is that our own culture favors these inequalities. That is, American values and beliefs support the economic status quo and hinder criticism of it.[14]

An important component of the American value system is a belief in what might be called *competitive individualism*. From the time we are children, we are taught that nobody gets or deserves a free ride in this society and that hard work, a willingness to strive, and winning out in competition against others will result in success. Appropriate attitudes toward work and economic rewards are typically instilled in the home as a part of childhood socialization. The schools also drill children in competitive individualism.[15] In both school and the labor market, individuals are encouraged to believe that they are fully responsible for their own economic fates.

In any truly competitive situation there will be both winners and losers. Not all can win in the competition for economic success—for high incomes and accumulation of wealth. Some will do much better than others. So we are encouraged to believe that economic success, or the lack of it, is almost totally an outcome of individual effort and competitive capabilities. The value system does not take into account the fact that the race may be rigged—that some start out just in front of the finish line, while others run the race wearing concrete boots.

When we internalize the belief in competitive individualism, we are simultaneously adopting an explanation of why economic rewards are unequally distributed. The affluent, we logically conclude, must deserve their privileged economic status or else they would not

[14] See Joan Huber and William M. Form, *Income and Ideology* (New York: The Free Press, 1973), and Michael Lewis, *The Culture of Inequality* (New York: New American Library, 1978).

[15] Scott Cummings and Del Taebel, "The Economic Socialization of Children," *Social Problems*, 26 (December 1978): 198–210.

have it. And the nonaffluent must equally deserve their plight.

Obviously, this explanation of economic inequality leaves much to be desired. It simplistically ignores some factors that result in generations of affluence for a few, hard-earned subsistence for most, and economic deprivation for all too many. We have already seen how, for example, inheritance and the tax structure help perpetuate the concentration of wealth and disparities in income over time. In the next section, additional inadequacies of our taken-for-granted beliefs will be suggested.

If we really believe that achieving economic well-being is like running a race, that the race is open and equally fair to all, and that people then get what they deserve, then we have no reason to be critical of the economic inequality that prevails in American society. Those at the very top, in the middle, and at the very bottom deserve their economic status. Possession of wealth and income becomes a measure of personal worth. If we believe all this, then we will not question inequality. But who benefits the most from our failure to engage in such questioning? Obviously, it is the ownership class, the most affluent—for so long as most members of American society accept economic inequality as natural and proper, the economic position of the most privileged is not threatened.

POVERTY AMIDST AFFLUENCE

According to the American system of values and beliefs, the poor are the losers in fair competition for economic rewards. So it is not surprising that most Americans believe that poverty is a result of supposed faults of the poor themselves.[16] Among these supposed faults are individual character deficiencies, lack of motivation to achieve, and unwillingness to strive to better their position. Some claim that the poor possess a unique set of cultural values that places little or no emphasis on hard work and economic success.[17] A less common explanation for poverty (but not as uncommon as one might expect) suggests that one's genes determine one's economic status. The poor, presumably, are those persons who are genetically inferior to everyone else.[18]

Beyond all this, the word *poverty* is often a synonym or code name for a racial or ethnic minority group. When someone says "the poor," many unknowledgeable persons immediately think of blacks, Puerto Ricans, American Indians, or Chicanos. The typical poor person is often inappropriately envisioned as a young, able-bodied nonwhite, living willingly (even happily) at the lowest income levels. Some people mindlessly suggest that the poor are really rather affluent in their poverty, living quite well on the welfare rolls. Many in ignorance think that the typical poor person chooses not to work, preferring public welfare benefits to employment.

This view of poverty, while fitting well with our system of values and beliefs about economic inequality, is out of step with reality. Poverty is a matter of economic deprivation, not character deficiency. Whatever the deficiencies of the poor, they do not include happy acquiescence in being poor. Sixty-five percent of the people who are poor in the United States are white. Rather than being able-bodied and available for employment, most members of the poverty population cannot hold full-time jobs because they are too old, too young, or disabled, or they are mothers who cannot readily leave their children. Only one in twenty-five welfare families has an

---

[16] Joe R. Feagin, "Poverty: We Still Believe That God Helps Those Who Help Themselves," *Psychology Today* (November 1972): 101 ff. See also Joe R. Feagin, *Subordinating the Poor* (Englewood Cliffs, N.J.: Prentice-Hall, 1975).

[17] The so-called culture of poverty is nicely handled by Charles Valentine, *Culture and Poverty* (Chicago: University of Chicago Press, 1968).

[18] Genetic theories are critiqued in Philip Green, *The Pursuit of Inequality* (New York: Pantheon Books, 1981), pp. 77–118.

able-bodied father in the house. Eligibility for welfare is quite restricted, and only 35 percent of all poor families receive cash welfare benefits. Those who are on welfare find that it provides a bare basis for survival as opposed to a life of comfort: recipients tend to feel humiliated and degraded by their dependence on it.

In this section, we examine poverty and the plight of the poor. We shall see that, just as there are mechanisms at work to ensure affluence and continued economic well-being for a privileged few, there are also mechanisms to provoke and perpetuate poverty for many millions.

What Is Poverty?

Poverty is first and foremost an economic state. Being poor means, essentially, lacking a means of subsistence capable of providing what—in this society and at this time—could be considered a secure and adequate standard of living. On the one hand, poverty is an absolute state—by any objective measure the poor are materially deprived to the point where survival often becomes an issue. And, on the other hand, poverty is a relative state—the poor are materially deprived in comparison with the majority of the population.[19]

For the purposes of discussion we will be using federal statistics on poverty. These statistics define poverty in a particular way. Since the 1950s the federal government has been measuring the extent of poverty in the population in accordance with the "thrifty food plan." This involves estimating the costs of a basic subsistence diet and then multiplying it by 3, under the assumption that poor people spend about a third of their incomes on food. The dollar amount calculated is considered the official poverty line; persons whose incomes fall below this dollar amount are considered poor. The dollar figure is adjusted for family size, and it is adjusted annually for changes in the costs of living. In 1964 the official poverty line for a family of four was about $3,000. In 1988 the line was drawn at $12,091. (See Figure 6.2.)

Critics have pointed out, and the federal government has admitted, that poor people typically must spend more than a third of their income to maintain a bare subsistence diet. An official poverty line that assumes otherwise is drawn too low and minimizes the extent to which there are people living in states of serious economic deprivation. Some would argue that poverty-level income should be considered to be that which falls more than 50 percent below the nation's income median. Such a statistic would add many more millions of people to the official poverty population.

Persons living in poverty typically have *some* means of subsistence. For some poor families it is public welfare, while most others who are poor or near-poor receive either a primary or partial source of subsistence from employment. For the employed poor, the income derived from working is too low to provide a secure and adequate standard of living. Thus, even though an individual may be eager to work, no one may want to employ him or her or the wages offered may be below the level necessary to move out of poverty. Being poor does not necessarily mean that the person is unwilling to embrace the notion of competitive individualism, but rather that the person's labor is not marketable.

Likewise, a person who is too old or too young to sell his or her labor, who is too disabled to go to work, or who must place the responsibilities of child care ahead of full-time employment may effectively be cut off from a secure and adequate standard of living. Apparently, unless one can contribute to the American economy as a worker, one is useless to it, no matter what the underlying reasons. Use-

[19] The measure for a statistical determination of poverty has long been the subject of debate. See articles in "Part II, Measuring Poverty," pp. 41–114 in Richard Goldstein and Stephen M. Sachs, eds., *Applied Poverty Research* (Totowa, N.J.: Rowman & Allanheld, 1983).

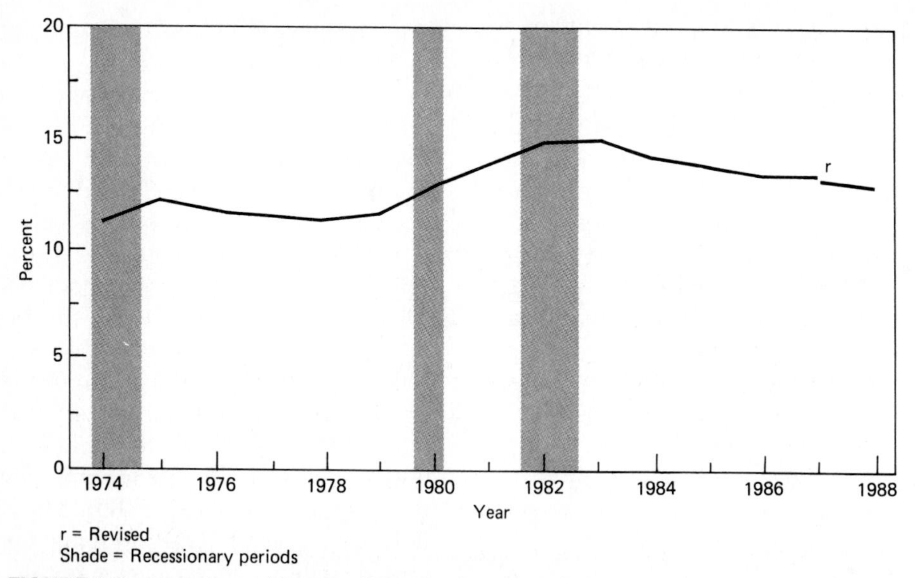

FIGURE 6.2 Percentage of Persons Below the Poverty Level
Source: U.S. Department of Commerce, Bureau of the Census, *Money Income and Poverty Status in the United States, 1988* (Washington, D.C.: U.S. Government Printing Office, 1989), p. 13.

lessness is underscored by according nonp-workers the most negligible share of the nation's economic resources. Consequently, many persons are also rendered useless as consumers.

The poor, in essence, are the tens of millions of people who are economically obsolete—those men, women, and children whose contribution to production and consumption is considered peripheral to the ongoing operation of the American economic system. Unable to produce or unable to demand sufficient rewards for their contributions to production, and thus unable to consume, tens of millions of Americans live out their lives in a state of economic deprivation. The promises of the consumer society remain well beyond their reach.

Who Are the Poor?

While the poor comprise a numerical minority within the United States, this minority is by no means an insignificant one. Census data for 1988, in which only the most destitute were considered poor, revealed that over 31.8 million persons were living in a state of poverty—one out of seven Americans. These 31.8 million poor people included 7 million families and an additional 7 million unrelated individuals.[20] (See Table 6.5.) The official definition of poverty used in this census varied for different categories of people; for example, a family of four was considered poor if its annual income was under $12,091. But in all cases the dollar definition of poverty encompassed those who were worst off both in absolute and relative terms. According to the census, another 11 million persons had incomes that placed them in the category of *near-poor*—that is, their incomes were so low that

[20] U.S. Department of Commerce, *Money Income and Poverty Status in the United States, 1988,* pp. 58 and 62.

TABLE 6.5 Number of Persons in Poverty, 1988 (in thousands)

Family Status	All races	White	Black	Hispanic origin*
Total	**31,878**	**20,765**	**9,426**	**5,379**
65 years and older	3,482	2,595	785	225
In families	24,173	15,045	7,718	4,721
Householder	6,876	4,471	2,090	1,141
Related children under 18	12,058	7,140	4,213	2,598
Other family members	5,240	3,434	1,415	982
In unrelated subfamilies	634†	404	199	61
Unrelated individuals	7,071	5,316	1,509	597

*Persons of Hispanic origin may be of any race, but over 90 percent are included in the white racial category in these data.
†Composed of persons related to each other but not related to the person or couple maintaining the household.
Source: U.S. Department of Commerce, Bureau of the Census, *Money Income and Poverty Status in the United States, 1988* (Washington, D.C.: U.S. Government Printing Office, 1989), pp. 57–61.

any slight drop (as a consequence of job loss, layoffs, serious illness, or disability) would place them below the official poverty line.

If we break down the poverty figures further, we get a better idea of which groups comprise the poverty population. Census data show that 40 percent of the poor are under eighteen years of age and that 11 percent are sixty-five and older. Thus, the majority of the poor (51 percent) are very young, school-age children and youth, and the elderly. To this we can add another 24 percent of the poor—females who are heads of families and unattached females. In other words, about 75 percent of the poor fall outside of the category of persons we usually think of as traditional breadwinners.

Though approximately two-thirds of poor persons in the United States are white, nonwhites are poor out of all proportion to their representation in the total population. Blacks comprise 12 percent of the population but are 30 percent of the poor. The prevalence of poverty among minority families contributes substantially to the white–minority income differential discussed earlier.

Data on the numbers of persons who are poor, collected annually by the Bureau of the Census, are somewhat misleading. Such data are not true indicators of the full extent to which poverty is experienced by Americans. Recent research focused on a representative sample of families whose economic status was followed over a ten-year period. Greg J. Duncan and his colleagues found that a *quarter* of all Americans experienced poverty at one time or another during the 1970s. That is, there is substantial turnover among the poverty population, as people's economic fortunes change for better or worse.[21]

Why Are They Poor?

As we saw earlier, poverty is very often considered the fault of the poor themselves. Our system of values and beliefs suggests that we must blame the victim for lack of economic success.[22] But poverty is an economic state. People are poor because they lack money. And they lack money because they are unable to sell their labor or because they are paid only very small incomes. In other words, the cause of poverty is not the victim but is instead the nature of the

[21] Greg J. Duncan et al., *Years of Poverty, Years of Plenty* (Ann Arbor: University of Michigan, Institute for Social Research, 1984).

[22] See William L. Ryan, *Blaming the Victim* (New York: Vintage Books, 1971).

American political economic system and the ways it deals with people.[23]

Business Practices Contributing to Poverty. Among the forces contributing to poverty has been *technological change*. Decisions by executives in business and industry to automate or increase mechanization of their operations—in order to increase efficiency and profits—have resulted in the displacement of many workers and have closed opportunities for new entrants into the labor force. Those most affected by technological change are unskilled and semiskilled workers. Thrown out of jobs or denied them in the first place, such persons have difficulty finding any work, not to mention work that pays enough to provide a secure and adequate standard of living.

Worker displacement is not limited to large industrial centers. Over the decades, the nation's farms have become large mechanized corporations, requiring fewer and fewer people to produce food for the population. Today some 3 percent of the work force feeds us all. As mechanization of agriculture has spread and intensified, millions of farm workers who lack the training and skills required to compete successfully in the urban labor market have found themselves economically obsolete. Displaced farm workers have contributed substantially to the size of the poverty population as a consequence of decisions over which they had no control.

Employers contribute to the creation and perpetuation of poverty in other ways as well. For example, many of our largest corporations have become international operations with plants around the world. To increase profits and thus reward stockholders, corporate executives have been channeling resources into other nations. Such investments are often undertaken because the costs of materials and labor are lower in these nations than in the United States. Many products that were once made by American workers are now being made elsewhere. In effect this has meant the export of jobs, increasing the competition for employment in this country and contributing to the high rates of unemployment that so often prevail.

The pay scales of business and industry also contribute to poverty. Some blue-collar workers have a certain amount of job security, somewhat higher wages, retirement pensions, and other worker benefits as a result of union membership. Yet only 17 percent of the U.S. labor force is unionized. For those millions of workers who do not belong to unions, wages are often so low as to place them near (if not in) a poverty situation. While federal and state governments have established minimum wages for a variety of occupational areas, the minimum wage is generally set so low that it does not provide families with a secure and adequate standard of living. Moreover, periodic upward revisions in the minimum wage have not been sufficient to offset cumulative effects of inflation and increases in the cost of living.

Government Benefits. Many members of the work force—particularly those in unskilled and semiskilled positions—are subject to periodic unemployment. Layoffs and seasonal unemployment most affect those with marginal skills. Contrary to popular belief, the *unemployment compensation* provided by government agencies for these and other workers does not necessarily prevent poverty. Unemployment compensation is not available to all members of the labor force, pays only a percentage of the wage formerly earned by the unemployed, and is cut off after a given period of time. Unless a worker can find a new job or get the old one back, welfare may be the next resort.

The rules concerning eligibility for *welfare* differ from state to state, as do the type and amount

---

[23] This section is based on Gabriel Kolko, *Wealth and Power in America* (New York: Praeger Publishers, 1962). See also the discussion of theories of poverty in Harold R. Kerbo, *Social Stratification and Inequality* (New York: McGraw-Hill, 1983), pp. 300–16.

of benefits available.[24] In no state does welfare provide more than a basis for subsistence well below the official poverty line. Potential recipients are subjected to a degrading screening process in which the state probes into virtually every area of their personal lives. Benefits are given grudgingly, and recipients are continually rechecked for eligibility and to make sure they do not have other sources of income. While welfare cheats have been found, only a tiny percentage of recipients cheat the system (despite the publicity accorded them).[25] Yet far more Americans have negative feelings about welfare recipients than about the "welfare benefits" the affluent routinely collect under the law.

Other Economic and Social Factors. As we have seen, *age* is closely linked to poverty. Many adults reach retirement age only to find that their savings and other economic resources are inadequate and that poverty is their future state. Senior citizens on fixed incomes (e.g., income from many insurance programs and pension plans, which does not increase with inflation) find that they cannot keep up with annual increases in the costs of living. Food costs, medical costs, rent, and utilities escalate—but incomes do not keep pace. For many, welfare is the only answer—and not much of an answer at that. Twelve percent of Americans who are sixty-five or older are poor, and many more are near-poor. Age, of course, works against finding or holding employment.

Like the aged, the young are confronted with the societal rule that people will be permitted to consume in accordance with their output (marketability), not in accordance with their requirements. Of the 40 percent of the poor under eighteen years of age, most are too young to work at all (even if jobs were available) and must depend on others to provide for them. A large proportion of those old enough to work are of school age, and sacrificing schooling for work typically means employment in the most low-paying, dead-end occupations. In general, the young are powerless to overcome poverty completely on their own volition; their situation is quite similar to that of the elderly poor.

Sex and *marital status* are also linked to the probability that one will be poor and will find it difficult to extricate oneself from poverty. (See Figure 6.3.) We are seeing the slow "feminization of poverty" as more women with young children are affected by it. Over time there has been an increase in the percentage of American families headed by women, and in 1988, some 52 percent of all poor families fell into this category. Employed women earn less than do men, on the average. This is partly a result of sex discrimination in hiring, which limits the types of jobs available to women. But even when women perform the same jobs as men, the women are often paid less. The woman who heads a household faces many problems, not the least of which is finding a job that will keep her family out of poverty. The serious shortage of reliable and inexpensive child-care facilities makes it even more difficult for female heads of households to avoid poverty.

To this add *racism*. Most poor people are white (two-thirds). But, for example, blacks are disproportionately represented among the low-income and poverty populations. For blacks a vicious cycle seems to be operating, involving educational discrimination and the failure of public schools to equip blacks to compete on an equal basis with whites for decent jobs; discrimination by employers, who hire whites over blacks and/or pay black workers less than whites for the same jobs; exclusion of black workers from union membership, particularly in the

---

[24] For a historical analysis of public welfare and some of its functions, see Frances Fox Piven and Richard A. Cloward, *Regulating the Poor* (New York: Vintage Books, 1971); see also Betty Reid Mandell, ed., *Welfare in America* (Englewood Cliffs, N.J.: Prentice-Hall, 1975).

[25] Physician Task Force on Hunger in America, *Hunger in America: The Growing Epidemic* (Middletown, Conn.: Wesleyan University Press, 1985), pp. 156–159.

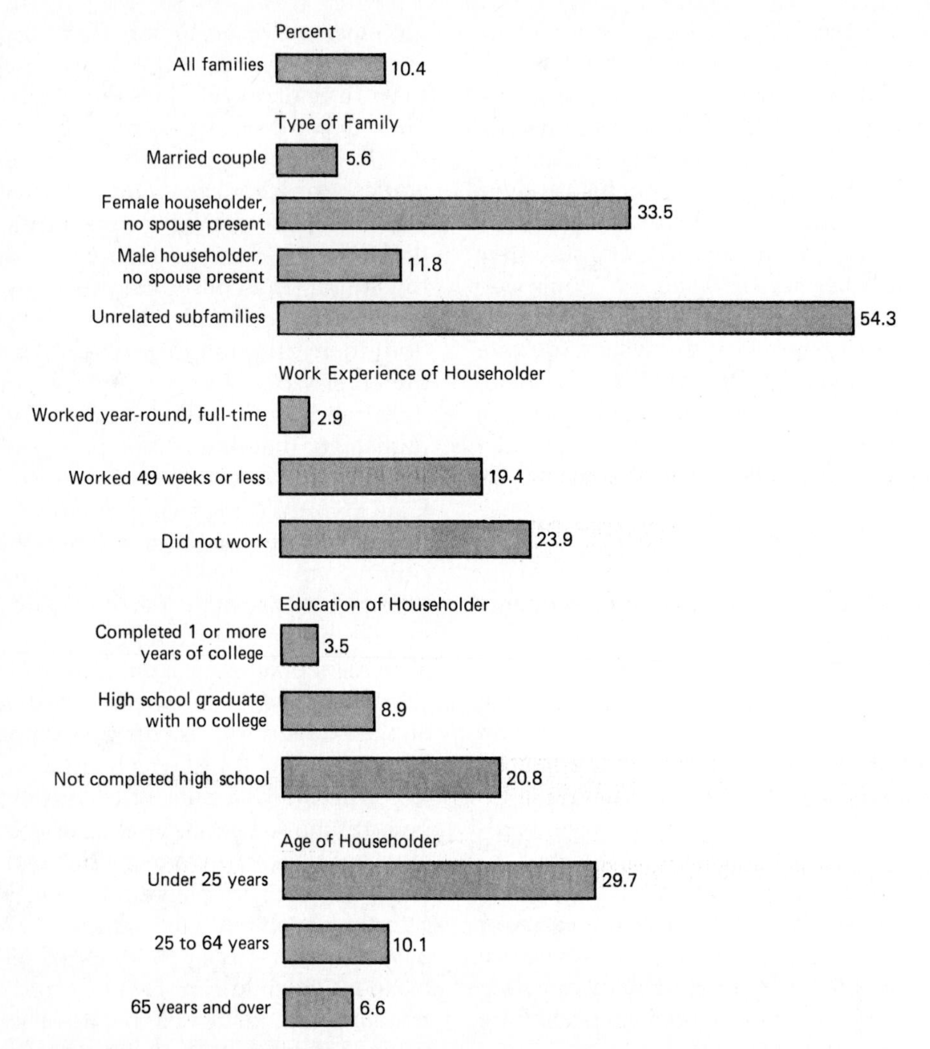

FIGURE 6.3 Poverty Rates for Families with Selected Characteristics, 1988
Note: Unrelated subfamilies are composed of persons related to each other but not related to the person or couple maintaining the household.
Source: U.S. Department of Commerce, Bureau of the Census, *Money Income and Poverty Status in the United States, 1988* (Washington, D.C.: U.S. Government Printing Office, 1989), p. 8.

skilled trades; and frequent unemployment, a reflection of the fact that the black worker is most likely to be in a job that is insecure and subject to either periodic layoffs or disappearance through mechanization. The black unemployment rate is normally twice that of whites. Finding that they cannot keep a job or earn enough while working to support a family, black men, like similarly situated white men, often define themselves as failures. Their sense of economic obsolescence, felt as personal worthlessness, often creates tensions in the home that contribute to family breakup. We then have a female-headed household, which, as we have seen, is quite likely to be poor or near-poor.[26]

As was implied previously, another factor that contributes to the creation and perpetuation of poverty is *education*. It is clear that without the kind and degree of education or training that will make one marketable, a decent-paying job is beyond one's reach. While it is questionable whether many jobs today really require the amount of schooling employers demand, a high school or college diploma is a necessity for marketability. But the dropout rates in schools serving poor children are enormous, and many children of the poor emerge from years of schooling as functional illiterates. Insofar as public schools fail to provide an adequate education or skills for children of the poor, the probability is increased that such children will replicate their parents' low-income position.

However, we should emphasize here that increasing the educational achievements of the poor and near-poor will not alone guarantee an end to poverty. The American economy must be capable of providing job opportunities for all—and at levels of remuneration above the poverty level—in order for increased education to be put to use. Without such changes in the employment picture, the reduction of poverty through education is bound to be thwarted.

The Structural Basis of Poverty. To answer the question "Why are they poor?" we must look well beyond the alleged personality characteristics, values, and genetic makeup of the poor. The organization of the economy and its machinations; the profit-oriented decisions made by top executives in business and industry; governmental policy; discrimination on the basis of age, sex, race, and ethnicity—all bear on the poor and tend to be outside their immediate control. The propensity to blame the victims for the economic deprivation under which they labor, while consistent with our values and beliefs regarding inequality, ignores all too many realities. Under the existing structure of our society, any of us could be poor if deprived of adequate means of subsistence by virtue of forces and decisions originating outside our control.

Just as our economic system perpetuates the privilege of the ownership class, so does it perpetuate the life situation of the poor. Many members of the ownership class earn more in one year than poor persons can reasonably expect to accumulate in a lifetime—a stark reflection of the extremes of economic inequality in the United States.

THE EFFECTS OF ECONOMIC INEQUALITY

Economic inequality is not simply an abstract intellectual concept. And the previous brief assessment of some of its dimensions and underlying causes barely begins to cover the topic. But at this point we turn away to suggest some of the consequences of economic inequality for American society. We then consider potential solutions.

Inequality and Life Chances

We live in a society in which wealth and income have an undeniable bearing on a citizen's life chances. To some extent, at least, we must "buy" life just as we purchase any other commodity. Our economic situation will determine whether we eat and whether we can afford nutritious foods. It will determine whether we are safely and comfortably housed and whether we can afford to buy quality health and medical care. Our economic situation will determine the area in which we can afford to live and the quality of educational opportunities available to our children. It will determine whether we have leisure time, how much we have, and how we

[26] See Carol B. Stack, *All Our Kin* (New York: Harper & Row Publishers, 1974).

can use it. It will determine whether our children live through birth, as well as the future life expectancy for us and them. Our economic situation will be inextricably linked to our sense of security, personal well-being, and self-worth. To the degree to which economic resources—wealth and income—are unequally distributed, life chances are also unequally distributed. By accident of birth and little more, a child born into the ownership class will be able to "buy" a life that is both longer and qualitatively different from that of a child born into poverty. While we all may have unalienable rights to "life, liberty, and the pursuit of happiness," economic inequality—with its impact on life chances—obviously stands in the way of the exercise of these rights.

Economic inequality also means that American society is incapable of harnessing and utilizing the potential talents and abilities of all its members. For example, educational opportunities closely correspond to economic position. It is the children of the affluent minority who most frequently go to private schools and academies, receive special tutoring, are "broadened" by travel, and are sent to elite colleges and universities. These advantages are conferred not because the children of the affluent deserve them more than anyone else, but because their parents can easily afford them. The children of the poor and of the average working family, on the other hand, must be happy with what little educational opportunity they receive in return for their parents' tax payments. Education, like color television, is a commodity; basically, you get what you pay for.

The denial of educational advantages means that much human talent remains hidden and repressed. Talent that goes unrecognized and insufficiently cultivated is not going to be utilized. The shortage of imaginative teachers, inventive medical practitioners, participants in the creative arts, and sensitive administrators and politicians is an arbitrary shortage. We have no real way of knowing how much potential talent goes to waste annually because millions of families lack the economic resources to ensure their children an opportunity to cultivate and demonstrate it. As a consequence, the whole society is poorer both culturally and materially.

Furthermore, economic inequality is becoming increasingly costly. How much does the United States devote to welfare relief, to unemployment compensation, and to paying the salaries of the armies of bureaucrats and workers who administer relief funds? How much do we devote to cleaning up the physical and mental damage done to those persons whose economic situation exerts a negative influence on their bodies and minds? How much do we devote to processing through the legal, judicial, and penal systems those who steal in order to secure temporary increases in their disposable incomes? The expenditures are enormous, and they are a result of the pervasiveness of economic inequality and poverty. In the absence of a shift in the distribution of wealth, income, and opportunity, the costs of maintaining the status quo can only be expected to continue to grow.

Some mention must also be made of the psychic costs of economic inequality. The competition for scarce economic resources, and thus life chances, leaves no one untouched. The thought of being a loser, of being or becoming economically obsolete, is a permanent nightmare for members of American society.[27] Competition separates people from one another and contributes to intergroup jealousies and hatreds, periodic conflicts, and tragic episodes of personal and collective strife. It means that the only people who are honored or revered are the winners—the affluent minority. And the anxieties, tensions, and frustrations economic inequality and competition generate

---

[27] Jules Henry, *Culture Against Man* (New York: Vintage Books, 1965).

may well be a contributing factor to many expressions of individual "deviance"—ranging from criminal behavior to mental illness. All these costs, though difficult to measure, are felt in real ways.

Homelessness

Among the most visible outcomes of economic inequality in the United States in recent years has been the growing numbers of men, women, children, and youth who have no homes. Homeless people have become an increasingly common sight as they seek shelter on the nation's streets, in bus and train stations, in parks and plazas, as well as in and around public buildings. The fastest growing segment of the homeless population consists of families, most often mothers and their children. There has been a dramatic decrease in the average age of the homeless, such that it is now reckoned to be in the midthirties. Hastily mobilized shelters for the homeless cannot keep up with the demands upon them; in extreme weather the homeless outside shelters sometimes die.

The mobility and transience of many of the homeless, along with the fact that people are continually entering or leaving this group, makes estimating their numbers difficult. Although observers agree that homelessness has been on the increase through the 1980s and into the 1990s, precise statistics remain a matter of dispute.[28] A study by the U.S. Department of Housing and Urban Development, suggesting the homeless population on any given day is 250,000–350,000 people, has been widely criticized as understating the situation. A more widely accepted estimate, one endorsed by the National Institute of Mental Health, is that 2 million to 3 million Americans are currently homeless.[29] The 1990 census is expected to provide additional information, but even there officials have acknowledged limitations on counting accuracy.

The U.S. Conference of Mayors, concerned about the increasing numbers of homeless and the growing costs localities face in helping them, initiated a study covering twenty-seven major cities. Their research helped to shed light on the characteristics of the homeless population. Half of the homeless in these cities were found to be single men. Thirty-four percent were families with children. The remaining were single women and youths unaccompanied by families. A quarter of the homeless were found to be employed.[30] Within the homeless population are people who suffer serious physical and mental disabilities, illness, and disease, as well as persons caught up in addictive substance abuse. All of the homeless need homes. Many need extensive care and services in addition to permanent shelter.

It would be an error, obviously, to view the homeless as an undifferentiated mass. Examined closely, the homeless are quite heterogeneous. In response to the question "Who are the homeless?," Leanne G. Rivlin answers:

> Single men and women and poor elderly who have lost their marginal housing, ex-offenders, single-parent households, runaway youths, "throw-away" youths (abandoned by their families or victims of family abuse), young people who have moved out of foster care, women escaping from domestic violence, undocumented and illegal immigrants, Native Americans leaving the reservation after Federal cutbacks and unemployment, alcoholics and drug abusers, ex-psychiatric patients, and the so-called "new poor" who are vic-

[28] A method of counting the homeless is described in Peter H. Rossi et al., "The Urban Homeless: Estimating Size and Composition," *Science*, 235 (March 13, 1987): 1336–41. See also Peter H. Rossi, *Without Shelter* (New York: Unwin Hyman, 1988).

[29] Constance Holden, "Homelessness: Experts Differ on Root Causes," *Science*, 232 (May 2, 1986): 569.

[30] Ifill, "Homelessness Takes Hold as National Issue," p. A4.

tims of unemployment and changes in the job market.[31]

These very different types of people have one thing in common, though. They either lack a source of income, or their incomes are so low—even if they are employed—that they cannot find affordable housing.

A major shift in housing costs that has been under way since the 1970s has made low-cost housing for families and individuals increasingly scarce. Between 1970 and 1983 rents tripled while renters' incomes only doubled. As this trend has continued, more and more people have been finding their incomes eaten up by the costs of shelter. It is said that 11 million families now spend over a third of their incomes in rent; 5 million actually spend more than *one-half* of their incomes in this way.[32] As rents have risen relative to incomes, the cost of purchasing a home has risen astronomically. Thus, many young people are unable to purchase their first homes and remain in competition for available rentals. This competition, along with altogether insufficient rates of new construction of low- to moderate-income rental housing, helps to drive rents up faster than incomes can increase.

Cheap housing has also been disappearing at a dramatic rate. Urban redevelopment projects have displaced low-income people from properties that have been converted into offices or condominium housing for the well-to-do. The renewal of property in and around the downtown areas of cities has frequently meant the destruction of single-room-occupancy hotels and rooming houses sheltering low-income individuals. Developers find it much more profitable to build office towers and luxury apartment buildings for the upscale life-style of high-income people than to address the housing needs of the economically deprived.

In New York City, for example, single-room-occupancy units declined from 170,000 in 1971 to 14,000 in the 1980s. Between 1978 and 1984 New York City suffered a loss of some 715,000 units renting at or below $300 per month.[33] As this trend has repeated itself across the nation, homeless people have literally been "manufactured" into existence.

In the meantime, publicly owned and government-subsidized housing, the last resort for low-income people who cannot compete in the private housing market, has been in decline.[34] About 2 percent of all housing units (or 1.4 million) are publicly owned. Each year 75,000 units are demolished; many more are in a state of dilapidation and terminal deterioration. Few new units are being built. The federal government all but abandoned its commitment to subsidized housing for low-income people during the 1980s. Expenditures for such housing went from $32 billion to $6 billion between 1981 and 1989. To suggest the priorities of those who govern, in 1981 federal officials spent $7 on defense for every dollar they spent on housing. By 1989 the ratio had changed to $46 on defense for each housing dollar. Government failure to support publicly owned and subsidized housing in the face of substantial and growing demand has contributed to homelessness. In most major cities there are waiting lists of up to two years for such housing; for the most part these waiting lists are closed.

In sum, costs of shelter in the private housing market have been outracing the ability of low-income individuals and families to pay. Housing costs have been going up dramatically at the same time, as we saw earlier in the chapter, the income of the poor has actually been declining and that of many others has been stag-

[31] Leanne G. Rivlin, "A New Look at the Homeless," *Social Policy*, 16 (Spring 1986): 4.

[32] Richard P. Applebaum, "The Affordability Gap," *Social Policy*, 19 (May/June 1989): 7.

[33] Ibid.

[34] Ibid.

nating. Low- to moderate-income housing is not being built to even remotely approach existing needs. Publicly owned and government-subsidized housing no longer provides a safety net for the desperate.

In one study done for the U.S. Congress, researchers predicted that by the year 2003 "the gap between the total low-rent housing supply (subsidized and unsubsidized) and households needing such housing is expected to grow to 7.8 million units."[35] This would mean that nationwide nearly 19 million people would be homeless. The incredible suffering already documented[36] would, if such predictions come true, be hellishly magnified.

Hunger and Malnutrition

> We learned that it is not uncommon for elderly people, living alone in apartments with no cooking facilities, to consume an evening meal of a tin of cat food and a raw egg.[37]

This quote, from a task force based at the Harvard School of Public Health, is an expression of yet another tragic consequence of economic inequality. Even as we function as one of the world's principal producers of grain and other foodstuffs, exporting to other nations and maintaining massive warehouses of surplus at home, an estimated 20 million people in the United States do not get enough to eat each day.[38] Simply put, the economic circumstances of these 20 million people are such that the amount and types of food they are able to consume leave them "chronically short of the nutrients necessary for growth and good health."[39]

In the decade of the 1970s America successfully fought to minimize hunger and malnutrition within the population. A public shocked by the discovery of the extent of such problems during the 1960s[40] pressured the federal government to act. As a consequence, the food stamp program, intended to permit low-income households to obtain a more nutritious diet, was expanded to cover many more needy people. New programs were set up and existing ones expanded to address needs of the isolated elderly, schoolchildren, pregnant women, and mothers and their infants. By the end of the 1970s the nutritional needs of low-income people were thought to have been pretty much taken care of.

Then, in the 1980s, hunger began to appear in the population much as did homelessness. The changing distribution of income, described earlier, meant that the real income of those in poverty went into decline. Poverty rates rose from where they had been in the 1970s. The purchasing power of cash benefits from welfare—benefits received by only a minority of those living under the official poverty line—fell by 40 percent. In effect, the poor began to become poorer.

In the midst of the growing economic adversity faced by those at the bottom levels of America's income structure, the federal government cut back on its nutrition programs in much the same way it dramatically reduced its commitment to making sure low-income people had access to affordable housing. Food stamp and school nutrition programs were substantially reduced. While well over 30 million Americans lived in poverty by the late 1980s, only about 19 million of them received food stamps. Not that the stamps guaranteed dietary opulence and

[35] MIT professor Philip Clay, quoted in Applebaum, "The Affordability Gap."

[36] Jonathan Kozol, *Rachel and Her Children: Homeless Families in America* (New York: Crown Publishers, 1988).

[37] Physician Task Force on Hunger in America, *Hunger in America,* p. 79.

[38] "20 Million in U.S. Said to Go Hungry," *New York Times* (October 27, 1987): A33.

[39] J. Larry Brown, "Hunger in The U.S.," *Scientific American,* 256 (February 1987): 37.

[40] *Hunger U.S.A.: A Report by the Citizen's Board of Inquiry into Hunger and Malnutrition in the United States* (Boston: Beacon Press, 1968).

Hunger and malnutrition are not phenomena found only in underdeveloped nations. Across the United States, many people are desperate for food, and local soup kitchens have become a necessity. Patronage of such services has been on the increase in recent years, as federal food programs have been cut back and eligibility for assistance has become more restricted. *(Jean-Louis Atlan/Sygma)*

gourmet eating: Their average benefit per meal for recipients is around half a dollar.[41] The billions of dollars in federal budget cuts, taken together with changes in federal regulations on eligibility for assistance by nutrition programs, came during a time when the need for this type of help was rising. The result? An epidemic of hunger.

Hunger is not always readily visible to the casual observer of everyday life. But in the 1980s suddenly social service agencies and religious organizations were beset by those in need of food. Physicians and hospital staffs began to see health problems associated with hunger and malnutrition. These included anemia, tuberculosis, and osteoporosis, as well as diseases ordinarily found only in underdeveloped nations where malnutrition is most advanced (e.g., kwashiorkor and marasmus). The inability of people to get enough to eat has become a major public health problem.

The consequences of nutrition-related problems tend to be most severe within certain groups. Pregnant women must eat well to avoid debilitating illnesses such as anemia and toxemia. Poor nutrition during pregnancy threat-

[41] Brown, "Hunger in the U.S.," p. 38.

ens the health and future prospects of the fetus, drastically increasing the likelihood of premature births and low birth weight babies. The latter have a higher than normal probability of mental retardation and developmental disabilities. Low birth weight is directly linked with infant mortality, the rates of which are very high in the United States. Malnourished children are highly susceptible to infections and disease and are unlikely to function effectively in school and in social relationships. Inadequate nutrition in old age leaves people vulnerable not only to chronic health problems but also to life-threatening ailments. In sum, women, children, and the elderly are at greatest risk when faced with hunger. In this respect the situation in the United States is not unlike that of the poorest nations of the world.

Most people do not choose to be hungry, any more than they choose to be homeless. It is a tragedy that befalls people for no other reason than lack of money. An elderly person on a fixed income may have to pay a rent increase, thus cutting back on money available for food. A mother may be faced with unexpected medical bills, thus forcing her to skip meals so her children may eat. An undocumented worker may be unable to seek out emergency food assistance for his children out of fear of being reported to immigration authorities and deported. An infant may find her formula watered down, as her jobless parents seek to find ways to economically survive. Such people "choose" to be hungry only in the most narrowly constricted sense.

In a society such as ours, hunger and malnutrition are not only an embarrassment but also unnecessary. The Physician Task Force on Hunger in America stated that we could virtually eliminate the situation by increasing federal expenditures on food programs annually by the amount of money we spend on two nuclear attack carriers.[42] The question to seriously ponder is why we don't.

The Need for Government Intervention

Economic inequality is a deeply rooted but by no means inevitable feature of American society. It is possible to reduce differences in personal wealth and income, thus making the life chances of all more nearly equal and enabling all to share more equitably in the goods and services being produced.

One of the first steps involves a change in attitudes toward economic inequality and poverty. Americans must become much more familiar with the facts about inequality and the harm stemming from it. Members of this society must also begin to reject the notion that extensive economic inequality is part of the natural order of things, and that therefore nothing meaningful can be done about it. Inequality can be attacked, but only if concerned people are willing to collectively press this issue in the national political arena.

The next major step is to work out precise mechanisms to redistribute wealth and income. The goal should be to provide a decent standard of living for all persons, while placing some restrictions on the senseless accumulation of wealth by a few. In recent years, various ideas on how to reduce inequality have been put forth by individual scholars and a few legislators. It is time that such proposals become a matter of public debate, so that members of this society can decide which show the most promise.

For example, one proposal involves providing a guaranteed minimum income through the *negative income tax* (NIT). Essentially, the NIT would be based on a periodic report on income, which each person or family would file with the federal government. If the income reported was above a set minimum amount, taxes would be paid on the excess above the minimum, with tax rates set low on earnings just above the minimum. If, on the other hand, the income re-

[42] Physician Task Force on Hunger in America, *Hunger in America*, p. 175.

PUBLIC PROBLEM, PRIVATE PAIN

The Crisis in Homelessness

Families with children are the fastest growing sector of the homeless population. Here a mother describes the hardship, suffering, and humiliation of being homeless in an appearance before a select committee of the U.S. Congress.

My name is Lisa McMullan. I am here with my husband, Guy, and my four children, Jamie, Ryan, Morgan and Ryder. The story of my family's experience with homelessness began in Mile City, Montana, early in 1986. My husband and I owned a house there, but when my husband's job was phased out due to the farm crisis, we could no longer make the mortgage payments so we gave the house back to the bank, sold everything and came East in the spring.

We first stayed with my mother-in-law, but that didn't work out because there wasn't enough room for all of us. There were seven of us living in the basement. After a few months we moved to Baltimore, and my husband and I both held a number of jobs. In November or December 1986, we began to have problems paying the rent on our apartment. [Lack of construction work; day care too expensive.] After several eviction notices, we found ourselves without a place to live and with no place to go.

I called around, with the help of Social Services, to several shelters in Baltimore, but no one would take us as a whole family. Finally, the Salvation Army offered us a room to stay in. The room was very small with six people in it. The conditions at the shelter were very stressful for me and my family and the children particularly became much more difficult to manage. The food was not that good as you can probably imagine.

It was very crowded, and there's a weird feeling that goes along with being there. You feel like you're nothing because you suddenly don't have a home. You know you've done all you can do and it isn't your fault, but the whole situation makes you feel like you must have done something wrong.

My family and I tried very hard to overcome these feelings. Especially because it really hurts the children. Children need to know and feel who has control over their lives. And suddenly they are living in a situation where they see their parents needing outside help, and they are all suddenly living with many other people they don't know and who frighten them.

To combat all this, and to keep our family life in order, we tried very hard to maintain a schedule. We made sure we went on walks with the children, we kept them in school, and did all we could do to make them feel we still had control over our lives and were still there for them.

But this was a real struggle for us. We were up every morning at 6 A.M. to get my husband to work on time and to take the two older children to school. In doing this, we missed breakfast at the shelter every day until they began giving us boxes of cereal to bring along to eat later. We were fortunate in still having a car to be able to keep that schedule. Not everybody does.

We were at the shelter between three and four weeks. Many of our experiences there were frightening and added a lot to the stress in our family. There was no door on the women's shower and one night I caught a man peeking into the women's bathroom watching my 10-year-old daughter. The man also lived in the shelter and I reported him, but nothing was done about it. Another time, a woman accused my daughter of trying to push her down the stairs. As it turned out, we learned that the woman was mentally disturbed and hated to be touched, so if you got too close to her, she got very upset.

These were the kind of things—overcrowding, hunger, lack of privacy and insecurity about the future—that really put stress on our children and our family. It was very hard on us all. My two oldest children, 10 and 7 years old, were in counseling, originally to help them deal with the loss of their younger sister to crib death when we were at my mother-in-law's house. But then I kept them in counseling all throughout this period because I knew that not having the security of a home and living in a shelter would be hard on them.

We recently found a small apartment, but it turns

out that our crisis was not over yet. A week after we moved in, my husband was laid off from his job at Bethlehem Steel. We are now both looking for jobs and are trying to get stability back in our children's lives. It is very, very difficult to maintain a family in this kind of insecure environment. I know that if it weren't for each other, we probably couldn't keep struggling to improve things.

Unfortunately, I know what great damage and harm that homelessness can do to a family, even when they're all trying to do their best to make everything work. Because of my family's painful experiences, I wanted to tell you our story today.

Source: U.S. House of Representatives, Select Committee on Children, Youth and Families, *The Crisis in Homelessness: Effects on Children and Families,* Hearings Before the Select Committee, February 24, 1987 (Washington, D.C: U.S. Government Printing Office, 1987).

ported was below the minimum, the federal government would issue a direct cash payment to make up the difference. The minimum must obviously be set high enough to move people out of poverty.

The NIT would provide an income floor for the most needy individuals and families. Its primary beneficiaries would be members of low-income groups, who would no longer have to struggle along on poverty-level wages or plead for welfare assistance. The present welfare system could be reduced in scope, at a substantial savings to taxpayers, and reoriented toward providing human services to anyone in need.

Mechanisms to eliminate poverty and enhance the standard of living of low-income groups must be accompanied by major changes in America's tax structure. In particular, income taxes must be made much more progressive in reality as well as in theory, so that those who have higher incomes are made to pay their fair share. Recent (1986) tax reforms notwithstanding, America's tax structure is tilted toward preserving the advantages of the rich at the expense of the average citizen. In general, all the loopholes that provide a form of welfare for the rich must be closed, and the tax structure should place some reasonable limit on the maximum levels of income and wealth that can legally be accumulated by an individual or family.

Ways must also be investigated to redistribute wealth and increase the net worths of the millions of Americans who own little or nothing. The federal government could, for example, place a *net worth tax* on millionaire families, of whom there are currently over 200,000. This tax would provide the federal government with sufficient revenue to permit special tax reductions for less affluent families who have put a certain amount of money into savings (thus accumulating an estate). The net result would be a gradual reduction in the concentration of wealth among the rich and greater economic independence for large numbers of Americans.

No matter which mechanisms are adopted to reduce inequality, any surplus tax funds that are generated must be used to expand the supply of *free or low-cost services* available to all members of this society. Such services include education and job-training, child-care facilities, efficient networks of public transportation, and health care. The purpose of attacking economic inequality is not simply to redistribute money, but also to improve the quality of living for all. Basic services should be readily available to all Americans by right, no matter what their economic circumstance.

The reduction of economic inequality will involve costs—but primarily for the most affluent, who will be most adversely affected by tax reforms aimed at the redistribution of income and wealth.[43] To the degree to which redistribution

[43] See Herbert Gans, "The Positive Functions of Poverty," *American Journal of Sociology*, 78 (September 1972): 275–89.

fosters increased equality in material terms, the economically derived status differences between the affluent and everyone else will be diminished. Such costs seem minor in comparison with the costs accompanying maintenance of the status quo, in which many millions are being forced to suffer.

As we have seen, the problem of economic inequality cannot be solved unless it is pressed in the national political arena. In Chapter 2 we analyzed the national political system and some of the political obstacles that must be overcome in dealing with inequality.

SUMMARY

In this chapter we have seen that the United States is a class-divided society. Wealth is heavily concentrated in a small ownership class, and a minority of family units receives the majority of the total annual family income. Gross economic inequality is perpetuated as wealth begets wealth, the taxation structure leaves inequalities largely untouched, and American cultural values provide a rationale for viewing such inequalities as natural and proper.

Those worst off within this class-divided society are the millions of poor and near-poor. While the vast majority are white, the poverty rate among racial and ethnic minority group members is far out of proportion to their numbers in the population. Contrary to myth, most poor people are very young, very old, disabled, and females who are heads of families. They are poor not because of individual deficiencies; rather, they are victims of decisions and circumstances outside of their immediate control. Just as social mechanisms help the rich maintain their affluence, there are economic, political, and social factors that render it difficult for people to escape poverty.

In a society in which one's opportunities and life-style are closely linked to having money, economic inequality translates into unequal life chances. As millions suffer in poverty, the potential talents and abilities of such persons go untapped—the entire society is poorer culturally and materially. The costs of poverty are also felt in the increasingly costly welfare, health care, and penal systems. More generally, the competition for scarce resources leaves no one untouched and is a source of individual anxiety and intergroup conflicts.

Gross economic inequality is not inevitable. It can be altered through government intervention. Mechanisms to change the distribution of wealth and income exist; for example, the Negative Income Tax and net worth tax. Such measures can be implemented. People must press the issue of economic inequality in the national political arena, or else the senseless suppression of talent and ability will simply continue.

DISCUSSION QUESTIONS

1. What is the probability that you or your children will ever become part of the ownership class (roughly the richest 2 percent of all American families)? What factors stand in the way?
2. Is it true that *anyone* can be economically successful if he or she really tries? Why?
3. What are your feelings about economic inequality? Should poverty be eliminated? If so, how should the costs of this be shared?
4. It is commonly held that any serious move toward the equalization of wealth and income will reduce people's incentive to work. What are the arguments for and against this view?
5. If you were a member of the ownership class, what arguments would you make against tax reforms that would take away much of your money to help eliminate poverty? If you were a member of the poverty population, what arguments would you make in favor of such tax reforms?
6. If America's economic growth seriously falters in the coming decades, job opportunities—even for college graduates—may undergo a marked decline. Moreover, oppor-

tunities for upward mobility may be restricted so that most workers are locked in place. Under such circumstances, what arguments might be made for the redistribution of wealth and income?

SUGGESTED READINGS

Block, Fred, et al. *The Mean Season: The Attack on the Welfare State* (New York: Pantheon Books, 1987).
Critiques of the conservative ideological attack on programs to assist poor people.

Brouwer, Steve. *Sharing the Pie* (Carlisle, Pa.: Big Picture Books, 1988).
A brief but informative overview of the increasing economic inequality in America and some reasons it is taking place.

Kozol, Jonathan. *Rachel and Her Children* (New York: Crown Publishers, 1988).
Highly acclaimed portrait of homeless families living on the streets and in dilapidated "welfare hotels."

Newman, Katherine S. *Falling from Grace* (New York: The Free Press, 1988).
The impact of downward mobility on Americans, as millions in recent years find they cannot remain middle class.

Sidel, Ruth. *Women and Children Last* (New York: Penguin Books, 1987).
The increasing concentration of women and children in the poverty population, and the need for a national family policy.

Wright, James D. *Address Unknown* (Hawthorne, N.Y.: Aldine de Gruyter, 1989).
The many causes of homelessness and possible solutions.

CHAPTER 7

Schooling and Unequal Educational Opportunity

Each individual must have ready and continuing access to the education and training needed to develop his or her interests and capabilities to the fullest extent.

In previous chapters, we examined macro problems that harm millions of Americans—such as economic inequality and the concentration of power. As we suggested, part of the reason these problems continue to plague our nation may be found in our educational system.

In this chapter, we will examine American ideals and beliefs about the educational system and evaluate their accuracy. We will consider the impact of schools on the socialization of children and on inequality in America. The chapter concludes with proposals for altering the educational system.

THE "GREAT SCHOOL LEGEND"

Historians of American education have generally provided a positive view of the contributions of the educational system. They claim that education has strengthened the American political system, that it has helped energize our economy, and that it has contributed to lessening class inequalities. In this section, we examine these claims and look at contrary views that suggest that the contributions[1] of the American educational system have not been totally positive.

Beliefs About American Education

When America's system of mass public education was established in the 1800s, the men and women who founded the various local school systems presumably wanted, among other things, to improve the readiness of people to participate in the political system. They felt—as do many today—that only with an educated citizenry could the United States function as a democracy. Since that time, the schools have sought to instill common political values in millions of members of our otherwise diverse population. Among these values has been respect for existing political institutions and procedures. American education, in the view of many historians, has contributed to political participation and has helped foster democratic ideals.

Historians have also pointed to the contribution made by our system of education to the economic development of the United States. Mass public education was introduced into America during a period of rapid industrialization. At this time, literacy and the creation and transmittal of new knowledge became more and more important to continued economic growth. Business and industry had to have people who could fill positions in the increasingly complex world of work. The schools responded by providing literacy and skills training, thus increasing our technological know-how and aiding the efficiency and productivity of America's economic system.

Finally, historians have suggested that mass public education has enhanced the ability of citizens to protect or better their socioeconomic positions. In the public schools, all children compete on the basis of individual merit, rather than on family position. This has made it possible for the poor to change their circumstances. We have, historians point out, moved a long way from the time when education—particularly higher education—was readily accessible only to the children of the affluent. Today almost all youngsters attend school. (See Table 7.1.)

There is certainly some truth to such historical generalizations. Our system of education has been handed vast responsibilities and has carried many of them out—often with very meager resources. But education has not only acted as a force for change and improvement. It has functioned as a conservative force as well. The positive picture of the contributions of education has been challenged by so-called revisionist historians.[2]

A Revisionist Critique

In recent years, some scholars have grown dissatisfied with the historical claims reviewed here. Revisionist historians have attempted to balance the picture, suggesting that there are aspects of the history of education not deserving of celebration.[3] It is important to look at some critical assessments of the history of education in the United States before considering the functions of education today.

In *The Great School Legend*, Colin Greer has taken a look at the belief that mass public education was developed in order to democratize the United States.[4] According to Greer, mass public education was an important part of the

---

[1] See, for example, Bernard Bailyn, *Education and the Forming of American Society* (New York: Vintage Books, 1960); and Lawrence A. Cremin, *The Genius of American Education* (New York: Vintage Books, 1965).

[2] For a more detailed overview of traditional versus revisionist views, see Daniel Selakovich. *Schooling in America* (New York: Longman, 1984), pp. 34–45.

[3] The need for historical revisionism is stressed in Marvin Lazerson, "Revisionism and American Educational History," *Harvard Educational Review*, 43 (May 1973): 269–83. The revisionists themselves are critiqued in Diane Ravitch, *The Revisionist Revised* (New York: Basic Books, 1978).

[4] Colin Greer, *The Great School Legend* (New York: Basic Books, 1972).

TABLE 7.1 Percentage of the U.S. Population 3–34 Years Old Enrolled in School,* by Race/Ethnicity and Age, October 1987

Age	All races	White	Black	Hispanic origin†
Total, 3–34 years	**48.6**	**47.7**	**51.7**	**45.3**
3 and 4 years	38.3	38.2	36.8	28.3
5 and 6 years	95.1	94.8	95.8	92.5
7–9 years	99.6	99.6	99.7	99.0
10–13 years	99.5	99.4	99.8	99.3
14 and 15 years	98.6	98.5	98.3	97.5
16 and 17 years	91.7	91.8	91.5	86.4
18 and 19 years	55.6	55.3	53.2	41.2
20 and 21 years	38.7	39.6	28.7	28.3
22–24 years	17.5	17.3	15.0	12.6
25–29 years	9.0	8.7	9.3	8.1
30–34 years	5.8	5.7	6.0	4.4

*Includes enrollment in any type of graded public, parochial, or other private school in regular school systems. Includes nursery schools, kindergartens, elementary schools, high schools, colleges, universities, and professional schools. Attendance may be on either a full-time or part-time basis and during the day or night. Enrollments in "special" schools, such as trade schools, business colleges, or correspondence schools, are not included.

†Persons of Hispanic origin may be of any race.

Source: National Center for Education Statistics, *Digest of Education Statistics, 1989* (Washington, D.C.: U.S. Government Printing Office, 1989), p. 14.

Americanization movement of the nineteenth century. This movement was aimed at indoctrinating the millions of people who immigrated to the United States, so that they would "fit into" the American political order. Wealthy and politically influential people encouraged the development of local school systems and adult education programs during the nineteenth century in the hope that schooling would head off political dissension and conflict. They felt that if poor and working-class immigrants could be brought to accept the elite-dominated political system and to work within it, class and ethnic grievances could be channeled into manageable directions. Citing historical documents and statements by nineteenth-century elites, Greer suggests that the mission of education "was to maintain and transmit the values considered necessary to prevent political, social, or economic upheaval."[5] In other words, instead of enhancing the democratic process, education was expected to function as a mechanism of social control that would protect the political and economic interests of the governing class.

Revisionist historians have also found documentary evidence suggesting that the role of education in industrialization was not exactly what earlier historians claimed. Nineteenth-century industrialization caused changes in the nature of work. In particular, more and more workers were becoming employees of enterprises owned by others. A way had to be found to smooth the transition into this new world of work. According to Samuel Bowles: "An ideal preparation for factory work was found in the social relations of the school, specifically in its emphasis on discipline, punctuality, acceptance of authority outside the family and individual accountability for one's work."[6] By organizing

[5] Ibid., p. 74.

[6] Samuel Bowles, "Getting Nowhere: Programmed Class Stagnation," *Society*, 9 (June 1972): 43. See also Samuel

One of the major goals of mass public education in the nineteenth century was to Americanize immigrants—to teach them to fit into the existing political and social order. This goal was met not only by developing curricula for the children of immigrants but also through a system of adult education in which citizenship was taught along with lessons on the English language. *(Library of Congress)*

mass public education to resemble the bureaucratic economic organizations of nineteenth- and early twentieth-century America, schooling was intended to foster a disciplined labor force—one that would not question managerial privileges and authority.[7]

The claim that American education has made a substantial impact on class inequalities has also been questioned. In a reexamination of the development of mass public education in the nineteenth century, historian Michael Katz showed that American public education has always been class biased.[8] Though it was introduced with the intention of opening up opportunities for all, education has both reflected and helped perpetuate class inequalities over time:

> It is the children of the well-to-do, not the children of the poor, who have benefited most from

Bowles and Herbert Gintis, *Schooling in Capitalist America* (New York: Basic Books, 1976).

[7] Regarding developments in the twentieth century, see Paul Violas, *The Training of the Urban Working Class* (Chicago: Rand McNally & Company, 1978).

[8] Michael Katz, *Class, Bureaucracy, and Schools* (New York: Praeger Publishers, 1971). See also Michael Katz, *The Irony of Early School Reform* (Cambridge, Mass.: Harvard University Press, 1968).

> public education. That is especially true of the higher levels of schooling, one important function of which has been to secure differential advantage to the children of the affluent.[9]

Furthermore, Katz observed that public schooling has historically functioned to secure such advantage primarily for children from affluent *white* families. Generations of black Americans, for example, were subjected to substandard education in racially segregated schools—a situation that has been addressed only in the last three decades.[10]

Thus the efforts to balance educational historians' celebration of American schooling have led to some critical findings.[11] If the American system of mass public education performed in the way the revisionist historians claim, what about education today? As we will see, there is evidence to suggest that not too much has really changed. Education still seems organized to foster political acquiescence, to nurture a compliant labor force, and to conserve existing economic inequality.

SCHOOLING AS AN AGENT OF SOCIALIZATION

Though laws pertaining to school attendance vary from state to state, most children are required by law to attend until the age of fifteen or sixteen. State governments dictate the number of hours and days per year that children must spend in school; indeed, state financial aid to local schools is often based on average levels of attendance. A local school system may lose money if absenteeism and truancy are high. Truancy is a crime, and parents may not withhold children from school attendance without providing a state-approved substitute.

Because of compulsory attendance, the majority of American children are exposed to schooling for many hours every year, whether they prefer to attend school or not. What are children expected to learn during these many hours? Sociologists of education generally agree that two distinct kinds of lessons are presented in the classroom.[12] First, there are the formal lessons—reading, arithmetic, history, and so forth. Second, certain standardized ways of thinking and behaving are also being encouraged. The second kind of lesson is often called the *hidden curriculum,* because of its subtle nature.

School systems differ from locale to locale, and community control over public schools ensures some measure of diversity across the nation.[13] Still, most school systems are organized bureaucratically. (The structure of elementary and secondary education, the route to higher education, may be seen in Figure 7.1.) Authority over children is vested in the hands of administrators and teachers, who are in turn responsible to an elected board of education. Students are urged to accommodate themselves to a system of administrative rules and regulations, and school authorities judge and reward students on the basis of how they respond to directions and commands. Such bureaucratic arrangements are said to be necessary in order to process large numbers of children each school day in a relatively impersonal, orderly, and efficient manner.[14] The same rationale for bureau-

---

[9] Katz, *Class, Bureaucracy, and Schools,* pp. 109–10.

[10] See John Ogbu, *Minority Education and Caste* (New York: Academic Press, 1978).

[11] A good overview may be found in Martin Carnoy and Henry M. Levin, *Schooling and Work in the Democratic State* (Stanford, Calif.: Stanford University Press, 1985), Chapter 4.

[12] See Christopher J. Hurn, *The Limits and Possibilities of Schooling* (Boston: Allyn & Bacon, 1978), Chapter 7.

[13] Efforts by the federal government to shape this diversity toward a national curriculum are described in Joel Spring, *The Sorting Machine* (New York: David McKay Co., 1976). See also his *American Education,* 2nd ed. (New York: Longman, 1982), Chapter 8.

[14] See Ann P. Parelius and Robert J. Parelius, *The Sociology of Education* (Englewood Cliffs, N.J.: Prentice-Hall, 1978), Chapters 4 and 5.

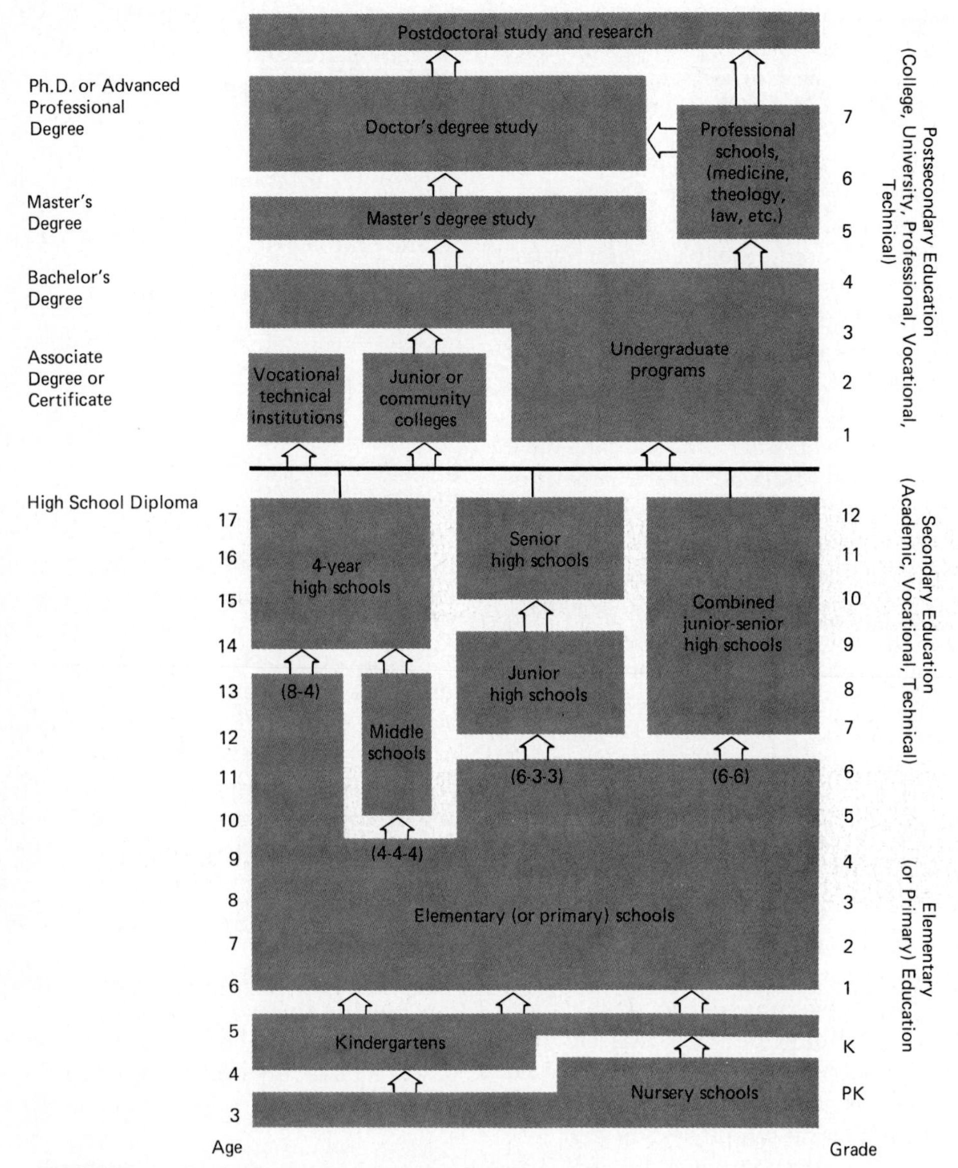

FIGURE 7.1 The Structure of Education in the United States
Note: Adult education programs, while not separately delineated above, may provide instruction at the elementary, secondary, or higher education level. Chart reflects typical patterns of progression rather than all possible variations.
Source: National Center for Education Statistics, *Digest of Education Statistics, 1989* (Washington, D.C.: U.S. Government Printing Office, 1989), p. 5.

cratic organization is often applied to prisons and mental hospitals.

In the late 1960s the Carnegie Corporation of New York sponsored an inquiry into the state of public education across the country. Charles E. Silberman, a well-known journalist and scholar, spent three years crisscrossing the country before presenting his findings in *Crisis in the Classroom*. His observations of school systems in action led Silberman to the conclusion that *docility* is being emphasized. Outbursts of spontaneity, originality, and nonconformity are commonly discouraged, while passivity and adherence to routine are stressed.[15]

A more recent in-depth study of schools by John I. Goodlad and associates seems to suggest that Silberman's observations continue to be valid today. In Goodlad's words,

> For the most part, the teachers in our sample of schools controlled rather firmly the central role of deciding what, where, when, and how their students were to learn.... When students played a role, it was somewhat peripheral, such as deciding where they sat.... The picture that emerges is one of students increasingly conforming, not assuming an increasingly independent decision-making role in their own education.[16]

Silberman and others have argued that compulsory participation in bureaucratic school settings fosters the formation of certain personality traits. Mass public education, it is said, promotes attitudes and habits of behavior that fit well with highly structured settings, those calling for rationality and predictability. While there has not been definitive research supporting such broad generalizations, several in-depth case studies of schooling do provide some evidence that this is the case.

[15] Charles E. Silberman, *Crisis in the Classroom* (New York: Vintage Books, 1970), pp. 113–57.

[16] John I. Goodlad, *A Place Called School* (New York: McGraw-Hill Book Company, 1984), p. 109.

The "Organization Child"

Sociologist Rosabeth Moss Kanter spent seven months studying a typical suburban nursery school located in the Midwest.[17] According to Kanter, the teachers in this school believed that children who followed orders and exerted self-control were mentally healthy children. As a result, the teachers constantly urged the children to adapt to the planned classroom routine, and they set up a round of activities each day conducive to promoting, in Kanter's terms, the *organization child*—the child who is most comfortable when those in authority provide supervision, guidance, and roles to be fulfilled. In requiring children to adapt to such experiences, Kanter concludes, the schools both reflect and support the trend toward bureaucratization of life in American society.

Similar conclusions have also been reached by Harry L. Gracey, a sociologist who studied classrooms in an eastern elementary school.[18] One part of Gracey's research focused on kindergarten, which he came to call *academic boot camp*. Kindergarten works to teach the student role to children not previously conditioned to organized schooling. The content of the student role is "the repertoire of behavior and attitudes regarded by educators as appropriate to children in school."[19] Such behaviors include willingness to conform to teacher demands and to perform the "work" at hand without resistance. Educators believe that children who have suc-

[17] Rosabeth Moss Kanter, "The Organization Child: Experience Management in a Nursery School," *Sociology of Education*, 45 (Spring 1972): 186–211.

[18] Harry L. Gracey, "Learning the Student Role: Kindergarten as Academic Boot Camp," in Dennis H. Wrong and Harry L. Gracey, eds., *Readings on Introductory Sociology*, 2nd ed. (New York: The Macmillan Company, 1972), pp. 243–54. Gracey examines elementary education in *Curriculum and Craftsmanship* (Chicago: University of Chicago Press, 1972).

[19] Gracey, "Learning the Student Role," p. 245.

cessfully learned the student role in kindergarten will function smoothly in the later grades.

Gracey found that school administrators best liked the teachers who most quickly and effectively produced order and routine. Such teachers elicited desired responses from the children with no more than a look, a few words, or a simple command signal. Gracey believed that these teachers were grooming the children to respond without question to officialdom and to follow orders without dissent. Even though many of the requests did not seem to make much sense to them, most of the children obeyed. Those who broke away from routines or resisted classroom authority were likely to be treated as "bad children" and to be sent to the school psychologist for guidance on how to adapt.

Both Gracey and Kanter concluded that the experience of organized schooling fosters certain personality traits. Since, if Silberman is correct, children are urged to conform for hours, days, and years on end, the outcome may be the *organization adult*—the team-oriented person who fits well into nonschool bureaucracies, such as corporations, the military, and the government. As Silberman puts it, "the teacher, although he may disclaim the title, is the students' first 'Boss.'"[20]

Of course, organized schooling is only one of the factors influencing personality traits and habits of behavior. Students—especially as they move into the advanced grades—often find enough strength in peer support to resist and sabotage the routines set up for them.[21] In his classic study *The Adolescent Society*, James Coleman found that the peer values of many young adults ran counter to those promoted by high school teachers and administrators.[22] In his view, the high schools often failed to motivate students into conformity with academic routine because educators did not understand how to counter peer influence.

In recent years, the matter of school discipline—enforcing school routine—has been a major issue in many city and suburban school systems. Violence and vandalism have plagued schools across the country. Teachers have been subject to physical attack and robbery. The most frightening trend is in the number of school-age children found carrying (and occasionally using) firearms in educational settings.[23] The response has been public outcries for greater surveillance and control practices, as schools struggle to maintain authority.[24]

Hence, the degree to which bureaucratically organized mass public education actually succeeds in producing adult prototypes of the organization child is open to question. Nonetheless, it seems that organized schooling today, as in the nineteenth century, is oriented toward doing so. "Good children" are presumably the sought-after result.

Learning to Participate in the Economy

Besides attempting to expose students to bureaucratic values, schools are said to promote attitudes and habits of behavior that are unique to a capitalist society. Jules Henry, a social anthropologist, conducted extensive field research

[20] Silberman, *Crisis in the Classroom*, p. 141.

[21] See Robert B. Everhart, "Classroom Management, Student Opposition, and the Labor Process," in Michael W. Apple and Lois Weis, eds., *Ideology and Practice in Schooling* (Philadelphia: Temple University Press, 1983), pp. 169–92.

[22] James Coleman, *The Adolescent Society* (New York: The Free Press, 1961). See also Arthur Stinchcombe, *Rebellion in a High School* (Chicago: Quadrangle Books, 1964).

[23] "Kids: Deadly Force," *Newsweek* (January 11, 1988): 18–19; Dennis Hevisi, "Schools Speed Their Efforts to Lock Violence Out of Classroom," *New York Times* (February 10, 1989): A14.

[24] See U.S. Department of Education, National Center for Educational Statistics, *Discipline, Order and Student Behavior in American High Schools* (Washington, D.C.: U.S. Government Printing Office, 1982).

on this topic over a period of years.[25] He compiled data for a case study by careful observation of a midwestern elementary school. On the basis of his research, Henry concluded that "school is an institution for drilling children in cultural orientations."[26]

Henry pointed out that public schools are faced with two incompatible tasks. On the one hand, they are expected to transmit dominant cultural values and beliefs; on the other hand, they are charged with liberating the minds of young people. Typically, according to Henry, they resolve this dilemma in favor of the first of the two tasks, keeping creativity—which may involve questioning and rejecting accepted ways of thinking about and doing things—under strict control. Henry's research indicated that the schools direct creative talent into certain channels, such as science and mathematics. Creative children generally are not encouraged to expend their energies on social studies, since this might require analysis and criticism of prevailing social and economic arrangements and conventional political and religious beliefs. Henry suggested that talent is pushed toward areas that serve the American technological economy and its ability to conduct sophisticated warfare.

In his research in the elementary grades, Henry was interested in what he came to call *noise*—that is, what children absorb in school aside from the formal subject matter. As part of his research, Henry recorded children's reactions to the games teachers introduced to make learning pleasurable. Whether involved in singing contests or spelling bees, children were constantly being pushed to compete against one another. On occasion, competition revolved around gaining the teacher's attention and winning the rewards only she or he could provide. Children quickly learned that their loss in a competitive arena meant someone else's gain. The winner's elation and excitement were, by definition, at the expense of the loser's depression and unhappiness.

Henry concluded that schooling teaches children (as noise) to be afraid of failure, to dislike themselves when they do fail, and to resent those who succeed at their expense. Children learn to compete at an early age and learn to see competition as natural. This, according to Henry, prepares them to compete with others throughout the course of their school careers and beyond. People learn to be motivated by the fear of failure and to be driven by the specter of personal obsolescence. They find themselves working hard to become a success—even if it means pushing others aside.

Children who fail to play competitive games, for whatever reason, are likely to be viewed as out of step with the expectations of school authorities. In the words of Edgar Friedenberg, a sociologist who has conducted research on the values of high school students:

> [The school] helps to see to it that the kinds of people who get ahead are those who will support the social system it represents; while those who might, through intent or merely by their being, subvert it are left behind as a salutary moral lesson.[27]

Again, one may question such broad generalizations, based as they are on very limited empirical evidence. But schools are arenas of competition—whether it be for grades, for dates, or for glory on the playing field. The noise is, in each such instance, "do not be a loser." It seems logical that such attitudes and values continue to guide people's behavior in adult life.

Some evidence has surfaced to indicate that the values of students include an uncritical acceptance of corporate capitalism, which is, af-

[25] Jules Henry, *Culture Against Man* (New York: Vintage Books, 1965), pp. 283–321.
[26] Ibid., p. 283.

[27] Edgar Z. Friedenberg, *Coming of Age in America* (New York: Vintage Books, 1965), p. 49.

ter all, only one way to organize an industrial society successfully. Scott Cummings and Del Taebel surveyed children from grades 3, 6, 9, and 12 in a major urban area of the Southwest.[28] The researchers were interested in assessing the attitudes and understandings held by children toward such topics as the organization of workers into trade unions, public ownership of large industrial enterprises, and government intervention into economic affairs. An uncritical acceptance of corporate capitalism would involve negative attitudes on each of these topics.

Cummings and Taebel found that while third and sixth graders are nonevaluative toward trade unions (as well as ignorant of their function), in the higher grades students progressively express attitudes unfavorable to unionization. In the view of twelfth graders, unions are "too big, too powerful, and jeopardize social stability."[29] This is, of course, the position typically taken by those espousing the cause of big business over and against that made on behalf of working people.

Children were also asked about private vs. public ownership of large industrial enterprises. Examples cited to them were oil and steel, two areas where a few major corporations monopolize economic activity. Again, while third graders are neutral, in the remaining grades students become progressively more negative toward the notion of public ownership.

Third and sixth graders, according to Cummings and Taebel, tend to view the state as benevolent and positive in its actions, and helpful in economic affairs (e.g., aid to the poor). Older students, on the other hand, see government intervention as politically disruptive, interfering with the natural laws of the marketplace, and posing the threat of socialism or communism. Sixth and twelfth graders also tended to explain the plight of poor people as resulting from alleged weaknesses in their character and motivation, skills, and training. Students thus were insensitive to the possibility that the workings of our economic system itself may create joblessness or that most of the poor (being children under eighteen and adults sixty and older) are unable to work.

In concluding, the researchers suggested that their data show

> the progressive development, in individual consciousness, of political ideals endorsing and legitimizing some of the more important features of capitalist economic thinking: private ownership of the means of production, individual striving and meritocratic explanations of inequality, and limited state intervention into business affairs. Conversely, children appear to develop explicitly anti-collective, anti-union and anti-socialist sentiments.[30]

To the degree to which students are armed with such values, they not only find it difficult to understand and appreciate other economic systems but also lack the ability to engage in critical reasoning and judgments about their own. The lack of such an ability is a sign of ideological dominance, not education.[31]

The Political Impact of Schooling

In the words of Joel Spring, contemporary mass public education is an "instrument of power." It prepares the young "for the acceptance of control by dominant elites."[32] To experience schooling is to be exposed to political indoctrination,

---

[28] Scott Cummings and Del Taebel, "The Economic Socialization of Children," *Social Problems*, 26 (December 1978): 198–210.

[29] Ibid., p. 203.

[30] Ibid., p. 208.

[31] Some sources of this ideological dominance are surveyed in Sheila Harty, *Hucksters in the Classroom: A Review of Industry Propaganda in the Schools* (Washington, D.C.: Center for Study of Responsive Law, 1979). See also Jean Anyon, "Workers, Labor and Economic History, and Textbook Content," in Apple and Weis, *Ideology and Practice in Schooling*, pp. 37–60.

[32] Joel H. Spring, *Education and the Rise of the Corporate State* (Boston: Beacon Press, 1972), p. 152.

for schools, whether consciously or unconsciously, make a contribution to the political outlook and behavior of the young.

Studies by political scientists have led them to conclude that public education functions to legitimate existing power relationships in America.[33] We should not be surprised that this is the case. Education in every known society—be it formal schooling or learning from one's parents—involves the transmission of the society's culture. That typically means transmission of the dominant cultural values, including the support of prevailing political arrangements. Or, as Ralph Miliband put it: "Educational institutions at all levels generally fulfill an important conservative role and act, with greater or lesser effectiveness, as legitimating agencies in and for their societies."[34]

Research shows that children develop political consciousness in stages.[35] At a very early age they are encouraged to have positive ideas about their society and government. In the first years of schooling, a simple form of patriotism is fostered. Children are taught to respect the symbols of government and political authority—from the American flag to the uniform of the police officer and the soldier.

As children slowly become capable of grasping more abstract political ideas, they are introduced to such concepts as democracy, voting, and civil liberties in their classes. They are taught about local, state, and national government. The political order is depicted largely in terms of political authority that should be respected and accepted in much the same way as children are expected to treat authority in the schools. Not surprisingly, the political status quo is presented as a given, not as an entity against which people might have valid reasons to struggle.

According to political scientist Jerry Tucker, students are encouraged to celebrate the political status quo as a rather idealized state of affairs. Tucker calls this kind of political education the *tooth fairy approach*.[36] His experience with college students leads him to believe that, by and large, public schools teach slogans and rhetoric instead of encouraging substantive inquiry. Children in classrooms are not only too often sheltered from controversial issues and from the often seamy underside of modern political life, but, even worse, are likely to be rendered politically ignorant. A review of research on political socialization revealed that the political knowledge of American youth is extremely limited.[37] Moreover, American secondary school graduates who have taken international tests on political systems and citizenship score near the bottom in comparison with other nations' graduates.[38] American students who study abroad are usually quite surprised at the depth of knowledge and enthusiasm with which their foreign counterparts approach political issues in routine conversation.

The tooth fairy approach to political education has also been noted in analyses of commonly used classroom materials:

> Textbooks generally present an unrealistic picture of American society and government. . . . In statements about democracy and the good life, text

[33] See Harmon Ziegler and Wayne Peak, "The Political Functions of the Educational System," *Sociology of Education*, 43 (Spring 1970): 129–42; and Edgar Litt, "Civic Education, Community Norms, and Political Indoctrination," *American Sociological Review*, 28 (February 1963): 69–75.

[34] Ralph Miliband, *The State in Capitalist Society* (New York: Basic Books, 1969), p. 239.

[35] See Richard E. Dawson, Kenneth E. Prewitt, and Karen S. Dawson, *Political Socialization*, 2nd ed. (Boston: Little, Brown & Company, 1977).

[36] Jerry Tucker, *The Experience of Politics* (San Francisco: Canfield Press, 1974), p. 133.

[37] Lee H. Ehman, "The American School in the Political Socialization Process," *Review of Educational Research*, 50 (Spring 1980): 99–119.

[38] Ralph W. Tyler, "The U.S. v. The World: A Comparison of Educational Performance," *Phi Delta Kappan*, 62 (January 1981): 307–10.

books often do not separate prescriptions from descriptions.[39]

Because they are led to confuse the political system as it should be with the political system as it is, according to Tucker, young people are likely to be bewildered and disillusioned when they run into political facts at variance with what they were taught.[40]

The daily experience of organized schooling also fails to encourage active political participation. We have noted that mass public education is both compulsory and bureaucratically organized. Students are drafted into school; they cannot choose to stay away. Once there, they are subject to rule from above and are likely to be punished if they resist the demands of authority. Much like inmates in a prison or mental institution, people in school are permitted little or no input into policies and decisions that directly affect them. Thus, though children are taught the rhetoric and slogans of democracy, they are simultaneously denied democracy in practice.

Consider, for example, the widespread phenomena of class elections and student governments. These activities are said to have educational merit. Yet, in reality, they are only an artificial exercise in political education, taking place in a vacuum. Elected student officers or representatives are rarely permitted a role in school decision making. At best, they may be invited to advise administrators and teachers. Student governments, ironically, exist only at the discretion and under the supervision of higher authorities. "Democracy" of this kind is an empty activity that does not prepare people to struggle in their own interests.

A similar situation exists with regard to the typical school newspaper. Freedom of the press, one of the principles underlying any truly democratic order, is usually sharply restricted. Censorship rights over student publications are reserved by school authorities. The right of censorship typically extends even to "creative" student publications, such as literary magazines, in which one might reasonably expect to find expressions of political discontent and heretical views. In the larger society, many newspaper publishers and other media groups have fought to maintain the concept of freedom of the press, but students are discouraged from doing so.

The Constitution of the United States guarantees freedom of assembly and speech. Public schools are tax-supported institutions—which means that they are paid for by citizens, including the parents of the students. But the use of school property is subject to approval and control by educational authorities, who alone determine what groups of students may gather and for what purposes. The assembly of large numbers of students, no matter what the official reason, is always carefully monitored (allegedly for safety reasons).

Politics is very much a part of schooling. For one thing, the tooth fairy approach to political education is itself a form of politics. Moreover, politics often directly intrudes into the conduct of public schooling through the actions of elected school boards. The members of such boards hold authority over administrators and teachers and may use this authority to impose their own views about proper educational experiences for children and young people.

In an environment so dominated by authority, it is highly unlikely that citizens' rights and responsibilities and political expertise could be taught. Rather, "Our schools teach passivity instead of responsible activism."[41] To the degree that the schools are successful in teaching this lesson, they are turning children into candidates

[39] Thomas R. Dye and L. Harmon Ziegler, *The Irony of Democracy*, 2nd ed. (Belmont, Calif.: Duxbury Press, 1972), p. 143.

[40] On the inaccurate and unrealistic treatment of American history, see Frances Fitzgerald, *America Revised* (Boston: Little, Brown & Company, 1979).

[41] Tucker, *The Experience of Politics*, p. 136.

for political manipulation. Never having been exposed to real-life political struggle, and armed largely with an unrealistic view of the political order, too many people are rendered impotent in the face of concentrated power. This is in large part the cause of the high levels of apathy, cynicism, and alienation from the prevailing political structure we saw in Chapter 2.

Once again, we do not wish to overstate the degree to which schools are successful in their intended or unintended socialization practices. Many factors—from peer influence to nonschool environmental forces—may function to undermine the effectiveness of such practices. Our knowledge of the ultimate impact of schooling on attitudes and behavior remains rather limited. We suggest, however, that the momentum of schooling lies in one direction: the encouragement of social conformity, fear of personal failure, and political passivity.

SCHOOLING AND INEQUALITY

Aside from and related to its role in socializing youngsters, the American educational system also functions as a *gatekeeper.* That is, it operates to guide people from and into one or another level of the class system—or to keep them at the same level. Where one stands in the class structure bears a direct relationship to the type, quality, and amount of formal education one is likely to receive. A person's class position is likely to be reaffirmed by the treatment received in school.[42]

Children from poverty-level areas face a real problem. They are most likely to attend public schools with a limited range of educational resources. Failure and dropout rates tend to be high in schools serving low-income populations. Many poor children, dissatisfied with their school experiences and/or drawn by the need to find employment to help their families, quit when they are legally old enough.[43] Nationally, 25 percent of high school students failed to graduate in the 1980s; most of them came from low-income backgrounds. Dropouts are most likely to wind up with low-paying blue-collar jobs. The relationship between years of school completed and income is readily visible in Table 7.2. Lacking the credentials that would help their marketability in the world of work (see Chapter 6), children from low-income families are likely to find themselves in the same position in the class structure as their parents. Mass public education, rather than helping low-income children change their class position, often functions to reaffirm their poverty.

By contrast, children who come from more affluent communities tend to have a more positive experience. They are likely to enter public schools with a built-in head start, since their parents are best able to provide the time, energy, and money to prepare their children for school. It is in affluent homes that expensive educational toys, games, and books are likely to be found. Children may gain experience from travel and preschool enrollment in enriched settings. They then enter schools whose structure and climate are in line with their childhood experiences.

Of equal importance is the fact that the public schools are ready for them. Schools serving middle- and upper-income populations tend to have the best teaching resources, the widest array of educational services, and high expectations for performance. Dropout rates are low, and movement into higher education is common. Thus, with the assistance of quality treatment, children of the affluent are channeled toward positions that replicate their parents' class standing.

A number of outside factors help keep the

[42] See Jeannie Oakes, *Keeping Track: How Schools Structure Inequality* (New Haven, Conn.: Yale University Press, 1985).

[43] Michelle Fine, "Dropping Out of High School: An Inside Look," *Social Policy,* 16 (Fall 1985): 43–50.

TABLE 7.2 Income Differences by Sex, Occupation, and Education, Median Incomes for Full-Time, Year-Round Workers, 1988

Variable	Men	Women
Occupation		
Executive, administrators, and managerial	$36,759	$23,356
Professional specialty	37,490	25,789
Technical and related support	30,369	21,039
Sales	27,022	15,474
Administrative support, including clerical	24,399	16,676
Precision production, craft, and repair	25,746	16,869
Machine operators, assemblers, and inspectors	21,382	13,289
Transportation and material moving	23,453	13,021
Handlers, equipment cleaners, helpers, and laborers	17,042	13,397
Service workers	18,648	11,032
Private household	*	7,299
Service workers, except private household	18,670	11,232
Farming, forestry, and fishing	14,300	9,926
Years of school completed		
Total, 25 years and over	29,331	19,497
8 years or less	17,190	11,358
High school		
Total	25,298	16,334
1–3 years	20,777	13,104
4 years	26,045	16,810
College		
Total	35,291	24,023
1–3 years	30,129	20,845
4 years or more	39,967	26,804
4 years	36,434	25,187
5 years or more	43,938	30,136

*Not calculated. Number of persons in category is not significant.

Source: U.S. Department of Commerce, Bureau of the Census, *Money Income and Poverty Status in the United States, 1988* (Washington, D.C.: U.S. Government Printing Office, 1989), pp. 44–45.

gatekeeper functioning. Expenditures on public education differ from state to state, depending on the state's economic well-being and the priority placed on school spending. Within each state, local per pupil expenditures differ among school systems. Though school systems receive state and federal funds, local school financing is based heavily on property taxes. Consequently, inequities abound. More affluent communities—in which property values are high—can provide a great deal of money for schooling at low tax rates. In communities in which property values are low, even very high tax rates will generate little money for education. Challenges have been brought against such inequities in a few state supreme courts, but a child's education often continues to reflect the worth of the land and buildings in his or her community.

Even where expenditures appear to be equal for all children, this may mask the fact that special outlays may be needed to aid children whose families were unable to get them ready for school success. Equal spending does not necessarily mean equal educational outcomes, given the damage that poverty-level living can do to the development of a small child. And children from low-income families are often faced with discriminatory treatment when attending school with more affluent children. Teacher expectations, the channeling of children into special groups for instruction, and the use of questionable testing devices are all part of the gatekeeping process.

In this section we shall go into more detail about the relationship between education and inequality. We shall be examining the mechanisms and processes through which organized schooling ensures that the class position of less affluent children is not appreciably altered.

Tracking and Testing—An Overview

When mass public education was introduced into the United States in the nineteenth century, increasing numbers of children enrolled in tax-supported school systems. Soon the population of the public schools began to be dominated by members of the poor and working classes.[44] This was particularly the case when school attendance became compulsory under the law. In general, however, the low-income children left school early to go to work. The higher grades primarily served those from affluent backgrounds.

But by the beginning of the twentieth century, a shift began to take place in the composition of the higher grades. Laws passed to keep children in school longer (and thus reduce the number of children in the labor pool) began to be effective. The occupational structure itself was changing, and new employment opportunities existed for people with literacy skills. More people could afford to let their children remain in school, instead of sending them out to find work at the first legal opportunity. Finally, there was a growing belief in education as a route to self-improvement and movement upward in the class system.

The result was that public high schools were faced with an influx of students from poorer families. Educators tried to find a solution to the problem of accommodating these students. They came up with the idea—deemed innovative at the time—of organizing high school curricula around a system of *tracks,* each geared to a different occupational or educational end. The tracks were set up to prepare students for what they would most likely be doing upon graduation. Educators assumed that children from economically disadvantaged backgrounds were destined for similar futures. Thus a *vocational track* was created for this group. The affluent were steered into an *academic track* on the assumption that they were likely to go on to college or to enter occupations in which academic skills would be useful.

Placement into one of these tracks was not only based on the socioeconomic standing of students' parents. Earlier performance in school was also taken into account. But since performance in academic subjects tended to reflect the environmental advantages associated with class background, the end result was the same. Placement in a vocational or academic track generally reflected class differences.

At the same time, educators were able to argue that all children were receiving an equal opportunity to be educated—that the schools had simply been organized more efficiently in order to take different abilities into account. In the early twentieth century, the notion of efficiency was of particular relevance, for public school systems were under political pressures to demonstrate that they were using tax funds

---

[44] This section draws heavily on the ideas of Samuel Bowles, "Unequal Education and the Reproduction of the Social Division of Labor," in Elizabeth L. Useem and Michael Useem, eds., *The Education Establishment* (Englewood Cliffs, N.J.: Prentice-Hall, 1974), pp. 17–43; David K. Cohen and Marvin Lazerson, "Education and the Corporate Order," *Socialist Revolution* (March–April 1972): 47–72; and Bowles and Gintis, *Schooling in Capitalist America.* See also Oakes, *Keeping Track.*

in a businesslike manner.[45] The track system was offered as proof that this was being done.

But despite the track system, the quest for efficiency, and other innovations, the dropout and failure rates in public schools were extremely high. By any real standard, mass public education was failing. In an examination of school surveys from a number of big-city school systems, Colin Greer found that, during the early part of this century, educators were more concerned with how many students were being enrolled than with what happened to them once they were in school. Greer argues that, ironically, the failures of American education were (and still are) signs that it has been succeeding in maintaining the status quo. High dropout rates, for example, have guaranteed a continuous source of labor for low-paying, low-status jobs.[46]

Shortly after World War I, another innovation began to spread through public school systems. Under the impetus of the newly developing science of psychology, special tests were developed that were said to be useful in measuring intelligence and native ability. Educators quickly grasped these tests. Here, presumably, were tools with which individual differences could be discovered among students. With testing, children could be guided to those educational programs for which they were most

[45] See Raymond Callahan, *Education and the Cult of Efficiency* (Chicago: University of Chicago Press, 1962).

[46] Greer, *The Great School Legend*, pp. 105–51.

Low-income white and minority students tend to have high dropout rates and thus are often poorly equipped to enter the job market. High school dropouts are likely to be eligible for only those jobs where pay is low and mobility upward very limited, such as entry-level positions in service firms. Performing unskilled work in a fast food establishment can be a dead end for a dropout, as opposed to a wayside stop for a graduate-to-be. *(Peter Menzel/Stock, Boston)*

suited—another step toward making schools efficient.

Needless to say, psychological testing fit well with the already accepted concept of tracking. And performance on the tests largely reflected the advantages associated with class background. Students from low-income backgrounds tended to perform poorly on the new tests, enabling school authorities to justify their placement in tracks demanding little in the way of academic work. The reverse tended to hold true for students coming from economically privileged backgrounds. The combined effects of testing and tracking were to further rigidify differential treatment of children on the basis of their class origins.

The logical accompaniment to the testing movement, and one that followed closely on its heels, was the growth of the guidance counselor profession. New experts were required to administer and interpret the results of the tests. Counselors trained in educational psychology and statistics were hired to work with students and parents. Not only did students from different class backgrounds continue to be channeled into different tracks; now the guidance counselor could show that they "deserved" the placement.

Today testing remains a common method of ascertaining the so-called intelligence and ability of students. Children from low-income families, both white and minority children, by and large perform poorly on IQ tests, for the forms of knowledge and the thought processes required by these tests are most likely to be acquired in middle-class homes and schools. But the use of IQ tests to measure intelligence is still widespread despite the generally acknowledged biases of the testing instruments.

In most public school systems, too, a track system still exists.[47] Guidance counselors continue to play the role of test administrators and help guide students into the appropriate curriculum. In sum, it is hard not to conclude, along with Colin Greer, that

> the fact of the matter is that American public schools in general, and urban public schools in particular, are a highly successful enterprise. Basic to that success is the high degree of academic failure among students. . . . The schools do the job today they have always done. They select out individuals for opportunities according to a hierarchical schema which runs parallel to existing social class patterns.[48]

If the public schools attempted to ensure academic success for every child, the supply of school- and self-defined losers would rapidly dwindle. In Greer's view, this would mean trouble, since there would be too many academically successful people from low-income backgrounds who would probably be very restive if forced to perform America's least desirable jobs.

An Elementary School Case Study

A case study that focuses on a group of children in an urban elementary school dramatically illustrates the impact of tracking and testing.[49] The study was conducted by Ray C. Rist, a student of the late Jules Henry, whose work on noise we discussed earlier. Rist followed the progress of a group of black children who were attending public school in St. Louis, Missouri. Teachers in the school likewise were black.

In the school Rist studied, teachers typically knew something about each child before the

---

[47] See Caroline Hodges Persell, *Education and Inequality* (New York: The Free Press, 1977), Chapter 6.

[48] Greer, *The Great School Legend*, p. 152.

[49] Ray C. Rist, "Student Social Class and Teacher Expectations," *Harvard Educational Review*, 40 (August 1970): 411–51. See also Rist, *The Urban School: A Factory for Failure* (Cambridge, Mass.: The M.I.T. Press, 1973), and "On Understanding the Processes of Schooling," in Jerome Karabel and A. H. Halsey, eds., *Power and Ideology in Education* (New York: Oxford University Press, 1977), pp. 292–305.

child began kindergarten. For example, they knew which children came from homes receiving welfare aid; they had met the mothers during preenrollment interviews; and they had heard about the experiences of other teachers with the children's brothers and sisters. None of this information, Rist notes, necessarily had anything to do with the talent or ability of the new kindergartners. But it did help create a certain set of expectations in each teacher's mind before the first day of class.

Rist observed that by the eighth day of kindergarten, the teacher in the class he was following had made permanent seating arrangements for each child. At the table closest to her (Table 1) were the well-dressed children who were not from welfare families, who seemed comfortable with classroom routine, and who spoke "school language" at all times (in other words, they spoke like the teacher). At the two remaining tables, farther away from the teacher's desk, sat children dressed in old, worn clothing. The Table 2 and Table 3 children were from welfare homes, seemed ill-at-ease in their surroundings, and rarely spoke. When they did speak, they often used a street dialect rather than "standard English."

The children at Table 1 were not only seated closest to the teacher; they also received most of her verbal and physical attention. Moreover, they were given special privileges and responsibilities by the teacher. Table 1 children were chosen to recite the Pledge of Allegiance, to read the weather calendar, to pass out class materials, and to take messages to the office.

Noting these seating arrangements and the positive treatment being accorded Table 1 children, Rist asked the teacher what was going on. The teacher told him that "the first table consisted of her 'fast learners' while those at the last two tables 'had no idea what was going on in the classroom.'"[50] Thus, by the eighth day of school, a process of labeling was already under way. On the basis of class bias, the teacher had effectively written off two tables of kindergartners as being uneducable.

Over time, Rist saw indications that the children at Table 1 were adopting the attitudes of their teacher. The so-called fast learners began to ridicule and belittle the Table 2 and Table 3 children. Within a few weeks, the low-income children had begun to sense that both the teacher and their more affluent peers were against them. In response, some of them became withdrawn, and others engaged in verbal and physical outbursts. This behavior confirmed the teacher's view that these children were different, troublesome, and not interested in learning. In reality, as Rist observed, the teacher herself had set the situation in motion, and the children's behavior was simply an outcome of her own.

The process Rist observed has often been called a *self-fulfilling prophecy*. Put simply, if one acts as if a situation is real, the situation may indeed become real. In this case, the teacher acted as if the low-income children could not learn, and as a consequence they did not learn. By her actions, the teacher's prophecy that the children were uneducable was fulfilled.

Most of the kindergarten children went on to the first grade. The kindergarten teacher had already given a dossier on each child to the first-grade teacher, who used the dossiers to make permanent seating arrangements. Not surprisingly, the seating plan closely resembled that of the kindergarten classroom. In the first grade, Table 1 children made rapid progress in reading—the kindergarten teacher had prepared them well. The first-grade teacher spent a good deal of time trying to teach the Tables 2 and 3 children the basics they should have learned earlier. Differential teacher expectations had become translated into differential academic performance, through no fault of the low-income children.

Almost all the children moved on to the second grade a year later. There, according to Rist,

[50] Rist, "Student Social Class and Teacher Expectations," p. 422.

PUBLIC PROBLEM, PRIVATE PAIN

A Child in the Lowest Track

Social psychologist Thomas J. Cottle has written extensively on children and youth. In pursuing research on how and why many poor children are excluded from receiving a quality education, Cottle recorded the following statement by a student attending elementary school. This youngster has just learned that he is being placed in the lowest academic track and that school officials consider his placement justified by his scores on so-called intelligence and capability tests. The child's words reveal his hurt and anger over this attack on his self-worth. According to Cottle, testing and placement in the lowest track contribute to poor performance, absenteeism, and high suspension and dropout rates among low-income children.

They told me in school that I'm stupid. I didn't know what they were talking about but they just kept saying it. Told me there was no use talking back to them because they had it in their tests, everything they wanted to know about me. I said I should be in the other group, because those kids were learning more and besides, they were getting all the best teachers in their classes. I didn't want them to put me in the class which they put me in. But they said it was not what they *wanted* to do, it was what they *had* to do 'cause they don't decide what classes to put the student in, the tests decide that for them. People don't decide.

I was thinking that maybe I should take a rest from school because if they're putting me in that worst class then I don't see any reason why I should be there at all. When you're in that class they don't even care if you go to school or not. All they care about is that their records are right. They got me tested the way I'm supposed to, 'cause you can't refuse it, you got to be tested if they say so. So now I'm tested. So now they know. They think I'm stupid. If they don't think so then all they have to do is go into that office and look inside my folder and then they can see. "We know you're a real smart guy," they'd say, "but the test knows better. We test everybody, and you're dumber than everybody except for all the nobodies we're putting in the same class with you."

I think you should be able to tell them whether you want to take those tests. Maybe if I said no way man, no way I'm going to answer any of your questions except the ones my teacher asks, maybe I could go and be with those other kids in the better class. I saw them testing one girl yesterday. They asked her politely, and she went with them. I followed them. You know why they were testing her? Because she talked too smart to be in the same class with the rest of us. She did talk smart too. I was thinking she was real smart, smarter than me.

They tested her 'cause they *wanted* to get her out of that class. That's why they did it. They wanted her to get out of there with us. But they don't want that with me. They don't want to teach me nothing at that school. They don't want me to get smarter 'cause if I get too smart they'll have to put me in a higher group like they did with that girl. They ain't helping me to read better or faster. All they do is keep testing me to see if I'm doing things any better. But how can anyone get smarter if nobody's teaching 'em nothing. How'm I suppose to read faster and then remember everything I'm reading too if everybody's running around testing everybody. Teachers are supposed to teach, not test! If they spent their time teaching they wouldn't have to test us all the time. Even if they don't teach us they could spend more time with us so if somebody asked them is that kid smart, they'd know. They'd know even without testing.

Thomas J. Cottle, *Barred from School: 2 Million Children!* (Washington. D.C.: New Republic Books, 1976). pp. 116–17.

students were assigned seats on the basis of their scores on reading tests. The second-grade teacher thus had a "scientific" basis on which to predict each child's performance in the classroom. Tables 1, 2, and 3 were almost totally reproduced in the second grade, but with a new element added. The best readers were the Tigers, the next best were the Cardinals, and the slowest readers were the Clowns. A number of the Clowns were repeating second grade.

The kinds of distinctions made among these children, the teachers' expectations for them, and their treatment by the teachers all fed into a system of tracking and testing. Academic retardation or failure, for the poorer children, quickly became cumulative. It seems reasonable to assume that when these children reach high school they will be persuaded that they deserve to enter a nonacademic track—assuming they have retained interest in education at all. (In many central city high schools the dropout rate is around 50 percent.) As Rist concluded:

> The public school system, I believe, is justifiably responsible for contributing to the present structure of society.... The picture that emerges from this study is that the school shares in the complicity of maintaining the organizational perpetuation of poverty and unequal opportunity.[51]

The High School Level

Tracking in other public elementary schools may be more subtle and informal than in the school Rist studied. But by the time a student gets to high school, the process typically becomes quite blatant and rigidified.[52] Walter E. Schafer and his colleagues studied two typical high schools, located in the Midwest, in an effort to document the impact of tracking in the higher grades.[53] One school was located in a middle-class, academic community, the other in a working-class, industrial area. Both high schools divided their programs into "college-prep" and "general" tracks. Students were assigned to one of the tracks upon entering the ninth grade.

The researchers had difficulty determining exactly *why* a student was assigned to a particular track, though they felt the guidance counselors played a key role. It became clear that "socioeconomic and racial background had an effect on which track a student took, quite apart from either his achievement in junior high or his ability as measured by I.Q. scores."[54] Students attending the high school located in the middle-class community and those from white-collar families in the working-class high school tended to enter the college-prep track. Students from blue-collar families, particularly if they were black, most often entered the general track. For the most part, the decision was permanent; students generally stayed in the same track through all four years of high school.

Track position was correlated with students' success in school. College-prep students had the highest grade average by senior year, and grade differences between this group and the general track students increased between grades 9 and 12. General track students were likely to graduate toward the bottom of their class. The dropout rate was 36 percent for general track students but only 4 percent for those in college prep. Finally, records indicated higher rates of delinquency and violation of school rules for youngsters in the general track than for college-prep students.

The problem facing the researchers was one of explaining these differences. Scores on the school achievement and IQ tests the students took in elementary school did not seem to be

---

[51] Ibid., p. 447.

[52] For an up-to-date overview, see Goodlad, *A Place Called School,* Chapter 5. See also James E. Rosenbaum, *Making Inequality: The Hidden Curriculum of High School Tracking* (New York: John Wiley & Sons, 1976).

[53] Walter E. Schafer et al., "Programmed for Social Class," *Trans-action,* 7 (October 1970): 39–46.

[54] Ibid., p. 40.

related to high school performance. The researchers finally reached a conclusion that seems to confirm Rist's findings—that differential academic performance and dropout rates were actually *promoted* by track assignment. That is, being placed in the general track or the college-prep track to some extent caused student behavior.[55]

Probing further, Schafer and his colleagues found that students felt stigmatized by not being assigned to college prep. Their placement in the general track negatively affected their self-esteem and eroded their belief in their own abilities. As a result, they did not work hard in school. Furthermore, the teachers and administrators expected little of general track students, and the students tended to respond accordingly. The self-fulfilling prophecy, mentioned earlier, was at work. The teachers felt justified in awarding low grades for the work performed by general track students, no matter how well the work was done. This practice contributed to low student motivation and a lack of commitment to school attendance—factors reflected in high dropout rates. General track students created a peer-group society in opposition to authority, leading to rule violation and delinquent acts in the community. Such phenomena were found in both high schools, despite the fact that they were located in quite different kinds of communities.

Once again, the outcome of differential treatment seems clear. Students from more affluent backgrounds, having been given preferential treatment in high school, will typically enter college. They will most likely get well-paying jobs and occupy a class position much like that of their parents. The students from low-income backgrounds, white and minority, have had their sense of self-worth attacked. They have been told by their track placement, by their treatment by teachers, and by the evaluation of their performance that they are not destined for success. It is unlikely that they will attend college. In such ways, the American system of education produces self-defined losers who, whatever their real talents and abilities, are likely to relive the experiences of their low-income families.

Higher Education

As we have seen, the American system of education does a good deal of sifting and sorting. Education also functions as a gatekeeper on the college and university levels. The question of who goes on to higher education is easily answered. If you have money, you go. Ability counts less than dollars. Thus, those from affluent backgrounds tend to have the highest number of years of education completed (see Table 7.3).

Since the end of World War II, an increasing percentage of high school graduates have gone on for further years of schooling. An important reason for this is that employers have progressively escalated their requirements for entry-level positions.[56] The educational attainment of the labor force has moved steadily upward. Another reason is the shortage of jobs. Many young persons have found enrolling in higher education—when they can afford it—preferable to being unemployed. Furthermore, there is more opportunity for students to continue their education, for the number and size of colleges and universities have (until quite recently) been undergoing substantial growth. Most noteworthy has been the creation of a massive network of two-year colleges. Today nearly half of all high

---

[55] On the impact of tracking, see also Barbara Heyns, "Social Selection and Stratification Within Schools," *American Journal of Sociology*, 79 (May 1974): 1434–51, and Karl Alexander and Edward McDill, "Selection and Allocation Within Schools," *American Sociological Review*, 41 (December 1976): 963–80.

[56] See Ivar Berg, *Education and Jobs* (New York: Praeger Publishers, 1970).

TABLE 7.3 Highest Level of Education Attained by 1980 High School Seniors, by Socioeconomic Status and Race/Ethnicity, Spring 1986

Socioeconomic status* in 1980 and race/ethnicity	Highest educational attainment of 1980 high school seniors in 1986						
	Total	No high school diploma†	High school diploma	License‡	Associate degree	Bachelor's degree	Graduate/ professional degree
Lower 25 percent							
White, non-Hispanic	100.0	0.9	75.1	12.2	5.0	6.6	0.3
Black, non-Hispanic	100.0	1.4	73.0	12.7	5.1	7.7	0.1
Hispanic	100.0	1.6	73.9	11.8	7.8	4.9	—§
Asian	100.0	—§	53.4	17.3	15.7	12.0	1.6
Middle 50 percent							
White, non-Hispanic	100.0	0.3	62.0	13.0	8.0	16.3	0.4
Black, non-Hispanic	100.0	0.3	67.5	14.7	6.5	10.7	0.3
Hispanic	100.0	1.0	67.0	14.7	6.5	10.7	0.2
Asian	100.0	—§	51.1	11.7	11.1	26.1	—§
Upper 25 percent							
White, non-Hispanic	100.0	—§	44.9	8.6	6.2	38.2	2.2
Black, non-Hispanic	100.0	—§	56.3	12.4	5.4	25.5	0.4
Hispanic	100.0	0.3	60.0	11.4	9.6	18.0	0.7
Asian	100.0	—§	42.9	6.5	4.8	40.0	5.9

Note: Because of rounding, percentages may not add to 100.0.
*Socioeconomic status was measured by a composite score on parental education, family income, father's occupation, and household characteristics in 1980.
†Seniors who dropped out of high school after spring 1980 survey and had not completed high school by 1986.
‡Includes persons who earned a certificate for completing a program of study.
§Less than 0.05 percent.
Source: National Center for Education Statistics, *Digest of Education Statistics, 1989* (Washington, D.C.: U.S. Government Printing Office, 1989), p. 278.

school graduates go on to some form of higher education each year, mostly to publicly supported institutions.

The gatekeeper function in higher education is seen most clearly in an analysis of which students go on to what kinds of institutions of higher learning.[57] High schools not only channel students to or away from further schooling; they also channel students to particular rungs on the status ladder of higher education. Again, class background of a student plays a determining role.

State systems of higher education are ordinarily made up of large universities, four-year colleges, and two-year ("community" or "junior") colleges. As one moves from the community college up to the university level—the most prestigious—the income backgrounds from which most students are drawn increase demonstrably. Since the level at which one enters the labor force is linked with the type of educational credentials one is able to gain, the multitiered system of higher education may be viewed as a part of the tracking process.

Whereas three-quarters of all adults aged twenty-five and over are high school graduates, only 20 percent of all adults have completed four

[57] See Samuel Bowles, "Contradictions in U.S. Higher Education," in Richard C. Edwards et al., eds., *The Capitalist System* (Englewood Cliffs, N.J.: Prentice-Hall, 1972), pp. 491–503; Jerome Karabel, "Community Colleges and Social Stratification," *Harvard Educational Review*, 42 (November 1972): 521–62; and L. Steven Zwerling, *Second Best* (New York: McGraw-Hill Book Company, 1976).

or more years of college.[58] Class background influences a student's chances of completing college. Since attendance at any institution of higher education costs money, the least affluent have the most difficult time remaining. Though public institutions tend to cost less than private ones, and though numerous grant and loan programs have been created to help needy students, costs continue to escalate. Those most likely to drop out completely, or to interrupt their studies for a period of time, come from low-income backgrounds.

Children from economically advantaged families are most likely to enter universities, not community colleges. Many will attend private elite institutions. From there they are likely to go on to graduate or professional schools. Because they, not the low-income students, stay in school longest, attend universities where per pupil costs are high, and go on to even more expensive graduate training, the affluent capture a disproportionate amount of the tax funds that go to support higher education. One might say that this is a special "welfare" subsidy available only to the children of upper-income groups, one that helps them remain at the class level of their families.

The Special Role of the Community College

Over 12 million students were enrolled in college in 1986—more than two and a half times as many as in 1960. This substantial rate of growth is largely a result of the importance of public two-year colleges. Community-college enrollment had grown to over 3.7 million by 1986. On the one hand, community colleges are evidence of the democratization of higher education; access to higher education has been made available to ever more people. On the other hand, community colleges have themselves been accused of playing a gatekeeping role.

Community colleges seem to have taken on two major tasks. First, they prepare students to go on to a four-year degree program at a state college or university. Second, they offer vocational programs for those who wish to (or must) pursue a two-year terminal degree. Vocational programs range from health services to data processing. Admission standards are usually very liberal, and students whose formal educational preparation might be cause for rejection by more exclusive institutions can easily get in. Unlike most four-year institutions, community colleges use a system of *open enrollment*, which means that they are consciously open to almost all comers.

Yet, while many of the students who enroll in community colleges may aspire to transfer to four-year schools, relatively few end up doing so. It has been suggested that many students who enroll in two-year schools are subjected to a "cooling out" process.[59] That is, testing and counseling practices may influence community-college students into lowering their academic aspirations by making these students doubt their ability to succeed in a four-year college or university. However, it could also be argued that the high costs of attending college, coupled with highly selective admissions practices at many four-year institutions, are what really lower aspirations. Those who place the blame on community colleges may simply be ignoring other factors that the staffs of such schools have no way of controlling.

According to Jerome Karabel, "community colleges are, in reality, a vital component of the class-based tracking system."[60] But in the ab-

---

[58] U.S. Department of Commerce, Bureau of the Census, *Educational Attainment in the United States* (Washington, D.C.: U.S. Government Printing Office, 1987).

[59] Burton R. Clark, "The 'Cooling Out' Function in Higher Education," *American Journal of Sociology*, 65 (May 1960): 569–77. See also Bowles, "Contradictions in U.S. Higher Education," p. 494, and Zwerling, *Second Best*.

[60] Karabel, "Community Colleges and Social Stratification," p. 555.

sence of such institutions, far fewer persons from low-income backgrounds would have the chance of receiving any higher education.

Literacy and Inequality

OVE
RCOM
INGIL
LITE
RACY

So reads the headline of a newspaper article on illiteracy.[61] The stress and disorientation one feels on being confronted by "words" that do not make any sense are familiar to the illiterate population. Also familiar are feelings of isolation and alienation. We live in a society that is knowledge-driven. The transmission and consumption of information in such forms as text, tables, figures, and maps are central to societal functioning. People who are unable to comprehend such information due to a lack of literacy are likely to live lives of social, economic, and political marginality.

The definition of illiteracy has been the subject of some debate.[62] The definition used is crucial, since it has implications for the size of the population about which we should be concerned. One traditional definition is simply the inability to write one's name. By this definition, few adults in the United States could be called illiterate. But when the criteria involve the ability to perform basic tasks in reading comprehension or fundamental mathematics, the vast dimensions of illiteracy in the United States stand revealed.

Consider the federal government's National Assessment of Educational Progress, a study of the literacy skills of young adults aged twenty-one to twenty-five. For the purposes of the study literacy was defined as "using printed and written information to function in society, to achieve one's goals, and to develop one's knowledge and potential."[63] The literacy skills assessed involved prose comprehension, use of information in nontextual materials (e.g., tables, schedules), and application of arithmetic operations to everyday tasks. The study revealed that 5 percent of young adults cannot read at a fourth-grade level of competency and 20 percent cannot read beyond an eighth-grade level.[64]

While ability to read at a certain grade level is an acceptable indicator of literacy to many experts, this study's emphasis on the ability to function in society produced some unexpected and troubling findings:

> For prose skills, almost all those tested could describe a job that they would like, but less than 40 percent could understand a somewhat difficult newspaper article and less than 10 percent could interpret a four-line poem.
>
> For ability to handle documents, all those tested could find the time of a forthcoming meeting on a memorandum, but less than 60 percent could read a paragraph and only 20 percent could effectively deal with a bus schedule.
>
> In quantitative skills, more than 90 percent could balance a checkbook, but less than 40 percent could calculate change they would be due when ordering a simple meal from a menu and less than 10 percent could properly fill out a catalogue order form.[65]

Such findings suggest that definitions of literacy based only on grade-level reading competency may mask some very fundamental deficiencies in the knowledge base of American adults.

---

[61] Catharine Foster, "OVE RCOM INGIL LITE RACY," *Christian Science Monitor* (September 8, 1988): 14–15.

[62] Ibid. See also Jonathan Kozol, *Illiterate America* (Garden City, N.Y.: Anchor Press/Doubleday, 1985), Chapter 2.

[63] U.S. Department of Education, National Center for Educational Statistics, *The Condition of Education* (Washington, D.C.: U.S. Government Printing Office, 1987), p. 30.

[64] Edward B. Fiske, "Literacy in America: Beyond the Basics," *New York Times* (September 26, 1988): A15.

[65] Leslie Maitland Warner, "U.S. Study on Adult Literacy Finds the Results Are Mixed," *New York Times* (September 26, 1986): D27.

That much having been said, data exist on adults of all ages to support the contention that 25 million people either cannot read at all or can read only at a level equivalent to the early elementary school years. Another 35 million adults read only as well as eighth-grade norms.[66] These 60 million people, termed "Illiterate America" by Jonathan Kozol, make up one-third of the U.S. adult population!

Who are the illiterate? In contrast to stereotypes held by many, most are white people born in the United States. However, by all accounts rates of illiteracy are disproportionately high among the native-born black and Hispanic populations. Immigrants from outside the United States make up only a small proportion of the illiterate; most of these are literate in their native language and need only to make the transition to functioning in English.

The presence of widespread illiteracy among people born in the United States and exposed to its system of educational opportunity should not be cause for surprise. We have seen how this society is divided along class lines and how such practices as tracking in schools often have a very negative effect on the education of those from poverty and working-class backgrounds. Illiteracy rates are little more than numerical indicators of the generation of school failures.

As illiterate children grow up and become illiterate adults, they may marry and have families. As parents they live with the constant knowledge that they are unable to help their own children learn how to read. Moreover, illiterate parents are in no position to monitor and appraise their children's school progress (or lack thereof). When such children find themselves in school settings that are subtly inhospitable and/or not responsive to their learning needs, the stage is set for the generation of yet more failures. The phenomena of "social promotion" (promotion from grade to grade without regard to a child's grade level skills) and of high dropout rates (25 percent nationally and up to 50 percent in some central cities) frequently involve illiterates being pushed through and finally out of schooling.

Some argue that the attention illiteracy has been receiving of late is a reflection of concern that the nation can no longer afford such lack of literacy in its labor force.[67] At the same time that the United States is facing sharp competition in world markets and is developing into a service economy based on complex technology and information exchange, it is being discovered that many in the adult population lack the skills to read a bus schedule or to calculate change due them when making a purchase.

It is estimated that 70 percent of the reading material used in a cross section of the nation's jobs requires comprehension at the ninth-grade level and higher. Some experts predict that abilities at the twelfth grade and beyond will be called for routinely in the new jobs generated in the twenty-first century. As the numbers of people incapable of performing higher than an eighth-grade level of comprehension increases each year, corporate and governmental elites are becoming disturbed over the adequacy of literacy skills in the U.S. labor force. Their concern is less for the problems faced by the illiterate individual than for potential declines in corporate profits and economic growth. Firms unable to depend on a stable supply of workers whose skill levels match job requirements confront inefficiencies and related expenses.

Such practical concerns ignore the crippling costs experienced by the individual who is trapped in a state of illiteracy.[68] Such persons suffer anxiety, embarrassment, and humiliation in the face of their disability; they may also be

[66] Kozol, *Illiterate America*, p. 10.

[67] Lee A. Daniels, "Illiteracy Seen as Threat to U.S. Economic Edge," *New York Times* (September 7, 1988): B8.

[68] Joseph Berger, "Price of Illiteracy Translates into Poverty and Humiliation," *New York Times* (September 6, 1988): A1, and Kozol, *Illiterate America*, Chapters 3–5.

While the majority of those disabled by illiteracy are white, members of minority groups are disproportionately represented in the illiterate population. There are volunteer tutorial and other programs for people who need help, no matter what their race or ethnic origins. But these programs are not large enough to help more than a small percentage of those in need. *(Alan Carey/The Image Works)*

paralyzed by feelings of powerlessness and wounded self-esteem. Imagine traveling into unfamiliar places unable to read maps, schedules, or street signs. Daily functioning can be a nightmare of stress when a person cannot comprehend employment applications, newspapers, landlords' leases and notices, labels on foods and medicines, warnings of hazards, restaurant menus, children's homework and teachers' messages, bills and bank notices, telephone directories, recipes, television program schedules, letters from friends and relatives, or even the names of candidates in a voting machine. At the same time as illiterate persons guard against discovery and thus the stigma of being cast as "stupid" by the literate, they are forced to forgo simple pleasures and freedoms that those able to read this textbook take for granted.

Thus, the production of illiterates as a byproduct of our system of education in the United States does more than create labor supply problems for employers. It produces men and women engaged in a continual struggle, overwhelmed by a sense of social, economic, and political marginality. Such persons reside in U.S. society but are blocked from full participation in it. Some 60 percent of the 440,000 people confined in federal and state prisons cannot read above the sixth-grade level.[69] At the risk of oversimplifying, one suspects that lack of literacy has something to do with the turns many of their lives have taken.

ALTERING THE EDUCATIONAL SYSTEM

Organized schooling both reflects and responds to the prevailing economic and political order. By preparing people to enter an adult world that already is, America's system of education plays socialization functions that help conserve the status quo. Though empirical evidence is scanty,

[69] Ibid.

research suggests that the schools fail to liberate children's minds and are as likely to deaden as to enliven human sensibilities. The bureaucratic nature of the school experience, together with the political indoctrination that goes on, may not produce robots. But neither does it produce people who are prepared to critically analyze American society and act collectively to bring about change. Economic inequality and concentrated political power cannot be blamed on public education. But to the degree to which socialization by schools fails to do more than legitimate the prevailing order, the schools cannot escape at least partial responsibility for the harm done to people within this order.

The gatekeeping function of organized schooling is both more complex and more obvious. On the one hand, America's system of education tends to affirm already existing inequalities. On the other hand, one must wonder whether our system of education could bring about a reduction of inequality in the absence of more fundamental changes in the prevailing order. Is education the "weak link" in the chain?[70] In other words, could the problem of inequality be best attacked through education? Or must economic inequality and the concentration of power be taken care of before we can hope to radically improve the organization and operation of education? In the long run, we believe the latter is the case. But in the short run, it is worth pushing the schools, those who run them, and the students who must survive in them toward changes that will minimize the harm being done to millions of children and young adults.

The first, and most basic, change goes to the heart of the American system of education. Whenever it becomes manifestly evident that a school is failing to teach, parents must be able to demand their children's placement in an alternative program of their choice. As it now stands, school attendance is mandatory even when the educational interests of children are not being met. The issue of compulsory attendance would be less critical if all schools were performing in ways that enhanced the development of children's human potential.

Changes are also long overdue in the organization of schools, specifically their bureaucratic and hierarchical nature. Obviously, rules are required to guide behavior whenever people must function in a group situation, but in many schools rules are used primarily to control and inhibit the freedom of children and youth. While such rules may serve the interests of the administrators and teachers who create and enforce them, they are not always in the best interests of students. Among the rules that deserve to be revised are those restricting students' freedom of physical movement, use of school facilities during and after school hours, and exercise of the rights of freedom of speech and of the press.

We have begun to see some movement away from the extreme bureaucratization of the school. Among the innovations tried by some schools are:

1. Open classrooms, which typically allow children freedom to move and talk within the classroom and provide a range of choices of learning tasks during at least part of the school day;
2. Individualized instruction, wherein curricular materials permit each child to work at some learning tasks at his or her own pace, and allow teachers to monitor the progress of individual children; and
3. Affective education, through which children are encouraged to recognize and understand their own and others' feelings, and their manner of relating to others.

The extensiveness of these innovations remains limited and their impact remains open to

---

[70] This is the position taken by Ivan Illich, *Deschooling Society* (New York: Harrow Books, 1971). See also Alan Gartner et al., eds., *After Deschooling What?* (New York: Harper & Row Publishers, 1973).

debate.[71] On the face of it, they would seem to be steps in the right direction. However, such classroom programs have been introduced *within* what remain bureaucratically organized institutions, dominated by educational authorities and subject to a wide array of rules and regulations.

What is needed is the democratization of educational institutions—itself an educational experience for those it would involve. Persons with a stake in school functioning—students, staff, and community representatives—should all freely participate in the formulation of rules. They should also collectively determine the division of labor and responsibilities that are to exist among those who fulfill different roles in the school setting. The point is to activate responsible involvement on the part of children and young people in shaping the decisions that affect them.

The implication is that schools must move toward becoming nonauthoritarian institutions, rather than settings for differential power and prestige. Along with this, schools should also become arenas for cooperation among all participants in the interests of meeting collective goals. The fear of failure is but one way—and a destructive one at that—to motivate young people to learn. Rather than encouraging children to compete, the schools should encourage them to cooperate. Individual learning experiences must be balanced by group efforts, to which all may contribute. Only in this way can the nightmare of personal obsolescence that competitive environments nurture be undercut.

Curricular changes that open up classrooms to the outside world must be implemented. Insulation from the world of work, from community problems, and from alternative political views runs counter to the ideal of human development through education. To function intelligently as adults, workers, voters, and taxpayers, students must be directly exposed to situations and issues with which they will have to deal. Rather than only reading about the world of work, students should be out talking to workers, union organizers, managers, and professionals. Instead of discussing current events, students should be creating or otherwise participating in political campaigns and social change movements. Any gap between the school and the real world is an artificial one, and there is no reason to permit it to exist.

Thus far we have dwelt upon changes in the organization of schools and in the kinds of socialization experiences to which students are exposed. An equally important feature of American education that must be altered is its gatekeeping function. Existing economic inequalities must be neither reflected in nor reinforced by the educational process.

The immediate goal is equality of opportunity for all children to develop their personalities, intellects, and manual skills to their fullest potential. Stark differences in the resources possessed by school systems must be minimized by reducing their financial reliance on local property taxes. Mechanisms to promote equitable funding of all systems through federal and state treasuries should be a top priority.

Within school systems, tracking must be abolished. More advanced students should routinely help less advanced students. The barriers between academic and vocational learning must also be abolished. All students should be developing interests and experiencing accomplishments that require skill with both head and hands. Testing, if used at all, should be used to diagnose progress, not as a device to channel students away from opportunities.

Educational professionals must be held accountable for their expected contributions to students during their careers in school. Those who

[71] For an assessment of the conflicting findings on the impact of open classrooms, see Hurn, *The Limits and Possibilities of Schooling*, pp. 237–47.

are not making a meaningful contribution to school programs should either be retrained or aided in finding some other line of work.

Finances should be no barrier to individuals who wish to go beyond high school—no matter at what point in their lives this decision is made. Free or low-cost tuition and flexible admissions policies can make higher education available to more people and can help meet the changing educational needs of people of all ages. Open enrollment must be implemented at all educational institutions that in any way benefit from public tax funds. That way, anyone who meets minimum educational requirements and who shows evidence of motivation will be assured entry into programs of his or her choice.

Rich educational opportunities from cradle to grave can be made available to all—but only if we are willing to press for change rather than moan about the existing system.

SUMMARY

Historians of education have tended to celebrate the positive contributions of America's system of mass public education. They have claimed that education has contributed to political democratization, economic growth, and the minimization of class inequalities. So-called revisionist historians have recently presented evidence that is somewhat contrary to such positive claims. The revisionists suggest that education has been looked to as a means of political indoctrination and social control, as a device to create a docile and compliant labor force, and as a mechanism to ensure that children of the affluent will retain their families' class position.

While we possess only limited knowledge about the impact of schooling on children today, a number of studies suggest that schools are important agents of socialization. Case studies point to the demands for conformity imposed on schoolchildren within bureaucratically organized institutions. It has been suggested that schools foster competition and fear of personal failure. And it is thought that schools function to render children politically unknowledgeable, unprepared for political struggle, and open to manipulation by elites. While the success of such socialization remains open to question, it appears that the momentum of schooling lies in such a direction.

Though mass public education has made schooling possible for everyone, it also performs a gatekeeping function. The resources of the affluent allow them to provide educational opportunities for their children that are qualitatively and quantitatively superior to those available to lower income groups. Moreover, systems of tracking and testing within school settings operate to place the less affluent in a position of educational disadvantage. A self-fulfilling prophecy operates when nonaffluent children are not expected to learn, are not taught, and thus do not perform at a level with their more affluent peers. Differential treatment in school translates into differential academic outcomes and helps keep class inequalities intact.

The gatekeeping function also operates at the level of higher education. Economically privileged families are best able to ensure that their children will attend college and remain until completion. Children from low-income families are less likely to attend and complete college. Those who do enroll are frequently forced to attend community colleges. Since where one enters the labor force is frequently linked to the type of educational credentials one possesses, children of the affluent possess a competitive advantage.

America's system of education can be altered in many ways. Parents must have the right to demand alternative school placement for their children when it is clear they are not being taught. Bureaucratic rules and regulations that are not in children's interests should be abolished, and efforts must be made to democratize educational institutions. Students must have a say in the decisions and policies affecting them. Moreover, schools must be turned into arenas of cooperation instead of competition. They must be opened up to the outside world, so that children can learn about the realities they will confront as adults.

Such changes must be accompanied by the abolition of practices that maintain the gatekeeping function of schools. Educational systems have to be equitably financed, and systems of tracking and testing that perpetuate differential treatment by class origin must be eliminated. The barriers between vocational and academic learning should be dropped, so that all students are able to maximize learning with their heads and hands. Educators must be held responsible for making a meaningful contribution to students throughout their school careers.

Finally, finances should be no obstacle to anyone who wishes to go beyond high school. Institutions of higher education must move toward open-enrollment policies and the reduction of tuition costs. Those who are motivated and possess the basic skills should be assured entry into programs of their choice.

DISCUSSION QUESTIONS

1. In what ways has going to school had an impact on your attitudes and behavior? Give examples.
2. What kinds of in-school behavior have you engaged in that was in violation of rules and regulations? Looking back, why do you think you engaged in such behavior?
3. What aspects of your school experience involved you in competition with others? How did you feel when winning or losing?
4. To what degree has your schooling provided you with the ability to analyze political issues and take a stand? Give examples.
5. Was there a tracking system in the schools you have attended? How was placement accomplished? How did students in different tracks view one another? What impact did being placed in a track have on you?
6. What alterations would you like to see in the organization and operation of the educational system? Why? Who or what stands in the way of such alterations?

SUGGESTED READINGS

Aronowitz, Stanley, and Henry A. Giroux. *Education Under Siege* (South Hadley, Mass.: Bergin & Garvey Publishers, 1985).
Conservative, liberal, and radical ideas on the functions of schooling.

Brint, Steven, and Jerome Karabel. *The Diverted Dream* (New York: Oxford University Press, 1989).
The historical role of two-year colleges in America and how they have functioned to foster and limit opportunities.

Cookson, Peter W., and Caroline Hodges Persell. *Preparing for Power: America's Elite Boarding Schools* (New York: Basic Books, 1985).
A behind-the-scenes look at prep school life and socialization for membership in the nation's elite.

Kozol, Jonathan. *Illiterate America* (New York: Anchor Press/Doubleday, 1985).
Data and personal accounts documenting the crisis of illiteracy for tens of millions in U.S. society.

Oakes, Jeannie. *Keeping Track: How Schools Structure Inequality* (New Haven, Conn.: Yale University Press, 1985).
Tracking practices in public schools and how they limit educational opportunity and achievement.

Rose, Mike. *Lives on the Boundary* (New York: Penguin Books, 1989).
Reflections on working with America's "educational underclass" and its members' enormous untapped strengths and talents.

CHAPTER 8

Racism

There should be no personal and institutional discrimination against individuals on the basis of race and ethnicity.

From the time the Plymouth settlement was founded by English colonists, the United States has been run by and in the interests of white people—and consciously so. Though men and women from a variety of other racial and cultural backgrounds have been major participants in the shaping of American history, most whites know little and care less about their roles. Alternately used, abused, and ignored by the white majority, Native Americans (Indians), black Americans, Hispanic Americans, Asian Americans, and other minority peoples have had a history of racial oppression.[1] Not only

[1] For a history of racism in the United States, see Paul Jacobs and Paul Landau (with Eve Pell), *To Serve the Devil* (New York: Random House, 1971). Though many white groups (for example, eastern and southern Europeans) have also experienced discrimination, this chapter focuses on those who are victims of discrimination based on race—or *racism*.

have the rights to "life, liberty, and the pursuit of happiness" historically been distributed along color lines; to a large extent, this is still the situation today.

Today, for example, there are over 1.5 million Native Americans. This group has suffered enormous injustice. Shortly after the European settlers arrived on this continent, they found it expedient to clear out the native peoples whose tribal societies stood in the way of territorial conquest and colonial expansion. The firm belief of whites in their own racial and cultural superiority (a belief without any real foundation) provided a ready rationale for their vicious treatment of "Indians." Native Americans were subjected to a continuing series of attacks: the takeover of ancestral lands, racially inspired killings, confinement on white-controlled reservations, bureaucratic manipulation by governmental agencies, and so on. Now, after generations of white domination, Native Americans are among the poorest and most oppressed minority groups in the United States. Their traditional patterns of living have been largely destroyed, and their life chances are almost completely subject to the whims of white-controlled institutions.[2] They were, and are, victims of racism.

The immediate territorial expansion of white American society involved pushing Native Americans back, aside, and under. And its early economic development to a large extent revolved around the wholesale purchase of human beings, their enslavement, and the use of their forced labor. Kidnaped and transported from the African continent, black men and women were forced to become a part of a white-run American society. Bought and sold, assaulted and bred, black slaves were worked relentlessly under a system of subjugation that was based on the assumption that they were not really human. When slavery in a society with democratic ideals began to present irreconcilable moral dilemmas (and, more important, when slavery became politically and economically questionable to maintain), it was cast aside as one outcome of a bloody Civil War. Yet the ingrained belief of whites in their own racial and cultural superiority did not significantly wither. Formal enslavement of black people was replaced by conscious racial segregation and other forms of discrimination that have functioned to keep black Americans "in their place." More than a century after the abolition of slavery, imposed inequalities continue to weigh upon many of the more than 29 million blacks living in the United States.[3]

Westward expansion was carried out at great cost to another group that was also made a part of the United States against its will. Prior to 1848 the southwestern portion of the United States was a part of Mexico. The people of Spanish and Native American ancestry occupying the territory had been there long before the colonists landed near Plymouth Rock. When white settlers began to "open up" the western frontier, the government of the United States precipitated a war against Mexico to "liberate" the rich agricultural lands and natural resources of the Southwest. Upon winning the war, the United States proceeded to annex half of Mexico's sovereign territory. Natives of Mexico who had occupied the lands for many generations were considered to have been conquered, and most landholdings were subsequently transferred into the hands of the victorious "Anglos." Once again the belief of whites in their own racial and cultural superiority came into play, conditioning the treatment of persons

[2] See Dee Brown, *Bury My Heart at Wounded Knee* (New York: Holt, Rinehart & Winston, 1970); Vine Deloria, Jr., *Custer Died for Your Sins* (New York: Avon Books, 1969); and Alvin M. Josephy, *Now That the Buffalo's Gone* (New York: Alfred A. Knopf, 1982).

[3] See John Hope Franklin, *From Slavery to Freedom*, 5th ed. (New York: Alfred A. Knopf, 1980); Harry Ashmore, *Hearts and Minds* (New York: McGraw-Hill Book Company, 1982); and Robert Staples, *The Urban Plantation* (San Francisco: Black Scholars Press, 1986).

of Mexican ancestry. Today 12.6 million Mexican Americans, most of whom reside in the Southwest, continue to struggle under Anglo control and domination.[4]

The American government's historical willingness to pursue territorial acquisition through conquest was responsible for pulling yet another group into this society's collection of minorities. Not too long after the annexation of the Southwest, the United States initiated a war against Spain—ostensibly to end Spanish colonial excesses in Cuba. After winning the war, the United States went on to claim the small Caribbean island of Puerto Rico. Spain ceded Puerto Rico to the United States, whereupon it fell—and remains today—under this society's political and economic control. Particularly in the years since World War II, Puerto Ricans—people whose ancestry includes mixtures of Spanish, African, and Taino Indian—have taken advantage of their American citizenship to migrate from the poverty-ridden island. Members of this group have settled primarily in the cities of the Northeast, especially in New York City. Mainland businesses, seeking cheap unskilled or semiskilled labor, have encouraged this migration. Once on the mainland, Puerto Ricans are just another racial minority so far as the dominant white population is concerned. The socioeconomic status of the more than 2 million Puerto Ricans on the mainland is severely depressed, and many are the victims of poverty and unemployment. Movement to and from the mainland is constant, as members of this group struggle for ways to deal with their difficult situation.[5]

The Hispanic population has been growing five times as fast as the rest of the country, according to census data. While people of Mexican origin comprise the numerically largest Hispanic-origin group, in the 1980s the fastest-growing sector of the Hispanic population was of Central and South American origin. They now number some 2.5 million people. Many Central and South American immigrants are in the United States after unsuccessful attempts to overcome crushing poverty conditions and harsh political repression by authoritarian governments. Often these regimes are financially and politically supported by the United States, as is the case with Guatemala and El Salvador. Such recent patterns of immigration, together with new births, have helped to establish Hispanic Americans as the second largest minority group in this country, now totaling over 20 million people.

But most of the groups mentioned to this point originally came within the domain of the United States and its white Anglo majority involuntarily. Native Americans were forcibly conquered and their homelands taken away. Black Americans were captured, transported to the United States, and enslaved. Mexican Americans and Puerto Ricans occupied areas taken over by the U.S. government as spoils of war. In contrast to the involuntary nature of these groups' original entry into this society, Asian Americans have typically been immigrants from abroad.[6] Nonetheless, the historical record shows that Asian Americans, living in the United States for well over 100 years, have suffered from racism. Subject to exploitation, violence, strict immigration quotas, and even mass imprisonment (in the case of 90 percent of all Japanese Americans during World War II),

[4] See Rodolfo Acuña, *Occupied America*, 3rd ed. (New York: Harper & Row Publishers, 1988), and Pastora San Juan Cafferty and William C. McReady, eds., *Hispanics in the United States* (New Brunswick, N.J.: Transaction Books, 1985).

[5] See Raymond Carr, *Puerto Rico: A Colonial Experiment* (New York: New York University Press, 1984), and Joseph P. Fitzpatrick, *Puerto Rican Americans*, 2nd ed. (Englewood Cliffs, N.J.: Prentice-Hall, 1987).

[6] See Harry Kitano and Roger Daniels, *Asian-Americans: The Emerging Minority* (Englewood Cliffs, N.J.: Prentice-Hall, 1988), and U.S. Commission on Civil Rights, *Civil Rights Issues of Asian and Pacific Americans* (Washington, D.C.: U.S. Government Printing Office, 1980).

Asian Americans have struggled against values of white supremacy. Today they comprise some 5 million people and are thought to be the fastest growing racial minority group, principally as a consequence of liberalization of immigration laws. It is a diverse group, largely made up of persons of Chinese, Filipino, Japanese, Asian Indian, Korean, Vietnamese, Cambodian, and Thai ancestry. All face barriers erected by racism, notable exceptions notwithstanding.

In this chapter we examine the major manifestations of racism that such minorities face, to one degree or another, in American society today. We point to reasons why racism exists, and we look at the mechanisms by which the white majority systematically subordinates minorities. Finally, we spell out some of the consequences of this macro problem and point to the need for change.

THE MEANING OF RACISM

The term *racism* is more than an abstract concept. It refers primarily to practices that harm people. Sociologist Robert Blauner provides us with the following definition:

> Racism is a principle of social domination by which a group seen as inferior or different in alleged biological characteristics is exploited, controlled, and oppressed socially and psychically by a superordinate group.[7]

Racism may serve a variety of functions. It may provide individuals with a group to use as a scapegoat or with whom to compare themselves favorably. It is often a means of limiting competition for scarce resources in society (e.g., desirable jobs, entrance into educational programs, preferable housing), and it may provide profit for some, at the expense of others, as when minorities are paid less than whites for the same work.

[7] Robert Blauner, *Racial Oppression in America* (New York: Harper & Row Publishers, 1972), p. 84.

There are two different types of racism.[8] The first type is *personal racism*. Individuals express negative feelings, by word and/or action, toward persons who are members of a minority group. The second type is *institutional racism*, wherein the routine operations of such institutions as business and the political system work to the disadvantage of minorities in general. We will examine both types of racism in this section. However, much of the remainder of this chapter focuses on institutional racism.

Personal Racism

Personal racism occurs when individuals hold attitudes of prejudice and/or engage in discriminatory or similar behavior. Among the manifestations of personal racism are stereotyping individuals on the basis of alleged racial differences; the use of derogatory names and references; discriminatory treatment during the course of interpersonal contacts; and threats and acts of violence against members of a group that is alleged to be racially inferior.

The following are some examples of personal racism cited by the U.S. Commission on Civil Rights.[9]

1. A personnel officer hires minorities only for low-level, low-paying jobs, based on stereotypes about minority abilities.
2. A teacher assumes that children in the class who are not members of the white majority cannot learn and therefore deserve little attention.
3. A real estate agent shows minority buyers only homes in minority neighborhoods un-

[8] See Louis L. Knowles and Kenneth Prewitt, eds., *Institutional Racism in America* (Englewood Cliffs, N.J.: Prentice-Hall, 1969).

[9] U.S. Commission on Civil Rights, *Affirmative Action in the 1980s: Dismantling the Process of Discrimination* (Washington, D.C.: U.S. Government Printing Office, 1981), pp. 8–9. See also Joe R. Feagin and Clairece B. Feagin, *Discrimination American Style*, 2nd ed. (Malabar, Fla.: R. E. Krieger Publishing Company, 1986), pp. 29–30.

The violence occasioned by a court-ordered school busing program in Boston during the mid-1970s demonstrates the extremes that expressions of personal racism can attain. Ironically, people who express personal racism often make use of the very symbols (the American flag, the U.S. Constitution) of the equality they are attempting to deny members of minority groups. (*Stanley Forman*/ Boston Herald American)

der the belief that people should live "with their own kind."

4. A parole official denies parole to minority prisoners more frequently than to whites imprisoned for the same crimes, believing that minority group members are more dangerous or unreliable.

Personal racism involves acts by individuals. Such actions may not be approved organizationally and may be so subtle that they go unnoticed.

On the other hand, personal racism may also take the form of overt acts of racial hatred. These often earn media attention, particularly when the acts are life-threatening or otherwise carry implications of violence. In recent years, for example, the Ku Klux Klan—a white supremacist group with a long history of terrorist violence—has become a focus of media attention. Largely muted in its activities since the passage of historic civil rights legislation in the 1960s, KKK rallies, marches, and recruiting efforts became highly visible once again in the late 1970s and 1980s.[10] Participation enables individual whites to communicate dramatically the contempt they have for minority peoples and thus to act out their personal racism in the company of like-minded individuals.

Although the Ku Klux Klan quickly comes to mind in any discussion of racism, a number of other white supremacist groups drew media attention in the 1980s. These include the National Alliance; Covenant, Sword, and the Arm of the Lord; Posse Comitatus; Aryan Nations; White Patriot Party; White Aryan Resistance; and The Order. Members of the latter, for example, attempted to pursue their racist goals through racketeering, counterfeiting, bank robbery, bombings, and murder.[11] Committed to establishing an independent white nation in the Pacific Northwest, The Order has found its members' criminal activities aggressively investigated and prosecuted. Yet, such violence-prone groups continue to pose serious threats.[12]

Clearly, personal racism may range broadly in intensity and visibility, but the purpose is always the same: to denigrate persons on the basis of their group membership. It is not surprising that some minority group members fight back on a similar level. Racial stereotyping, use of derogatory names and references, acts of interpersonal discrimination, and threats and acts of violence are at times aimed at members of the white majority. Indeed, one of the costs of being white in America is to be seen as a member of the group that has historically engaged in oppression and exploitation of minorities.

However, as the numerical majority and as the group that monopolizes positions of political power in U.S. society, whites are far freer than minority individuals to express personal racism without undue fear of retribution. There are certainly minority group members who engage in acts of personal racism, but they are far fewer in number and at far greater risk when doing so than members of the white majority.

When we think of racism, often it is only personal racism—and its most visible forms at that—that comes to mind. But the damage that is done by personal racism, as tragic and painful as it may be, in no way has the same impact as institutional racism. It is to this second form of racism that we now turn.

Institutional Racism

Institutional racism is our major concern in this chapter. The term *institution,* as used here, refers to an organizational structure created to perform certain services or functions within a society. Business and industry, unions, the political system, education, the mass media, the legal system—all may be thought of as institutions. Ideally, such organizational structures can be made to function so as to take the interests of all social groups into account. In reality, of course, they can be made to perform so as to provide advantages or benefits to some groups over and above others. We have already seen in earlier chapters how a few of these institutions operate to the distinct advantage of the

---

[10] See "The Violent Rebirth of the Klan," *New York Times Magazine,* 130 (December 7, 1980): 150–56, and Philip Finch, "Can the Klan Ride Again?", *New Republic,* 189 (September 5, 1983): 18–20.

[11] Cheryl Sullivan, "Racists Take Violent Path," *Christian Science Monitor* (January 12, 1987): 1.

[12] Dan Freedman, "Hate Groups Reorganizing, Experts Warn," *San Francisco Chronicle* (August 30, 1988): 1. Regular updates on KKK and other white supremacist organizations may be obtained from the Klanwatch Project, Southern Poverty Law Center, in Montgomery, Alabama.

economically affluent and to the disadvantage of those who lack economic power. Institutional racism involves the treatment accorded specifically to minority peoples at the hands of such institutions.

The term *institutional racism* draws attention to the fact that groups such as Native Americans, black Americans, Hispanic Americans and Asian Americans—by virtue of their historical exclusion from key institutional policymaking and decision-making roles—frequently find themselves victimized by the routine workings of such organizational structures. Unlike some forms of personal racism, the racism that occurs through the day-to-day and year-to-year operation of large-scale institutions is often difficult to detect without careful investigation. It is a form of racism that *only* whites can express, since it is they who fill command positions in such institutions.

Let us look at some examples of institutional racism provided by the U.S. Commission on Civil Rights. These include:[13]

1. Seniority rules applied to jobs for which only whites historically had been hired, which now make recently hired minorities more subject to layoffs than whites (i.e., "last hired, first fired").
2. Use of standardized tests or academic credentials to screen potential employees when such tests or credentials are not relevant indicators of future job performance and are geared to knowledge and experience most likely to be possessed by members of the white middle class.
3. Credit policies of banks and other financial institutions that make it difficult to obtain mortgages or loans for home improvements in minority neighborhoods, thus promoting housing decline.
4. Preference in law and medical school admissions given to the offspring of influential and wealthy alumni, the latter of whom are almost always white, because of past discriminatory admissions practices.

As can be seen from the preceding examples, institutional racism need not involve acts or policies that directly or intentionally discriminate against minority group members. Institutional operations may be neutral or "color-blind" on the surface, appear justifiable or even "fair." But they are racist if they have the ultimate effect of placing minorities at a disadvantage vis-à-vis whites.

> Whatever the motivation behind such organizational acts, a process is occurring, the common denominator of which is the denial of equality of opportunity to large numbers of minorities. ...When unequal outcomes are repeated over time and in numerous societal and geographical areas, it is a clear signal that a discriminatory process is at work.[14]

Institutional racism is a societal phenomenon that only whites can set in motion and sustain. The key element is *power* over organizational structures and their operations. Since minority group members generally lack access to positions of power in the key institutions that affect them, they are incapable of discriminating against whites at this level. One can talk, for example, about incidents of "black racism" at the personal racism level. But it should be remembered that minorities have never had, and do not have today, the means to practice racism on the same institutional scale and thus with the same broad effects as whites.

The Myth of Innate Racial Inferiority

As we mentioned earlier, majority white domination over Native Americans, black Ameri-

[13] U.S. Commission on Civil Rights, *Affirmative Action*, pp. 9–11.

[14] Ibid., p. 11.

cans, Hispanic Americans, and Asian Americans has long been accompanied by beliefs in the racial and cultural superiority of whites.[15] Such beliefs have frequently taken the form of so-called scientific theories that postulate the innate inferiority of racial minorities due to genetic factors. Such theories have not only purported to explain why minorities, on the whole, lag behind whites in terms of educational achievement and economic success; they have also served to justify *actions* against minority peoples by whites. Thus, theories of genetic inferiority are more than abstract systems of ideas or academic exercises. They provide an intellectual climate for the perpetuation of personal and institutional racism.

A few psychologists and other academicians have rekindled the longstanding controversy over the bases of human intelligence: the "nature versus nurture" debate.[16] The theories they have put forth rest on the claim that intelligence is determined primarily by genes rather than by environmental influences on learning. These theorists have based many of their conclusions on the results of IQ tests, which they consider devices capable of measuring intelligence. (We mentioned the biases of such tests in Chapter 7.) Since, in terms of group averages, minorities lag behind whites on test results, the theorists suggest that the genetic characteristics of members of racial minorities limit their learning potential. Innate genetic differences, it is alleged, interfere with achievement in schooling. The obvious implication of such theories is that the money spent on the education of minorities is wasted. To the degree to which these kinds of ideas receive acceptance by the whites who are in charge of political and educational institutions, the stage is set for cutbacks in the already inadequate educational opportunities provided minority children.

Such theories and their policy implications are in and of themselves racist. They are forms of ideological thinking that support inequalities along color lines as natural and, therefore, inevitable. That such theories are based on unproven assumptions and faulty premises renders them even more distasteful.

The claim that human intelligence is determined primarily by genes is just that—a claim, not a fact.[17] Most geneticists will readily admit that little is known about the relationship between genes and human behavior, and that there is no scientific evidence that genes play the major role in determining intelligence. In fact, there is not even agreement today about what the concept *intelligence* really means. Thus, there is no consensus on how to measure it validly. If there is any explanation for the economic, political, and educational subordination of minority peoples in American society, it does not rest with genes. Subordination is imposed by racism.

ECONOMIC DEPRIVATION AND EXPLOITATION

In Chapter 6, "Economic Inequality and Poverty," we saw that the United States is a class society, divided along economic lines. Political and economic power and the privileges of material affluence are closely tied to property ownership and high income. Native Americans, black Americans, and Hispanic Americans, for example, are unlikely to own income-producing property. Only a small percentage of each of

---

[15] Thomas F. Gossett, *Race: The History of an Idea in America* (New York: Schocken Books, 1965). These beliefs are closely related to the beliefs behind the social pathology approach discussed in the introduction to this text.

[16] See, for example, Arthur R. Jensen, "How Much Can We Boost I.Q. and Scholastic Achievement?," *Harvard Educational Review,* 39 (Winter 1969): 1–123. Critiques of this position may be found in the Spring and Fall 1970 issues of the *Harvard Educational Review.*

[17] See Allan Chase, *The Legacy of Malthus* (New York: Alfred A. Knopf, 1977); Philip Green, *The Pursuit of Inequality* (New York: Pantheon Books, 1981); and Richard C. Lewontin, Steven Rose, and Leon J. Kamin, *Not in Our Genes: Biology, Ideology, and Human Nature* (New York: Pantheon Books, 1984).

these groups has been able to gain entry into occupations and professions that pay well. These facts, along with the disproportionate presence of racial minorities in the poverty and low-income sectors of the American population, can best be explained by institutional racism.

Employment and Income

Native Americans, black Americans, and Hispanic Americans are far more likely to be unemployed or sporadically employed than members of the white majority. They are far more likely to be underemployed—that is, to be overqualified for the jobs they hold.[18] And they are far more likely to occupy positions with the lowest income, benefits, security, and status. How does one explain the marginal occupational situation of racial minorities as compared to the general white population? Though there are many reasons, institutional racism plays a key role.

First, the handicap of inadequate schooling must be examined. Census data show that dominant group–minority group differentials in years of education completed have been narrowing. Black Americans especially have made some notable gains. (See Table 8.1.) But aggregate statistics on years of school completed do not say anything about the *quality* of educational experiences to which many minority children and teenagers continue to be subjected. Some limited insight may be gained by examining performance on nationwide achievement tests (in reading, mathematics, etc.). Scores on such tests continue to indicate that whites, on the average, are being taught more.[19]

Achievement or "aptitude" tests are often used as screening devices by public and private employers. The failure of educational systems to prepare many minority students—even high school graduates—to compete on an equal basis with whites on such tests directly limits their occupational opportunities. The use of such tests especially affects groups whose native language is not English—for example, Puerto Ricans and Mexican Americans. Employers have claimed that the use of such tests is fair and nondiscriminatory (although there are obviously cases in which the tests have little to do with the work to be done). Yet, insofar as such screening devices function to the direct disadvantage of minorities, the tendency toward discrimination along racial lines is institutionalized.[20]

Nor does high performance on tests necessarily guarantee employment and occupational mobility for minority persons. White employers often react negatively to distinguishing physical features, dress, accent, and other characteristics associated with minority background and culture. They prefer employees who will "fit in." In a predominantly white establishment, this renders minority membership a deficit in and of itself.

Direct discrimination means that even objectively qualified minority candidates have often needed far more in the way of educational credentials than whites in order to get the same kinds of jobs. If statistics on employment can be believed, many employers routinely pay minorities less than whites for similar work and block the advancement of minority group members (with the exception of "token success models").[21] In business and in government, white monopolization of positions with the highest pay and the most authority remains largely unchallenged. Moreover, many of the

---

[18] U.S. Commission on Civil Rights, *Unemployment and Underemployment Among Blacks, Hispanics, and Women* (Washington, D.C.: U.S. Government Printing Office, 1982).

[19] The most comprehensive national survey to date is James S. Coleman et al., *Equality of Educational Opportunity* (Washington, D.C.: U.S. Government Printing Office, 1966). Findings regarding white–minority achievement test score differentials continue to remain valid.

[20] See James J. Kirkpatrick et al., *Testing and Fair Employment* (New York: New York University Press, 1968). See also Feagin and Feagin, *Discrimination American Style*, pp. 58–60.

[21] U.S. Commission on Civil Rights, *Unemployment and Underemployment.*

TABLE 8.1 Years of School Completed by Persons 25 Years Old and Older, by Race, Hispanic Origin, and Sex, 1970–87

		Percent of population completing:							
		Elementary school			High school		College		
Year, race, Hispanic origin,* and sex	Population (in thousands)	0–4 Years	5–7 Years	8 Years	1–3 Years	4 Years	1–3 Years	4 Years or more	Median school years completed
1970, total persons†	**109,899**	**5.5**	**10.0**	**12.8**	**19.4**	**31.1**	**10.6**	**10.7**	**12.1**
White	98,246	4.5	9.1	13.0	18.8	32.2	11.1	11.3	12.1
Male	46,527	4.8	9.7	13.3	18.2	28.5	11.1	14.4	12.1
Female	51,718	4.1	8.6	12.8	19.4	35.5	11.1	8.4	12.1
Black	10,375	14.6	18.7	10.5	24.8	21.2	5.9	4.4	9.8
Male	4,714	17.7	19.1	10.2	22.9	20.0	6.0	4.2	9.4
Female	5,661	12.0	18.3	10.8	26.4	22.2	5.8	4.6	10.1
Hispanic	3,946	19.5	18.6	11.5	18.2	21.1	6.5	4.5	9.1
Male	1,897	19.1	18.0	11.3	18.1	19.9	7.6	5.9	9.3
Female	2,050	19.9	19.2	11.6	18.3	22.3	5.4	3.2	8.9
1980, total persons†	**132,836**	**3.6**	**6.7**	**8.0**	**15.3**	**34.6**	**15.7**	**16.2**	**12.5**
White	114,290	2.6	5.8	8.2	14.6	35.7	16.0	17.1	12.5
Male	53,941	2.8	6.0	8.0	13.6	31.8	16.4	21.3	12.5
Female	60,349	2.5	5.6	8.4	15.5	39.1	15.6	13.3	12.6
Black	13,195	8.2	11.7	7.1	21.8	29.3	13.5	8.4	12.0
Male	5,895	10.0	12.0	6.7	20.5	28.3	14.0	8.4	12.0
Female	7,300	6.7	11.6	7.3	22.9	30.0	13.2	8.3	12.0
Hispanic	6,739	15.5	16.6	8.1	15.8	24.4	12.0	7.6	10.8
Male	3,247	15.2	16.2	7.7	15.5	22.6	13.4	9.4	11.1
Female	3,493	15.8	17.1	8.4	16.1	26.0	10.6	6.0	10.6
1987, total persons†	**149,144**	**2.4**	**4.5**	**5.8**	**11.7**	**38.7**	**17.1**	**19.9**	**12.7**
White	129,170	2.0	4.1	5.9	11.0	39.2	17.2	20.5	12.7
Male	61,678	2.1	4.2	5.8	10.6	35.6	17.2	24.5	12.8
Female	67,492	2.0	4.0	6.0	11.4	42.6	17.3	16.9	12.6
Black	15,580	5.0	8.0	5.3	18.2	37.1	15.7	10.7	12.4
Male	6,919	5.9	8.6	5.2	17.2	36.5	15.5	11.0	12.4
Female	8,661	4.3	7.6	5.4	19.0	37.5	15.8	10.4	12.4
Hispanic	9,449	11.9	15.2	8.1	13.9	29.0	13.3	8.6	12.0
Male	4,614	11.8	14.8	7.4	14.2	28.0	14.2	9.7	12.1
Female	4,835	12.0	15.6	8.8	13.6	30.0	12.5	7.5	12.0

*Hispanic persons may be of any race.
†Includes other races, not shown separately.
Source: U.S. Department of Commerce, Bureau of the Census, *Statistical Abstract of the United States, 1989* (Washington, D.C.: U.S. Government Printing Office, 1989), p. 131.

very top institutional positions in the public and private sectors (e.g., boards of directors, cabinet and agency heads, judgeships) are typically gained through appointment. Those in a position to do the appointing are likely to be white men, and they tend to choose persons like themselves.

Minority group members who aspire to move upward have also found that denial of their cultural backgrounds—that is, becoming operationally "white" on the job—may be a prerequisite to employment security and success. The conflict between "selling out" and freely maintaining and expressing consciousness of minority identity is a forced one. It stems primarily from the need to please white superiors in order to gain acceptance and get ahead in majority-dominated institutions.[22]

In the labor market as a whole, according to social scientists, there is a division along racial lines.[23] The *primary labor market* consists of the higher paying, more secure, and most desirable occupations for which employers recruit white workers. For example, white-collar jobs are predominantly filled by white workers. The *secondary labor market* consists of the lower paying, least secure, and most undesirable jobs. It is within this secondary market that most minority group members are likely to find work. For example, within the blue-collar job market, blacks are mostly found as nonfarm laborers and operatives. They also make up a high percentage of service workers. (See Table 5.2, p. 160.) A competitive threat occurs when minority groups attempt to move up and out of the sector of the labor market in which they have long been believed to "belong"—a threat felt whenever equal treatment is demanded in employment practices. To the degree to which Native Americans, black Americans, Hispanic Americans, and Asian Americans fall or are pushed aside in the competition for primary labor market positions, whites have an open field.

Minority group members have made their greatest gains in the American occupational structure when there has been a labor shortage, as during periods of war. When there is work to be done, when there is no other way to get it done, employers have dropped some of their normal procedures for screening, hiring, and promoting employees—a situation that provides opportunities otherwise unavailable. On the other hand, during a period of labor surplus—for example, an economic recession and slowdown—minority group members tend to be the hardest hit. In many sectors of the economy, layoffs are carried out on the basis of seniority; the last to arrive leave first. And those with the most seniority are the first to be rehired. This process at least partially accounts for the extraordinary unemployment rates among minorities during economic slumps. (See Figure 8.1.)

In recent years, individual minority members have been permitted to move upward in the occupational structure as pressures have increased against blatant discrimination. These individuals tend to be highly visible, giving the impression that great gains are being made. But in *group* terms, most of America's minorities have tended to remain "in place," a situation verified by continuing lags in income.[24] (See Table 8.2.)

Other factors also influence the occupational situation of many minority group members. Minorities have become residentially concentrated in central city areas, while business and industry have been migrating out of large cities to suburbs and smaller towns that offer attractive tax rates and white labor pools. Locked into central city areas by housing segregation, the expense of alternative housing, and the inadequacy or cost of transportation to outlying jobs, urban-dwelling minorities have found it increasingly difficult to find satisfactory employment. The "white flight" of business and industry, while not necessarily intended to work to the disadvantage of minorities, effectively does so.

---

[22] See George Douns and Glegg Watson, *Black Life in Corporate America* (New York: Anchor Press, 1982), and Lena Williams, "For the Black Professional, the Obstacles Remain," *New York Times* (July 14, 1987): A16.

[23] See Michael Reich, Richard Edwards, and David Gordon, *The Segmentation of Labor in U.S. Capitalism* (New York: Cambridge University Press, 1981).

[24] See, e.g., David Swinton, "The Economic Status of Black Americans," in Janet Dewart, ed., *The State of Black America 1989* (New York: National Urban League, 1989).

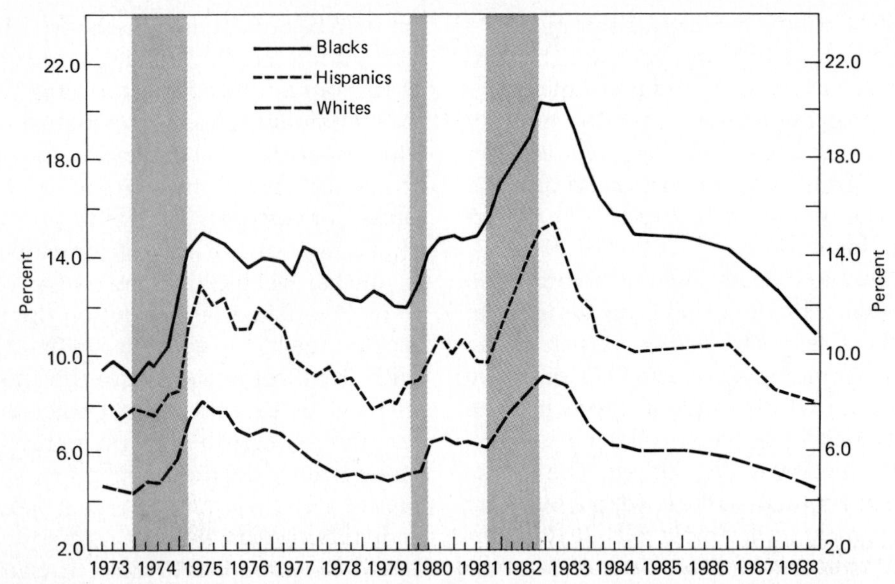

FIGURE 8.1 Unemployment Rates of Blacks, Hispanics, and Whites, Quarterly Averages, Seasonally Adjusted, 1973–88
Note: Shaded areas indicate recessions as designated by the National Bureau of Economic Research.
Source: U.S. Department of Labor, *Monthly Labor Review*, 108 (February 1985): 13, and *Monthly Labor Review*, 112 (January 1989): 90.

Technological changes, which have altered the makeup of parts of the occupational structure, also work against minority employment. In recent years, new job areas calling for training and skills of an extensive and often esoteric nature have been created. Since educational resources and opportunities are disproportionately available to whites, whites are in a privileged position to compete for such jobs. At the same time, technological advances have enabled some employers to cut back on or even eliminate certain positions, typically those that require limited skills. One sociologist has argued that automation, for example, will render much of the labor performed by minorities obsolete and exacerbate their employment problems.[25]

Just as neither business nor government has seen fit to eliminate the employment difficulties facing minorities, so has organized labor served as an impediment.[26] Union membership and long apprenticeships are requirements for entry into many occupations—particularly the higher paying skilled crafts and trades. But members of racial minority groups often have been—and still are—denied membership in white-dominated unions. Discrimination in this area has meant that minority individuals, even if they possess the skills, are locked out of contractual opportunities that would enable them to demand as much for their time and labor as unionized whites. Union resistance to minority enrollment is by no means total. In fact, a higher percentage of black workers than white workers belongs to unions today. But for the better

[25] Sidney Willhelm, *Black in a White America* (Cambridge, Mass.: Schenkman Books, 1983).

[26] William B. Gould, *Black Workers in White Unions* (Ithaca, N.Y.: Cornell University Press, 1977).

TABLE 8.2 Money Income of Families: Percent Distribution by Income Level in Constant (1987) Dollars, by Race and Hispanic Origin of Householder, 1970–87

Year	Number of families (in thousands)	Percent distribution of families, by income level								Median income (dollars)
		Under $5,000	$5,000–$9,999	$10,000–$14,999	$15,000–$19,999	$20,000–$24,999	$25,000–$34,999	$35,000–$49,999	$50,000 and over	
					All families					
1970	52,227	3.5	7.6	9.1	9.9	11.3	22.0	21.2	15.4	28,880
1975	56,245	2.9	8.1	10.0	10.2	10.4	20.9	21.0	16.4	28,970
1980	60,309	3.7	8.2	9.8	10.2	10.2	20.0	20.5	17.5	28,996
1983	62,015	4.8	8.4	10.3	10.1	10.2	19.0	19.2	17.9	28,147
1984	62,706	4.5	8.3	9.7	10.0	9.7	18.4	19.7	19.6	28,923
1985	63,558	4.4	8.0	9.7	9.9	9.9	18.3	19.2	20.6	29,302
1986	64,491	4.5	7.5	9.2	9.6	9.5	17.7	19.8	22.2	30,534
1987	65,133	4.4	7.3	9.1	9.5	9.2	17.5	20.2	22.9	30,853
					White					
1970	46,535	2.9	6.7	8.5	9.5	11.3	22.6	22.2	16.4	29,960
1975	49,873	2.3	6.9	9.5	10.0	10.3	21.5	21.9	17.6	30,129
1980	52,710	2.7	6.9	9.2	10.0	10.3	20.6	21.5	18.7	30,211
1983	53,890	3.7	7.1	9.9	10.1	10.4	19.5	20.2	19.2	29,474
1984	54,400	3.4	7.0	9.2	9.9	9.8	19.0	20.7	21.0	30,294
1985	54,991	3.5	6.9	9.1	9.6	10.0	18.8	20.1	22.1	30,799
1986	55,676	3.3	6.5	8.6	9.4	9.5	18.2	20.8	23.7	31,935
1987	56,044	3.2	6.1	8.6	9.3	9.1	18.1	21.2	24.4	32,274
					Black					
1970	4,928	9.0	16.7	14.6	14.3	12.0	15.6	12.0	5.7	18,378
1975	5,586	7.4	19.0	15.2	12.2	11.7	16.1	12.5	6.1	18,538
1980	6,317	10.7	18.5	15.1	12.0	9.3	15.6	12.0	6.9	17,481
1983	6,681	13.5	19.2	14.1	11.1	9.4	15.1	10.9	6.9	16,610
1984	6,778	13.3	18.4	14.2	11.6	9.4	14.3	10.9	8.0	16,884
1985	6,921	12.4	16.8	14.1	12.4	8.8	15.0	12.2	8.3	17,734
1986	7,096	13.4	15.9	13.5	10.6	9.7	14.5	13.0	9.5	18,247
1987	7,177	13.5	16.5	12.5	11.8	10.0	13.6	12.8	9.5	18,098
					Hispanic*					
1975	2,499	5.8	14.9	15.8	13.0	12.2	19.8	12.8	5.8	20,168
1980	3,235	6.5	14.1	15.5	13.5	11.4	17.3	14.1	7.5	20,297
1983	3,788	8.3	16.0	14.1	13.6	11.4	16.3	12.3	7.9	19,313
1984	3,939	8.6	14.5	13.9	12.7	9.9	17.5	14.1	9.0	20,606
1985	4,206	7.4	16.0	14.8	11.7	11.1	16.6	13.0	9.6	20,102
1986	4,403	8.2	14.3	14.8	11.8	10.6	16.1	13.3	11.0	20,726
1987	4,588	8.6	14.4	14.7	11.7	10.2	15.7	14.0	10.9	20,306

*Hispanic persons may be of any race.

Source: U.S. Department of Commerce, Bureau of the Census, *Statistical Abstract of the United States, 1989* (Washington, D.C.: U.S. Government Printing Office, 1989), p. 445.

paying, more highly skilled jobs, exclusionary practices by organized labor are another form of institutional racism.

The United States has a work force of 116 million people. As one moves down the occupational and professional hierarchy, the percentage of persons with dark skin increases. As one moves up, it decreases. If we look only at the very top positions in business and government, we could hardly think that ours is a multiracial society. Through institutional racism, minorities are effectively kept at and toward the bottom of the employment ladder.

Business Ownership

As a result of white domination of high-level positions, the concentration of members of minority groups at the bottom of the economic ladder, and the reluctance of white employers to hire them, there has been much interest in setting up minority-owned businesses as a means of improving the economic situation of minorities. After all, one way to make money and to struggle toward an improved economic position is through the ownership of a business. Minority business owners, so the theory goes, could hire minority workers and thus improve the situation of the entire group.

But despite the interest in and excitement about minority-owned business, business ownership has not resulted in *group* improvement. When we examine business ownership in the United States, it quickly becomes evident that whites prevail. Surveys by the U.S. Department of Commerce, conducted periodically since the late 1960s, continue to substantiate the same facts.[27] In terms of their percentage representation in the population, minority group members own few businesses. Moreover, minority-owned enterprises are likely to be small and to employ few people. All such enterprises taken together account for only a tiny percentage of the nation's total annual business income.

A number of rationales have been offered to explain the relative absence of minority entrepreneurs and the economic insignificance of most of the firms owned by minorities. Some blame the victim, suggesting that minority group members lack the interest and motivation necessary to succeed in the competitive world of profit-making. Such explanations are clearly inadequate. It is not minority inability but instead institutional racism that has been responsible for the low rates of minority business ownership.[28]

Starting a new business or expanding an ongoing one requires cash and credit. Unless an individual has a very substantial income and a large amount of savings, it becomes necessary to deal with banks. In the American economy, the financial sector has always been overwhelmingly controlled and staffed by whites. The aspiring minority entrepreneur may be faced with direct rejection by unsympathetic banking officials, simply on the basis of group membership. But institutional policies—which are said to be totally unrelated to discrimination against minorities—often result in the same kind of negative outcome. Banks and other lending institutions have a plentiful supply of competing white and minority applicants. They are most likely to extend loans to individuals whose economic success in the past renders them excellent credit risks, to those to whom money and credit have successfully been extended before, to those who possess property that can be put up as collateral against loans, and to those who can most easily demonstrate the probable profitability of their business project. On the average, these criteria are met more readily by whites than by minorities.

[27] The first nationwide study was U.S. Bureau of the Census, *Minority-Owned Business: 1969* (Washington, D.C.: U.S. Government Printing Office, 1971).

[28] See, for example, William F. Haddad and G. Douglas Pugh, eds., *Black Economic Development* (Englewood Cliffs, N.J.: Prentice-Hall, 1969).

In recent years, the federal government's Small Business Administration has worked with members of the corporate and banking communities to aid minority entrepreneurs. The government has also made limited attempts to purchase more products and services from minority businesses and has urged its large corporate suppliers to do so as well. But these forms of aid, while receiving a great deal of publicity, have not resulted in any dramatic change in the magnitude of minority business ownership. In fact, limited federal loans for minority-owned businesses were further reduced in the 1980s.

In the absence of a first chance to become involved in the business world, minorities are likely to remain shut out. It is like being turned down for a job because of lack of formal experience when one can only gain such experience by getting the job. The effect is that one goes nowhere, an experience many minority group members have grown to anticipate in dealing with financial institutions.

POLITICAL POWERLESSNESS

In Chapter 2, "Concentration of Political and Economic Power," we stressed the close relationship between economic power and political clout on the national level. As we have seen, minority groups are economically disadvantaged in comparison with the overall white population. Even more than most whites, they are light-years away from competing with the economic and political power wielded by the ownership class—the small segment of the population among whom wealth and income are concentrated. If, as we saw in Chapter 2, many members of the white majority feel powerless to affect national decision making, minority group members must feel even more helpless. Minority groups are almost totally dependent on white power-holders for the initiation and enforcement of policies that might improve their life chances. To varying degrees, this situation of political powerlessness prevails right down to the state and local levels of government.

Government Employment

At the national level, blacks and members of some other minority groups are currently well represented in terms of government employment. But whether we are speaking of the executive, legislative, or judicial branch of the federal government, this representation lies primarily in the lower paying, nonpolicymaking positions. In 1986, for example, blacks held less than 5 percent of the top-level presidential appointments in the executive branch.[29] Other minority groups have not fared nearly as well. Periodically, the U.S. Commission on Civil Rights (an independent federal watchdog agency) has castigated various bodies of the national government for discrimination in the operation of their programs and in their hiring and promotion practices. One of the commission's targets has been the White House itself. Over 1,000 presidential appointments may be made during a president's term in office. These include cabinet-level secretaries, undersecretaries, and assistant secretaries; other executive branch agency heads; U.S. attorneys; judges; and ambassadors. The commission noted that few members of minority groups "have been included in these top Federal Government policymaking positions during this Nation's history."[30]

Minorities are underrepresented in key elected positions at the national level. While black leader Jesse Jackson sought to break the pattern in 1984 and 1988, all American presidents have been white, and white-dominated

[29] Robert Pear, "Number of Blacks in Top Jobs in Administration Off Sharply," *New York Times* (March 22, 1987): A1.

[30] U.S. Commission on Civil Rights, *Equal Opportunity in Presidential Appointments* (Washington, D.C.: U.S. Government Printing Office, 1983).

political parties have persistently avoided any attempts to alter that trend. As of 1990 only a handful of blacks had been appointed to the presidential cabinet. There are few minority members of the U.S. Senate or House of Representatives. Those who are there find that their numbers are far too small to allow them to wield much influence in the face of an overwhelmingly white majority of lawmakers. Although often expected to represent minority concerns, there is little they can do without the support of their white colleagues.

The situation is similar on the state and local levels. For example, between 1965 and 1982 the number of black elected officials increased tenfold—from about 500 to 5,100.[31] By early 1988 the number was over 6,700 (see Table 8.3). This is undeniably a significant improvement over past figures. But most of these officials serve in small southern communities in which the black population is numerically predominant. And blacks are only 1.5 percent of the nation's elected officials. The situation facing other

[31] Joint Center for Political Studies, *Black Elected Officials and Their Constituencies* (Washington, D.C.: JCPS, 1983), p. 1.

TABLE 8.3 Black Elected Officials, by Office, 1970–88, and by Region, 1988

Year and region	Total	U.S. and state legislatures	City and county offices	Law enforcement	Education
1970 (Feb.)	1,479	179	719	213	368
1971 (Mar.)	1,870	216	909	274	471
1972 (Mar.)	2,275	224	1,112	263	676
1973 (Apr.)	2,635	256	1,268	334	777
1974 (Apr.)	3,007	256	1,607	340	804
1975 (Apr.)	3,522	299	1,885	387	951
1976 (Apr.)	4,006	299	2,284	415	1,008
1977 (July)	4,342	316	2,509	451	1,066
1978 (July)	4,544	316	2,616	458	1,154
1979 (July)	4,636	315	2,675	491	1,155
1980 (July)	4,963	326	2,871	534	1,232
1981 (July)	5,109	343	2,914	559	1,293
1982 (July)	5,241	342	3,017	573	1,309
1983 (July)	5,719	386	3,283	620	1,430
1984 (Jan.)	5,865	396	3,367	657	1,445
1985 (Jan.)	6,312	407	3,689	685	1,531
1986 (Jan.)	6,384	410	3,800	676	1,498
1987 (Jan.)	6,646	428	3,949	727	1,542
1988 (Jan.)	6,793	424	4,089	738	1,542
Region					
Northeast	695	73	275	104	243
Midwest	1,285	93	733	139	320
South	4,446	227	2,980	392	847
West	367	31	101	103	132

Source: U.S. Department of Commerce, Bureau of the Census, *Statistical Abstract of the United States, 1989* (Washington, D.C.: U.S. Government Printing Office, 1989), p. 255.

Minority group members have yet to make significant gains in achieving top governmental positions at the state and national levels. The election of L. Douglas Wilder to the governorship of Virginia is the first time a black citizen has reached this high state office. In this photograph he is shown at the January 1990 swearing-in ceremonies. *(P. F. Gero/Sygma)*

groups—for example, Native Americans, Hispanic Americans, and Asian Americans—is even worse.

In the last decade or so several major cities across the country—from Los Angeles to Chicago to New York and Atlanta—have voted black mayors into office. To some this is evidence of the existence of growing minority political power. Indeed, it does reflect one outcome of the changing color of many of America's central cities, where many minority group members have come to reside. Yet the signs of political arrival of groups long out of power must be placed in their full context.

Black mayors are arriving in office in an era when very few resources are available from state and federal governments to help deal with city problems. Moreover, mayors, no matter what their color, must often deal with the reality of an existing urban power structure that acts as a "hidden government." This urban power structure is typically composed of whites who hold command positions in local (or locally based) corporate and financial institutions. City governments are often highly dependent on this urban power structure to get anything substantial done, and such dependency limits the ability of mayors to be responsive to minority concerns and needs.[32]

This brief overview suggests the kinds of problems minorities confront in getting their concerns expressed and dealt with. Yet we have left aside the whole question of the *quality* of the representation minorities have achieved. As

[32] For an overview of research on the role of corporate actors in urban politics, see Scott Cummings, ed., *Business Elites and Urban Development* (Albany: State University of New York Press, 1988).

in the area of employment generally, at least some of those who manage to make their way into key political positions progressively lose identification with their minority constituencies. Fearing that failure to adapt to majority views or practices will result in the loss of newly achieved power and prestige, they often let themselves become coopted by or assimilated into the white-dominated political and governmental system. Minority officeholders may find themselves forced to mute their race-related concerns in the interests of accommodation and compromise with more powerful representatives of the white majority. If they press minority concerns too vigorously and are too unyielding, they may see their overall political effectiveness jeopardized. This too contributes to the dilution of minority political power.

Voter Participation

The forces generating political powerlessness also include the lack of voter participation. For years exercise of the franchise by minority group members lagged behind that considered normal for whites, a situation that has slowly been undergoing change. A common explanation of this fact blames the victim. Persons of low socioeconomic status and limited formal education—minority or not—tend to have little desire and energy to get involved in institutionalized political activity, especially because they believe that it is dominated by the more affluent and highly educated. This common phenomenon is exacerbated in the case of minorities, whose members disproportionately fall in the lower depths of the class structure.

More to the point is the fact that many minority group members have been faced with extraordinary resistance to their participation in the political system at any level—including voting. Blacks and others have faced white-controlled election laws and rules designed to impede voter registration and the exercise of the franchise. Among these rules have been insistence that Native Americans and Hispanics take literacy tests in English, the imposition of poll taxes on people who cannot afford to pay them, and threats and acts of economic reprisal. Gerrymandering has also been common—that is, white decision makers have altered district boundaries so as to keep minority peoples from making up a majority of voters and thus influencing the outcome of elections. Federal voting rights laws have, in recent years, eliminated many such formal practices.

As a consequence, many minority group members have long approached the idea of voting with cynicism. Only recently have representatives of numerically large, urbanized groups—such as black Americans and Mexican Americans—successfully attempted to get more minority candidates into elected office. And only recently have agencies of the government provided protection for those who had been manipulated or harassed out of the franchise for many years.

In 1965 the U.S. Congress, appalled by flagrant violations of minority voting rights and under pressure from a militant civil rights movement, passed the Voting Rights Act. Since then the act has been extended three times—in 1970, 1975, and 1982—based in part on evidence that discrimination continued to exist against those who would seek to exercise their citizenship. The act prohibits various procedures and devices intended to discourage registration and voting, provides for examiners and observers to keep an eye on local voting processes, and sets up channels through which minority citizens may seek redress when their rights are violated. Yet despite the existence of the Voting Rights Act, the U.S. Commission on Civil Rights has expressed concern that all of its provisions are not being implemented or adequately enforced.[33]

---

[33] U.S. Commission on Civil Rights, *State of Civil Rights, 1957–1983* (Washington, D.C.: U.S. Government Printing Office, 1983), pp. 5–17.

In sum, important decisions affecting the life chances of minorities are made *for* them, not *by* them. One outcome of institutional racism in the political structure is the continuing, sporadic outburst of militant discontent directed against the abuses of the white power structure. Such outbursts can be seen as indications of the failure of this structure to incorporate or adequately respond to minority concerns.

Minorities and the Law

Existing laws, and provisions for the enforcement of these laws, have all been created by representatives of the white majority. In the past, law has actually been used to deprive minorities of rights taken for granted by white citizens. Discriminatory practices have continued even as such laws have slowly been repealed, and it has taken years of struggle by minorities and their allies to get new laws guaranteeing protection of their rights passed. The struggle to get such laws enforced is still going on in such areas as education, employment, and housing discrimination. It is no wonder, then, that many minority group members have little confidence in law as a facilitator of their interests.

Minority discontent has been especially noteworthy in the area of criminal law and its enforcement. State and local police forces are overwhelmingly controlled by whites. Discrimination in police recruitment, hiring, and promotion has been rampant. (This situation has slowly begun to change as minorities press for enforcement of antidiscrimination laws.) Furthermore, members of racial minorities have long felt themselves to be the prime victims of police misconduct and brutality. Most police forces are not under the supervision of civilian review boards through which allegations of misconduct and brutality could be investigated by concerned citizens. The police investigate themselves when charges are levied, and in most cases this accomplishes little. Hence, predominantly white police forces have an inordinate amount of freedom to exercise power over minorities—including the indiscriminate use of force—without a great deal of accountability.[34]

Discriminatory treatment of minority persons by white police officers may involve both personal and institutional racism. Personal contact with police in ghettos, barrios, and reservations has led to widespread hostility and distrust on the part of minorities. For example, in the aftermath of the black urban rebellions of the 1960s, investigators found that the major grievance voiced by ghetto residents was police brutality and harassment.[35] Similar complaints were documented in U.S. Civil Rights Commission investigations of the treatment of Mexican Americans.[36]

The problem is not limited to the actions and attitudes of individual police officers. Racism in the administration of justice, as elsewhere, is an institutionalized process. Prosecutors, judges, juries, prison personnel, members of parole boards—all tend to be white. Minority individuals are accused of crimes, placed under arrest, detained in jail before trial, forced to rely on public defenders for legal assistance, prosecuted, found guilty, given severe sentences, and denied early parole more than whites. While in prison, minorities may be subject to racial denigration by guards and other staff. Once out of prison, they are handicapped not only by an arrest record, but also by the extra burden of discrimination in the labor market that even those minority group members

[34] U.S. Commission on Civil Rights, *Who Is Guarding the Guardians?* (Washington, D.C.: U.S. Government Printing Office, 1981).

[35] *Report of the National Advisory Commission on Civil Disorders* (Washington, D.C.: U.S. Government Printing Office, 1968), Chapter 11.

[36] U.S. Commission on Civil Rights, *Mexican Americans and the Administration of Justice in the Southwest* (Washington, D.C.: U.S. Government Printing Office, 1970). See also Ernie Sotomayer, "Police Abuse: The Most Volatile Issue," *Perspectives: The Civil Rights Quarterly*, 13 (Winter 1982): 29–35.

who have never been arrested must face. All of this is made possible by minority political powerlessness and the continued exclusion of minorities from institutional positions from which more just and equitable policies could be fashioned.

EDUCATIONAL DEPRIVATION

Formal education is not a guarantee of employment or security in our competitive, hierarchical society. But the lack of quality formal education, coupled with experiences of denigration and school failure, is likely to leave an individual in an untenable economic position. This is true both for whites and minorities, but more so for the latter, given discrimination in the world of work. The burden of school failure disproportionately falls on minority children. Political powerlessness also means that minority parents have little or no control over how, what, and how much their children are encouraged or permitted to learn.

In considering institutional racism in education, we again come back to the question of power. Who holds the command positions through which decisions about education are made and resources allocated? In general, at the federal, state, and local levels, decisions regarding education are made by representatives of the white majority. Minorities thus find it enormously difficult to pressure educational systems to make them provide learning experiences commensurate with their children's needs. School segregation, limited educational programs and teaching resources, alienating curricula, and racist practices by school personnel contribute to the poor education of millions of minority children.

The Battle Against Segregation

Not too long ago, racially segregated public schools were maintained by whites with support from the society's legal system.[37] Tens of millions of minority children passed through "their own" schools, while whites went elsewhere. Typically, fewer resources were allocated to the schools that served minority children, since it was not expected that they would go on to higher education or get jobs that required education. North and South, East and West, rural and urban, inequalities in school expenditures operated in the interests of children of the white majority, particularly the more affluent whites.

In 1954, after decades of legal battling by minority representatives and their white allies, the nation's courts were persuaded to address the question of whether school segregation was a denial of equal rights under the law. Court decisions such as *Brown* vs. *Board of Education of Topeka* called for an end to dual school systems. They were followed up by civil rights legislation in the 1960s. The focus was primarily on educational systems in the southern and border states. Since then, white and minority children have slowly been brought together under the same school roofs.

At first, court decisions and antisegregation legislation had little impact in the northern and western states. Only recently have the courts begun to move against segregation in these regions, and there has been less progress than in the South. Where dual school systems have been found to exist, particularly in urban areas, white school officials have blamed this on uncontrollable population shifts and the movement of minorities into racially homogeneous ghettos and barrios. In most central city school systems, segregation has noticeably *increased* since 1954. Urban minority populations have grown; many whites have fled to the residentially segregated suburbs; and city "neighborhood school" policies have continued to perpetuate the racial isolation of minorities. Cities in the

[37] U.S. Commission on Civil Rights, *With All Deliberate Speed, 1954–19??* (Washington, D.C.: U.S. Government Printing Office, 1981).

southern and border states have begun to develop in similar directions, even while denying intentional segregation practices.

Obstacles to Equal Education

Segregation is an important concern not only because it separates white and minority children into two different worlds. The real problem regarding segregation involves the quality of education received by minorities as compared with whites. As we saw in Chapter 7, "Schooling and Unequal Educational Opportunity," public school systems rely heavily on local property taxes for their money. The flight of affluent families to the segregated suburbs, the failure of government to take steps to control urban blight, and the movement of business and industry out of central city areas have all contributed to school fiscal crises. Educational costs—like everything else in recent years—have steadily gone up, and the revenues needed to meet these costs have failed to keep pace. Thus the city schools that serve minority children often find that they cannot afford the kinds of programs and services commonly available in affluent white suburbs. Instead, they must make do with outdated physical plants and equipment, overcrowded classrooms, and limited curricular offerings.

Despite the increasing minority enrollment in central city schools, whites predominate in the running of most schools. From the school board, to superintendent, to principals, and often on down to teachers and counselors, minorities are underrepresented, and procedures for input from minority groups are the exception rather than the rule. Members of the dominant white majority administer education to children whose backgrounds, cultures, and everyday life experiences in racially isolated communities are too often little understood and viewed as alien. Learning is unlikely to take place when understanding and respect are lacking.

Until quite recently, textbooks and other curricular materials were produced primarily for the children of the white Anglo majority and did not reflect the multiracial character of American society and of the world population generally. Social studies texts either ignored the history and present status of minorities or implied that such topics were unimportant by their brevity of coverage. The implication was that only whites have said or done anything worth learning about. This encouraged and reinforced minority feelings of racial isolation and even of inferiority. Shortcomings in curricula have also extended to the ways in which peoples who live outside the white, Western world are treated. The history and cultures of the predominantly nonwhite Third World, for example, are still rarely dealt with fully and equitably, thereby again suggesting the notion of white superiority.[38]

As we saw in Chapter 7, the commonly used IQ tests favor those students who have best mastered the vocabulary common in middle-class homes. Yet minority children are often channeled into one or another school program on the basis of their performance on such tests. Testing is used to place children in ability groups. On the average, minority children tend to perform less well on the tests than do those for whom they were originally designed, so minority children are generally shunted into groups set up for those with low measured ability.

Marion Wright Edelman has noted that black children, for example, are disproportionately routed into public school classes for the "educable mentally retarded," or "EMR." As many as one in thirty black children are in such classes. According to Edelman,

> A white child is twice as likely to be placed in a class for gifted students as in an EMR class; a black

[38] U.S. Commission on Civil Rights, *Characters in Textbooks* (Washington, D.C.: U.S. Government Printing Office, 1980).

child is almost three times as likely to be placed in an EMR class as in a class for gifted students.[39]

Ability groups are no secret to the children placed in them. Minority children are likely to take their placement seriously and doubt their own potential and intelligence. School personnel also tend to view children in low-ability groups as inferior. Such a view may be expressed through attitudes toward the children or through the use of curricular materials that demand very little of them. The result is a self-fulfilling prophecy (see Chapter 7), as white school personnel demand little from minority children, teach little, and find that their students learn little.[40]

Institutional racism in education fosters failure. The performance of minority children, on the average, tends to be below grade level when compared with children of the white majority. Minority children have higher suspension, expulsion, and dropout rates than their white counterparts. Proportionately fewer minority students go on to higher education. The inadequate educational preparation many receive along with family financial problems contributes to lower rates of college completion for those who do manage to go on. All these outcomes, in turn, intensify the economic disadvantage that minority group members face in the labor market, and the circle closes.

RACISM AND SOCIETY

The economic deprivation, political powerlessness, and educational inequality fostered by institutional racism have consequences for the society as a whole as well as for members of racial minorities. In this section we shall spell out some of the costs white America pays for its institutionalization of racism. We shall then look at minority responses to racism and their effect on American society. Finally, we will consider some proposals for change.

The Costs of Racism

It is obvious that institutional racism makes it extremely difficult for members of racial minorities to achieve in economic, political, and educational spheres. But racism also has negative consequences for *whites*, whether they are active practitioners of or allegedly innocent bystanders to minority subordination.[41]

Because of institutional racism, minorities have been regularly denied resources and excluded from opportunities through which they could more fully develop and display their human capabilities. That is, racism arbitrarily restricts the development and utilization of vast amounts of human talent. This talent could be mobilized in the interests of society as a whole, and its restriction means a loss to us all.

Racism ultimately translates into monetary costs as well. Much of the tax money paid by both whites and minority peoples is used to improve or otherwise deal with conditions that institutional racism has helped create and perpetuate. Since unequal educational opportunities and employment discrimination have meant high levels of joblessness and depressed wages for minorities, tax money must be diverted to pay for family assistance and other forms of aid. The ghettoization of minorities and the abandonment of central city areas by whites are components of what has been called the urban crisis. A great deal of tax money must go into central cities just to keep them functioning. De-

[39] Marion Wright Edelman, "Growing Up Black in America," in Jerome H. Skolnick and Elliott Currie, eds., *Crisis in American Institutions*, 7th ed. (Glenview, Ill.: Scott, Foresman and Company, 1988), p. 154.

[40] Morris Rosenberg and Roberta G. Simmons, *Black and White Self* (Washington, D.C.: American Sociological Association, 1971).

[41] Benjamin P. Bowser and Raymond G. Hunt, eds., *Impacts of Racism on White Americans* (Beverly Hills, Calif.: Sage Publications, 1981).

spite their flight, whites cannot escape paying for the urban stagnation afflicting cities across the country.

Then there are the unmeasurable psychic costs to whites. Historians of slavery have commented that the slaveholder's own sense of security and freedom was circumscribed so long as he restricted the freedom of others. Knowing that rebellion and acts of retribution were constant possibilities, he always had to look over his shoulder and remain ready to protect himself or his property. More than a century after the formal abolition of slavery, majority–minority relations in this society still give rise to white anxiety and fear. Racial conflict—and the possibility of racial conflict—has led to massive investments in police forces and other instruments of social control.

Racism divides our society. It provides a channel through which members of the white majority can release their frustrations. Minority groups have been said to play the role of lightning rods for the dissatisfactions that whites feel they must somehow express. Since minorities are disadvantaged in terms of ability to fight back freely, they provide a relatively easy target. But the problems that frustrate many members of the white majority—economic difficulties, political powerlessness, and so on—are similar to those minorities face. Racism prevents whites from seeing how much they have in common with minorities; it obscures the fact that all might gain by cooperating and uniting. Intergroup conflict and distrust along racial lines mean that the dissatisfactions of many whites are expressed downward—toward powerless groups that are not responsible for the problems. In the meantime, the handful of whites who hold economic and political power and who make decisions affecting *all* those below them benefit from racial disunity. Through a conscious or unconscious divide-and-conquer strategy, societal elites can subtly use racism to the disadvantage of everyone else.

The Inspiration of Minority Responses

Americans have long believed that "white is beautiful." People who neither look nor act as if they are full-fledged members of the dominant white majority have continuously been kept aware of their "disability." To be permanently stigmatized by virtue of color and culture, to be dealt with as inferior and systematically subordinated, may easily cause individuals to doubt their own self-worth. If such doubts are internalized, they lend support to white dominance by making minority group members believe that they deserve inequitable treatment.[42]

In the past some social science literature has portrayed minority peoples as mentally crushed by racism.[43] In many individual cases, this is no doubt true. But the portrayal of such peoples as mentally or spiritually crushed is a distortion of reality when applied to minority groups as a whole. It is another version of blaming the victim—of considering racially oppressed groups as incapable and thus responsible for their continuing economic, political, and social disadvantage vis-à-vis whites.

In fact, of course, we can hardly help but be inspired by the emotional and spiritual health of members of racial minorities in the face of racism. Millions of men, women, and children have revealed the extraordinary ability of human beings to endure imposed hardships. Though many individuals have been crushed by these hardships, overall Native Americans, black Americans, Hispanic Americans, and Asian Americans have survived generations of subordination, denigration, and material disadvantage and have organized and struggled to

[42] See Thomas F. Pettigrew, *A Profile of the Negro American* (Princeton, N.J.: D. Van Nostrand Company, 1964), Chapter 1.

[43] One of the best examples of this literature is William H. Grier and Price M. Cobbs, *Black Rage* (New York: Basic Books, 1968).

PUBLIC PROBLEM, PRIVATE PAIN

Old Forms of Resistance

All Americans are familiar with the Reverend Jesse Jackson, whose contributions to the civil rights movement, politics, and public discourse have drawn respect across the nation. In this selection from a commencement address given at the University of Massachusetts Medical School in 1981, Jesse Jackson comments on the continuing burden of powerlessness in a predominantly white society.

This anti-black personality of the American culture is nothing new, and neither is its denial of the depth and dimensions of the problem. America has never acknowledged the uniqueness of the experience of blacks in this country. We were the only people brought here against our will, rather than as immigrants seeking a thrill or a new way of life. No other group endured 250 years of slavery and was characterized in the Constitution as three-fifths human. No other group endured 100 years of illegal apartheid, and no other group endures to this very hour the degree of daily denial, indignity, and discrimination that is heaped on black people. The old forms of denial were, relatively speaking, simple. They were clear-cut laws of denial and rejection: slavery; the extermination of the Native American; the expropriation of life and land through terrorism, downward land assessment, and eminent domain; the annexation of Hispanics against their will; and the raw exploitation of workers by private businesses where workers were forced to work long, dirty, and dangerous hours for slave wages. This was the period when the very laws were stacked against us. No thought was given to training those to heal whom the Constitution declared to be only three-fifths human. Medical education was not for those "who had no laws which a white man must respect." For black people, then, there was no legal protection under the law, much less equal protection under the law.

The struggle that has dominated the over three and a half centuries of our presence on this continent has been one to gain first the recognition of the law and then equal protection under the law. Thus we fought for the Thirteenth, Fourteenth, and Fifteenth Amendments to the Constitution, a struggle which we championed—but all benefited. That is why, in this century, we have continued to fight for the 1954 *Brown* decision, ending the "separate but equal" legal principle and providing for equal educational opportunity by law. It is why we fought for the 1964 Civil Rights Act, providing us equal access to public accommodations; the 1965 Voting Rights Act, assuring us by law of our right to vote—which must be fought for again and renewed in 1982; and it is the reason we fought for a 1968 Open Housing Act—*to provide equal protection under the law.*

As we struggled, and won, equal protection under the law, a new dimension of the problem began to manifest itself. The historic struggle had been a horizontal one, seeking access to areas where we formerly, by law, had been locked out. But the struggle shifted from an essentially horizontal one to an essentially vertical one. Upward mobility, not just access, became the key. It was a shift from equal protection under the law to equal protection within the law. In many instances we were legislated in but "regulated" or "costed" out. What real difference does it make to have the right to live in any neighborhood but not have the money to pay the house note? What is the fundamental difference in having the right under law to enroll in any medical school but not have the ability to pay the tuition? When the shift from citizenship rights to economic rights, from access to equality, began to take place, some of our former allies, rather than making the adjustment and growing into the new dimensions of the struggle, chose instead to become our adversaries.

There has been a lot of controversy around desegregating the nation's schools, busing, affirmative action, and minimum quotas, but most people have missed the crux of the matter. The fundamental problem is fairly simple. The same people who were in charge of segregation are now in charge of desegregation. We have shifted teachers and principals and children and some money, but we have not shifted power. The power—which schools get closed, who gets bused and where, who gets admitted to law and medical school and for what reasons—the power to plan, to decide, to appraise, and to define is still fundamentally in the same old hands. Until we learn to share power within our various institutions, not merely grant access paternalistically, our progress toward racial reconciliation will continue to be at a snail's pace.

Source: From Jesse L. Jackson, *Straight from the Heart,* pp. 105–106.

assert their worth. Despite all that has been done to them historically, such groups have continued to battle for even the smallest gains toward equality with whites.

Ironically, one rarely considered consequence of racism in the United States has been the development of social movements that continue to inspire many persons who seek social change, no matter what their color. The contemporary women's movement and environmental movement, for example, have drawn inspiration from minority struggles for civil rights, as did the antiwar movement of the late 1960s and early 1970s.

The Civil Rights Movement

The most famous minority struggle against racial discrimination is the black civil rights movement of the 1950s and 1960s.[44] In 1954 the efforts of such groups as the National Association for the Advancement of Colored People (NAACP) culminated in a Supreme Court decision outlawing segregated public schooling. Although it would be years before the decision would begin having any substantial impact on the education of racial minorities, it did signal a new era in American race relations. Once the Supreme Court ruled that segregated schools denied blacks their constitutional rights, it was obvious that discriminatory voting laws and segregated public facilities, housing, transportation systems, and workplaces had to go.

One day in 1955, in Montgomery, Alabama, a seamstress named Mrs. Rosa Parks refused to give up her seat in a segregated city bus so that a white man could sit. Inspired by her arrest, over 50,000 blacks soon joined a boycott of segregated public transportation in that city; and after a year-long struggle, the buses were desegregated. This protest demonstrated that segregation could be fought by grassroots collective action. And it turned a leader of the Montgomery protest, Dr. Martin Luther King, Jr., into a national civil rights figure.

Inspired by the success in Montgomery, groups of blacks and their supporters slowly began to test resistance to desegregation both in the South and in the North. By the early 1960s, this testing had begun to take on the characteristics of a national social movement, led by such groups as the NAACP, the Congress of Racial Equality (CORE), the Student Nonviolent Coordinating Committee (SNCC), and Dr. King's Southern Christian Leadership Conference (SCLC). Peaceful marches, boycotts, and sit-ins against segregationist practices captured public attention nationwide. The response to civil rights demonstrations was frequently violent. Incidents of harassment and terrorism were directed at both black and white civil rights advocates, in some cases resulting in tragic deaths. Many Americans were outraged, and the incidents thus resulted in increased public support for civil rights.

In 1963 over a quarter million supporters of the civil rights movement staged a dramatic march in Washington, D.C. There, movement leaders such as Dr. King called on the American people and federal officials to support new legal measures that would force an end to segregation. The immediate outcome was the passage of new federal civil rights legislation—most notably the Civil Rights Act of 1964 and the previously discussed Voting Rights Act of 1965. Blacks could now appeal to the law when faced with discrimination.

Unfortunately, the new legislation did little for blacks who resided in the nation's urban ghettos. If anything, the sense of isolation and hopelessness among many ghetto blacks was inflamed. It had become clear to many that outlawing discrimination was not the same as upgrading ghetto schools, eliminating poverty and inferior housing, reducing police brutality, and providing decent employment opportunities. In

---

[44] See Franklin, *From Slavery to Freedom*, and Ashmore, *Hearts and Minds*.

Civil rights demonstrations in the late 1950s and 1960s resulted in considerable public support for legislation to protect the rights of minorities in the United States. Dr. Martin Luther King, Jr., shown helping to lead a march, was a central figure in the civil rights movement. His death by assassination in 1968 shocked people around the world. *(AP/Wide World)*

the mid-1960s ghetto communities began to erupt in riots. America's "race problem" took yet another turn as the civil rights movement began to splinter.

Groups that had long battled for desegregation and integration, such as the NAACP, maintained their commitment to such goals and continued to solicit white support. CORE and SNCC, on the other hand, began to reject white participation in their activities and called for "Black Power."[45] Basically, this meant that black

[45] Black power and other outcomes of the 1960s civil rights movement are critically analyzed in Robert L. Allen, *Black Awakening in Capitalist America* (Garden City, N.Y.: Doubleday & Co., 1969). See also Stokely Carmichael and

people should collectively strive to take over those white-dominated institutions that directly affected their lives. It meant community control of schools, local political apparatus, police departments, economic endeavors, and social services. As CORE and SNCC began to mobilize support for Black Power, more militant black organizations began to emerge in ghetto areas. The most well known was the Black Panther Party. To the Panthers, racism was the immediate enemy, but its roots were to be found in the capitalist makeup of American society. The ultimate goal to be pursued was not desegregation or even community control. The goal was the abolition of capitalism and the creation of a socialist alternative.[46]

The ghetto rebellions that rocked the nation each year from 1965 to 1968 and the growing political militancy of segments of the civil rights movement alienated many whites. At the same time, the more moderate elements of the movement lost the one charismatic leader with white support. Dr. Martin Luther King, Jr., was assassinated in 1968. In the wake of his death, the already segmented civil rights movement began to founder.

Between the mid- and late 1960s, the federal government used a carrot-and-stick approach to ghetto discontent. Limited funds were poured into new federal programs, like the War on Poverty and the Model Cities Program, that were designed to foster the impression that ghetto problems were being addressed in concrete ways. Simultaneously, federal agencies such as the FBI—along with local police departments—began to systematically harass and disrupt both the militant and moderate civil rights groups.[47]

Charles V. Hamilton, *Black Power* (New York: Random House, 1967).

[46] Philip S. Foner, ed., *The Black Panthers Speak* (Philadelphia: J. B. Lippincott Company, 1970).

[47] Nelson Blackstock, *Cointelpro: The FBI's Secret War on Political Freedom* (New York: Vintage Books, 1976). See also David J. Garrow, *The FBI and Martin Luther King* (New York: Penguin Books, 1983).

By the early 1970s the civil rights movement was in a state of disarray. Members of the white majority had lost interest in the continuing plight of racial minorities. Other national issues, such as military involvement in Southeast Asia and economic recession, overshadowed racism. The gains of the civil rights movement were substantial—especially when measured against the harsh treatment of the recent past. But since the early 1970s, little has been done to further improve the life chances of minorities.

In the last decade, civil rights organizations that remain committed to desegregation have concentrated on two key issues, neither of which has drawn a great deal of support from whites. Attacks on employment discrimination through legal efforts to bring about "affirmative action" in hiring have proven threatening to many whites. Attacks on urban school segregation have also aroused white concern, if not outright resistance.

After an era of conflict and minority advance, black–white relations seem to have settled into an uneasy holding pattern. The subordinate position of the black population, as well as that of other minorities, has only been eased by the successes of the civil rights movement, not eliminated.

Toward a More Equal Society

The elimination of personal and institutional racism will benefit racial minorities and the white majority. Racism and its consequences ultimately harm everyone.

Attacks against racism must take place on two levels. First, racist ideas must be attacked and discredited. Ideas alleging the inferiority of minority peoples, no matter how subtly they are stated, are inevitably used to justify their denigration or to rationalize minority disadvantage.

Second, attacks must also be made on practices that—whether intended to do so or not—contribute to the subordinate status of minorities. This means fighting discrimination and exploitation wherever they appear and pushing for affirmative institutional practices that will upgrade and enhance opportunities for minority group members. Movements to end school and housing segregation and to put an end to discrimination in employment must once again become as energized as the 1960s civil rights movement. More people must join or create collective efforts against racism, if only out of a self-interested desire to avoid sharing in its costs.

We must not lose sight of the fact that many of the problems facing minority group members are matters afflicting tens of millions of white people as well. Poverty, substandard schooling, unemployment, and poor housing are not solely or even primarily minority problems. By pushing for societal changes, such as a reduction in economic inequality and the expansion of free or low-cost services, the plight of many whites as well as minorities can be measurably improved.

Under the prevailing order, improvement in the economic and political position of minorities is often seen as a threat to whites. The assumption is that whites will sustain losses if minorities make gains in employment, education, and politics. This will continue to be a problem so long as we believe that competition for existing resources and opportunities is part of the "natural order." We need to begin ignoring the color line, so that all people with common wants and needs can develop strategies for change through which all can gain. The only losers should be those whose inordinate power and privilege depend on maintaining racial antagonisms and preserving the status quo.

SUMMARY

Native Americans, black Americans, Hispanic Americans, and Asian Americans are among the minorities that have been subjected to harm by the dominant white majority. Members of such groups have experienced personal racism, as expressed by individual whites. And they have been victimized by institutional racism. The routine operations of white-dominated institutions continue to function to minority disadvantage. This treatment of minorities has often been rationalized by so-called scientific theories that allege minority genetic inferiority. Such theories have no basis in fact, but they provide an intellectual climate for the perpetuation of personal and institutional racism.

Institutional racism operates in the area of employment. Hiring and promotion practices are often subtly discriminatory—for example, the use of tests that favor whites (due to the educational advantages the latter enjoy). Those who hire or appoint people to key positions are usually white men, and they tend to choose people who are like themselves and who will "fit in." Consequently the labor market is divided along racial lines. The primary labor market, consisting of the more desirable occupations, is largely populated by whites. The secondary labor market, where wages are low and jobs least secure, is the one in which minorities are most likely to find work.

As antidiscrimination laws have begun to bring blatant discrimination to an end, individual minority group members have been permitted to move upward in the job hierarchy. But in *group* terms, Native Americans, black Americans, and Hispanic Americans have not made significant gains. Factors other than those mentioned help account for this. The white flight of business and industry out of central cities has made it increasingly difficult for ghettoized minorities to find satisfactory employment. Technological changes threaten the existence of unskilled and semiskilled jobs in which minorities are concentrated, while opening up jobs requiring specialized skills for which whites are disproportionately prepared. Exclusionary practices by white-dominated unions have helped keep minority group members out of the better paying skilled crafts and trades. Finally, minorities who want to open their own businesses have been subjected to discrimination by banks and other financial institutions. The limited efforts to aid minority entrepreneurs in recent years have not resulted in any dramatic improvement in minority business ownership.

Institutional racism also operates in the political sphere. Minority employment in government is primarily in the lower paying, nonpolicymaking positions. At the national level, few minority members have been appointed to public office, and few hold elected office. Minority political officials find themselves outnumbered and pressured to limit expression of race-related concerns. Some progressively lose identification with their minority constituencies, thus further diluting minority political power. Until quite recently, minority group members were even discouraged from voting by racist practices. Now that voting rights are protected by law, minority voter activity has been on the increase. But important decisions affecting the life chances of minorities continue to be made *for* them, not *by* them.

In comparison to the dominant white majority, minorities are educationally deprived. Segregated schooling continues, and urban fiscal crises exacerbate the problem of financing education for the ghettoized on a level with that of white suburbs. Whites continue to dominate in the administration of educational programs at the federal, state, and local levels. Within educational systems, minority children are often taught by persons who have little understanding of or respect for their culture and experiences. Curricular materials have suggested white superiority by their failure to reflect the multiracial character of society, a situation only recently undergoing change. Testing practices that favor the environmental advantages experienced by many whites have been used to assign minorities to low-ability classes. Once there, differential treatment leads to differential learning and performance. School failure intensifies the disadvantages that minority members face in the labor market.

Institutional racism harms minorities, and it hurts whites as well. Racism restricts the pool of talent from which society as a whole could benefit. It forces up tax expenditures to counter the effects of unequal educational opportunities, unemployment, and poverty. Racism leaves whites with anxiety and fear in relating to minority group members, and stirs the possibility of racial conflicts against which investment in police forces and other forms of social control must be made. Finally, racism divides our society. The common problems both whites and minorities face tend to be obscured. Those whites who hold economic and political power benefit from racial disunity, consciously or unconsciously using a divide-and-conquer strategy to the disadvantage of everyone else.

Despite the harm done them, minorities have not been mentally or spiritually crushed. Indeed, their historic struggles for survival and equality with whites have revealed the extraordinary ability of human beings to endure imposed hardships. One consequence of racism has been the development of social movements—for example, the civil rights movement of the 1950s and 1960s—that have inspired many persons who seek to bring about changes in American society. The gains of the civil rights movement were substantial when measured against the past, but much more effort is needed to eliminate the subordination of minorities.

Attacks must be made against racist ideas, as these are inevitably used to justify the denigration of minorities or to rationalize their situation of disadvantage. Moreover, attacks must be made on personal and institutional practices that—intended or not—subordinate minorities. Many of the problems facing minority group members are faced by millions of whites as well. Efforts to deal with poverty, substandard schooling, unemployment, and poor housing will relieve the plight of many whites—not just minority group members. The only whites who stand to lose from attacks against racism are those whose power and privilege depend on maintaining racial antagonisms and preserving the status quo.

DISCUSSION QUESTIONS

1. A childless white couple wishes to adopt a child. The demand for healthy white infants has outstripped the supply, but several children from minority backgrounds are available. What arguments could be made for and against the adoption of a minority child by whites?
2. Two applicants—one white and one a minority group member—are equally qualified for a professional job opening. What arguments could be made for and against giving preference to the minority applicant? If preference is not given, how will minority underrepresentation in the professions ever be altered?
3. If you are white, discuss your feelings about being in a social situation in which you are the only white present. If you are of minority background, discuss your feelings about being in a social situation that is wholly white. In both cases, discuss the sources of your feelings.
4. At predominantly white campuses across the country, it is common to see minority students clustered among their racial peers. For example, all-black tables in cafeterias are not uncommon. How does one account for this informal segregation? Is it desirable or undesirable? How so?
5. Some years ago, a movie depicted changes in the life of a white man who woke up one morning and found he had turned black. If you are white and this were to happen to you, what would your reactions be? If you are a minority group member and you were to wake up white, what would your reactions be? In both cases, discuss the change in life chances and opportunities that your color alteration could entail.
6. If, as we noted in this chapter, racism harms whites, why do not more whites see the struggle against personal and institutional racism as in their self-interest? Under what conditions could this situation change?

SUGGESTED READINGS

Blauner, Bob. *Black Lives, White Lives: Three Decades of Race Relations in America* (Berkeley: University of California Press, 1990).
Blacks and whites speak candidly on their perception of race and changing opportunities in recent decades.

Green, Philip. *The Pursuit of Inequality* (New York: Pantheon Books, 1982).
Critique of various theories of group superiority (e.g., that whites are "racially superior" to racial minorities).

Omi, Michael, and Howard A. Winant. *Racial Formation in the United States from the 1960s to the 1980s* (New York: Routledge, Chapman & Hall, 1986).
Analysis of the central role race has come to play in our contemporary culture and everyday life.

Schaefer, Richard T. *Racial and Ethnic Groups,* 4th ed. (Glenview, Ill.: Scott, Foresman & Company, 1990).
Comprehensive overview of America's major racial and ethnic minority groups, their struggles, and their achievements.

Williams, Juan. *Eyes on the Prize* (New York: Penguin Books, 1987).
Popular history of the civil rights movement, 1954–65.

Wilson, William J. *The Truly Disadvantaged* (Chicago: University of Chicago Press, 1987).
How racism and class barriers combine to entrap low-income blacks in an unending struggle for economic survival.

CHAPTER 9

Sexism

There should be no personal and institutional discrimination against individuals on the basis of sex.

In earlier chapters we examined several distinct patterns of inequality, each of which is an integral feature of the overall structure of this society. We saw that the unequal distribution of wealth, income, and educational opportunity divides Americans into separate classes. Political power is concentrated in the hands of a few, and decisions about the nature and course of American society generally serve the interests of the dominant economic class. Institutional racism creates further cleavages within the population, subordinating minority peoples and obscuring the problems many different groups have in common. Such macro problems adversely affect the life chances of millions of persons, young and old.

Yet another pattern of inequality limits life chances—the pattern of sex inequality. Women are a majority in numbers, comprising slightly over 50 percent of the American population; but they are a minority group in treatment, in that they are socially, economically, and politically disadvantaged in comparison to men. The fact that women are collectively disadvantaged and are thus a minority group is still not fully accepted.[1] Many men and some women greet this idea with derision, even while acknowledging that there are certain costs associated with being born female.

In this chapter we look at the minority status of women in America. We first consider the phenomenon of sexism and the myths that back it up. The chapter then goes into the economic and political effects of sexism—for both women and men. Finally, we consider the goals, gains, and future hopes of the women's movement as it attempts to liberate women from their subordinate status.

THE MEANING OF SEXISM

Sexism is the systematic subordination of persons on the basis of their sex. In the United States, sexism limits females to very circumscribed roles, based on the belief that biology is destiny.[2] This belief has been perpetuated and instilled in women through everyday socialization practices, and the subordination it calls for has been carried out in male-dominated institutions.

Male Chauvinism Versus Institutional Sexism

In Chapter 8, we drew a distinction between personal and institutional racism. A somewhat parallel distinction can be drawn between male chauvinism and institutional sexism. *Male chauvinism* is exhibited at the level of interpersonal relationships. The term refers to attitudes and actions through which individual males display their sense of superiority over women. For example, by using such slang terms as *chick, fox,* and *bitch,* men place women metaphorically on the level of animals. Other terms, such as *broad* for *woman,* refer to things, or properties, rather than human beings. Statements such as the male-to-male query "Are you getting any?" segment human relations into genital relations, a process more directly expressed when women are entertained (or paid) for the sole purpose of sexual exploitation.

Within the home, male chauvinism is expressed in other ways. Many men refuse to perform routine housekeeping tasks, such as cooking and cleaning. After all, they worked hard all day (the implication is that their wives or lovers did not), and besides, such activities are women's work. Women who work outside the home commonly find that they are expected to bear the burdens of housework as well. It is also not uncommon for a man to insist that a woman bear full responsibility for contraception, or that she be at her mate's beck and call to satisfy his sexual whims. In our culture, "a man's home is his castle," and since few households have paid servants, the "little woman" must often suffice.[3]

Women who work outside the home are often expected to be cheerful coffee-brewers and desk-top straighteners for busy men. Working women may have to put up with being eyed and ogled or subjected to pats and chucks under the chin by friendly males.[4] At annual office Christmas parties, the real reason behind the year's paternal or playful pats is sometimes expressed more directly. To refuse to play along or to get upset can put a woman's job in jeopardy. Men may dismiss a woman's outbursts of fury and resentment over being subjected to

[1] The idea that women comprise a minority group was voiced in sociology some forty years ago, but it went largely ignored until the late 1960s. See Helen M. Hacker, "Women as a Minority Group," *Social Forces* 30 (1951): 60–69.

[2] This belief is expressed by Steven Goldberg, in *The Inevitability of Patriarchy* (New York: William Morrow & Company, 1973), and by Daniel Amneus, in *Back to Patriarchy* (New Rochelle, N.Y.: Arlington, 1979). An excellent critique of such beliefs is found in Philip Green, *The Pursuit of Inequality* (New York: Pantheon Books, 1981), pp. 119–62.

[3] Arlie Hochschild and Anne Machung, *The Second Shift: Inside the Two-Job Marriage* (New York: Penguin Books, 1989).

[4] On the treatment of women in nontraditional jobs, see Jean R. Schroedel and Ronnie J. Steinberg, eds., *Alone in a Crowd* (Philadelphia: Temple University Press, 1985).

these indignities (which few men would silently endure) with the cavalier explanation: "It's just like a woman," or "It must be that time of the month." Women who aggressively challenge expressions of male chauvinism are likely to be accused of being sexually frustrated, frigid, or lesbians.

Chauvinist attitudes and actions reduce women to objects or to servants catering to the self-defined physical and emotional needs of men. Not all men are chauvinists. Some chauvinists do not recognize themselves as such. Others freely admit their chauvinism but seem not to understand that their attitudes and actions degrade women as people. On the other hand, not all women chafe under the separate and unequal role into which chauvinists place them. The definition of male chauvinism as sexist (and, indeed, the term itself) is a relatively recent phenomenon. It is attributable largely to the consciousness-raising effects of the women's movement, wherein women sensitive to sexism have encouraged such sensitivity among others.

As annoying and difficult as male chauvinism is, *institutional sexism*—the subordination of women built into societal institutions—has far greater implications. Institutional sexism has proven to be just as, if not more, pervasive than male chauvinism. While male chauvinism operates at the level of interpersonal relations, institutional sexism is more on the level of ongoing, organizational routine. In the economy, in politics, and in education, women are systematically treated in a manner that institutionalizes and increases their disadvantage vis-à-vis men. Often quite subtle, institutional sexism is less amenable to direct confrontation and attack than is chauvinism.

Is Biology Destiny?

Both male chauvinism and institutional sexism are based on and justified by the ideology that biology is destiny. According to this ideology, basic biological and psychological differences exist between the sexes. These differences require each sex to play a separate role in social life. Women are the weaker sex—both physically and emotionally. Thus, they are naturally suited, much more so than men, to the performance of domestic duties. A woman's place, under normal circumstances, is within the protective environment of the home. There biologically determined physical limitations and emotional sensitivity are not deficits. Nature has decreed that women play nurturant, caretaker roles such as wife and mother, homemaker and confidante. On the other hand, men are best suited to go out into the competitive world of work and politics, where serious responsibilities must be borne. Men are to be the providers; women and children are "dependents."

This view assumes that men will work and support women and children who remain in the home.[5] It makes no provision for single, widowed, divorced, or abandoned women and their families. The ideology thus ignores the reality of demands faced by millions of such women, not to mention those whose husbands' earnings are so low as to force wives' participation in the labor force.

The ideology also holds that women who wish to or must venture outside the household should naturally fill those jobs that are in line with the special capabilities of their sex. It is thus appropriate for women, not men, to be employed as nurses, social workers, elementary school teachers, household helpers, and clerks and secretaries. These positions are simply an extension of women's domestic role as a supportive adjunct to men and their labor. Informal distinctions between "women's work" and "men's work" in the labor force, according to the ideology, are simply a func-

[5] Sometimes referred to as the "domestic code," the view is explored in Alice Kessler-Harris, *Women Have Always Worked: A Historical Overview* (New York: Feminist Press, 1980).

tional reflection of the basic biological differences between the sexes. If women venture outside these working roles into male-dominated occupations and professions, they are often under pressure to renounce wifely and motherly opportunities.

The ideology suggests that nature works in another significant way. For the human species to survive over time, its members must regularly reproduce. Sexual attraction between potential mates is the first step in this necessary process. Thus, women must strive to fill the role of sex object to men. Whether at home or in the labor force, women must make the most of their physical appearance. The role of sex object (and, ultimately, full-time mother) is biologically allocated to women and cannot be lightly dismissed.

Finally, the ideology ignores the possibilities of homosexuality and assumes a fully heterosexual world. It sidesteps the reality that in our own society an estimated one in ten persons is homosexual, while irrationally implying that homosexuals are violators of nature. It is such views that help to encourage and perpetuate homophobia, that is, hatred or fear of homosexuals and homosexuality.

It is, of course, not true that basic biological and psychological differences between the sexes require each to play such sex-delineated roles in social life. Here it is appropriate to make a distinction between two concepts: *sex* and *gender*. When social scientists refer to sex, they are referring to the genetic and physical characteristics of persons that identify them as either male or female. Gender, in contrast, is a concept referring to the culturally accepted behaviors and ways of relating to others expected of the two sexes. Gender is learned, whereas sex is biologically given. There is ample evidence that male and female gender roles vary from society to society, and those role differences that do exist are largely learned.[6] Since this is the case, they can be changed.

But to the degree people actually believe that biology is destiny and that nature intended for men and women to make different contributions to society, rigid sex-delineated gender roles will be seen as totally acceptable. Expecting women to remain in their place in the home, to limit their aspirations to "women's work" in the labor force, and to preoccupy themselves with sexual attractiveness to men will not be seen as oppression. Instead, such matters will be viewed as part of nature's grand design. Women who question their biological fate—who demand liberation from the roles they are given on the basis of sex—are likely to be seen as deviants.[7]

Socialization and Self-concept

Women make up a numerical majority in American society. Why have they, in general, accepted sexist treatment and allowed its ideology to be perpetuated? The answer lies in everyday patterns of socialization.

Early personality development hinges largely on experiences in one's family, and the meaning attached to sex group membership—both for men and women—begins in the home.[8] At birth, children typically are dressed in either pink or blue—the initial uniform that sets girls and boys apart. Although infants cannot discern the message of these colors, adults can,

---

[6] For gender role origins and their variation among societies, see M. Kay Martin and Barbara Voorhies, *Female of the Species* (New York: Columbia University Press, 1975). The processes by which female gender roles are learned are found in Hilary M. Lips, "Gender-Role Socialization: Lessons in Femininity," in Jo Freeman, ed., *Women: A Feminist Perspective*, 4th ed. (Mountain View, Calif.: Mayfield Publishing Company, 1989), pp. 197–216. See also Candace West and Don Zimmerman, "Doing Gender," *Gender and Society*, 1 (June 1987): 125–51.

[7] Edwin M. Schur, *Labeling Women Deviant: Gender, Stigma, and Social Control* (New York: McGraw-Hill, 1983).

[8] Some researchers would disagree. See Eleanor Maccoby and Carol Jacklin, *The Psychology of Sex Differences* (Stanford, Calif.: Stanford University Press, 1974).

and it is at this point that gender role differentiation begins. Parents actively impart their own sense of what it means to be male or female to their children, thereby *creating* many personality and behavioral differences that would not otherwise exist. These differences, as they receive subsequent reinforcement through school and exposure to the mass media, help both men and women define their "place" in adult society.

Even such mundane aspects of the child's world as toys and games promote separate gender roles. Girls usually receive dolls (which they can "mother"), cooking and tea sets (to practice "housework"), and cast-off handbags and cosmetic kits (to practice being a "sex object"). Most parents encourage their daughters to develop traits associated with femininity. Aggressive behavior and fighting are discouraged; crying is acceptable. It is all right to be cute, coy, and flirtatious—an operational definition of what it means to be "daddy's little girl."

Conversely, boys are typically given tool kits and building equipment (to practice "work") and sports paraphernalia (so that they might develop masculine "toughness"). So-called feminine traits, such as emotional sensitivity, are discouraged. Aggressiveness, competitiveness, and a drive to excel are prized. The worst insult to a little boy is to say that he acts, sounds, looks, or smells like a girl. Most boys (and girls, for that matter) find it easier to live up to their parents' gender role expectations than to question or resist them. Fortunately, many parents are themselves becoming conscious of the negative impact of gender role stereotyping.

Parental influence is quickly supplemented by the experience of schooling. It is in school that children will have their first in-depth exposure to segregated toilet facilities and single-sex team sports (softball for girls, hardball for boys). In many schools, girls get lessons in home economics while boys take shop. In the upper grades, girls wave pompoms in support of the team; the boys bear the responsibility of fighting for athletic glory.

Throughout the schooling experience, curricular materials remind children of gender role differentiation.[9] Numerous studies of sex stereotyping in children's books and school texts have found women portrayed as mothers and housewives to such an extent that one would never guess that there are well over 52 million women currently employed in the labor force. History tends to be the history of men's accomplishments; social studies, the story of how men govern; and English, the literature and poetry of men. Girls cannot help but get the impression that women are not very important, at least not outside of the home.[10]

By adolescence, girls—having been sensitized to their gender identity by their parents and their school experiences—begin to have their first fears of human obsolescence.[11] They begin to ask: "Will/do/why don't boys like me?" The drive for social acceptability, popularity, and recognition is constantly tempered by concern with what boys will think. Looks attract. But competitive accomplishments—physical or intellectual—can be interpreted as masculine and are likely to repel. It seems safest just to be a woman, a member of the "weaker sex"—a sexually attractive, sensitive, nurturant, supportive companion. Girls thus slip into "woman's place" as defined by the biology-is-destiny ideology. Since successful performance of the female gender role requires them to avoid competing with men, they can see themselves only as something less than men.

---

[9] See Hilary M. Lips, "Gender-Role Socialization," in Freeman, *Women: A Feminist Perspective*, pp. 202–5.

[10] An effort to write women back into history was undertaken by Elise Boulding, in *The Underside of History* (Boulder, Colo.: Westview Press, 1976).

[11] See Jules Henry, *Culture Against Man* (New York: Vintage Books, 1965), Chapter 6.

THE ECONOMIC EFFECTS OF SEXISM

The biology-is-destiny ideology might view the ideal American woman as an industrious, happy housewife concerned only with laundry, dishes, children's snacks, and personal cleanliness. But this "ideal" is far from reality. Over the last several decades an ever-increasing percentage of the adult female population has been taking on part-time or full-time employment outside the home. By 1989 some 55 million women were in America's labor force—57 percent of all women over sixteen. (Over 52 million were actively employed, with another 2.8 million seeking work.)[12] Many of the women working part-time were doing so because of an absence of full-time employment opportunities.

For the most part, women work outside the home because of *economic necessity*. In 1988, some 56.5 percent of all married women were in the labor force. Most of these women were working in order to supplement their husbands' earnings and provide for adequate family support. This was particularly the case for minority women, whose families are, as we saw earlier, disproportionately represented in low-income categories. Among women who were divorced from their mates, 75.7 percent were in the labor force. Most of them had no choice but to become breadwinners for themselves and their families.[13] Finally, 65.2 percent of all single women were in the labor force; they needed some means of self-support or had to contribute to their families' earnings. Thus, the beliefs that American women are not serious participants in the labor force and that they work primarily for "pin money" are clearly erroneous. The labor performed by women outside the household makes a significant contribution to our capitalist economy.

Nor has having children blocked millions of women from seeking work, despite the responsibilities of motherhood. (See Figure 9.1.) Most working mothers have families still living at home. In 1988 some 65 percent of married women with children under eighteen and over half of those with children under six were in the labor force. It seems silly to argue about whether mothers should be in the labor force—for they are there. The number of mothers employed would probably be higher if many women did not feel guilty about leaving the home (because they have internalized the biology-is-destiny ideology), if there were more decent-paying employment opportunities for women, and if adequate and inexpensive child-care facilities were more widely available. The latter two factors particularly hamper women who are heads of households, forcing reluctant dependence on poverty-level public assistance programs.

A number of forces promise to propel more and more women into the search for employment in future years. Women are marrying later, so it seems likely that a higher percentage of single women will be looking for means of support. More effective means of contraception and a trend toward smaller family size mean that a higher percentage of married women will find it possible to break away from home and/or extend their stay in the labor force. Since divorce and separation rates have been very high in recent years, and since women, on the average, outlive men, an increasing percentage of women will find themselves living without a mate at some period during adult life. Many will require employment to sustain themselves and perhaps their children. In sum, women's involvement in the American labor force is not only here to stay; it can be expected to grow—despite the ideology that woman's place is in the home.

---

[12] Statistics in this section are from issues of *Employment and Earnings* and *Monthly Labor Review* (periodicals published by the federal government). See also Francine D. Blau and Anne E. Winkler, "Women in the Labor Force: An Overview," in Freeman, *Women: A Feminist Perspective*, pp. 265–86.

[13] See Terry Arendell, *Mothers and Divorce* (Berkeley: University of California Press, 1986).

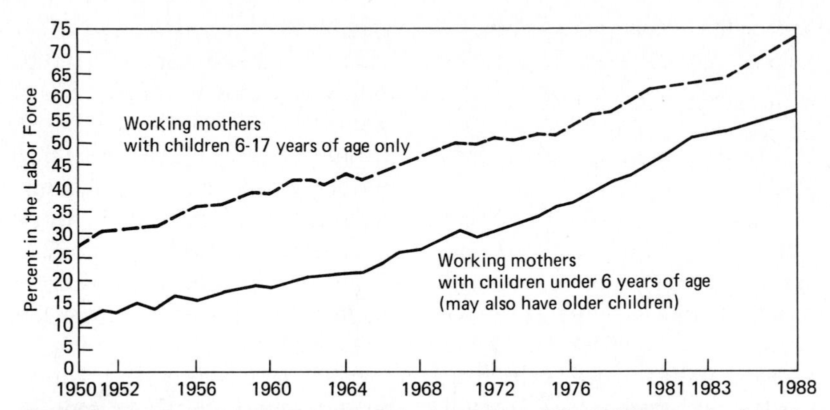

FIGURE 9.1 Civilian Labor Force Participation Rates of Married Women, by Age of Children, 1950–88
Source: U.S. Department of Labor, *Time of Change: 1983 Handbook on Women Workers* (Washington, D.C.: U.S. Government Printing Office, 1984), p. 21; U.S. Department of Commerce, Bureau of the Census, *Statistical Abstract of the United States, 1985* (Washington, D.C.: U.S. Government Printing Office, 1984), p. 399; and U.S. Department of Labor, Bureau of Labor Statistics, *News*, September 7, 1988.

Earnings and Job Opportunities

By 1989 over 122 million persons were in the American civilian labor force; some 45 percent of them were women. What do women receive in return for their labor? By all indications, they get much less in return than do men.

We can, for example, examine the median weekly incomes of full-time, year-round workers. When workers' incomes are broken down according to sex, we find that women, on the average, earned $326 a week to men's $468 a week in early 1989. This huge gap between the median earnings of full-time male and female workers has been in existence for decades and shows little sign of dramatic change. Thus, at the same time women's participation in the labor force has been on the increase—primarily out of economic necessity—their economic standing has remained severely disadvantaged.

A further indication of the vast discrepancy between the earnings of the sexes arises if we group the median weekly earnings of full-time workers by occupation and sex. In early 1989 female managers and professionals earned only $487 per week compared to their male counterparts' $675. Females in technical, sales, and administrative (including clerical) positions received $314, whereas males received $482. Women work, but they get little in return.

For the most part the low incomes of women are a result of the *types* of positions women hold. (See Table 5.2, p. 160.) U.S. Labor Department statistics regularly show that women are grossly overrepresented in low-status, low-paying jobs—for example, clerical work and service occupations. In 1989, for example, 58.3 percent of all working women were in jobs with the lowest median earnings (clerical, service, sales). Conversely, women are underrepresented in the better paying occupations. In 1989 only 18.3 percent of employed women held technical and professional jobs, and only 11.2 percent were in managerial, executive, or administrative positions.

Within occupational categories, the earnings of women are adversely affected by patterns of less work experience than men and less time in the position held than men. Nonetheless, it has been estimated that discrimination probably accounts for *over half* of the male–female pay differences.[14] These differences can be substantial. (See Table 9.1.)

The high concentration of women workers in low-paying and often menial positions and the gap between their earnings and those of men holding similar jobs are not consequences of female biology. Clearly, not all women in the United States perform menial work at discriminatory wages. And in other countries women are far better represented in so-called men's occupations. Nor can these matters simply be attributed to differences in the educational attainments of women compared with men. For it seems that women in the labor force have, as a group, completed approximately the same number of years of schooling as men. Women's investment in education does not pay off as much as does men's. (See Figure 9.2.)

The disadvantaged position of women workers can be explained only in terms of institutional sexism. Women are the losers in a labor market that is segregated along sex lines. Employers—for the most part men—have taken advantage of the biology-is-destiny ideology, treating women differently from men. Direct discrimination in employment, promotion, and pay works to keep women down, often despite their capabilities.

[14] Blau and Winkler, "Women in the Labor Force," p. 273.

TABLE 9.1 Median Weekly Earnings of Full-Time Wage and Salary Workers by Occupation and Sex, 1989

	Median weekly earnings	
Occupation	**Men**	**Women**
Managerial and professional specialty	$675	$487
Executive, administrative, and managerial	670	456
Professional specialty	678	505
Technical, sales, and administrative support	482	314
Technicians and related support	543	394
Sales occupations	484	281
Administrative support, including clerical	435	313
Service occupations	305	213
Private household	*	179
Protective service	458	386
Service, except private household and protective	266	214
Precision production, craft, and repair	467	302
Mechanics and repairers	452	366
Construction trades	448	*
Other precision production, craft, and repair	494	293
Operators, fabricators, and laborers	361	241
Machine operators, assemblers, and inspectors	369	240
Transportation and material moving occupations	403	317
Handlers, equipment cleaners, helpers, and laborers	294	217
Farming, forestry, and fishing	249	203

*Not calculated. Number of persons in category is not significant.
Source: U.S. Department of Labor, *Employment and Earnings*, 36 (April 1989): 72.

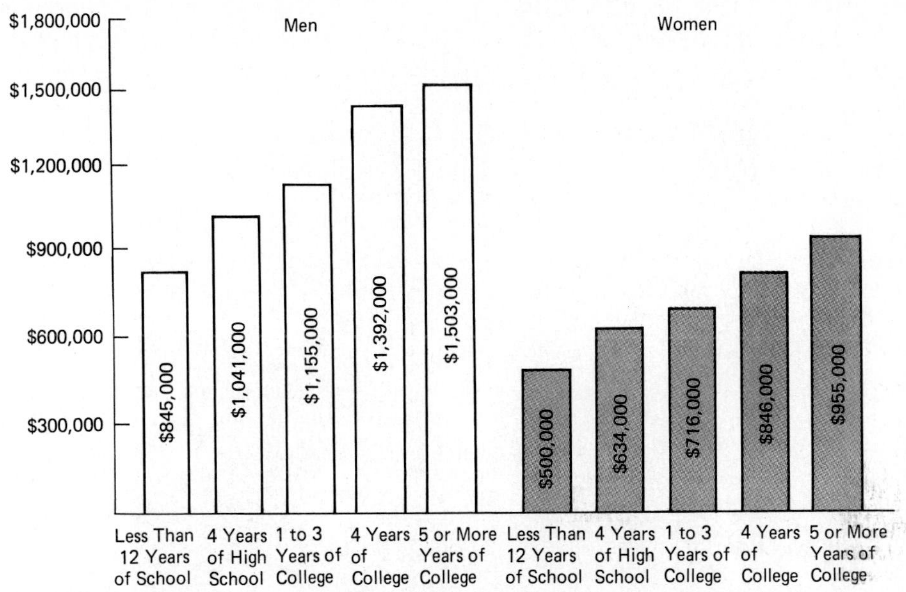

FIGURE 9.2 Expected Lifetime Earnings for Year-Round, Full-Time Workers, by Sex and by Years of School Completed: United States, 1979 [in 1981 Dollars]
Note: Earnings are from age 18 through age 64.
Source: National Center for Education Statistics, *Digest of Education Statistics, 1983–84* (Washington, D.C.: U.S. Government Printing Office, 1984), p. 192.

Forces Favoring Economic Subordination

The inferior economic position of women workers is obviously not to their advantage. On first glance, however, it appears to work to the advantage of men in the labor force. The direct employment discrimination that channels women into low-status, low-paying jobs and/or restricts their job mobility also lessens the competition men face for the better positions. In the absence of unlimited occupational opportunities (an absence exacerbated in periods of economic slowdown), there simply is not room for all at the top.

But it is more likely that men are hurt by institutional sexism in the world of work.[15] For example, discrimination against married women with children reduces family income potential and sustains the pressures on men to achieve economically. In this situation, men are certainly not benefiting from the continuation of sexist employment practices. Neither do they benefit when they must pay their divorced wives child support and/or alimony because the wives cannot earn enough to support themselves and their children. Such payments are a source of economic hardship for many men.

The presence of a large pool of low-paid women who could replace men for cheaper wages acts as a depressant on men's wages. Male workers are aware that they are not totally indispensable; if they are threatened with displacement by women who—out of financial need—are willing to work for less, they must temper their own wage demands. In addition,

[15] See Barbara Ehrenreich, *The Hearts of Men* (Garden City, N.Y: Anchor Doubleday, 1983).

Because existing laws and court orders have made it possible for some women to enter "men's jobs," many Americans believe that occupational discrimination against women has pretty much become history. But the presence of a small number of female police officers, corporate executives, and jet pilots does not change the fact that sexist employment practices are still the norm in many fields and work settings. *(Rhoda Sidney/Stock, Boston)*

men who enter occupations presently dominated by women—for example, nursing, secretarial work, elementary school teaching—are likely to find themselves forced to accept the going rates for women's work. Thus, while on one level men generally enjoy benefits from restricted job competition and the subordination of women within the labor market, on another level they must pay the price for sexist practices.

But some men do benefit in this situation. By channeling women into certain types of jobs, restricting their mobility, and keeping their pay low, employers can keep their labor costs down. Insofar as the cost of labor can be kept down, profits are enhanced. Since profit is the key objective requirement of economic institutions operating within America's capitalist economy, the exploitation of women's labor (like that of other minorities) cannot simply be ended without disrupting many businesses and industries. Employers thus have a positive incentive—aside from whatever feelings they may have about women—to perpetuate sexist practices.

The fact that so many women work out of necessity also plays into the hands of employers. In the absence of full-time work opportunities and/or because they must care for their children, millions of women must take part-time jobs. This means being dependent on periodic, temporary, and often seasonal jobs, for which it is too costly to maintain a ready reserve of full-time workers. In hiring women on a part-time basis, employers save money on such employee benefits as vacation pay, sick pay, and pension plans that full-time workers expect almost as a matter of right. They are thus able to exploit the fact that women comprise a large reserve labor pool, to be drawn upon at will and sent home when not needed.

In sum, institutional sexism in the labor market is an important force sustaining the success of our economy. As we have seen in past chapters, the benefits of this economy are appropriated to a disproportionate degree by the dominant economic class—primarily those who own

Though the occupation of registered nurse requires considerable training and skill, and though it has a great deal of importance to our society, nursing carries relatively low wages and relatively little prestige. This is a result of the belief that nursing is "women's work." Women have generally been forced to compete against one another in the handful of job categories open to them, and wages for these occupations have generally remained low. *(Lee Trail)*

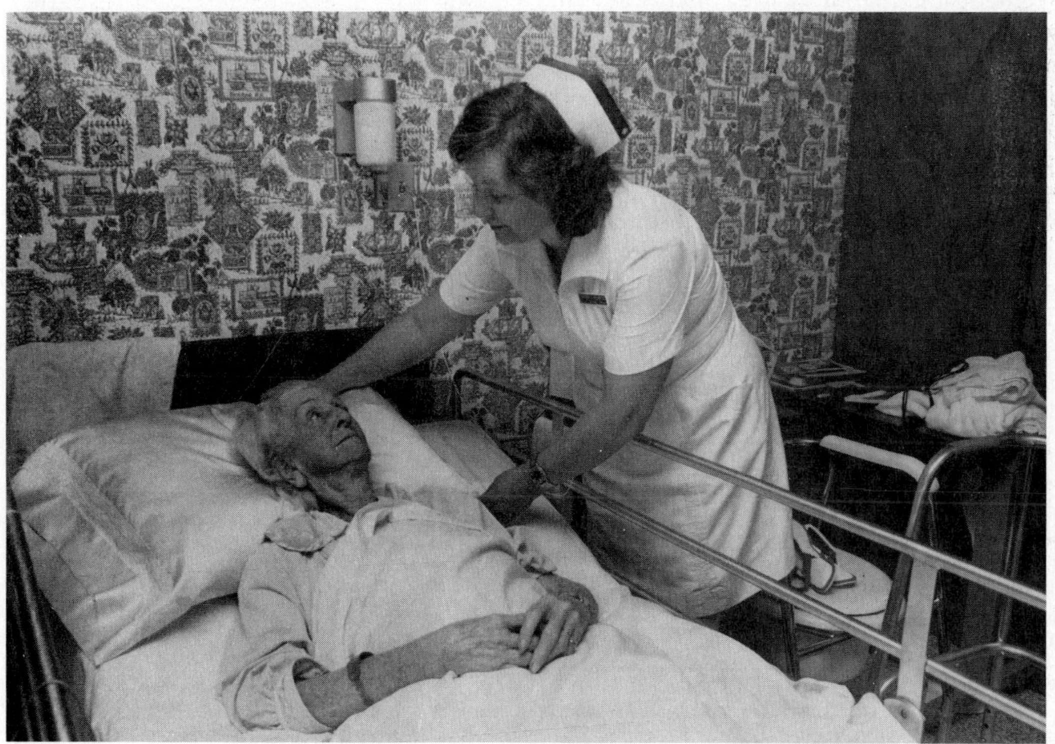

and control business and industry. Sexism, then, harms women and has dubious advantages even for most male workers. But it is profitable to the dominant few, who are an important obstacle to its elimination.

The Issue of Comparable Worth

While women and men receive different returns for their labor outside the home, under federal law persons who do the same work must receive the same pay regardless of their sex. This principle, established by the Equal Pay Act of 1963, has resulted in a number of lawsuits against employers and back pay to women employees. Between 1965 and 1976 over $135 million is said by the U.S. Equal Employment Opportunity Commission to have been due women who were underpaid in comparison with their male co-workers. However, because of lax enforcement less than a quarter of this amount was restored to the women during that period.[16] Although it has not made much of an economic impact, the Equal Pay Act has heightened awareness of discrimination against women in the area of pay.

As we have seen, the major obstacle to equal pay for women in the work force is segregation into low-paying positions. These positions are "sex-typed," in that few men are employed in them. Most women hold jobs in which 70 percent or more of their co-workers are female, and 40 percent of all women who are working hold one of the following sex-typed jobs: secretary, typist, cashier, waitress, nurse, bookkeeper, seamstress, household worker, or elementary school teacher.[17] Table 9.2 lists some occupations in which women are likely to be found.

Those who would seek to improve the pay of women in sex-typed positions have come to argue that women's work is underpaid in comparison with men's work by any neutral standard. In 1981 the U.S. Supreme Court acknowledged the legal validity of a theory that stated that "pay be equal not just for the same job but, for any given employer, for all jobs that call for comparable skills, effort and responsibility."[18] That is, jobs that have "comparable worth" must be paid the same.

It is important to emphasize that comparable worth means much more than simply equal pay for equal work, such that men and women in identical jobs would be paid equally. This is already the law of the land, as stated earlier.

> Comparable worth rests on the additional assumption that the work traditionally labeled "women's work" or associated with supposed special talents of women ought to be valued equally with those labors traditionally associated with men. For example, caretaking jobs, such as daycare workers, teachers, and nurses, ought to earn at least as much as jobs requiring the lifting of heavy objects or handling of machinery, such as digging ditches, driving trucks, and hauling garbage.[19]

In effect, comparable worth means raising the pay for those positions into which women have traditionally been channeled and segregated. Jobs that are comparable in terms of skill, effort, and responsibility would be paid the same whether men or women filled them. Under comparable worth, employers would have to develop job classifications free of gender bias and

---

[16] See Marcia Greenberger, "The Effectiveness of Federal Law Prohibiting Sex Discrimination in the United States," in Ronnie S. Ratner, ed., *Equal Employment Policy for Women* (Philadelphia: Temple University Press, 1980), pp. 108–28.

[17] Mary Frank Fox and Sharlene Hesse-Biber, *Women at Work* (Palo Alto, Calif.: Mayfield Publishing Company, 1984), p. 211. See also Barbara F. Reskin and Heidi I. Hartmann, eds., *Women's Work, Men's Work: Sex Segregation on the Job* (Washington, D.C.: National Academy Press, 1986).

[18] Robert D. Hershey, Jr., "Women's Pay Fight Shifts to Comparable Worth," *New York Times* (November 1, 1983): A15.

[19] Rita Mae Kelly and Jane Bayes, "Comparable Worth and Pay Equity: Issues and Trends," in Rita Mae Kelly and Jane Bayes, eds., *Comparable Worth, Pay Equity, and Public Policy* (Westport, Conn.: Greenwood Press, 1988), p. 4.

TABLE 9.2 Women as a Percentage of All Full-Time Workers and Relative Earnings of Women, 1979 and 1986

Occupation	Women as a percentage of all full-time workers		Ratio of female to male earnings (full-time workers)	
	1979	1986	1979	1986
Secretaries	98.8	99.2	.58	NA
Registered nurses	94.6	92.7	.82	NA
Bookkeepers, accounting and auditing clerks	88.1	93.0	.66	.74
Nursing aides, orderlies, and attendants	85.1	88.3	.72	.81
Cashiers	77.7	79.8	.71	.75
Computer operators	56.6	63.8	.69	.73
Assemblers	47.2	42.1	.71	.75
Accountants and auditors	34.0	44.7	.60	.72
Computer programmers	28.0	39.7	.80	.81
Supervisors and proprietors, sales occupations	22.4	26.6	.57	.55
Managers and administrators, n.e.c.*	22.1	28.9	.51	.61
Computer systems analysts	20.4	29.7	.79	.83
Janitors and cleaners	15.3	21.0	.74	.69
Lawyers	10.4	15.2	.55	.63
Sales representatives, mining, manufacturing and wholesale	10.1	13.4	.62	.72
Electrical and electronic engineers	4.4	9.4	.75	NA
Truck drivers, heavy	1.5	1.5	.71	NA
Carpenters, except apprentices	1.1	0.5	.71	NA
Automotive mechanics, except apprentices	0.9	0.6	.86	NA

Key: NA, not available.
*Not elsewhere classified.
Source: U.S. Department of Commerce, Bureau of the Census, *Male–Female Differences in Work Experience, Occupation, and Earnings: 1984* (Washington, D.C.: U.S. Government Printing Office, 1987), p. 5.

rank order them in terms of their worth and appropriate pay.

Job segregation involving differentially paid "women's work" and "men's work" exists in both the government and private sectors. To date, efforts to push the principle of equal pay for jobs of comparable worth have focused on government, which is more vulnerable to pressures for internal policy changes on salary issues than are business and industry. Government officials must contend with taxpayers and voters, many of whom are women. Moreover, the public sector is more likely than the private to be unionized and unions have taken an interest in pay inequities suffered by their female members.

Whereas the federal government has thus far successfully ignored or resisted pressures to address comparable worth in its own work force, the same is not true at the state level. Many state governments have begun to study the principle of comparable worth and its applicability to their particular situations; some states have actually gone ahead and implemented policy changes.[20] Women working for Washington, Minnesota, Connecticut, Iowa, New York, Massachusetts, Wisconsin, and other states, have

[20] Keon S. Chi, "Comparable Worth in State Government," in Kelly and Bayes, *Comparable Worth, Pay Equity, and Public Policy*, pp. 109–23.

been the beneficiaries of progressive policies. Yet other states remain hostile to the principle.

The drive to upgrade the pay allocated to so-called women's work has just begun. The demand for equal pay for jobs possessing comparable worth in terms of skills, effort, and responsibility has far-reaching implications. Private-sector employers can be expected to battle and seek to channel this demand into directions that do not attack their vested interest in cheap labor.[21]

Given the current trends, the U.S. poverty population may be made up almost wholly of women and children by the year 2000. The failure of our political system to deal with job segregation and pay inequities on a national scale not only helps to generate poverty. This failure also ensures many will find it extremely difficult—much more so than need be—to climb out of poverty circumstances through gainful employment. Widely implemented comparable worth policies will not eliminate poverty, but they will help those women who are able to work outside the home and who are able to find jobs.

Laboring in the Home

Though married women have been entering the labor force at an increasing rate in recent years, about 42 million, or 44 percent, still remain at home during the work week. In some cases, women prefer not to work, believing that a woman's place is in the home. But many of the millions of women who call themselves "just a housewife" do not do so out of preference.

We are all familiar with the daytime television version of being a housewife. TV commercials typically show young, fresh-faced, fashionably dressed starlets exuding enthusiasm over a product that has perfected the already immaculate state of their beautifully decorated homes. Mothers are shown in total control of their well-behaved, healthy children, blissfully enjoying their biological mission and accomplishing light tasks with playful ease (and the occasional help of a quick-acting drug). The imagery tells us that work is really something that takes place outside the home.

What this imagery ignores is the labor entailed in housework and its unrecognized value to the American economy.[22] We can get a good idea of what is involved by imagining how much a husband would have to pay persons to perform the tasks that a wife and mother does for free. He would probably have to hire a cook, a cleaning person, a chauffeur, and a baby-sitter or other child-care worker. He might require the services of a nurse, a psychologist, or an accountant. This husband would quickly find that his take-home wages were rapidly depleted when payday came for all his employees. He would have to conclude that his wife's work has monetary value when someone other than a wife does it.

Domestic and child-care workers get paid for such tasks because, contrary to television imagery, they are not much fun. Most persons do not dream of being domestics—and for good reason. In the labor market, household workers are of low social status and receive the minimal economic rewards associated with the performance of "dirty work."

Husbands who do not think of housework as a form of labor usually change their minds when, for some unexpected reason, they must temporarily take over the "little woman's" role. For it is not that housewives do not work.

[21] The issues are well presented in Michael Evan Gold, *A Dialogue on Comparable Worth* (Ithaca, N.Y.: Cornell University ILR Press, 1983). Data supporting comparable worth are found in Donald J. Treiman and Heidi I. Hartmann, eds., *Women, Work, and Wages* (Washington, D.C.: National Academy Press, 1981).

[22] Myra Marx Ferree, "Housework: Rethinking the Costs and Benefits," in Irene Diamond, ed., *Families, Politics, and Public Policy* (New York: Longman, 1983), pp. 148–67.

Rather, they labor *outside* the mainstream economy within which work is defined as an activity you are paid to do. Women who call themselves "just a housewife" implicitly recognize the secondary importance attributed to their labor.

In essence, housewives are contributing unpaid labor to the economy. This unpaid labor is a boon to employers. In its absence, husbands would be forced to demand far higher wages than they presently receive in order to pay for housekeeping and child-care services. They would have to take more time off work, and they would be unable to work overtime. They would be less able to travel frequently, if their jobs demanded travel. So long as wives perform household and child-care tasks for free, employers directly benefit. By maintaining that housewives do not really perform useful work, and certainly not work that deserves wages, employers effectively get *two* employees for the price of one. Should housewives demand wages for the work that allows business and industry to have their husbands each day, the pursuit of profit would be seriously undercut. Again, economic success is sustained by women's separate and unequal status, a status celebrated by the biology-is-destiny ideology.

The Consumer Role

It has been estimated that women are responsible for 75 percent of consumer expenditures annually. Business and industry recognize this and gear billions of dollars in investments toward the production of commodities it is hoped women will buy. Commercial advertising is used to stimulate and elicit consumption, to convince women that they and/or their households simply cannot do without "Product Z." Whether women really need these commodities, or if instead they are being manipulated into wanting them, is not a concern of business and industry. No matter what the reason, business and industry profit when commodities sell.[23]

Sales appeals to women take place on two levels: subtle attacks on their sense of personal adequacy and messages designed to suggest ways to relieve the burdens of housework and further adorn the home. The appeals tend to be written by men and to play upon the roles allocated to women by the biology-is-destiny ideology.

Attacks on women's sense of personal adequacy revolve around the idealization of the role of sex object. Advertisers encourage women to worry about their skin, eyes, lips, hair, weight, shape, clothing, and odor. Commercial appeals both create and exploit women's doubts and fears regarding loss of sexual attractiveness. Simultaneously, manufacturers and advertisers provide solutions to the anxieties to which they contribute: Purchase more beauty aids and appliances, clothing, rejuvenating drugs, diet foods. Immense profits ride on the comparisons women make between themselves and other women. For the woman who sees herself as "just a housewife" or who is functioning as a near-robot in the labor force, consumption promises a way to gain a sense of self-worth and identity—at least she can try to emulate commercial standards of sexual attractiveness.[24] If women were to discard such concerns and ignore commercial appeals, a whole sector of the economy would be disrupted.

The dissatisfactions caused by the burdens of housework provide another basis for consumption in the interests of private profit. By promoting doubts about the adequacy and efficiency of products and appliances currently in use and by singing the glories of new home commodities, advertisers take advantage of the

[23] For a historical analysis, see Stuart Ewen, *Captains of Consciousness* (New York: McGraw-Hill Book Company, 1976), pp. 159–84.

[24] See Diane Barthel, *Putting on Appearances: Gender and Advertising* (Philadelphia: Temple University Press, 1988).

The use of females as sex objects to capture the attention of males continues to be a mainstay of advertising. In this photograph automobiles are the product being marketed, though one would not necessarily know this from the expressions on some of the audience drawn to the advertising display. *(Barbara Alper/Stock, Boston)*

wish to reduce housekeeping time and effort. They also push the idea that "other people do not live like you do" ("Whose wash is whiter?"), suggesting that women can gain self-esteem through improved performance of household labor or the purchase of home adornments that everyone supposedly has.

Advertising does not itself create roles for women. Rather, it serves to reinforce conventional gender roles and to then take advantage of the roles. Women are not the only targets of sexist advertising. The "macho" appeals to purchase "men's products" both promote and exploit male chauvinism. Such products are often sold by using women as sex objects to capture attention, implying to men that they can overcome doubts about their gender role performance through acts of consumption.

THE POLITICAL EFFECTS OF SEXISM

The exploitation of women at work and at home, wherein they are cast into separate and unequal gender roles, is closely linked with women's collective exclusion from political power. We have seen in past chapters that political power is associated with wealth and economic influence and with being white. Political power is also associated with being male, and women's rights suffer as a result.

Women's Rights and the Law

The American legal system only peripherally recognizes women's economic plight and their rights as citizens. A case in point is the Civil Rights Act of 1964. This piece of federal legislation was introduced into Congress in order to put the approval of the national government behind efforts to end discrimination against persons on the basis of race. Before the act was passed, a congressman who hoped to sabotage the bill jokingly added the word *sex*.[25] His effort to defeat the bill by making it ludicrous failed, and the provision against discrimination on the basis of sex became law. That a bill pertaining to civil rights should almost *accidentally* include women is an indication of how little lawmakers cared about the status of women even as late as the mid-1960s.

The difficulties women face in gaining legal recognition of their rights through the political system are most obvious in the efforts to add the Equal Rights Amendment (ERA) to the U.S. Constitution. This amendment would state: "Equality of rights under the law shall not be denied or abridged by the United States or by any state on the basis of sex." The Fourteenth Amendment to the Constitution has long guaranteed all American citizens—regardless of race, creed, or color—equal rights under the law (the extension of these rights in practice is another question). But the Constitution does not protect persons who are treated differently under the law just because of their sex group membership. After fifty years of effort by women's rights groups, ERA was finally proposed by Congress in 1972. In order to become law, it had to be ratified by thirty-eight states. Organized resistance to ERA has been widespread, and ratification by the required number of states has not occurred. Quite a few women are against ERA, fearing that it means an end to alimony and the start of drafting women in times of war. As of this writing, the U.S. Constitution guarantees equal rights under the law to all Americans, so long as they are male.[26]

Laws that specify different treatment for men and women remain in force in states and localities across the country. Many of these laws deal with employment and allegedly exist as forms of protective legislation—for example, there are laws restricting the hours and working conditions for women. Such laws contribute to the economic subordination of women discussed in the previous section, for they are used as excuses to keep women out of better paying jobs and job opportunities.

In recent years the need to further women's legal rights has drawn ever-increasing concern. Take, for example, the rights of rape victims. Rape involves the infliction of physical and psychological damage upon the female victims—ranging in age from infants to the elderly—as men seek to demonstrate power over them in the rawest terms.[27] Legal obstacles with sexist overtones can make it difficult for many women to prove they were raped, particularly in cases where men are free to interpret women's behavior so as to claim the victim invited and/or willingly participated in the sex acts in question.

The phenomenon of "date rape" has drawn attention to the fact that it is fairly common for rapists and victims to know one another. Studies on college campuses, for example, reveal that rape is more common than one could imagine. In one study of 600 students, 15 percent of the women and 7 percent of the men reported being on a date where sexual relations took place against the woman's will.[28] Few of these date rapes are ever reported and prosecuted, so there is little to deter the rapists from

[25] Caroline Bird, *Born Female* (New York: Pocket Books, 1969), Chapter 1.

[26] For an analysis of why political mobilization on behalf of the ERA has not been effective, see Jane J. Mansbridge, *Why We Lost the E. R. A.* (Chicago: University of Chicago Press, 1986).

[27] The classic analysis of rape as an extension of sexism is Susan Brownmiller, *Against Our Will* (New York: Simon & Schuster, 1975).

[28] "Date Rape: Familiar Strangers," *Psychology Today* (July 1987): 10. See also Julie K. Ehrhart and Bernice R. Sandler, *Campus Gang Rape: Party Games?* (Washington, D.C.: Association of American Colleges, 1985).

breaking the law again. Women students victimized by such sexual violence may even drop out of school.

Another women's rights issue is sexual harassment. Most research and efforts at intervention have focused on the harassment of women workers as well as women students. One definition is as follows:

> Sexual harassment (1) is physical or verbal behavior that is sexual in nature (i.e., it makes the victim's sex salient over her occupational or other statuses); (2) is unwanted; and (3) implicitly or explicitly is experienced as a threat to the woman's job or ability to perform her work or educational activities.[29]

Although declared a form of sex discrimination and thus illegal by the courts and the U.S. Equal Employment Opportunity Commission, such harassment is extremely widespread. Enforcement of laws and policies against it remains weak, punishment of those engaged in harassment is rare, and women must cope with fears of reprisal should they attempt to secure their right to be left alone. Thus, once again, even when legislation and court rulings are on the side of women, it may not be sufficient to deter sexist practices.

A further issue bearing on women's rights involves prostitution. In cities and towns across the United States women who are "in the life" must confront the threats of sexually transmitted disease, violence, and arrest. Prostitution is a job, but one with some of the most hazardous and degrading working conditions. Most women who become prostitutes are forced to do so due to financial desperation, drug addiction, and/or coercion by sexually domineering and economically exploitative males. And it is an alienating job, one of any number of service occupations that women hold which require they feign pleasure with male customers for whom they may actually feel contempt. Yet even here women's rights are secondary to those of men. Women are arrested for prostitution; their male clients are likely to go free without charge. Women's suffering is the price of men's enjoyment, courtesy of the law.

The multi–billion-dollar industry of pornography provides an additional arena in which women's rights must be considered. Within this industry women are exploited by men for profit, as crass economic greed is harnessed to the gender role of women-as-sex-objects. In many cases what would otherwise pass as erotica includes an emphasis on violence against women, thus suggesting to consumers that there is something sexy about physically mistreating women. Pornography, protected by law, helps to contribute to an overall societal environment in which all women must live in fear of assault.[30]

Finally, there is the particularly controversial issue of women's reproductive rights under the law.[31] The right to have an abortion anywhere in the United States was granted by the U.S. Supreme Court in the 1973 *Roe* vs. *Wade* decision. Women who choose to do so not only have been able to end unwanted pregnancies, but through abortion have protected themselves from serious threats to their health and even their lives. In recent years women's reproductive rights have been under direct attack, particularly by those who share the biology-as-destiny ideology pertaining to women's "proper" gender roles.[32] The loss of reproductive rights would have massive ramifications for women and their life chances, as well as for male–female relations in this society. Abortion represents an arena in which women may lose

---

[29] Susan Ehrlich Martin, "Sexual Harassment: The Link Joining Gender Stratification, Sexuality, and Women's Economic Status," in Freeman, *Women: A Feminist Perspective*, p. 58.

[30] See Margaret T. Gordon and Stephanie Riger, *The Female Fear* (New York: The Free Press, 1988).

[31] See Kristin Luker, *Abortion and the Politics of Motherhood* (Berkeley: University of California Press, 1984).

[32] See Rebecca E. Klatch, *Women of the New Right* (Philadelphia: Temple University Press, 1988).

PUBLIC PROBLEM, PRIVATE PAIN

The Lecherous Professor

Sexual harassment has become a major issue in recent years, the subject of legislative actions as well as court decisions. Protection is now extended to those harassed in their places of work and education. The following examples of harassment, drawn from college campuses, underscore the demeaning and exploitative nature of sexist practices.

A group of men faculty—from the math department—were standing in the hallway outside their offices. A fairly attractive girl went up to one of them, apparently her professor, and asked about an assignment. He put his arm around her shoulders, walked a few steps with her, and said, loudly, so everyone could hear, "Let's go in my office and talk about it—and you can take your clothes off." Everyone—except the girl—laughed. One professor asked sarcastically, "Is that harassment?" And someone wisecracked, "Not unless she thinks it is."

...

I knew that this prof chased his students so when he started flirting with me in class, I just ignored it. I didn't want anything to do with all that and it made me nervous. But one day after class he sort of cornered me as I was leaving. He backed me up against the wall and was touching me and telling me that he wanted me. He was almost shaking and very intense. I was trying to figure out how to get out of there without an awful scene. He started telling me how his wife didn't like oral sex and he felt frustrated because he had so much to give and wanted to give it to me. He was sweating and shaking and said, "I have a magic tongue. That used to be my nickname." I couldn't believe it. I was frightened by him and wanted to laugh at the same time. I pulled away and ran out of the classroom. It still seems a little funny, but he stalks me in the halls and it's still scary to me.

...

Dr. ______ asked me to come to his office to help him rearrange his books. Maybe it was my fault for going in the first place. He has these high bookcases, and the only way you can reach them is to stand on this little stool. I remember I had on this blue tight skirt that made it hard for me to step off and on that stool, but the skirt was pretty long. After a while, he got up and walked over and started bumping the stool. At first I thought he was just kidding around, and I laughed. Then I got sort of scared because he almost knocked me over. I told him to be careful and that I didn't think he knew I was really scared. "I know you are, but the only way to keep from falling is for you to go about your business while I lay down on the floor here and watch you." I think that's exactly how he said it. I didn't know what else to do. I was afraid to leave, so I just kept on taking books down while he laid on the floor and looked up my dress at my underpants. Then I left, and he said thank you and never ever mentioned anything about it again. I guess I should have reported him to somebody, but I didn't know who. No one would have believed it anyway.

...

I met Dr. ______ accidentally at a social function we'd both been invited to. I had a dress that was cut in a low V-neck. I guess he would say I bought it to entice men. I thought I bought it because it looked good on me. Anyway, he kept following me around all night even though his wife was there and asking me if I was wearing a bra. I don't know what it was supposed to prove if I wasn't, but I just kept changing the subject. He kept getting more and more personal until finally I asked my fiancé to take me home. When I saw him two days later at a meeting of my [doctoral] committee, he was horrible to me. He challenged everything I said and acted as if he was getting some sort of thrill out of putting me down. I'd never seen him behave like that before, and it took over two days for me to figure out that he really did want to put me down—literally. He couldn't screw me physically, so he made up his mind he was going to do it academically.

Source: From Billie Wright Dziech and Linda Weiner, *The Lecherous Professor: Sexual Harassment on Campus*, pp. 10, 18, 46.

rights only recently won, as opposed to those we have mentioned in which women's rights under the law are in need of sensitive revision.

The trend toward restriction of women's access to legal abortions is being facilitated by the U.S. Supreme Court, a majority of whose members no longer consider this access a fundamental constitutional right. In 1989 the Court ruled in *Webster* vs. *Reproductive Health Services* to allow each state to determine its own restrictions when it came to abortion policy. While falling short of overturning *Roe* vs. *Wade*, the 1989 decision represents a fundamental shift in Court thinking about women's reproductive rights.[33] This, combined with the fact that many doctors are bowing to pressure groups against the practice of performing abortions,[34] means that women who wish to terminate unwanted pregnancies will find it more difficult to do so. Already in some parts of the country women must travel hundreds of miles to obtain an abortion. Women who are ill or poverty-stricken are most likely to find the legal barriers being erected against abortion difficult to overcome. But all women will find their freedom to make choices restricted.

In an environment in which women's access to abortion is significantly restricted by law, those who cannot end unwanted pregnancies will find it more difficult to pursue needed education and training as well as work opportunities. The shortage of quality, affordable child care, the monetary costs associated with child rearing, and conscription into an undesired parental role will weigh heavily on many more women than now. Single women, including teenagers, will be at the greatest disadvantage in facing the competing demands of parenting while attempting to be economically self-supporting. Fewer married women will be able to work outside the home and more will be forced into part-time employment when full-time work actually is needed. The economic power of many women will be lowered, and they will be thrust into greater dependency on welfare assistance or husbands' earnings. As women are weakened economically, the gains they have made in recent years toward more independence and autonomy—particularly in breaking away from traditional biology-is-destiny gender roles—are likely to erode. Thus the barriers being erected to abortion are not simply a challenge to women's reproductive rights, but to women's human rights more generally.

Political Participation

The failure of this society's legal system to protect women's rights fully is due to institutional sexism in the political system.[35] We need only examine the composition of key political institutions to see one reason why the momentum of sexism continues.

On the federal level women fare poorly in terms of representation in those institutional positions through which the collective interests of women could be pursued. There has never been a woman president, nor have the Democratic and Republican parties ever seriously considered a female candidate. The vice presidency has also steadfastly remained a male post, although the choice of Geraldine Ferraro as the Democratic vice-presidential candidate in 1984 was an unprecedented lowering of the sex barrier. Throughout American history, and as of 1988, only ten women have been appointed to White House cabinet-level positions. One woman has served on the U.S. Supreme Court.

[33] Linda Greenhouse, "Supreme Court, 5–4, Narrowing *Roe v. Wade*, Upholds Sharp State Limits on Abortions," *New York Times* (July 4, 1989): A1.

[34] Gina Kolata, "Under Pressures and Stigma, More Doctors Shun Abortion," *New York Times* (January 8, 1990): A1.

[35] An excellent discussion of the failure of women to achieve equal rights with males is found in Joan Hoff-Wilson, "The Unfinished Revolution: Changing Legal Status of Women," *Signs*, 13 (Autumn 1987): 7–36.

In the House and Senate women are grossly underrepresented in terms of their proportion of the American population. In 1988, there were two women senators and only twenty-five women representatives. All together, women comprise 5 percent of Congress. The few women who manage to get elected to Congress find themselves handicapped by the informal "male locker-room" nature of legislative wheeling and dealing, from which they are easily excluded. Most women in Congress have served relatively short terms (many temporarily replacing husbands who died in office); their lack of seniority has blocked them from attaining such powerful positions as heading important committees.

At the lower levels of the federal government, the picture remains similar to that of racial and cultural minorities. Both in appointed offices and in high-level career civil service posts, women are most notable for their absence. As might be expected, they are more than fully represented in the lowest employment positions, for example, as clerks and secretaries.

One cannot expect a male-dominated federal government, which *itself* appoints, hires, and advances men over women, to be deeply concerned about women's social and economic position in the society at large. The exclusion of women from central positions in the national political system renders them the weaker sex when it comes to having their concerns taken seriously and acted upon.

The conspicuous absence of women continues on the state level. Only eight women have ever been governors. Three of the eight succeeded their husbands, and thus did not gain the post solely in recognition of their own merits. Today women hold less important elective and appointed posts in state executive branches, but nowhere near their representation in the population. The same can be said with regard to state legislatures and judicial bodies. In 1987 women made up only 15.5 percent of state legislators. But when there is typing to be done, there are plenty of women in evidence.

Finally, on the local level, the political presence of women improves somewhat. While, as of 1987, only 14.3 percent of the nation's mayors and municipal council members were female, some posts have been "reserved" for women. For the most part, these are the poorly paid or volunteer positions on local boards deemed "appropriate" for women and found unattractive by many men.

But women do vote; the right was extended to them in 1920, after a long battle. Unfortunately, women are still not using the franchise to the fullest possible degree. Indeed, it was only in 1980 that the percentage of eligible women voting became similar to that of men.

Racial minorities and the poor tend to view politics as being dominated by the white and affluent (a realistic assessment); thus many have avoided political activity, including voting. In a somewhat parallel vein, women have been encouraged to view politics as part of man's world, and many have restricted or narrowed the range of their involvement in it. But given the fact that women make up 53 percent of the voting population, the possibility of their making some impact through electoral power far exceeds that of other minority groups. It remains to be seen whether women can successfully mobilize this power by putting forth and electing candidates for office who will be more responsive to women's needs—particularly at the national level.

THE WOMEN'S MOVEMENT

With the development of the women's movement, women's economic and political subordination has come under attack. Earlier in this chapter, we saw some of the reasons why this attack has been so long in coming. Women have tended to see themselves as separate and unequal. Attainment of economic and political equality with men requires the mobilization of personality traits and behaviors that girls have been taught are unwomanly. Women have, in effect, been participants in their own oppression. But in the last two decades, under the stimulus of the women's movement, gender role differentials have begun to be questioned by increasing numbers of women.

The Development of the Women's Movement

Viewed historically, there have really been two women's movements in the United States.[36] The first movement essentially entailed a seventy-year struggle for the right of women to vote, culminating in 1920 with the passage of the Nineteenth Amendment to the Constitution. The women who led that protracted struggle often differed over other issues concerning women's place in a male-dominated society, including the treatment of women within the institution of marriage and within the world of employment. The one issue they were able to coalesce around and agree on was the desirability of women's suffrage. Once the vote was won, this first manifestation of collective political activism among women died off, leaving a period of quietude that lasted all the way up to the mid-1960s. The contemporary women's movement, of which we shall take note here, took up an agenda of issues that had been left unresolved in the past.

Analyses of the contemporary women's movement often start by pointing to the stresses that educated, middle-class women had begun to experience by the 1960s. Increasing numbers of women had been going on for higher education in the post–World War II period but either ended up becoming housewives or taking low-level positions because they were barred from access to men's jobs. Whether at home or at work, women found themselves limited by male dominance—a situation they were expected to endure.[37]

Events in the 1960s helped transform the generalized discontent of many women into overt forms of political expression. In the opening years of the decade, female college students became involved in the civil rights movement, the student movement, and other political change activities. In spite of their energetic contributions, female political activists found themselves routinely relegated to subordinate roles in male-dominated organizations. By the mid-1960s, many movement women had been struck by the irony: Here they were participating in struggles for minority civil rights and societal changes that were intended to better the life chances of others, while the conditions under which America's women were forced to suffer were being ignored. Female activists bridled under the gap between the progressive political rhetoric espoused by their male cohorts and the indifference of movement men to their own sexism.[38]

The resentments of politically active women were given impetus by the emergence of a new organization, one primarily aimed at advancing the interests of educated, middle-class professionals. The National Organization for Women (NOW), founded in 1966, became instrumental in focusing nationwide attention on the subject of sexist discrimination. NOW became, if not the voice of a women's movement, a key consciousness raiser of political issues with which women could easily identify.

From the mid-1960s onward, the women's movement has consisted of a wide assortment of groups, ranging from NOW to entirely localized women's organizations. All share common concerns with regard to the treatment of women in American society. But beyond this,

[36] See Eleanor Flexner, *Century of Struggle* (New York: Atheneum Publishers, 1973); and Betty Friedan, *The Second Stage* (New York: Summit Books, 1981).

[37] See Betty Friedan, *The Feminine Mystique* (New York: Dell Publishing Company, 1984).

[38] See Sara Evans, *Personal Politics: The Roots of Women's Liberation in the Civil Rights Movement and the New Left* (New York: Random House, 1980).

such groups reflect a wide spectrum of political perspectives as to just what women should be seeking.

Issues and Goals

In some ways, the term *women's movement* is a misnomer, for there is not one unified movement—rather, there are several.[39] Just as other minorities who have struggled in recent years to fashion goals and strategies for change have often split into different factions, so it is with women.

There is, first, the liberal feminist faction, perhaps best represented by such organizations as the National Organization for Women. NOW is a predominantly white, middle-class group whose goals revolve around increasing the participation of all women in economic and political life. The focus is on integrating women into existing institutions and opening up more opportunities in education and employment. The liberal feminist faction accepts the prevailing societal order but seeks an end to discrimination against women within it. The strategists of NOW, for example, have concentrated their resources on political lobbying, legal battles against discrimination, and educational campaigns to awaken women's and men's consciousness and gain public support.

There is also another, much smaller, faction of the women's movement. Here one may identify two distinct groups that see the need for far-reaching changes. The first group, the "radical feminists," consists of women who define men as a collective "enemy" and seek liberation from all roles associated with male dominance. Marriage is considered a particularly oppressive social arrangement for women, placing debilitating restrictions on their potential for human self-realization. Thus, one goal of many radical feminists is the redefinition of the meaning of "family," making it possible for women to enter into relationships with other adults and children on their own terms. The emphasis is on the conscious creation of new roles by and for women—rather than acquiescence to those imposed by and in the interests of men.

A second group, Marxist or socialist feminists, sees American capitalism, not men, as the enemy to be fought. Both women and men are viewed as victims of an economic system that exploits the labor of both sexes and that serves only the interests of the ownership class. From this perspective, to seek integration into the prevailing order is to accept and strengthen an economic system that deserves to be abolished; to see men alone as the enemy is to divert energies in the wrong direction. Thus, the goal of this group is to call the entire capitalist political economy into question, exposing its faults and encouraging men and women to join in the struggle for a socialist alternative. This goal flows out of the belief that sexism is an integral part of capitalism—in other words, that sexism is a requirement of a society in which those holding power put profit interests before the needs of people. This being the case, sexism cannot be abolished within the prevailing order nor can women truly be liberated within its confines.

The very existence of these factions within the women's movement points out a number of deeply felt concerns among a growing proportion of America's female population.[40] Women are reacting to a sense of economic, political, legal, and social exclusion. Many are highly dissatisfied with present male–female and family relationships, within which women

[39] See Jo Freeman, "The Origins of the Women's Liberation Movement," *American Journal of Sociology*, 78 (January 1973): 792–811. See also Margaret L. Andersen, *Thinking About Women*, 2nd ed. (New York: The Macmillan Company, 1988), pp. 287–361, and Myra Marx Ferree and Beth B. Hess, *Controversy and Coalition: The New Feminist Movement* (Boston: Twayne Publishers, 1985).

[40] Our discussion of the factions and their philosophies is by necessity brief and simplified. For an extended treatment, see Alison M. Jaggar, *Feminist Politics and Human Nature* (Totowa, N.J.: Rowman and Allanheld, 1983).

have been made to play separate and unequal roles. And there is a concern with the direction of American society as a whole, a society to which both sexes contribute but from which neither seems to receive full human satisfaction. All told, the women's movement has raised issues that bear on the future roles and well-being of all adults and children—male and female.

The Gains of the Movement

Institutional sexism—the systematic subordination of persons on the basis of their sex—simultaneously has been sustained by and has helped sustain the ideology that biology is destiny. The social, economic, and political disadvantages women face in comparison to men have begun to be addressed, however, and the ideology has begun to lose its power.

The women's movement has made some notable gains. It has succeeded in making millions of people conscious of sexist ideas and practices. More and more women have become sensitized to the harm done them in a sexist society and have been objecting to the gender-delineated roles in which they have traditionally been placed. Partly as a consequence, male–female relations—both outside of and within marriage—have begun to change. To some extent, socialization practices in the home and in school have begun to reflect this new consciousness of sexism. Finally, the women's movement has produced an ongoing struggle against sexism in the world of work and in the mass media.

But the forces that continue to promote sexism are impressive, and there is some question as to just how much change the existing women's movement can bring about. This question is particularly relevant with regard to the position of women in the economy, within which sexist practices thrive under the incentive of the pursuit of profit. Insofar as concentrated economic power is crucial to the exercise of political power at the national level, the subordinate position of women in the economy is a major political handicap—just as it is for racial minorities.

In response to the women's movement, women may well have gained increased verbal support of their rights. But this is not the same as granting an end to their collective subordination. Again, the struggle of racial minorities is instructive: laws and constitutional amendments have done little more than legitimate their right to struggle for improved life chances; they have not granted such groups control *over* their life chances.

Once more we return to the variable of power. Insofar as economic and political power continues to be concentrated in the hands of a few; insofar as women's separate and unequal position serves, for example, profit interests; and insofar as women are unable to wring concessions from those who benefit from their disadvantage—the movement to eliminate sexism from American society is unlikely to go very much further than it now has.

But unlike the civil rights movement, the women's movement has not yet withered away, even though its limited successes are far outweighed by the continuing presence of institutional sexism and male chauvinism. Since women comprise over half the American population, there remains a large pool of uninitiated recruits available to become future movement activists. And because the women's movement embraces a lengthy agenda of issues, it maintains the potential of offering an outlet for the expression of grievances by women and many male allies from all walks of life.

The Question of Men's Liberation

Criticisms of male chauvinism and institutional sexism have also, if somewhat belatedly, brought a number of men to question their own gender roles.[41] According to the biology-is-destiny ideology, men are supposed to be aggressive, competitive, achievement-oriented, and decisive. They are expected to hide their emotions in favor of an impression of strength and toughness. As we have seen, socialization in the family and in school tends to encourage the development of personality traits and behavioral orientations appropriate to the male gender role.

But despite the opportunities and benefits that accrue to men in a sexist society, the role-playing expected of them can be highly demanding. Not all men are equally capable of fulfilling the demands; not all men feel comfortable when playing the role. The responsibilities associated with "manhood" can be a source of stress, and many men feel doubts about their adequacy as lovers and providers. The requirement that they bottle up their fears, anxieties, and emotionality means that the tensions accompanying the male gender role may be difficult to dissipate.

Hence, while some men may find themselves threatened by the changing consciousness and more positive self-concepts being promoted by the women's movement, others would no doubt be relieved to give up acting out the pretense of male superiority. More equalitarian interpersonal relationships, in which both sexes share in confronting the problems of living in American society, should ideally *reduce* the burdens of being a man—not increase them.[42]

Hopes for the Future

Any approach to the elimination of sexism in America must be multifaceted. Not only must more women get involved in attacking sexism; more men must also join the battle, if only to reduce the costs that sexism exacts from them.

The economic disadvantages suffered by women still remain to be aggressively addressed. Women, along with racial minorities, have historically made their greatest gains in the work force during periods of labor shortage (unfortunately, this has tended to be during times of war). Revamping the American economy through governmental strategies to expand nonhousehold job opportunities is imperative. Expanding job opportunities would also mean a reduction of men's fear of competition as more and more women enter the workplace.

Accompanying these expanded opportunities must be an expansion of the availability of low-cost child-care facilities. Critics have argued that access to such facilities would contribute to family breakup by encouraging women to abdicate their motherly responsibilities. This is nonsense. Family well-being is more likely to be threatened by the inability of women to make use of child-care facilities so that they can help relieve economic burdens facing their families or so that they can escape the monotony of housework. Moreover, the shortage of child-care facilities places an enormous burden on women who are already heads of broken households and who must either work outside the home or live in poverty on public assistance.

The contribution of those women who must or wish to remain in the home must be recognized—in a more material way than simply celebrating Mother's Day once a year. It would not be unreasonable to alter the tax structure to provide annual family allowances to women, based perhaps on the full-time versus part-time nature of women's household responsibilities and the number of persons being cared for. It has been proposed that we recognize housework as an occupation for the purpose of bringing women who are laboring in the home into America's social security system. This alone would be a major step toward recognizing

[41] See Michael S. Kimmel, "From Pedestals to Partners: Men's Responses to Feminism," in Freeman, *Women: A Feminist Perspective*, pp. 531–94.

[42] See Michael S. Kimmel and Michael A. Messner, eds., *Men's Lives* (New York: The Macmillan Company, 1989).

housewives' economic contributions. It would also help women of advanced age who cannot live on the benefits accrued by their husbands.

Expanding job opportunities and child-care facilities will not automatically end discrimination against women in the labor force. As with other minorities, a much more aggressive attack on discrimination and exploitation is required. At the national level, the U.S. Equal Employment Opportunity Commission has the responsibility for handling complaints from around the country from women and other minorities. The resources allocated to this commission are so meager that aggrieved persons may have to wait *years* before any actions are taken. There are also heavy backlogs of cases in state equal employment commissions. There is no point in having antidiscrimination laws if they are not going to be enforced quickly and effectively. The current situation ultimately discourages women, since those suffering discrimination may assume that little good is likely to come from complaining about it.

The foregoing economic questions are clearly political ones as well, and it is thus important for more women and men to press for greater representation of women in America's political institutions. For starters, pressure must be placed on federal and state governments to practice what they preach and to ensure that women are appointed to top-level decision-making positions. More tax money (increasingly provided through women's labor force participation) must be allocated to programs for the improvement of the status of women. Over half the American population is female, and women's collective disadvantage is surely significant enough to justify the allocation of such resources.

The relatively few women who run for public office at the state and national levels often seem hesitant to stress the issue of sexism in their campaigns. Thus, an important opportunity to generate discussion and further educate the public is being missed. In the long run, underplaying what must be done by and for women contributes to the maintenance of institutional sexism. More discussion of the issue of sexism could also help persuade male candidates and incumbent politicians to take a more positive stand on women's rights.

America's schools and colleges are an important source of knowledge about and attitudes toward sexism. Though more and more children and youth are being taught that biology is not destiny, students are not being taught how to struggle against sexism. Schools could be part of the women's movement, but they are not. Struggling to make them so will, at the very least, rejuvenate and stimulate discussion of sexism—a prerequisite to change.

SUMMARY

While women are a majority in numbers, they are a minority group because of their social, economic, and political disadvantage in comparison to men. Women are victims of *sexism*—the systematic subordination of persons on the basis of their sex. Sexism is displayed on one level through *male chauvinism.* This term refers to attitudes and actions through which males display their sense of superiority over women. On another level is *institutional sexism,* wherein the subordination of women is built into societal institutions. Institutional sexism involves ongoing organizational routine in such areas as the economy, politics, and education.

Male chauvinism and institutional sexism are justified by an ideology that says that biology is destiny. This ideology holds that there are basic biological and psychological differences between the sexes which require that men and women play quite different roles in social life. Women, allegedly the weaker sex, belong in the home or performing women's work in the labor force. In order for the human species to reproduce, they must strive to fulfill the role of sex object. Despite the claims of this ideology, it is not true that differences between men and women require each to play such sex-delineated roles in social life. Gender roles vary from society to society, and role differences are largely learned rather than biologically based.

Women's acceptance of unequal treatment and the biology-is-destiny ideology has primarily been due to everyday socialization practices. From birth, girls and boys are treated differently in the family as parents impart their own sense of what it means to be male or female. Gender role differentiation by parents helps create personality and behavioral differences that would not otherwise exist. Parental influence is supplemented by the experience of schooling. From sports activities to curricula and textbooks, children are reminded of gender role differences. In the classroom and in dating relationships, girls are likely to find that successful performance of the female role requires them to avoid competing with men and to see themselves as something less than men.

Institutional sexism has economic effects. More and more women have been entering the labor force. Many are married; some have children at home; others are widowed, divorced, separated, or single. Despite their labor-force participation, women earn substantially less than men. They are overrepresented in low-status, low-paying jobs. Even when they are in more desirable professional and technical positions, women earn less than men on the average. The labor market is divided along sex lines as employers take advantage of the biology-is-destiny ideology and treat women differently from men. The main beneficiaries of sexism in this case are employers, who are able to profit by keeping labor costs down. The drive toward pay on the basis of comparable worth could greatly improve women's status in the labor market.

Millions of women remain homemakers. The economic value of their labor goes largely unrecognized. In the absence of their unpaid labor, men would be forced to demand far higher wages to pay for housekeeping and child-care services and would be more restricted in their hours and work-related travel. Employers benefit from this unpaid labor, for in essence they get two workers for the price of one. Meanwhile, business and industry appeal to the spending ability of housewives (and women working outside the home as well) by stressing consumption. Sales appeals attack women's sense of personal adequacy and play on dissatisfactions imposed by the burdens of housework. Advertising reinforces stereotyped sex roles and seeks to take advantage of these roles. While such activities may be profitable, they contribute to the biology-is-destiny ideology.

Institutional sexism operates in the political system, where women are collectively excluded from positions of power. The American legal system only peripherally recognizes the economic plight of women and their rights as citizens. The composition of the political system helps account for this. At the federal level, women are grossly underrepresented in key policymaking positions—from the White House, to Congress, to the courts. The situation is similar at the state and local levels. The exclusion of women from central positions in politics renders them the weaker sex when it comes to having their concerns taken seriously and acted on.

With the development of the women's movement in the mid-1960s, women's economic and political subordination has come under attack. The women's movement has consisted of a variety of groups and factions, all concerned with the treatment of women but reflecting a range of political perspectives. The liberal feminist faction has sought increased participation of all women in economic and political life. The radical feminists see men as the enemy and are concerned with liberating women from roles associated with male dominance—for example, within marriage. Socialist feminists hold that sexism stems from and is crucial to the operation of capitalism; they argue that men and women must struggle together for a socialist alternative.

The women's movement as a whole has made

many gains, particularly in raising people's consciousness of sexism and encouraging women to struggle against social, economic, and political domination. However, its gains are still outweighed by the continuing presence of male chauvinism and institutional sexism. In recent years a number of men have also begun to question their sex-delineated roles. These roles can be highly demanding, despite the opportunities and benefits that often accrue to men in a sexist society. The responsibilities of manhood can be a source of stress. More equalitarian interpersonal relationships, in which both sexes share in confronting problems, should ideally reduce the burdens of being a man.

Both men and women stand to benefit from joining in the battle against sexism. Women's economic disadvantage must be addressed by expanding job opportunities and child-care facilities. The economic contributions of homemakers must be recognized in material terms. Employment discrimination must be more directly and aggressively attacked, and antidiscrimination laws more quickly and efficiently enforced. Pressure must be put on government to employ and appoint more women to top positions, while women and men should do more to make sexism an issue in election campaigns. Finally, schools and colleges have an important role to play. Though more and more children are being taught that biology is not destiny, they are not being taught how to struggle against sexism. It is worth making schools part of the women's movement.

DISCUSSION QUESTIONS

1. In your experience, what are the most common ways in which male chauvinism is expressed? How do you feel about being subjected to or witnessing expressions of male chauvinism?
2. Make a list of all the advantages of being male that you can think of. Make a list of all the advantages of being female. Which list is longer? Compare and discuss your lists with the lists your classmates made.
3. Two applicants—one male and one female—are equally qualified for a professional job opening. What arguments could be made for and against giving preference to the female applicant? If preference is not given, how will female underrepresentation in the professions ever be altered?
4. Should women be paid for the work they do as housewives? Why? If you think they should be paid, who should pay them, and how should the value of their labor be determined?
5. Obtain a selection of men's, women's, and general circulation magazines from your home, dorm, or library. Examine the advertisements—photographs and texts—and discuss the attitudes they project toward male and female sex roles.
6. If sexism has dubious benefits for, and may even harm, many men, why do not more men see the struggle against sexism as in their self-interest? Under what conditions could this situation change?

SUGGESTED READINGS

Andersen, Margaret. *Thinking About Women*, 2d ed. (New York: The Macmillan Company, 1988).
Sociological examination of the position of women in a range of institutional settings and movements for change.

England, Paula. *Comparable Worth* (Hawthorne, N.Y.: Aldine de Gruyter, 1990).
The need for predominantly female jobs to be paid equitably through policies of comparable worth.

Ferree, Myra Marx, and Beth B. Hess. *Controversy and Coalition: The New Feminist Movement* (Boston: Twayne Publishers, 1985).
An overview of women's struggles to respond to sexist policies and practices.

Freeman, Jo, ed. *Women: A Feminist Perspective*, 4th ed. (Mountain View, Calif.: Mayfield Publishing Company, 1989).
Like earlier editions, contains comprehensive re-

views of issues reflecting the (mal)treatment of women in our patriarchal society.

Jaggar, Alison Mary, and Paula S. Rothenberg, eds. *Feminist Frameworks: Alternative Theoretical Accounts of the Relations Between Men and Women*, 2d ed. (New York: McGraw-Hill Book Company, 1984).
Presentation of a variety of different feminist viewpoints and their applications.

Schur, Edwin M. *Labeling Women Deviant: Gender, Stigma, and Social Control* (New York: McGraw-Hill Book Company, 1983).
How women are victimized when they depart from norms maintained by and in a male-dominated society.

CHAPTER 10

Ageism

There should be no personal and institutional discrimination against individuals on the basis of age.

From the moment of birth each of us is involved in the process of aging. That is one thing we can all count on. As we live on, our bodies inevitably undergo some subtle and often visible changes. Somewhere along the way we are deemed "old," based on popular social definitions held by those who are chronologically younger. Often such social definitions bear little relation to our objective capacities to contribute to and draw enjoyment from the society of which we are a part.

Census statistics show a dramatic increase in the proportion of persons who have entered "old age" in this century. (Old age is arbitrarily, but commonly, considered to commence at age sixty-five.) Statistics on life expectancy have led to predictions of further dramatic increases in the number and proportion of the population who will enter old age by the year 2000 and beyond. "The graying of America" is a development that carries significant social, economic, and political ramifications that we are only beginning to appreciate and confront.

For most persons the fact of aging is not in and of itself an overwhelming problem. Aging is, after all, natural and inevitable. It is instead the treatment one receives that is problematic. Thus, in this chapter we consider older Americans as members of a "minority group," subject to personal prejudice and institutional discrimination. Myths and stereotypes about those who have entered later life are common and help to contribute to an environment in which ageism quietly flourishes and turns many older Americans into second-class citizens. Social science theory, as we shall see, has contributed to this process, suggesting that it is necessary for aging persons to disengage from important life roles for the good of society. In practice a substantial (and growing) segment of the American population is denied or discouraged from participation in a variety of arenas of life, prompting dependency and physical decline often well before they occur as a result of biological processes.

As they are encouraged to disengage, many older Americans are confronted simultaneously with a variety of conditions that may speed their demise. Among these conditions, to be reviewed in this chapter, are involuntary unemployment and permanent loss of economically productive roles; economic strain, often to the point of poverty or near-poverty; lack of adequate assistance in maintaining physical and mental health; inadequate housing and transportation; victimization by criminals; and abuse by caregivers. Such conditions render growing old the worst part of life for millions of people now, and many more millions will be affected similarly in the future.

As you read these lines you are growing older and are coming closer to joining a "minority group" that, sociologically, should never exist. Since we all will probably belong to this group, we all have a stake in how aging Americans are treated. If only for this reason we should be more than a little concerned about this macro problem.

BIOLOGICAL AND SOCIAL DEFINITIONS OF AGING

Aging is a natural and inevitable biological process, one that begins at birth. With increases in chronological age, all people undergo physiological changes—some visible, others hidden—that precede an end to life. Physical appearance undergoes a marked alteration with time, including the loss of skin elasticity, the appearance of wrinkles, the graying of hair (because of pigment loss), and signs of frailty. Hidden changes may affect sight and hearing. The circulatory, respiratory, and other major body systems lose their operating efficiency. Susceptibility to illness and disease increases, and aging persons may lose their ability to combat sickness as well as when they were younger.

The rate of biological aging varies among individuals. Thus, a given chronological age does not automatically dictate when the types of changes involved in aging will occur. As yet poorly understood genetic factors may contribute to variations in the aging process among different persons. Certainly environmental influences play a role. One's life-style, dietary and nutritional practices, exercise habits, amount of exposure to physically harmful conditions and substances, access to adequate health care services, and degree of contact with psychologically stressful experiences are thought to affect the biology of aging. Hence, older persons are in reality a heterogeneous group in physiological terms.

Despite this heterogeneity and the wide differences in mental and physical capacity associated with it, members of society tend to share a common view of when old age commences. This social definition of old age is largely chronologically based and is accompanied by a set of often erroneous assumptions about persons who are reaching their later years. In general, old age is thought to commence at age sixty-five. This view has been encouraged by the institutionalization of sixty-five as the age of eligibility for certain federal social insurance benefits, such as social security and (until very recently) the age of mandatory retirement from employment. While an individual may be no different at age sixty-five than at age sixty-four, except in chronological years, by social definition this one year arbitrarily signals old age.

Even more arbitrary is the fact that entering old age carries with it certain widespread assumptions about what people sixty-five and beyond are like. Robert N. Butler cogently describes what many persons who are chronologically under sixty-five seem to believe about their older counterparts:

> An older person thinks and moves slowly. He does not think as he used to or as creatively. He is bound to himself and to his past and can no longer change or grow. He can learn neither well nor swiftly and if he could, he would not wish to.... He enters a second childhood, caught up in increasing egocentricity.... He becomes irritable and cantankerous, yet shallow and enfeebled. ... Indeed, he is a study in decline, the picture of mental and physical failure.[1]

While this description may well depict some small segment of the older population accurately, it does a grave injustice to the bulk of this population by ignoring the heterogeneity we have discussed. Reaching chronological age sixty-five does not automatically mean entering into a state of "mental and physical failure," a fact to which we shall return in our discussion of myths and stereotypes about old age.

The social definitions bearing on old age also differ by gender. While gray hair for a man who is aging is likely to give him a "distinguished appearance," for a woman it is a sign of "getting old." Because of our social and cultural emphasis on women's role as a sex object (see Chapter 9), any movement away from the artificial mass-media ideal of youth and feminine beauty is widely considered a step toward old age, as well as a step down. Whole industries (cosmetics, hair styling, clothing, and footwear) thrive on women's commercially induced fear of age obsolescence. The mass media do not maintain an artificial ideal of youthful beauty for males with anywhere near the intensity that they do for females. Socially, women are informally defined as old at an earlier age than men.

This dual standard has a variety of ramifications. Older men may freely marry women who are chronologically much younger without drawing social criticism, but older women may not marry younger men with such freedom. Since, as we shall see, the proportion of women in the population is greater than that of men in advanced age groups, widowed, divorced, or never-married older women are at a distinct disadvantage in locating marital partners. Older men face far less of a problem in this regard.

The social definition of women as being old chronologically earlier than men also has significance in the sphere of employment. Despite legal strictures against age discrimination, there is widespread subtle discrimination toward the hiring of women whose appearance is within or not far from the artificial mass-media ideal of youthful beauty. This is particularly the case in situations where employed women are expected to have extensive public contact by virtue of the work performed. But it is also the case that many male employers believe it is within their prerogative to include "decorating the office" as one unspoken criterion for who will be hired. Many older women face difficulty in finding employment, and this difficulty is not necessarily related to their job skills or record of work experience. Again men have an advantage in not being as constrained in employment opportunities by such invisible, discriminatory standards.

---

[1] Robert N. Butler, *Why Survive? Being Old in America* (New York: Harper & Row Publishers, 1975), pp. 6–7.

The social definitions of *old age* arbitrarily set the beginning of old age at sixty-five, lump a heterogeneous group of older persons together as "mental and physical failures," and treat women as old at earlier ages than men. These social definitions affect millions of people. In the next section we examine the victims of such social definitions.

THE GRAYING OF AMERICA

Population Trends and Projections

Census figures for 1988 indicate that some 30 million Americans are sixty-five or older, a number that represents over 12 percent of the population.[2] There has been a dramatic increase in the number of older Americans since the turn of the century. In 1900 only 3.1 million persons, representing 4.0 percent of the population, were sixty-five or older. In every decade from the 1930s through the 1960s the number of older Americans grew by a third.

Until early in this century the percentage of the population that was sixty-five or older remained low. This was primarily due to high birth rates among families, the relative youth of much of the large incoming immigrant population, and limited life expectancies among the aging. Since then birth rates have gone down and life expectancy has increased, largely because of medical advances and improved health practices. Immigration continues but at nowhere near the rate of earlier years.

Birth rates and changes in life expectancy both will play a role in determining the future age composition of America's population. Population experts presently estimate that the sixty-five-and-older population could increase as follows (see Table 10.1): by 1990, to 31.6 million persons, or 12.6 percent of the total population; by 2000, to 35 million, or 13 percent; by 2010, to 39.4 million, or 13.9 percent. By the year 2020 there could be a substantial increase to 52.1 million, or 17.7 percent of the population. The jump between 2010 and 2020 is forecast because that is the period when the members of the post–World War II "baby boom" will reach sixty-five and thus "old age." By the year 2030 the percentage of the population that is sixty-five or older could move up to over 20 percent. Much depends on whether the present low rates of birth continue. Members of the baby boom are in their childbearing years. A sizable increase in the birth rate due to childbearing by baby boom members could have the effect of slowing the rate of percentage increase of persons sixty-five and older in the twenty-first century.[3]

Just as changes in the birth rate could affect current projections, so might increases in life expectancy. As it now stands, life expectancy has risen to 74.8 years for those persons born in 1987, the highest it has ever been. (The average life expectancy in 1900 was 49 years.) White females born in 1987 have a life expectancy of 78.8 years, and black females have one of 73.8 years. White males have a shorter life expectancy of 72.1 years, while black males lag far behind at 65.4 years (see Figure 10.1).

According to William W. Lammers, "the fairly steady increases in the life expectancy of the aging will increase more rapidly in the next two decades."[4] Earlier medical advances in this century helped to reduce infant mortality. More modern advances promise to extend old age further in chronological time. The two leading causes of death in the sixty-five-and-older group are heart disease and cancer. Preventive and curative practices in recent years, as well as innovations and discoveries expected in the future,

---

[2] Population statistics are drawn from U.S. Department of Commerce, Bureau of the Census, *Projections of the Population of the United States, by Age, Sex, and Race: 1988 to 2080* (Washington, D.C.: U.S. Government Printing Office, 1989).

[3] See Stephen Crystal, *America's Old Age Crisis* (New York: Basic Books, 1982), pp. 23–25.

[4] William W. Lammers, *Public Policy and the Aging* (Washington, D.C.: CQ Press, 1983), pp. 7–8.

TABLE 10.1 Projected Population and Percent Distribution of the Population, by Age, 1960–2080

		Age (years)									
Year	Total	Under 5	5–13	14–17	18–24	25–34	35–44	45–64	65 and over	85 and over	100 and over
					Number						
1990	250,410	18,408	32,393	13,237	26,140	43,925	37,897	46,851	31,559	3,254	56
1995	260,138	17,799	33,864	14,510	24,281	40,962	42,336	52,622	33,764	3,912	76
2000	268,266	16,898	33,483	15,332	25,231	37,149	43,911	61,381	34,882	4,622	100
2005	275,604	16,611	31,980	15,491	26,918	35,997	40,952	71,381	36,275	5,331	131
2010	282,575	16,899	31,001	14,746	27,155	37,572	37,202	78,637	39,362	6,115	171
2020	294,364	17,095	31,697	14,074	25,018	39,100	37,591	77,722	52,067	6,651	266
2030	300,629	16,305	31,282	14,574	25,290	36,464	39,092	72,018	65,604	8,129	363
2040	301,807	16,217	30,214	14,036	25,408	37,147	36,525	74,151	68,109	12,251	446
2050	299,849	15,900	30,093	13,771	24,411	36,875	37,168	73,098	68,532	15,287	775
2080	292,235	14,971	28,348	13,089	23,288	34,763	35,586	70,559	71,631	16,966	1,440
					Percent						
1990	100.0	7.4	12.9	5.3	10.4	17.5	15.1	18.7	12.6	1.3	—
1995	100.0	6.8	13.0	5.6	9.3	15.7	16.3	20.2	13.0	1.5	—
2000	100.0	6.3	12.5	5.7	9.4	13.8	16.4	22.9	13.0	1.7	—
2005	100.0	6.0	11.6	5.6	9.8	13.1	14.9	25.9	13.2	1.9	—
2010	100.0	6.0	11.0	5.2	9.6	13.3	13.2	27.8	13.9	2.2	0.1
2020	100.0	5.8	10.8	4.8	8.5	13.3	12.8	26.4	17.7	2.3	0.1
2030	100.0	5.4	10.4	4.8	8.4	12.1	13.0	24.0	21.8	2.7	0.1
2040	100.0	5.4	10.0	4.7	8.4	12.3	12.1	24.6	22.6	4.1	0.1
2050	100.0	5.3	10.0	4.6	8.1	12.3	12.4	24.4	22.9	5.1	0.3
2080	100.0	5.1	9.7	4.5	8.0	11.9	12.2	24.1	24.5	5.8	0.5

Source: U.S. Department of Commerce, Bureau of tne Census, *Projections of the Population of the United States, by Age, Sex, and Race: 1988 to 2080* (Washington, D.C.: U.S. Government Printing Office, 1989), pp. 7 and 8.

are likely to increase the average life expectancy beyond what it is today.

No one disagrees that the "graying of America" is taking place and that the number of people reaching old age will be substantial in the twenty-first century. Statistical projections are, however, somewhat tentative because of uncertainty over what actual birth rates and life expectancies will be.[5]

[5] See Jacob S. Siegel and Cynthia M. Tauber, "Demographic Perspectives on the Long-Lived Society," *Daedalus*, 115 (Winter 1986): 77–117.

Characteristics of Older Americans

Earlier we noted that the rate of biological aging varies and that this creates a degree of heterogeneity among older Americans in terms of their physical and mental capacities. The heterogeneity exists on many other levels as well, making it even more erroneous to refer to "old people" as if they were all the same. In this section we describe further sources of difference.

Financial Status. Older Americans have long been forced to function under severely strained

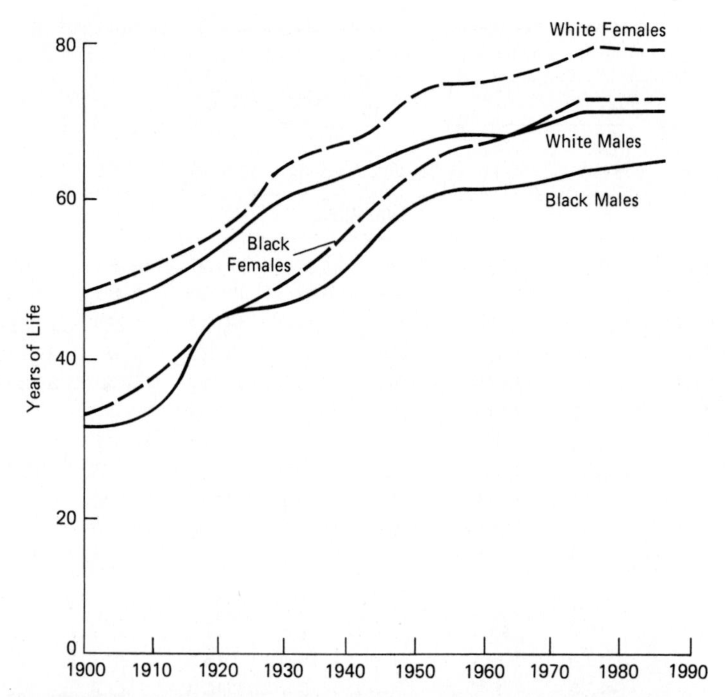

FIGURE 10.1 Expectation of Life at Birth, by Race and Sex: 1900–87
Source: Cynthia M. Tauber, *America in Transition: An Aging Society*, Bureau of the Census (Washington, D.C.: U.S. Government Printing Office, September 1983), p. 5; National Center for Health Statistics, *Monthly Vital Statistics Report*, 33 (December 20, 1984): 3; and U.S. Department of Health and Human Services, *Health, United States, 1988* (Washington, D.C.: U.S. Government Printing Office, 1989), p. 53.

economic conditions.[6] Until fairly recently, the percentage of elderly falling within the federal government's official definition of poverty was very high. According to James H. Schultz, "the economic status of the elderly has changed dramatically in recent years, primarily as a result of rising social security, private pension, and government employees' pension income."[7] Nonetheless, in 1988 some 12 percent of the sixty-five-and-older population, a figure representing 3.5 million people, was officially considered poor. Those who were "near-poor" (with incomes no higher than 125 percent of the official poverty line) constituted another 2.2 million. Thus, in 1988 almost one in five of those sixty-five and older were deemed poor or near-poor. (We shall return to poverty among older Americans in a later section.)

Ethnic and Racial Composition. Many older Americans today (perhaps 15 percent) are foreign-born, largely as a consequence of migration from European countries early in this century until World War I. The majority of persons sixty-five and older are white, but because

[6] For a historical overview, see David H. Fischer, *Growing Old in America* (New York: Oxford University Press, 1981).

[7] James H. Schultz, *The Economics of Aging*, 2nd ed. (Belmont, Calif.: Wadsworth, 1980), p. 46.

Members of U.S. society who are in their "old age" are a very heterogeneous group, contrary to popular stereotypes. It is erroneous to make broad generalizations about older Americans without keeping many qualifications and exceptions in mind. The ages of the runners pictured here, 83 and 77, help to remind us that the aging process is not uniform for all. *(Jaye R. Phillips/The Picture Cube)*

the life expectancy of racial minorities is lower than that of the white majority, a smaller percentage reaches old age than would be expected on the basis of their representation in the overall population. In 1987 the percentage of black Americans who were sixty-five and older was 8.2; in contrast, 13.1 percent of whites were in this group. For Hispanic Americans the rate was 5 percent. Any significant developments in increased life expectancy for minorities would be important to projections regarding the overall size of the sixty-five-and-older population in the next century.

Sex Composition. The life expectancy differences between men and women noted earlier clearly affect the sex composition of the sixty-five-and-older population. Women in this population outnumbered men in 1987 by over 5 million. In that year the census found 17.7 million older women and 12.1 million older men. As one moves up chronologically in the sixty-five-and-older grouping, the ratio between men and women changes (see Table 10.2). While overall there are 68 men for every 100 women, by age seventy-five this ratio is down to about 55 men for every 100 women. Since older women infrequently marry younger men, this disparity underscores the high probability that a married woman, reaching old age, will spend a number of years without her spouse. There is little opportunity for remarriage. Among the widowed elderly in America, some 80 percent are women.

Educational Attainment. When today's older Americans were born, completion of a high school education was not yet the norm. Moreover, many were foreign-born and had little contact with American schooling. Thus, the sixty-five-and-older group has, on the average, fewer years of formal education than the general population. This situation will change, because persons born since World War I, and especially since World War II, have found progressively greater educational opportunities and reasons to pursue them. Hence, persons reaching old age in coming decades will have far greater levels of formal education than do many of their present-day counterparts. The difference between this group and the general population in this regard will become minimal.

Labor Force Participation. Since the turn of the century the proportion of persons sixty-five years of age and older who continue to work has dropped markedly. In 1900 two-thirds of all males in this age group worked, as did one in twelve females. While the female rate of labor force participation has remained about the same, the male rate has declined. By 1950 less than half of all older American males were in the labor force. This number has since dropped to approximately 16 percent. Thus, in a relatively short period retirement from the labor force by age sixty-five has become a norm. In fact, over a third of those in the sixty- to sixty-four age category are no longer working. In the sixty-five-and-over group, two out of five retirees claim to have left work involuntarily. Those who remain working past sixty-five are concentrated in low-pay, often part-time, positions.

Geographical Distribution. While early in this century older Americans were uniformly distributed throughout the country, this pattern has changed. Since World War II, members of this group have become concentrated in relatively few states. A quarter of the sixty-five-and-older group now lives in New York, California, and Florida. If we add to this Pennsylvania, Illinois, Ohio, Michigan, and Texas, half of this age group are accounted for. In general, older Americans are likely to live either in the nation's central cities or in small, rural towns.

Comment on Diversity. Clearly, the sixty-five-and-older population is far from being a homogeneous social entity. While some may be economically comfortable or even affluent, one in five are poor or near-poor. While predominantly a white population, non–native-born and minority group persons are an important segment. Females dominate proportionately and in numbers, and this is progressively true as we look at age categories beyond age sixty-five. The older American male is much less likely to be living alone without a spouse than his female age counterpart. Most older Americans have, on the average, less formal educational attainment than the general population, but this difference is undergoing change. Older Americans tend to be either small-town or central city residents. Perhaps the one thing most of those sixty-five and older are coming to share is lack of labor force participation—for example, only 16 percent of males are working.

TABLE 10.2 Persons Sixty-Five Years Old and Over by Sex, 1987

Characteristic	Male	Female
Total (million)	**12.1**	**17.7**
Percent of total population	10.2	14.2
White (million)	10.9	16.0
Black (million)	1.0	1.5
Age		
65–69 years (percent)	3.8	4.3
70–74 years (percent)	2.8	3.6
75–79 years (percent)	1.9	2.8
80 years and over (percent)	1.7	3.5
Percent below poverty level		
Family householders	6.1	13.0
Unrelated individuals	19.6	26.8
Percent Distribution		
Marital status		
Single	4.5	5.5
Married	77.1	41.0
Spouse present	74.9	39.2
Spouse absent	2.2	1.8
Widowed	14.0	49.2
Divorced	4.3	4.3
Family status		
In families	81.9	56.7
Nonfamily householders	16.6	41.8
Secondary individuals	1.6	1.5
Residents of institutions	(NA)	(NA)
Living arrangements		
Living in household	99.7	99.5
Living alone	15.6	40.9
Spouse present	74.9	39.2
Living with someone else	9.2	19.4
Not in household	.3	.5
Years of school completed		
8 years or less	34.4	31.8
1–3 years of high school	14.8	16.8
4 years of high school	27.7	33.0
1–3 years of college	10.4	10.5
4 years or more of college	12.8	7.9
Labor force participation		
Employed	15.9	7.2
Unemployed	.4	.2
Not in labor force	83.7	92.6

Source: U.S. Department of Commerce, Bureau of the Census, *Statistical Abstract of the United States, 1989* (Washington, D.C.: U.S. Government Printing Office, 1989), p. 36.

Yet despite their diversity—both in where they stand in terms of biological aging and in their mixed social and economic characteristics—older Americans are victims. They are victims of myths and stereotypes, personal prejudice and institutional discrimination. In short, they are victims of "ageism": ideas and practices that have negative consequences for persons who are socially defined as "old." In the next section these topics are examined in some detail.

MYTHS AND STEREOTYPES

In the words of Robert N. Butler,

> We have shaped a society which is extremely harsh to live in when old. The tragedy of old age is not the fact that each of us must grow old and die but that the process of doing so has been made unnecessarily and at times excruciatingly painful, humiliating, debilitating and isolating through insensitivity, ignorance and poverty. The potentials for satisfactions and even triumphs in late life are real and vastly unexplored. For the most part, the elderly struggle to exist in an inhospitable world.[8]

Part of this inhospitableness is the prevalence of myths and stereotypes, in reality expressions of insensitivity and ignorance, that are inflicted on older Americans.[9]

"Old People Are All the Same." Older Americans are as highly differentiated as individuals as are members of any other age group. After all, they were once young, and people tend to carry their unique personal characteristics with them into their later years. Older people bear the mark of their accumulated personal experiences throughout life and perhaps become more different from one another with age, since the different experiences each has had are more numerous.

Moreover, there are invisible "generational" differences in the life-forming experiences of those sixty-five and older. For example, today's sixty-five-year-olds had no direct experience with World War I. This is not the case for today's eighty-five-year-olds. The latter group had to live with the impact of the Depression in the 1930s precisely when they were grappling with major adult work and child-rearing responsibilities. In that era today's sixty-five-year-olds were but dependent children and youths. Such generational differences among older Americans accentuate their diversity.

"Old People Are Unproductive." With advancing age, people leave the labor force. Their childbearing activities are long over, and there is typically an end to the assumption of any major responsibility for the children raised in their homes. But to view older persons as "unproductive" in such contexts is a form of blaming the victim for his or her personal situation. As we shall see later, older workers have been both ejected involuntarily and economically enticed into retiring. Moreover, change in roles and responsibilities vis-à-vis children in families is a natural outcome of family life-cycles; most young people can barely wait to "be on their own."

Most older Americans are indeed productive. Even if they do not continue to work outside the home, most remain socially active in a wide range of settings, politically involved at a level higher than that of most other age groups (as indicated, for example, by voting practices), and active as key supporters and patrons of culture-disseminating institutions. If older persons are less engaged in such self-activity than they could be, it is because of younger persons. Older persons are expected to "act their age," meaning that they may be admonished or ridiculed when they strive to continue many of the activities and behaviors arbitrarily reserved for and by those who are chronologically younger.

---

[8] Butler, *Why Survive?* pp. 2–3.

[9] See Jack C. Horn and Jeff Meer, "The Vintage Years," *Psychology Today,* 21 (May 1987): 76–90. Misconceptions about the aging are summarily covered in Erdman Palmore, "Facts on Aging: A Short Quiz," *The Gerontologist,* 17 (1977): 315–20.

Aging does not mean an end to the physical expression of love and affection, something of importance to all human beings. Our elders may be sexually active in the absence of poor health and lack of partners. The discomfort this thought causes many younger persons reflects common stereotypes about growing old. *(Frank Siteman/Stock, Boston)*

"Old People Are Senile." Because some older persons exhibit psychological and behavioral deviations from what is socially defined by those younger as normal, it is often assumed that all do or someday will. In reality, relatively few persons age sixty-five and older exhibit such deviations, and in many cases "senility" is treatable and reversible. To a degree, senility is induced by the treatment accorded older persons in this society.

There are two sources of medically untreatable senility, both involving brain damage. In one case, there is a hardening of the arteries to the brain. But in recent years much more attention has been directed at what is known as Alzheimer's disease, wherein neurons (nerve cells) in the brain are steadily lost or become degraded. (See Chapter 11.)

Alzheimer's disease currently affects an estimated 4 million people in the United States, most of them elderly. Each year over 100,000

TABLE 10.3 Percentage of Persons Aged 65 and Over in Selected Age Groups, 1960–2080

Year*	Percent aged: 65–74 years	75–84 years	85 years and over	Median age of 65-and-over population
1960	66.3	28.1	5.6	71.9
1965	64.4	29.7	5.9	72.3
1970	62.1	30.7	7.1	72.6
1975	61.3	30.7	8.0	72.5
1980	60.9	30.3	8.8	72.8
1985	59.6	31.0	9.4	73.0
1987	59.2	31.2	9.6	73.1
1990	58.2	31.5	10.3	73.3
1995	56.1	32.3	11.6	73.8
2000	52.3	34.4	13.3	74.5
2005	50.8	34.5	14.7	74.2
2010	53.4	31.0	15.5	74.2
2020	59.5	27.7	12.8	73.0
2030	54.9	32.8	12.4	74.0
2040	45.2	36.8	18.0	76.1
2050	46.1	31.6	22.3	76.1
2080	44.6	31.7	23.7	76.4

*1960–87, estimates; 1990–2080, projections.
Source: U.S. Department of Commerce, Bureau of the Census, *Projections of the Population of the United States, by Age, Sex, and Race: 1988 to 2080* (Washington, D.C.: U.S. Government Printing Office, 1989), p. 9.

people die from its progressive effects.[10] Some have referred to Alzheimer's disease as an "epidemic,"[11] for it is a disease estimated to strike 10 percent of those 65 and older. The disease will pose even more of a problem in the future as the median age of those 65 and over increases and the percentage of "old-old" (85 and over), among whom the disease is most prevalent, grows (see Table 10.3).

Unfortunately, the cause of Alzheimer's disease is unknown. Correct diagnosis is usually not possible until symptoms are severe and debilitating. These include memory loss and disrupted thought processes, reflections of brain degeneration and shrinkage. There currently is no cure or way to halt the slow death that often results.

Still, it is important to emphasize that much of what is popularly called senile activity involves expressions of anxiety and depression that have no known physiological cause but are no doubt linked to problems in living faced by many aging people. Misuse of drugs and alcohol can produce similar symptoms. Thus, much so-called senility is not only treatable but avoidable. This fact has only recently been recognized in the health arena and has not yet entered the public mind to counter the senility stereotype.

"Old People Are in a State of Deterioration and Decline." This myth often is found in a variety of areas. Older Americans are stereo-

[10] Richard J. Wurtman, "Alzheimer's Disease," *Scientific American*, 252 (January 1985): 62.
[11] See Robert Bazell, "The Infancy of Aging," *New Republic* (December 22, 1986): 17.

typically viewed as an extremely unhealthy group, stricken by disabling illnesses and handicaps that force them into a state of dependency. In fact, most older persons are quite healthy until their very final years, and the vast majority live independently in their own homes. At any one time, only 5 percent of those sixty-five and older are to be found in "old age homes" or nursing homes.

The notion of deterioration and decline is commonly directed at the intelligence of older persons. "Intelligence" is a slippery concept, but recent studies that have measured the mental traits of individuals repeatedly as they aged have found no significant evidence of decline. Indeed, depending on what trait is being measured, there is evidence that intelligence increases with age.

Finally, the socially taboo topic of sexual interest and activity on the part of older persons is worthy of mention. There is supposedly a period in life often referred to as the "sexless older years." While sexual interest and activity do tend to decline among many older persons, the rate at which this takes place, and whether it takes place at all, is highly variable. For the most part, older people do remain sexually active, barring serious physical ailments or the inability to find a sexual partner.

DISENGAGEMENT VERSUS ACTIVITY THEORY

While popular myths and stereotypes about old age abound, social science has certainly not been neutral with regard to the role of those who grow old. For some thirty years debate has gone on between those who see old age through "disengagement theory" and those who approach old age through "activity theory."

The debate was touched off by Elaine Cumming and William E. Henry, whose *Growing Old: The Process of Disengagement* continues to generate discussion today. The researchers proposed a theory that was intended to shed light on the withdrawal, or "disengagement," of many aging persons from active roles in society. Cumming and Henry suggested that disengagement was "an inevitable process in which many of the relationships between a person and other members of society are severed and those remaining are altered in quality."[12] While they note that total disengagement occurs with death, "the fully disengaged condition of the living can be considered to exist when only those bonds necessary to sustain life remain."[13] The process of disengagement was said to be a social response to the biological and psychological decline that Cumming and Henry assumed was an intrinsic part of growing old. It was also, in effect, a response by and to the old-ager in anticipation of his or her death.

Cumming and Henry suggested that disengagement behavior was undertaken both by the aging individual and by the larger society. This mutual disengagement was thought to be functional (i.e., to serve certain functions). For example, as older people retired from their work roles (voluntarily or involuntarily), this served the function of opening up occupational opportunities for younger persons. The latter were likely to suffuse their work roles with new energies and talents, to the benefit of society as a whole. Moreover, as older people routinely withdrew from such roles, society avoided the disruption and disharmony that could occur were aging role incumbents always being unpredictably stricken with debilitating disease or death. Finally, disengagement was thought to function in the interests of aging individuals as well. Withdrawal from work and other roles was said to be an appropriate way for such individuals to shed responsibilities and relationships that would be burdensome to persons in a state of biological and psychological decline.

[12] Elaine Cumming and William E. Henry, *Growing Old: The Process of Disengagement* (New York: Basic Books, 1961), p. 211.

[13] Ibid.

Disengagement was thus theorized to be the way to a more comfortable and "successful" old age. In sum, according to Cumming and Henry, growing old necessitated changes in life-style and levels of involvement with others.

Disengagement theory has spawned a host of critics and has been the impetus to a good deal of research.[14] A typical response to Cumming and Henry's point of view is as follows:

1. Research findings do not support the notion that old age inevitably means decline and that this characteristic causes disengagement. Older persons are often sufficiently healthy and capable of filling important social roles until shortly before death.
2. Disengagement, rather than contributing in a positive way to societal functioning, often has a negative impact. Persons with valuable knowledge and wisdom based on years of experience are often cut off from making contributions, thus depriving society. Lack of concrete roles for older persons to play may provide a basis for prejudiced attitudes and treatment by younger people, thus contributing to differential distribution of self-esteem and unnecessary intergroup tensions within society.
3. While early retirement from work roles may open up opportunities for younger workers, the shortage of such opportunities should not be blamed on the old, nor should mandatory retirement be considered natural. The availability of work opportunity for younger persons is a function of elite-made economic and political decisions over which aging workers have no control. The main beneficiaries of mandatory retirement policies (largely eliminated under current federal law) have been employers, who usually pay younger workers less in wages and benefits.
4. Aging individuals who are "disengaged," particularly involuntarily (e.g., through mandatory or informally forced retirement), may face many serious problems as a consequence—problems that impose a cost on society. Such problems may include poverty or near-poverty, impaired physical and mental health, isolation, and loneliness. For all too many, disengagement is a route to an uncomfortable and unsuccessful old age.

Opponents of disengagement theory sometimes view it as an ideology justifying the exclusion of older persons from active participation in society. This exclusion actually creates much of the psychic and physical decline. This thinking has been characteristic of those who adhere to an *activity theory* of old age.

Disengagement theory, in viewing old age as a period requiring changes in life-styles and especially reduced levels of involvement with others, rejected the notion that the activities enjoyed in middle age can be carried on. Activity theory, on the other hand, argues not only that activities enjoyed in middle age can be carried on by most older persons, but that they should be. In the words of Jack Levin and William C. Levin,

> Activity theory suggests that there is a positive relationship between activity and life-satisfaction and that the greater the role loss, the lower the life-satisfaction. Thus, those who wish to enjoy their last years of life should continue to live as they had during their middle years right to the time death or illness stops them.[15]

This, of course, assumes that the middle years were indeed a source of enjoyment. In many cases, persons who faced problems in living in the middle years will continue to face them when older. For example, poor middle-aged per-

[14] See Jack Levin and William C. Levin, *Ageism: Prejudice and Discrimination Against the Elderly* (Belmont, Calif.: Wadsworth, 1980), pp. 44–54 and 84–85.

[15] Ibid., p. 53.

sons may well be poor elderly persons. Still, it is said that "most of the methodologically sound research tends to support activity theory."[16]

What kinds of difficulties hinder the ability of the aged to be active participants in society? What kinds of problems plague many older Americans, turning the notion of the "golden years" into an absurdity? In the next section some responses to these questions are explored.

INCOME AND POVERTY STATUS

> Income is a crucial determinant of how the aged live. The level, the adequacy, and the maintenance of income affects other aspects of the lives of the elderly: the maintenance of physical and mental health, transportation utilization, housing and nutrition adequacy, vulnerability to crime, level of social participation and the general quality of life.[17]

In light of the preceding quote, it becomes significant that as recently as 1988 some 12 percent of all persons sixty-five and older, over one in ten, were officially considered poor. Counting those who were "near-poor" (i.e., with incomes no more than 125 percent of the official poverty line), 19 percent, or nearly one out of five persons sixty-five and older, were living on severely restricted incomes. The poverty threshold for a two-person household whose members are sixty-five and older was a mere $7,158 in 1988.[18]

It is true that the poverty rates for older Americans have declined significantly over the years. For example, almost one-third of those sixty-five and older were considered poor in 1960. This figure dropped to 24.5 percent in 1970, to 15.3 percent in 1975, and to 12 percent in 1988. Yet while the poverty rate has been in decline, indicating improvement in the position of older persons in absolute terms, the relative economic status of this group has not improved. That is, there has been no significant increase in the income of the sixty-five-and-older group relative to the incomes of other age groups.[19]

The 1988 poverty rate of 12 percent (involving 3.5 million persons) is an overall figure, and one that masks the distribution of poverty within the sixty-five-and-older population. For example, in 1988 the rate for whites was 10 percent, but for black Americans it was three times as high—32.2 percent. There were also sex differences, with older women more likely to be poor than older men. In 1987, for example, the rate for women was 14.9 percent; for men it was 8.5 percent. Yet even these figures do not tell the whole story of the range of distribution. While white men sixty-five and older have a poverty rate of 6.8 percent, black women have a rate of 40.2 percent! Female black households in which no husbands were present had an astounding poverty rate of 49.4 percent!

Lori Girshick and John Williamson point out that over 90 percent of older Americans receive social security benefits from the federal government and that the majority of persons in this age group depend on government programs as their principal income source.[20] However, they are quick to note that such benefits do not necessarily mean that one lives above the poverty line. This is particularly the case for those older persons whose earlier lives had been conducted at low-income levels. Persons who were poor

[16] Erdman Palmore, "United States of America," in Erdman Palmore, ed., *International Handbook on Aging* (Westport, Conn.: Greenwood Press, 1980), p. 45.

[17] Charles S. Harris, *Fact Book on Aging: A Profile of America's Older Population* (Washington, D.C.: National Council on the Aging, 1978), p. 36.

[18] Statistics in this section come from U.S. Department of Commerce, Bureau of the Census, *Money Income and Poverty Status in the United States: 1988* (Washington, D.C.: U.S. Government Printing Office, 1989, and from the 1987 version of the report.

[19] See Lori Girshick and John A. Williamson, "The Politics of Measuring Poverty Among the Elderly," in Richard Goldstein and Stephen M. Sachs, eds., *Applied Poverty Research* (Totowa, N.J.: Rowman and Allanheld, 1984), pp. 64–76.

[20] Ibid., p. 67.

PUBLIC PROBLEM, PRIVATE PAIN

The View in Winter

Our elders often reflect on their lives, looking both to the past and to the present. For many, the present is clouded with a sense of isolation, loneliness, and loss because of the deaths of those to whom they were close. The past, in contrast, can be savored for remembered pleasurable experiences. In this selection a very proud and dignified woman in her eighties shares some of her feelings about old age.

The eighties are difficult. You wonder how you'll manage them. You do feel a difference. Then, half-way through them, you begin to take them for granted. Everything is infinitely harder, that's all. I spend my day trying to read. At odd times. That magnifying-glass is growing unsuitable but I've got another one coming. I can't read very well and it was the reading which I liked most. I go on crying all the time. That is what I mostly do now, cry. I try to meet things. I think that is what one must do now. You can't say that "I can't like this" or "I won't like that." When you are old you must meet a situation—there is no other alternative. I certainly feel very isolated—I do feel that. It is a strange thing, really. They've all passed away. All the real friends are gone. There are none left of the friends of my life-time. The greatest friend was the last to go. There are cousins, but I don't know these cousins because I was away so long. But there are cousins. . . .

My day has quite gone. It is over. Quite gone. It is all very different now and difficult to understand. There is nothing I can do here, although everybody is kind. It is too steep to walk to the library and hard to walk anywhere. I need to be somewhere where I can do more things. I certainly want to walk. There is a bus here, but I can't manage it. There are no cars to hire. The world belongs to the young.

The world is so different, isn't it? But it is difficult to say whether it is worse or not. Although we find the children very erratic, it could be that they ought to be like that for their times. It is useless complaining about how they behave. We don't know what they'll have to meet when they get older. It will all be very, very different, and we won't know. They must be able to meet what is coming, and so it is useless to say whether now they are right or wrong. How can I know what they will have to meet or face? How useless it is for the old to say anything at all about the young. How can I know what they will see or they know what I have seen? It is pointless comment.

As for old age, you are expected to accept it. You know you are a back number. I don't resent it. I don't expect what I expected when I was young. I don't even think of it. You take a simple thing such as whether somebody likes you or they don't. It doesn't cross your mind when you are very old. I don't expect to be liked or disliked. I don't expect *anything*. I don't expect anyone to do anything for me, but when they do I say, "How kind they are," and mean it. It is all so different, you see.

I don't take medicines. People have a way of taking them just to go to sleep! I won't do that. I don't sleep well, but one should never do that. It is a very unfortunate thing to do. They are to relieve pain, and that is different. But to take them just because one can't sleep, well really! The doctor says rest. Rest. I was gardening and walking very long distances until [my greatest friend's] death. I've always been very busy. I was very strong. Then her death and this weakness from grief came in the end suddenly. But my memory stays extremely good, and I've never failed mentally in what I've had to do. Which I think is a great boon. I treasure my brain-power. I hoard it. You really must have memories. They are all you have left, and if you didn't have them you would think about what is happening now, and it would be fatal. It would not be the wonderful past which would be inside you, but the dreadful now.

What I have complete faith in is that there is another life. I've got total faith in that. I don't hesitate at all. So there is a greater experience soon. Everybody is going on the same journey. I think of death, but I don't say that I am prepared to die. But I'm prepared to leave. Ever since I got to this place, I have been writing out what I want done when I leave. I've got everything arranged. But whether I

PUBLIC PROBLEM, PRIVATE PAIN (continued)

myself am prepared—that's a very different matter! Towards the end, when one is old, I shouldn't think that many people consider dying. They would prepare for it but not consider it. I've had a lovely life, really. I shouldn't have had the same life at all, if I hadn't met my friend. She was a good help. I think there are a lot of wonderful things in life now, but whether they are better I don't know. As for myself, I have to say, "Well, you've had your day and now sit and rest and think about it." But when I say this I remember that it was *our* day, and then I weep.

Source: From Ronald Blythe, *The View in Winter: Reflections on Old Age*, pp. 193–95. Copyright © 1979 by Ronald Blythe. Reprinted by permission of the publisher, Harcourt Brace Jovanovich, Inc.

or near-poor before reaching sixty-five generally continue to be so in old age. Since black and other minorities are disproportionately represented in the overall poverty population (see Chapter 6), it should be no surprise that this holds true in the so-called golden years of life as well.

EMPLOYMENT AND RETIREMENT

A key factor determining income for all families is the movement of a member into or out of the paid labor force. Most older persons live with a spouse or alone, and the loss of income from employment can have a significant impact on quality of life in the household. Consider that in 1988 the median income of a household whose members were sixty-five and over was only $14,923.

In an earlier section we noted that since 1900 a smaller proportion of the sixty-five-and-over population has remained employed, until today only 16 percent of males and even fewer females in this age group are holding down jobs. Moreover, retirement before sixty-five is becoming increasingly common. These trends are expected to continue, even while a larger proportion of the U.S. population enters old age.

Withdrawal from the labor force is voluntary for most older Americans, but for many it is not. For perhaps as many as 40 percent of retirees, involuntary retirement has been a reality. For some it was a matter of responding to episodic or seemingly permanent unemployment. Not only are unemployment rates high for older workers, but durations of unemployment tend to be longer than those for their younger counterparts. They tend to be longest for those fifty-five to sixty-five or older. Insofar as permanent withdrawal from the labor force at least renders one eligible for bare survival-level government benefits (usually social security), it becomes a reluctant alternative to the stress and humiliation of unemployment.

But it is not only the unemployed worker who involuntarily retires. Employers' rules for mandatory retirement (until fairly recently set at age sixty-five) forced millions of able, willing, and financially vulnerable persons into a limbo of joblessness. While federal legislation of 1986 largely outlawed mandatory retirement (partly out of a desire to slow the growing budgetary burden of paying out social security benefits), it is likely that much retirement will remain involuntary and continue to take place at sixty-five, if not before. Let us suggest some reasons for this:[21]

1. Job dissatisfaction, particularly among blue-collar workers, is an incentive to early retirement. Moreover, jobs held by the latter work-

[21] Levin and Levin, *Ageism: Prejudice and Discrimination Against the Elderly*, pp. 122–23; see also Anne Fone and Karen Schwab, *Aging and Retirement* (Monterey, Calif.: Brooks/Cole Publishing Co., 1981), pp. 45–54.

ers are often dangerous, physically punishing, or otherwise conducive to ill health, thus forcing persons to retire because of physical disability or the fear of it.

2. Although laws against discrimination in employment on the basis of age exist, such discrimination on the part of employers continues. Subtle informal pressures to retire are difficult and frequently expensive to fight in private legal suits. Government agencies charged with antidiscrimination enforcement are poorly funded, short-staffed, and backlogged with years of complaints.
3. Social and cultural expectations in general support withdrawal from the labor force. Thus, many workers, faced with real or internalized pressures to disengage from their work role, simply do so. They may believe what so many falsely allege: When you reach sixty-five (or earlier) you are supposed to move over and let someone younger take your place. They are simply fulfilling what they see as others' expectations.
4. Our system of social security, begun in 1935 to supplement income but now heavily relied on as a primary source by so many, encourages labor force withdrawal. Since its benefits are linked only to reaching the chronological age of sixty-five, and not to disability or unemployment, persons reaching that magic age are faced with the incentive of retiring to receive social security benefits. Private pension plans may offer similar incentives to stop work at sixty-five, or special provisions for retirement even earlier.

While retirement means the acceptance of reduced income on a permanent basis—ordinarily half or less of what one might have earned while employed full time—its impact goes beyond income restrictions. The loss of a work role may affect self-esteem and self-image, reduce social contacts and enjoyment gained from peer and friendship groups, and in general lower morale. Involuntary loss of a work role in many cases may help increase vulnerability to mental and physical health problems, as well as self-destructive behavior (from alcoholism or other forms of drug abuse to suicide).

HEALTH AND HEALTH CARE

Earlier we addressed the stereotype that depicted persons sixty-five and older as all living in a state of mental and physical failure. While this is an incorrect depiction of older Americans, increasing age does bring with it a greater vulnerability to and hence probability of certain health problems. Many variables enter into the determination of health status, including income level, dietary and nutritional practices, behavior known to be associated with health problems (e.g., smoking and alcohol abuse), exercise routines, degree of exposure to dangerous conditions and polluting substances, experiences of psychological and physical stress, and access to (and ability to obtain) adequate health care when needed.

A major reason that our sixty-five-and-over population is growing is the successful eradication of illness and disease that resulted in many people dying in their younger years. Hence, more persons have the opportunity today to be afflicted with health problems long experienced by segments of the aging population. For the most part, when health problems do exist among older Americans, they are chronic (i.e., of relatively long duration). Examples of such conditions are arthritis and rheumatism, hearing and vision impairment, and high blood pressure. Such health problems may slow people down, but ordinarily they do not require institutionalization. In summing up physical health care problems, one expert put the situation this way:

> With advancing age, the basic health care requirements of the population become greater than those in younger age categories; with advancing age, the basic health requirements become different

from those in younger age categories because of their chronic nature.[22]

Despite the preceding situation, health care for aging Americans is widely acknowledged as inadequate.[23] Among the problems is the fact that health in one's later years is so greatly affected by what the individual experiences while younger. If one's environment and environmentally associated behaviors are not health-enhancing all through life—as is particularly the case for so many poor and working class people—health problems can be expected in one's later years. In essence, health care for the aging American is a process that should begin before birth and go on from there, and it should include preventive policies that maximize the probability of good health in old age. Needless to say, America's health care system does not fit this model very well. It is far more attuned to responding to experiences of illness after the fact than it is to helping alter environments that facilitate the development of such illnesses.

But more than the preceding is involved in the inadequacy of health care available to older Americans:

1. Physicians are not trained to specialize in the problems of older persons, despite the fact that a substantial part of their time is spent with them. Geriatric medicine is not a recognized specialty in the United States (although it is elsewhere), and few medical schools require their students to take work in this area.
2. Many persons in the medical field share the stereotypes about and prejudices toward older Americans. This cannot help but affect their interest and effectiveness in dealing with them. Moreover, chronic health problems are often considered medically uninteresting and routine, in comparison to "acute" illnesses. The latter are often serious, demand urgent attention, and usually can be quickly resolved with proper medical procedures. The rate of acute illness among older persons is very low.
3. For many persons health and related services are simply inaccessible. This can be the case for diverse reasons. There are gaps in government programs that assist older persons in paying for care and services (Medicare and Medicaid), thus making them too expensive for many persons to afford. In some cases, serious illness results in expenses that propel persons into poverty. Today there are the "new poor" who become so by divesting themselves of assets (such as homes and savings) acquired while members of the working or even the middle class. Rural areas and lower income urban neighborhoods where many older persons reside have very limited medical services, thus hampering accessibility for those who are not geographically mobile.

HOUSING AND TRANSPORTATION

At first glance older Americans appear to be in good shape with regard to housing. Some 70 percent of those sixty-five and older live in housing they own. Eighty percent of the housing owned by older Americans is held without a mortgage. Yet a true picture must go beyond such superficial information.

For most elderly homeowners, housing is both the largest and the only significant asset they possess. Yet it is a nonliquid asset; as long as they want to hold on to their property and remain in their homes, the money value of the housing is unavailable for day-to-day living expenses. Yet it is these expenses—property taxes, utilities, energy costs, housing maintenance—that have routinely gone up over the past years.

[22] Harris, *Fact Book on Aging*, pp. 111–12.
[23] For a penetrating analysis, see Laura K. Olson, *The Political Economy of Aging* (New York: Columbia University Press, 1982), pp. 128–64.

Most older persons face highly restricted and relatively fixed incomes on retirement. One in five of those sixty-five and older are poor or in near poverty. Many older Americans cannot afford to stay in the houses they own; some find they are forced to cut back on expenditures in such areas as food and medical services in order to pay heating bills.

Those older Americans who live in apartments, boarding houses, and hotels tend to live in even more economically precarious positions than do those in owner-occupied housing. Yet they too face increased costs, reflected in high rents and utilities. Since for some years there has been a serious shortage of rental properties to accommodate the housing needs of the population in general, not to mention older persons, demands in the face of shortage allow landlords to charge higher rents than might otherwise be the case. Owners of such properties are increasingly finding it more profitable to either abandon them (when the rising costs outrun the ability of occupants to pay higher rents) or convert them to private condominiums. The sales prices of the latter are ordinarily well beyond the ability of elderly renters to pay; thus, they cannot stay in their homes.

There are other problems as well. An estimated 9 percent of the housing units occupied by older Americans are substandard. But much of the housing owned by members of this group is old and thus needs more repair and heat than newer housing in which younger people tend to reside. Since the elderly are likely to be housed in the nation's central cities, where lower income neighborhood decline and deterioration are common, the environment surrounding their housing is often unattractive, unsafe, and a source of stress. In both blighted central city neighborhoods and the rural small towns in which older Americans also are likely to live, services that are supportive of their particular needs and life-styles are likely to be lacking. These kinds of difficulties lead Laura K. Olson to conclude:

> Given their poor neighborhood conditions, inaccessibility of essential supportive services, higher maintenance and rental costs relative to income, and other housing-related problems, the vast majority of older persons lack adequate housing.[24]

While the housing situation of many if not most older Americans could stand significant improvement, the same may be said of transportation. According to a study commissioned by the National Council on the Aging,[25] like others, older Americans are dependent on automobile transportation. Yet as this dependency increases, the likelihood that one can afford to keep an automobile, as well as the ability to drive one, decreases. Some 40 percent of households headed by persons sixty-five and older do not own a car (a rate twice that of younger households). There are numerous reasons for this. The rising costs of car ownership, maintenance and repair, fuel, licensing, and insurance become too much for persons on relatively fixed incomes. Older persons pay more than younger persons for car insurance and may have their insurance policies canceled when a certain age is reached. Finally, for some, health-related disabilities may make driving a private vehicle a risky endeavor if not an impossibility.

This situation would not be so serious if it were not for the paucity of adequate and affordable public transportation. In many cases (e.g., rural areas) such transportation is either very limited or nonexistent. In central city areas the situation is often somewhat better, but rising costs, fear of criminal victimization, and the at times intimidating physical demands associated with using public transportation restrict its use. The result is geographic immobility, isolation, and barriers between older Americans and the medical, recreational, educational, and social services they frequently must have to sustain a decent way of life.

---

[24] Ibid., p. 164.

[25] See Harris, *Fact Book on Aging,* pp. 211–31.

CRIMINAL VICTIMIZATION

One would like to think that security against criminal victimization is possible for older Americans, yet they do not escape the ravages of property crimes and crimes of violence. As we shall see, the impact of criminal victimization may weigh more heavily on the old than on the young.

Crime statistics must always be taken with caution. Official statistics on crimes reported to the police tend to be underestimates of the amount of crime actually taking place (see Chapter 13, "Criminal Behavior"). With respect to the elderly and crime, our knowledge is limited by the fact that until fairly recently data were not collected or organized to provide knowledge about the sixty-five-and-older group.

At the national level, overall criminal victimization rates appear to be somewhat lower for the older population than for the younger population. This may be a matter of underreporting; it may also be that certain segments of the sixty-five-and-older population successfully isolate themselves from the risk of victimization. Yet, looking at particular crimes and at older persons living in particular locales, some have argued that older Americans are *more* likely to be crime victims than younger persons.[26] Further inquiry is needed to clarify the question of victimization rates and their relation to old age.

Leaving aside the adequacy of official statistics, it seems fair to say that older Americans are most likely to be victims of property crimes as opposed to crimes of violence. Yet both types of crime are held to have more severe effects on the old than on the young. Robbery on the street, burglary in the home, and victimization through fraud or confidence games often have a devastating impact on older Americans. Many older Americans are living on relatively fixed incomes and cannot afford to lose their meager social security or pension payments or small accumulated savings. Since persons sixty-five and older are unlikely to be working, cars and material possessions often cannot be replaced. A property loss that a younger person might angrily shrug off is likely to be a major blow to the more vulnerable older American.

Similarly, while victimization by crimes of violence is far less frequent than by property offenses, older persons are at a disadvantage. As aging may slow down physical agility, so may it slow down rates of recuperation. With advanced age for some comes physical frailty, so that a severe blow or fall can readily result in serious trauma and even death. In the words of Charles S. Harris,

> The problem of crimes against older Americans must be measured by the effect of crime on the victim rather than by the frequency of assault.[27]

Some social scientists have been surprised that fear of criminal victimization is very high among older Americans, even while overall statistics suggest that victimization is less frequent than for younger persons. This fear is itself a form of injury. Many older persons, particularly in densely populated central cities, are virtually immobilized by their fear of crime and the likelihood that they will be singled out as easy marks by local predators. As Alan Malinchak puts it:

> Soft-core sentiment and emotions play no part in the hard-core dealings of criminal activity. A criminal cannot afford to be generous. Crime involves the element of risk. It is only natural for the criminal to prey upon the elderly, for there is less risk in being apprehended and suffering the consequences of a prison term.[28]

[26] See, for example, Alan A. Malinchak, *Crime and Gerontology* (Englewood Cliffs, N.J.: Prentice-Hall, 1980), pp. 13–16 and 41–46.

[27] Harris, *Fact Book on Aging*, p. 260.

[28] Malinchak, *Crime and Gerontology*, pp. 41–42.

Such fear may even be a source of some of the disengagement from active participation in social roles and relationships with others of which we spoke earlier. Living in a state of nervous isolation behind locked doors, afraid to venture out on the street, potential victims are denied normal lives in what are supposed to be the "golden years." Crime and fear of crime alter the life-styles and adversely affect the mobility of the old much more than of younger Americans.

ELDER ABUSE

For most older Americans, the struggle to lead happy lives in a society afflicted with ageism is relatively successful. Yet, a significant minority is held hostage to physical and/or mental abuse by members of their own households. Elder abuse has become what one champion of the aged, the late U.S. Representative Claude Pepper, called "a national disgrace." He was responding to figures in a 1985 House subcommittee report estimating that 1.1 million Americans over age sixty-five suffer such abuse annually.[29] With the proportion of the population sixty-five and over growing, the numbers of elders at risk could easily rise.

There appear to be two views or schools of thought on how to account for elder abuse.[30] One view emphasizes the stresses and burdens placed on those who care for infirm and incapacitated older people. Caregivers are often adult children or spouses who, it is believed, grow resentful and angry over the dependency of another upon them. In response to the demands they must suffer, caregivers may respond with abuse. In effect, this view is suggesting normally nonabusive people are being driven by circumstances into negative behaviors. The characteristics of the elderly bring on the abuse.

The second school of thought focuses instead on the characteristics of the abusers. It has been suggested that abusers of the elderly are *themselves* likely to be dependent people. The persons for whom they are caring may be supporting them financially in whole or part, responsible for their shelter, health insurance, and so on. Further, abusers—more than nonabusive caretakers of the elderly—are thought to be people with troubles. They are, it is argued, more likely to have mental difficulties, problems with alcohol or drugs, and law violations involving them with the police.

Until recently there were few data to help sort out which of these two views was most likely the case. Now, however, research appears to lend support to the view that it is the dependent, troubled caregiver who abuses. Based on the first large-scale random-sample survey on this question, in this case conducted in the greater Boston area, researchers Karl Pillemer and David Finkelhor concluded:

> The picture of maltreatment that emerged from the present study [shows] relatively well-functioning elderly who have responsibility for, or are at least required to interact with, ill and socioemotionally unstable relatives. The abuse appears to be a reflection of the abuser's problems and dependency rather than the elderly victim's characteristics. . . . Instead of well-meaning caregivers who are driven to abuse by the demands of an old person, elder abusers appear to be severely troubled individuals with histories of antisocial behavior or instability.[31]

As Pillemer and Finkelhor point out, their findings undermine any tendency we might have to "blame the victim," that is, to suggest that aging people are so stressful and hard to care for that their abuse is understandable if not

[29] "Abusing the Elderly," *Newsweek* (September 23, 1985): 75.

[30] Karl Pillemer and David Finkelhor, "Causes of Elder Abuse," *American Journal of Orthopsychiatry*, 59 (April 1989): 179–87.

[31] Ibid., p. 186.

forgiveable. As they argue, just as we have come to understand that rape victims, battered spouses, and victims of incest and child abuse can hardly be viewed as having in some way "asked for it," so also should we understand the victims of elder abuse. Although this research does not put the discussion to rest, and although there may well be other contributing factors to elder abuse (see the discussion of family violence in Chapter 12), the attention such abuse is receiving harbors well for those who may be at risk.

OLD AGE AND POLITICAL POWER

With one in eight members of the American population at age sixty-five or over and an even larger proportion forecast, older Americans can play a much more significant political role than they do today.[32] As we have seen, there are a variety of areas within which transformations are required to mitigate harmful conditions facing this age group—from economic deprivation to elder abuse. However, few experts agree on just what the political implications are of an aging population.

Here are some facts stemming from social science research that may bear on the role of older Americans in politics as we look into the future:

1. In general, rates of political participation (e.g., voting behavior, expression of opinions on political issues) rise with increased age.
2. The commonly held view that political attitudes grow more conservative with age does not appear to be true; aging per se seems not to systematically affect political outlooks.
3. Too little is known to be able to predict whether in the future older Americans are likely to become a major political force—whether through acting as an effective voting bloc or through taking part in militant social movement activities revolving around age-related policy issues.

[32] This section draws on Douglas Dobson, "The Elderly as a Political Force," in William P. Browne and Laura Katz Olson, eds., *Aging and Public Policy* (Westport, Conn.: Greenwood Press, 1983), pp. 123–44. See also Henry J. Pratt, "National Interest Groups Among the Elderly," pp. 145–79 in the same volume.

Item 3 relates to the question of whether older Americans are likely to develop "age consciousness." That is, will older Americans come to see themselves as possessing important political and economic interests in common, and seek to advance these interests through society-wide mobilization? There are different points of view on such questions.

Among the factors that may help to promote age consciousness are an increase in the proportion of the population made up of older people; the trend toward residential segregation, whereupon older Americans live apart from younger kin (increasingly in "retirement communities"); the presence of government programs and publicly financed services that bring older people together and increase opportunities for group interaction; higher levels of educational attainment and political sophistication among future elderly Americans; and possible resistance on the part of persons who are not old to continuing demands for taxation stemming from the growing needs of an aging population. As the numbers of aging persons who find themselves dependent upon those younger increase, will the burden become such that the younger rebel? Such age-based conflict is frequently portrayed as both a possible cause and a possible outcome of age consciousness.

Yet others are doubtful that such "age consciousness" is likely to occur to any great degree or that older Americans will mobilize on a society-wide basis. The emphasis in this point of view is on the heterogeneity that will continue into the future. Diversity—whether it be economic, ethnic or racial, geographic or sexual—serves to splinter the older population and

Just as sexism and racism have stimulated protest, so has ageism. Pictured here is Maggie Kuhn, founder of the Gray Panther Party. This organization was begun in the early 1970s and currently has some 70,000 members. The Gray Panthers are dedicated to building a political coalition of persons from all age groups to fight ageism and are frequently quite militant in their efforts to stop age discrimination. *(Elizabeth Crews/Stock, Boston)*

reduce the probability that it might come to function as a unified political force. Moreover, the sixty-five-and-over population is not static but is undergoing constantly changing membership as new persons enter old age and still others die. Fluctuation in group membership is seen as another force undermining effective political unity.

Still, even with heterogeneity and the transiency of old-age group membership, it is conceivable that attacks on the well-being of our elders in the future could galvanize a far-reaching response. Alarmed by the treatment of older Americans today and the economic threat to the non-old that swelling numbers of elders may pose, Jack Levin and Arnold Arlucke suggest that our society may be heading toward a "final solution." They state:

> A *de facto* mass extermination may already be taking place. Many elders suffer a social death in which they are removed from the main stream of life.... Elders are also the victims of benign neglect: They are deprived of the food, shelter and health care needed to survive.... The intellectual justification for a final solution can already be observed in our changing attitudes toward aging and death.[33]

Levin and Arlucke see a subtle movement toward writing off the old, in effect "exterminating" many of them through indifference and negligence—a movement that could escalate in the future. Surely, we would presume, any such steps will generate a substantial reaction from older persons, and many of their younger counterparts as well.

SUMMARY

In the words of Simone de Beauvoir,

> By the way in which a society behaves toward its old people it uncovers the naked and often carefully hidden truth about its real principles and aims.[34]

If the preceding words are true, then our treatment (or maltreatment) of those who have served U.S. society longest is a sad commentary on our principles and aims. In the preceding pages we have seen that myths and stereotypes, often quite derogatory and harmful, have been inflicted on those who enter the arbitrarily

[33] "Our Elderly's Fate," *New York Times* (September 29, 1983): A31.

[34] Simone de Beauvoir, *The Coming of Age* (New York: Warner Books, 1973), p. 131.

defined period of "old age." Such myths and stereotypes, along with questionable social science theory that calls for older persons to disengage from life roles for the good of society, promote minority group status for millions in their later years. Such ideas also justify ignoring the numerous problems the aging face, problems that pose direct harm to the quality, if not the length, of their lives. As a consequence, one in five older Americans are poor or near-poor. For many, retirement is an involuntary removal from an important work role, or escape from chronic job dissatisfaction and unemployment, rather than a retreat into the "golden years" of life. Economic vulnerability is, as well, linked to problems of physical and mental health. So are the stresses connected with inadequate housing and immobility because of lack of transportation. As if this were not enough, older Americans silently suffer fear of criminal victimization as well as its reality, and they may be abused in their homes.

There is no sign that these problems will go away and that the lives of our elders will be transformed. Yet, as the sixty-five-and-over segment of the population grows, conditions could well become such that old-agers will be a far more potent and unified political force in this society than they are at present. With "age consciousness" could come the mobilization of a rather heterogeneous group to attack ageism. This group could include younger persons as well.

In Irving Rosow's view,

> The crucial people are *not* the aged, but the *younger* groups. It is *we* who determine the status and position of the old.[35]

As we, through action and inaction, determine the status and position of the old in society, we are determining what *we* shall be allowed to become when we reach "old age."

[35] Irving Rosow, "And Then We Were Old," in Beth B. Hess, ed., *Growing Old in America* (New Brunswick, N.J.: Transaction Books, 1976), p. 54.

DISCUSSION QUESTIONS

1. Discuss the differences and the similarities between ageism, on the one hand, and racism or sexism, on the other hand.
2. Suppose medical discoveries make it possible for Americans' average life expectancy to go from 75 years (about where it is now) to 100 or more years. Discuss the consequences of such a change for U.S. society.
3. What, typically, are older people doing when you somehow feel they are not "acting their age"? Why are you made uncomfortable by their actions?
4. Older people are often the butt of jokes and the subject of humor. What characteristics of older people are commonly communicated through jokes and humor? To what degree are these characteristics stereotypical and degrading?
5. Make a list of what you are likely to do in the course of a typical day after you turn sixty-five. Compare the lists produced by males in your class with those produced by females. What conclusions may be drawn?

SUGGESTED READINGS

Butler, Robert N. *Why Survive? Being Old in America* (New York: Harper & Row Publishers, 1975).
Classic indictment of discriminatory and dehumanizing treatment of the elderly.

Fischer, David H. *Growing Old in America* (New York: Oxford University Press, 1981).
Traces the treatment of elders historically, suggesting how and why their status has changed.

Levin, Jack, and William C. Levin. *Ageism: Prejudice and Discrimination Against the Elderly* (Belmont, Calif.: Wadsworth, 1980).
Critical discussion of social science theories that contribute to the segregation, stereotyping, and victimization of older Americans.

Margolis, Richard J. *Risking Old Age in America* (Boulder, Colo.: Westview Press, 1990).
Probing analysis of government programs and their relationship to poverty and dependency among our elders.

Olson, Laura Katz. *The Political Economy of Aging* (New York: Columbia University Press, 1982).
Problems confronting the elderly in U.S. society, with particular attention to housing and health care issues.

Vladeck, Bruce C. *Unloving Care* (New York: Basic Books, 1980).
An analysis of the forces that produce institutional warehousing, as opposed to humane care, in nursing homes.

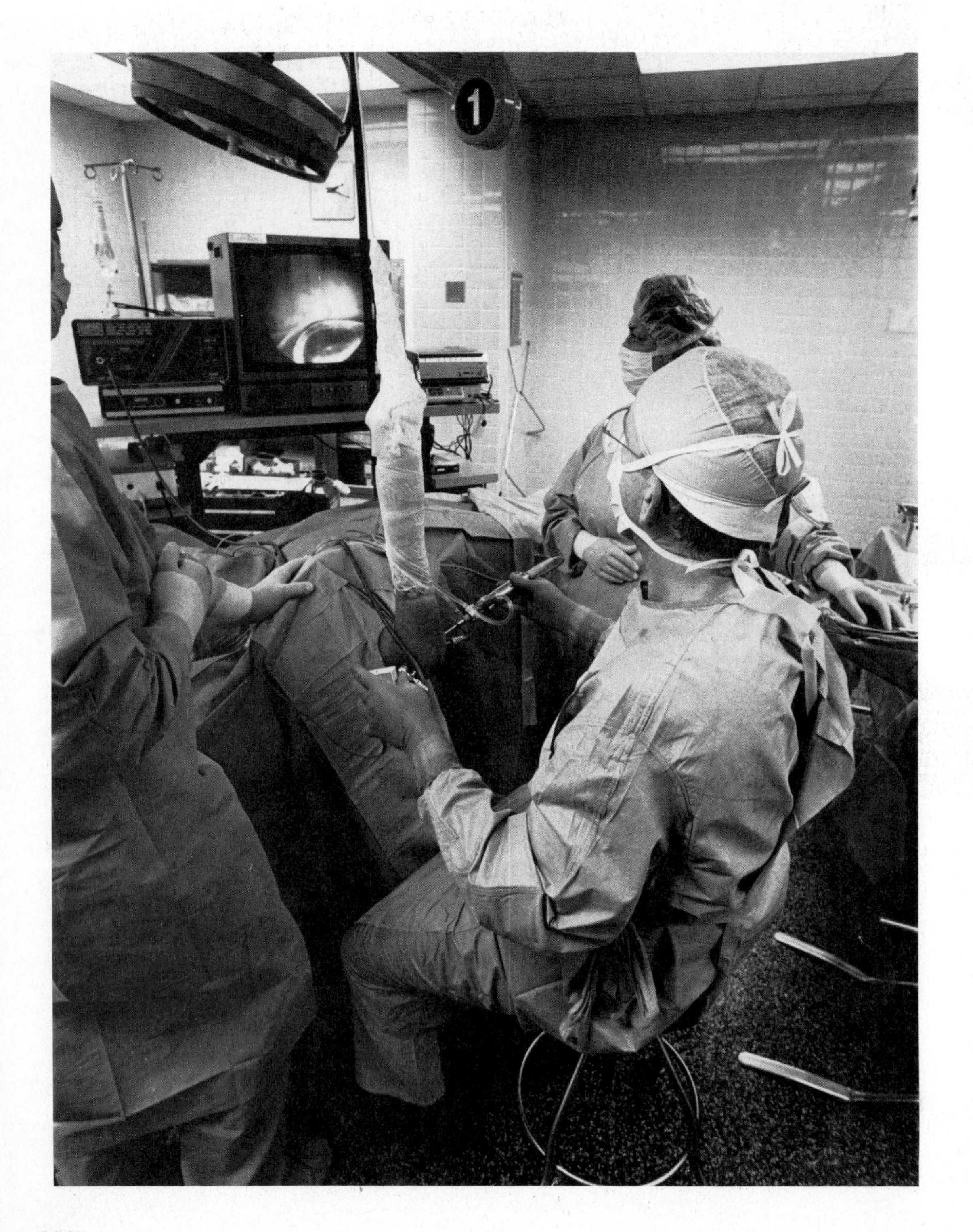
1

CHAPTER 11

Health Care

Adequate health care should be a human right and made accessible and affordable to all.

In the preceding chapters we analyzed a long list of macro problems, defined in the Introduction as organizational features of society that stand in the way of our individual and collective development as human beings. To put it another way, these features of society are harmful to millions of people. In this chapter we add America's system of health care to the list.

As we shall see, Americans are not necessarily as healthy as persons living in similarly well-developed nations. Moreover, major differences in health status by class and race abound in the United States. Our system of health care tends to be oriented toward responding to people's problems, rather than helping to prevent problems in the first place. Moreover, ready access to health care is not available to everyone. Health care costs have skyrocketed in recent years and many persons are unable to afford treatment. And the demands on our already inadequate system will increase dramatically as we seek to cope with the AIDS epidemic and the chronic health needs of an aging population. These are the matters we consider in this chapter.

THE HEALTH STATUS OF AMERICANS

When sociologists assess the health status of a population they use a variety of measures or indicators. One commonly used indicator is life expectancy: How long is the average person born in a given year expected to live? In the case of the United States, by this measure we have grown ever more healthy. A person born in the year 1900 was expected to live about forty-nine years. In contrast, life expectancy for persons born today is about seventy-five.[1]

How does one account for this 50 percent increase in life expectancy? To a large extent, increased life expectancy reflects improvements in diet, personal hygiene, housing, and public sanitation.[2] Modern medicine has also found ways to directly combat infectious diseases and their effects.[3] In 1900 people regularly died from tuberculosis, pneumonia, and influenza. Children were hard hit by such diseases. With the advent of immunization and the development of antibiotics, many more people were able to live into middle and old age. Thus, the causes of death today are largely noninfectious diseases that are associated with longevity: heart disease and cancer. Relatively few people lived long enough in 1900 to contract the latter.

Another measure of a population's health status is the infant mortality rate. This is the number of newborns who die in a given year per 1,000 live births. The statistic encompasses those who die before their first birthday. Again, using this measure, it appears that Americans have certainly grown healthier over time. In 1900 the infant mortality rate was 143 per 1,000 newborns. In recent years this has dropped to a little over 10 per 1,000. Improved sanitation and nutrition, the medical advances mentioned, and changes in prenatal, neonatal, and obstetric practices have contributed to this sharp (and welcome) decline in infant deaths.

Since 1957 the federal government has sponsored national surveys in which respondents are asked to assess their own health and that of family members in their household. In 1988 almost 67 percent made an assessment of "excellent" or "very good," and about 23 percent said "good." Only 10 percent answered "fair" or "poor."[4] This subjective indicator of Americans' overall health status would seem quite positive.

Yet, although the data mentioned thus far paint a rather positive picture, there is cause for concern. In the next section we dwell at length on the fact that good health is unequally distributed within the U.S. population. Here we wish to note that the United States does not compare particularly well on health status indicators with other industrialized nations. Indeed, this is the case despite the fact that we spend more per capita on health than they do.

For example, people born in Japan, Sweden, the Netherlands, Switzerland, and Norway live longer than those born in the United States. And our infant mortality rate, low compared to what it was in 1900, is worthy of national shame. In the mid-1980s twenty-one other nations had rates of infant death lower than ours! (See Table 11.1.) Among these other nations are those just mentioned as well as Canada, Spain, and Singapore.[5] Clearly something is very wrong when in this day and age so many tragic and preventable deaths occur.

---

[1]Data in this section are from the National Center for Health Statistics.

[2]William C. Cockerham, *Medical Sociology,* 4th ed. (Englewood Cliffs, N.J.: Prentice-Hall, 1989), Chapter 1.

[3]There is evidence public health and social change measures, as opposed to medical advances, are most responsible for reduced mortality rates in twentieth-century America. See John B. McKinlay and Sonja M. McKinlay, "Medical Measures and the Decline of Mortality," in Peter Conrad and Rochelle Kern, eds., *The Sociology of Health and Illness,* 3rd ed. (New York: St. Martin's Press, 1990), pp. 10–23.

[4]National Center for Health Statistics, *Vital and Health Statistics, Current Estimates from the National Health Interview Survey, 1988* (Hyattsville, Md.: U.S. Department of Health and Human Services, 1989), p. 115.

[5]U.S. Department of Health and Human Services, *Health, United States, 1988* (Washington, D.C.: U.S. Government Printing Office, 1989), p. 59.

TABLE 11.1 Infant Mortality Rates and Average Annual Change for Selected Countries, 1980 and 1985

	Infant mortality rate*		
Country	**1980**	**1985†**	**Average annual percent change**
Japan	7.5	5.5	−6.0
Iceland	7.7	6.1	−4.6
Finland	7.6	6.3	−3.7
Sweden	6.9	6.8	−0.3
Switzerland	8.5	6.9	−4.1
Hong Kong	11.2	7.5	−7.7
Canada	11.9	7.9	−7.9
Denmark	8.4	7.9	−1.2
Netherlands	8.6	8.0	−1.4
France	10.0	8.3	−3.7
Norway	8.1	8.5	1.0
Spain	14.3	8.5	−9.9
Ireland	11.1	8.8	−4.5
Federal Republic of Germany	12.6	9.0	−6.5
Luxembourg	11.5	9.0	−4.8
Singapore	11.7	9.3	−4.5
Belgium	11.0	9.4	−3.1
United Kingdom	12.1	9.4	−4.9
German Democratic Republic	12.1	9.6	−4.5
Australia	11.0	9.9	−2.1
Italy	14.6	10.3	−6.7
United States	12.6	10.6	−3.4
New Zealand	12.6	10.9	−2.9
Austria	14.3	11.2	−4.8
Israel	15.1	11.9	−4.7
Malta	14.6	13.2	−2.0
Czechoslovakia	16.6	14.0	−3.3
Greece	17.9	14.1	−4.7
Bulgaria	20.2	15.4	−5.3
Cuba	19.1	16.5	−2.9
Portugal	23.9	17.8	−5.7
Costa Rica	20.2	18.3	−2.4
Kuwait	27.7	18.4	−7.9
Poland	21.3	19.2	−2.1
Chile	33.0	19.5	−10.0
Hungary	23.2	20.4	−2.5

*Infant mortality rate is defined as the number of infant deaths per 1,000 live births.

†Data for Costa Rica are for 1984. Data for all other countries refer to 1985; of these, Belgium and Spain are provisional and all others are final.

[Rankings are from lowest to highest infant mortality rates based on the latest data available for countries or geographic areas with at least 200,000 population and with "complete" counts of live births and infant deaths as indicated in the United Nations *Demographic Yearbook, 1985.*]

Source: U.S. Department of Health and Human Services, *Health, United States, 1988* (Washington, D.C.: U.S. Government Printing Office, 1989), p. 59.

CLASS AND HEALTH STATUS

In an earlier chapter we saw that the United States is a class-divided society. Data were provided showing that wealth and income are distributed highly unequally, and by all indications this situation has been worsening in recent years. Health status is highly correlated with position in the class structure. As one goes down this structure, good health becomes less frequent.

Let us go back to the federal survey in which people were asked to assess their health and that of family members with whom they live. Table 11.2 examines the responses of people by family income level. At the highest income level ($35,000 or more) 78 percent say they are in "excellent" or "very good" health, and only 4 percent report "fair" or "poor." The corresponding percentages for the lowest income level (under $10,000) are 49 percent excellent or very good and 22 percent fair or poor.[6] An inspection of Table 11.2 clearly establishes that people assess their health status differentially by economic well-being.

But subjective evaluations aside, there are many objective indicators of the correlation between class and health status.[7] Let us return to infant mortality. One of the reasons the United States ranks so shamefully in infant mortality rates is poverty. Rates are substantially higher among the poor than among the non-poor. Indeed, death rates for small children in general—not only infants below the age of one—are higher. Because of this and other factors we shall discuss, the overall life expectancy is less at lower levels of the class structure. To say that poverty kills is no exaggeration.

Infectious diseases, we noted previously, took a major toll on people early in this century. For the poor today, the toll goes on. For example, cases of pneumonia and influenza, and other infectious diseases such as tuberculosis and diphtheria, are much more routinely diagnosed among the poor than among the more affluent. The principal reason pneumonia and influenza rank sixth among the leading causes of death in the United States (the only infectious diseases among the top ten causes) is their association with poverty conditions.

Chronic disabling diseases are disproportionately found in lower income groups. These include heart disease, cancer, stroke, and diabetes—all among the leading causes of death in America. Impairment of speech, motor skills, and vision are prevalent. Other sources of disability such as arthritis affect the poor more than others.

Low-income people are more likely than others to find their daily activities restricted by both chronic (long-lasting) and acute (severe, but not long-lasting) conditions of illness, injury, or impairment. The results of a federal survey bearing on this are seen in Table 11.3. Respondents were asked how many days in 1988 they found their activities restricted by such conditions and the types of restrictions involved. The least affluent reported more days lying disabled in bed and suffered the most days lost from work or school. Again, Table 11.3 shows a direct correlation between economic well-being and health status.

Diane B. Dutton draws our attention to a controversy of some interest:

> There has been a longstanding debate about whether the worse health of lower socioeconomic groups should be attributed primarily to the material conditions of poverty and the biological and emotional stresses they create or to aspects of the

[6] National Center for Health Statistics, *Vital and Health Statistics*, p. 115.

[7] See Diane B. Dutton, "Social Class, Health, and Illness," in Linda H. Aiken and David Mechanic, eds., *Applications of Social Science to Clinical Medicine and Health Policy* (New Brunswick, N.J.: Rutgers University Press, 1986), pp. 31–62. This section draws heavily on this source.

TABLE 11.2 Number of Persons and Percent Distribution by Respondent-Assessed Health Status, According to Sociodemographic Characteristics: United States, 1988

Age	All persons* (number in thousands)	Respondent-assessed health status—percent distribution				
		Excellent	Very good	Good	Fair	Poor
		Under $10,000				
All ages	**28,400**	**25.8**	**23.1**	**28.9**	**14.6**	**7.5**
Under 5 years	2,590	41.5	23.4	27.0	6.6	1.6
5–17 years	5,186	36.0	26.0	31.1	6.0	0.8
18–24 years	5,039	38.1	30.7	24.7	6.0	0.6
25–44 years	5,905	23.7	25.5	31.4	14.2	5.2
45–64 years	3,523	10.3	14.2	25.1	27.8	22.7
65 years and over	6,157	11.7	17.2	31.1	25.0	15.0
		$10,000–$19,999				
All ages	**42,163**	**31.3**	**27.0**	**27.5**	**10.4**	**3.9**
Under 5 years	3,393	47.7	28.1	20.9	2.8	0.5
5–17 years	7,409	43.7	28.4	24.1	3.3	0.5
18–24 years	5,038	37.7	32.7	24.2	4.7	0.7
25–44 years	11,723	33.2	30.1	26.9	7.7	2.1
45–64 years	6,919	19.5	21.2	32.0	18.4	8.8
65 years and over	7,682	15.5	21.7	32.5	21.3	9.0
		$20,000–$34,999				
All ages	**59,615**	**39.9**	**30.2**	**22.6**	**5.7**	**1.7**
Under 5 years	4,995	54.4	29.7	13.3	2.3	0.3
5–17 years	11,723	53.8	28.0	16.0	1.9	0.2
18–24 years	5,397	44.9	33.6	18.5	2.7	0.3
25–44 years	21,531	39.6	33.5	21.9	4.0	1.0
45–64 years	10,777	26.7	27.4	31.4	10.8	3.8
65 years and over	5,193	18.2	23.5	34.9	17.0	6.4
		$35,000 or more				
All ages	**74,869**	**49.7**	**28.4**	**17.9**	**3.2**	**0.8**
Under 5 years	5,249	63.9	22.8	11.3	1.5	0.5
5–17 years	14,910	63.0	24.2	11.7	0.9	0.1
18–24 years	6,549	53.5	27.5	16.6	2.3	0.2
25–44 years	28,017	49.1	31.2	16.9	2.6	0.3
45–64 years	16,668	38.1	30.2	24.8	5.5	1.4
65 years and over	3,476	25.1	25.8	30.9	11.9	6.3

[Data are based on household interviews of the civilian noninstitutionalized population.]

*Includes unknown health status.

Source: U.S. Department of Health and Human Services, National Center for Health Statistics, *Current Estimates from the National Health Interview Survey, 1988* (Washington, D.C.: DHHS, 1989), p. 115.

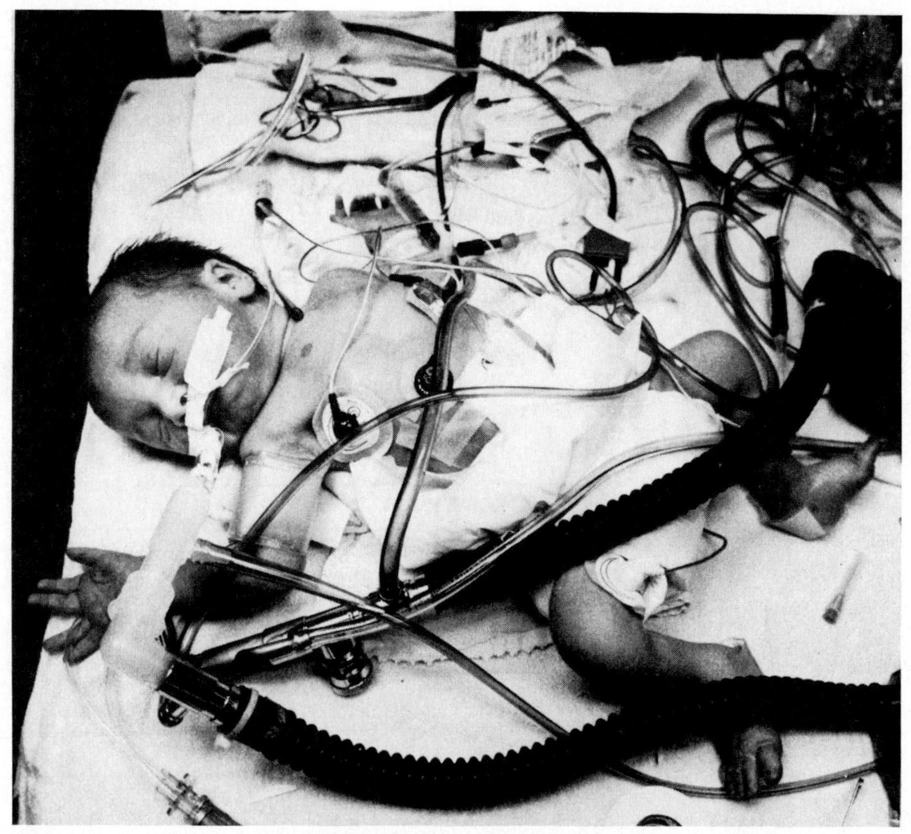

Twenty other nations have lower rates of infant mortality than does the United States. Many of the infants who die in their first year of life are born premature, such as the little boy shown in this photograph who is hospitalized in an intensive care unit. Widespread poverty and lack of access to affordable, quality health care help keep U.S. rates of infant mortality high. *(AP/Wide World)*

> lifestyle of the disadvantaged (e.g., cultural values and individual behavior).[8]

In other words, are low-income people to be blamed for their ill health and premature deaths, or are external factors—largely outside their control—responsible?

Most Americans are mentally and physically capable of taking some steps, no matter how minor, to enhance or protect their health status. Indeed, we have witnessed a striking increase of public interest in ways to maintain health and prolong life.[9] The prevalence of cigarette smoking and consumption of hard liquor have gone down. People have been making dietary changes (e.g., eating less red meat and more vegetables). Engagement in exercise such as walking, running, and aerobics has become more frequent. More people are monitoring their blood pressures, cholesterol levels, and weight. Yet despite the publicity we see in the mass media, not everyone is equally involved.

---

[8]Ibid., pp. 37–38.

[9]See Barry Glassner, *Bodies* (New York: Putnam Publishing Group, 1988).

TABLE 11.3 Number of Days per Person per Year and Number of Days of Activity Restriction Due to Acute and Chronic Conditions, by Type of Restriction and Sociodemographic Characteristics: United States, 1988

	All restrictions		Bed disability		Work or school loss*	
Age	Days per person	No. of days (in thousands)	Days per person	No. of days (in thousands)	Days per person	No. of days (in thousands)
	Family Income: Less than $10,000					
All ages	**26.6**	**754,378**	**12.2**	**346,753**	**7.1**	**86,589**
Under 5 years	14.3	37,158	8.1	20,910	—	—
5–17 years	11.6	60,054	5.9	30,343	7.2	37,167
18 years and over	31.9	657,165	14.3	295,500	7.1	49,422
18–24 years	11.9	60,116	5.4	27,098	4.7	11,454
25–44 years	23.1	136,624	10.3	10,653	8.8	26,078
45–64 years	54.0	190,116	26.3	92,601	8.1	90,038
65 years and over	43.9	270,309	18.7	115,149	6.3	2,853
	$10,000–$19,999					
All ages	**17.8**	**750,829**	**7.9**	**333,922**	**6.1**	**150,587**
Under 5 years	9.2	31,083	5.2	17,679	—	—
5–17 years	9.5	70,293	4.4	32,389	5.2	38,289
18 years and over	20.7	649,452	9.1	283,853	6.5	112,297
18–24 years	10.4	52,488	4.3	21,794	5.0	17,883
25–44 years	17.1	200,179	6.9	80,858	7.0	62,953
45–64 years	26.1	180,772	11.2	77,451	7.1	26,639
65 years and over	28.1	216,014	13.5	103,750	5.5	4,822
	$20,000–$34,999					
All ages	**12.3**	**733,602**	**4.9**	**292,823**	**5.4**	**229,949**
Under 5 years	9.9	49,530	4.6	22,950	—	—
5–17 years	8.2	96,579	3.6	42,187	4.6	54,438
18 years and over	13.7	587,492	5.3	227,687	5.7	175,511
18–24 years	9.2	49,776	3.6	19,160	5.2	22,096
25–44 years	11.1	239,414	4.2	91,090	5.5	100,715
45–64 years	16.2	174,994	6.0	65,108	6.4	48,228
65 years and over	23.7	123,309	10.1	52,329	5.5	4,471
	$35,000 or more					
All ages	**9.7**	**725,634**	**3.8**	**287,547**	**4.3**	**250,988**
Under 5 years	10.6	55,751	4.9	25,745	—	—
5–17 years	8.6	128,114	3.9	57,785	4.4	66,115
18 years and over	9.9	541,769	3.7	204,018	4.2	184,873
18–24 years	6.9	45,067	2.6	16,859	3.9	20,474
25–44 years	8.9	250,122	3.1	87,363	4.2	102,679
45–64 years	10.7	177,728	3.6	60,422	4.3	56,856
65 years and over	19.8	68,851	11.3	39,374	5.7	4,864

[Data are based on household interviews of the civilian noninstitutionalized population.]

*Sum of school-loss days for children 5–17 years of age and work-loss days for currently employed persons 18 years of age and over. School-loss days are shown for the age group 5–17 years; work-loss days are shown for the age group 18 years and over and each older age group.

Source: U.S. Department of Health and Human Services, National Center for Health Statistics, *Current Estimates from the National Health Interview Survey, 1988* (Washington, D.C.: DHHS, 1989), p. 113.

Tens of millions of poor and near-poor Americans of all ages are largely outside of and unengaged in such activity. Perhaps they should not be, but they are.

However, holding those with low incomes to blame for their health status can easily be a form of "blaming the victim."[10] It implies they bring their own lower life expectancies and higher rates of infant mortality on themselves; thus, they could be collectively healthier with some simple changes in life-style. This would be fine were it not for a growing body of evidence showing the direct link between income level and the nature and quality of the work and living environments to which people are daily exposed. To put it bluntly, the more money you make, the better able you are to avoid exposure to the kinds of hazards and stresses that affect your health negatively. As will become evident, the kinds of life-style alterations that have grown popular among more affluent Americans fail to address the underlying causes of health problems for millions.

Consider the work environment. Those jobs that provide the lowest economic returns tend to be the most physically taxing and hazardous in terms of what workers are exposed to. Imagine going to work in the kinds of jobs where over 14,000 employees die each year, another 100,000 die prematurely, and an additional 400,000 suffer illness from occupationally related diseases. These kinds of tragedies should elicit outrage because they are largely preventable. But neither private-sector employers nor government agencies have seen fit to take the necessary steps toward prevention.[11] The results of this negligence are inflicted on low-status, low-wage workers in factories and other work sites across the country.

Low-wage workers are also more likely than others to be in the least secure jobs, for example, seasonal positions and those subject to reductions in force with the shifting economic climate. In an earlier chapter we commented on some of the impacts of unemployment. Not only is the experience of unemployment associated with health problems—from cardiovascular difficulties to ulcers—the loss of income often has an impact on the unemployed workers' ability to afford adequate health care. As we shall see later, the jobless are among the 37 million Americans with no health care insurance to help pay for treatment for themselves and their families.[12]

But it is not only the work setting that is more problematic for the health status of low-income people than that of the more affluent. Living conditions, too, can be fraught with dangers. Workers exposed to hazardous substances on the job can bring them home on their clothing or bodies, thus endangering others in the household, including children. People living in areas subject to particularly concentrated levels of air pollution (e.g., urban poverty dwellers) are put at high risk for such diseases as lung cancer, emphysema, and bronchitis. The failure of absentee landlords to take an interest in the health and safety aspects of their housing property contributes to lead poisoning from paint chips, the spread of disease by rats and insects, sanitation problems due to inadequate waste disposal, fires, and accidents.

The serious shortage of affordable housing for low-income people not only discourages tenant complaints and household moves; it also forces many families to double and even triple up so that they can afford shelter (even at the risk of eviction). Overcrowded living conditions contribute to stresses that lower immunity to illness as well as facilitate the spread of infectious diseases.

The abuse of alcohol and other drugs is for

---

[10]See William Ryan, *Blaming the Victim* (New York: Random House, 1972).

[11]See Daniel Berman, *Death on the Job* (New York: Monthly Review Press, 1978).

[12]See "Forgotten Patients," *Newsweek* (August 22, 1988): 52–53.

some a way to cope with the reality of the kind of living environment we have been describing. It is a reality that often is also permeated by the threat of criminal victimization. It can be a depressing reality, filled with grayish images of dirt, trash, and physical decline. It may be a reality that imposes a sharp sense of social isolation and alienation from the wider society. Substance abuse may offer an escape from all this, but it carries negative ramifications for health. Users' health may be endangered. The violence against others in and outside of the home, stemming from the abuse of alcohol and certain illegal drugs (e.g., amphetamines, "crack" cocaine, PCP), is now considered a major public health issue.

Our homes are supposed to be places where we can go to be emotionally replenished, and nutritionally replenished as well. As we saw in an earlier chapter, for millions of Americans the home provides little in the way of nutritional replenishment. Insufficient food, or the ability to afford only foods that are minimally balanced nutritionally, is a fact of life for too many low-income people. Obesity, a health-threatening condition, often afflicts those whose diets are overloaded with inexpensive starches and carbohydrates. On the other hand, the absence of food in homes has produced the hunger described in shocking reports in recent years. Most at risk are women (including pregnant women), small children, and the elderly.[13]

But we also know that not all Americans have homes. And the estimated 2 million to 3 million homeless are beset by serious health problems. Many of these problems stem from malnutrition, stress, fatigue, contact with others' infectious diseases, exposure to unsanitary conditions, and difficulty maintaining personal hygiene. Injury from accidents or others' violent behavior and illness from exposure to the elements are among the environmental threats faced by homeless people. Increasingly the homeless include women and their children. Even AIDS victims, too ill to work, evicted from their dwellings, and shunned by family and friends, are being found on America's streets! The failure of this society to provide affordable housing for all its members, and the inability of the homeless to do anything about their situation, demonstrates how health problems are organized into existence at the lower levels of the class structure.

People whose home environments, neighborhoods, and work settings are hostile to psychological and physical well-being require more than superficial life-style changes if their health status is to improve. The homeless are unlikely to find that jogging or aerobics addresses the sources of their health difficulties. The hungry are unlikely to be concerned with keeping their cholesterol levels down and will understandably eat anything they can get their hands on. While the affluent can afford to take steps to avoid even minor maladies, many low-income people are trying to figure out how to survive life-threatening environments. Until such conditions are changed, the sharp class differences in health status will continue unabated.

A NOTE ON HEALTH AND RACE

Minority group members in this society are subject to serious maltreatment and disadvantage, as we saw in Chapter 8, "Racism." As we consider the unequal health status of Americans, it is important to note that not only class but race as well is correlated with health status. This is clear if we take our society's largest racial minority, black Americans, as an example.

If America's infant mortality rates are higher than they have any reason to be, then the rates for black Americans are most shocking. For whites the rate is 10 infant deaths per 1,000. It is twice as high for black infants! Equally saddening and disturbing are data indicating sharp

[13]See Larry J. Brown and H. F. Pizer, *Living Hungry in America* (New York: New American Library, 1989).

racial differences in life expectancy. White females born in 1986 can expect to live 78.8 years, compared to 73.5 years for black females. In contrast to white males' life expectancy of 72 years, black males can expect only 65.2 years of life. Available data indicate that from 1984 to 1986 the life expectancy of black males actually went down, rather than up as was the case with other groups.[14]

The life expectancy rate of black Americans is lowered by inclusion of their higher rates of infant mortality. But reports provided by the National Center on Health Statistics, a federal agency, reveal that blacks have higher rates of death than whites from almost all causes. To some degree this may be explained in terms of the disproportionate presence of black Americans in the lowest income levels of the class structure. However, some would argue that treatment of people by race, apart from their class position, exacts an additional toll.[15]

AMERICA'S HEALTH CARE SYSTEM

The United States has the most expensive health care system in the world. It consumes over 11 percent of our gross national product (GNP) at this time, up from 7.4 percent in 1970.[16] (See Table 11.4.) No other nation spends as much per capita as we do. Yet, as has been discussed, our health status falls short of what we might expect given these expenditures. This cannot be explained wholly with reference to failings in our life-styles or even the harsh environmental circumstances endured by many low-income people. We must examine what role America's health care system itself plays in all this.

Among all industrialized societies in the Western world, only the United States and South Africa have no comprehensive system of national health insurance or national health service providing care for all. Other nations—from Canada to West Germany—take the position that health care is a basic human right and provide universal coverage to all their citizens. Only in the United States is the task of securing health care left up to the individual to such an extent. Our system is oriented largely around a "pay-as-you-go" mentality, and health care is considered a commodity that must be purchased if it is to be consumed. Unfortunately, not all Americans are in a position to buy. (Table 11.5 summarizes this situation.)

Three-quarters of Americans under age sixty-five, some 160 million people, are covered by some type of private health insurance. Typically it is obtained through one's employer, who shares part of the costs. Where this is not the case, the individual must pay the full insurance premium. Insurance costs have gone up significantly in recent years, as health care itself has grown more and more expensive. Employers, faced with inroads on their profit margins due to rising insurance costs, have been struggling to shift a greater share of the costs to employees.

It is also the case that most private insurance plans are very limited in terms of their coverage—for example, some do not cover the children of employees. Nor do such plans cover the full costs of different medical services that may be called for by doctors and hospitals. In all such cases, individuals must pay for part of their expenses out of their pockets. Americans are now finding it increasingly difficult to afford the type and quality of care they need. Many have no choice but to exhaust their savings, go heavily into debt, or even sell their homes. In the United States, unlike other West-

[14]U.S. Department of Health and Human Services, *Health, United States, 1988,* p. 53.

[15]Wornie L. Reed, "Suffer the Children: Some Effects of Racism on the Health of Black Infants," in Peter Conrad and Rochelle Kern, eds., *The Sociology of Health and Illness,* 2d ed. (New York: St. Martin's Press, 1986), pp. 272–80.

[16]U.S. Department of Health and Human Services, *Health, United States, 1988,* p. 151.

TABLE 11.4 National Health Expenditures, 1970–86

	Total*			Health services and supplies							
				Private				Public			
					Direct patient payments			Total‡		Medical payments	
Year	Total (billions of dollars)	Per capita (dollars)	Percent of GNP	Total† (billions of dollars)	Total (billions of dollars)	Percent of total private	Insurance premiums (billions of dollars)	Total (billions of dollars)	Percent of total health expenses	Medicare (billions of dollars)	Public assistance (billions of dollars)
1970	75.0	349	7.4	44.7	26.5	59.3	16.9	24.9	33.2	7.5	6.3
1971	83.5	384	7.6	48.9	28.1	57.4	19.3	28.4	34.0	8.3	8.1
1972	94.0	428	7.7	55.3	30.6	55.4	22.2	32.1	34.1	9.1	9.1
1973	103.4	467	7.6	60.7	33.3	54.8	24.7	35.8	34.6	10.1	10.3
1974	116.1	521	7.9	65.8	36.2	55.0	27.9	42.9	36.9	13.1	12.1
1975	132.7	590	8.3	73.0	38.1	52.2	33.2	51.3	38.6	16.3	15.1
1976	150.8	665	8.5	84.5	42.0	49.8	40.4	57.3	38.0	19.3	16.9
1977	169.9	743	8.5	96.7	46.4	48.1	48.0	64.0	37.7	22.5	18.9
1978	189.7	822	8.4	106.6	50.7	47.6	53.6	73.3	38.7	25.9	21.1
1979	214.7	921	8.6	120.4	55.8	46.4	62.0	83.8	39.0	30.3	24.3
1980	248.1	1,054	9.1	138.7	63.0	45.5	72.6	97.5	39.3	36.8	28.1
1981	287.0	1,207	9.4	160.6	72.6	45.2	84.4	113.2	39.4	44.8	32.3
1982	323.6	1,348	10.2	182.2	79.6	43.7	98.7	127.1	39.3	52.4	34.9
1983	357.2	1,473	10.5	202.8	88.7	43.7	109.7	138.9	38.9	58.9	37.7
1984	391.1	1,597	10.4	224.7	98.4	43.8	121.5	150.8	38.6	64.4	38.3
1985	422.6	1,710	10.6	240.7	105.3	43.7	130.1	166.5	39.4	72.3	42.2
1986	458.2	1,837	10.9	262.5	116.1	44.2	140.7	179.5	39.2	77.7	45.8

[Includes Puerto Rico and outlying areas]
*Includes medical research and medical facilities construction.
†Includes other sources of funds, not shown separately.
‡Includes other programs, not shown separately.
Source: U.S. Department of Commerce, Bureau of the Census, *Statistical Abstract of the United States, 1989* (Washington, D.C.: U.S. Government Printing Office, 1989), p. 90.

TABLE 11.5 Health Care Coverage for Persons Under 65 Years of Age as a Percentage of the Population, by Type of Coverage and Selected Characteristics: United States, 1980, 1982, and 1986

	Private Insurance			Medicaid*			Not covered†		
Characteristic	1980	1982	1985	1980	1982	1986	1980	1982	1986
Total‡,§	**78.8**	**77.3**	**75.9**	**5.9**	**5.6**	**5.9**	**12.5**	**14.7**	**15.3**
Age									
Under 15 years	74.7	72.7	71.4	10.2	9.8	10.4	12.8	15.8	16.1
Under 5 years	70.3	69.7	68.0	12.0	11.4	12.0	15.2	17.0	17.5
5–14 years	76.7	74.2	73.1	9.4	8.9	9.5	11.7	15.2	15.3
15–44 years	79.3	77.6	75.8	4.2	4.1	4.1	14.2	16.5	17.4
45–64 years	83.6	83.1	82.4	3.1	2.7	3.0	8.6	9.7	10.3
Sex‡									
Male	79.5	78.0	76.4	4.7	4.5	4.8	12.7	14.8	15.8
Female	78.2	76.7	75.4	7.1	6.6	6.8	12.2	14.5	14.9
Race‡									
White	81.9	80.4	79.1	3.9	3.6	4.0	11.4	13.5	14.0
Black	60.1	59.6	57.0	17.9	17.2	17.4	19.0	21.2	22.6
Family income‡,¶									
Less than $10,000	38.6	38.3	31.3	27.6	24.9	28.4	31.0	35.0	37.0
$10,000–$14,999	61.1	67.6	58.1	9.2	4.4	8.8	25.9	24.7	31.3
$15,000–$19,999	79.0	81.3	72.6	3.0	2.0	2.7	15.0	14.2	21.2
$20,000–$34,999	90.2	91.8	88.3	1.1	0.7	1.0	6.2	5.7	8.4
$35,000 or more	93.7	93.8	93.7	0.6	0.5	0.4	3.9	4.1	3.9

[Data are based on household interviews of a sample of the civilian noninstitutionalized population. Percents do not add to 100 because the percent with other types of health insurance (e.g., Medicare, military) and unknown health insurance are not shown, and because persons with both private insurance and Medicaid appear in both columns.]

*Includes persons receiving Aid to Families with Dependent Children or Supplemental Security Income or those with current Medicaid cards.

†Includes persons not covered by private insurance, Medicaid, Medicare, and military plans.

‡Age adjusted.

§Includes all other races not shown separately and unknown family income.

¶Family income categories for 1982 and 1986. Income categories in 1980 are less than $7,000; $7,000–$9,999; $10,000–$14,999; $15,000–$24,999; $25,000 or more.

Source: U.S. Department of Health and Human Services, *Health, United States, 1988* (Washington, D.C.: U.S. Government Printing Office, 1989), p. 171.

ern industrialized nations, citizens who suffer from poor health may be allowed to plummet into poverty.

Those able to secure private health insurance are among the fortunate. Some 37 million Americans have no health insurance at all, not even the limited coverage provided certain categories of people under government programs (to be discussed shortly). And the ranks of these uninsured people have been growing. The figure of 37 million represents an increase of 11 million over the last decade.[17] Most of these people are workers and their families. Their employers tend to be smaller businesses that do not provide any health benefits. Others of the uninsured are self-employed persons who cannot afford to pay the premiums. Still others have no jobs or are between jobs and have lost their insurance. The poor, minority group mem-

[17]"Forgotten Patients," p. 52.

bers, young adults, and rural dwellers are disproportionately represented among the uninsured.[18]

The result of having one in six Americans walking around completely responsible for paying for their health care is predictable. If people cannot afford to pay for care, they will ignore symptoms and likely end up in even greater distress. A study by the Robert Wood Johnson Foundation found that insured people experiencing chest pain or unexplained bleeding are likely to seek out medical help. Uninsured people are not.[19] One can only imagine the results of "toughing it out."

In 1965 the U.S. government agreed to finance a health insurance plan for Americans aged sixty-five years and older. Known as Medicare, this plan now covers some 32 million people. As older Americans are quite aware, Medicare falls far short of paying the full costs of health care. There are restrictions on just what services will be covered by insurance (e.g., the length of hospitalization). As a consequence, the elderly have found themselves squeezed by rising health care costs just like all other Americans. Most must supplement their Medicare coverage with private insurance in a quest for some semblance of protection in their "golden years." For many persons sixty-five and older, health expenses have become an increasing burden each year.

Also in 1965 the federal government adopted a plan in which it would, in cooperation with the states, jointly fund a program aimed at addressing the health needs of the poor. This program is called Medicaid, and it is riddled with serious problems that get in the way of meeting these needs. For example, since by law physicians may not charge poor patients more than Medicaid is willing to pay for services, and since this amount can be low, many doctors refuse to take Medicaid patients! Other problems stem from eligibility criteria, which vary across the individual states. In 1988 a family of four living in the state of New York could not have an annual income over $7,704 (substantially below the official poverty line) and still be eligible for Medicaid. In Alabama, an income over $4,248 would disqualify such a family.[20]

Medicaid coverage is extended automatically to adults and children participating in Aid to Families with Dependent Children, more commonly known as "welfare." But many persons below the official poverty line—out of lack of knowledge, ineligibility, or principle—are not welfare recipients and are thus cut off from this route to Medicaid coverage. The net result of all this is that only a minority of the poor in this country participate in the Medicaid program, and those who do participate find it hard to locate physicians willing to treat them.

Many of those who go uninsured or inadequately covered are women and children. Concerned about the high rates of infant death in the United States, the U.S. Congress created a National Commission to Prevent Infant Mortality. The Commission reported that 26 percent of those women who are of childbearing age have no maternity insurance coverage. Millions of infants and young children go uncovered by insurance even when a parent in the home works. This is a recipe for disaster, a disaster clearly reflected in the statistics described earlier in this chapter.

The pay-as-you-go system of health care, as we have seen, weighs heavily on the backs of individual citizens. And those who suffer the worst health status—persons at the bottom levels of the class structure—are least able to afford care. Economic disadvantage effectively functions as a barrier to access to the existing health care system. But what of the system itself? In ways we shall address, attributes of the health care system form barriers to its utilization.

The core of America's health care system, at

[18]Ibid.
[19]Ibid.
[20]Ibid.

least in this century, has traditionally been the private physician.[21] Active physicians number some 500,000 today, most functioning in individual and group practice (others work for government agencies or business employers). Most private physicians are affiliated with hospitals that are available to assist them in patient care. This group of people—one physician for every 500 Americans—on the face of it seems adequate in size to take care of everyone's health needs. Yet there exists what we shall call an "artificial doctor shortage." Let us explain.

With some qualifications, we can say that in general physicians in our pay-as-you-go system of health care are out to make money. If the average incomes they receive are any indicator, they are quite successful in reaching this goal. To be successful they must, like any other businessperson, locate a profitable market for their services. Running a medical practice alone or in concert with others is an expensive undertaking (not to mention the need of new physicians to pay off education debts). Making money means going to those areas where people's income levels and private insurance plan coverage are high, and where affiliation with a quality hospital or clinic is easily accomplished. As physicians flock to these areas, they in effect create an artificial doctor shortage in other areas. Rural communities, small towns, and inner-city poverty areas suffer the most from this shortage. Much like underdeveloped countries, America suffers an internal "brain drain" of medical talent away from areas of need and to areas where physicians prefer to locate.

This brain drain operates in another dimension as well. Particularly since World War II there has been a trend for physicians to become specialized within the medical profession. Today, only a minority function as general practitioners, or "family doctors." In part this has occurred due to the explosion of knowledge and growth of advanced technology available for use in the health field. No one can keep up with everything, and specialization has occurred just as in many other fields (including sociology).

Yet other factors have been at work as well in promoting the specialization trend. The number of physicians has been on the increase, particularly since the 1970s. We have 500,000 today; in 1970 there were only 279,000. Even higher figures are projected into the future. With the growth in numbers of physicians, the threat of competition among them has increased. Specialization is in part a way of sidestepping this threat. (See Table 11.6.) Physicians who specialize lay claim to providing unique services for which they are able to command respectable fees. But this skewing of physicians toward "limited practice" involving their technical specialties means that far fewer Americans today have access to primary care by physicians interested in their overall well-being.

Victor and Ruth Sidel define a primary care physician as

> a physician based in the community rather than in a hospital; a physician people first turn to, who does not regularly see referrals from other physicians; who provides continuing care rather than episodic care; and who serves the function of integrating the work of referral specialists and other community resources in relation to the patients' care.[22]

Most physicians today are not engaged in primary care but are pursuing their specialties. They treat a particular part of the body of those who appear before them, often with the assistance of extremely expensive and complex technology that is more and more likely to be hospital-based. This situation simply aggravates the artificial doctor shortage confronted by those whose needs first and foremost lie with primary care.

---

[21] Paul Starr, *The Social Transformation of American Medicine* (New York: Basic Books, 1982).

[22] Victor W. Sidel and Ruth Sidel, "Health Care and Medical Care in the United States," in Conrad and Kern, *The Sociology of Health and Illness*, p. 175.

TABLE 11.6 Physicians, by Sex, Specialty, and Major Professional Activity, as of December 31, 1970–86 (Numbers in Thousands)

	1970					1986						
						Total		Patient care				
										Hospital-based		
Specialty	Total	Percent	1975, total	1980, total	1985, total	Number	Percent	Total	Office-based	Full-time	Residents*	Other professional†
Total‡	**334.0§**	**100.0**	**393.7§**	**467.7§**	**552.7§**	**569.2§**	**100.0**	**462.1**	**327.0**	**46.4**	**88.7**	**43.6**
Male	(NA)	(NA)	358.1§	413.4§	472.0§	482.5§	84.8	391.8	289.4	37.6	64.8	37.2
Female	(NA)	(NA)	35.6§	54.3§	80.7§	86.7§	15.2	70.3	37.6	8.8	23.9	6.5
General practice	57.9	17.3	54.6	60.0	67.1	67.7	11.9	65.6	54.1	4.0	7.5	2.1
Internal medicine	41.9	12.5	54.3	71.5	90.4	91.3	16.0	81.2	52.5	6.9	21.8	10.2
Pediatrics	17.9	5.4	21.7	28.3	35.6	36.5	6.4	33.1	22.6	3.2	7.3	3.4
General surgery	29.8	8.9	31.6	34.0	38.2	37.2	6.5	35.6	23.6	2.7	9.3	1.6
Obstetrics, gynecology	18.9	5.7	21.7	26.3	30.9	31.4	5.5	30.2	23.6	1.7	4.9	1.1
Orthopedic surgery	9.6	2.9	11.4	14.0	17.2	17.7	3.1	17.2	13.1	1.0	3.2	.4
Ophthalmology	9.9	3.0	11.1	13.0	14.9	15.2	2.7	14.7	12.1	.6	2.0	.5
Psychiatry	21.1	6.3	23.9	27.5	32.3	32.7	5.7	29.4	18.3	5.8	5.3	3.3
Anesthesiology	10.1	3.0	12.9	16.0	22.0	23.1	4.1	22.1	15.3	2.6	4.2	1.1
Pathology	10.3	3.1	11.7	13.4	15.5	15.5	2.7	12.4	6.6	3.2	2.7	3.1
Radiology	10.5	3.1	11.5	11.7	10.1	8.3	1.5	7.8	6.1	1.3	.3	.6

Key: NA, not available.
[Includes Puerto Rico and outlying areas.]
*Includes interns and, beginning 1986, clinical fellows (10,761).
†Medical teaching, administration, research, and other.
‡Includes other specialties not shown separately.
§Includes physicians who are inactive, not classified, or with address unknown.
Source: U.S. Department of Commerce, Bureau of the Census, *Statistical Abstract of the United States, 1989* (Washington D.C.: U.S. Government Printing Office, 1989), p. 99.

One consequence is that poor people use the health care system less than they should, given their actual health needs. Unable to afford to pay private physicians for care, lacking adequate health insurance, and faced with a shortage of doctors oriented toward primary care, those with low incomes often put off contact with physicians until their conditions are seriously disabling. Many have no choice but to use the hospital emergency room in lieu of any other alternative, enduring long delays, assembly-line treatment by overworked and rushed staff, and lack of follow-up after treatment. The hospitals are strained by the poor—they had to provide $13 billion in uncompensated care in 1986 alone. These "charity" costs are then passed on to private insurance providers in the form of higher costs for services provided to the insured. The private insurance providers in turn raise their rates. In this way the plight of the poor is passed on to employers and employees who are already beleaguered by rising health care costs.

Other barriers to quality care facing the poor include corruption. Some medical practitioners of few scruples have chosen to milk government programs like Medicaid for as much money as they can get, no matter what effect this has on their patients. Since physicians customarily receive a fee for every service provided a patient, and since the government pays for every fee submitted, abuse of the system has occurred. Some physicians have made a practice of rad-

PUBLIC PROBLEM, PRIVATE PAIN

Caring for the Poorest

Many Americans today lack access to even basic health care services. In this selection we learn of a physician who is struggling valiantly to help the rural poor, even while government programs in support of such efforts are allowed to dwindle.

There aren't many doctors like Ronald Myers, a jazz-playing, Baptist-preaching family practitioner whose dream has always been to practice medicine in the kind of place most other doctors wouldn't even stop for a tank of gas.

But there are plenty of places like Tchula, a forlorn patch of Mississippi Delta poverty where it is hard to find a street that's not rutted, a sign that's not crooked, a paint job that's not peeling or a life that's not perched on the brink of economic ruin.

Dr. Myers's story—how hard it has been for him to get here and how hard it may be for him to stay—provides a dispiriting look at health care in rural America. The situation is worsening because the Government's program to provide doctors for the nation's neediest areas is being dismantled as health care needs continue to grow.

"Working in Tchula, Miss., is like working in a third world country," said Dr. Myers, who became Tchula's only doctor when he opened a clinic this month in an abandoned restaurant next to an empty liquor store. "The needs are that great. So how is it that here's a well-trained physician who wants to come to an area that's desperately poor, and I can't get any assistance? I can't get a loan. I'll take a tongue depressor if someone will give me one. There's a problem somewhere."

In poor rural areas, particularly in the South, regular medical care is seldom more than a distant dream. In areas like Tchula and nearby Belzoni, where Dr. Myers previously worked, infant mortality rates are three times the national average, most women receive little if any prenatal care and people usually see a doctor only when they have no choice.

"The health problems in this area are staggering," said Dr. Henry Bartee, who operated a practice here before giving it up two years ago and now practices 12 miles away in Lexington. "I would say 70 percent of the people who walk through the door are either hypertensive or they have diabetes. Many have significant heart disease and their cholesterol levels are all sky high. A lot of people have never had a Pap smear, a breast examination or a pelvic or rectal exam."

It is a common story, especially in the South. In Tennessee, the state says, more than a third of the 95 counties have no doctors who deliver babies and almost half do not have enough doctors to provide adequate basic health care. In South Carolina, all but 9 of the 47 counties have doctor shortages, and the state says it needs 225 family practitioners, obstetricians and pediatricians.

'I FEEL RIGHT BEING HERE'

Dr. Myers is rare in his profession, a physician who went to a good deal of trouble to practice where no one else would. A 33-year old Milwaukeean who graduated from the University of Wisconsin Medical School, an accomplished jazz pianist and an ordained Baptist minister, he said coming to the rural South was always his goal in medicine.

Tchula has 2,000 people, and the population of the area served by Dr. Myers's clinic is 4,500. Mayor Jessie D. Banks says 70 percent of the town is unemployed in winter, when there is no agricultural work to be found.

Dr. Myers began work in Belzoni a year and a half ago as part of his agreement with the National Health Services Corps, which pays a year's worth of medical school costs for each year the recipient agrees to serve in an underserved area.

While he served at a clinic there, he saw that the need was even greater in Tchula, 21 miles away, where there was no doctor at all. He decided to set up his own clinic in Tchula, using money he had made working overtime at emergency rooms, and to work there in the evening after spending his days at Belzoni.

The Federal Public Health Service, which oversees the program, told him he was not authorized

PUBLIC PROBLEM, PRIVATE PAIN (continued)

to practice in Tchula and ordered him to stay in Belzoni. Officials told him that they did not think a medical practice could survive in Tchula and that doctors fare better when they can take advantage of existing health care organizations.

TOO POOR TO SUPPORT A PRACTICE?

Undeterred, Dr. Myers took his fight to elected officials and the Mississippi news media, winning so much attention that the Public Health Service relented. He now operates full-time in Tchula while living in a double-wide trailer in Belzoni.

But getting permission to be in Tchula was only half the battle. To cobble together his clinic, he has had to rely on makeshift financing, advances from medical suppliers and his own wits. He has no lab equipment and does his own urinalysis under a microscope.

Dr. Bartee thinks that all this is in vain, that Tchula may be too poor to support a physician. "The patients he will be seeing will primarily be indigent, Medicare-Medicaid patients, and it's almost impossible to make a living just seeing those patients," Dr. Bartee said. "He's got to have some outside help."

Dr. Myers wonders why the Government does not encourage the doctors it brings to rural areas to stay there by helping them set up practices. But increasingly, the problem is not keeping rural doctors but getting them there in the first place.

Started in 1972, the National Health Services Corps has placed more than 13,000 doctors in the nation's most underserved communities. But its financing has been slashed from $79.5 million in the 1980 fiscal year to $7.5 million in 1990, and six doctors leave the program for every one who enters it. Now it is unclear whether the program will survive at all. Its plight reflects both the Reagan-era budget cutbacks and an assumption that turned out to be erroneous: that because there was a nation-wide oversupply of doctors, large numbers would stay in the rural areas where they were placed.

"It was hoped that natural diffusion would take care of a lot of our needs," said Joseph Hayden, the corps's associate director. "But it didn't." Today's needs, he went on, "are just as great now as they were in 1980."

Source: Peter Applebome, "Rural Doctor's Struggle to Care for the Poorest," *New York Times* (February 12, 1990): A1 and B11.

ically escalating the number of patients they see daily, spending only a few cursory minutes with each. They have insisted on unnecessary return visits, ordered hosts of tests, and written prescriptions that were not needed. In effect, they have exploited the vulnerability and medical powerlessness of the poor for private gain. The tragedy is compounded when one realizes that many such patients have access to the health care system only through these white-collar criminals.

Should they require hospitalization, those without insurance or with the kind of limited coverage provided by Medicaid face new barriers to the best care. Privately owned hospitals, an increasing percentage of which are turning into for-profit institutions, do not want such patients in their beds. There is pressure within such settings to transfer them—even out of emergency rooms—to public hospitals or those affiliated with university medical schools. In the case of public hospitals, staffing, facilities, and level of technology are prone to be in need of improvement due to severe financial strains in the face of rising costs. A number of public hospitals have simply had to close down in recent years, unable to maintain acceptable standards on the budgets they had to work with. The level of care in public hospitals, then, is likely to be less adequate than in more fiscally prosperous private institutions.

Low-income people often do not have ready access to affordable health care, and in many cases must use hospital emergency rooms like the more affluent use their family doctor. There is, of course, likely to be an enormous difference between the quality of the care experiences involved. For many individuals and families there is no choice in the matter. *(David Powers/ Stock, Boston)*

In the case of university-affiliated hospitals, poor patients frequently are informally segregated and treated by doctors in training, medical school graduates working extraordinarily long hours for little pay simply to gain experience with different types of cases. If a low-income person presents a case that is "interesting" or "unusual," he or she probably will get special attention. Otherwise this may not be the situation. In neither kind of hospital is the low-income patient likely to receive the personalized care and expressions of concern expected from one's own private doctor by more affluent, appropriately insured people.

Thus, the economically disadvantaged often must use hospitals (due to health conditions grown serious and lack of primary-care physicians) that offer an unpleasant experience, to say the least. The world of health care for low-income people is often disjointed, confusing, frustrating, and alienating. Lacking transportation, in need of child care, unable to leave work for erratic medical appointments, and faced with the possibility of second-rate treatment, even people who know they should seek help are discouraged from doing so. The results appear in the sanitized government statistics that are made public each year.

In the words of Karen Davis and Diane Rowland,

> It strains our image as a just and humane society when significant portions of the population endure avoidable pain, suffering, and even death because of an inability to pay for health care.[23]

Ironically, while these avoidable outcomes continue, the American health care system is evolv-

[23]Karen Davis and Diane Rowland, "Uninsured and Underserved: Inequities in Health Care in the United States," in Conrad and Kern, *The Sociology of Health and Illness*, p. 251.

ing into what some call a "medical–industrial complex."[24] Given the enormous amounts of money spent on health, now over $500 billion annually, it is understandable that astute businesspeople (including many doctors) would seek new ways to capitalize on this.

The elements of the medical–industrial complex are still in the process of emerging, but they include:

Increases in the number of investor-owned private hospitals;

Growth in the size of firms that lease or own hospitals that are run as chains;

Private investor and corporate expansion into nursing homes, home health services, and local surgical centers and clinics;

Movement by investor-owned hospitals into such areas as private health insurance.

Arnold S. Relman asks an obvious question:

> When a single investor-owned corporation sells the insurance, owns all the facilities and services covered by the insurance, and employs or contracts with the physicians who deliver the services, what will happen to the quality, accessibility, and cost of health care?[25]

Some predict that by the mid-1990s large hospital-owning firms, operating for profit, will control 30–60 percent of all hospitals in the United States, up from 6 percent in 1975.[26] This means more than the "McDonaldization" of health care. Such moves toward concentrated ownership hold dangers for those already ill served by America's health care system. Investor-owned health care corporations are not charitable organizations; they are motivated by the same bottom-line profit goals as Ford Motor Company or Philip Morris. Thus, there is a tendency for health care corporations to avoid involvement in services that are least profitable (e.g., emergency rooms for the poor) and to expand into those services most in demand in market locations where affluent, insured people are heavily concentrated. There is no law that says for-profit firms must behave charitably toward the uninsured or those dependent on Medicaid. Cost–benefit analyses can be used to determine the kinds of health technology the firms will invest in, with that most likely to generate the most favorable "fees for service" preferred. In other words, it may come to where it doesn't matter what people's health needs are: The corporations will go where the money is. This is just the opposite direction from the philosophy of all other Western industrialized societies. Their systems are aimed at serving the citizenry; people's health misfortunes are not treated as an occasion to enrich the privileged few.

The emergence of the medical–industrial complex throws the traditional power of the medical profession into question. Long in a position of professional dominance and monopoly over medical practice,[27] they are now being challenged by the "corporatization of medicine."[28] Many doctors are in response becoming part of the process itself, through their own private investments and ownership ties to the complex. How this process can bring more equity into America's health care system remains to be seen.

AIDS AND HEALTH CARE

Since 1981, when the first cases were diagnosed, people in the United States and elsewhere around the world have come to fear a new deadly infectious disease syndrome: AIDS (ac-

[24]See Arnold S. Relman, "The New Medical–Industrial Complex," in Howard D. Schwartz, ed., *Dominant Issues in Medical Sociology*, 2d ed. (New York: Random House, 1987), pp. 597–608, and Mimi Abromovitz, "Privatizing Health Care," *The Nation* (October 17, 1987): 410–12.

[25]Relman, "The New Medical–Industrial Complex," p. 607.

[26]Abromovitz, "Privatizing Health Care," p. 410.

[27]See Eliot Freidson, *Professional Dominance: The Social Structure of Medical Care* (New York: Atherton Press, 1970).

[28]Starr, *The Social Transformation of American Medicine*.

quired immune deficiency syndrome). Although the United States leads all other nations in the number of documented cases, AIDS is believed to be potentially far more devastating to populations in underdeveloped nations.[29] At this writing some 112,000 cases have been diagnosed in this country. Since the number of new cases doubles every fourteen to sixteen months, by the time this text is in the hands of users there will likely be a quarter million cases, and a half million by the mid-1990s. The spread of AIDS has justifiably been described as epidemic.

The epidemic is a deadly one. Between 1943 and 1956 the United States was swept by a polio epidemic which killed 22,000 people. Already, in a far shorter time—from 1981 to 1990—over three times as many Americans have died from diseases associated with AIDS. Between 1963 and 1975 some 56,000 Americans were killed in the Vietnam War. More than that have already died because of AIDS. Unchecked, this epidemic could kill millions in the United States. The World Health Organization estimates that tens of millions will die worldwide.[30] Understandably, seven in ten Americans surveyed identify AIDS as the most serious health problem we face today.[31]

As most Americans now know, AIDS is spread by the human immunodeficiency virus (HIV). This virus is readily transmittable from person to person through intimate sexual contact, the sharing of needles by drug users, and less commonly through blood transfusions. Pregnant women who are infected with HIV may pass it on to the fetus, and there are growing numbers of "AIDS babies" being born in American hospitals. The virus can be carried unknowingly and transmitted to others without any party being aware. The symptoms of AIDS often do not appear until five or more years after HIV is passed on. People with the virus may be perfectly healthy until these symptoms begin to occur. A person with HIV does not have AIDS, but it is believed that all such persons will eventually become disease victims.

The virus causing AIDS also causes ARC (AIDS-related complex), a milder but often debilitating syndrome. The symptoms of AIDS and ARC differ primarily in their duration and severity. These symptoms include chronic fatigue, fevers, unexplained weight loss, diarrhea, enlarged lymph nodes, coughs and sore throat, easy bruising, and unusual skin bumps and blotches. Full-blown cases of AIDS are recognized as such when it becomes apparent that a person's natural ability to fight off disease and infection has broken down. Those with AIDS become susceptible to diseases that most people simply never get. Four-fifths of AIDS patients contract such rare illnesses as *Pneumocystis carinii* pneumonia, a parasitic infection of the lungs, or Kaposi's sarcoma, a type of cancer.

The AIDS virus is currently carried by perhaps 1 million to 1.5 million people. In the absence of a national program of screening for HIV infection, these figures are speculative. But the number of new AIDS cases that are appearing each year makes scientists apprehensive about the number of persons with HIV. As the death toll has grown, increasing amounts of money have been going into research related to AIDS. Unfortunately, this has occurred only after a good deal of foot-dragging and delay on the part of federal officials, who resisted acknowledging there was indeed a serious problem meriting national concern.[32]

At present, most of those with AIDS are men who have had sexual relations with other men.

---

[29]Lester R. Brown, *State of the World, 1988* (New York: W. W. Norton & Company, 1988), p. 160.

[30]Lori Heise, "AIDS: New Threat to the Third World," *World Watch* (January–February 1988): 19–27.

[31]Hal Quinley, "The New Facts of Life," *Public Opinion* (May/June 1988): 53–55.

[32]See Randy Shilts, *And the Band Played On: Politics, People, and the AIDS Epidemic* (New York: St. Martin's Press, 1987).

Primarily these are persons whose sexual orientation is either homosexual or bisexual. It is believed that the rate of spread of HIV has slowed among this group, largely due to fear-induced changes in their sexual practices. (We should note that in America's prison population unsanctioned, high-risk, male-to-male sex remains rampant, and the prevalence of HIV is exceptionally high.) The second major group in which AIDS is found all too frequently is in need of much more intervention. This group is made up of intravenous drug users, principally users of cocaine and heroin, who share needles with one another (see Chapter 17, "Drug Abuse"). Although media publicity and even street-level outreach programs have been under way to discourage needle sharing, it remains common.

The view that AIDS is a "gay disease" ignores an important reality: heterosexuals are at risk. The rate at which new AIDS cases are developing among heterosexuals is now identical to the rate for gay people. In both groups the number of cases doubles every fourteen to sixteen months. In most cases the infected heterosexual is an intravenous drug user, has had sexual contact with such a user, or is the child of a user. Families in which someone uses intravenous drugs have been hard hit, and people who patronize drug-using prostitutes are open to infection. In other instances of heterosexual transmission no drug use may be involved; for example, bisexual males may pass HIV on during sexual contact with females. The virus can also be passed on in connection with sexual assaults, including date and acquaintance rapes. Once infected with HIV, persons unknowingly can contribute to expanding the spread of infection within the heterosexual population. Men who patronize prostitutes can bring HIV home to their wives. Women unknowingly infected by bisexual men or as a consequence of sexual assaults can infect other sex partners. In short, HIV is loose in the general population and AIDS is not a "gay disease."

The AIDS epidemic has raised significant issues central to our concern with health care. In some cases the issues are dividing the medical community. For example, there are physicians who are unwilling to work with AIDS patients, thus denying health care to people who desperately need it. This of course is contrary to the professional ethics that we expect physicians to heed. Moreover, some 80–90 percent of medical education to which physicians are exposed as students is publicly financed. Many would ask, "Is not something owed the public in return?" In contrast, those who have chosen to treat and minister to AIDS victims confront the problem of "burnout" from the stress and emotional drain of knowing one's efforts are ultimately useless and watching these predominantly young members of society prematurely die. Both the issue of "freedom not to treat" and that of dealing with burnout are likely to grow ever more central as the number of AIDS patients escalates and the health care system is put under increasing pressure to respond.

But an even larger concern should be the kind of response AIDS victims are likely to get from a system organized around the principle of pay as you go. The handling of AIDS cases thus far appears to underscore the weaknesses in the system to which we alluded earlier.[33] About 40 percent of the persons treated for AIDS have had private health insurance, and another 40 percent have had Medicaid. Twenty percent—a much higher proportion than is true of adults in the general population—have been uninsured. Thus, 60 percent of AIDS patients have had limited or no assistance in paying their medical bills, which can be very substantial. Consequently, most have had to rely on the charity of public hospitals. With AIDS cases growing at a rapid rate, particularly among nonaffluent segments of the population such as inner-city drug abusers, the demands on such

[33]Charles J. Mosely, "AIDS Update," *Editorial Research Reports*, 2 (December 16, 1988): 640–41.

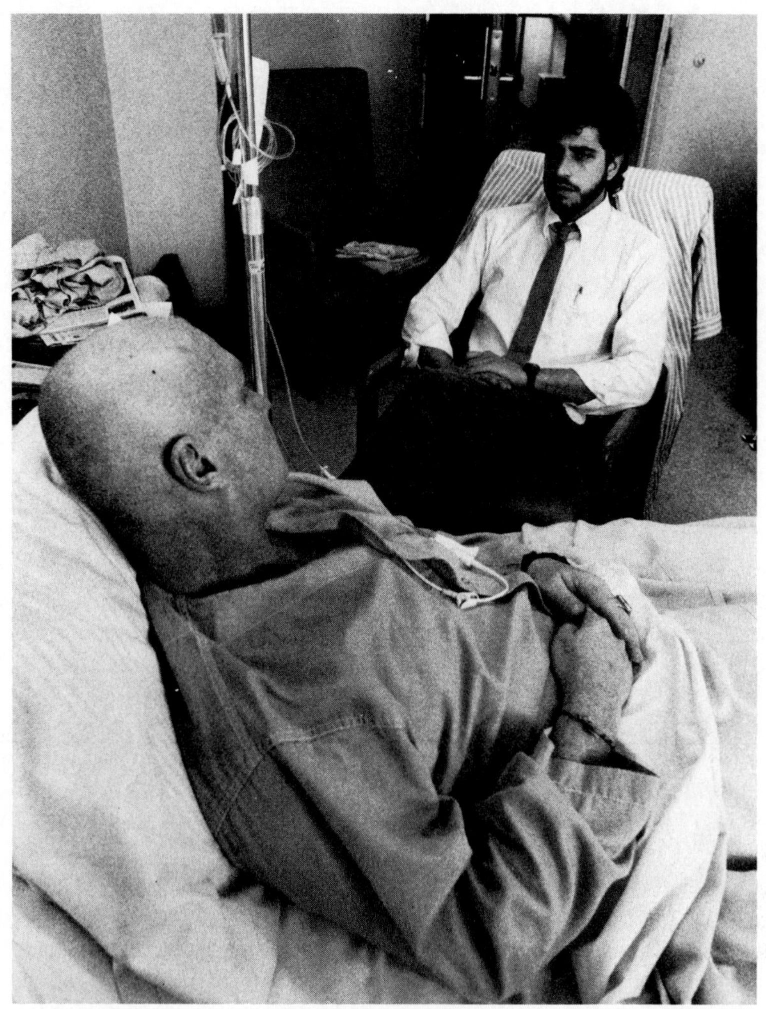

A psychologist counsels an AIDS patient in a New York veterans' hospital. The AIDS epidemic is already taxing the medical resources available in those states that are particularly hard hit, such as New York and California. The epidemic promises to underscore some of the fundamental weaknesses and limitations of our system of health care. *(John Griffin/The Image Works)*

institutions is bound to grow. How public hospitals will find the money, staff, and other resources to meet these demands is not known. Unless they receive outside assistance, or other types of hospitals agree to share the burden, public hospitals in areas in which AIDS cases are highly concentrated (New York and California, for instance) will be faced with irresolvable fiscal crises. This is all aside from the issue of the quality of care AIDS patients can reasonably expect in such hard-pressed surroundings.

Private health insurance providers are not helping the situation. Insurance companies are attempting to avoid coverage of persons who have AIDS or who are infected with HIV. There is now no way they can avoid covering workers whose employers include them in group insurance policies, but the insurance companies are seeking to do so in the case of those applying for individual policies. In some cases applicants must take tests for the presence of HIV, answer questions on applications about AIDS-related matters, or have a physician produce testimony about their health and likelihood of being at risk. Similarly, employers who "self-insure" their workers—that is, pay their medical bills—may rule out paying for AIDS if they wish. Many workers would be negatively affected by such a policy.

Thus, there are growing signs that the private sector is trying to get out of the health care system when it comes to AIDS, in sharp contrast to other deadly diseases. Persons who get too sick to work because they are debilitated by AIDS-related diseases lose their health insurance when they leave their jobs. Given the posture of private insurance providers, they are then unable to purchase individual policies (assuming they can afford them, given unemployment) to help meet their medical expenses. They must then join the ranks of the uninsured or seek eligibility for Medicaid. (It is possible for AIDS patients to qualify as disabled and obtain assistance under Medicare, but the two-year waiting period for eligibility means they may die first.)

People who want assistance from Medicaid must, as we have seen, be indigent. Given what we have said about the income limits that govern eligibility for Medicaid coverage, an AIDS patient must be almost destitute to take advantage of the program. Many are. Many more will be forced into destitution as they exhaust their savings and assets in response to requests that they pay their bills before they die.

Ironically, it may well be that the tragedy of AIDS will contribute to a crisis in health care delivery that will cause the needed reassessment of the entire system. If AIDS does not do it alone, the reassessment may be pushed along by another growing phenomenon, the "graying of America." The changing age composition of our population, involving an ever-increasing percentage of persons being age sixty-five and older, promises to render the inadequacies of America's health care system even more blatant than at present.

HEALTH CARE FOR OUR ELDERS

In Chapter 10, "Ageism," we dwelt at length on the problems facing many older Americans. By and large they are a healthy lot and remain so until their final years. Many do, however, frequently suffer various chronic problems that limit their range of activities. This is particularly true for elderly at the lower income levels. Such chronic problems include heart conditions, arthritis and rheumatism, hypertension, and impairments of the lower extremities and hips. Visual and hearing impairments are also common. Treating all these conditions places demands on America's health care system. The demands are expected to dramatically increase, given the projected growth in the sixty-five-and-older population. The projected growth is from 12.2 percent of the U.S. population in 1987 to 17.7 percent in the year 2020 when the baby boomers push the sixty-five-and-older population sharply upward. In the next thirty years or so we will see the graying of America escalate.

The demands on the U.S. health care system are expected to be exacerbated by yet a new epidemic, one affecting our elders. This is Alzheimer's disease, now the fourth leading cause of death in this country. As mentioned in Chapter 10, this is a disease involving the degeneration of the brain. Brain cells are progressively destroyed, memory loss occurs, personality changes and socially inappropriate behaviors are exhibited, cognitive processes are adversely affected, physical functioning declines, and finally there is death. Over 100,000 people die from this epidemic annually at this point, after an average of ten years of deterioration and decline. There is no cure for the disease; scientists do not know what causes it.[34]

The disease went unrecognized until the 1970s. Until recently it was thought to affect no more than 1.5 million to 2 million older Americans. However, research now suggests that as many as 4 million elders—10 percent of those sixty-five and older, and almost 50 percent of those eighty-five and older—may currently have Alzheimer's disease.[35] As more and more Americans reach and pass age sixty-five, the size of the eighty-five-and-older population grows. Given current projections on the age composition of the U.S. population, we could have 14 million Alzheimer's patients to care for in the year 2050. An official of the National Institute on Aging, reflecting on the dimensions of the problem, stated that the disease is "one of the biggest public health dilemmas we've ever encountered." Yet, while we spend over a billion dollars a year on cancer research, at present we spend about a tenth of that studying Alzheimer's disease.[36]

Most people with this disease live and are cared for at home, but perhaps 30 percent must be cared for in hospitals and nursing homes. There is a serious shortage of quality affordable care settings, which is predicted to reach crisis proportions in the future. Indeed, were so many Alzheimer's patients not being cared for by family members, the crisis would be overwhelming right now. As we shall see, one of the reasons families are assuming responsibility to such an extent is not only the shortage of nursing homes, but their high cost and the failure of health insurance plans to cover the kind of long-term care that chronic sufferers of the disease require. Nonetheless, the costs of care even today are enormous. In 1985 alone the United States spent $88 billion to care for persons with Alzheimer's disease and other debilitating dementias (e.g., stroke-related mental impairment).[37]

Many of those providing care in the home are themselves elderly and the effort is a source of both physical and emotional strain. It is now believed that stress from caring for Alzheimer's patients actually makes caregivers more vulnerable than usual to infectious diseases. Since these people may not be in the best of health in all cases anyway, their own demise may be hastened. Hence the growing numbers of elderly in need of long-term care may tragically produce new victims—those who sacrifice to help them. This multiplicative effect puts even more pressure and strain on the U.S. health care system than would be the case if the caregivers had more in the way of respite and support.

Americans aged sixty-five and older are eligible for Medicare, but we have already seen that coverage is restricted and those in need of health care are required to pay for certain services either wholly or in part. Medicare does not cover chronic-care costs such as those necessary to keep people in their homes ($18,000–20,000 per year) or in nursing-home settings ($25,000 per year, on average). On the other hand, Medicaid, once again, requires that recipients of assistance be indigent. As in the case of AIDS patients, getting care for the elderly may require that they exhaust all their assets first, then sink into poverty and reliance on public hospitals and nursing homes catering to poor people. Again, the issue of the quality of care becomes pertinent. As is true throughout much of the health care system, you get what you are able to pay for.

How will we deal with the growing numbers of our elders in need of health care now and in

[34]See Robert J. Wurtman, "Alzheimer's Disease," *Scientific American*, 252 (January 1985): 62–74.

[35]"The Brain Killer," *Newsweek* (December 18, 1989): 54–56.

[36]Ibid., p. 54.

[37]Lien-Fu Huang et al., "The Economic Cost of Senile Dementia in the United States, 1985," *Public Health Reports*, 103 (January–February 1988): 3–7.

the years ahead? Will older Americans (including us) be left to struggle within a pay-as-you-go system that allows some people to fall through the cracks altogether and leaves tens of millions dependent on charity care? Or will we reassess our health care system and bring it more into line with what other Western industrialized nations are doing?

SOME ALTERNATIVES FOR THE FUTURE

As the limitations of America's health care system become ever more evident, and as the health status of millions of citizens is increasingly jeopardized by this system, pressures for change will mount. Two general alternatives to the present system are possible: (1) national health insurance and (2) a national public health service system.

National health insurance is the most common route taken by other industrialized countries—from Japan to Canada. Under such a system all citizens are covered by comprehensive health insurance, typically paid for by some combination of taxes and contributions by employers and employees (for those working). The medical profession serves people in response to their health care needs and then bills the insurance system, which is run by or under the supervision of government.

The pay-as-you-go system now existing in the United States could be maintained under national health insurance, the difference being that all citizens would be in a position to have payments made on their behalf. There would be no uninsured men, women, or children. Nor would there be persons whose insurance coverage was more lavish than that of others. Whether you were rich or poor, you would be guaranteed insurance payments for the same quality of treatment in the health care system. The coverage gaps and state-to-state variations in eligibility requirements that currently exist would disappear.

The success of a national health insurance system in the United States would not only rest on the expansion of coverage and services to those presently in need. It would also require aggressive measures by our government to keep health care costs down. Government would have to curb the excesses of the growing medical–industrial complex with its profit-maximization tendencies. With appropriate government controls, the United States could have a national health care system that is simultaneously affordable and dramatically more attentive to the health status of the least affluent of its citizens.

A more radical alternative, and perhaps the one that is most alien to our current system, is a public health service. As in Great Britain, health care workers (including doctors) would become public employees. Hospitals would be public institutions. In effect, health care would become the responsibility of government and not be left to the whims of the private economic marketplace. Resources would be directed where most needed and equal access for citizens of all social classes would be guaranteed. As can be imagined, the idea of a public health service (or "socialized medicine" as some call it) draws intense opposition from the medical profession in the United States. Because the other alternative, national health insurance, provides leeway for physicians to remain private entrepreneurs and for health care organizations to remain in the profit-making sector, this is most likely to be the direction in which any changes that occur will take place.

SUMMARY

America's health care system falls far short of any imaginable ideal. It serves lower income people and members of racial minorities less well than other segments of the population, as indicated by their second-class health status. When epidemics occur, as in the case of AIDS and Alzheimer's disease, the health care system is incapable of responding in a way that would provide high-quality, affordable care to all in need. The health care system is, in short, a feature of the way in which we have organized our society that does the reverse of what we ask it to do: it harms people. Despite the enormous sums we lavish upon it each year, it limits people's life chances. Practically no other macro problem cries out so much for change.

DISCUSSION QUESTIONS

1. Consider the on-the-job health risks to which office-bound professionals (e.g., business executives, engineers, lawyers, accountants) are likely to be exposed. How do these risks differ from those faced by adults you know who work in blue-collar, manual jobs?
2. Thirty-seven million Americans, including many young people, lack any type of health insurance. Assume you are in this group. Make inquiries to find out how much an insurance company would charge you annually for an individual policy that would provide you with comprehensive medical care and hospitalization coverage.
3. While the U.S. population has many health care needs, physicians are permitted to choose specialties that leave some needs poorly addressed. What arguments could be made for and against greater public control over (a) the overall supply of physicians and (b) the specialty areas in which they are permitted to practice?
4. Should the United States adopt some form of national health care plan? If not, why not? If so, what do you think its most prominent features should be?
5. Physicians are pretty much free to choose not to treat certain categories of patients, e.g., AIDS victims or chronically ill elders. What arguments might be made on behalf of this situation? What do you think of these arguments?
6. The AIDS virus is currently carried by perhaps 1 million to 1.5 million people in the United States. Presently there is no national program of screening for HIV infection. Should there be such a program? Should it be mandatory? What should be done with the knowledge when certain individuals test positive for the virus? Why?

SUGGESTED READINGS

Brown, Phil, ed. *Perspectives in Medical Sociology* (Chicago: The Dorsey Press, 1989).
An overview of the health field and the many issues in which it is embroiled today.

Ratcliff, Kathryn S. *Healing Technology: Feminist Perspectives* (Ann Arbor: University of Michigan Press, 1989).
Assessment of health care problems facing women as a consequence of male domination of the medical profession and major health technology institutions.

Shilts, Randy. *And the Band Played On: Politics, People, and the AIDS Epidemic* (New York: St. Martin's Press, 1987).
An account of the politics and human suffering accompanying the struggle to gain recognition of AIDS as a major health epidemic.

Sidel, Victor W., and Ruth Sidel, eds. *Reforming Medicine: Lessons of the Last Quarter Century* (New York: Pantheon Books, 1984).
Accounts by medical reformers of their successes and failures in seeking changes in America's inadequate health care system.

Starr, Paul. *The Social Transformation of American Medicine* (New York: Basic Books, 1982).
Award-winning history of the medical profession and health care in the United States that helps put current issues in context.

U.S. Department of Health and Human Services. *Health, United States, 1988* (Washington, D.C.: U.S. Government Printing Office, 1989).
Annual report on the nation's health status.

PART II

Micro Problems

In Part I we examined a number of macro problems, key features of society that do harm to millions of people. Our major point of focus was U.S. society, although attention was drawn to the tragic conditions in underdeveloped nations, where most of humanity dwells.

Problems also exist at the individual level. We call problems at this level *micro problems*. Micro problems involve behavior by individuals that has an adverse effect on others and/or that is self-harmful. The reasons individuals engage in such behavior are often complex and a challenge to sociological understanding.

Nearly everyone is, at some point in his or her life, a member of a family. Family-related problems have gained much attention in recent years. In Chapter 12 we examine changes in family life due to premarital teenage pregnancies and marital dissolution; violent behavior by family members against one another, as well as sexual abuse directed at children; and children who flee from or are pushed out of their homes. These behaviors have varying degrees of adverse effect on those involved.

Crime is another micro problem that has caused considerable concern in recent years. The definition and pervasiveness of criminal behavior shifts with changes in the law and its application (Chapter 13). Though some categories of crimes against people and property seem to be decreasing, data on how many crimes are actually committed are difficult to obtain. Sociologists and other social scientists continue to pursue the causes of criminal behavior of all types. On the practical side, however, our system (courts, police, correctional institutions) for handling law violators faces a number of operational problems. At present, this system seems to have only a marginal impact on many of the more common forms of criminal behavior.

The micro problem of mental illness (Chapter 14) is highly complex. Millions of people are mentally troubled, but there is controversy over whether the behavior of such persons should be categorized as "illness." Some feel that no disease is involved and that the behavior should not be treated as if it were a medical problem. Some critics of the medical perspective suggest that such behavior could be a normal, even healthy, way for persons to react to intolerable life situations. Nonetheless, sociologists have contributed a great deal of knowledge to help determine correlates of mental distress, the effects of institutionalization, and the impact of labeling people mentally ill.

One of the most dramatic and mysterious micro problems is suicide (Chapter 15). While it is commonly assumed that persons who commit or attempt suicide are mentally ill, this may not be the case. Sociologists have long been intrigued by this question and, together with other social scientists, have made substantial contributions to a now vast literature on why people kill themselves. Such knowledge helps to provide some guidance to those who seek to prevent suicides. Recently, the notion that people have a right to die in this way has evoked considerable controversy.

Drug abuse, which includes the abuse of alcohol, is a form of self-harm in which many Americans are engaged (Chapters 16 and 17). In innumerable cases strangers, friends, or family members have become the victims of abusers' behaviors. The use of consciousness-altering substances, both legal and illegal, is extremely widespread. Why so many people seek to alter their state of consciousness, even at the risk of serious illness or death, is a significant sociological question. The knowledge acquired through research can only enhance current efforts to intervene against this behavior and control its harmful effects.

On one level it seems easier to change individual behavior that may be harmful to others and/or self-harmful than to change key features of society as a whole that are harmful. In ways that we do not yet fully understand, many of the macro problems discussed in the first part of this book and the micro problems we are about to discuss may be interrelated. From time to time such interrelations will emerge in these final chapters where we feel empirical evidence merits it. Teasing out the relationship between societal features and individual behaviors is a central concern of sociology. The success of sociologists in this effort will help clear the way toward a better understanding of, and solutions to, the micro problems that plague us.

CHAPTER 12

Family-Related Problems

Special attention and support should be freely given to troubled families and their members, including single-parent households. Moreover, the bases for violence and abuse within families of all types should be absent.

Sociologists have traditionally viewed the family as a multifunction unit, central to the stability and continuity of human society. Among its functions are economic production, intimacy and nurturance, sexual reproduction, and socialization of the young. Viewed in the abstract, the family may be seen as a social collectivity that protects and aids the individual in confronting the often challenging and sometimes stressful demands of daily life.

In recent decades the nature of the family in the United States has been undergoing change, and a variety of problems related to the family have emerged. There have been significant increases in premarital births and in the numbers of unwed teenage mothers. Rates of marital dissolution also have risen sharply, thus adding to the unprecedented numbers of single-parent households. Researchers have uncovered an unexpectedly high volume of violent behavior within families, most notably in the form of spouse abuse as well as violence and sexual abuse directed at children. One response of children to discord and victimization in the home has been to flee—to become runaways. There are also indications that many children are becoming "pushouts," being made to leave home.

In this chapter we examine these family-related problems. Our attention focuses on the nature of these problems as well as on their extent, causes, and consequences. We begin by looking at premarital births and single teenage mothers.

PREMARITAL BIRTHS AND TEENAGE MOTHERHOOD

The typical image that comes to mind when we hear the term *family* is likely to be mother, father, and children living together in a household. This image belies the reality of what has been taking place in America in recent decades, particularly the surge in the percentage of families living in single-parent households. While much of the change in family composition has occurred as a consequence of increased rates of divorce (a topic addressed later in this chapter), increasing numbers of families *begin* with a single parent.

In 1986 some 3.8 million births were recorded in the United States. As Table 12.1 indicates, 23.4 percent of these births were to unmarried mothers (as compared with 4.0 percent in 1950).[1] While persons under age twenty accounted for only 12.6 percent of all births recorded in 1986, in well over half of these births the under-twenty mother was unmarried. In the under-twenty group the likelihood that the young mother giving birth was unmarried decreased with age: The vast majority of mothers sixteen or under were unmarried, while about half of all eighteen-year-olds were unmarried. In sum, while one in five births in 1986 was to an unwed mother, for teenagers the rate was one in two. Such high rates of premarital births—involving 290,000 births to teenagers in 1986 alone—often have harmful consequences.

Before assessing these consequences we might ask why premarital birth rates are so high, especially among teenagers. A variety of factors seem to be at work.[2] The age of beginning menstruation (and thus susceptibility to becoming pregnant) has been going down over the years, presumably because of overall improvements in the U.S. population's nutrition and health. Thus, the size of the group of young persons at risk for pregnancy has grown.

Perhaps more important is the fact that the percentage of teenagers who are sexually active has been on the upswing in recent years, at least since the mid-1960s. The data available suggest that sixteen is now the average age for a youth's first experience with sexual intercourse. The likelihood of having intercourse has been increasing at all age levels during the teen years, and by age nineteen some four-fifths of all males and two-thirds of all females have had intercourse.[3]

Technology has, of course, provided both males and females with means of pregnancy prevention. One would expect unmarried young people to take advantage of birth control measures, a few of which are highly effective, to reduce the risk of premarital pregnancy; too often, however, they do not do so. Survey data on young unmarried females indicate that a quarter of those who are sexually active *never* use contraceptives, and an additional 45 percent use them only from time to time.[4] Contraceptives frequently are not used by those who are having their first experiences with intercourse, a time when many pregnancies occur.

[1] These and more recent data relating to recorded births may be found in *Monthly Vital Statistics*, a federal government publication. See also U. S. Bureau of the Census, *Fertility of American Women: June 1988* (Washington, D.C.: U.S. Government Printing Office, 1989).

[2] See *Teenage Pregnancy: The Problem That Hasn't Gone Away* (New York: Alan Guttmacher Institute, 1981).

[3] Ibid.

[4] Ibid. See the data presented in Melvin Zelnick and John F. Kantner, "Sexual and Contraceptive Experience of Young Unmarried Women in the United States, 1976 and 1971," *Family Planning Perspectives*, 9 (March/April 1977): 55–71.

TABLE 12.1 Births to Unmarried Women, by Race of Child and Age of Mother, 1970–86

Race of child and age of mother	1970	1975	1980	1985	1986
Number (in thousands)					
Total live births*	**398.7**	**447.9**	**665.7**	**828.2**	**878.5**
White	175.1	186.4	320.1	433.0	466.8
Black	215.1	249.6	325.7	365.5	380.3
Under 15 years	9.5	11.0	9.0	9.4	9.4
15–19 years	190.4	222.5	262.8	270.9	280.7
20–24 years	126.7	134.0	237.3	300.4	316.2
25–29 years	40.6	50.2	99.6	152.0	165.7
30–34 years	19.1	19.8	41.0	67.3	74.9
35 years and over	12.4	10.4	16.1	28.2	31.6
Percent distribution					
Total*	**100.0**	**100.0**	**100.0**	**100.0**	**100.0**
White	43.9	41.6	48.1	52.3	53.1
Black	54.0	55.7	48.9	44.1	43.3
Under 15 years	2.4	2.5	1.4	1.1	1.1
15–19 years	47.8	49.7	39.5	32.7	32.0
20–24 years	31.8	29.9	35.6	36.3	36.0
25–29 years	10.2	11.2	15.0	18.4	18.9
30–34 years	4.8	4.4	6.2	8.1	8.5
35 years and over	3.1	2.3	2.4	3.4	3.6
Births to unmarried women as percent of all births in racial groups					
Total*	**10.7**	**14.2**	**18.4**	**22.0**	**23.4**
White	5.7	7.3	11.0	14.5	15.7
Black	37.6	48.8	55.2	60.1	61.2
Birth rate†					
Total‡	**26.4**	**24.5**	**29.4**	**32.8**	**34.3**
White	13.8	12.4	17.6	21.8	23.2
Black	95.5	84.2	81.4	78.8	80.9
15–19 years	22.4	23.9	27.6	31.6	32.6
20–24 years	38.4	31.2	40.9	46.8	49.7
25–29 years	37.0	27.5	34.0	39.8	42.0
30–34 years	27.1	17.9	21.1	25.0	26.9

*Includes other races not shown separately.
†Rate per 1,000 unmarried women (never-married, widowed, and divorced) estimated as of July 1.
‡Covers women aged 15–44 years.
Source: U.S. Department of Commerce, U.S. Bureau of the Census, *Statistical Abstract of the United States, 1989* (Washington, D.C.: U.S. Government Printing Office, 1989), p. 66.

Ignorance and misinformation expose millions of sexually active, unmarried teenagers to the risks of pregnancy. In recent years efforts have been under way to provide counseling and effective means of contraception to teenagers, but much more must be done if their startlingly high premarital pregnancy rate is to be reduced. *(Ellis Herwig/The Picture Cube)*

If technology to prevent pregnancy is widely available, why is it so underutilized? The reasons are many.[5] There is still widespread lack of knowledge and misinformation regarding birth control measures and the conditions under which pregnancy may occur. Much of this ignorance stems from the paucity of education on these matters provided to young people, whether by parents, schools, or religious institutions. Sex education (but particularly education in birth control practices) remains a controversial subject in U.S. society. Fears are often expressed that young people will be encouraged into premature sexual activity by such information.

Yet teenagers are already sexually active. Failure to combat lack of knowledge and misinformation thus allows the premarital pregnancy rate to remain high. One study has demonstrated that sex education does not increase the rate of those having intercourse but that it does increase the probability that contraceptives will be used by sexually active teenagers.[6] Yet empirical data along these lines have not begun to be acknowledged by those who see sex education as contributing to teenage sexual activity and the pregnancies that so often follow.

[5] Melvin Zelnick and John F. Kantner, "Reasons for Nonuse of Contraception by Sexually Active Women Aged 15–19," *Family Planning Perspectives,* 11 (September/October 1979): 290–96. Also, in the same issue, see Melvin Zelnick, "Sex Education and Knowledge of Pregnancy Risk Among U.S. Teenage Women."

[6] Melvin Zelnick and J. Kim Young, "Sex Education and Its Association with Teenage Sexual Activity, Pregnancy, and Contraceptive Use," *Family Planning Perspectives,* 14 (May/June 1982): 117–26.

While lack of knowledge and misinformation may contribute to high premarital pregnancy rates, other personal and social factors can get in the way of the utilization of effective birth control measures. Intercourse may occur in an unplanned way, perhaps without original intention. It may also be unplanned in the context of what has been called "date rape," wherein the teenage female is sexually coerced or abused, often while under the influence of alcohol or drugs.

Persons who are struggling over guilt about becoming sexually active may avoid seeking birth control measures, thinking that to do so is to make a concrete commitment to future activity. There may be concern too over comfort or side effects of some contraceptives. There may be a lack of communication between sexual partners over who is responsible for protection. For some teenagers, obtaining and using contraceptives may appear inconvenient, embarrassing, or dangerous (if parents find out). In addition, some simply cannot afford adequate contraceptive measures.

Finally, and often with unhappy results, there are some who *want* to get pregnant—in the hope of coercing the father into marriage or of demonstrating maturity and arrival into "adulthood" or out of a need to have someone to love and who will give love in return.

It is important to note that failure to make effective use of contraceptives has implications for the growing rates of abortion among young females.[7] In 1985 there were 1,588,600 legal abortions reported to government statistical agencies. (The actual rate of abortion may be 10–20 percent higher.) Over a quarter of these abortions occurred in the under-twenty age group. Most persons having abortions are unmarried.[8]

Thus far we have delayed discussion of the consequences of premarital births and teenage motherhood.[9] The evidence shows that to be put into this situation may be self-harmful to the mother and/or harmful to others (in particular to the newborn child). Health implications are the first of many concerns. The younger the age at which pregnancy occurs, the higher the probability that both mother and child will have serious health problems. Young mothers may face complications in giving birth. Newborn children of teenage mothers often have low birth weights and a higher than average incidence of serious birth defects. Infant mortality rates are also high among children born to very young mothers.

To a large extent these health problems are exacerbated by the fact that a disproportionate percentage of premarital births occur among teenagers from low-income households. Such youths have least ready access to sex education and effective contraceptive measures and are least able to afford abortions or marriage to the male sexual partner. (Low-income teenage couples cannot afford to set up households.) Health services to poor or near-poor young people often preclude proper prenatal care. Economic deprivation frequently has negative effects on dietary and nutritional practices important to the health of the mother and unborn child. Postnatal and "well-baby" care may also not be readily available or affordable.

Aside from health problems, teenage pregnancy commonly restricts the life chances of mother and child in other ways. While public education institutions cannot refuse to serve pregnant unwed girls of eligible school age, many teenagers quit school when they become pregnant. Even more leave upon the births of their children as they face the demands of child care and/or the need for some kind of employment. Once they drop out of school, they are unlikely to return and earn their diplomas, thus

---

[7] See data in *Monthly Vital Statistics*.

[8] Aida Torres and Jacqueline D. Forrest, "Why Do Women Have Abortions?," *Family Planning Perspectives*, 20 (July/August 1988): 169–76.

[9] *Teenage Pregnancy*.

reducing the likelihood of obtaining jobs that provide adequate pay and security. With this process under way, the probability of living in poverty or near-poverty is very high. Consequently, the children of such unions are likely to suffer the often harsh demands of low-income life. Welfare benefits for the children may become a necessary bare means of survival for the most economically desperate. For the fortunate, family and friends (and, less frequently, the biological father) provide a network of support that enables teenage unwed mothers to manage.

All of these demands and responsibilities of teenage parenthood, it should be underscored, are being borne by young persons who have not yet reached physical, emotional, or intellectual maturity. Many are barely out of childhood, even while they struggle to be parents and providers. The result can be serious psychological stress in the face of newfound pressures. The frustrations reveal themselves over time in a number of ways, from ill-conceived attempts at marriage and involvements that may incur additional pregnancies to child abuse and self-harmful behaviors.

At this point it may be obvious that practically nothing has been said about the male partner. This is because in most cases of premarital pregnancy and birth among teenagers the male drops out of sight quickly. The likelihood that marriage will occur in such cases has diminished over the years, as the tradition of forced, or "shotgun," marriages has largely broken down (see Table 12.2). Given the enormous difficulties male teenagers face in supporting a wife and family today and the probability that this means dropping out of school and limiting employment prospects for the foreseeable future, teenage fathers are reluctant to enter into a marital relationship. Moreover, teenage mothers are often unlikely to push them, understanding perhaps that a marriage initiated in such circumstances is unlikely to last.

The public outcry in the last decade or so over teenage pregnancy—termed by some an epidemic—appears to focus on two main concerns. First, such pregnancies objectively announce the fact that teenagers are indeed sexually active. This is a fact that many adults would prefer not to know or would like to see reversed.[10] Second, and perhaps of equal importance, is concern over the costs of teenage pregnancies and their aftermath. This concern is largely voiced in the context of more general antipathy toward persons who must call on public assistance for family support. The increasing proportion over the last twenty years of welfare recipients who are members of female-headed households in which the mother is unmarried seems to be deeply resented. This resentment arises not only out of moral condemnation of unwed motherhood, but also out of concern over the tax burden posed by welfare families.[11]

Yet the public outcry largely neglects the causes of premarital pregnancies as well as the massive problems many teenage mothers face in trying to further the life chances of their children. Moreover, condemnation and resentment of unwed mothers apparently are having little effect on teenage pregnancy rates or decisions by young people to be sexually active.[12]

MARITAL DISSOLUTION

Marital dissolution is a second major contributor to the growing number of families in which only one parent is present. While most persons whose marriages end in divorce do eventually remarry, the problems leading to and flowing from family breakup can be harmful to those involved.

---

[10] "Gallup Poll Shows More Americans Say Premarital Sex Is Wrong," *Family Planning Perspectives*, 20 (July/August 1988): 180–81.

[11] Katherine Bradbury, "Income Maintenance Alternatives and Family Composition," *Journal of Human Resources*, 13 (Summer 1978): 305–31.

[12] See *Teenage Pregnancy in the United States: The Scope of the Problem and State Responses* (New York: Alan Guttmacher Institute, 1989).

TABLE 12.2 Women with a Premaritally Conceived First Child Who Married Before the Birth of the Child, 1970–74 to 1985–88 (Numbers in Thousands)

Race and period of first birth*	Total, 15–24 years		Age at first birth					
			15–17 years†		18 and 19 years		20–24 years	
	Number	Percent	Number	Percent	Number	Percent	Number	Percent
All races								
1985–88	1,359	26.2	214	17.3	422	27.3	723	28.2
1980–84	2,347	36.6	608	27.0	754	35.4	985	43.5
1975–79	2,140	38.6	694	26.7	674	46.6	772	42.4
1970–74	2,132	45.9	732	38.4	766	50.7	634	48.9
White								
1985–88	877	37.5	101	36.6	289	34.6	487	39.4
1980–84	1,647	44.0	417	34.8	521	44.1	709	49.4
1975–79	1,437	52.5	409	42.5	484	60.3	544	52.9
1970–74	1,440	58.1	447	53.7	534	60.5	459	59.7
Black								
1985–88	445	4.7	109	—	124	8.1	212	5.2
1980–84	623	14.8	181	7.7	209	12.4	233	22.3
1975–79	651	8.1	274	2.9	172	9.9	205	13.7
1970–74	636	18.7	268	13.8	208	28.4	160	14.4
Hispanic‡								
1985–88	129	25.6	9	(B)	36	(B)	84	17.9
1980–84	336	27.4	104	26.0	94	4.3	138	44.2
1975–79	262	36.3	76	18.4	74	(B)	112	38.4
1970–74	199	30.7	61	(B)	69	(B)	69	(B)
Not Hispanic								
1985–88	1,230	26.3	204	15.7	387	26.4	639	29.6
1980–84	2,013	38.1	505	27.1	662	39.9	846	43.3
1975–79	1,879	38.9	618	27.7	601	45.9	660	43.0
1970–74	1,934	47.5	672	40.0	697	51.8	565	51.2

Key: B, base too small to show derived statistic.
*Periods are for complete calendar years with the exception of the 1985–88 period, which is for January 1985 to June 1988.
†Excludes births to women who were never married and were 15–17 years old in June 1988.
‡Persons of Hispanic origin may be of any race.
Source: U.S. Department of Commerce, Bureau of the Census, *Fertility of American Women: June 1988* (Washington, D.C.: U.S. Government Printing Office, 1989), p. 9.

America's "divorce rate" can be expressed in different ways.[13] In 1985, some 2,413 million couples were married. In that same year 1,190 million already existing marriages ended in divorce, for a rate of 493 divorces for every 1,000 marriages. This ratio increased from 258 per 1,000 in 1960 and 328 per 1,000 in 1970. In expressing the divorce rate in this way one must remember that the marriages include persons who were formerly divorced.

A second way to approach the divorce rate is in terms of the number of divorces per 1,000 persons in the population. Viewed in these

[13] Data are from U.S. Bureau of the Census.

This scene is a familiar one, repeated again and again annually in the United States with varying degrees of ceremony. The probability that such couples will experience divorce seven years on average after marrying is very high. *(Jerry Howard/Stock, Boston)*

terms, the rate was 5.0 divorces per 1,000 persons in 1985. (See Table 12.3.) The rate was up from 2.2 in 1960 and 3.5 in 1970. This approach must be used cautiously because changes in the age composition of the population affect the numerical divorce rate.

The third and most common way of expressing the divorce rate is to look at the number of divorces per 1,000 married women. Table 12.3 indicates that in 1965 there were 10.6 divorces per 1,000 married women. This rate rose to 20.3 in 1975 and has leveled off since 1980. In 1985 the rate was 21.7.

However the divorce rate is expressed, it is clear that marital dissolution has been on a dramatic upswing over the last three decades. Longitudinal statistics show that these recent increases are in reality the extension of a much longer upward trend in divorce rates. Nonetheless, the extent to which this trend has gone of late is having an impact on millions of people. For example, in the last two decades some 19 million children under age eighteen have seen their parents enter into a divorce.

Before turning to the consequences of marital dissolution, let us consider some of the factors that may help to account for the more recent acceleration of the divorce rate. Social scientists continue to debate these factors and the weight to be attributed to them.[14]

1. Laws pertaining to divorce have changed in recent years. While the upward climb in rates of divorce began well before 1970, prior to that year states would grant a divorce only on such grounds as adultery, cruelty (physical or mental), or desertion. One or the other

---

[14] See Mary Joe Bane, *Here to Stay: American Families in the Twentieth Century* (New York: Basic Books, 1976), and Robert S. Weiss, *Marital Separation* (New York: Basic Books, 1975).

TABLE 12.3 Marriages and Divorces, 1960–85 (Numbers in Thousands)

	Marriages*						Divorces and annulments		
		Rate per 1,000 population						Rate per 1,000 population	
					Unmarried women				
Year	Number	Total	Men 15 years old and over	Women 15 years old and over	15 years old and over	15–44 years old	Number	Total	Married women 15 years old and over
1960	1,523	8.5	25.4	24.0	73.5	148.0	393	2.2	9.2
1965	1,800	9.3	27.9	26.0	75.0	144.3	479	2.5	10.6
1970	2,159	10.6	31.1	28.4	76.5	140.2	708	3.5	14.9
1975	2,153	10.0	27.9	25.6	66.9	118.5	1,036	4.8	20.3
1980	2,390	10.6	28.5	26.1	61.4	102.6	1,189	5.2	22.6
1981	2,422	10.6	28.4	26.1	61.7	103.1	1,213	5.3	22.6
1982	2,456	10.6	28.4	26.1	61.4	101.9	1,170	5.0	21.7
1983	2,446	10.5	28.0	25.7	59.9	99.3	1,158	4.9	21.3
1984	2,477	10.5	28.1	25.8	59.5	99.0	1,169	5.0	21.5
1985	2,413	10.1	26.9	24.8	57.0	94.9	1,190	5.0	21.7

*Beginning 1980, includes nonlicensed marriages registered in California.
Source: U.S. Department of Commerce, Bureau of the Census, *Statistical Abstract of the United States, 1989* (Washington, D.C.: U.S. Government Printing Office, 1989), p. 85.

partner in a marriage had to be found at fault by divorce courts. In 1970 California instituted a no-fault divorce law that allowed married couples to dissolve their marriages in court by mutual agreement. Over half of all states have since adopted a similar law or added no-fault grounds to existing laws. Such legal changes may represent and facilitate more permissive attitudes toward divorce among married persons.

2. The availability of effective means of contraception to married couples is also believed to have had an impact on divorce. Contraception can make extramarital affairs less risky than they otherwise would be—indeed, infidelity is a major source of breakup in first marriages. Moreover, such contraceptive advances as "the pill" have enabled many couples to exert control over the number of children they wish to have. To the degree to which having children mitigates against marital dissolution, not having them may make divorce a more viable option than it otherwise would be. The average number of children involved in divorce has fallen from 1.33 per divorce in the late 1960s to less than 1.0 at present. (Yet as noted earlier, the number of children affected by divorce over the last twenty years is still substantial. More than half of all divorces involve children even now. See Table 12.4.)
3. Women's participation in the labor force (discussed in Chapter 9) is also a factor to be considered. As women have gained more control over childbearing through contraceptive advances and as they have moved into paid positions outside the home—usually from necessity, but often out of choice—their dependence on the husband-as-supporter has diminished somewhat. As their roles in the family have undergone change, many women locked into unhappy marriages have looked to their work as a way of escape. It is also possible that men, seeing their wives in

TABLE 12.4 Divorces and Annulments—Median Duration of Marriage, Median Age at Divorce, and Children Involved, 1970–85

Duration of marriage, age, and children involved	1970	1975	1977	1978	1979	1980	1981	1982	1983	1984	1985
Median duration of marriage (years)	6.7	6.5	6.6	6.6	6.8	6.8	7.0	7.0	7.0	6.9	6.8
Median age at divorce											
Men (years)	(NA)	32.2	32.4	32.0	32.5	32.7	33.1	33.6	34.0	34.3	34.4
Women (years)	(NA)	29.5	29.9	29.7	30.1	30.3	30.6	31.1	31.5	31.7	31.9
Children involved in divorce (in thousands)	870	1,123	1,095	1,147	1,181	1,174	1,180	1,108	1,091	1,081	1,091
Average number of children per decree	1.22	1.08	1.00	1.01	1.00	0.98	0.97	0.94	0.94	0.92	0.92
Rate per 1,000 children under 18 years of age	12.5	16.7	16.7	17.7	18.4	17.3	18.7	17.6	17.4	17.2	17.3

Key: NA, not available.
Source: U.S. Department of Commerce, Bureau of the Census, *Statistical Abstract of the United States, 1989* (Washington, D.C.: U.S. Government Printing Office, 1989), p. 87.

a position of being able to pursue economic independence, have become less reluctant to dissolve an unhappy marriage.

4. Stresses faced by today's families are likely to exacerbate everyday problems in living and the normal tensions of family life. For example, since the late 1960s U.S. society has experienced economic downturns that have been accompanied by cycles of high inflation; unemployment and a loss in the value of wages have hit moderate- and low-income groups especially hard. Official poverty rates have shown an increase. While economic adversity may bring some families closer, and while others may find divorce a financially unsound option, for still other families economic adversity creates a climate in which divorce takes place. The availability of welfare assistance and other forms of government aid to poverty-stricken female-headed households has probably made divorce more thinkable for some. Divorce rates are highest at lower income levels.
5. Finally, changing attitudes toward marriage may help to account for the upsurge in divorce rates. Investigators such as Robert Weiss suggest that marriage is less likely to be viewed as a sacred, permanent institution than it was only a few decades ago. Persons entering marriage are more likely to seek self-fulfillment and personal pleasure out of marriage, as opposed to seeing it as an avenue through which to pursue interpersonal commitment and cooperation in meeting social responsibilities. When self-fulfillment and personal pleasure ebb for one or both partners, there may no longer be much reason to stay married. Nor is there likely to be much public pressure on couples to remain together. The subject of divorce remains the focus of much public hand-wringing, but in reality divorce is usually dismissed as reflecting a relationship that just did not "work out."

The consequences of marital dissolution are many. Sharon Price-Bonham and her colleagues have reviewed existing literature on its impact on adults.[15] They point out that divorce involves far-reaching consequences, involving as it does a major life transition. Price-Bonham and col-

[15] Sharon Price-Bonham, David W. Wright, and Joe F. Pittman, "Divorce: A Frequent 'Alternative' in the 1970s," in Eleanor D. Macklin and Roger H. Rubin, eds., *Contemporary Families and Alternative Lifestyles* (Beverly Hills, Calif.: Sage Publications, 1983), pp. 125–46.

leagues found that the time of separation prior to formal divorce is often extremely stressful. Depression and psychosomatic symptoms associated with it (e.g., loss of appetite, sleep problems, increased drinking) are quite common. The separation period may be experienced as especially stressful because of such factors as increased parental responsibilities, sudden economic dislocation, change in familiar habits, and grief over the loss of a love object. Compared with married persons, those who are in the process of divorcing and who are newly divorced have been found to have higher rates of mental disturbance, suicide, homicide, accidents, and diseases leading to death.[16]

Adjustment to divorce is a process sometimes described in terms analogous to adjustment to a death. Price-Bonham and colleagues suggest that adjustment requires a variety of conditions, including "breaking away from the former marriage, accepting new roles, building a new lifestyle, and regenerating one's sense of self-concept and trust of others."[17]

The ability to adjust to divorce is influenced by numerous factors. The person who initiated the divorce may experience less stress and readier adjustment, as he or she at least has the advantage of some sense of control over the emerging situation. Economic strain is likely to make adjustment difficult. Having a network of friends and relatives who are supportive in times of need during the pre- and postdivorce period makes adjustment easier. Finally, dating and establishing positive relationships with members of the opposite sex is important to the adjustment process. It should be noted that most persons who divorce also remarry, thereby perhaps signaling an end to the adjustment.

The impact of divorce on children has been much debated. Some social scientists have held that the impact is wholly negative. Others have suggested that children are better off in a single-parent household than in one where the relationship between the parents has obviously fallen apart. Our understanding of the impact on children has been advanced by the research of Judith S. Wallerstein and Joan B. Kelly.[18] These researchers examined a group of 131 children from 60 families who came into contact with a California counseling agency. Meeting with the children at the time of the divorce, eighteen months after, and five years after, Wallerstein and Kelly gained unique data on the impact of divorce on children over time.

At the time of the divorce between their parents, the children were found to be very upset. Younger children expressed fright and confusion over the divorce, often seeing themselves as somehow at fault. Older children were found to be angry and concerned over what this situation might mean for them. Five years later, according to the investigators, the psychological effects of the divorce still lingered for most. While a third of the children were evidently happy and well adjusted, another third showed some signs of unhappiness and the remaining third were seriously dissatisfied.[19]

Andrew J. Cherlin concludes that while all children are likely to be emotionally upset when divorce occurs, most do adjust in a year or two. A minority have long-term psychological problems that can be attributed to the dissolution of their parents' marriage.[20] Yet, considering that 19 million children have seen their parents divorce in the last twenty years, the sheer numbers of those who have been emotionally impaired by this process are substantial.

[16] Ibid., pp. 126–27.

[17] Ibid., p. 131.

[18] Judith S. Wallerstein and Joan B. Kelly, *Surviving the Breakup* (New York: Basic Books, 1980).

[19] The researchers were able to interview most of the study's children in a ten-year follow-up. For all too many, the divorce continued to have a troubling impact. See Judith S. Wallerstein and Sandra Blakeslee, *Second Chances* (New York: Ticknor & Fields, 1989).

[20] Andrew J. Cherlin, *Marriage, Divorce, Remarriage* (Cambridge, Mass.: Harvard University Press, 1981), p. 79.

Cherlin does note that the probability of children's successful adjustment to divorce is enhanced by three factors: (1) regular contact with the parent who does not have custody of the children; (2) parental avoidance of involving the children in their differences, so that the latter are not forced to choose sides; and (3) structured, orderly household routine, coupled with an emotionally supportive custodial parent.[21]

Perhaps the most difficult task faced by the parent who is left with the major responsibility for child care is economic. After all the psychological and social adjustments are made and even while they are being attempted, money is frequently a central concern. The fact that the custodial parent is ordinarily the mother adds to the burden, given the subordinate and second-class role women continue to occupy in the labor force (see Chapter 9).

Divorce almost always has a negative economic impact on the single-parent household. The bulk of economic support for the family is typically provided by the husband in intact marriages. When this suddenly disappears or lessens, the standard of living of mothers and children suffers. In most cases of divorce, the father provides little or no child-support money. Even when they are ordered by the courts, child-support payments are received by fewer than half of the women to whom they have been awarded. In 1985, out of the 8.8 million women living with children under twenty-one with no father present, 5.4 million were expecting to receive court-ordered child-support payments. Only 48.2 percent of these women received full payment. In a quarter of the cases the father simply refused to pay. The amount provided to those receiving payments in 1985 averaged $2,220 annually, hardly a boon to most families who have lost a key wage earner.[22]

The economic impact of divorce has been explored in a study by Lenore J. Weitzman.[23] Calculating the incomes of divorced women in relation to their needs in contrast to those of men, Weitzman finds:

> Just one year after legal divorce, men experience a 42 percent improvement in their postdivorce standard of living, while women experience a 73 percent decline.... Divorce is a financial catastrophe for most women.[24]

The women's own words give meaning to Weitzman's statistics.

> We ate macaroni and cheese five nights a week. There was a Safeway special for 39 cents a box. We could eat seven dinners for $3.00 a week.... I think that's all we ate for months.
>
> I applied for welfare.... It was the worst experience of my life.... I never dreamed that I, a middle class housewife, would ever be put in a position like that. It was humiliating... they make you feel it.... But we were desperate, and I had to feed my kids.
>
> You name it, I tried it—food stamps, soup kitchens, shelters. It just about killed me to have the kids live like that.... I finally called my parents and said we were coming... we couldn't have survived without them.
>
> Sometimes when you are so tense about money you go crazy... and you forget what it's like to be twelve years old and to think you can't live without Adidas sneakers... and to feel the whole world has deserted you along with your father.[25]

Many divorced mothers are thus forced into the labor market on a full-time basis and/or

---

[21] Ibid., p. 80

[22] U.S. Bureau of the Census, *Child Support and Alimony: 1985* (Washington, D.C.: U.S. Government Printing Office, 1989), p. 3.

[23] Lenore J. Weitzman, *The Divorce Revolution: The Unexpected Consequences for Women and Children in America* (New York: The Free Press, 1985).

[24] Ibid., p. 339.

[25] Ibid., pp. 339 and 340.

[26] See Terry J. Arendell, "Women and the Economics of Divorce in the United States," *Signs*, 13 (Autumn 1987): 121–

forced to rely on welfare assistance to provide for their families.[26] Divorce and failure to receive adequate child support have contributed to the so-called feminization of poverty (see Chapter 6). Almost 50 percent of the children living in households headed by women are poor. The figure for children in intact husband–wife households is 8 percent.[27] In Andrew Cherlin's words, "the most detrimental aspect of the absence of fathers from one-parent families is not the lack of a male presence but the lack of a male income."[28]

Fortunately, most persons who divorce do remarry—some three-fourths of all divorced women and an even higher percentage of divorced men. Remarriage usually takes place three to four years after divorce. It can ease the economic burden carried by divorced mothers, for many of whom this is the only viable solution. Yet the divorce rate among the remarried is slightly higher than that for those in their first marriage, a fact that should underscore the fragility of marriage as an institution in contemporary times.

VIOLENCE IN THE FAMILY

Ideally, one's family should always exist as an oasis, a place that is safe and satisfying, where one can seek relief from and aid in dealing with the often stressful demands of the outside world. In too many cases today, however, the family setting is just the opposite; it contains levels of tension, conflict, and violence from which flight might be the only rational response. Many persons now admit to being aware of victims of family violence (see Table 12.5.)

Consider this statement by researchers considered experts in their subject matter: "Americans run the greatest risk of assault, physical injury, and even murder in their own homes by members of their own families."[29] Such statements are based not on alarmist rhetoric but on empirical research that has revealed startling rates of husband and wife abuse, parental abuse of their children, and children's abuse of their parents and one another. (By *abuse* we mean acts of physical violence.)[30]

Prior to research by Murray A. Straus and his colleagues, our knowledge of violence in the family was limited. Families in which abuse took place were commonly believed to be abnormal and pathological, their members perhaps victims of mental illness. It was also commonly thought that episodes of violence in the family were almost entirely restricted to the poor. Straus and colleagues have systematically destroyed these views as myths.[31]

The researchers examined 2,143 families who were carefully chosen to be representative of approximately 47 million families in America. The families were not known to have any mentally ill members, and they reflected a broad cross section with regard to age, class, race, and region of the country. An adult from each of the 2,143 families was interviewed and asked a variety of questions bearing on violence in the home. The purpose was to establish, for the first time, the "incidence rate" of family violence. (The incidence rate in this case refers to the frequency with which acts of violence occurred in the year prior to the interviews.) Violence was defined as "an act carried out with the inten-

35, and her *Mothers and Divorce* (Berkeley: University of California Press, 1986).

[27] U.S. Bureau of the Census, *Poverty in the United States, 1987* (Washington, D.C.: U.S. Government Printing Office, 1989), p. 11.

[28] Cherlin, *Marriage, Divorce, Remarriage*, p. 81.

[29] Murray A. Straus, Richard J. Gelles, and Suzanne K. Steinmetz, *Behind Closed Doors: Violence in the American Family* (Garden City, N.Y.: Anchor Books, 1980), p. 4.

[30] See Richard Gelles, "Family Violence," *Annual Review of Sociology*, 11 (1985): 347–67.

[31] The data and discussion that follow are drawn from Straus, Gelles, and Steinmetz, *Behind Closed Doors*, and from Murray A. Straus, "A Sociological Perspective on Violence in the Family," in Maurice R. Green, ed., *Violence and the Family* (Boulder, Colo.: Westview Press, 1980), pp. 7–31.

TABLE 12.5 Child Maltreatment Cases Reported, 1976–85

Item	1976	1977	1978	1979	1980	1981	1982	1983	1984	1985
Number of children reported (in thousands)	**669**	**838**	**836**	**988**	**1,154**	**1,225**	**1,262**	**1,477**	**1,727**	**1,928**
Rate per 10,000 children	101	128	129	154	181	194	201	236	273	306
Type of maltreatment										
Deprivation of necessities	70.7	64.0	62.9	63.1	60.7	59.4	62.5	58.4	54.6	55.7
Minor physical injury	18.9	20.8	21.2	15.4	19.8	20.4	16.8	18.5	17.7	15.4
Sexual maltreatment	3.2	6.1	6.6	5.8	6.8	7.5	6.9	8.5	13.3	11.7
Emotional maltreatment	21.6	25.4	23.8	14.9	13.5	11.9	10.0	10.1	11.2	8.9
Unspecified physical injury	0.5	0.4	0.4	2.5	3.1	3.2	4.7	5.2	3.6	4.1
Major physical injury	3.1	3.7	3.5	4.4	3.9	4.1	2.4	3.2	3.3	2.2
Other maltreatment	7.6	7.5	7.4	8.9	7.7	11.7	9.2	8.3	9.6	10.2
Characteristics of child involved										
Age, average (years)	7.7	7.6	7.4	7.5	7.3	7.2	7.1	7.1	7.2	7.1
Sex										
Male	50.0	49.9	49.4	49.5	49.8	49.2	49.5	48.9	48.0	48.1
Female	50.0	50.1	50.6	50.5	50.2	50.5	50.5	51.1	52.0	51.9
Race/ethnicity										
White	61.1	67.7	67.1	65.7	69.4	67.8	64.9	67.5	67.0	(NA)
Black	19.8	19.1	21.1	22.2	18.8	21.7	21.7	19.7	20.8	(NA)
Hispanic	11.1	6.8	8.0	9.2	9.7	8.6	10.9	9.9	9.6	(NA)
Other	8.0	6.3	3.8	2.9	2.0	1.9	2.4	2.9	2.6	(NA)
Characteristics of caretaker										
Age, average (years)	32.6	32.0	32.0	31.9	31.7	31.6	31.4	31.6	31.9	(NA)
Sex										
Male	38.9	39.1	38.0	37.6	37.5	36.8	36.5	36.9	38.5	(NA)
Female	61.1	60.9	62.0	62.4	62.5	63.2	63.5	63.1	61.5	(NA)
Race/ethnicity										
White	65.3	71.5	70.4	72.1	72.7	73.0	70.8	73.1	74.5	(NA)
Black	17.0	15.9	17.2	17.5	16.6	18.6	19.1	17.5	17.5	(NA)
Hispanic	10.0	6.4	9.6	4.9	5.1	4.7	6.1	6.8	5.5	(NA)
Other	7.7	6.2	2.8	5.5	5.6	3.7	4.0	2.6	2.5	(NA)
Family characteristics										
Single-female–headed families	38.5	38.7	40.7	41.8	39.3	43.1	43.4	40.3	37.4	(NA)
Children in household, average (number)	2.3	2.3	2.2	2.2	2.2	2.2	2.2	2.2	2.2	2.3
Families receiving public assistance	45.0	46.5	43.9	48.3	44.2	43.4	43.4	47.4	48.3	(NA)
Characteristics of perpetrator										
Age, average (years)	32.3	31.7	31.7	32.0	31.4	33.8	31.2	31.3	31.5	31.5
Sex										
Male	39.0	39.2	39.0	38.1	41.2	39.3	38.6	40.4	43.0	40.6
Female	61.0	60.8	61.0	61.9	58.8	60.7	61.4	59.6	57.0	59.4
Race/ethnicity										
White	65.1	71.2	71.2	71.2	72.0	71.1	69.0	69.5	69.9	(NA)
Black	17.7	16.5	18.4	19.1	17.6	19.7	19.7	18.7	19.1	(NA)
Hispanic	9.5	6.3	7.4	7.2	8.3	7.5	9.2	9.8	9.3	(NA)
Other	7.7	6.0	3.0	2.5	2.1	1.7	2.1	2.0	1.9	(NA)

[In percent, except as indicated. Total number of children reported is generally a duplicate count in that a child may be reported and therefore enumerated more than once each year. Because of differences in enumeration methods, a relatively small number of states (5 to 10) can provide only unduplicated reports, whereas most states provide only duplicated counts.]

Key: NA, not available.

Source: U.S. Department of Commerce, Bureau of the Census, *Statistical Abstract of the United States, 1989* (Washington, D.C.: U.S. Government Printing Office, 1989), p. 172.

tion of, or perceived as having the intention of, physically hurting another person."[32]

Spouse Abuse

The interviews revealed that incidents of violence between husband and wife had occurred in one in six families in the previous year. While most incidents were relatively minor, involving slapping, shoving, pushing, or throwing things at a person, some were far more serious in terms of real or potential physical harm. In 6 percent of the families, the incidents involved such acts as punching, kicking, biting, hitting with an object, or using a knife or gun. Husbands beat up their wives only slightly more frequently than wives beat their husbands, although it was thought that violence by wives out of self-defense could help to account for this particular finding. What this means is that some 3 million families experience serious acts of spouse abuse each year. Seven and one-half million experience violence of some sort annually.

Child Abuse

The interviews that Straus et al. conducted revealed rates of child abuse that were even higher than rates of spouse abuse. Seven out of ten parents used some form of physical violence on their children in the year prior to the interviews. Again, in most cases this was relatively minor (e.g., spanking). But 14 percent of the children suffered serious attacks. Overall, approximately 6.5 million children in a single year were subject to abuse by being punched, kicked, bitten, hit with an object, beaten up, or attacked with a knife or gun.

Child-initiated Violence

Findings of the research suggest that perhaps one in five children hit a parent the previous year, including a parent who was elderly. One in ten used a method in which the risk of physical injury was high. Children also attack one another, at rates higher than their physical attacks on anyone else in the family.

Comment on the Findings

Straus and colleagues readily admit that their findings may underestimate the rate of family violence to an unknown degree. There are several reasons for this. Some of those interviewed may not have recalled or not have chosen to reveal violent incidents. The 2,143 families studied represent only intact families, thus omitting child abuse data for single-parent households. The research also did not examine violence between parents and their children under age three. Finally, the families studied represented 65 percent of those originally selected. It is conceivable that those who chose not to participate in the study may have functioned in families that were more violent than the families willing to be interviewed.

Nonetheless, the data reveal that violence in the family is widespread. Mental illness does not seem to be a major factor among those involved in violent acts; perhaps no more than 10 percent of the family violence that occurs is linked to psychological problems. While rates of violence were found to be highest among low-income families, the researchers' data revealed that violence is common across all income lines.

The next question is "Why?" How does one account for family violence? If mental illness and the ravages of poverty fail to provide more than partial answers, what are the causes of behavior that can leave adults and children injured and even result in loss of life?

According to Straus and colleagues, violence in the family has been around for a long time. Family life may have been even more violent in the past, although this is difficult to ascertain firmly. The reasons underlying family violence cannot be reduced simply to psychological prob-

[32] Straus, "A Sociological Perspective on Violence in the Family," p. 29.

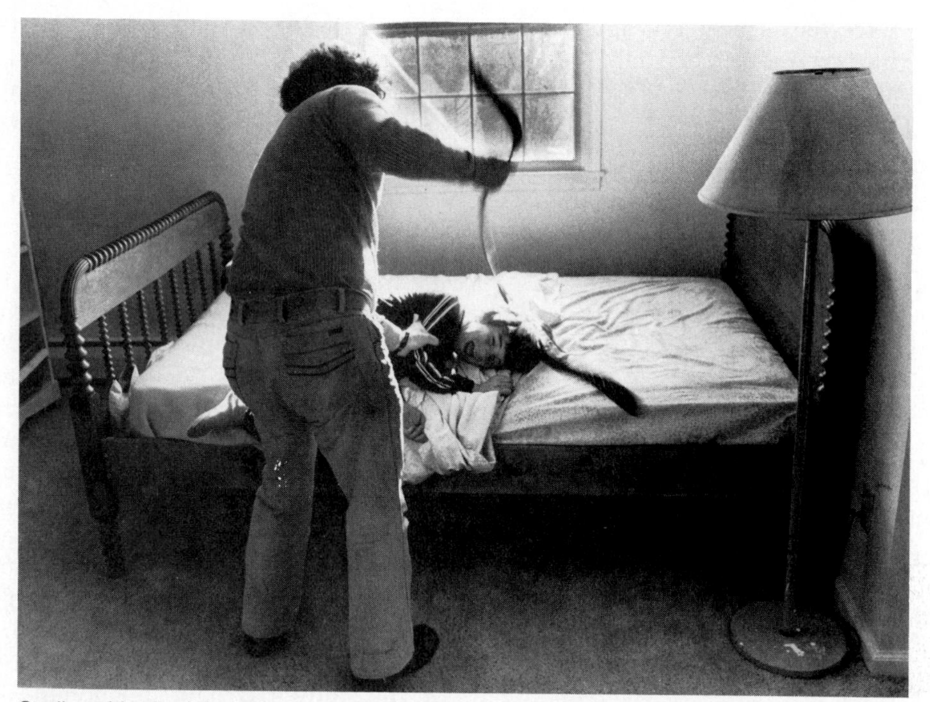

Studies of family violence have revealed that the rate of child abuse is higher than many people realize. Fortunately public awareness has been on the increase and more cases of abuse are being reported. Still, it is difficult to know of all such cases. This father, shown beating his son with a belt, may never have to answer to authorities for his actions. *(Robert Kalman/The Image Works)*

lems; instead they seem to be rooted largely in the nature of the family itself and influenced by other features of American society as a whole. This is not to say that persons who physically abuse other family members are somehow blameless for their actions. But much family violence is thought to be "situational": There are social and cultural influences that may propel persons toward the use of violence, and in many cases this violence is widely tolerated. What are these social and cultural influences?

First, persons may entertain the use of violence in the family setting as an option partially because they themselves were physically abused or because they observed other family members' violence. Thus, the use of violence to solve interpersonal problems becomes part of the outlook on life of clinically "normal" people. The use of violence is also constantly reinforced and subtly sanctioned in books, movies, and television shows, as well as through celebration of the activities of society's military forces and police agencies. In this sense the types of data being generated on violence in the family reflect both direct and indirect socialization into the larger culture and the behavior it often tolerates.

A second social and cultural influence pertains to social norms. Norms are rules or standards that define what is socially acceptable behavior. Thus, according to Straus and colleagues, some family violence can be termed *normal violence* in that it is tolerated and accorded legitimacy. As an example of such norms, Straus offers the following: "If someone is doing something wrong and 'won't listen to reason,' it is o.k. to hit."[33]

On the other hand, some violence is seen as socially unacceptable. Termed *abusive violence* by Straus and colleagues, this usually has the potential for inflicting the most serious physical harm. According to Straus, police may define what is considered abusive violence in accordance with the "stitch rule." In many cities police informally observe a norm that holds that unless family disputes result in more than a certain number of stitches, arrests are unlikely to be made. In sum, social norms influence the acceptance or nontolerance of violence within the family.

A third facet of the phenomenon of violence rests with the way in which the family itself is organized. According to Straus and colleagues, family organization can generate conflict between members that may result in incidents of violence. Conflict may be built into the family setting as a consequence of differences in age and sex of family members or differences in roles to be played (e.g., husband vs. wife, parents vs. children). Moreover, when differences do arise they may be felt far more intensely than differences between persons in nonfamily settings, because family members are very involved with one another emotionally.

Family units consider themselves to be collectivities whose business is theirs alone, and others usually share this view. The privacy demanded by and allowed families means that behavior in the home is subject to less public scrutiny and control than is behavior in other institutional settings (e.g., a place of employment, worship, schooling).

Finally, families are subject to a great deal of stress that may help to propel persons into violent behavior. This is particularly the case for low-income families, among whom rates of violence tend to be highest. During their life cycles most families suffer stressful events; at the same time they may be faced with substantial social responsibilities. Husbands and wives, facing stressful life conditions, may include violence in their repertoire of coping mechanisms—hitting out at others who may not even be the cause of the anger they feel. Children, caught up in a situation in which the use of violence may have become a norm, may know of no other way of dealing with their own stressful experiences.

In a study sponsored by the U.S. Department of Justice, researchers found that many of the victims of family violence brought to the attention of the courts continue to be victimized for months or even years after the original case is resolved.[34] The fact that court intervention does not necessarily provide protection for abused family members only serves to underscore the importance of the various social and cultural forces contributing to family violence that social scientists have endeavored to identify.

SEXUAL ABUSE OF CHILDREN

The attention given to violence in the family in recent years, and particularly to child abuse, has inevitably led to concern with what Florence Rush has called "the best kept secret": sexual abuse of children.[35] Long considered not a topic to be discussed in polite company, social scientists have finally begun to explore it in a small-scale way. The little research that has been done indicates that the sexual abuse of children is more widespread than most of us would prefer to believe.[36]

[33] Ibid., p. 16.

[34] See "A Study of Patterns in Family Violence," *New York Times* (June 8, 1983): C14.

[35] Florence Rush, *The Best Kept Secret: Sexual Abuse of Children* (New York: McGraw-Hill Book Company, 1980).

[36] Stefanie Doyle Peters, Gail Elizabeth Wyatt, and David Finkelhor, "Prevalence," in David Finkelhor et al., eds., *A*

In one study David Finkelhor surveyed 796 college students. Of 530 female students, 19 percent admitted to having been sexually victimized during childhood. For males, the percentage was lower—8.6 percent.[37] If the victims' experiences were to be projected to the U.S. population as a whole, this would mean that over 30 million persons will have had a sexual encounter with an adult while in childhood. Although our ability to generalize to the population at large from a survey of college students is doubtful, other research is beginning to confirm the widespread incidence of child sexual abuse.

In a more recent study, Finkelhor interviewed parents in 521 Boston families. This carefully selected sample of families had a total of 1,428 children between the ages of six and fourteen. Among the reported findings are these:[38]

1. Nine percent of the parents said one of their own children had been a victim or attempted victim of sexual abuse. (Finkelhor believes the actual rate could be double the 9 percent, given that children frequently do not report it.)
2. Children from every social class and ethnic and racial background were equally vulnerable to sexual abuse.
3. Forty-seven percent of the parents knew of a child who was a victim of sexual abuse; in 37 percent of these cases the victim was six years old or younger.
4. Fifteen percent of the female parents and 6 percent of the male parents had themselves been sexually abused as children. In only a third of the cases were the abusers strangers; 67 percent of the abusers were relatives, acquaintances, or their own parents.

Sourcebook on Child Sexual Abuse (Beverly Hills, Calif.: Sage Publications, 1986), pp. 15–59.

[37] David Finkelhor, *Sexually Victimized Children* (New York: The Free Press, 1979).

[38] David Finkelhor, *Child Sexual Abuse* (New York: The Free Press, 1984), Chapter 6.

Many of the cases of abuse fail to come to the attention of authorities. In the preceding study, only 56 percent of the parents interviewed reported their children's abuse. What is reported thus is no doubt simply the tip of the iceberg. For example, a quarter of all rapes reported to authorities involve victims who are under twelve. Sexual assault centers and hospitals commonly see children who have been sexually abused, and many children served by youth shelters, runaway services, and juvenile facilities have had such experiences.

Not all cases of child sexual abuse involve such violent acts as rape. Not all come about through the use of force or physical coercion. Nor is sexual intercourse always involved. The bulk of the offenders are thought to be members of the victims' families or family friends. Almost all offenders are male. Faced with demands for sexual activities that many children may not even understand, demands posed by persons who are usually known and trusted, children often simply comply. They may not know they have the right to refuse, or they may be afraid to do so. Abuse may last for long periods of time, even years.

Florence Rush argues that most of the adults who engage in sexual activity with children are not mentally disturbed. They seek out a child for sexual pleasure

> because a child, more than a woman, has less sexual experience, less physical strength, is more trusting of and dependent upon adults and therefore can be more easily coerced, seduced, lured, or forced.[39]

Difficulties arise in dealing with child sexual abuse within the circles of family and friends. Adults to whom complaints are made may not believe the victim, or they may even blame the victim. Children may be reluctant to complain in the first place, feeling confused and power-

[39] Rush, *The Best Kept Secret*, pp. 2–3.

PUBLIC PROBLEM, PRIVATE PAIN

The Secret Trauma

We have come to learn that incest is far more common in our society than anyone had realized. Child sexual abuse within families most frequently involves father or stepfather abuse of daughters. This selection illustrates the impacts such abuse may have (impacts that victims can help to heal through counseling, no matter when the abuse took place in their lives).

The most upsetting experience was when I was fourteen. My parents were alcoholics and would stay up till 4 or 5 A.M. drinking and fighting. When my mother would pass out, my father would get my sister and me out of bed for "family discussions." He thought my mother was sexually inhibited and he said he was going to help my sister and me through it so we wouldn't be inhibited too. One night I got up to go to the bathroom and my father was still up. He picked me up bodily, sat me on the table and kissed me. Because he was so drunk and couldn't stop me, I got off the table and after fifteen minutes of argument, I managed to leave and go to bed.

(What about other times?) Right after they were married, when I was about eight and my mother was out, I asked if I could go to bed with him. Being young and without a father, I wanted to be close to him. He said yeah, but when in bed, he asked me if I knew the difference between boys and girls. He said, "Give me your hand." He was going to put it on his penis. I said, "I'd better go to my bed."

(Did you have other sexual experiences with him?) Yes. He'd do little things like say "Give me a kiss," then he'd turn his face so I'd have to kiss him on the mouth. I was careful around him at all times, and tried to avoid physical contact with him. My sister and I never wore just robes or underwear around him.

(What ended it?) I left home at sixteen. (Upset?) Extremely upset. (Effect on your life?) A great effect. It had a much greater effect than being raped by a stranger—someone you'll never see again. I never told my mother. It would have broken her heart and I don't know if she would have believed me. It's so awful on Christmas, birthdays, and especially Father's Day. I have to send the bastard a card for her sake, and I spend hours in card shops looking for a card that's not mushy—that doesn't say "what a wonderful father you are."

I wanted a father—someone to be close to—not someone I had to be afraid of every moment I was with him. It's very, very sad. My own father left us, so my father image is bad. Because of my father and my stepfather, I felt all men were rotten. It became really hard to relate to men and to trust them. However, I've discovered they have feelings and they're not all bad.

It inhibited me sexually for a long time. There has to be a certain kind of trust for me to have sex with a male. Every time anyone makes a sexual comment or yells at me on the street, I ask myself, "What kind of image am I projecting? Is it the way I walk, or dress, or look? There must be something about me—an aura—that brings that out in people that pass by. Or is it just chance?" The thing that's kept me going is I've been a strong person. I left home early and put myself through school. I'm a fighter. I can't spend the rest of my life brooding about this. I can't jump off bridges, so I just move on.

I've thought of another effect and this is a biggy! My mother is a very sexually inhibited person. She became an alcoholic and thereby avoided it [sex]. After marrying my stepfather, my mother gained an incredible amount of weight and became unattractive to my stepfather. I realize that I did the same thing; I gained about fifty pounds and still can't get rid of the extra weight. I ate constantly also to make myself unattractive to men and to not have to deal with them.

(What did you find most helpful in dealing with the experiences with your stepfather?) Myself. Getting away from the household. And I took psychology courses in college to get more understanding of what had happened.

Source: Diana E. H. Russell, *The Secret Trauma: Incest in the Lives of Girls and Women*, pp. 246–47.

less. Concerned adults may interpret the incidents as less than serious, often to avoid rupturing interpersonal relationships with the offenders for personal, social, or even economic reasons.

Father or stepfather and daughter incest, found to be the most common form of child sexual abuse in David Finkelhor's study of college students, is a case in point. In many families in which incest takes place, the mother is helpless. Ashamed to reveal what is happening to others, fearful of involving law enforcement officials, often ignorant of other sources of assistance, and dependent on her husband for economic support for herself and other family members, the mother often withdraws and is frequently depressed. As a consequence, most offenders in cases of incest go undetected by outside authorities and are rarely elevated to the status of criminal.

Perhaps one of the most revealing pieces of research on incest and nonfamilial sexual abuse of children is that conducted by Diana Russell in San Francisco.[40] A carefully selected sample of 930 women residents was interviewed and asked about their experiences as victims of such abuses. The women were first asked if they had ever experienced "incestuous abuse," which

> includes any kind of exploitative sexual contact or attempted sexual contact that occurred between relatives, no matter how distant the relationship, before the victim turned eighteen years old.[41]

Russell found that 16 percent of the women had had at least one experience with incestuous abuse (e.g., sexual propositions, unwanted touching or kissing, forced intercourse) with a relative. In three-fourths of these cases, the incestuous abuse had taken place before the victim was fourteen years of age.

Russell also asked whether the women had been victims of sexual abuse apart from that involving relatives (and also omitting unwanted sexual behavior from a partner in the teenage dating years). If we add these cases to those noted in the preceding paragraph, the experiences of abuse are greatly magnified. Russell found that *38 percent* of the women had had at least one experience with incestuous and/or nonfamilial sexual abuse before reaching age eighteen. And in two-thirds of all the cases, the abuse was experienced before age fourteen.

We do not know if Russell's study has produced results that can be safely generalized to America's female population at large. But it seems safe to say that both incestuous and nonfamilial sexual abuse of children and teens are much more common than many of us would like to believe.

Amazingly, there are a few professionals in the mental health field who argue that adult sexual encounters with children are in many cases harmless and in some cases even positive.[42] That such views are in the minority is largely due to evidence on the often harmful consequences of sexual abuse.[43] These consequences include genital injury, venereal disease, and pregnancy. Moreover, there are emotional effects. These may be expressed in a variety of ways, including loss of appetite, nightmares, bed-wetting, depression and inability to function, and even suicide. Residues of guilt and anger may last long after the occasion of abuse.

While child sexual abuse may be our "best kept secret," in recent years our cultural environment has been one in which children are portrayed in erotic terms. There has been a flowering of attention to child and youth sexuality in films and pornographic materials (so-called kiddie porn).[44] Advertisements for such pop-

---

[40] Diana E. H. Russell, *The Secret Trauma: Incest in the Lives of Girls and Women* (New York: Basic Books, 1986).

[41] Ibid., p. 59.

[42] Ibid., pp. 38–39.

[43] For views of some who have been sexually abused as children, see Ellen Bass and Louise Thornton, eds., *I Never Told Anyone* (New York: Harper & Row Publishers, 1982).

[44] David Finkelhor, "Sexual Abuse: A Sociological Perspective," *Child Abuse and Neglect*, 6 (1982): 99.

ular consumer items as blue jeans have used young girls in adultlike seductive poses to invite attention to the product. Such efforts, motivated by nothing more than a crude quest for profit, may help to legitimate the unspoken and generally unacceptable notion that children can be treated as sex objects. The role of the media in this regard remains speculative, since there is little research on this topic.

RUNAWAYS AND HOMELESS CHILDREN

One response to neglect or abuse within the family is to flee, even if only temporarily. Since the mid-1970s the federal government has provided limited funds to assist runaways through support of youth shelters and telephone hotlines that encourage children to initiate contact with their families. Yet as more has been learned about the runaways, it has become increasingly apparent that many have not simply fled home but have been made to leave. So-called pushouts or "throwaway children," as they have been termed, are effectively homeless. The pushout phenomenon may be viewed as yet another variant of the overall spectrum of child abuse. Runaways ordinarily can go home; they have a home to return to. Pushouts cannot.[45]

At least 1 million children, mostly between the ages of ten and seventeen, leave home each year. As many as half may be pushouts. Some of the pushouts are "economic refugees," evicted by parents facing financial crises who find they cannot support their children. Of the million or more children who leave their homes annually, perhaps half have been victims of some form of parental abuse.[46]

Much of what is known about such children is based on surveys of those served by federally funded youth shelters, of which there are presently 166 around the country. Generalizations about the total runaway–pushout population on the basis of shelter surveys must be made with caution. The shelters serve only about 45,000 children annually, or approximately 5 percent of all who leave home. In any event, it is estimated that the average age of this group is fifteen and that some 60 percent are female. Seventy percent are white. While perhaps 40 percent are school dropouts, most have never been in any kind of trouble that brought them to the attention of juvenile authorities.

What happens to the children who leave home? Runaways are likely to return, usually within twenty-four to forty-eight hours of their disappearance. Of those who do not return in a short period, some will find their way to youth shelters. Others will be picked up by police and placed in jail, either because they must be held for legal disposition as homeless minors or because they have been charged with illegal acts. The latter frequently occur as children away from home struggle to cope with problems of economic survival. Survival may be possible only through such acts as theft and prostitution. Prostitution involves boys as well as girls, and it is estimated that one out of ten homeless children engage in it. Often prostitution results from coercion by adults to whom the children have turned for assistance and protection.[47]

In 1986 police around the nation arrested 138,586 persons under eighteen years of age because they were runaways. The characteristics of those arrested may not reflect the runaway population in general, it should be noted. Of those taken into custody, 55,984 were under age fifteen; 2,210 were under ten. The vast majority (84 percent) were white, and most (58 percent) were female.[48] By 1988, the number of those

[45] U.S. Senate, Committee of the Judiciary, *Homeless Youth: The Saga of Pushouts and Throwaways in America* (Washington, D.C.: U.S. Government Printing Office, 1980).

[46] Arlene Rubin Stiffman, "Physical and Sexual Abuse in Runaway Youths," *Child Abuse and Neglect*, 13 (1989): 417–26.

[47] See "A Nation of Runaway Kids," *Newsweek*, 100 (October 18, 1982): 97, and "An Endless Parade of Runaway Kids," *U.S. News & World Report*, 94 (January 17, 1983): 64.

[48] Timothy J. Flanagan and Katherine M. Jamieson, eds., *Sourcebook of Criminal Justice Statistics, 1987* (Washington,

arrested increased 20 percent, to 166,900.[49]

Social science research on children who leave home is limited. However, there is evidence to suggest that, at least for runaways, a variety of factors are influential in determining the decision to flee home. First, children who run away are likely to face a lot of stress within their families.[50] In the words of Tim Brennan and colleagues, families of runaways frustrate "important youth needs and satisfactions, such as the need for security and belonging, the need for autonomy, the need for feelings of competence and self-esteem, the need to be understood."[51] The families of runaways are likely to combine displays of power (e.g., physical punishment, denial of privileges) with apparent withdrawal of love and parental remoteness. Often these processes occur simultaneously with family disruption resulting from death, divorce, or job loss. In all, families of runaways provide little in the way of role models for their children.

Brennan and colleagues have also found that school experiences typically add to the stresses experienced by children who run away. Runaways are more likely than nonrunaways to experience "negative labeling by teachers, blocked access to rewarding roles, low grades, failure tracks, expulsions, suspensions, being beaten by teachers and so on."[52] Thus, bonds to school as well as family are weakened. While there are no doubt some children who leave home simply for adventure and a quest for excitement, these cases are clearly in the minority.

As stated earlier, most runaways return home. The situation of pushouts is much more serious, because they are homeless. A U.S. Senate study, commenting on pushouts and throwaway children, warns of the severity of this family-related problem:

> There is no reason to doubt the numbers of homeless youth will increase. Certainly the wasted lives and talents of these youngsters represent a tremendous loss of human potential to our society. As the size of the homeless population grows, there will be an even larger underclass of bitter, defeated, or angry people in this country.[53]

WHAT IS TO BE DONE?

The picture painted in this chapter is very bleak. One must place these problems in perspective; it is clear that most American families are harmonious and enriching, with children who develop nicely.

With regard to the family-related problem of premarital births and teenage motherhood, some very sensitive issues must be confronted. Youths must be accepted as sexual beings, even if they are only in the process of becoming personally, socially, and intellectually mature. As such, many will make the decision to become sexually active and to engage in intercourse, although the rates will no doubt fluctuate. Knowing this, it seems that the only rational response is to seek to reduce risk of pregnancy. This can be done only by giving teenagers knowledge about contraception and contraceptive devices and seriously promoting birth control as an inviolable prerequisite to premarital sexual behavior. The costs of not doing this—to the unwed mother and child, and to the rest of society—far outweigh the costs of possibly encouraging a small percentage of youths to become sexually active who might not otherwise have done so.

Still, pregnancies will occur. Some teenagers—even when armed with knowledge and

D.C.: U.S. Department of Justice, Bureau of Justice Statistics, 1988), Tables 4.5 and 4.6.

[49] U.S. Department of Justice, *Uniform Crime Reports for the United States, 1988* (Washington, D.C.: U.S. Government Printing Office, 1989), p. 168.

[50] Paul G. Shane, "Changing Patterns Among Homeless and Runaway Youth," *American Journal of Orthopsychiatry*, 59 (April 1989): 208–14.

[51] Tim Brennan, David Huizinga, and Delbert S. Elliott, *The Social Psychology of Runaways* (Lexington, Mass.: Lexington Books, 1978), p. 303.

[52] Ibid.

[53] U.S. Senate, *Homeless Youth*, p. 83.

having ready access to contraceptive resources—will ignore it all. Accidents will occur. Nor is the technology of contraception 100 percent effective. Abortion will no doubt continue to be a highly charged moral and political issue and an avenue rejected by many pregnant teenagers (as well as adults). Some may opt to place their babies for adoption; many will not. If nothing else is done for those who do become mothers, current efforts to provide guidance and support in parenting skills, health assistance, and help in completion of formal education must be greatly expanded. The meager and begrudging help presently offered to young persons who are locked into the responsibility of mothering young babies is a shocking comment on the level of Americans' concern for human life.

Marital dissolution cannot be avoided. In many cases divorce is a solution as well as a problem. The two major areas of deepest concern should be those of (1) adjustment to divorce by adults and children, and (2) economic security for those left most vulnerable by family breakup (commonly the wives and children). The limited steps that are taken to hold fathers to financial responsibility can only be improved. The notion that men who father children have little or no responsibility for the standard of living and life chances of the children after divorce deserves full condemnation.

As for adjustment to divorce, the resources presently available to adults—from professional guidance to self-help groups—should be utilized more fully. The trend toward joint custody, where the divorced parents both play a continual role in parenting, is a positive way of fostering children's emotional adjustment and should be further encouraged. The decline in the number of children on average that are involved in divorce actions is a welcome trend.

Violence in the family seems unstoppable. It is really only in the last few years that family violence has been systematically revealed and widely acknowledged as a problem. The same can be said for the sexual abuse of children. It has been argued that such phenomena have long existed in this society and that the widespread attention they are presently receiving represents shifting attitudes that could well be necessary for behavioral change. Concern with the rights of persons within a family setting is perhaps an extension of concern over the rights of other categories of persons whose treatment is often harmful (e.g., racial minorities, women, the old, the disabled).

The identification of hidden and often tolerated acts in family settings as abuse, outside of the realm of socially acceptable behavior, is at least a start. Such a normative shift is at the very least likely to mean that situations involving violence and other forms of serious abuse are more likely to be brought to the attention of law enforcement and social service agencies. However, the ability of such agencies to respond and successfully alter the behaviors in question will have to be considerably expanded. At present social service agencies are overwhelmed with "business," and they are—far more than law enforcement agencies—understaffed and precariously funded. None of this, unfortunately, addresses the broader social and cultural determinants of family turmoil and abuse. Attitudinal shifts and increased intervention efforts are thus likely to do little more than stem the tide, barring more radical transformations in the self-concept of the American family (and of American society in general).

So long as families are troubled, children will run away. The runaway phenomenon is best understood as an indicator of the existence of child abuse and/or neglect. Thus, our comments regarding the desirability of attitude shifts and increased intervention to aid families are again applicable. But the pushout phenomenon is something else again. Ideally, there would be reason and opportunity for intervention *before* parents deny children their homes. Yet it is likely that many children will have no choice but to try and make a life outside their family setting. For most, youth and economic circumstance virtually dictate that they find their way to families who want them. An expansion of foster family care and small-group homes is required to meet the immediate needs of pushouts.

SUMMARY

Family-related problems have attracted widespread attention in recent years. The rising rates of premarital pregnancy and teenage unwed motherhood have contributed to an increase in single-parent households. Teenage pregnancies reflect the fact that more teenagers are sexually active than in the past, along with their frequent failure to employ effective contraceptive measures. Teenage mothers and their children are at higher than average risk for health-related problems, and their life chances are frequently diminished.

Rates of marital dissolution have also been on the increase and have made a contribution to the number of single-parent households. Divorce rates may have gone up because of more permissive divorce laws; contraceptive advances that permit women more control over childbearing; female participation in the labor force and the possibility of economic independence from a husband; stresses faced by families, particularly economic ones; and changing attitudes toward marriage. Divorce, which involves a major life transition, requires difficult emotional adjustments on the part of adults and children. It almost always has a negative economic impact on the single-parent household. The failure of women to receive adequate child support from their former husbands has contributed to the "feminization of poverty."

Recent research has also revealed high levels of violence within American families, including spouse abuse, child abuse, and violence by children against their parents and against one another. The reasons for such violence cannot be reduced to individual psychological problems in most cases, but lie more with social and cultural factors. Persons learn by observation that violence is often used to solve interpersonal problems and that it is frequently tolerated or accepted as a norm. Conflict that may escalate into violent acts may be built into family life, because of differences that arise between members. Families are permitted a great deal of privacy in handling their own affairs and thus are not subject to much control from without that would impede the expression of violence. Finally, there is the contribution of stress on the family, to which violence may be a response.

As such family-related problems as child abuse have become more widely recognized, the often hidden problem of sexual abuse of children has come to light. Child sexual abuse is more common than we might prefer to believe and commonly involves children and adults (almost always male adults) who are either relatives or family acquaintances. For the most part, offenders are thought to be psychologically undisturbed people who take advantage of the vulnerability and trust of children for their own needs. Most cases of abuse fail to come to the attention of law enforcement and social service agencies. While a few mental health professionals have tried to suggest that children's sexual encounters with adults may in many cases be harmless or even positive, reports of harmful physical health and emotional outcomes suggest otherwise. The treatment of children as possible sex objects by the mass media and in pornography may contribute to child sexual abuse.

One response by children to family turmoil, abuse, or neglect is to run away. Not only are runaways likely to have experienced ill treatment by their families, but they—more than nonrunaways—have negative experiences with teachers and schooling. While runaways usually return to their homes, many other children have no homes to return to. So-called pushouts, or throwaway children, are made to leave by their families. Pushouts and runaways who remain away from home face problems of economic survival that can propel them into such illegal activities as theft and prostitution.

What is to be done? The family-related problem of premarital births and unwed teenage motherhood makes apparent the need for sex education and encouragement of the use of effective contraceptive measures as a norm for sexually active youth. Greater support in such areas as parenting, health, and completion of formal education for pregnant teenagers who decide to be mothers is imperative.

The two areas of major concern with regard to divorce are adjustment to it and the economic stabilization of the custodial parent (commonly the mother) and children. Ways must be found to hold fathers financially responsible for children involved in divorces. The trend toward joint custody—wherein divorced mothers and fathers continue to share in parenting—is a positive step in the adjustment area. The fact that fewer children are involved in divorces (although the number is still substantial) is also a positive trend that may help ease adjustment and economic strains.

As violence in the family and child sexual abuse have become recognized as serious, widespread problems, there has been reduced tolerance of these problems; this may help bring about behavioral change. At the very least it is becoming more likely that family violence and child sexual abuse will be brought to the attention of law enforcement and social service agencies. More resources that would allow such agencies to respond and successfully alter the behaviors in question are needed.

Such intervention may also help to reduce the number of children who flee their homes as runaways; it may also reduce the number of pushouts. The latter, because of their youth and economic circumstances, do need alternative homes where they are wanted. Expanded networks of foster family care and small-group homes are required to meet the immediate needs of such homeless children.

DISCUSSION QUESTIONS

1. Despite lip-service paid to the need for sex education, many parents and religious officials continue to protest and resist its implementation in public schools. Simulate a dialogue between those for and those against school sex education.
2. Alarmed by the increasing rate of divorce, some experts have advocated a mandatory trial marriage period. For those who wished to remain together, a permanent license would then be issued and this marriage would be legally very difficult to dissolve. Discuss the pros and cons of such a policy.
3. Children seem to have fewer rights than adults in general, and this lack extends to their ability to avoid or end abuse. What additional rights do you think should be extended to children under the law? What might be the positive and negative outcomes of doing this?
4. As widespread as child and spouse abuse has become, it is time to raise questions about how to better deter it. What further deterrents are there? What are the obstacles to implementing these deterrents?
5. Running away from home is widely treated as a juvenile "status offense" and is punishable by court action. What arguments could be made for and against eliminating treatment of this behavior as a crime?

SUGGESTED READINGS

Edelman, Marian Wright. *Families in Peril* (Cambridge, Mass.: Harvard University Press, 1989).
Examination of the impact of family instability and poverty on children.

Russell, Diana E. H. *The Secret Trauma: Incest in the Lives of Girls and Women* (New York: Basic Books, 1986).
Incest and its impacts, as told by victims of this sexual abuse.

Teenage Pregnancy in the United States (New York: Alan Guttmacher Institute, 1989).
Overview of the teenage pregnancy problem and state programs designed to intervene.

Wallerstein, Judith S., and Sandra Blakeslee. *Second Chances* (New York: Ticknor & Fields, 1989).
A ten-year follow-up of an original set of interviews of young persons whose parents went through divorce.

Weitzman, Lenore J. *The Divorce Revolution: The Unexpected Consequences for Women and Children in America* (New York: The Free Press, 1985).
Legal issues surrounding divorce and child custody, and the economic hardships into which women and children are thrust.

Zinn, Maxine Baca, and D. Stanley Eitzen. *Diversity in American Families* (New York: Harper & Row Publishers, 1987).
The state of the family in America and the changes it has been undergoing.

CHAPTER 13

Criminal Behavior

Members of American society should be at peace with themselves and with one another. The vicarious rewards associated with crime and violence must have no attraction.

Periodically, pollsters ask a representative sample of Americans to list and rate the social problems they consider most serious. No list looks exactly like any other, as new issues are added and older ones receive different ratings. But crime shows up in every poll.

There is a very realistic basis for our concern with crime. National data reveal that one out of four households was touched by crime in a recent twelve-month period.[1] Most are victims of

---

[1] U.S. Department of Justice, Bureau of Justice Statistics, *Report to the Nation on Crime and Justice*, 2nd ed. (Washington, D.C.: U.S. Government Printing Office, 1988), p. 14.

property offenses rather than crimes of violence. In central city areas, particularly in and around low-income neighborhoods, the rates of victimization are even higher.

For the most part, the phrase *crime problem* primarily means larceny, burglary, robbery, auto theft, assault, rape, and murder to Americans. These crimes touch people very personally. In several, the victims come face to face with the perpetrators. Such experiences are often terrifying, if not dangerous or fatal.

The public is far less concerned about certain other categories of crime, perhaps because these seem rather distant and remote. White-collar crime, which costs billions of dollars more per year than common theft, arouses little public ire. Organized crime is more frequently a subject of entertainment programs than a threat to public sensibilities. Political crimes—whether engaged in by dissident groups or government officials—seem incomprehensible to many Americans and are easily ignored. Only the most spectacular incidents or revelations are likely to evoke widespread public concern about these types of crime, and even this is often quite temporary.

Thus, most Americans take a narrow view of the crime problem, focusing only on prospects or memories of personal victimization. This lack of concern about other types of crime is also found in the official crime statistics produced by law enforcement agencies. These statistics regularly focus on types of criminal behavior Americans fear. When publicized by the news media, official crime statistics reaffirm the legitimacy of public concern. The meaning and reliability of these statistics are rarely questioned, except perhaps by sociologists. Nor do most Americans ordinarily notice that certain categories of crime, such as many white-collar offenses, are absent from official reports.

Because of their concern over the crime problem, Americans support policies and expenditures that claim to be able to restore "law and order." Yet we need to understand more about the *causes* of criminal behavior. In the absence of an adequate understanding of the causes, America's system of criminal justice remains only partially effective in curbing the crime problem.

In this chapter we examine crime and criminal behavior in American society today. We try to answer the question "What is crime?" and look at sources of crime statistics and their limitations. With these limitations in mind, we assess the extent and significance of various categories of crime. The chapter then considers some physiological, psychological, and sociological explanations for criminal behavior. Finally, we look at the workings of the criminal justice system.

WHAT IS CRIME?

As we have seen, most Americans define *crime* as behavior that turns individuals into victims, posing a direct threat to their personal safety or property. The behaviors that are defined as criminal in this sense are considered evil in and of themselves—*mala in se*—such as murder and burglary. No one should have to live in constant fear of harm or loss of personal belongings. No society could continue to function if its members were free to attack one another or take others' property at will. Such acts are condemned in virtually every society. In short, there is universal agreement that certain offensive behaviors are not to be tolerated—they are "wrong" and thus criminal.

But this popular definition of crime as *mala in se* acts does not account for all types of criminal behavior. To define crime, we must examine the society's system of law. Legally, the concept of crime encompasses many more acts than the average American has in mind when discussing the crime problem. In the United States, the legal definition of crime is also very precise, referring to acts that are intentional, inexcusable or indefensible, in violation of an existing law, and punishable by the state.

The popular and legal definitions of crime do not always coincide. Americans frequently engage in behaviors that are crimes under the law, but that they do not necessarily think of as crimes. For example, workers often remove supplies or tools from their places of employment without realizing that they are committing property offenses. An estimated 65 million Americans have tried marijuana, but most would not describe themselves as drug offenders. Laws against fornication and adultery are broken daily, but the individuals involved are unlikely to see themselves as sex criminals. Not until agencies of law enforcement attempt to confer criminal status on individuals engaging in such acts are most Americans fully conscious of violating the law. Whether people are aware of or agree with the legal definition of crime, it is ultimately the law that makes an activity a crime and allows sanctions to be imposed on violators.

Elements of the Legal Definition

Let us look more closely at the legal definition of crime and the various elements involved in this definition. First, in order to be defined as a crime, an act must have been *intentional.* Although the concept of intention is somewhat vague, the law assumes that most people are capable of regulating their behavior and avoiding illegal acts. Hence, those who engaged in law-violating behavior must have intended to do so. While intentions are addressed by prosecutors in court, and accused individuals are given the opportunity to defend themselves, the burden of proving an act to be unintentional is placed squarely on the shoulders of the accused.

The legal definition of crime also involves the idea that the act in question is *inexcusable or indefensible.* One of the few excuses is that the individual had no control over the illegal behavior. Thus, individuals are unlikely to be accorded criminal status if they can prove that they were acting under duress—that is, if they were forced by others to violate the law. Likewise, age is considered to be relevant to the issue of control over, and thus responsibility for, criminal behavior. Ordinarily, children under seven years of age are not held responsible for their actions. Special judicial treatment is accorded individuals between seven and sixteen or eighteen years of age, because *juvenile delinquents* are ordinarily considered to be less responsible for their behavior than are adults. Finally, individuals may defend their illegal behavior by claiming insanity. In this case, accused persons may claim that they were mentally incapable of avoiding the act in question or incapable of differentiating between right and wrong at the time the law violation took place. (For a discussion of the insanity defense, see Chapter 14.)

Ultimately, however, the key element of the legal definition of crime is the *law* itself. The law enables the state to *punish* those whose acts are considered intentional, inexcusable, and in violation of a law by conferring the status of criminal on them. It is not too much of a truism to say that in the absence of law, criminals would not exist. Without law there is no such thing as crime—at least in the legal sense.

Defining Behavior as Criminal

Why do some acts get defined by law as crime while others do not? There are conflicting answers to this question. According to some, law is formulated in response to the will of the people. Members of the society, it is said, share common values. Law is the product of a societal consensus about what forms of behavior are to be allowed and what forms are to be condemned and punished. In this view, we live in a democratic, pluralistic society (see Chapter 2), in which equally powerful interest groups compete to direct and express the public will. The state responds by passing laws that serve the self-defined best interests of society's members. The state itself is neutral. It is not under the sway of any dominant group, for there is no such group in American society.

An alternative view holds that law is formulated in response to the interests of the dominant economic and social class. In a society like ours, wealth, status, and political power are unequally distributed. The dominant class—that which is most advantaged in terms of this distribution—is said to be in the best position to influence actions of the state. This class seeks to protect its economic resources and general well-being through the force of law. In this view, the state is not neutral—either in the formulation of law or in practices of law enforcement. Rather, the state acts in the interests and is an instrument of the dominant class.

Sociologist William Chambliss has suggested that the real state of affairs lies somewhere in between these two views.[2] According to Chambliss, there is evidence that some laws are indeed expressions of public opinion and are responses to pressure by interest groups. Examples include laws limiting pollution and statutes protecting minorities against discrimination. Other laws, however, clearly work to the advantage of the economically advantaged. Examples here are tax loopholes and the absence of severe legal penalties for many white-collar crimes. Thus, says Chambliss, there is evidence that members of the dominant class actively use their political power to influence the formulation of law so as to protect themselves.

Chambliss has proposed a third view of why acts are defined as crimes. He calls this view a *conflict theory of legal change*. This theory begins by recognizing that American society is composed of competing classes and interest groups that seek favors from the state. Since these classes differ in their wealth, power, and prestige, conflicts (e.g., over the control of economic resources) will and do take place. These conflicts ultimately cause acts to be defined as crimes:

> It is in the course of working through and living with these inherent conflicts that the law takes its particular content and form. It is out of the conflicts generated by social class divisions that the definition of some acts as criminal or delinquent emerges.[3]

Chambliss notes that the dominant class wins only some of these conflicts. Class-based conflicts are often resolved by the state through compromise legislation or legal decisions that seem fair to most if not all.

Meanwhile, according to Chambliss, a variety of interest groups that are not class-based are also competing for favors from the state. Bureaucracies want their interests protected or advanced. "Moral entrepreneurs"—groups with particular moral concerns that they would like to see translated into law—likewise compete for attention. Again there is winning, losing, and compromise as the state responds.

Chambliss suggests that the formulation of law, and thus the creation of the legal definition of crime, is a dynamic, historical process. This process is not totally democratic—in other words, law does not automatically emerge from and serve the interests of all members of society. Nor is the process totally manipulated by a dominant class. It is, however, a political process:

> What gets defined as criminal or delinquent behavior is the result of a political process within which rules are formed which prohibit or require people to behave in certain ways.... Nothing is inherently criminal, it is only the response that makes it so. If we are to explain crime, we must first explain the social forces that cause some acts to be defined as criminal while others are not.[4]

---

[2] William J. Chambliss, "The State, the Law, and the Definition of Behavior as Criminal or Delinquent," in Daniel Glaser, ed., *Handbook of Criminology* (Chicago: Rand McNally & Company, 1974), pp. 7–43.

[3] Ibid., p. 39

[4] Ibid.

Sociologists like Chambliss do research on how laws are formulated and how this leads to the "creation" of crime.[5] Clearly, the answer to the question "What is crime?" must go beyond a legal definition. The answer must include attention to the sources of any such definition.

CRIME STATISTICS

This chapter primarily considers crime as it is legally defined. In the United States, our perception of the crime problem is to a large extent based on official reports, such as the *Uniform Crime Reports* issued annually by the U.S. Department of Justice. Data in this report and from other sources as well must be approached with caution.[6]

Official Statistics

The Justice Department's *Uniform Crime Reports* is a summary of data submitted by almost 16,000 police departments around the country. These agencies of law enforcement are in a position to gather several types of crime statistics, including the number and kinds of crimes reported to or observed by local police, arrest statistics, and statistics on cases in which conviction took place. To assess the amount of crime taking place in the United States, one begins with data on the number of crimes reported to police or otherwise officially detected.

Sociologists have long been aware that the statistics accumulated by police departments and reported by them are of questionable accuracy. Many crimes simply are not brought to the attention of police and thus do not get counted. Murder is almost always reported; but perhaps several times as many rapes occur as are brought to police attention. While most people will report the theft of an automobile, far fewer will report the theft of personal property that is worth relatively little. A woman who is beaten up by a stranger on the street is likely to call the police; one who is assaulted by her husband is far less likely to do so.

In some cases, crimes are not reported to law enforcement agencies because the victims know the perpetrator and want to handle the problem informally. This often occurs for minor offenses. In other cases, people may feel that a crime is not worth reporting because it is unlikely that the police will handle it satisfactorily or solve it. In still other cases, the victims may fear retribution or revenge if they report offenses to the police. Finally, some crimes are simply never detected—or the illegal acts in question are not defined as crimes by those in a position to do the reporting. Whatever the reasons involved, we know that statistics on crime reported to the police grossly underestimate the extent of crime.

Official crime statistics are also subject to distortion by the actions of police themselves. Police departments differ in their vigilance and in the degree to which they are actively concerned with particular categories of crime. Attention to public complaints and police reaction to observed law violations may vary among police departments at different times. Police departments and individual officers have considerable discretion in making arrests. If they choose to avoid arresting individuals, the amount of crime will look smaller than it actually is. Alternatively, police activism may create the appearance of statistical increases in criminal behavior.

A case in point is the way police handle persons possessing illegal drugs. There has been an upward trend in arrests for possession and sale of illegal drugs in recent years. Part of this increase can be attributed to the fact that drug use was not considered an important problem during most of the 1960s, so police rarely made arrests, or else concentrated on certain segments

---

[5] For examples of such research, see Don C. Gibbons, *Society, Crime, and Criminal Behavior*, 5th ed. (Englewood Cliffs, N.J.: Prentice-Hall, 1987), pp. 56–69.

[6] Sue Titus Reid, *Crime and Criminology*, 5th ed. (New York: Holt, Rinehart & Winston, 1988), pp. 45–61.

of the population, such as the poor, when looking for drugs. From the late 1960s on, however, drug use became both more widespread and a matter of societal concern, and police became more vigilant. Nonetheless, police today continue to ignore many minor drug offenders—one need only go to a rock concert to see drug laws violated with impunity, often right in front of the police. Such crimes do not find their way into crime statistics.

Furthermore, individual police departments have different procedures for collecting and reporting crime statistics. The U.S. Department of Justice has been making notable efforts to encourage standardized procedures across the country, but it has not been totally successful. Moreover, as departments change their procedures to conform with federal standards, statistics on incidence may change even if the same amount of crime is occurring. There is also evidence that some police departments do not report all the crimes they know of. For example, in the 1960s the President's Commission on Law Enforcement found that a number of large city police departments kept separate records on crimes that they did not follow up and on those they wanted to keep from the public for political reasons.[7]

There is also the question of just what police are counting. A violation may involve one offender or many; it may also involve more than one law. For example, if two teenagers kill someone in a fight, escape by stealing a car after assaulting the driver, and are finally stopped after numerous traffic offenses, who and what is to be counted? When confronted with such dilemmas, police departments are likely to work out their own formulas. They may count crimes by the numbers of victims involved. Or they may count only the most serious crime (in terms of the probable penalty for conviction) committed by each offender. This and other inaccuracies in counting distort official statistics.

If trying to figure out what to make of official statistics is made difficult by such factors, trying to compute crime *rates* is even worse. Crime rates are important for a number of reasons. They make it possible to compare crime in different locales or over periods of time. Sociologists use comparative crime rates in the search for explanations of crime and criminality. Knowledge of changing rates is also of practical importance to officials interested in evaluating the effectiveness of efforts to prevent or control crime. The public wants to know whether the taxes they pay for law enforcement are being used wisely. People also use crime rates as a barometer of the quality of life in their communities.

Crime rates are calculated in terms of the ratio between the number of crimes officially recorded and the size of the population. For example, the murder rate is expressed in terms of the number of known murders per 100,000 people. One would assume that, since most murders become known to police, the murder *rate* is reliable. But there are problems other than the lack of reliability of police statistics. We only count the number of people in the American population every ten years. Even then, the Bureau of the Census misses millions—for example, inner-city residents, members of minority groups, the homeless, and persons in the country illegally are generally undercounted. This means that the population figures so crucial to computing crime rates are estimates. Crime rates can be no more reliable than the statistics that go into them, which means they should be treated with caution.

Another complication involves the changing composition of America's population. What may appear to be a shift in criminality may simply be a reflection of changing population charac-

[7] President's Commission on Law Enforcement and Administration of Justice, *The Challenge of Crime in a Free Society* (New York: Avon Books, 1968), p. 112. See also David Seidman and Michael Conzens, "Getting the Crime Rate Down: Political Pressure and Crime Reporting," *Law and Society Review*, 8 (Spring 1974): 457–93.

teristics. For example, young people are responsible for a disproportionate amount of such common crimes as robbery. A decrease in the rates for these crimes may simply be a result of a decreased proportion of young people. Such changes create problems. Do we know all the factors that must be taken into account in order to compare crime rates among locales or over time? How much weight should be given to those factors we do know about in order to interpret rates and compare them?

At best, official crime statistics provide an approximation of the actual amount of crime. Attempts to refine the methods of gathering, reporting, and interpreting such statistics continue, but substantial problems remain. Criminal codes defining what is a crime differ somewhat from state to state. Political considerations in a particular locale will probably always affect police activity and patterns of law enforcement. Individuals will probably never report each and every crime they know about. While the Justice Department can encourage and demand valid, standardized statistics from local law enforcement agencies, it cannot really do anything about such sources of error—except estimate the biases they introduce in crime data.

Victimization Studies

In an attempt to develop more satisfactory data on the extent of crime, some researchers have gone to the real or potential victims. Beginning in 1972, the U.S. Department of Justice began funding National Crime Surveys of victimization in which annual interviews are held with a national sample of people aged twelve and over.[8] In these interviews, individuals are asked whether they had been victims of rape, robbery, assault, or larceny in the past year. Data are also collected on burglary, larceny, and auto theft experienced by households. (See Table 13.1.)

The National Crime Surveys have shown that many crimes are not reported to police and thus never appear in official police statistics. Further, the reporting of crimes to police varies, depending on the type of crime. The findings of the surveys are consistent, in general, with the more limited studies carried out by sociologists in the 1960s.[9]

Besides the striking evidence of underreported crimes, the National Crime Surveys also reveal some interesting facts about crime victims. In the case of violent crime, for example, the rates of victimization are highest among those who are young, male, black, divorced or separated or never married, and unemployed and who are from families with annual incomes under $7,500.[10]

Victimization surveys can be criticized. One has to assume that the sample of people being interviewed is representative of the population as a whole. One must also assume that those interviewed are providing accurate information—that they are neither consciously distorting nor unintentionally forgetting information.[11] But even with such possible sources of error, victimization studies have opened up a whole new way of measuring the extent of crime in the United States. The most serious limitation of the surveys is their very narrow focus on certain categories of crime to the exclusion of others. For example, nothing is asked about consumer fraud as a victimization of people.

---

[8] See, for example, U.S. Department of Justice, Bureau of Justice Statistics, *Criminal Victimization in the United States 1986* (Washington, D.C.: U.S. Government Printing Office, 1988).

[9] See Albert D. Biderman et al., *Report on a Pilot Study in the District of Columbia on Victimization and Attitudes Toward Law Enforcement* (Washington, D.C.: U.S. Government Printing Office, 1967).

[10] U.S. Department of Justice, *Report to the Nation on Crime and Justice*, p. 26.

[11] James Levine, "The Potential for Crime Over-Reporting in Criminal Victimization Surveys," *Criminology*, 14 (November 1976): 307–30.

TABLE 13.1 Estimated Percent Distribution of Personal and Household Victimizations, by Type of Victimization and Reporting to Police: United States, 1986*

		Reported to police		
Type of victimization	Number of victimizations	Yes†	No	Not known and not available
All crimes	**34,118,310**	**37.2%**	**61.4%**	**1.4%**
All personal crimes	18,750,640	34.4	64.0	1.6
Crimes of violence	5,515,450	49.6	49.3	1.1
Completed	2,049,310	60.0	39.0	0.9
Attempted	3,466,140	43.4	55.4	1.2
Rape	129,940	48.1	49.9	1.9‡
Completed	45,640	39.3	55.1	5.5‡
Attempted	84,310	52.9	47.1	0.0‡
Robbery	1,009,160	58.3	41.5	0.2‡
Completed	621,730	69.7	30.0	0.3‡
With injury	233,900	81.5	17.7	0.8‡
From serious assault	109,640	80.9	19.1	0.0‡
From minor assault	124,270	82.1	16.4	1.5‡
Without injury	387,830	62.5	37.5	0.0‡
Attempted	387,430	40.2	59.8	0.0‡
With injury	116,560	49.5	50.5	0.0‡
From serious assault	54,420	70.8	29.2‡	0.0‡
From minor assault	62,150	30.9	69.1	0.0‡
Without injury	270,870	36.2	63.8	0.0‡
Assault	4,376,350	47.6	51.1	1.3
Aggravated	1,542,870	58.9	40.0	1.0‡
Completed with injury	561,650	63.3	35.2	1.5‡
Attempted with weapon	981,220	56.4	42.8	0.8‡
Simple	2,833,480	41.4	57.2	1.4
Completed with injury	820,290	51.7	47.5	0.8‡
Attempted without weapon	2,013,190	37.3	61.1	1.7
Crimes of theft	13,235,190	28.0	70.1	1.9
Completed	12,401,860	28.4	69.7	1.9
Attempted	833,330	21.7	76.3	2.0
Personal larceny with contact	536,290	38.4	57.8	3.8
Purse snatching	163,280	56.5	41.2	2.3‡
Completed	133,940	66.3	32.4	1.3‡
Attempted	29,350	11.9‡	81.2	6.8‡
Pocket picking	373,000	30.5	65.1	4.4
Personal larceny without contact	12,698,900	27.6	70.6	1.8
Completed	11,894,920	28.0	70.3	1.8
Less than $50	5,515,920	11.8	86.6	1.5
$50 or more	5,730,640	43.7	54.3	2.0
Amount not available	648,350	26.0	71.9	2.2‡
Attempted	803,980	22.0	76.1	1.9‡
All household crimes	15,367,670	40.6	58.3	1.1
Completed	13,064,150	41.2	57.8	1.0
Attempted	2,303,520	36.9	61.6	1.5

TABLE 13.1 *(Continued)*

		Reported to police		
Type of victimization	Number of victimizations	Yes†	No	Not known and not available
Burglary	5,556,600	52.3	46.4	1.4
Completed	4,307,160	56.3	42.3	1.3
Forcible entry	1,812,780	75.8	22.7	1.5
Unlawful entry without force	2,494,380	42.2	56.6	1.2
Attempted forcible entry	1,249,440	38.2	60.3	1.5
Household larceny	8,455,220	27.7	71.5	0.8
Completed	7,869,350	27.6	71.6	0.8
Less than $50	3,434,300	12.7	87.0	0.3‡
$50 or more	3,883,560	40.6	58.4	1.0
Amount not available	551,490	29.1	68.8	2.1‡
Attempted	585,870	28.7	70.2	1.1‡
Motor vehicle theft	1,355,860	73.0	25.4	1.6
Completed	887,640	88.5	10.2	1.3‡
Attempted	468,210	43.7	54.1	2.2‡

*Subcategories may not sum to total because of rounding.
†Represents the rates at which victimizations were reported to the police, or "police reporting rates."
‡Estimate is based on about ten or fewer sample cases.
Source: Timothy J. Flanagan and Katherine M. Jamieson, eds., *Sourcebook of Criminal Justice Statistics, 1987* (Washington, D.C.: U.S. Department of Justice, Bureau of Justice Statistics, 1988), p. 215.

Self-report Studies

Another way researchers attempt to measure the extent of crime is to ask people to report on their own law-violating behavior. In numerous studies, people have been invited to fill out anonymous questionnaires or submit to confidential interviews.[12] In many cases, researchers have made efforts to validate their interview or questionnaire data against official police records.

The major findings of these self-report studies support common sense. Just about everyone has violated the law at one time or another, committing offenses for which he or she could have been jailed or at least fined. Most of the illegal acts were undetected, at least by law enforcement officials. Most law violators admit to committing only a few minor offenses. A small minority admits to numerous minor offenses and/or some serious crimes.

One of the obvious contributions of self-report studies is that they disprove the belief that only certain types of people (e.g., the poor, minorities, and the mentally ill) engage in criminal acts. Such studies also suggest that we cannot generalize about the characteristics of those who commit crimes on the basis of knowledge about persons who are caught.

The findings of self-report studies on the distribution of criminality by age, sex, race, and class are of doubtful validity. For example, some studies suggest that common crimes are disproportionately committed by lower-class people, while others throw doubt on such findings. The two most important limitations are that we do not know if the people who answer questionnaires and submit to interviews are providing accurate information and that we cannot trust

[12] Reid, *Crime and Criminology*, pp. 57–60.

the validity of the official police records against which the results of such inquiries are checked. In addition, self-report studies have frequently been undertaken without much concern over the representativeness of the sample of persons studied, so the generalizability of their findings is difficult to judge.

More revealing, perhaps, are the occasional self-reports of individuals who are *not* the subjects of research attention. When, for example, an organized crime figure decides to "sing" during a congressional investigation, a whole new world of crime and criminal intrigue may be revealed.[13] Such dramatic self-reports underscore the shallowness, if not the questionable accuracy, of official crime statistics.

EXTENT AND DISTRIBUTION OF CRIME

Criminal behavior, as legally defined, takes a wide variety of forms. In this section we examine a number of different forms of serious crime and look at official statistics on their extent. As we have noted, such statistics are known to underestimate the actual amount of crime in the United States. We also look at victimless crime, illegal activity people engage in voluntarily, in which allegedly there is no victim. Since certain types of criminal behavior—white-collar, organized, and political crime—do not show up adequately in official statistics, our coverage of these types of crime is descriptive rather than statistical.

Traditional Crime

Despite the problems associated with official crime reports, they are still the best existing source of statistics on common or *traditional crime*. In the vernacular of the U.S. Department of Justice's *Uniform Crime Reports*, we shall address the extent and significance of *index offenses*.[14] Index offenses are serious law violations which, in the view of the Justice Department, indicate the gravity of America's crime problem. They are criminal homicide, forcible rape, robbery, aggravated assault, burglary (breaking and entering), larceny (theft), and motor vehicle theft. In 1988 a total of 13,923,100 index offenses were reported by police departments. On the average, this comes out to one offense every two seconds (see Figure 13.1). While increasing steadily up to 1980, the index offense rate has since leveled off. However, in most crime categories the rate is still higher than a decade ago (see Table 13.2).

Murder and Nonnegligent Manslaughter. Murder and nonnegligent manslaughter refer to the willful killing of another person, as determined by police investigation. In 1988, 20,680 persons were victims, a 3.6 percent decrease from 1979. Three-quarters of the victims were males, and a third were in their twenties. Half were white, meaning that the murder of minorities occurs far more frequently than their percentage representation in the population would lead one to predict. Over half of the deaths were either within the confines of the family or involved people who knew one another. Such factors render murder a difficult offense to prevent. Nonetheless, 70 percent of all known criminal homicides were solved by arrest in 1988—a higher percentage than that for any other crime. Of those arrested, most were males of the same race as the victim, and 35 percent were in the eighteen-to-twenty-four-year age group. (There has been a notable trend toward criminal homicide among the young in recent years.) Most of those killed died by being shot—in 1988, 60 percent of the criminal homicides

[13] See, for example, Peter Maas, *The Valachi Papers* (New York: G. P. Putnam's Sons, 1968).

[14] Data in this section are from U.S. Department of Justice, *Uniform Crime Reports for the United States, 1988* (Washington, D.C.: U.S. Government Printing Office, 1989). This is updated annually.

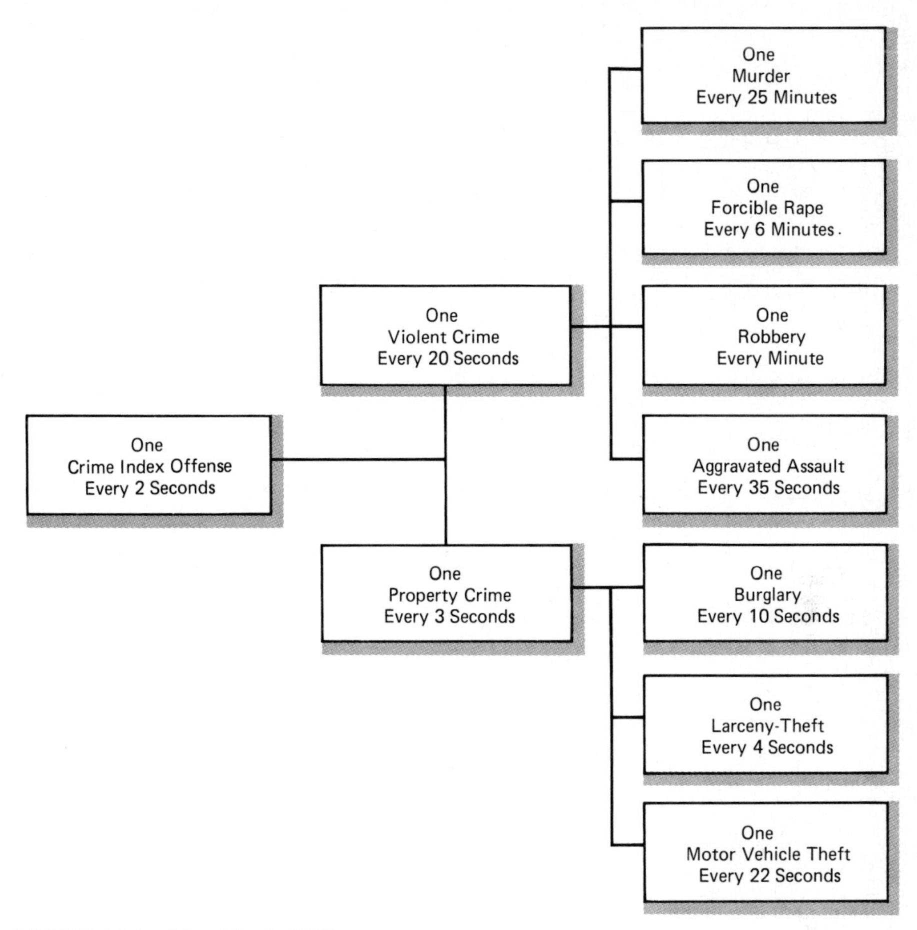

FIGURE 13.1 Crime Clock, 1988
Source: U.S. Department of Justice, *Uniform Crime Reports for the United States, 1988* (Washington, D.C.: U.S. Government Printing Office, 1989), p. 7.

involved some type of firearms, and in 45 percent of the cases handguns were involved.

Aggravated Assault. Serious assaults involve attempts to kill or to inflict severe bodily injury. Police departments reported 910,090 cases of aggravated assault in 1988, up 44.6 percent from 1979. In most instances, assault takes place either within the family or between neighbors and acquaintances. Unlike criminal homicide, which mainly involves the use of firearms, the weapons employed in aggravated assaults vary greatly. In 1988, 57 percent of the assaults known to the police were solved by arrest. Since the victim, perpetrator, and witnesses are likely to be related to or acquainted with one another, witnesses and victims are often reluctant to testify. According to official statistics, most of those arrested in 1988 were eighteen or older.

Forcible Rape. Rape is one of the most underreported offenses in the United States. None-

TABLE 13.2 Index of Crime: United States, 1979–88

Population*	Crime index total†	Violent crime‡	Property crime‡	Murder and non-negligent man-slaughter	Forcible rape	Robbery	Aggra-vated assault	Burglary	Larceny–Theft	Motor vehicle theft
Number of offenses										
1979: 220,099,000	12,249,500	1,208,030	11,041,500	21,460	76,390	480,700	629,480	3,327,700	6,601,000	1,112,800
1980: 225,349,264	13,408,300	1,344,520	12,063,700	23,040	82,990	565,840	672,650	3,795,200	7,136,900	1,131,700
1981: 229,146,000	13,423,800	1,361,820	12,061,900	22,520	82,500	592,910	663,900	3,779,700	7,194,400	1,087,800
1982: 231,534,000	12,974,400	1,322,390	11,652,000	21,010	78,770	553,130	669,480	3,447,100	7,142,500	1,062,400
1983: 233,981,000	12,108,600	1,258,090	10,850,500	19,310	78,920	506,570	653,290	3,129,900	6,712,800	1,007,900
1984: 236,158,000	11,881,800	1,273,280	10,608,500	18,690	84,230	485,010	685,350	2,984,400	6,591,900	1,032,200
1985: 238,740,000	12,431,400	1,328,800	11,102,600	18,980	88,670	497,870	723,250	3,073,300	6,926,400	1,102,900
1986: 241,077,000	13,211,900	1,489,170	11,722,700	20,610	91,460	542,780	834,320	3,241,400	7,257,200	1,224,100
1987: 243,400,000	13,508,700	1,484,000	12,024,700	20,100	91,110	517,700	855,090	3,236,200	7,499,900	1,288,700
1988: 245,807,000	13,923,100	1,566,220	12,356,900	20,680	92,490	542,970	910,090	3,218,100	7,705,900	1,432,900
Percent change: number of offenses										
1988/1987	+3.1	+5.5	+2.8	+2.9	+1.5	+4.9	+6.4	−.6	+2.7	+11.2
1988/1984	+17.2	+23.0	+16.5	+10.6	+9.8	+12.0	+32.8	+7.8	+16.9	+38.8
1988/1979	+13.7	+29.7	+11.9	−3.6	+21.1	+13.0	+44.6	−3.3	+16.7	+28.8
Rate per 100,000 inhabitants										
1979	5,565.5	548.9	5,016.6	9.7	34.7	218.4	286.0	1,511.9	2,999.1	505.6
1980	5,950.0	596.6	5,353.3	10.2	36.8	251.1	298.5	1,684.1	3,167.0	502.2
1981	5,858.2	594.3	5,263.9	9.8	36.0	258.7	289.7	1,649.5	3,139.7	474.7
1982	5,603.6	571.1	5,032.5	9.1	34.0	238.9	289.2	1,488.8	3,084.8	458.8
1983	5,175.0	537.7	4,637.4	8.3	33.7	216.5	279.2	1,337.7	2,868.9	430.8
1984	5,031.3	539.2	4,492.1	7.9	35.7	205.4	290.2	1,263.7	2,791.3	437.1
1985	5,207.1	556.6	4,650.5	7.9	37.1	208.5	302.9	1,287.3	2,901.2	462.0
1986	5,480.4	617.7	4,862.6	8.6	37.9	225.1	346.1	1,344.6	3,010.3	507.8
1987	5,550.0	609.7	4,940.3	8.3	37.4	212.7	351.3	1,329.6	3,081.3	529.4
1988	5,664.2	637.2	5,027.1	8.4	37.6	220.9	370.2	1,309.2	3,134.9	582.9
Percent change: rate per 100,000 inhabitants										
1988/1987	+2.1	+4.5	+1.8	+1.2	+.5	+3.9	+5.4	−1.5	+1.7	+10.1
1988/1984	+12.6	+18.2	+11.9	+6.3	+5.3	+7.5	+27.6	+3.6	+12.3	+33.3
1988/1979	+1.8	+16.1	+.2	−13.4	+8.4	+1.1	+29.4	−13.4	+4.5	+15.3

[All rates were calculated on the offenses before rounding.]

*Populations are Bureau of the Census provisional estimates as of July 1, except April 1, 1980, preliminary census counts, and are subject to change.

†Because of rounding, the offenses may not add to totals.

‡Violent crimes are offenses of murder, forcible rape, robbery, and aggravated assault. Property crimes are offenses of burglary, larceny–theft, and motor vehicle theft. Data are not included for the property crime of arson.

Source: U.S. Department of Justice, *Uniform Crime Reports, 1988* (Washington, D.C.: U.S. Government Printing Office, 1989), p. 47.

theless, police departments reported 92,490 cases of forcible rape in 1988, a 21.1 percent increase from 1979. Like other official crime statistics, those on forcible rape are hard to interpret. The apparent increase could be partially due to greater willingness on the part of women to report rape, which they have been urged to do by advocates of the women's movement and by police officials. The presence and proliferation of sexual assault and rape crisis centers, which provide counseling and legal advice to rape victims, may also stimulate increased reporting. Yet, only half of all forcible rapes and attempted rapes are said to have been reported to police (see Table 13.1).

Forcible rapes were even less likely to be solved by arrest than aggravated assaults. Only 52 percent resulted in arrests in 1988. These statistics indicate that forcible rape is one of the easiest crimes to get away with, given the low likelihood of ultimate conviction. In 1988, 43 percent of those arrested were under twenty-five years of age; half were white and half were racial minorities. Contrary to popular stereotypes, virtually all forcible rapes take place within racial groups. Victims frequently are acquainted with the rapist, which helps account for the relatively low rates of arrest and prosecution, since it is sometimes difficult for victims to prove that they were indeed assaulted forcibly and against their will. Sexist attitudes on the part of police and prosecutors often work to give accused rapists the benefit of the doubt, although this is beginning to change.

Robbery. Robbery involves stealing, during which force and violence (or the threat of violence) are employed. Police departments reported 542,970 robberies in 1988, an increase of 13 percent over 1979. Over half the robberies known to police were committed on the street; the remainder occurred within households and business establishments. Only 26 percent of robberies were solved by arrest. Victims are unlikely to know the law violators, and it is relatively easy to get away with the crime. If we assume that those who are arrested are representative of robbers, young people are very much involved in this index offense. In 1988, 59 percent of those arrested were under twenty-five years of age. Most of the arrests involved males, and 63 percent of those arrested were black. According to Justice Department estimates, money and goods valued at $343 million were stolen from robbery victims in 1988.

Burglary. Burglary involves unlawfully breaking into or entering a structure (e.g., a home or business), with the intent of committing theft or some other serious crime. Burglary is a far more common crime than is robbery. In 1988 an estimated 3,218,100 burglaries were reported by police departments, down 3.3 percent from 1979. Sixty-six percent involved residences, and most took place at night. Losses were estimated at $3.3 billion. Despite the volume and costs of burglary, only 13 percent of reported burglaries were solved by arrest in 1988. Of those arrested, 67 percent were under twenty-five years of age, and 18 percent were under eighteen. Sixty-seven percent of those arrested were white, and almost all were male.

Larceny. In 1988, police departments reported 7,705,900 cases of larceny, making it the most frequent of the index offenses. This number represented an increase of 16.7 percent from 1979. Larceny, which does not include motor vehicle theft, involves taking or removing property that belongs to another. In 1988, larceny cost its victims an estimated $3.3 billion. Only 20 percent of all cases of larceny known to the police were solved by arrest. Of those arrested, 30 percent were under eighteen years of age. Significantly, almost a third of the arrests involved females—they are arrested far more frequently for larceny than for any other single index crime. In 1988 arrests of whites outnumbered arrests of blacks by two to one.

When people worry about the crime of assault, they generally are thinking of the terror of being accosted on the street by strangers. However, most cases of aggravated assault take place within the family and between acquaintances. (J. Berndt/Stock, Boston)

Motor Vehicle Theft. In 1988 police reported 1,432,900 cases of motor vehicle theft. This is up 28.8 percent from 1979. While most stolen vehicles were eventually recovered and returned to their owners, only 15 percent of such thefts were solved by arrest. Most of those arrested were young; 58 percent were under twenty-one, and 40 percent were under eighteen. Most of those arrested were male, and 59 percent were white. As with the other index offenses, one can only cautiously assume that those arrested are representative of those who have committed this particular law violation. Stolen vehicles involved losses of some $7 billion in 1988.

A Note on Crime and Gender

In reviewing the preceding official crime statistics, occasional note was made of the proportional arrests of males and females. It is clear that most arrests involve males, and this is particularly true with regard to crimes of violence. Male dominance of arrest figures has been the case since the Justice Department began collecting these data some fifty years ago.

There has, however, been a visible increase in female arrest rates. The U.S. Department of Justice has compiled data on arrest rates by sex of the offender, covering the period 1971–85.

During that period the overall arrest rate for men charged with index offenses rose 6 percent; for women, the increase was 37 percent.[15] Women's share of America's prison population has likewise been on the increase, although not as dramatically.

There has been debate over the meaning of such increases.[16] Rita James Simon has argued that the increasing arrest rates for women reflect more involvement on the part of women in criminal activity. Although much of the increase that has taken place involves property offenses as opposed to crimes of violence, to Simon this represents a movement toward sex equality in criminal behavior. Increased labor force participation of women and related breakdowns in traditional patterns of sexist treatment have begun to open up new opportunities for women and to put them under new kinds of pressures as well.[17] As this occurs, Simon argues, we should expect to see changes in the volume and types of criminal behavior involving women.

A somewhat different approach to interpreting trends in female criminal behavior has been taken by Frieda Adler.[18] She argues that what we are seeing is the rise of "the new woman criminal," a variant of the aggressive, competitive female inspired by the women's movement. As traditional gender roles blur, as women enter realms of activity always reserved for men and considered "masculine," this shift toward androgyny is carrying over into criminal pursuits. Critics of Adler's notion of the new woman criminal point out that most of the increase in criminal behavior—if arrest rates are the indicator—is in property crime, not crimes of violence. The latter are still eminently a man's domain. Moreover, the statistical changes in question apparently began early in the 1960s, before the women's movement made its appearance and thus could have affected criminal behavior. Finally, critics have suggested, the rise in both female arrest and imprisonment could simply mean that the police and others who are part of the criminal justice system have had their attitudes altered by the women's movement. Perhaps women are being treated more equally (and severely) by the system.[19]

Victimless Crime

The seven index offenses are considered by the Justice Department to be the most serious crimes in America, in terms of both the damage they inflict and their extensiveness. In its *Uniform Crime Reports,* the Justice Department also presents data on offenses ranging from arson to loitering. Of the 13.8 million arrests made by local police departments in 1988, 80 percent were for crimes other than index offenses (see Table 13.3). A high percentage of these arrests were for alcohol- and drug-related offenses, gambling, sex offenses and prostitution, pornography offenses, vagrancy, and curfew and loitering violations.

Those crimes, which are entered into voluntarily and do not involve crime victims, are called *victimless crimes.* Victimless crimes are difficult to measure and are a matter of substantial controversy. Though arrest statistics on many victimless crimes are compiled in the Justice Department's *Uniform Crime Reports,* there are no official figures on their extent. Arrest statistics grossly understate the extent of such crimes.

Controversy surrounds victimless crimes for

---

[15] U.S. Department of Justice, *Report to the Nation on Crime and Justice,* p. 46.

[16] For an overview of these issues, see Carol A. Whitehurst, "Women and the Commission of Crime: A Theoretical Approach," in Delos H. Kelly, ed., *Deviant Behavior,* 2nd ed. (New York: St. Martin's Press, 1984), pp. 614–27.

[17] Rita James Simon, *Women and Crime* (Lexington, Mass.: D. C. Heath & Company, 1975).

[18] Frieda Adler, *Sisters in Crime* (New York: McGraw-Hill Book Company, 1975).

[19] Darrell Steffensmeier and Michael Cobb, "Sex Differences in Urban Arrest Patterns, 1934–1979," *Social Problems,* 29 (October 1981):37–49.

TABLE 13.3 Total Estimated Arrests, United States, 1988*

Total†	**13,812,300**
Murder and nonnegligent manslaughter	21,890
Forcible rape	38,610
Robbery	149,100
Aggravated assault	416,300
Burglary	463,400
Larceny–theft	1,571,200
Motor vehicle theft	208,400
Arson	19,700
Violent crime‡	625,900
Property crime§	2,262,700
Crime Index total‖	2,888,600
Other assaults	901,800
Forgery and counterfeiting	101,700
Fraud	366,300
Embezzlement	15,500
Stolen property: buying, receiving, possessing	166,300
Vandalism	295,300
Weapons: carrying, possessing, etc.	221,800
Prostitution and commercialized vice	104,100
Sex offenses (except forcible rape and prostitution)	106,300
Drug abuse violations	1,155,200
Gambling	23,600
Offenses against family and children	69,900
Driving under the influence	1,792,500
Liquor laws	669,600
Drunkenness	818,600
Disorderly conduct	760,500
Vagrancy	36,500
All other offenses (except traffic)	3,078,900
Suspicion (not included in totals)	14,000
Curfew and loitering law violations	72,200
Runaways	166,900

*Arrest totals based on all reporting agencies and estimates for unreported areas.

†Because of rounding, figures may not add to totals.

‡Violent crimes are offenses of murder, forcible rape, robbery, and aggravated assault.

§Property crimes are offenses of burglary, larceny–theft, motor vehicle theft, and arson.

‖ Includes arson.

Source: U.S. Department of Justice, *Uniform Crime Reports, 1988* (Washington, D.C.: U.S. Government Printing Office, 1989), p. 168.

two reasons. First, many people believe that the state has no right to impose its version of morality on certain types of behavior. For example, they argue, if people want to enjoy hard-core pornography, possess and use marijuana, purchase sexual enjoyment, or gamble, they should be free to follow their own moral standards without interference by the state. However, others strongly feel that such behaviors should not be permitted under the law.

The second reason victimless crimes are controversial relates to their impact on the criminal justice system. Enough arrests are made for such crimes to clog the system and overwhelm the capacity of the police, courts, and penal institutions. Many experts believe that a new approach to victimless crimes would make the criminal justice system more efficient and less costly. One suggestion is to decrease penalties. In a number of states and localities, for example, possession of a small amount of marijuana for personal use is punishable by a summons (similar to a traffic ticket) and a small fine. This frees the criminal justice system while implicitly recognizing the moral argument against unlicensed freedom to use this particular drug.

Some would argue that the term *victimless crime* is a misnomer and that significant costs are involved.[20] For example, gambling profits often help to sustain the activities of organized crime, as do prostitution, drug sales, and pornography. Prostitution may be an occasion for robbery, crimes of violence, and the spread of disease. Drug sales contribute to drug abuse, as well as habitual criminal behavior on the part of some users (e.g., addicts in need of funds to support their habits). Both intravenous drug use and prostitution have been implicated in the spread of AIDS. Financial transactions accompanying such offenses are ordinarily hidden from taxation and thus represent a loss to government treasuries. Finally, the inability or failure of the criminal justice system to make headway in the control of such forms of criminal

[20] Edwin M. Schur and H. A. Bedeau, *Victimless Crimes: Two Sides of a Controversy* (Englewood Cliffs, N.J.: Prentice-Hall, 1974).

behavior calls the credibility of the system itself into question, thus reducing general citizen respect for it. This is particularly true whenever it is revealed, as it so often is, that some "victimless crimes" go on with police indifference or even cooperation.

We might also mention juvenile "status offenses" as further examples of victimless crime. Status offenses are acts deemed illegal if performed by juveniles but legal if performed by adults. Age status determines the illegality. Examples would include running away from home, sexual promiscuity, being beyond the control of one's parents, or chronic truancy from school. Such offenses may result in juveniles being placed in jail-like detention centers. While the victimless crimes may seem quite harmless in comparison with those discussed earlier (e.g., gambling, prostitution, etc.), the costs to the juvenile who gets caught up in the criminal justice system can be enormous.[21]

White-Collar Crime

The term *white-collar crime* was made popular in the 1940s by criminologist Edwin H. Sutherland.[22] Sutherland believed that researchers were not paying enough attention to criminal practices on the part of business executives and other high-status individuals. In his view, explanations for crime had to encompass the full range of law violations—not just the actions of lower-class people that come to the attention of local police. To Sutherland, white-collar crime was "crime committed by a person of respectability and high social status in the course of his occupation."[23]

When Sutherland examined the practices of seventy American corporations over a forty-five-year period, he found that each corporation had a record of one or more law violations. These included false advertising, restraint of trade, unfair labor practices, and financial fraud. Other researchers have since probed various aspects of white-collar criminality, but in a rather piecemeal fashion.[24] Information is often very difficult to obtain. The offices of executives and professionals are not readily accessible to researchers, and the types of behavior in question are carried out in great secrecy. Often the victims do not know they are being victimized. Moreover, to prove that white-collar crimes are being committed, researchers may need skills in law, accounting, and economics. Sociologists usually lack this kind of expert knowledge. As a consequence, most of what we know about white-collar crime comes from court cases or occasional government investigations. The information so gained is typically fragmentary and may not be representative in terms of the overall scope of white-collar criminality.

In recent years the narrowness of Sutherland's definition of white-collar crime has come under attack. Scholars have pointed out that individuals other than high-status jobholders also commit acts that are not traditional or common crimes in the course of their occupations. One attempt to expand the definition was proposed by Herbert Edelhertz, a former official of the U.S. Department of Justice. Edelhertz included as white-collar crimes all illegal acts committed by nonphysical means and by concealment and guile, whose purpose is to obtain money or property, to avoid their loss, or to obtain business or personal advantage.[25] This definition focuses on the crime, rather than on the characteristics of the law violator. It not only encompasses financial fraud by corporate executives

[21] Patrick T. Murphy, *Our Kindly Parent . . . The State* (New York: Viking Press, 1974).

[22] Edwin H. Sutherland, "White-Collar Criminality," *American Sociological Review*, 5 (February 1940): 1–12.

[23] Edwin H. Sutherland, *White Collar Crime* (New York: Dryden Press, 1949), p. 9.

[24] For an excellent overview, see James William Coleman, *The Criminal Elite: The Sociology of White Collar Crime*, 2nd ed. (New York: St. Martin's Press, 1989).

[25] Herbert Edelhertz, *Nature, Impact, and Prosecution of White Collar Crime* (Washington, D.C.: U.S. Government Printing Office, 1970), p. 12.

but also fraud by such lesser mortals as veterans who receive payments enabling them to continue their education under the GI Bill but who do not attend school.

Sociologists still disagree about how to define white-collar crime and what acts the definition should encompass. The law is often quite hazy and ambivalent with regard to criminality. For example, during the 1970s a number of large corporations used secret funds to bribe important officials in other countries into doing business with them. These acts were legal until passage of the Federal Corrupt Practices Act in 1977.

Many law violations never reach criminal courts. For example, false advertising and restraint of trade by corporations are often investigated and adjudicated by governmental review boards or other administrative bodies. When a company is proven to have engaged in false advertising, it may be asked to "cease and desist" its illegal activities. Once it does, the case is closed—there is no "conviction" and no "criminal" insofar as the law is concerned. But has not a white-collar crime been committed?

Difficulties in studying white-collar criminality and the complexities in defining it hamper attempts to estimate its extensiveness. Moreover, like traditional or common crimes, white-collar crimes, however defined, are underreported to an unknown degree. Nonetheless, various estimates point to significant economic costs that far outweigh the dollar losses from common property crimes such as burglary, larceny, and robbery. For example, the Judiciary Committee of the U.S. Senate has looked into the costs of corporate activities such as production of faulty goods, monopolistic practices, and other violations. The Committee estimates such activities cost the consumer from $174 billion to $231 billion annually.[26] Yet such "corporate thievery," costly though it may be, is the subject of little public uproar in comparison to more readily perceived crime in the streets.

Because of the ambiguities surrounding white-collar crime, we can only offer illustrations of the directions it frequently takes. Through media reports in recent years, Americans have been made aware of congressmen accepting bribes while agreeing to influence the letting of government contracts; misrepresentation by doctors about services provided people in order to get more money from government medical programs; computer-related thefts of money or information; union leaders' use of pension funds for questionable purposes; and environmental crimes involving the illegal dumping of toxic wastes. The list could be expanded indefinitely, even holding to the definitions of white-collar crime offered by Sutherland and Edelhertz.[27] It should be emphasized that the penalties for these white-collar crimes and others are generally far less severe than those for traditional property crimes.[28]

Organized Crime

Like white-collar crime, *organized crime* is pervasive in the United States and is more costly to the public than traditional crime.[29] Organized crime is a cooperative endeavor involving thousands of law violators. Its basic focus is on supplying goods and services illicitly to members of the public. Such goods and services include gambling opportunities, loans, drugs, stolen commodities, pornography, and prostitution. Beyond this, organized crime has successfully

[26] Marshall B. Clinard and G. C. Yeager, *Corporate Crime* (New York: The Free Press, 1980).

[27] See the detailed inventory of white-collar crime in Coleman, *The Criminal Elite*. See also Craig B. Little, *Understanding Deviance and Control* (Itasca, Ill.: F. E. Peacock Publishers, 1983), Chapter 6.

[28] Penalties frequently involve probation and fines. For example, on federal offenses see U.S. Department of Justice, Bureau of Justice Statistics, *White Collar Crime, Special Report* (Washington, D.C.: U.S. Government Printing Office, September 1987).

[29] See Donald R. Cressey, *Theft of the Nation* (New York: Harper & Row Publishers, 1969).

infiltrated some legitimate businesses and labor unions. In virtually all facets of its activity, the main objective of organized crime is to make money. Some of this money is used to buy power, including protection from politicians and from agencies of law enforcement.[30]

A major source of income for organized crime is illicit gambling, including numbers games and off-track betting. Since more money is paid in by gamblers than is paid out to winners, high profits are assured. Estimates place annual gambling profits at $12 *billion*.[31]

Another major source of income is the interest received on loans made to individuals who need funds and cannot get them legally. Organized crime is engaged in loansharking, in which loans have much higher interest rates and shorter repayment periods than permitted under the law. Borrowers include individuals with gambling debts, narcotics users, and even merchants and business executives who find themselves in financial need. Organized crime encourages borrowers to repay loans and interest on time by the threat or use of force—from murder and beatings to property destruction. No one knows how much money is involved, but it is estimated that annual profits run into the billions of dollars.

The importation and wholesale distribution of illegal drugs—heroin in particular—is another significant source of profit for organized crime. The heroin trade requires international connections and the ability to lay out large sums of money for large-scale importation of the drug. In the early 1980s it was estimated that $16 billion changes hands each year in connection with America's heroin usage, at least $11 billion of which is pure profit for organized crime.

Although relatively little is known about the matter, law enforcement agencies report that organized crime has invested heavily in legitimate businesses. Organized crime figures gain a thin veneer of public respectability and a visible source of legal income through their involvement in such enterprises. Not all business involvement comes about through direct investment. Firms may be secretly acquired in lieu of full repayment of loans or gambling debts or through extortion. Once in business, organized crime figures may use extralegal tactics to ensure high profits. Such tactics range from strongarming other firms into becoming customers or suppliers to driving competitors out of business. The impact of such business involvement by organized crime remains a matter of speculation. It is often claimed that this involvement has driven up the prices of many goods and services.

It is also claimed that organized crime has infiltrated and gained control over segments of organized labor. Among the results are the limitation of unionization in certain industries and the negotiation of union contracts favorable to business owners—all in return for financial or other favors. Unions collect a great deal of money from their members, and control over union funds permits organized crime to divert money into its business investments. When organized crime controls a union, companies must look the other way when merchandise is stolen if they wish to gain union cooperation or avoid labor problems. Stolen goods can then be channeled to firms controlled by organized crime or sold to legitimate businesses at an easy profit.

If law enforcement agencies were vigilant and active in investigating organized crime and intent on prosecuting violations of the law, these activities would be more difficult to carry out. So it is to the advantage of organized crime to bribe and threaten politicians and law enforcement officials. No one knows how widespread such corruption is. Its effect is to make interference by agencies of the state less likely. Thus, even when persons complain about known law

---

[30] President's Commission on Law Enforcement, *The Challenge of Crime*, pp. 446–47.

[31] Pennsylvania Crime Commission, *A Decade of Organized Crime, 1980* (St. Davids: Commonwealth of Pennsylvania, 1980), p. 5.

violations, little may be done. Moreover, complainants never know whether their "tips" to law enforcement agencies may lead to retribution. This helps reduce complaints, and thus the need for corruption.

How extensive is organized crime? No one is certain. In the late 1960s the President's Commission on Law Enforcement surveyed police departments in over seventy major cities. Using the responses of those cities that cooperated along with other sources of information, the Commission concluded that organized crime operates in 80 percent of cities with a population of over a million.

The Commission also reported that there were twenty-four groups across the country that were operating as well-organized "criminal cartels" and whose activities were coordinated by a small group of top-level overseers. These groups were said to have a total of at least 5,000 core members, and their activities were assisted by thousands more who were not officially members. Each of the groups was said to be organized in a hierarchical manner, structured like a combination family and business corporation. Policies were made by individual "bosses," and the day-to-day operations were monitored by underlings of different ranks. Those on the very bottom often did not know where orders and directives originated. Group discipline was strictly enforced from within, with systems of internal surveillance used to control members. Membership was restricted, so as to keep out possible informers. The groups were held together by common regional and ethnic ties and by a code of conduct that placed a premium on loyalty and obedience. Collectively, organized crime is popularly referred to as the "Mafia" or "Cosa Nostra," reflecting the stereotype that most members are of Italian-American origin.

It is important to emphasize that it is largely incorrect that organized crime is carried out only by highly structured, hierarchical Italian-American groups. In the first place, such crime involves people of many ethnic and racial groups, including nonwhites.[32] Second, organized crime appears to vary in the degree to which participants formally structure their activities and relationships.[33] Finally, by focusing on so-called Mafia groups and their activities, certain highly organized and bureaucratic forms of white-collar crime tend to be ignored. For example, systematic criminality within and between business and government could be viewed as "organized crime."[34]

Because of the extent and effects of organized crime, the President's Commission concluded:

> In many ways organized crime is the most sinister kind of crime in America. The men who control it have become rich and powerful by encouraging the needy to gamble, by luring the troubled to destroy themselves with drugs, by extorting the profits of honest and hardworking businessmen, by collecting usury from those in financial plight, by maiming or murdering those who oppose them, by bribing those who are sworn to destroy them.[35]

But despite this indictment, federal, state, and local law enforcement agencies allocate relatively few resources to the destruction of organized crime. Leaders of organized crime have rarely been prosecuted for violations of the law (although there are signs that this is now changing). Perhaps they have been too smart to get caught. Perhaps corruption has effectively safeguarded them from the law. Certainly, they have been able to use legal safeguards of con-

---

[32] Francis A. J. Ianni, *Black Mafia* (New York: Simon & Schuster, 1974). See also August Bequai, *Organized Crime* (Lexington, Mass.: Lexington Books, 1979).

[33] Albert K. Cohen and James F. Short, Jr., "Crime and Juvenile Delinquency," in Robert K. Merton and Robert Nisbet, eds., *Contemporary Social Problems*, 4th ed. (New York: Harcourt Brace Jovanovich, 1976), pp. 80–90.

[34] See Dwight C. Smith, *The Mafia Mystique* (New York: Basic Books, 1975).

[35] President's Commission on Law Enforcement, *The Challenge of Crime*, p. 485.

stitutional rights to impede investigations of and prosecution for their activities.

Political Crime

The term *political crime* refers to illicit acts undertaken with the intention of affecting political policies or the political system as a whole.[36] The term is most often used when the powerless challenge the political status quo. Far less frequently is criminal status bestowed by the state on people who misuse the power they possess, such as high government officials. In the latter case, the state is prosecuting its own officials, a difficult business. This is well illustrated by the approach taken by the U.S. Department of Justice to revelations that Central Intelligence Agency operatives had been opening citizens' mail for twenty years, illegally violating the rights to privacy of tens of thousands of Americans. In 1976 the Justice Department recommended that none of those involved be subjected to criminal prosecution, as they were acting on the basis of directives from government officials at higher levels. Yet higher-level government officials remained rather hazy about where such directives came from.[37]

Probably the most common situation in which criminal status is conferred on people in connection with political activity occurs when citizens engage in protest and dissent. For example, during the 1960s and 1970s, civil rights and antiwar activists were routinely charged with crimes in connection with acts of peaceful civil disobedience. The federal government even passed special laws designed to restrain the leaders of political change organizations. For example, the so-called Rap Brown Law of the 1960s makes it a federal offense to cross state lines for the purpose of inciting a riot. This law was intended to restrict the mobility of popular activists and to make them individually responsible for disruptions involving any assembly of people with whom they might have had the remotest contact.

The threat or reality of prosecution can be a potent weapon against those who want to change the political status quo, even those who use legal channels. There has been reason to believe that government agents have framed dissident individuals to entangle them in legal troubles. In 1972, antiwar priest Father Philip Berrigan and six others were charged with conspiring to kidnap Henry Kissinger (who at the time was President Nixon's foreign affairs adviser) and to bomb government buildings by sneaking into underground heating pipes.[38] The key witness was a paid Federal Bureau of Investigation (FBI) informer. Though the government was unable to prove these charges in court, Father Berrigan was found guilty of smuggling letters out of the federal prison in which he was confined. The person carrying the letters was the FBI informer.

During the 1970s it was revealed that the FBI had been engaging in secret intelligence activities aimed at disrupting protest groups, discrediting dissidents, and generating activities that could lead to arrests. For example, the FBI's COINTELPRO (counterintelligence program) was responsible for hundreds of break-ins and burglaries aimed at political organizations and protest leaders; the spread of "disinformation" designed to create divisions within and between protest groups; use of agents to incite acts of violence; and harassment of individuals through anonymous derogatory letters to spouses and employers of persons involved in political dissent.[39]

[36] See Martin R. Haskell and Lewis Yablonsky, *Criminology* (Chicago: Rand McNally & Company, 1974), pp. 187–236.

[37] See Frank Donner, *The Age of Surveillance* (New York: Alfred A. Knopf, 1980).

[38] Jack Nelson and Robert Ostrow, *The FBI and the Berrigans* (New York: Coward, McCann & Geoghegan, 1972).

[39] Nelson Blackstock, *COINTELPRO* (New York: Vintage Books, 1976). See also David J. Garrow, *The FBI and Martin Luther King* (New York: Penguin Books, 1983).

Political crimes often involve acts by public figures that are spectacular in their audacity and disregard for the law. In this photograph Lt. Col. Oliver North (U.S.M.C.) consults with his attorney during testimony before a Joint Congressional Committee investigating the "Iran–contra Affair." Lt. Col. North was eventually tried for criminal acts allegedly undertaken in the service of his country. *(AP/Wide World)*

While two FBI officials were finally convicted in 1980 in the wake of investigations into such activities, they were given light fines and ended up being pardoned by President Ronald Reagan in 1981.

Again in the 1980s "political police" activity on the part of the FBI emerged. A public interest organization, the Center for Constitutional Rights, obtained government documents revealing that the FBI carried out an intensive campaign (from 1981 to 1985) aimed at neutralizing groups critical of U.S. involvement in Central America. Some 138 groups were targeted, ranging from the American Federation of Teachers to the Southern Christian Leadership Conference.[40] The FBI used illegal harassment and surveillance techniques that had been widely condemned after revelations of similar activities in the 1970s.

Not all persons who engage in protest and dissent do so nonviolently. In recent years the United States has experienced political protest that has ranged from mass uprisings in the nation's ghettos to acts of terrorism by "underground" left- and right-wing groups. While such activities have gone outside the boundaries of the law, in many instances so has the response of the state.[41] Among the illegal governmental responses have been "police riots" involving the indiscriminate use of force and the extensive violation of constitutional rights during criminal investigations. When government agencies use extralegal means to contain those engaged in

[40] *New York Times* (January 28, 1988): A1.

[41] See David Wise, *The American Police State* (New York: Random House, 1976).

extralegal forms of political expression, it is difficult to tell who the political criminals are.

Perhaps one of the most shocking examples of the illegal use of governmental power for political purposes in the 1980s is the "Iran–contra Affair." U.S. Marine Lieutenant Colonel Oliver North, evidently with the blessing and knowledge of top officials in the White House and Central Intelligence Agency, set up a hidden underground government with its own foreign and military policy. Colonel North proceeded to sell some $25 million worth of military arms to Iran, a nation the U.S. government had publicly denounced for involvement in political terrorism.[42] Still proceeding in secrecy, Colonel North then diverted sales profits to the "contras," CIA-backed paramilitary units intent on overthrowing the Sandinista government in Nicaragua.[43] The reason this deal had to be secret was its illegality: The U.S. Congress had prohibited the use of U.S. funds for such a purpose. Although Colonel North was brought to trial and eventually found guilty of a variety of charges, the roles played by Ronald Reagan, George Bush, and other high officials remain obscured. Upon appeal, Colonel North was able to reverse most of the guilty verdicts on legal technicalities.

Political crimes reflect the existence of an unequal distribution of power within the society. They are an important indicator of the degree to which a society is meeting the needs of its members. Despite their significance, neither the public nor the FBI's *Uniform Crime Reports* considers political crimes important enough to categorize as part of America's crime problem.

Violence Deterred? Gun Control and Capital Punishment

Among the forms of criminal behavior most feared by Americans, and understandably so, are crimes of violence. Often such crimes involve the use of weapons, principally firearms and knives. Firearms are commonly involved in cases of murder—indeed, 59 percent of all homicides result from gunshots. Firearms also play a role in 11 percent of all reported rapes, 23 percent of robberies, and 12 percent of assaults.[44]

The connection between firearms and crime has helped to feed an ongoing debate over the desirability of adopting new policies aimed at "gun control." This debate periodically intensifies when a crime occurs that is particularly heinous in the public's view. For example, in recent years we have witnessed attempted and successful assassinations of celebrities and important political figures, as well as multiple murders in homes, workplaces, restaurants, and even college and public school grounds. Such crimes not only involve handguns; some assailants have been found with military assault weapons capable of firing over 1,000 rounds per minute.

The United States has the highest rate of gun-related criminal offenses of any Western industrialized nation. Some would argue that this has a great deal to do with the ready, legal access people have to weapons. In addition, firearms are available in the underground economy of stolen and bartered goods in which the criminally prone often participate. There are no definitive data; however, research by James D. Wright and Peter H. Rossi suggests that in the

---

[42] Ironically, many of the activities in which the United States itself engages are condemned as terrorism elsewhere. See Edward S. Herman, "U.S. Sponsorship of International Terrorism: An Overview," *Crime and Social Justice*, 27–28 (1987): 1–31.

[43] The Iran–contra Affair is but one of a long series of extralegal activities by the United States aimed at crippling Nicaragua. See Donald R. Pfost, "Reagan's Nicaraguan Policy: A Case Study of Political Deviance and Crime," *Crime and Social Justice*, 27–28 (1987): 66–87.

[44] U.S. Department of Justice, *Report to the Nation on Crime and Justice*, p. 20.

late 1970s there were 120 million firearms in private hands in the United States. Some 30 percent of these, it is estimated, were handguns.[45] The production and sale of such weapons is a multi–billion-dollar business. New weapons enter the marketplace by the millions each year from both domestic and foreign sources. Acquiring a firearm, whether a cheap "Saturday-night special" handgun or a high-powered military assault rifle, is a matter accomplished with relative ease in most states and locales.

Proponents of gun control vary in their policy proposals. Some would like to see all owners of firearms required to register their weapons with government authorities and made to report any that are lost or stolen to police. Often registration proposals are accompanied by calls for more stringent screening of the backgrounds of firearms purchasers, as well as tougher restrictions on weapons transportation, storage, and legal use.

Those who would go further with gun control question whether such policies will have sufficient impact on the use of guns for criminal purposes, suggesting the ante must be increased for gun-related crimes. Stiff fines and imprisonment for unauthorized weapon possession or possession of a stolen weapon have been proposed, as have drastic increases in penalties for crimes in which firearms play a role. A few gun control proponents would go even further, calling for a gun-free society. Citizens would be asked to voluntarily surrender their firearms or be subject to their confiscation with penalty.

Although many members of the public (and the police) are sympathetic to one or another gun control measure, the political reality is that relatively little headway has been made in halting the proliferation of weaponry. Powerful lobbying groups such as the National Rifle Association and the firearms industry have managed to block or divert efforts to legislate major changes in law at the federal and state levels. Meanwhile, the U.S. Department of Justice routinely reports such facts as these:[46]

> Handguns are involved in 43 percent of all homicides (with rifles, shotguns, and other firearms accounting for an additional 16 percent).
>
> Offenders armed with a gun have shot victims in about 4 percent of all violent crimes and attempted to do so in 21 percent of such incidents.
>
> An offender armed with a gun is more likely to be able to complete rapes or robberies.
>
> In 1985, seventy-eight police officers died in the line of duty. Of these, seventy were shot to death (fifty-eight by handguns).

In the United States violent crimes such as murder and rape have frequently exposed offenders to the possibility of the death penalty, which is thought by many to have a deterrent effect. In recent years the death penalty, although seldom imposed, has become a matter of much controversy. Based on current evidence, many social scientists are skeptical of claims that it has value as a deterrent.[47]

Since 1622 there have been over 12,000 legal executions of convicted offenders in this society, insofar as historians have been able to determine. The federal government has kept official statistics on capital punishment only since 1930. Between 1930 and 1967, 3,859 people were put to death by civilian authorities. In 1967 challenges to the death penalty led to the blocking of further executions until the Supreme Court could review charges it was unconstitutional, in violation of the Eighth Amendment stricture against "cruel and unusual punishment." In a

[45] See James D. Wright and Peter H. Rossi, *Weapons, Crime, and Violence in America* (Washington, D.C.: National Institute of Justice, 1981).

[46] U.S. Department of Justice, *Report to the Nation on Crime and Justice*, p. 20.

[47] Gibbons, *Society, Crime, and Criminal Behavior*, pp. 469–75.

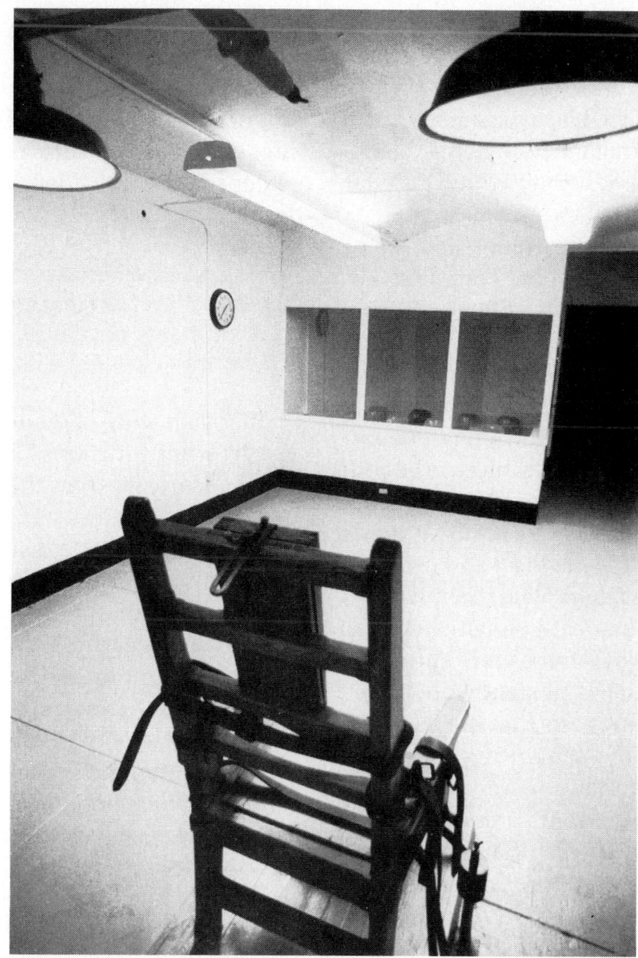

Capital punishment has become a topic of considerable controversy in recent years. While public opinion now leans toward it, some view capital punishment as a form of state-sanctioned murder. The electric chair and witness box await many of those presently confined to "death row." *(AP/Wide World)*

1972 decision (*Furman* vs. *Georgia*) the Court narrowly ruled that the death penalty itself was not subject to question, but it had been applied to offenders in arbitrary and often discriminatory ways. This ruling had the effect of striking down all state death penalty laws and setting aside the death penalties of the 633 prisoners who were on "death row."

The arbitrary and discriminatory application of the death penalty has been well documented by social scientists.[48] For example, of the 3,859 people executed between 1930 and 1967, 54 percent were black. Of all those executed, 455 had been convicted of rape; 89 percent of those executed for rape were black. Whereas blacks who

[48] See Michael L. Radelet and Margaret Vandiver, "Race and Capital Punishment: An Overview of the Issues," *Crime and Social Justice*, 25 (1986): 94–113.

raped whites were routinely exposed to the death penalty, no known cases exist in which a white man was executed for raping a black woman. Violent acts by blacks against whites invite executions; similar acts against blacks (whether by other blacks or by whites) are far less likely to do so.

After the 1972 Supreme Court decision, states began passing new death penalty statutes designed to avoid the Court's objections to the earlier laws. In the new statutes the jury renders its verdict as to guilt separately from decisions on sentencing. Specific guidelines for judges and juries have been adopted, listing "mitigating" and "aggravating" circumstances to be considered in sentencing decisions. The Supreme Court upheld such approaches as constitutional in 1976 (e.g., in *Proffitt* vs. *Florida*) and over 100 executions have since taken place. Some thirty-seven states now have a death penalty in place. As of 1987 over 1,900 prisoners were sitting on death row. The fact that 44 percent were blacks and other minorities suggests that the question of bias in conviction and sentencing continues to deserve serious attention.

What about the deterrent effect of capital punishment? Economist Isaac Ehrlich claimed to have evidence that the more frequently the death penalty was carried out, the less frequent were homicides.[49] But his research has come under strong criticism.[50] There just does not seem to be evidence supporting capital punishment's alleged deterrent effect.[51] Criminologist Don C. Gibbons has pointed out that homicide rates in adjoining states with similar social and economic characteristics are typically about the same, even when one state has the death penalty and the other does not. Moreover, he notes that when states adopt, abolish, or reintroduce capital punishment, homicide rates do not change in ways that believers in deterrence might expect. Finally, Gibbons observes that killings of police officers are no less frequent in states that have the death penalty than in states that do not.[52] Overall, he concludes:

> One point seems clear enough from the studies of the death penalty and homicide: The deterrent effects, if any, of criminal sanctions are extremely difficult to identify with precision.[53]

In the absence of evidence as to its deterrent effect, what functions does the death penalty play? Clearly it serves the function of removing convicted offenders permanently from society (including, of course, some who have been erroneously convicted). Does it do more? David Bruck argues that the reemergence of the death penalty in the early 1970s, after a period of waning public support in the 1950s and 1960s, was no accident.[54] The death penalty reemerged in the context of post-1960s economic recession and inflation, military failure in Southeast Asia, loss of public confidence in government exacerbated by such scandals as Watergate, and the demise of the civil rights movement and other organized initiatives against discrimination and poverty. Bruck points to the fact that the death penalty is most common in societies that use repression to deal with insecurities and lack of direction. Countries like South Africa, Iran, and China execute criminals; Western democracies have little need to pursue this route to reaffirming national resolve and self-confidence. The fact that the United States stands practically alone among such democracies in the implementation of capital punishment is, in Bruck's view, a sign that we have lost our way: The death penalty becomes a "potent social

---

[49] Isaac Ehrlich, "The Deterrent Effect of Capital Punishment," *American Economic Review*, 65 (1975): 397–417.

[50] William J. Bowers and G. L. Pierce, "The Illusion of Deterrence in Isaac Ehrlich's Research on Capital Punishment," *Yale Law Review*, 85 (1975): 187–208.

[51] See William C. Bailey and Ruth D. Peterson, "Murder and Capital Punishment," *American Sociological Review*, 54 (October 1989): 722–43.

[52] Gibbons, *Society, Crime, and Criminal Behavior*, pp. 473–74.

[53] Ibid., p. 472.

[54] David Bruck, "Decisions of Death," *The New Republic*, 189 (December 12, 1983): 18–21.

symbol'' that has little or nothing to do with the problem of crime.

Nor does the death penalty play an important economic function, in terms of saving taxpayers' money by avoiding lengthy, perhaps life imprisonment for offenders. Because capital punishment typically carries with it a variety of opportunities for persons facing the death penalty to appeal, and because the state must pick up the costs of these appeals by the typically indigent prisoners (as well as the costs of fighting the appeals), it actually ends up costing the taxpayers much *more* than would life imprisonment. This again leads one to wonder whether the death penalty exists for reasons other than the common wisdom would provide.

EXPLANATIONS FOR CRIMINAL BEHAVIOR

As we have seen, many kinds of behavior are considered crimes under the law. Why do people engage in these behaviors? Why do they murder, falsely advertise products, steal, or illicitly repress dissent? *No single explanation can account for all crime.* The factors involved in any type of criminal behavior are extraordinarily complex, and explanations tend to focus on different aspects of crime and criminality. They are often, at best, partial explanations of criminal behavior. In this section we look at some of the explanations that have been put forth.

Physiological Explanations

Efforts to explain criminal behavior as a result of the physiological traits of criminals have a long history. Since the nineteenth century, serious attempts have been made to identify such traits.[55] An Italian physician, Cesare Lombroso, conducted research on soldiers and inmates of Italian military prisons in order to show that the propensity for criminal behavior was inborn and that there were physical differences between criminals and law-abiding citizens. Criminals, in his view, were throwbacks to earlier versions of the human species and were often distinguishable by their primitive head shapes, among other stigmatizing features. Lombroso claimed to have found proof for these ideas. His research was harshly criticized for not recognizing that the Italian citizens who were most likely to be involved in criminal activity came from a subsector of Italian society in which such activity was often tolerated for historical and cultural reasons. While members of this subsector—Sicilians—frequently did possess physical features that distinguished them from other Italians, critics observed that these physiological differences could not be accepted as a *cause* of crime since important historical and cultural factors could also be responsible. Lombroso later altered his studies to include such factors.

Lombroso's explanation was further discredited by research conducted in the early twentieth century on English convicts.[56] Charles Goring compared a group of convicts with a group of Cambridge University students and found no significant physical differences between the two groups. But Goring's research did reveal a high correlation between imprisonment of fathers and imprisonment of sons and a correlation between fathers' and sons' physical characteristics. Thus, he concluded that criminality was inherited. Critics pointed out that Goring had no way of taking into account the full range of environmental influences that might have accounted for his findings.

Efforts to demonstrate physiological bases for crime continued. In the 1940s, William Sheldon posited a relationship between body build, per-

[55] See Saleem A. Shah and Loren H. Roth, "Biological and Psychophysiological Factors in Criminality," in Glaser, *Handbook of Criminology*, pp. 101–73.

[56] Charles Goring, *The English Convict* (London: H. M. Stationery Office, 1913).

PUBLIC PROBLEM, PRIVATE PAIN

Strange Fruit

Few people in America have been nominated for the Nobel Peace Prize; the Reverend Joseph Ingle is one of them. He directs the Southern Coalition on Jails and Prisons, a criminal justice reform group, and is a United Church of Christ minister. Joseph Ingle is a formidable opponent of capital punishment, as indicated in this interview.

Congratulations on your nomination for the Nobel Peace Prize. Tell us: What can be done internationally to bring about the abolition of capital punishment in the United States?

Sending telegrams, letters and all that stuff is fine—keep sending them. But we gotta up the ante and I am advocating three things. One: I am askin' all the western European countries, starting with my friends in Sweden, to launch an economic boycott against those states in the United States that have the death penalty. If they are going to open up a Volvo plant in the United States, it shouldn't be in a state that has the death penalty. They can put it in Kansas, Minnesota, Michigan or New York. Somewhere where there is no death penalty. They ought to make a public statement. You know if we are going to boycott South Africa for their racial policies.... my God, we are killing our citizens too! We need to be held accountable for this.

Secondly: We need help monetarily. Not just my organization but all of us. There are two thousand people on death row and one thing we know is that they are all poor. You take every organization in the country that is working against the death penalty, add up all their budgets, and it's probably less than a million dollars. Hell, most states spend several million dollars to kill one person.

Thirdly: We have to make the American people see how totally out of step we are, as a nation, in comparison with our democratic allies. We have to speak out.

There are many corrections officers and prison officials speaking out against capital punishment....

...They may be speaking out, they may be good men, but hell, they've killed people! How can you be against executions and still kill people? This is the politics of the death penalty, that's all it is. So don't tell me about these men.... I know them.

Don't you think it is a good thing that they are coming forward however late?

Who cares?

But at least some of the people you are trying to reach may listen to them, rather than you.

Oh sure, they'll listen to them. But where were they when it was time to make a decision? Now they say, "Hey, I'm against the death penalty." But what difference does it make? What honest-to-God difference does it make? I mean, Jesus said, "By your fruits you will know them," and I have seen the fruits from all the so-called progressive liberals and it stinks. It is rotten fruit.... as Lillian Smith wrote, "It's strange fruit."

Wasn't she referring to the bodies hanging off the trees?

Exactly. Now you must understand me here, it is not a question of bad people, or bad versus good people. We have devised a political, judicial system to murder our citizens. You minimize the horror of this whole problem when you try to say it's this governor or this warden because the primary issue here is these are individuals in a *system.* We have a *system* designed to exterminate our citizens.

To me, the parallel is with the early days of Nazi Germany. We can sit here and say, "Well, Eichmann was a bad guy and Hitler was a bad guy." Well, let's face facts, the German people participated and allowed that to happen. It is exactly what is going on in this country.

Every day American citizens are participating and allowing murder to be officially carried out in their names. Sure it is concentrated in power, no doubt about it. The warden who actually gives the order to pull the switches is more powerful than the ordinary citizen, but the guilt and the responsibility go all the way down the line. It is not just a matter of a few DAs or a few wardens who are angry and want to see people killed, it is a whole *system* in this country. That's why it is so evil.

Why do you feel the American public needs to have the death penalty?

Well, the death penalty is a confession of failure. When you say as a society that you have to kill people, then that means that you have no other way to deal with them. So it is really an admission of failure. But it is also a lie, because there *are* other ways of dealing with murder. I mean, look at all the European nations. Somehow they manage to deal with people who commit murder without executing

PUBLIC PROBLEM, PRIVATE PAIN (continued)

them and it certainly hasn't sent them back into the twelfth century.

So you get down to it in the South, that's all I know about, that's my bailiwick, and you talk about the death penalty and, to me, you are talkin' about race. Race of victim is paramount in all these cases. Nine out of ten times you are going to find a white victim. Second thing you are talkin' about is class. All these people are poor. They are the refuse of our society and this is how we handle it.

There are people on death row in other states too, for example, over 200 in California. Do you think they will start to execute again in these other states where one has not occurred in over 20 years and, if so, do you feel there will be a backlash?

I appreciate what you are saying. Tom Wicker [*New York Times* columnist] and I had a discussion in 1976, and he brought up the same point. He was saying that we will kill maybe two or three people and then we will get outraged and sickened with it and stop it. And I said, "Tom, you don't know how mean this thing is. You really don't know how entrenched and how mean it is." The reality is that America, Southern Americans, Western Americans, wherever, in this country... well Alexis de Tocqueville described it best in *Democracy in America.* De Tocqueville had one major concern and his concern was what he called "tyranny of the masses." Tyranny of the majority is what happens in America when the majority decides to do away with a minority, and he pointed to slavery and he pointed to the American Indian. He was exactly right. Well, it's the same mindset that we bring to the death penalty. We have a minority that we are going to exterminate and it's all nice and legal, set up in the laws. Everybody is saying, "Yeah, yeah, we've got the death penalty, we gotta do it." But the process of thinking here is that psychologically we have dehumanized the men on death row. Once you think people on death row are not human, you can do anything you want to them. You can give them a number. You can send them to a place to wait for their extermination and then you can exterminate them, because they are not like you and me, they are murderers. Just so happens that not only are they murderers but they are probably poor, black, and convicted of killing a white person. They are not like us. You see, de Tocqueville was right. When the majority of the American people set up laws to implement that kind of psychology, then you have mass murder. That's what we had with the Indians. That's what we had with the slaves. And that's what we've got now. It's mass murder. It's two thousand people being exterminated for beginners. We are starting right where the Third Reich started. Look at death row, look who's there. Retarded people, minors, and all these so-called bad murderers. Did you know a third of Florida's death row is there for its first offense? First offense, and they are on death row. What's goin' on here?

Why do you think there is so much violence in the American culture?

Well, we are a very violent culture, especially when you talk about the South. Lord have mercy, we are so violent. The South has the highest per capita incarceration rate in the country, and our country ranks right up at the top of the western world. So a movie like *Rambo* is nothing out of the ordinary, it's just another day at the shop as far as we're concerned. There's a bumper sticker that you'll see that says: "GOD, GUNS, AND GUTS, THAT'S WHAT MADE AMERICA GREAT." That sums up the whole mentality.

What is the effect on a society that condones state executions?

I think that what happens is that you become a society of murderers. When that happens that leads to more and more people getting murdered. Once you have removed the barrier and allowed the state to kill people, where do you stop? Where do you stop this? Do you stop it with people who commit murder? Maybe we will just stop it there for twenty years, then open the gate a little wider and bring it back for people who commit rape, and then maybe a little wider and kill people who commit armed robbery, and the next thing you know you are killing thousands of people a year.

But again it's that whole psychological mechanism. Once you regard people as non-human, subhuman, less than you, you can do anything you want to them, and that's what we're doing. That's what we're doing!

Source: From Ian Gray and Moira Stanley, *A Punishment in Search of a Crime*, pp. 142–45. Copyright © 1989 by the authors. Used by arrangement with Avon Books.

sonality type, and delinquent behavior.[57] Sheldon classified people into three categories. Ectomorphs are thin and fragile, with introverted personalities; endomorphs are soft and fat, with submissive personalities; and mesomorphs are muscular and tough, with assertive personalities. Sheldon then examined 200 American reform school youths. He found that 60 percent of them were mesomorphs. From this he concluded that body build, which has a hereditary basis, was connected with criminality. Sheldon was roundly criticized for weaknesses in his research design and data. Common sense alone tells us that police officers, athletes, and others with muscular builds are not unusually prone to crime. Subsequent studies have not been able to establish the validity of Sheldon's conclusions without confronting similar criticisms.

More recently, research has focused on a possible relationship between genetics and criminality.[58] In recent years, several researchers have claimed that an unusually large proportion of male prison inmates have an extra Y chromosome and that the presence of this extra Y chromosome causes criminal behavior. (Males generally have one X and one Y chromosome; females generally have two X chromosomes.) This theory has been highly controversial—especially since no one knows what proportion of noninmates (or noncriminals) also possess this extra chromosome. Nor does such an explanation help clarify the causes of female criminal behavior.

Only one conclusion can be drawn about physiological explanations: We have no scientifically acceptable evidence that heredity—either in terms of inherited bodily features or genetic characteristics—plays a significant role in causing criminal behavior. In concentrating on physiological traits, researchers continue to engage in what sociologists call *reductionism.* That is, they are isolating individuals and their behavior from the larger context and are reducing explanations to one very basic variable. There is a sharp parallel between physiological approaches and the explanations for criminal behavior that were popular in the Middle Ages. Then such behavior was commonly attributed to demons or evil spirits inflicting the souls of the unfortunate. Demon theories also ignore the larger context in which people's behavior takes on meaning and is defined in criminal terms. Physiological explanations are almost ludicrous when one recalls that self-report studies typically find that almost everyone admits to having committed a criminal act. Unless we are ready to claim that almost the entire American population is physiologically marred, such explanations must be rejected out of hand.

Psychological and Social–Psychological Explanations

Psychological explanations are those that focus almost entirely on the personality traits of individuals. Social–psychological explanations relate personality traits to the individuals' immediate social environment.

A major psychological approach is the psychoanalytic explanation, based on the work of Sigmund Freud. Most psychoanalytic viewpoints see crime as the outcome of unconscious motivations arising within certain troubled individuals.[59] These motivations, in turn, stem from the workings of components of the personality: the id, ego, and superego. Briefly, the id represents the drive for pleasure and self-gratification; it is present at birth. The ego, which develops later, governs the id's urges, directing the search for pleasure within the lim-

[57] William H. Sheldon, *The Varieties of Delinquent Youth* (New York: Harper & Row Publishers, 1949).

[58] See Shah and Roth, "Biological and Psychophysiological Factors in Criminality," pp. 134–39, and Lee Ellis, "Genetics and Criminal Behavior," *Criminology,* 20 (May 1982): pp. 43–66.

[59] See, for example, Walter Bromberg, *Crime and the Mind* (Philadelphia: J. B. Lippincott Company, 1948).

its of surrounding reality. The superego is the guardian of right and wrong; its development marks the emergence of a sense of conscience or guilt over violating the wishes of others in the search for pleasure. In psychoanalytic theory, criminal behavior commonly stems from the failure of the ego and the superego to control the urges of the id. Also, the inadequate development of any of the three personality components may result in emotional problems—from neuroses to psychoses. These problems hamper the ability of individuals to function "normally" and render them prone to crime.

While this explanation may seem compelling, one must remember that the id, ego, and superego are theoretical constructs. Even some professional psychoanalysts do not agree that these components exist. Among those who believe they exist, there are disagreements over their functions and their relationship to behavior. Sociologically oriented critics would suggest that psychoanalytic explanations for criminal behavior place too much emphasis on individual personality factors and not enough on factors that are external to the individual. Such critics would also point out that known criminals do not in general appear to be any more psychologically troubled than noncriminals.

A second type of psychological explanation involves the belief that criminal behavior is *learned*.[60] In this view, people learn to engage in or to avoid such behavior on the basis of *reinforcement*—rewards and punishments. It is assumed that human beings by nature try to seek pleasure and avoid pain. If people are rewarded for criminal behavior, either by other people or by the results of their acts, criminal behavior will have been reinforced as pleasurable. On the other hand, punishment, or the threat of punishment, renders criminal behavior painful and to be avoided.

To an overwhelming degree, this explanation of criminal behavior has been based on experiments with animals, such as pigeons and rats. There are no data on its relevance to actual criminal behavior. One of the major problems lies in the specification and measurement of reinforcers and the meaning of particular reinforcers to different individuals. Moreover, this explanation—like so many others—is always applied after the fact. That is, it is assumed that persons who engage in criminal acts were somehow reinforced into doing so. No one has identified such reinforcers with the precision that would enable predictions of who will commit a crime and under what conditions.

An important social–psychological explanation, one that relates learning more directly to social factors, has been called *differential association theory*.[61] According to this theory, criminal behavior is learned during the course of communication and interaction with criminals or delinquents. When individuals associate with the criminally prone, they learn the techniques of crime and the motives, attitudes, and rationalizations for criminal behavior. The neophyte criminal then adopts definitions of the legal codes that favor law violation over law-abiding behavior.

Differential association theory has been criticized on a number of counts. It does not explain who is likely to become associated with criminally prone people, or why. Nor does it address the question of exceptions—those whose exposure to criminals leads them to reject criminal behavior. Finally, as with so many other explanations, differential association theory is at best a partial explanation. The individual who cheats on income tax, who secretly patronizes a prostitute, or who murders a family member may have *no* history of association with criminally prone people.

Another social–psychological explanation

---

[60] See Ronald L. Akers, *Deviant Behavior* (Belmont, Calif.: Wadsworth, 1973).

[61] Edwin H. Sutherland and Donald R. Cressey, *Criminology*, 9th ed. (Philadelphia: J. B. Lippincott Company, 1974), pp. 75–77.

that relates psychological characteristics to the social environment is called *containment theory*.[62] Containment theory starts with the premise that not all individuals are equally tempted to engage in criminal behavior and asks why this is the case. The answer is that some people are "contained" or controlled and avoid crime because of outer controls and/or inner controls. Outer controls are social pressures that condemn criminal acts, such as community standards. Inner controls are a result of socialization. Family, school, church, and peers may encourage self-control in the face of temptations to engage in crime. Indicators of self-control are said to include a positive self-concept, an orientation to realistic and legitimate goals, the ability to tolerate frustration, and favorable attitudes toward law and law enforcement agencies. On the other hand, those who commit crimes are uncontained and lacking in self-control. Containment theory is extremely broad. We know little about the kinds of social pressures or community standards that help "contain" crime; nor do we fully understand the conditions under which individuals are socialized to develop inner controls.

The preceding explanations all have one common feature. They attempt to infer what goes on in the minds of individuals, and these inferences are then taken to be the causes of criminal behavior. In more general sociological explanations greater attention is given to the features of the larger society and how these might relate to the generation of behavior that comes to be proclaimed criminal.

Sociological Explanations

One of the most famous sociological explanations for criminal behavior is *anomie theory*, developed by Robert Merton.[63] Merton observed that our culture places a great deal of emphasis on material success and that materialistic values are thus shared by members of this society. But, Merton points out, success in material terms is not readily achievable by all. Opportunities are denied certain groups more than others—for example, minorities and the poor. There is, in Merton's terms, a dysjunction or gap between cultural success goals and the availability of means to pursue them. This dysjunction creates stress, which takes the form of *anomie*, a sense of disorientation or normlessness. Those affected by anomie may respond in one of several ways. They may simply scale down their success goals and go about their daily lives in a ritualistic manner. They may engage in illegal ventures, pursuing goals of material success by illegitimate means. They may simply reject such goals entirely, and retreat from participation in the mainstream of society. Or they may rebel and attempt to alter the society whose cultural emphases are unacceptable and unattainable.

Merton's theory is highly suggestive, but it remains rather vague in specifying who is likely to experience anomie and how such persons are likely to respond. Moreover, some crimes appear to have little to do with blocked opportunities for material success. One example that immediately comes to mind is the illegal pursuit of financial advantages by the already rich. Having already achieved material success, and with access to legal channels to achieve more, why commit crimes?

Other sociological explanations have focused on particular segments of the American population, suggesting that criminal behavior is more closely linked to certain subcultures than to American culture as a whole. Overall, such ex-

[62] Walter C. Reckless, *The Crime Problem* (New York: Appleton-Century-Crofts, 1961).

[63] Robert K. Merton, *Social Theory and Social Structure* (New York: The Free Press, 1957), pp. 131–60. Anomie theory is also discussed in the Introduction to this text.

planations have limited their attention to crime among low-income groups.

For example, according to sociologist Albert Cohen, lower-class youth possess a distinct subculture within which delinquent behavior has special meaning.[64] Feeling unfairly discriminated against by middle-class society, these youngsters suffer from "status frustration," which they act out in delinquent forms. Low-income boys engage in delinquent behavior precisely because it is abhorrent to middle-class behavioral standards. Much delinquency takes place by youth gangs, which Cohen sees as collectivities within which such behavior receives support and legitimation.

Richard Cloward and Lloyd Ohlin have also concerned themselves with lower-class gang behavior, drawing on Merton's ideas to explain it.[65] In their view, the gap between cultural success goals and opportunities to pursue them cause lower-class youths to form delinquent subcultures. Cloward and Ohlin have identified three types of delinquent subcultures: criminal, wherein property crimes are a main activity; conflict, involving a preoccupation with violence; and retreatist, where drug use predominates. In their judgment, lower-class communities provide support for one or another of these subcultures. If the adults in a community are involved in property crimes, a criminal subculture will emerge to act as a training ground for delinquent youth. In communities in which such adult models are lacking, youngsters are likely to turn to violence for status. Finally, those who are unable to make it in either of the two other types of subcultures tend to band together in retreatist groups and engage in heavy drug use.

Walter Miller has posited the existence of an autonomous lower-class culture within which members are socialized into a unique set of values, or "focal concerns."[66] Among these focal concerns are toughness, smartness, trouble, and excitement. The lower-class culture, in Miller's view, automatically brings its adherents into conflict with the law. By contrast, Miller suggests, middle-class subcultural values are more in congruence with behavior required by the legal system.

Such subcultural explanations for crime and criminal behavior have limitations. They address such phenomena only among the nonaffluent. Yet we know—if only from self-report studies—that similar behavior takes place outside the lower class. Moreover, not all sociologists agree on the existence of distinct class subcultures. Among those who do, there is disagreement about whether these subcultural variations *cause* behavior in and of themselves.

Other sociological explanations focus not so much on the groups involved in law violation as on the ways in which people are designated as criminals or delinquents. *Labeling theory* is one such explanation.[67] This theory suggests that criminal behavior exists only if and when certain acts are labeled as criminal. It does not address the origins of the acts in question. But in a way, the labeling process may be considered a "cause" of criminal behavior. For example, when the courts identify certain people as criminals, a whole chain of events may be set into motion. Community members, families, and employers may act as if they expect further criminal behavior. In a kind of self-fulfilling prophecy, the newly labeled may be driven toward the behavior expected by others.

A somewhat related explanation is Richard Quinney's *theory of the social reality of crime*.[68] Like

---

[64] Albert K. Cohen, *Delinquent Boys* (New York: The Free Press, 1955).

[65] Richard A. Cloward and Lloyd E. Ohlin, *Delinquency and Opportunity* (New York: The Free Press, 1960).

[66] Walter B. Miller, "Lower Class Culture as a Generating Milieu of Gang Delinquency," *Journal of Social Issues*, 14, No. 3 (1958): 5–19.

[67] Edwin Lemert, *Human Deviance, Social Problems, and Social Control* (Englewood Cliffs, N.J.: Prentice-Hall, 1967).

[68] Richard Quinney, *The Social Reality of Crime* (Boston: Little, Brown & Company, 1970), pp. 15–25.

those sociologists who are interested in the labeling process, Quinney has focused on processes of crime definition. In a simple form, his theory is as follows:

1. Crime is a product of law, and law is determined for the most part by legislative action.
2. Legislatures are greatly influenced by the most powerful segments of society.
3. Acts that are in conflict with the interests of the most powerful segments of society are most likely to be addressed under the law.
4. Segments of the society that are not influential in law creation have a high probability of having their behaviors defined as criminal.
5. The behaviors so defined are an outcome of structured opportunities, learning experiences, interpersonal relations, and self-conceptions.
6. Those whose behaviors are defined as crimes come to see themselves as criminals, and to act in response to the expectations that they will fulfill criminal roles.

Thus, Quinney is saying that crime is a social reality that is *constructed*—behavior that is in conflict with the interests of the powerful is declared unlawful. The behavior in question has a variety of underlying causes. In effect, Quinney has not so much come up with a totally new explanation as he has drawn together what he sees as useful parts of other explanations. His theory thus must stand or fall on the strengths of the latter.

THE CRIMINAL JUSTICE SYSTEM

America's system of criminal justice is made up of three interrelated components: the police, the courts, and correctional institutions.[69] As an arm of the state, the main function of this system is to handle those who have violated the law.

Ideally, the criminal justice system operates smoothly and efficiently. The police are supposed to apprehend and arrest those suspected of illegal acts. The accused are to be brought into courts of law, where their guilt or innocence is determined. Those found guilty should be turned over to correctional institutions for supervision and rehabilitation. Needless to say, the system does not always work this way. In this section we look at some of the reasons.

The Police

The presence of police helps deter crime in America's communities. Indeed, police spend a good deal of time trying to head off situations in which criminal acts might occur. But an equally important police responsibility is the apprehension and arrest of those suspected of illegal acts. It is at this point that the system first fails to work as it is supposed to.

Of the 13.9 million serious crimes (index offenses) reported by local police departments to the Justice Department in 1988, only 21 percent were solved by arrests. Of the 13.8 million arrests made in 1988, most were for relatively minor offenses. For example, a third were for law violations related to alcohol. In most large cities, the jails and courts are clogged with persons arrested by police for minor crimes.

There are many reasons that arrest rates for many serious crimes are so low. (See Figure 13.2.) The sheer volume of crimes known to the police is overwhelming, and there are not enough officers to investigate them all. While many serious offenses are reported to police departments, there is often no way for police to identify the law violators. This is particularly the case with regard to property crimes. Thus, the police generally can apprehend and arrest only persons who violate the law right before their eyes or for whom there is strong suspicion or evidence of criminal behavior.

The whole question of arrest is itself a difficult one for police. On the one hand, police have

[69] President's Commission on Law Enforcement, *The Challenge of Crime*, pp. 70–81.

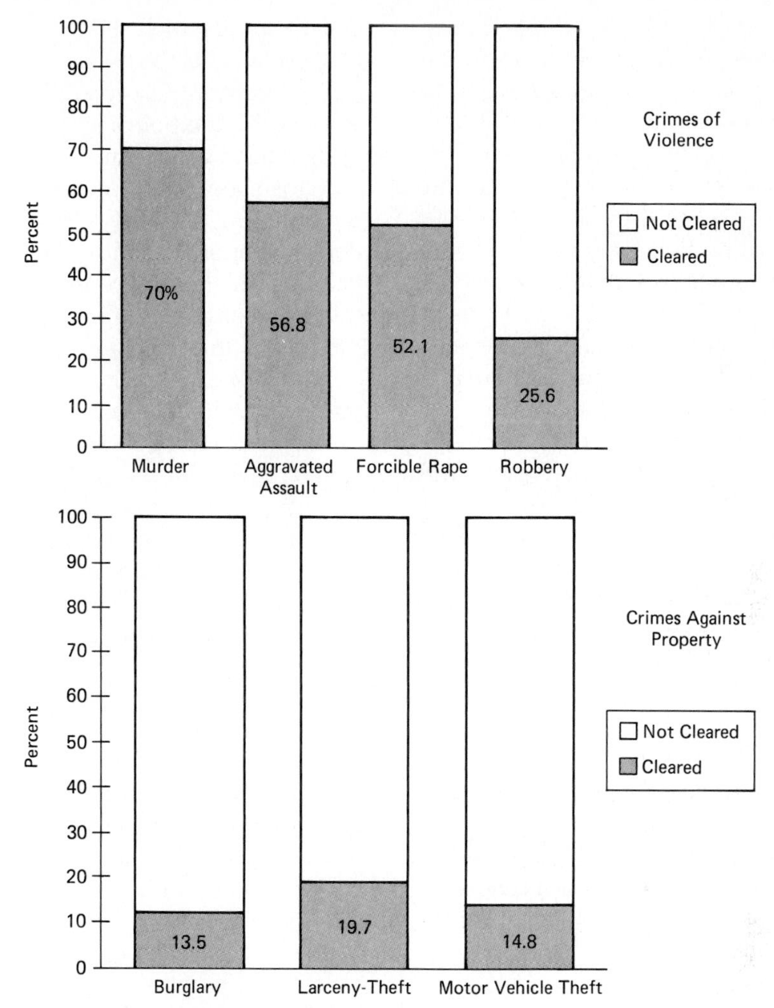

FIGURE 13.2 Crimes Cleared by Arrest, 1988
Source: U.S. Department of Justice, *Uniform Crime Reports for the United States, 1988* (Washington, D.C.: U.S. Government Printing Office, 1989), p. 158.

a great deal of discretion in exercising their arrest powers; at the same time, they are restricted by legal rules in their handling of suspects. Legal restrictions are intended to protect the innocent from the violation of their rights. The police must advise suspects that they have the right to remain silent and to obtain the assistance of an attorney. Police are not allowed to use unnecessary force in making arrests, and they must obtain evidence legally. Although many police officers violate such restrictions, they do so at the risk that those arrested may be set free if the violations become known.

The arrest activity of police is often hampered by corruption among police themselves. In most locales, the police are underpaid. They are expected to do the "dirty work" of society, often at a risk to their own lives. In cities around the country, police have been found accepting bribes and payoffs from law violators, selling confiscated drugs, and even engaging in burglaries. While there is no way to know the extent of such corruption, its existence represents a partial breakdown of the criminal justice system. When even a few police become law violators, the credibility of all police as upholders of the law is diminished. Since the police need the cooperation of the public in apprehending and arresting those suspected of law violations, corruption inhibits police work.

The Courts

After individuals have been arrested, they are ordinarily brought before a prosecutor or other official who draws up the charges that will be presented in court. At this stage, problems frequently crop up, effectively undoing the work of the police. Prosecutors may detect or suspect that arrests were made illegally. They may decide that witnesses and/or evidence would not stand up under examination in court. Many prosecutors are faced with a large backlog of cases, and they generally prefer to draw up charges only when they expect those involved to be found guilty. They thus serve as gatekeepers for the courts.

Prosecutors' decisions place many persons arrested by the police back on the streets—often to police and victims' dismay. The conflicts that arise between prosecutors and police over the handling of those arrested represent a further source of breakdown in the criminal justice system. Police are likely to lose their enthusiasm for arrests when they have to guess at the results that will stem from their efforts.

The courts, especially those in large cities, are faced with far more criminal cases than they can handle. The backlogging of cases has given rise to the routine use of the practice of *plea bargaining,* in which prosecutors offer accused persons the opportunity to plead guilty to a lesser crime. The prosecutor may, for example, offer to reduce a charge of aggravated assault to one of simple assault if the accused will plead guilty. While plea bargaining is intended to lighten the load of the courts and eliminate the need for time-consuming trials, this practice has some serious side effects. Those who are suspected of serious crimes, in the view of victims and police, too often get off lightly. Those who are innocent of violating the law, but who are faced with possible punishment for crimes they did not commit, may be coerced into accepting criminal status and the stigma that goes with it.

Even when accused individuals have their day in court, the criminal justice system often proves to operate inequitably. When there is a backlog of cases, those arrested frequently have to spend a lengthy period in jail before the trial. Affluent persons often can obtain freedom before their trials by raising money for bail. Low-income people have much more difficulty raising bail money, so it is primarily the poor who populate the jails while awaiting trial. Furthermore, in order to convince a judge to grant release on bail, it helps to have a lawyer who has plenty of time to prepare the case. Again, it is the affluent who are likely to be advantaged in this regard.

The resources available to the accused often affect what happens when cases finally go to court. The nonaffluent usually must rely on attorneys provided them by the courts. These attorneys often handle so many cases that they can give little attention to preparing a defense for any one individual. To expedite matters, they may advise their clients to take advantage of opportunities for plea bargaining. The affluent, on the other hand, can afford legal talent tailored to their interests and needs.

Judges and trial jurors are typically middle-class people, "respectable" members of the community. Though guilt and innocence are supposed to be determined solely on the basis of the evidence presented rather than on personal prejudices, class, race, and other differences do enter into determinations. Accused individuals who are most "like" the jury members are likeliest to receive gentle treatment. They may be found not guilty, or if found guilty may receive light sentences and probation. Guilty verdicts and harsh punishments, consequently, weigh most heavily on the poor and members of racial minorities. The poor and minorities predominate in jails and prisons across the country, and it is not because they commit the majority of crimes.

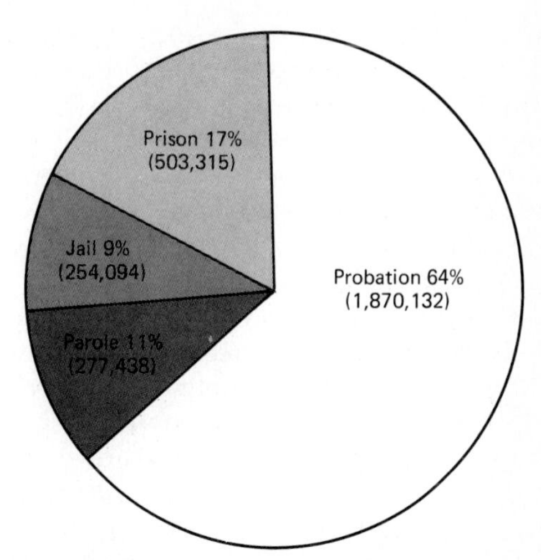

FIGURE 13.3 Persons under Correctional Supervision, by Type of Supervision, 1985
Source: U.S. Department of Justice, Bureau of Justice Statistics, *Report to the Nation on Crime and Justice*, 2nd ed. (Washington, D.C.: U.S. Government Printing Office, 1988), p. 104.

Corrections

Persons who plead guilty to crimes or who are found guilty by the courts may be handled in a variety of ways. They may be fined, imprisoned, or allowed to remain free during a supervised period of probation. (See Figure 13.3.) We shall deal here with imprisonment, which—aside from the death penalty—is the most severe penalty the state can impose on law violators.

Sending people to jail or prison is supposed to serve several different functions. (Jails hold minor offenders serving short sentences, as well as those awaiting trial. Prisons hold those convicted of more serious offenses and serving longer sentences.) Imprisonment removes law violators from society, thus protecting the public from any further threats they might pose. By taking away freedom, imprisonment serves as a form of punishment and retribution for the offenses committed. The threat of such punishment is intended to serve as a deterrent to anyone tempted to engage in criminal behavior. Finally, imprisonment is intended to place convicted law violators in a controlled environment in order to rehabilitate them.

Prisons are very effective in removing people from society and inflicting punishment. But the threat of imprisonment does not seem to be a major crime deterrent. Given the low likelihood of arrest—even for many serious offenses—criminals have a good chance of avoiding prison. Nor does imprisonment do much to rehabilitate those who experience it. The vast majority of prisoners either have been there before or can be expected to return in the future.

The failure of prisons to turn law violators into law-abiding citizens represents the final stage in the breakdown of the criminal justice system.

The basic problem seems to be the contradictory functions imprisonment is supposed to serve. Isolating law violators and taking away their freedom clearly run counter to goals of rehabilitation. On the other hand, the public does not want criminals to be "coddled." Those who violate the law, it is commonly felt, deserve to pay for it. Criminals deserve punishment, not therapy, or else no one would feel any qualms about engaging in criminal acts. In practice, this view prevails in prisons. Only a small percentage of the resources allocated to correctional institutions goes toward anything that could even loosely be called therapy. Most money is spent to maintain security and to keep inmates under careful control.

In response, the inmates develop their own informal society—a subculture with its own set of rules. Prisons have been called schools for crime, as inmates trade knowledge about their techniques of violating the law. Some inmates use physical force or force of personality to exploit others. Crime is rampant inside prisons. Drug use, rape, assault, murder, theft, and extortion are common. From the perspective of most inmates, the prison experience is not only brutal, it is purposeless. Few come out in better shape than when they went in. Whatever the reasons inmates had for violating the law, these reasons are not eradicated by locking individuals up.

Imprisonment has increasingly been employed in the handling of offenders. Consequently, prisons are vastly overcrowded. The imprisoned population cannot be decently housed and more prisons are being constructed. Conditions within America's prisons can only be described as highly dangerous, unhealthy, oppressive, and demoralizing. Given these conditions, prisoner revolts periodically occur.

SUMMARY

Americans rate crime as one of the societal problems they consider most serious. Public concern over the crime problem is essentially focused on personal victimization, such as robbery and assault. Less concern is expressed over white-collar, organized, and political crime, perhaps because these seem rather distant or remote.

Crime is linked to a society's system of law. Whether people are aware of or agree with the legal definition of crime, it is ultimately the law that makes an activity a crime. Under the legal definition, a crime is an act that is intentional, inexcusable, in violation of a law, and punishable by the state.

Why do some acts get defined as crimes, while others do not? Some people believe that law is the product of pluralist democracy and consensus on acts that should be outlawed. Others hold that law is formulated in response to the interests of the dominant economic and social class. Somewhere between these views is the conflict theory of legal change, which sees law creation as the product of conflict between classes and among a variety of interest groups that are not class-based. Sociologists are just beginning to expand research into how laws are formulated and how this leads to the "creation" of crime.

People's perception of the crime problem is to a large extent based on official reports of crime statistics. Such statistics are known to be inaccurate for a number of reasons. Many crimes are not reported to law enforcement agencies. Police may either be lax or be extremely vigilant and aggressive in their handling of certain crimes. The reporting procedures of law enforcement agencies may affect the statistics compiled. Crime rate statistics are also affected by the requirement that they be calculated in conjunction with very accurate population statistics—which we do not possess. At best, official crime statistics, such as those presented in the Justice

Department's *Uniform Crime Reports* each year, provide an approximation of the actual amount of crime.

Efforts to develop more satisfactory data on the extent of crime have taken different forms. For example, researchers have carried out victimization studies wherein people are asked if they have recently been crime victims and whether they reported the crimes to police. Data from such studies indicate that official statistics understate the crime problem to a large extent. Researchers have also conducted self-report studies, in which people are asked about their own law-violating behavior. Data disprove the notion that only certain kinds of people commit crimes and suggest that we cannot generalize about criminal characteristics on the basis of those who get caught.

Criminal behavior takes a wide variety of forms. We have official statistics on common or traditional crime, which includes the serious offenses the Justice Department calls index offenses: criminal homicide, aggravated assault, forcible rape, robbery, burglary, larceny, and motor vehicle theft. According to official statistics, serious crime recently has leveled off. Most arrests are for less serious offenses, including victimless crimes. These are crimes entered into voluntarily that allegedly do not involve crime victims, like prostitution or gambling, and status offenses by juveniles. Many people feel that the state should not impose its moral standards on individuals for certain types of behavior. The magnitude of arrests for victimless crimes affects the efficiency of the criminal justice system.

White-collar crime is both widespread and difficult to define. It and organized crime are thought to be far more economically costly to Americans than traditional property crimes. Political crimes, like white-collar and organized crime, receive little public concern. Political crime reflects the existence of an unequal distribution of power within society.

Why do people engage in criminal behavior? No single explanation can account for all crime. Researchers have put forth explanations based on alleged physiological traits of criminals. They have offered explanations referring to alleged personality traits. And they have offered explanations suggesting that certain features of society cause the generation of behavior that comes to be proclaimed criminal. Sociologists continue to seek knowledge about the causes of criminal behavior. In the absence of an adequate understanding of the causes, America's system of criminal justice is hampered in curbing the crime problem.

The criminal justice system is made up of three interrelated elements: the police, the courts, and correctional institutions. The system does not always work smoothly and efficiently, but instead suffers from breakdowns at a number of different points. For example, it catches only a minority of those who break the law; of those it does catch, most will violate the law and probably be caught again.

DISCUSSION QUESTIONS

1. Have you ever been the victim of a crime? Why do you think this particular type of crime occurs in America? Based on your explanation of why the crime occurs, what do you see as the most appropriate and effective solution?
2. Have you ever knowingly violated the law? Who or what led you to do so? What factors would have had to be present to keep you from violating the law? Based on the importance of such factors, what are solutions to this type of crime?
3. Choose a victimless crime. Develop arguments for and against substantially lowering the penalties for this crime. What arguments could be made for and against making this behavior totally legal?
4. Go to your local police station, courthouse, and jail. Talk with as many people as you can and observe the handling and disposi-

tion of those accused of violating the law. What changes in this process do you think are needed? Why?

5. In the United States, people are presumed to be innocent of law violation until proven guilty. If the principle were to be reversed (i.e., guilty until proven innocent), what problems would this give rise to? Which principle is most desirable?
6. If you blew up a bridge, set fire to homes and other buildings, and took lives by the score, you would no doubt be accused of crimes. If you did all these things in time of war, you might be called a hero. What does this tell you about the relation of law and crime "creation"?

SUGGESTED READINGS

Coleman, James William. *The Criminal Elite: The Sociology of White Collar Crime*, 2nd ed. (New York: St. Martin's Press, 1989).
Cases and analyses of criminal behavior by government and corporate officials.

Garrow, David J. *The FBI and Martin Luther King* (New York: Penguin Books, 1983).
The story of the FBI's illegal harassment of the civil rights movement and its best known leader.

Gray, Ian, and Moira Stanley. *A Punishment in Search of a Crime* (New York: Avon Books, 1989).
Attorneys, prisoners, families of crime victims, and others, speak out against the death penalty.

Katz, Jack. *The Seductions of Crime* (New York: Basic Books, 1988).
An unusual effort to theorize about the attractions of criminal behavior as a way of understanding why people engage in it.

"Our Crowded Prisons," *The Annals of the American Academy of Political and Social Science*, 478 (March 1985). Special edition.
Issues surrounding the high rate of criminal incarceration and prison overcrowding in the United States.

Reiman, Jeffrey H. *The Rich Get Richer and the Poor Get Prison*, 2nd ed. (New York: John Wiley & Sons, 1984).
Exploration of class bias in America's criminal justice system.

CHAPTER 14

Mental Illness

Members of American society should be at peace with themselves and with one another. The social factors that provoke mental troubles should be absent.

During the 1972 presidential campaign, the issue of mental illness was brought before the public in dramatic fashion. Democratic candidate George McGovern's running mate, Thomas Eagleton, admitted that he had been hospitalized for nervous exhaustion three times in the 1960s.[1] Eagleton had twice undergone electroshock treatments, which are commonly employed during therapy for mental depression.

Though Eagleton and McGovern insisted that this was all in the past and that the vice-presidential candidate was in excellent health,

[1] See "Crisis Named Eagleton," *Newsweek*, 80 (August 7, 1972): 12–16; and "Eagleton's Own Story of His Health Problems," *U.S. News & World Report*, 73 (August 7, 1972): 16–17.

the news generated great public concern. If the two men were elected, what would happen if Eagleton had to take over presidential duties? Could the presidency—with its power over domestic, foreign, and military affairs—be entrusted to a person with a history of mental illness? Did the choice of such a running mate reflect badly on McGovern's judgment? As public discussion became increasingly intense, Eagleton withdrew from the campaign. McGovern and his new running mate, Sargent Shriver, lost the 1972 election to the Nixon–Agnew team, perhaps in part because of the "Eagleton affair."

On one level the Eagleton affair was simply an unfortunate moment in America's complex and often fast-paced political history. But on another level, it was extremely revealing about American attitudes toward mental illness. The Eagleton affair made it clear that Americans harbor deep fears and anxieties about mental problems. There was every reason to believe that Eagleton could meet the demands of high executive office. But there was also sufficient public apprehension about his mental state to deny him the opportunity to prove his capabilities. The vice-presidential candidate, for all practical purposes, was treated as if he were *still* mentally troubled. This suggests that, even if psychiatrists and other mental health practitioners do not feel that an individual is "ill," he or she may be labeled as such by others.[2]

How common is mental illness in American society? Just what is meant by the term *mental illness?* How does labeling fit into the definition of who is ill? What factors are thought to be associated with, or to cause, mental troubles? What happens to people who are confined in mental institutions? We address such questions in this chapter.

[2] Empirical evidence is provided in Bruce G. Link et al., "The Social Rejection of Former Mental Patients: Understanding Why Labels Matter," *American Journal of Sociology,* 92 (May 1987): 1461–1500.

THE EXTENT OF MENTAL ILLNESS

How mentally troubled are Americans? Numerous attempts have been made to discover, first, the total number of cases of mental illness existing at any one time and, second, the number of new cases occurring over time. Findings of both types of research have been inconclusive.

The Prevalence of Mental Illness

Most of the attempts to measure the *prevalence* of mental illness—that is, the total number of cases existing at a given time—have involved surveying a sample of people and then generalizing from the findings. The best known empirical inquiry is the Midtown Manhattan study, conducted by sociologist Leo Srole and his associates.[3] These researchers interviewed a sample of adults in New York City, asking questions bearing on their mental state. The data were then turned over to psychiatric experts, who rated each case on a scale ranging from mentally well to incapacitated. The psychiatrists rated only 18.5 percent of those surveyed as mentally healthy. Almost 25 percent were found to be incapacitated or were said to show severe or marked symptoms of mental impairment. According to the psychiatrists, the remainder of those sampled had moderate or mild symptoms of mental illness. If these findings were valid, it would mean that the majority of New York City residents showed some symptoms of mental illness!

The findings of similar studies conducted in other communities, from Baltimore to Houston, have varied enormously.[4] Prevalence rates have been found that range from 1 to 60 percent of those surveyed. The most commonly quoted figure is around 10 percent, but many would ar-

[3] Leo Srole et al., *Mental Health in the Metropolis* (New York: McGraw-Hill Book Company, 1962).

[4] For an overview of many such studies, see Howard B. Kaplan, *The Sociology of Mental Illness* (New Haven, Conn.: College & University Press, 1972), pp. 49–64.

gue that this figure is conservative. One presidential commission concluded the national rate was closer to 15 percent.[5] A study sponsored by the National Institute of Mental Health, a federal agency, came up with close to 19 percent.[6]

Why is there no precise information on the prevalence of mental illness? The main reason is the lack of agreement among researchers on the appropriate diagnostic measures. Existing studies use different criteria for identifying the mentally ill, a variety of survey instruments, and various means for classifying cases. This makes comparisons between studies very difficult. Consequently, no one really knows with any precision how prevalent mental illness is among the American people. Most experts accept the rough figure of 10 percent, or over 24 million troubled Americans.

The Incidence of Mental Illness

Efforts to identify the *incidence* of mental illness—the number of new cases occurring over time—have primarily been based on statistics on treatment. For example, one may examine the number of persons receiving aid through outpatient facilities and the number confined in hospitals.

Over 6 million persons (many of them children) currently receive treatment in mental health facilities each year. About a third of them undergo confinement; most are handled as outpatients. The number of people receiving treatment has risen steadily over the last thirty years.[7] This might mean that the incidence of mental illness has been on the increase. But it could also mean that people feel more comfortable about seeking help for mental troubles than they did in the past. Or it could be that more people are defining themselves as ill, having no other way to understand or articulate things that are bothering them. We do know that treatment has become more accessible to Americans. (See Table 14.1.) Since the mid-1960s, the federal government has provided funds for mental health centers in local communities. This has been done in order to provide alternatives to large, often isolated, residential institutions. However, the trend toward increased use of treatment facilities began before such community centers started to proliferate.[8]

The question of incidence is further muddied when other factors bearing on treatment statistics are considered. Obviously, not all persons who are mentally troubled seek out or are brought to treatment. For example, many of those interviewed by Srole and his associates were considered mentally impaired but were not or had never been under treatment. Furthermore, some troubled individuals who seek aid may not be counted in treatment statistics. This would be the case for those who consult religious figures or school counselors. Still others—particularly the affluent—rely on private psychiatrists, who generally do not release information about their patients. Thus, these cases do not show up in treatment statistics. For such reasons, it seems likely that estimates of the incidence of mental illness underreport the number of new cases occurring each year.

In the last thirty years, there has been a noticeable drop in the number of persons confined in mental hospitals at any given time. (See Table 14.2.) If we limited our attention to the number confined, we might conclude that mental illness—or at least serious mental illness—is on the decrease. However, while this drop has been going on, the actual number of new *admissions*

[5] President's Commission on Mental Health, *Report to the President* (Washington, D.C.: U.S. Government Printing Office, 1978).

[6] National Institute of Mental Health, *Mental Health, United States, 1985* (Washington, D.C.: U.S. Government Printing Office, 1985), p. 4.

[7] General statistics are available from the National Institute of Mental Health.

[8] See Franklin D. Chu and Sharland Trotter, *The Madness Establishment* (New York: Grossman Publishers, 1974), p. 30.

TABLE 14.1 Mental Health Facilities: Summary by Type of Facility, 1987 (Numbers in Thousands)

Type of facility	Number of facilities	Inpatient beds		Inpatients		Average daily inpa-tients	Inpatient care epi-sodes†	Expenditures		Patient care staff§
		Number	Rate*	Number	Rate*			Total (millions of dollars)	Per capita (dollars)‡	
Total	**4,747**	**267.6**	**111.8**	**237.9**	**99.4**	**228.5**	**2,052**	**18,460**	**77**	**346.6**
Mental hospitals										
State and county	285	119.0	49.7	111.1	46.4	107.1	442	6,326	26	119.0
Private‖	751	54.7	22.9	47.8	20.0	46.1	305	3,607	15	60.6
General hospitals#	1,351	45.8	19.1	34.5	14.4	34.4	883	2,878	12	61.1
Veterans Administration**	139	26.9	11.2	24.3	10.2	21.2	204	1,338	6	23.6
Freestanding psychiatric outpatient services††	773	(NA)	(NA)	(NA)	(NA)	(NA)	(NA)	518	2	9.2
Other‡‡	1,448	21.2	8.9	20.2	8.4	19.7	218	3,793	16	73.1

[Facilities and beds as of January 1987; inpatients as of year end 1986; other data are for calendar year or fiscal year ending in a month other than December since facilities are permitted to report on either a calendar or fiscal year basis. Excludes private psychiatric office practice and psychiatric service modes of all types in hospitals or outpatient clinics of federal agencies other than Veterans Administration. Excludes data from Puerto Rico, Virgin Islands, Guam, and other territories.]

Key: NA, not applicable.

*Rate per 100,000 population. Based on Bureau of Census estimated civilian population as of July 1.

†"Inpatient care episodes" is defined as the number of residents in inpatient facilities at the beginning of the year plus the total additions to inpatient facilities during the year.

‡Based on Bureau of the Census estimated civilian population as of July 1.

§Full-time equivalent.

‖ Includes residential treatment centers for emotionally disturbed children.

#Nonfederal hospitals with separate psychiatric services.

**Includes Veterans Administration (VA) neuropsychiatric hospitals, VA general hospitals with separate psychiatric settings, and VA freestanding psychiatric outpatient clinics.

††Includes mental health facilities which provide only psychiatric outpatient services.

‡‡Includes other multiservice mental health facilities with two or more settings, which are not elsewhere classified, as well as freestanding partial care organizations, which only provide psychiatric partial care services. Number of facilities, expenditures, and staff data also include freestanding psychiatric day/night facilities.

Source: U.S. Department of Commerce, Bureau of the Census, *Statistical Abstract of the United States, 1989* (Washington, D.C.: U.S. Government Printing Office, 1989), p. 109.

TABLE 14.2 Patient Care Episodes, by Type of Mental Health Organization: United States, Selected Years 1969–83

Type of organization	1969	1975	1979	1981	1983
Number of inpatient episodes					
All organizations	**1,710,372**	**1,817,108**	**1,779,587**	**1,720,392**	**1,860,613**
State and county mental hospitals	767,115	598,993	526,690	499,169	459,374
Private psychiatric hospitals	102,510	137,025	150,535	176,513	180,822
Nonfederal general hospitals with separate psychiatric services	535,493	565,696	571,725	676,941	820,030
VA medical centers*	186,913	214,264	217,507	205,580	170,508
Federally funded community mental health centers	65,000	246,891	254,288	—	—
Residential treatment centers for emotionally disturbed children	21,340	28,302	33,729	34,426	32,544
All other organizations†	32,001	25,937	25,113	127,763	197,335
Percent distribution of inpatient episodes					
All organizations	**100.0%**	**100.0%**	**100.0%**	**100.0%**	**100.0%**
State and county mental hospitals	44.9	33.0	29.6	29.0	24.7
Private psychiatric hospitals	6.0	7.5	8.5	10.3	9.7
Nonfederal general hospitals with separate psychiatric services	31.3	31.1	32.3	39.4	44.1
VA medical centers*	10.9	11.8	12.2	11.9	9.2
Federally funded community mental health centers	3.8	13.6	14.3	—	—
Residential treatment centers for emotionally disturbed children	1.2	1.6	1.9	2.0	1.7
All other organizations†	1.9	1.4	1.4	7.4	10.6
Inpatient episodes per 100,000 civilian population					
All organizations	**859.1**	**859.6**	**812.1**	**755.7**	**799.1**
State and county mental hospitals	385.3	283.3	236.4	219.3	197.7
Private psychiatric hospitals	51.5	64.8	67.6	77.5	77.8
Nonfederal general hospitals with separate psychiatric services	269.0	267.6	266.3	297.3	351.3
VA medical centers*	93.9	101.4	101.3	90.3	73.4
Federally funded community mental health centers	32.6	116.8	114.1	—	—
Residential treatment centers for emotionally disturbed children	10.7	13.4	15.1	15.1	14.0
All other organizations†	16.1	12.3	11.3	56.1	84.9

[The population used in the calculation of these rates is the January 1 civilian population of the United States for the respective years.]

*Includes VA neuropsychiatric hospitals, VA general hospital psychiatric services, and VA psychiatric outpatient clinics.

†Includes freestanding psychiatric partial care organizations and multiservice mental health organizations.

Source: U.S. Department of Health and Human Services, *Mental Health, United States, 1987* (Washington, D.C.: U.S. Government Printing Office, 1987), p. 34.

to mental hospitals has remained high (Table 13.2). Though more persons are being admitted, the length of confinement is decreasing. One reason is that the extensive use of drugs enables people to function outside of confinement.[9] Second, community mental health facilities make it possible for more individuals to be treated as outpatients. Third, there has been an ongoing effort to move the aged out of mental institutions and into nursing homes or geriatric hospitals. In the past, elderly persons who could not care for themselves were often left to languish in such institutions. Finally, it costs more to care for the confined. Moving persons out of confinement helps hold down the costs of running tax-supported public hospitals.

One could argue that the incidence of mental illness is increasing. More people are seeking treatment, and the rate of admission to hospitals is high. But because of the problem of interpreting available statistics, one must advance such an argument with caution. As with prevalence, the incidence of mental illness remains a topic of debate.

DEFINING MENTAL ILLNESS

Thus far we have used the term *mental illness* rather freely. After all, everyone seems to know what it means. However, there is some disagreement over whether the term means anything at all. We discuss the problems of definition in this section.

The Medical Model

Only since the nineteenth century have troubled persons been designated as "ill."[10] Prior to that time, they were more likely to be considered "possessed" by spirits, the victims of witchcraft, morally defective, or otherwise afflicted by unknown and unsavory problems. During the nineteenth century, medical practitioners advanced the theory that mental troubles were actually matters of health. They argued that persons exhibiting such troubles should not be harassed and punished or locked up in jails and asylums. Instead, said the doctors, they should be cured and made well.

This approach is usually called the *medical model* or disease model of mental illness.[11] It is based on the belief that just as one's body is subject to injury or disease, so is one's mind. Unusual forms of behavior and/or signs of psychological disturbances are the warning symptoms of the illness. Psychiatrists and other mental health practitioners (e.g., psychotherapists, psychologists, psychiatric social workers) use the symptoms to diagnose the nature of the illness afflicting the troubled individual. Depending on the diagnosis and on the treatment preferences of the practitioner, a method of cure will be prescribed. The cure may involve the intensive probing of a person's thoughts, drug or electroconvulsive therapy, or group meetings attended by similarly ill people. The mentally ill individual is expected to assume the role of patient and to rely on the expertise and advice of the mental health professional.

The evolution of the medical model has been accompanied by the adoption of a system of diagnostic terms. These terms are used to categorize the various types of mental illness that have been discovered by psychiatrists and to help standardize treatment of individuals exhibiting similar symptoms. In the United States,

---

[9] See William Gronfein, "Psychotropic Drugs and the Origins of Deinstitutionalization," *Social Problems*, 32 (June 1985): 437–54.

[10] See, for example, Michel Foucault, *Madness and Civilization* (New York: Random House, 1965), and George Rosen, *Madness in Society* (Chicago: University of Chicago Press, 1968).

[11] See Peter Conrad and Joseph W. Schneider, *Deviance and Medicalization* (St. Louis, Mo.: C. V. Mosby Company, 1980), pp. 38–72.

the American Psychiatric Association publishes a guide to this diagnostic system.[12]

In actuality, the American Psychiatric Association has issued several editions of its guide—in 1952, 1968, 1980, and more recently in 1987. Each has involved changes in terminology and the addition or subtraction of various forms of behavior, reflecting a changing consensus among psychiatrists of exactly what constitutes mental illness.

The 1987 guide provides the following system of classification (here examples are indicated in parentheses):

1. Disorders usually first evident in infancy, childhood, or adolescence (retardation, hyperactivity, stuttering, eating problems as in anorexia nervosa).
2. Organic mental disorders (brain damage, senility).
3. Substance use disorders (alcohol and drug abuse).
4. Schizophrenia (loss of contact with reality, paranoia).
5. Delusional disorders (feelings of grandiosity).
6. Mood disorders (mania, depression).
7. Anxiety disorders (phobias, anxiety, compulsive behavior).
8. Somatoform disorders (hypochondria).
9. Dissociative disorders (amnesia, multiple personality).
10. Sexual disorders (exhibitionism, fetishism, loss of sexual desire).
11. Sleep disorders (insomnia).
12. Factitious disorders (intentionally produced physical symptoms).
13. Other disorders of impulse control (pathological gambling, kleptomania).
14. Adjustment disorders (maladaptation to stress).

The preceding classification drops two categories that have entered into popular usage: psychosis and neurosis. Schizophrenia and mood disorders most commonly comprise what had been classified as psychosis. Anxiety disorders do the same for most of what had been called neurosis. However, these older, more familiar terms will be employed here for purposes of discussion.[13]

Psychosis. According to mental health practitioners, the *psychoses* are a very severe form of mental illness. Individuals diagnosed as psychotic frequently have their own versions of reality and thus are often unable to perform the roles expected of them in everyday life. Consequently, treatment of the psychoses commonly involves voluntary or involuntary confinement.

Psychotics may suffer from hallucinations, deep changes in mood, or an inability to think, speak, or remember. While psychiatrists have found that some psychoses are *organic*—that is, a result of actual physical damage to the brain or of chemical imbalances in a person's system—they claim that most types of psychosis are *functional*. In other words, in most psychoses there is no known physical reason for the symptoms of illness that are displayed. The mind itself is unwell and in need of cure.[14]

One of the more common psychoses is called *schizophrenia*. This term is used for people who are extremely withdrawn from their surroundings or who act as if they were living in another world. Schizophrenics' thoughts may appear disorganized and bizarre, their emotions inap-

[12] American Psychiatric Association, *Diagnostic and Statistical Manual of Mental Disorders*, 3rd ed., rev. (Washington, D.C.: APA, 1987).

[13] See Bernard J. Gallagher III, *The Sociology of Mental Illness* (Englewood Cliffs, N.J.: Prentice-Hall, 1980), pp. 35–127.

[14] Some argue that many forms of mental illness are biologically or genetically influenced. See Peter McGuffin and Theodore Reich, "Psychopathology and Genetics," in Henry E. Adams and Patricia B. Sutker, eds., *Comprehensive Handbook of Psychopathology* (New York: Plenum, 1984), pp. 47–75.

propriate for the situation, and their behavior unusual. Various types of schizophrenia have been identified and categorized. Persons who exhibit delusions of being persecuted by others are called paranoid schizophrenics. Catatonic schizophrenics act in an excessively excited manner or, alternatively, exist in a mute vegetative state. Childhood schizophrenia, or autism, is marked by withdrawal and repetitive, occasionally self-harming, motor behavior.

In the view of psychiatrists, schizophrenia primarily involves difficulties in thinking. *Mood disorders,* on the other hand, mainly involve changes in emotion. In mood disorders, people may become extremely elated or deeply depressed for no apparent reasons. One type of mood disorder, melancholia, is characterized by unrelenting signs of worry. Manic-depressive disorders, by contrast, take the form of sudden and severe changes in mood. The person may be gleefully boisterous in the manic state and may seriously contemplate self-destruction in the depressed state.

In everyday language, a person designated as psychotic by a psychiatrist is likely to be considered "mad," "nuts," "cuckoo," or "crazy." These terms are not used by those embracing the medical model. To mental health practitioners, such persons are ill and in need of professional healing.

Neurosis. Persons suffering from one or another type of *neurosis,* a second major category of mental disorder or illness, are typically capable of functioning in everyday life. Unlike the psychoses, the neuroses generally do not involve distortions of reality. Moreover, neurotics typically know that there is something wrong with their thinking or behavior.

The principal symptom of neurosis is evidence of anxiety. In mild cases of neurosis, anxiety may be expressed directly. In some severe cases, a person may appear to be in a state of panic. According to psychiatrists, anxiety may also be expressed indirectly, showing up as a variety of other problems—such as blindness, deafness, exhaustion, inexplicable fear of objects or particular situations, and compulsive activity (e.g., hand washing).

In most cases, individuals who are diagnosed as neurotics do not require hospitalization. In fact, mental health practitioners often find it hard to tell if someone is indeed suffering from an anxiety-produced neurosis—that is, is "ill"—or is merely very temporarily responding to pressures that anyone might find distressing.

Problems of Classification

While the American Psychiatric Association has come up with an elaborate classification system, there continue to be many problems with it. Application of the various categories, each of which is accompanied by a list of symptoms to guide diagnosis, remains difficult. Psychiatrists often disagree among themselves on the most appropriate diagnostic label to apply, not to mention treatment.

The fact that categories and behaviors identified as disorders change raises questions about the reliability of the system. For example, in the mid-1970s members of the American Psychiatric Association decided that homosexuality, which had been classified as a mental disorder, should be dropped from the classification scheme. Was homosexuality *ever* a mental disorder—a form of illness deserving treatment?[15]

There has been a tendency in subsequent editions of the APA guidelines to add various forms of behavior to the list of disorders, but health insurance companies have tried to fight this tendency. As the list of "illnesses" expands, so do the numbers of persons seeking treatment and health insurance payments.

Fundamental questions have been raised, not only about the classification system generally accepted by psychiatrists, but about the utility of the medical model itself. It is to this that we now turn.

---

[15] Conrad and Schneider, *Deviance and Medicalization,* pp. 192–93.

The Utility of the Medical Model. The problem mental health practitioners have in determining who is ill and who is well has led some critics to question the whole concept of *mental illness*. How accurate and valid are the judgments made by the most prestigious mental health professionals, the psychiatrists? According to David L. Rosenhan: "There are a great deal of conflicting data on the reliability, utility, and meaning of such terms as 'sanity,' 'insanity,' 'mental illness,' and 'schizophrenia.'"[16] Prevalence surveys and treatment statistics indicate that many people are mentally troubled. But whether their mental states are best viewed and treated as forms of illness is another issue. Could it be that illness is simply a label routinely applied by believers in the medical model?

Rosenhan set up an ingenious experiment in order to pursue this question. He recruited eight people who had no history of mental troubles and were, in the language of the medical model, mentally healthy. At Rosenhan's direction, each of them sought admission to a mental hospital. The staffs of these institutions had no inkling that Rosenhan's associates were "pseudopatients."

Upon arriving at the hospitals, the eight pseudopatients claimed that they had been hearing voices and that they had come to see whether anything was wrong with them. Aside from this deception, they truthfully answered all questions pertaining to their medical backgrounds, life-styles, and relationships with others. Seven were immediately diagnosed as schizophrenic, and the eighth was judged to be manic-depressive. Their deception was not discovered by psychiatrists. Even though they were healthy, they were diagnosed as ill.

Once they were assigned to psychiatric wards, all eight pseudopatients stopped faking the symptoms that had gained them admittance. They behaved in a friendly and cooperative manner and answered questions about their health by saying they felt fine. But no one—except other patients—doubted that their illnesses were real. After hospitalizations ranging from seven to fifty-two days, the eight pseudopatients were released, their illnesses officially diagnosed as in remission. In other words, they were still considered to be mentally ill, but the symptoms of their illnesses were said to have subsided.

To further test the ease with which people are termed ill or well, no matter what their true mental state, Rosenhan carried his experiment one step further. He told the staff of one mental hospital—where his pseudopatient trick had become known—that he would seek to admit more such persons to their wards. In effect, he dared the psychiatric staff to uncover his pseudopatients. Following his dare, the staff screened 193 individuals. Of these, 41 were alleged to be Rosenhan's pseudopatients, and many others were considered suspect. Rosenhan had *not* sent anyone to that hospital!

On the basis of his experiment, Rosenhan concluded that "any diagnostic process that lends itself so readily to massive errors of this sort cannot be a very reliable one."[17] His work helped feed the contemporary controversy over the meaning of mental illness and the utility of the medical model. It lends credence to critics who have urged rejection of the medical model.

Mental Illness as a Myth

The principal critic of the medical model, Thomas Szasz, is himself a psychiatrist. In his writings, Szasz acknowledges the evidence that links brain damage to certain behavior and/or thinking difficulties.[18] Severe cases of syphilis,

[16] David L. Rosenhan, "On Being Sane in Insane Places," *Science*, 179 (January 19, 1973): 250. See also David L. Rosenhan, "The Contextual Nature of Psychiatric Diagnosis," *Journal of Abnormal Psychology*, 84 (October 1975): 462–74.

[17] Rosenhan, "On Being Sane in Insane Places," p. 252.

[18] See Thomas S. Szasz, *The Myth of Mental Illness* (New York: Delta Books, 1961). His position is most succinctly

the excessive use of alcohol, and physiological changes sometimes accompanying aging, for example, can cause people to behave or think in unusual ways. Szasz also acknowledges the effect of chemical imbalances on mental functioning. In such cases, Szasz tells us, it is correct to state that a person is ill. Moreover, such illnesses are most appropriately handled within a medical context.

But Szasz reminds us that most of the illnesses treated by mental health practitioners are *functional* rather than organic in origin. He contends that these functional disorders are actually individual traits that may deviate from what is considered culturally, socially, ethically, or legally normal. When psychiatrists compare their own standards of what is normal with the traits exhibited by their clients, they are making value judgments about which norms people should follow. They call the people who depart from these norms ill and in need of treatment. Szasz believes that there is a contradiction between judging people as deviant on the one hand and offering them medically oriented diagnoses and treatments on the other:

> Since medical interventions are designed to remedy only medical problems, it is logically absurd to expect that they will help solve problems whose very existence have been defined and established on nonmedical grounds.[19]

According to Szasz, the symptoms many psychiatrists associate with mental illness are really no more than styles of communication. People designated as ill are simply saying something about themselves, others, and the world around them: "What people now call mental illnesses are, for the most part, *communications* expressing unacceptable ideas, often framed in an unusual idiom."[20] These communications are expressed because people find that life is a difficult struggle. Their relations with other people and their contacts with societal institutions are accompanied by a great deal of personal stress and strain. Often their needs, values, and aspirations are going unmet. They are disturbed by the lack of harmony in American society and by unavoidable conflict with others. In Szasz' terms, people face "problems in living." They are not sick or diseased; they are trying to communicate the difficulties with which they are burdened in everyday life.

By calling individuals with problems in living ill, we are implying that there is something wrong with *them* and that they must change. This is why troubled people are encouraged to become patients and to become dependent on professional care (even against their will). The medical model, in Szasz' view, is an ideology that

> has succeeded in depriving vast numbers of people—sometimes it seems very nearly everyone—of a vocabulary of their own in which to frame their predicament without paying homage to a psychiatric perspective.[21]

People who face problems in living are encouraged by the medical model to look primarily within themselves for the sources of their difficulties. Only if they accept the fact that they are indeed sick and in need of help can they get better. They must adjust and accommodate their thinking and behavior to that considered normal by psychiatrists.

Those who reject the medical model and the treatments flowing from it still must confront the question of what—if anything—might be done for persons who are mentally troubled.

---

put forth in "The Myth of Mental Illness," *American Psychologist,* 15 (February 1960): 113–18.

[19] Thomas S. Szasz, *Ideology and Insanity* (New York: Anchor Books, 1970), p. 17. This is also the theme of his article "Power and Psychiatry," *Society,* 18 (May/June 1981): 16–18.

[20] Szasz, *Ideology and Insanity,* p. 19.

[21] Ibid., p. 5. For elaboration on this theme, see Martin L. Gross, *The Psychological Society* (New York: Random House, 1978).

In our major cities, there are some men and women whose daily lifestyles may seem unusual, leading people to label them as deviant and sometimes as mentally ill. The man in this photograph works as a junk picker. On what grounds can we justify calling unusual behavior "sickness" and deserving of medically oriented treatment? *(Alan Carey/The Image Works)*

Szasz believes that the latter *can* be helped to deal with problems in living without being told that they are sick. In his view, therapists must establish open, humane relationships with such people. Such relationships should be entered into and maintained purely on a voluntary basis and must not place troubled persons in the subordinate role of patient.

Mental Illness as a Sign of Health

Another well-known critic of the medical model, British psychiatrist R. D. Laing, felt that "humanity is estranged from its authentic possibilities."[22] Laing used the term *alienation* to characterize the relations that exist among family members, generations, sex groups, classes, and races:

> The "normally" alienated person, by reason of the fact that he acts more or less like everyone else, is taken to be sane. Other forms of alienation that are out of step with the prevailing state of alienation are those that are labeled by the "normal" majority as bad or mad.[23]

The abnormally alienated are most likely to be noticed, to seek or be brought to treatment, and to be designated as ill under the medical model.

Laing suggested that one of the more severe forms of mental illness, schizophrenia, has noth-

[22] R. D. Laing, *The Politics of Experience* (New York: Ballantine Books, 1967), p. 12.

[23] Ibid., pp. 27–28.

ing to do with disease. Instead, according to Laing:

> The experience and behavior that gets labelled schizophrenia is a special strategy that a person invents in order to live in an unlivable situation. In his life situation the person has come to feel he is in an untenable position. He cannot make a move, or make no move, without being beset by contradictory and paradoxical pressures and demands, pushes and pulls, both internally from himself, and externally from those around him.[24]

Serious disorders, to Laing, are efforts on the part of an individual to escape from alienating societal arrangements. Laing suggested that these efforts to escape existing realities might actually be considered a sign of health. They are certainly a healthier response than would be living with the problems. "The perfectly adjusted bomber pilot may be a greater threat to species survival than the hospitalized schizophrenic deluded that the Bomb is inside him."[25]

Likening the schizophrenic experience to an LSD drug "trip" or spiritual journey, Laing felt that psychiatric efforts to cure schizophrenia are more often harmful than helpful. He believed that experienced psychotics should be used to guide those who are in the process of embarking into another level of reality. Needless to say, Laing's ideas—like those of Szasz—are unpopular among those who remain committed to the medical model.

Nonetheless, Laing's observations suggest ways of approaching those who are troubled. His stress on empathy and understanding, implied by the suggestion of using persons who have "been there" to help others, offers an alternative to telling troubled people that there is something wrong with them.

[24] Ibid., pp. 114–15.
[25] Ibid., p. 120.

The Labeling Process

Like Rosenhan and Szasz, Laing emphasized that mental illness is a label bestowed on people whose thinking and/or behavior is judged unacceptable. The bestowal of such a label is, according to Laing, a *political event*, in which those with medical, legal, and moral authority are in a position to cast an individual into the role of sick person. This labeling process has been spelled out by sociologist Thomas Scheff.[26]

Scheff notes that members of society have handy categories in which to place those who violate commonly accepted rules or norms. Persons who violate the law are "criminals"; those who eat peas with their knives are "ill-mannered." But some forms of behavior are so unusual or unthinkable that they cannot be easily categorized. Such *residual deviance* is likely to be allocated to a catchall category: mentally ill.

Unlike Szasz and Laing, Scheff is not too concerned with pinning down the initial reasons why persons may express unusual thinking and/or behavior. Instead, he simply states that the deviant behaviors called mental illness may arise from diverse sources ranging from the physiological to the socioeconomic.

Scheff contends that the rate of residual deviance is extremely high, and that only a small amount comes to be treated as mental illness. Much deviance is either ignored, unrecognized, or rationalized away. Moreover, much of it is transitory. But at least some is labeled mental illness and is treated. The crucial variable, according to Scheff, is *societal reaction*. The label must be imposed by society for mental illness to exist.

[26] Thomas J. Scheff, *Being Mentally Ill* (Chicago: Aldine Publishing Company, 1966). See also a critique by Walter R. Gove, "Societal Reactions as an Explanation of Mental Illness: An Evaluation," *American Sociological Review*, 35 (October 1970): 873–80. More recent work by Scheff includes *Labeling Madness* (Englewood Cliffs, N.J.: Prentice-Hall, 1975) and *Being Mentally Ill*, 2nd ed. (Hawthorne, N.Y.: Aldine de Gruyter, 1984).

When does society impose the label? Scheff posits that we learn stereotypes of what it means to "act crazy" in early childhood. These stereotypes are then reaffirmed, for example, by the mass media and even in everyday conversations. When residual deviance becomes publicly noticed, such stereotypes are mobilized, and the individual is told that he or she is ill.

An individual who has been labeled mentally ill is encouraged to accept this label and to display the traits stereotypically expected of a sick person. Once this occurs, the illness becomes "stabilized": Mental disorder becomes a social role. The individual impersonates illness by accepting and acting within the diagnostic labels of the medical model.

Scheff observes that persons may actually be rewarded for playing the illness role. Psychiatrists, for example, are pleased when someone accepts their diagnosis and treatments. Conversely, persons may be punished for attempting to shed the role. Once labeled, so-called mentally ill people—even if pronounced cured—may find it difficult to escape discriminatory treatment (as did Thomas Eagleton, whose experiences were discussed at the start of this chapter). Any additional episodes of residual deviance are likely to be interpreted as signs of continued illness. Individuals thus may be caught up in a *career* of being mentally ill, filling this role in response to societal reactions to them.

In sum, there is a controversy over whether most mentally troubled persons are in fact ill. As critics of the medical model contend, such individuals may face problems in living or be alienated from existing societal arrangements. As they respond to their situations with unusual expressions of behavior and/or thinking, they may be labeled as ill and subjected to treatment in a medical context. The critics question the wisdom of such treatment for persons whose troubles are essentially rooted in the societal environment in which they find themselves.

Mental Illness and Criminal Justice

On March 30, 1981, young John W. Hinckley shot President Ronald Reagan and three other persons during an assassination attempt in Washington, D.C. A shocked nation soon learned that Mr. Hinckley, who had been under treatment by a psychiatrist prior to the shooting, was claiming a bizarre motive for his action—the desire to court the favor of Jodie Foster, a movie star. There was no denying his involvement in the assault, as it was recorded on film and widely disseminated on television. A year later, however, Mr. Hinckley's fate was decided: "Not guilty by reason of insanity." He was remanded to a federal mental hospital for treatment and presumably eventual release.

Although pleas of not guilty by reason of insanity are relatively rare and defendants are seldom successful in raising the insanity defense, widely publicized trials such as Hinckley's raise serious issues. *Insanity* is a legal term, and involves problematic psychiatric judgments and labeling around which disagreements may occur. Moreover, there is the question of the standard that should be applied to determine when a person should be relieved of responsibility for a criminal act. This question has occupied legal minds for centuries, and to date no resolution has been reached that meets with widespread satisfaction.[27]

To be found guilty of a serious offense, a defendant ordinarily must be shown to have had criminal intent. The law, in such circumstances, is interested in finding fault and thus establishing individual responsibility. An insanity plea in essence denies individual responsibility. Psychiatric judgments are brought into play by both the prosecution and the defense to provide "expert opinion" to guide decision making by a jury of citizens. Often the judgments of the psychi-

[27] For an overview of legal and clinical issues, see Seymour L. Halleck, *The Mentally Disordered Offender* (Washington, D.C.: U.S. Government Printing Office, 1986).

atrists representing the two sides conflict, as they did in the Hinckley case, thus providing little guidance to a jury. In such cases the rather "inexact science" of psychiatry is highlighted and its credibility is likely to suffer.

Efforts to establish a standard to determine the criteria for legal insanity have resulted in a couple of major variations.[28] The first, the M'Naghten Rule, resulted from a legal decision in England in 1843, and presently is used in twenty states. Legal insanity is said to exist if "at the time of the committing of the act, the party accused was laboring under such a defect of reason from disease of the mind as to not know the nature and quality of the act he was doing, or if he did know it, that he did not know he was doing what was wrong."[29] This standard focuses only on the cognitive side of mental illness: What did the defendant know about what he or she was doing? As knowledge of mentally troubled persons has grown, this standard has seemed too narrow to many psychiatrists. It does not give attention to the possibility that the accused may have known what he or she was doing but lacked the ability to control the criminal behavior.

Subsequent court decisions have produced an alternative standard of legal insanity that now guides most state and federal courts. "A person is not responsible for criminal conduct if at the time of such conduct as a result of mental disease or defect he lacks substantial capacity either to appreciate the wrongfulness of his conduct or to conform his conduct to requirements of law."[30] The problem is one of applying this wider standard—particularly when psychiatric experts give contradictory views of a defendant's mental state.

In the wake of the verdict of not guilty by reason of insanity in the Hinckley trial, there have been calls for a new verdict to be made available to juries: "Guilty, but mentally ill." At present, eight states are experimenting with this verdict. Those found guilty are sentenced as criminals, evaluated for psychiatric treatment needs, and sent for treatment until such time as they are no longer judged "mentally ill." At that point they complete their sentence in a prison setting. The opportunity to render this verdict is being watched to make sure it does not create further confusion for juries and that the party found guilty is indeed provided with adequate treatment. The latter may be most problematic, along with the mental health impact of imprisoning a supposedly "cured" mental patient.

In the words of federal judge Irving R. Kaufman, "In the final analysis the key question facing society is this: What should be done with mentally disturbed offenders?"[31] Given the difficulties mental health professionals still face in evaluating, diagnosing, and providing effective treatment to the mentally troubled—including noncriminals—this key question continues to await a humane and wise answer. In the meantime, public dismay and outrage over cases such as that involving John W. Hinckley are not likely to abate.[32]

FACTORS ASSOCIATED WITH MENTAL ILLNESS

Who are the persons whose behaviors are most likely to set the labeling process into motion? Four factors seem to have a lot to do with being defined as mentally ill. These factors are class, economic disruption, racism, and sexism.

[28] Irving R. Kaufman, "The Insanity Pleas on Trial," *New York Times Magazine*, 131 (August 8, 1982): 16–20.
[29] Ibid., p. 18.
[30] Ibid.
[31] Ibid., p. 20.
[32] An even-handed treatment of many of these issues is found in "The Insanity Defense," special edition of *The Annals of the American Academy of Political and Social Science*, 477 (January 1985).

Class

Because of their economic disadvantage, low-income groups face daily problems in living. Thus we should expect many members of such groups to display signs of being mentally troubled. The impact of class on mental functioning has long been recognized. In the 1930s, sociologists Robert E. L. Faris and H. Warren Dunham probed this issue in their research on mental hospitals in Chicago.[33] Faris and Dunham looked at the records of 35,000 persons who had been admitted to the city's private and public mental institutions, checking not only the diagnostic labels that psychiatrists applied to each patient, but also the part of the city each came from. They found that the highest rates of hospitalization were for persons residing in unstable low-income areas. Moreover, the most seriously troubled people—those diagnosed as schizophrenic—tended to come from these same areas.

The study by Faris and Dunham could be criticized for concentrating only on the hospitalized. A more comprehensive inquiry that avoided this pitfall was conducted during the early 1950s in New Haven, Connecticut.[34] This study, which was conducted by August Hollingshead and Fredrick Redlich, covered not only the hospitalized but also persons treated in clinics and by private psychiatrists. Hollingshead and Redlich identified the total population of all persons receiving treatment over a five-month period. They divided this group into five classes, based on area of residence, occupation, and amount of education. The classes ranged from Class I (business and professional people) down to Class V (unskilled laborers and welfare clients). This division corresponds with differential economic status—Class I being the upper middle class and Class V the poor.

The findings of Hollingshead and Redlich's study were consistent with those of the Chicago study. The severely troubled—those designated as psychotic—most frequently came from Class V. Both the incidence and prevalence of serious mental troubles were highest for this group. Those suffering from less serious problems—that is, the neuroses—were most likely to come from Class I. In fact, Hollingshead and Redlich found that the top four classes contributed fewer patients than one would expect, given their numerical representation in the New Haven population.

Beyond this, Hollingshead and Redlich noted that the *type* of treatment patients received varied in accordance with their class membership. People from the lower classes were most likely to be served by public institutions, most of which provided little more than custodial care. Members of the more affluent classes, particularly Class I, most frequently patronized private psychiatrists; if hospitalization was required, they were likely to enter expensive private institutions. Such differential treatment, it has been suggested, may influence statistics on the high rates of serious disorders among the poor.[35] The prospects for personalized attention and quick release are lower in public, as opposed to private, hospitals. Moreover, the lower classes are more likely to be diagnosed as seriously ill than the more affluent, even when they display the same symptoms—an indication of class bias in the application of psychiatric labels.

Both the Chicago and New Haven studies

[33] Robert E. L. Faris and H. Warren Dunham, *Mental Disorders in Urban Areas* (Chicago: University of Chicago Press, 1939).

[34] August B. Hollingshead and Fredrick C. Redlich, *Social Class and Mental Illness* (New York: John Wiley & Sons, 1958). See also Jerome K. Myers and Lee L. Bean, *A Decade Later: A Follow-up of Social Class and Mental Illness* (New York: John Wiley & Sons, 1968).

[35] S. M. Miller and Eliot G. Mishler, "Social Class, Mental Illness, and American Psychiatry," *Milbank Memorial Fund Quarterly*, 37 (April 1959): 1–26.

were limited to persons undergoing treatment, which means that they cannot be generalized to any larger population. However, the Midtown Manhattan study, discussed earlier in this chapter, provides some information about the nontreated sector.[36] In this study, the cases were not only classified on the basis of the degree of mental impairment, but were also ranked in terms of the socioeconomic background of the residents. Almost half of the persons who came from the lowest economic stratum were found to have severe or marked symptoms of impairment, or to be incapacitated. By contrast, little more than 10 percent of those from the highest stratum were judged to be so troubled.

Many other studies have been conducted, and their findings are generally consistent: The highest rates of mental illness, particularly of serious mental difficulties, seem to be found in the lowest economic strata.[37] The affluent may be afflicted with anxieties, which are relatively minor illnesses within the framework of the medical model. But the poor often respond to problems in living by fleeing from reality. Lacking the finances to pursue private, individualized attention from psychiatrists, poor people who are troubled generally must fall back on the tax-supported institutions reserved for them. There, within a medical context, the poor are told that something is the matter with *them*—not with a society whose organization presents them with problems in living.

Economic Disruption

There is little information about the impact of large-scale societal change on the mental well-being of Americans. One of the few studies was conducted by sociologist M. Harvey Brenner. Brenner hypothesized that "mental hospitalization will increase during economic downturns and decrease during upturns."[38] To test this hypothesis, he examined data on hospitalization and economic conditions in New York State, covering a period of nearly thirteen decades, from before the Civil War to 1971.

Using sophisticated statistical techniques, Brenner found evidence to support his hypothesis. He discovered that the functional mental illnesses were extremely sensitive to adverse changes in the American economy. Most of the organic illnesses were not sensitive to changes, with the exception of psychoses following excessive alcohol consumption. Evidently, many people try to lose themselves in drink in times of great economic stress. Brenner noted that the people admitted to mental hospitals were typically workers whose occupations were most vulnerable to unemployment or loss of income.

Through his research, Brenner was also able to show that several other factors had nothing to do with changes in hospitalization levels and rates. Among these unrelated factors were the availability of bed space, changing treatment practices, population changes, differences in state treatment facilities, and shifting public and psychiatric definitions of who is ill. By rejecting these alternative explanations, he demonstrated that "the destiny of the individual is to a great extent subject to large-scale changes in the social and economic structure that are in no way under his control."[39]

In discussing the implications of his findings, Brenner questioned the effectiveness and appropriateness of psychiatric treatment. Since many causes of mental illness lie outside the individual, society—not the patient—must be changed in order to reduce mental troubles. Furthermore, he contended:

---

[36] Srole et al., *Mental Health in the Metropolis*.

[37] Such studies are reviewed in Bruce P. Dohrenwend and Barbara S. Dohrenwend, *Social Status and Psychological Disorder* (New York: John Wiley & Sons, 1969).

[38] M. Harvey Brenner, *Mental Illness and the Economy* (Cambridge, Mass.: Harvard University Press, 1973), p. 10.

[39] Ibid., p. x.

> Hospitalization is not only a psychiatrically inappropriate response to economic stress; it actually compounds the social impact of economic stress enormously.... The patient's economic and social careers can be very seriously damaged.[40]

What Brenner was alluding to here is the fact that individuals who have been hospitalized for mental troubles are frequently stigmatized by the hospitalization.[41] Their "histories" of mental problems make it difficult for them to find economic security, for they are suspected of still being "sick." This, of course, is akin to Thomas Scheff's concept of mental illness careers.

Beyond this, according to Brenner, mental hospitals are vehicles for social control. They function like prisons in that they remove troubled, and possibly troublesome, people from the population and act as safety valves for the society. Since the systemic sources of mental troubles are rarely acknowledged, the very existence of mental hospitals supports the status quo.

Brenner's empirical findings have been underscored by observations during the 1970s and early 1980s, when the national unemployment rate periodically soared. Staffs at mental health facilities across the country reported a rise in the number of individuals and families seeking help. Families in high-unemployment areas experienced "an increased level of severe quarrels, wife beating, child abuse, depression, suicide attempts, excessive alcohol use, insomnia, and fatigue."[42] Mental and other health troubles are clearly a part of the human toll taken by economic adversity.[43]

Racism

As we saw in Chapter 8, racism is a source of harm for millions of Americans. Thus, we would expect to find that minority group members experience mental troubles more frequently than whites. However, studies and data relating to race and mental illness are limited and are confused by the impact of class on minorities. Members of minority groups are overrepresented in the most economically disadvantaged strata, where mental illness is more prevalent. Moreover, most of the focus of literature on mental health and racism is on black Americans, not on all minority groups.[44]

Case studies on the impact of racism are of limited utility. One of the best known studies was conducted in the early 1950s by Abram Kardiner and Lionel Ovesey. In *The Mark of Oppression*, these researchers concluded that black Americans suffer from extremely low self-esteem and from self-hatred.[45] They reached this conclusion on the basis of interviews with twenty-five people who were thought to be psychologically disturbed. Though Kardiner and Ovesey's study had an impact on social science thinking about black problems, it was criticized for stereotyping an entire minority group on the basis of limited data.

A similar study was published in the late 1960s by two black psychiatrists, William Grier and Price M. Cobbs. In their book *Black Rage*, Grier and Cobbs suggested that blacks who live in a predominantly white society develop "cul-

---

[40] Ibid., pp. 228–29.

[41] Their families may also suffer stigma. See Otto F. Wahl and Charles R. Harman, "Family Views of Stigma," *Schizophrenia Bulletin*, 15, No. 1 (1989): 131–39. The *Bulletin* is a publication of the National Institute of Mental Health.

[42] Bryce Nelson, "Despair Among Jobless," *New York Times* (April 2, 1983): 25.

[43] Increases in unemployment are associated with increased physical illness as well as increased mental illness. See M. Harvey Brenner, "Personal Stability and Economic Security," *Social Policy*, 8 (May/June 1977): 2–4. Also Ramsey Liem and Paula Rayman, "Health and Social Costs of Unemployment," *American Psychologist*, 37 (October 1982): 1116–23.

[44] See Alexander Thomas and Samuel Siller, *Racism and Psychiatry* (New York: Brunner/Mazel, 1972), pp. 122–34, and Morton Kramer et al., "Definitions and Distributions of Mental Disorders in a Racist Society," in Charles V. Willie et al., eds., *Racism and Mental Health* (Pittsburgh: University of Pittsburgh Press, 1973), pp. 353–459.

[45] Abram Kardiner and Lionel Ovesey, *The Mark of Oppression* (Cleveland: World Publishing Co., 1951).

tural paranoia" in response to racism.[46] Every white is an enemy until proven otherwise. In dealing with their minority status, blacks develop distorted psychological functioning. Behind all this, according to Grier and Cobbs, black Americans are filled with rage. Critics were quick to point out that Grier and Cobbs largely based their claims on contact with black psychiatric patients—people unable to function in American society. The millions of blacks—and all others victimized by racism—who do function were ignored. *Black Rage*, it was noted, failed to shed any light on the mental state of the majority of minority group members. Moreover, as in *The Mark of Oppression*, Grier and Cobbs' emphasis on the pathology of black mental functioning clearly failed to address the equally important question of strengths that have enabled such groups to survive racial oppression.[47]

If such case studies fail to shed much light on the mental state of minorities, investigations of prevalence and incidence are at least as difficult to interpret. Social psychologist Thomas Pettigrew noted that the overrepresentation of minorities in low-income categories makes it difficult empirically to single out racism as an independent source of mental troubles.[48] Minority group members who suffer from serious disorders often cannot afford to patronize private hospitals. Since they are unlikely to have much faith in white-dominated public facilities, they may avoid seeking help until troubles grow severe. These factors may lead to institutionalization of the most deeply disturbed, inflating statistics on, for example, the frequency of psychoses among minorities.

Pettigrew also points out that in some regions of the country, minority group members are more likely than whites to be involuntarily committed to institutions. Once in large public hospitals, many of which are informally segregated, a lack of quality care and racist practices may result in prolonged stays. Frequent readmissions may follow. All this is to say that estimates of minority mental troubles based on treatment statistics may be biased by factors that do not impinge on whites.[49]

Thus, for example, statistics for admissions to mental hospitals (Table 14.4) indicating that blacks have higher rates of admission than whites are not easy to interpret. Similarly, the facts that blacks have higher admission rates for schizophrenia than whites (Table 14.3) and that first admission rates for neuroses are higher for whites are also hard to interpret. It could be that racial minorities simply ignore mental disorders that are not incapacitating, so that only the most seriously troubled are likely to come into contact with treatment agencies.

Furthermore, it is possible that white mental health practitioners may designate minority group members as ill more frequently than they apply this label to whites. Not only may there be class bias; there may also be ignorance of minority life pressures and ethnic characteristics. Simple things like language barriers may impede understanding the troubles of such groups as Spanish-speaking Americans.

Whatever the facts about the impact of racism on the mental state of minorities and on patterns of treatment, we must remember that the medical model calls for finding fault with the victims. It does not call for fighting the systemic sources of minority mental troubles.

---

[46] William Grier and Price M. Cobbs, *Black Rage* (New York: Basic Books, 1968).

[47] See John McCarthy and William Yancey, "Uncle Tom and Mr. Charlie: Metaphysical Pathos in the Study of Racism and Personal Disorganization," *American Journal of Sociology*, 76 (January 1971): 648–72; and Ronald L. Taylor, "Psychosocial Development Among Black Children and Youth," *American Journal of Orthopsychiatry*, 46 (January 1976): 4–19.

[48] Thomas F. Pettigrew, *A Profile of the Negro American* (Princeton, N.J.: D. Van Nostrand Company, 1964), pp. 73–82.

[49] See Max Seham, *Blacks and American Medical Care* (Minneapolis: University of Minnesota Press, 1973).

TABLE 14.3 Percent Distribution of Admissions to Selected Inpatient Psychiatic Services, by Race, Hispanic Origin, and Primary Diagnosis: United States, 1980

	Inpatient psychiatric services			
Race, Hispanic origin,* and primary diagnosis	State and county mental hospitals	Private psychiatric hospitals	Nonfederal general hospitals	VA medical centers
Total, all races	369,049	141,209	666,300	158,931
Alcohol-related disorders	21.7%	9.3%	7.6%	34.5%
Drug-related disorders	4.8	2.9	2.9	5.1
Organic disorders	4.2	3.5	3.3	2.5
Affective disorders	13.4	42.9	31.1	14.4
Schizophrenia	38.0	21.2	25.2	29.9
Personality disorders	5.7	4.8	4.6	4.7
All other	12.3	15.4	25.2	8.9
White	265,442	123,051	552,679	125,966
Alcohol-related disorders	23.8%	9.4%	7.8%	36.7%
Drug-related disorders	5.3	2.8	2.8	3.5
Organic disorders	4.2	3.4	3.1	2.6
Affective disorders	15.6	44.5	33.9	16.4
Schizophrenia	31.5	19.2	22.7	26.4
Personality disorders	6.5	5.1	4.7	4.8
All other	13.1	15.5	25.0	9.6
Black	96,299	16,633	102,212	31,245
Alcohol-related disorders	15.5%	8.8%	6.4%	25.1%
Drug-related disorders	3.1	3.7	3.3	11.2
Organic disorders	4.2	4.7	4.1	2.1
Affective disorders	7.7	30.8	16.8	6.4
Schizophrenia	56.3	35.7	38.0	44.5
Personality disorders	3.5	2.4	4.6	4.5
All other	9.8	14.0	26.8	6.2
All other races	7,308	1,525	1,409	1,720
Alcohol-related disorders	27.2%	—†	8.0%	45.2%
Drug-related disorders	7.3	—†	—†	—†
Organic disorders	3.6	—†	6.5	—†
Affective disorders	10.1	39.1	23.9	15.1
Schizophrenia	32.4	27.2	31.3	21.0
Personality disorders	4.1	—†	—†	—†
All other	15.4	24.6	21.9	9.1
Hispanic origin	21,231	4,998	33,017	6,410
Alcohol-related disorders	18.4%	4.3%	6.0%	21.7%
Drug-related disorders	7.5	—†	—†	10.2
Organic disorders	2.7	—†	2.5	—†
Affective disorders	15.2	40.4	27.4	20.8
Schizophrenia	43.9	27.2	36.7	26.6
Personality disorders	7.2	3.2	2.0	9.0
All other	5.1	22.6	24.2	11.5

Note: Because of rounding, percentages may not add to 100.0.
*Hispanic persons may be of any race.
†Five or fewer sample cases; estimate not shown because it does not meet standards of reliability.
Source: U.S. Department of Health and Human Services, *Mental Health, United States, 1987* (Washington, D.C.: U.S. Government Printing Office, 1987), p. 79.

TABLE 14.4 Rate of Admission to Selected Inpatient Psychiatric Services, per 100,000 Civilian Population, by Race, Hispanic Origin, and Sex: United States, 1980

	Inpatient psychiatric services			
Race, Hispanic origin,* and sex	State and county mental hospitals	Private psychiatric hospitals	Nonfederal general hospitals	VA medical centers
Total, all races	163.6	62.6	295.3	70.4
Male	219.8	61.9	276.4	141.9
Female	111.1	63.3	313.1	3.7
White	136.8	63.4	284.9	64.9
Male	182.2	61.7	265.0	130.1
Female	94.1	65.0	303.6	3.6
Black	364.2	62.9	386.6	118.2
Male	512.7	70.4	369.4	247.1
Female	233.5	56.3	401.6	4.7
American Indian or Alaskan native	306.4	41.2	371.6	99.5
Male	381.1	46.0	450.8	192.9
Female	234.1	36.5	295.0	—†
Asian or Pacific Islander	75.4	25.0	161.0	6.6
Male	104.2	15.7	159.1	11.8
Female	48.8	33.6	162.8	—†
Hispanic origin	146.0	34.4	227.0	44.1
Male	206.3	35.2	234.3	87.1
Female	86.8	33.6	219.9	1.9

*Hispanic persons may be of any race.
†Based on five or fewer sample cases; rate not shown because it does not meet standards of reliability.
Source: U.S. Department of Health and Human Services, *Mental Health, United States, 1987* (Washington, D.C.: U.S. Government Printing Office, 1987), p. 77.

Sexism

Until quite recently little attention was paid to the mental state of American women. Under the impetus of the women's movement, sexism and the problems in living to which it gives rise have become more widely discussed. (See Table 14.4) Nonetheless, as psychologist Phyllis Chesler tells us: "Contemporary psychiatric and psychological theories and practices both reflect and influence our culture's politically naive understanding and emotionally brutal treatment of women."[50]

[50] Phyllis Chesler, "Patient and Patriarch: Women in the Psychotherapeutic Relationship," in Vivian Gornick and Barbara K. Moran, eds., *Woman in Sexist Society* (New York: Mentor Books, 1971), pp. 362–63.

Chesler notes that men have long dominated the mental health profession. Though women are well represented among psychiatric social workers, men generally hold the more prestigious positions of psychiatrist, psychoanalyst, and psychologist. Thus men have determined how women's mental difficulties will be explained and treated. Women with problems in living who seek help from mental health practitioners are likely to be told that they are at fault, "and this by men who have studiously bypassed the objective fact of female oppression."[51]

Chesler points to studies indicating that women who exhibit—or wish to exhibit—some

[51] Ibid., p. 363.

of the personality traits of mentally healthy men are likely to be thought ill. That is, women who want to be assertive, independent, and aggressive—traits stereotypically associated with the male sex role—may be seen as abnormal. She suggests that there is a masculine ideology in mental health practice, in which the "healthy" woman is one whose personality does not depart from traditional concepts of femininity.[52]

In *Women and Madness,* Chesler draws attention to statistics indicating that, when all modes of treatment are taken into account, women undergo treatment for mental troubles far more frequently than men.[53] Moreover, women have been making up an increasing proportion of those undergoing treatment since the mid-1960s. While there are probably many reasons for this, it seems likely that, as women are growing increasingly aware of and sensitive to their position of subordination, they are searching for ways to cope with the unhappiness they feel. Viewing herself as mentally ill, ironically, may be one of the ways a woman can find someone who will listen to her troubles.

What kinds of symptoms do women undergoing treatment most frequently display? Reviewing literature on female patients, Chesler notes they are often "self-deprecatory, depressed, perplexed, suffering from suicidal thoughts, or making suicide attempts."[54] (Fewer women than men actually commit suicide, however.) These are the kinds of symptoms one would expect among a group that suffers from male chauvinism and institutional sexism.

Marriage, long considered to be the proper "place" for women in this society, seems to be a particular source of unhappiness for many. Jessie Bernard, in her review of the many studies that suggest that wives are less satisfied with their marriages than husbands, underscores the dilemma of many married women. While "their happiness is more dependent upon marriage than men's,"[55] women are expected to do the adjusting to their husbands' demands. According to Bernard, the psychological costs of such adjustments are often considerable and "may greatly impair mental health."[56]

TREATING MENTAL ILLNESS

As we have seen, millions of Americans are mentally troubled. Men, women, and children of all races and classes face problems in living that may well be linked to the organization of American society. Some of them respond to these problems by behaving in ways that are labeled mental illnesses.

According to the medical model, which dominates the mental health profession, mentally troubled individuals are sick. Private psychiatric care, community mental health centers, and mental hospitals are used to treat the mentally ill and to foster their adjustment to the societal status quo.

When we include lost productivity due to mental disorders, treatment of mental illness costs tens of billions of dollars each year. One out of three hospital beds in the United States is reserved for the mentally troubled. More money and resources are used for the treatment of mental illness than for the elimination of some of the sources of mental anguish. For example, while government programs in the field of mental health care have expanded in recent years,

---

[52] Phyllis Chesler, *Women and Madness* (Garden City, N.Y.: Doubleday & Co., 1972), pp. 67–69.

[53] Ibid., pp. 306–33. See also Bruce P. Dohrenwend, "Sociocultural and Social-Psychological Factors in the Genesis of Mental Disorders," *Journal of Health and Social Behavior,* 16 (December 1975): 365–92, and Marcia Guttentag et al., eds., *The Mental Health of Women* (Orlando, Fla.: Academic Press, 1980).

[54] Chesler, "Patient and Patriarch," p. 371.

[55] Jessie Bernard, "The Paradox of the Happy Marriage," in Gornick and Moran, *Woman in Sexist Society,* p. 149.

[56] Ibid. See also Janice M. Steil, "Marital Relationships and Mental Health: The Psychic Costs of Inequality," in Jo Freeman, ed., *Women: A Feminist Perspective,* 4th ed. (Mountain View, Calif.: Mayfield Publishing Company, 1989), pp. 138–48.

this has not been the case with programs to eliminate poverty, unemployment, and discrimination.

In this section we look at a common treatment given the seriously mentally ill—confinement in large public institutions. We consider the issue of involuntary confinement and its implications for civil liberties. Finally, we discuss the possibility of alternatives to confinement.

Mental Hospitals as Total Institutions

As we have seen, not all people who are defined as mentally ill are confined in large public institutions. Who are the people most likely to be confined? According to sociologist Robert Perrucci:

> They are victims of families and communities who can no longer tolerate rule-breaking and problematic behavior. They are victims of poverty, powerlessness, and discrimination and the resulting individual-psychological explanations for their plight as people with a mental illness. They, moreover, are often willing victims insofar as they accept and adopt the roles of madness in order to "solve" the problems of living which they are experiencing. In short, they are not in the hospital because they are mad, but because they have been rejected by society and have no suitable place in it.[57]

In Perrucci's words, mental hospitals function "as a dumping ground for societal rejects."[58]

Large public mental hospitals appear to have a great deal in common with one another. Erving Goffman calls them *total institutions.*[59] Mental institutions are total institutions in that eating, sleeping, work, and play all occur within a schedule set up by hospital administrators and staff. Every patient is required to do certain things at certain times, usually in the company of fellow patients, under a system of rules imposed from above. Some, however, might say this is helpful in that patients are relieved of the burden of decision making.

To Goffman the total institution has a great impact on the individual who is confined there.[60] People enter mental hospitals with what Goffman calls a "presenting culture" based on their way of life and the routines they took for granted prior to confinement. They also have a conception of who they are, based on their past participation in social arrangements and interaction with family members, co-workers, and friends and neighbors. According to Goffman, the patients' presenting cultures are ignored in the mental institution; and patients are forced to live in accordance with the demands of institutional authority. In addition, their self-concepts are attacked and altered.

The attack on patients' self-concepts is done through a process of *mortification*. From the moment they enter the institution, patients are cut off from contact with the outside world. They may be photographed, fingerprinted, weighed, measured, undressed, searched, bathed, and disinfected. Personal belongings and clothing may be taken away, and institutional garments provided. The patient may be assigned a number, living arrangements, and a list of regulations. According to Goffman:

> In thus being squared away, the new arrival allows himself to be shaped and coded into an object.... This object can be fed into the administrative machinery of the establishment, to be worked on smoothly by routine operations.[61]

The staff carefully observes individuals' willingness to accept being "squared away." Patients who resist may be viewed as troublemakers who deserve punishment. Goffman notes

[57] Robert Perrucci, *Circle of Madness* (Englewood Cliffs, N.J.: Prentice-Hall, 1974), p. 30.
[58] Ibid., p. 31.
[59] Erving Goffman, *Asylums* (Garden City, N.Y.: Anchor Books, 1961), p. xiii.
[60] Ibid., pp. 12–74.
[61] Ibid., p. 16.

that the staff may actually test new arrivals to see how far they can be pushed. By doing this, the staff gets to demonstrate punishments to the newcomers while simultaneously reminding other patients what happens when someone refuses to defer to staff demands.

Goffman felt that the result of the mortification process is to undermine the patient's sense of autonomy and adult self-determination, placing the individual in a position of childlike dependency on the institutional staff. The staff can then more easily maintain order and routine.

Furthermore, the mortification process fits well with the medical model, which sees the inmate as sick. As Perrucci puts it:

> The self that existed prior to hospitalization is defined as having been in some way the cause of the patient's present condition. Thus, the old self must be destroyed, and a new self incorporated through a resocialization process.[62]

Perrucci tells us that the mortification process occurs in a "world of unfreedom." Patients have little control over what happens to them in the institution, so they cannot choose to remain unaffected by it. Perrucci found that patients respond to the pressures in various ways. Some "withdraw" from relations with patients and staff but comply with institutional routines. Others engage in "accommodation," trying to be perfect patients. Still others respond with "conversion"—imitating the staff's way of relating to other patients. Finally, some "resist":

> Patients operating under this mode are greatly concerned with maintaining their own self-respect and dignity. In this respect, they resist all efforts to place them in the general category of patient.[63]

Novelist Ken Kesey memorialized the resisters—and speculated on their fate—in *One Flew Over the Cuckoo's Nest*.[64] The novel recounts the experiences of McMurphy, a man who chose confinement in a mental hospital over jail. McMurphy's attempts to humanize his ward by organizing such forbidden activities as gambling and parties run into resistance from a staff member named Big Nurse, who ultimately gains control over McMurphy by forcing him to undergo a frontal lobotomy (a brain operation that can replace aggressiveness with meekness). Kesey's depiction of the struggle between institutional authority and a patient who refused to adapt to it was inspired by his observations in a mental hospital.

There is one more response to confinement. In *Methods of Madness*, psychologist Benjamin Braginsky and his associates found patients who were content to remain confined.[65] They had been in confinement for so long that they could not even bear to think of leaving the institution. Such patients manipulated the staff by affecting symptoms that would bar their release. Through such "impression management," they gained some control over their fate. In Braginsky's view, such behavior was not a result of illness; it was an outcome of the effects of institutionalization itself.[66]

In recent years there have been limited reforms in the administration of large public mental hospitals. And, as we mentioned earlier, the costs of maintaining people in long-term confinement—together with the adoption of drugs that alter the behavior of patients—have decreased the average length of a stay in such institutions. While admission rates have gone up in recent years, so have release rates. Still, the large public mental hospital remains a major fo-

---

[62] Perrucci, *Circle of Madness*, p. 53.

[63] Ibid., p. 64.

[64] Ken Kesey, *One Flew Over the Cuckoo's Nest* (New York: Signet, 1962).

[65] Benjamin Braginsky et al., *Methods of Madness* (New York: Holt, Rinehart & Winston, 1969).

[66] To "deinstitutionalize" such patients, hospitals have experimented with simulations of nonhospital life in the wards. See Kenneth J. Neubeck, "Capitalism as Therapy?," *Social Policy*, 8 (May/June 1977): 41–45.

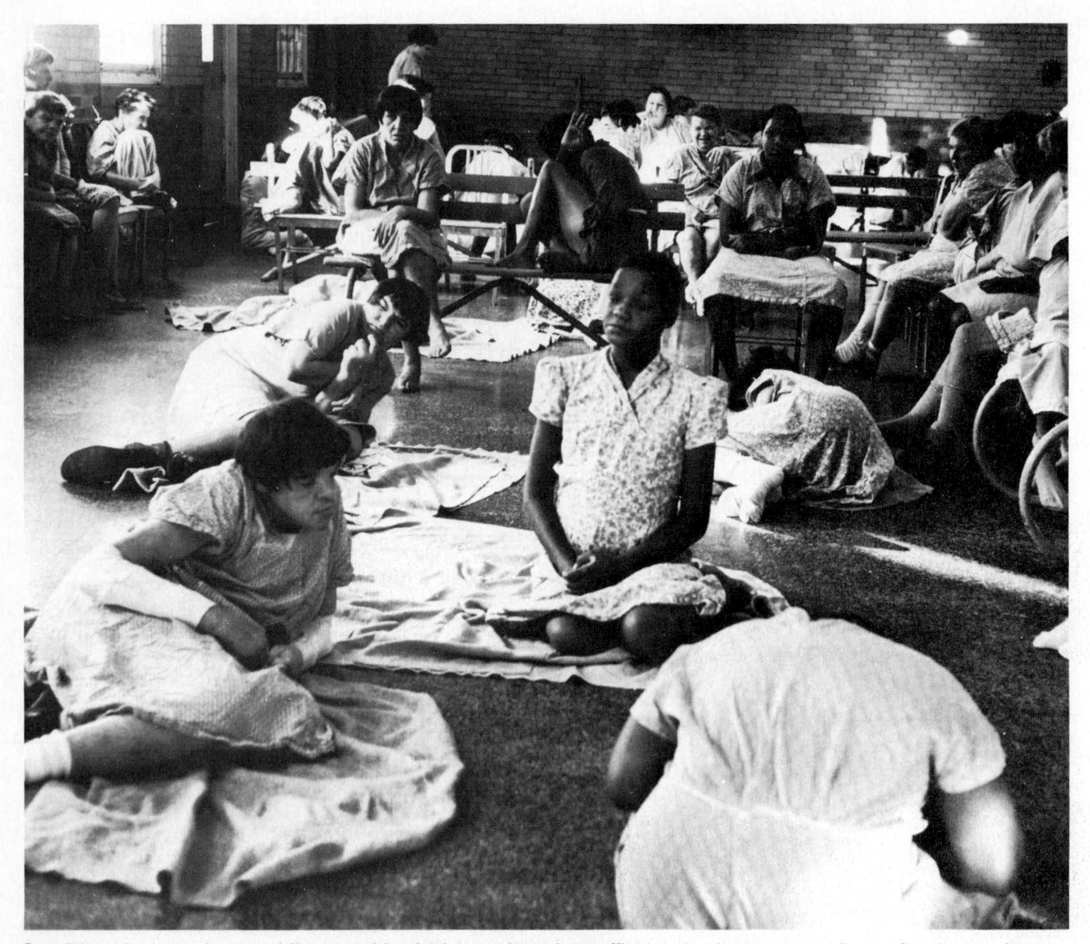

Conditions in many large public mental institutions, where less affluent people are generally confined, are often dismal. Inmates are given tranquilizing drugs and often receive little or no therapy. Confinement in such institutions can be extremely harmful. *(Steve Deutch)*

cal point for the treatment and mental rearmament of persons who are troubled.

The Politics of Involuntary Confinement

At several points we have alluded to the fact that people may be involuntarily confined to mental institutions.[67] All states have legal procedures that make it possible to hospitalize individuals who refuse to accept the illness label. These procedures often involve having a judge rule that individuals are a danger to themselves and/or others.

[67] This section draws heavily on David Mechanic, *Mental Health and Social Policy* (Englewood Cliffs, N.J.: Prentice-Hall, 1969), pp. 123–35. See also Thomas S. Szasz, *Law, Liberty, and Psychiatry* (New York: The Macmillan Company, 1963).

PUBLIC PROBLEM, PRIVATE PAIN

The Voices of Bobby Wilde

Bobby Wilde was only nine years old when he heard "voices." From that point on he lived the life of a paranoid schizophrenic, struggling to hold on to jobs and friends, and ultimately succumbing to harsh poverty and the wary loneliness of the chronically troubled. His story, as it opens here, suggests that we look with utmost compassion on those whose internal processes are so little understood.

The first "voice" I ever heard assaulted me when I was a third-grade schoolboy. I was in an uneasy frame of mind because I had told a lie to get out of going to school. I was at home, on the landing between two flights of stairs that led to the second floor. This landing was a favorite place of mine. There was a blackboard there, and a window with a windowseat, and it was a cozy spot for me to go with my books. I was sitting there, reading, the house was perfectly quiet—and of course *I always* was quiet—and I heard the voice.

"I've got you."

The voice was plain as broad open daylight and terrifying as pitch black night. It was a man's voice—not one I recognized—and its quality was appallingly definite. I didn't then know words like sinister and ominous, but it was both of these to an unbearable degree. It wasn't a loud voice, not at all a loud voice; but it was harsh and emphatic, and the sound told me that it was the voice of a man who hated me and would surely get me. And I knew with the most chilling certainty that for a man with a voice like that to get me, I'd be done for. It spoke just the once. "I've got you."

I sat stock-still, absolutely incapable of moving a muscle. I guess this lasted just a moment or so, and then I leapt up and hurled myself down the stairs. Momma was somewhere downstairs, and I was frantic to get to her. By the time I was halfway down, my own voice returned and I started screaming bloody murder. When I found Momma, I told her somebody upstairs had said, "I've got you." She was concerned when she first saw me, because of the screaming; but when I told her this, she brushed it right aside. She said, "Oh, no. You heard somebody outside, talking to somebody else."

From that moment until my early middle years, I never told anybody about that voice or any of the other voices that have bedeviled me with very brief letups. I saw no reason to tell anybody, and every reason not to tell. I thought I was hearing real voices, and I attached them to persons present or within earshot when I was hearing them. Why should a boy or a man tell anybody about accusations being made to his very face, some by people who knew him? Loss of what few friends I had would have been a certainty. If they had heard these voices themselves, I surely wasn't going to bring it up. If they hadn't, I certainly wasn't going to tell them. This kept me off balance all the time and with everybody. I naturally thought that the voices could be heard by anybody present when I heard them, and I continued to think this for many years. The voices attacked me in every public or social situation I was ever in, and finally in seclusion too. This evolved into a condition of stark aloneness. No matter how many people were around me—friends, acquaintances, strangers—I was always alone, in the most desolate sense of the word.

Source: From Elizabeth Kytle, *The Voices of Bobby Wilde, pp. 3–4*.

The procedures leading to involuntary confinement raise serious civil liberties issues. Relatives, social welfare agencies, police, or private citizens may start the process, often when they become aware of individuals who communicate their alienation from the status quo in unusual or disruptive ways or of children or the elderly who do not seem to be able to care for themselves. In other words, the initial judgments about such individuals' mental states are typically made by "accusers" who have no medical or psychiatric training. The judgments are made in terms of value-laden views about what is normal and what is deviant.

In most states, police are empowered to take the "accused" into temporary custody, where he or she may be forced to undergo examination by medical practitioners. Sometimes the examining doctors have no training in psychiatry. Even when they do, as we saw earlier, professional judgments about mental health are not always accurate. Nevertheless, the examining doctor may recommend to the court that hospitalization take place. Since court personnel are not likely to be trained in assessing mental capabilities, they are likely to routinely accept the judgments of medical experts. According to sociologist David Mechanic, "the commitment process has the form of due process of law but is actually vacuous since the decision tends to be predetermined."[68]

Court personnel seem to assume that a person would never have been brought into commitment proceedings unless there was something wrong with him or her. Consequently, many people whose behavior is said to be unacceptable—but who pose no harm to themselves or others—are confined. Even confining those who *may* be dangerous poses civil liberties issues, since there often is no way to predict such behavior. Hospital administrators generally admit that very few of their patients would harm others if released on the spot.

Further, commitment proceedings assume that hospitalization—even involuntary commitment—will help those who are mentally troubled. We have already seen that the impact of confinement in a total institution may actually be harmful. We have also noted that the stigma of hospitalization may plague persons after release. Moreover, since the sources of problems in living may not necessarily reside within the individual, removal from the community may be a questionable solution.

Can't confinement be replaced by some other type of treatment procedure? David Mechanic does not feel that reforms will lead us in this direction:

> Even if we assume adherence to due process in the use of commitment procedures and even if the quality of treatment undergoes impressive improvement, the community will still demand that certain individuals be removed and treated despite no desire on their part for such care.... Misfits will always frighten or threaten others, and people will always feel that the interests of the community are best served by placing such deviants in custody. Inevitably what is thought to be in the interests of some is not in the interests of others.[69]

Mechanic's pessimism may cause us to conclude that the tendency to place "misfits" in confinement is traceable to human nature. In reality, not human nature but *power* plays the central role. The label of deviant or "misfit" is forced on individuals who are mentally ill due to physical causes or who may be simply alienated from society. Sociologist Howard Becker has raised and answered the key question:

> Who can, in fact, force others to accept their rules and what are the causes of their success? This is, of course, a question of political and economic power.[70]

Parents may exercise their power to have a troublesome child confined. Children may dispose of their aging parents in the same way. The local ne'er-do-wells whose presence and behavior annoy the "solid citizenry" may be taken away or pressured into voluntary surrender to a mental hospital. In such cases, the ability of the accused to resist confinement may be minimal. Resistance itself, ironically, may be inter-

[68] Mechanic, *Mental Health and Social Policy*, p. 127.

[69] Ibid., p. 135.

[70] Howard S. Becker, *Outsiders* (New York: The Free Press, 1963), p. 17.

preted as further evidence of illness and may be used to justify confinement. On the other hand, high-status people may most easily avoid the label of mental illness and confinement against their will.

We must not forget that there is much money to be made from the mental health industry. Private psychiatrists often receive one hundred dollars or more an hour for their services. Companies profit from the demand for drugs and equipment utilized by the mental health profession. These people have a vested interest in maintaining today's treatment procedures. Were extensive changes to be made, the status and jobs of many such professionals would be jeopardized.[71]

The Deinstitutionalization Movement

In the early 1960s the federal government began to provide funds to encourage the creation of community-based treatment centers for the mentally troubled. The intent was that these centers would grow in number and ultimately replace most of the large-scale residential institutions in which so many persons were then confined.[72]

The "deinstitutionalization" of the mentally troubled was to be facilitated by the availability of new drugs that allowed mental patients to be released into local communities. There they were to obtain treatment and rehabilitation services from the planned network of community mental health centers. Deinstitutionalization in conjunction with community-based treatment was seen as an enlightened and effective way of helping the mentally troubled. Politicians were attracted to this approach by the prospect of cost savings.[73]

Earlier in this chapter we noted that the total resident populations of mental hospitals have decreased significantly over the last three decades. (See also Figure 14.1.) This is one indicator of the deinstitutionalization process that has been going on. Although perhaps praiseworthy in its intent, the process has been accompanied by severe problems—hundreds of thousands of mentally troubled people have been ill served.[74]

The original federal goal of fostering some 1,600 community mental health centers has long gone unmet. To date, fewer than half this number exist, and many of these are suffering from inadequate funding and insufficient staffing. Hence many of those persons who have been deinstitutionalized have failed to link up with community-based treatment or have found inadequate assistance. Too often former mental patients have floundered in the community, only to find themselves reconfined in still-existing residential institutions for repeated durations—a kind of "revolving door" situation.[75] The latter is reflected in the fact that while the patient populations in residential institutions have gone down overall, annual new admissions for short-term treatment have gone up. An unknown number of these new admissions are really readmissions of the deinstitutionalized who lack community-based care.

The failure of community-based treatment to grow to meet the needs of released mental patients is painfully evident in towns and cities across the nation. Severely disturbed persons, along with others who are mentally disabled, have come to comprise a new and highly vis-

[71] See Peter Schrag, *Mind Control* (New York: Pantheon Books, 1978).

[72] For background see Murray Levine, *The History and Politics of Community Mental Health* (New York: Oxford University Press, 1981).

[73] See Andrew T. Scull, *Decarceration* (Englewood Cliffs, N.J.: Prentice-Hall, 1977), pp. 77–160.

[74] Ellen L. Bassuk and Samuel Gerson, "Deinstitutionalization and Mental Health Services," *Scientific American*, 238 (February 1978): 46–53.

[75] For an autobiographical account, see Susan Sheehan, *Is There No Place on Earth for Me?* (New York: Vintage Books, 1983).

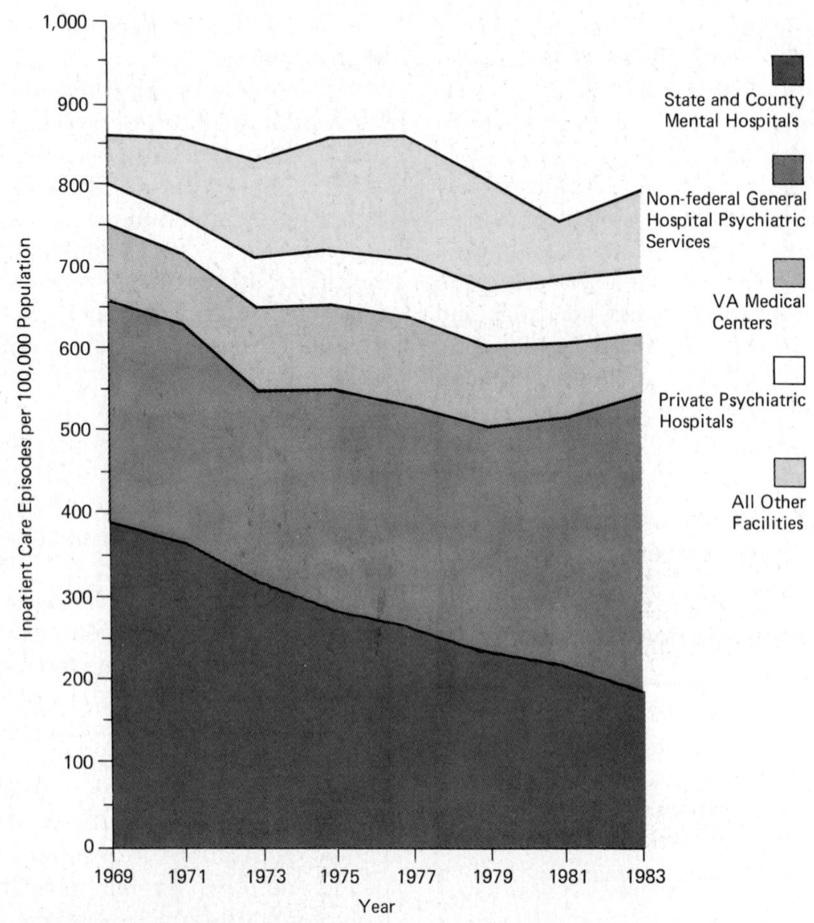

FIGURE 14.1 Inpatient Care Episodes per 100,000 Civilian Population, by Type of Facility: United States, 1969–83
Source: U.S. Department of Health and Human Services, *Mental Health, United States, 1987* (Washington, D.C.: U.S. Government Printing Office, 1987), p. 19.

ible minority group in low-income central city areas. There they often settle in single-room-occupancy hotels and rooming houses. Others among this group are among the nation's estimated 2 million to 3 million homeless persons. Subject to local hostility, fear, and ridicule and frequently preyed on by criminals, deinstitutionalized persons find their plight made worse by living in a "community" setting.

The Need for Change

So long as the mentally troubled are automatically defined as being at fault for their plight, the features of American society that provoke problems in living are likely to remain unquestioned. It is far easier to pour money and resources into treating the sick minds of individuals than to confront the prospects of altering

One alternative to routinized care through an institution or reliance on a mental health practitioner is participation in a self-help group. Groups exist to help people deal with almost every imaginable problem in living, offering support from others who have "been there." *(David Grossman/Photo Researchers)*

society so that humanity is no longer estranged from its authentic possibilities.

But we cannot afford to wait for large-scale societal changes while doing nothing to help the millions who are troubled now. The ideas of Szasz and Laing offer some alternatives to confinement. In fact, Laing's idea of having people who have been troubled help others has become widely accepted. In many cities, people who face common problems in living can join self-help groups and pool their knowledge and experiences to provide one another with mutual support. Those groups that operate outside the medical model, stress voluntary participation, and offer positive, nonalienating relationships can be expected to make an important contribution.[76]

[76] See Judi Chamberlin, *On Our Own* (New York: Hawthorne Books, 1978).

Moving people out of confinement in public institutions and into the community must be speeded up. This has been taking place, often simply for budgetary reasons because of the rising costs of inpatient care. But the newly released are too frequently set adrift and left to fend for themselves. Many end up isolated and alone and/or suffering from the stigmatization of their confinement. Many are among America's homeless. Trained volunteers might be organized to be special friends and companions to such persons in their home environments. Some of the newly released may like to be placed in the homes of persons who would guide them in their transition to full community participation.

Ultimately, however, the societal factors that seem to give rise to problems in living—from poverty to sexism—must be confronted if mental troubles are to be mitigated.

SUMMARY

Millions of Americans are mentally troubled. We do not know the prevalence of mental illness—that is, the total cases existing at a given time—because of problems of definition and measurement. A rough estimate is that 10 percent of the population—over 24 million people—are ill. The number of new cases occurring over time—the incidence of mental illness—appears to be on the increase. But because of the problem of interpreting available data, most of which are based on treatment statistics, one must advance such an argument with caution. Many factors bear on whether or not troubled people seek out and receive treatment.

The dominant approach to the treatment of the mentally troubled is called the medical model. Psychiatrists and other mental health practitioners commonly assume that troubled people are ill and in need of cure. Two major illness categories are the psychoses and the neuroses. Psychoses are considered very severe forms of illness wherein individuals have their own versions of reality and are often unable to perform expected roles. The neuroses are considered less severe forms of illness and typically involve expressions of underlying anxieties.

The medical model has come under criticism and is a source of controversy. Critics point to problems in classifying mental disorders and symptoms. Questions have been raised as to the accuracy of the judgments made by mental health practitioners in their diagnoses. Critics of the medical model have questioned the very concept of mental illness. It has been contended that the sometimes unusual forms of behavior and/or thinking of the mentally troubled are actually communications in response to problems in living. So-called mental illness has even been interpreted as a sign of health, a strategy invented by people to allow them to live in an unlivable situation. Finally, it has been pointed out that the mentally troubled are often subject to labeling. Those whose behavior is deemed deviant may be designated as ill, forced to accept the role of patient, and given treatment within the confines of the medical model. Problems in diagnosis and labeling plague the legal arena as well, as experts struggle over definitions of insanity in relation to criminal behavior.

Various factors seem to be associated with what the medical model labels mental illness. The impact of class on mental functioning has long been recognized, as the highest rates of illness—particularly severe disorders—seem to be found in the lowest income strata. Large-scale economic disruption that adversely affects individuals has been found to be related to increased hospitalization rates. While data are hard to interpret due to the intrusion of class and other factors, minorities seem to suffer from serious illnesses more frequently than whites. Moreover, women undergo treatment for mental illness far more frequently than do men.

While the treatment of most troubled people is through outpatient facilities, many enter confinement in mental hospitals. Such hospitals have been called total institutions in recognition of authorities' control over almost every aspect of inmates' living conditions and routine. The mental hospital is said to have a great impact on those confined, attacking their self-concepts and encouraging dependency on institutional staff. People who are confined may respond in any number of ways—from withdrawal to resistance. Some, confined so long that they cannot bear the thought of leaving, manipulate the staff by pretending to be ill.

The process of deinstitutionalization, whereby more and more persons have been released into local communities, has also resulted in problems. Lack of follow-up and community support has left many such persons adrift, even homeless. People may be involuntarily confined to mental hospitals. The procedures involved raise serious civil liberties issues, particularly regarding due process. There is a need for change. Mental troubles are typically treated as if the individuals are at fault, despite indications that large-scale societal factors have a bearing on such troubles. Ultimately, such societal factors must be confronted. Meanwhile, self-help groups for the troubled and community support for persons newly released from confinement can be useful.

DISCUSSION QUESTIONS

1. Have you ever wondered whether you were mentally ill? Have you ever been convinced of it? What was the basis for your concern? Did you trace the sources of your feelings to something wrong with you or to the life circumstances confronting you?
2. What are the attitudes of your friends and family toward persons who are thought to be mentally troubled? In your view, are their attitudes realistic and appropriate? Why?
3. On most college campuses, utilization of mental health facilities by students is thought to have been on the increase since the 1970s. Speculate on the possible reasons for this.
4. According to Jessie Bernard, many studies suggest that women are less satisfied with their marriages than men, and the circumstances of marriage may impair women's mental health. In terms of your own experiences and/or observations, is this often the case? Why?
5. Develop a set of criteria that would allow the courts to determine who among the mentally troubled should be involuntarily confined for examination and possible treatment. Compare your criteria with those of others.
6. Prepare a defense for an individual who faces involuntary confinement in a mental hospital because he or she may be dangerous to the community, based on your understanding of people's rights under the law.

SUGGESTED READINGS

Goffman, Erving. *Asylums* (New York: Doubleday-Anchor Books, 1961).
Classic analysis of a large public mental institution, its routines, and its impact on those subject to its demands.

"The Insanity Defense," *The Annals of the American Academy of Political and Social Science,* 477 (January 1985). Special edition.
Issues and problems surrounding judicial consideration of the mental state of those accused of committing crimes.

Scheff, Thomas J. *Being Mentally Ill,* 2nd ed. (Hawthorne, N.Y.: Aldine de Gruyter, 1984).
Challenge to the medical model of mental illness, which is viewed as a form of rule violation.

Sheehan, Susan. *Is There No Place on Earth for Me?* (New York: Vintage Books, 1983).
Story of a chronically troubled woman who is shuffled through a "revolving door" of treatment institutions.

Szasz, Thomas S. *The Myth of Mental Illness,* rev. ed. (New York: Harper & Row Publishers, 1984).
View of mental illness as behaviors stemming simply from "problems in living."

Torrey, E. Fuller. *Nowhere to Go* (New York: Harper & Row Publishers, 1989).
Traces the suffering of mentally troubled people abandoned to homelessness in local communities.

DAY
5 IMPAC 558-3034
2 AMBULANCE 431-2800
3 SEARCH 553-1145
2 CAB 626-4400
NIGHT
6 MINISTER 621-8282
5 MIS. EM. 648-8200
3 SEARCH 553-1506
1 TRACE
PSYCH. 5
SEX 10
RELIG. 6
LONE-BORED 13
WORK 17

CHAPTER 15

Suicide

Members of American society should be at peace with themselves and with one another. The social factors that provoke suicide should be absent.

By the time you finish reading this chapter, two or three Americans will have killed themselves. According to official statistics, almost 31,000 Americans committed suicide in 1986.[1] Perhaps ten times more attempt but fail to do so. Many of those who attempt suicide will try again in the future.

Means of suicide range from the straightforwardly grim to the unexpectedly bizarre. People shoot and slash themselves, ingest poisonous substances, overdose on drugs, asphyxiate themselves with gas, jump from high places, hang themselves, leap in front of trains, electrocute and drown themselves, swallow dangerous objects, tear themselves apart with explosives, pilot speeding vehicles into crashes, and burn themselves. Those who survive suicide attempts are often maimed or disabled.

Most of us think of suicide, in the abstract, as an unnatural act, probably related to mental illness. How could a sane person choose death over life? The whole idea is distasteful to con-

[1] U.S. Department of Commerce, Bureau of the Census, *Statistical Abstract of the United States, 1989* (Washington, D.C.: U.S. Government Printing Office, 1989), p. 84.

template and difficult to condone. As with many other forms of socially unpleasant behavior, people tend to blame the victim for his or her own plight.

In more concrete situations, where the suicidal individual is known, friends and family are likely to react with shock and self-blame. Asking themselves whether there was something they could have done to avert the tragedy, they try to assuage their sense of guilt and rationalize what has happened. Family members attempt to limit public attention to the death, for in this society suicide is considered a shamefully unfortunate affair.

When Americans are confronted with suicide, the first question they ask is "Why?" This same question has preoccupied social scientists for decades; it is a central concern of this chapter. In the following pages we focus on the nature and extent of suicide, efforts to explain suicide, and approaches to suicide prevention.

THE NATURE AND EXTENT OF SUICIDE

Before any social phenomenon can be explained, it must be carefully defined. We have already seen the problems involved in defining such phenomena as crime and mental illness. Similar difficulties arise in any discussion of suicide.

The Concept of Suicide

What exactly should someone interested in explaining suicide choose to study? Should suicide research be limited to those who succeed in killing themselves? Or should researchers also study those who attempt to kill themselves but fail? Furthermore, many persons threaten to kill themselves and, at least in some cases, follow such threats with suicide attempts. Others express, directly or indirectly, suicidal thoughts. Should these forms of behavior be of major concern to someone interested in explaining suicide?

As a result of such questions, social scientists have attempted to categorize various forms of suicidal behavior, believing that there must be some relationship among them.[2] But such categorization creates other questions. One of these is the issue of *intent.* Is it not important to understand the intentions of persons who engage in one or another form of suicidal behavior? For example, researchers believe that some completed suicides are actually accidental deaths caused by errors of judgment. This would be the case when a person who takes an overdose of drugs, expecting to be discovered and saved from death, is not found in time. Shouldn't such deaths be distinguished from suicides in which the intent to die is clear? Or, to take another example, some attempted suicides are staged events. An attempt may be superficial or ambivalent, involving a method of self-harm that is unlikely to cause death. Shouldn't such attempts be distinguished from those that appear serious and potentially lethal?

Intent is closely related to the issue of *consciousness.* Here the question is whether individuals realize that their actions may bring about their demise. Many suicides are both intentional and consciously planned; the person carefully chooses the method, time, and circumstances. In other cases the degree of consciousness is less clear. For example, when individuals kill themselves while under the influence of alcohol or other drugs, we may have no way of knowing whether they are really conscious of the possible outcome of their actions.

To complicate things even more, many people die as a consequence of taking risks with their own personal welfare.[3] For example, medical experts claim that heavy cigarette smokers are slowly killing themselves. While the average person may not categorize heavy smoking

---

[2] See, for example, Louis Wekstein, *Handbook of Suicidology* (New York: Brunner/Mazel, 1979), pp. 24–35.

[3] See Norman L. Farberow, ed., *The Many Faces of Suicide* (New York: McGraw-Hill Book Company, 1980).

TABLE 15.1 Death Rates from Accidents and Violence, 1970–86*

	White						Black					
	Male			Female			Male			Female		
Cause of death	**1970**	**1980**	**1986**	**1970**	**1980**	**1986**	**1970**	**1980**	**1986**	**1970**	**1980**	**1986**
Total	**101.9**	**97.1**	**85.8**	**42.4**	**36.3**	**33.2**	**183.2**	**154.0**	**131.1**	**51.7**	**42.6**	**37.4**
Motor vehicle accidents	39.1	35.9	29.2	14.8	12.8	11.5	44.3	31.1	28.6	13.4	8.3	8.5
All other accidents	38.2	30.4	25.7	18.3	14.4	12.8	63.3	46.0	36.4	22.5	18.6	14.5
Suicide	18.0	19.9	22.3	7.1	5.9	5.9	8.0	10.3	11.1	2.6	2.2	2.3
Homicide	6.8	10.9	8.6	2.1	3.2	3.0	67.6	66.6	55.0	13.3	13.5	12.1

*Rates per 100,000 population.
Source: U.S. Department of Commerce, Bureau of the Census, *Statistical Abstract of the United States, 1989* (Washington, D.C.: U.S. Government Printing Office, 1989), p. 83.

as suicidal behavior, social scientists must deal with this phenomenon in terms of its potential lethality for the individuals involved. Is it suicidal behavior? If so, is it intentional? Is it conscious self-harm?

In sum, those interested in explaining suicide continue to face difficulties in categorizing suicidal behavior and in figuring out how to take the issue of intent into account. For the most part, sociologists have focused on completed suicides, frequently using official statistics gathered by agencies of government. In the next section we look at some of the limitations of these statistics as well as some of the patterns of suicidal behavior.

Suicide Statistics

As in the areas of unemployment and crime, statistics on suicide are collected by agencies of government. The government calculates the frequency of deaths by suicide, as compared to deaths from other causes (see, for example, Table 15.1). Government data also include information on the age, sex, and race of persons who take their own lives.

In this society, cause of death is ordinarily ascertained by a physician. When there is doubt about the cause of death, a coroner or medical examiner usually conducts an inquiry. In all cases, the death certificate classifies the death as natural, accidental, homicide, or suicide. Death certificates provide the basis for official statistics.

Social scientists have long been concerned about the reliability of official statistics, suspecting that they underestimate the frequency of suicide.[4] The cause of death listed on death certificates reflects the judgment of the physicians and other medical professionals assigned to ascertain causes of death. Social scientists do not know how these individuals choose to define suicide or whether they agree on a common definition. Moreover, it is suspected that doctors classify some suicides as deaths from other causes to spare the feelings of the victims' families or even to assist their heirs in avoiding problems with life insurance companies.

Often, it is extremely difficult to be positive that suicide is the cause of death. For example, an individual is found dead from an overdose of drugs. Was this an accident or a suicide? Could it have been a homicide, set up to look

[4] Jack D. Douglas, *The Social Meanings of Suicide* (Princeton, N.J.: Princeton University Press, 1967), pp. 163–231. See also Wekstein, *Handbook of Suicidology*, pp. 38–42. For a rebuttal to the critics of official statistics, see Bernice Pescosolido and Robert Mendelsohn, "Social Causation or Social Construction of Suicide?", *American Sociological Review*, 51 (February 1986): 80–101.

like a suicide? A person is found shot to death. It looks accidental, but perhaps the family concealed a suicide note. Or did the victim purposely manage the circumstances of death to make it look accidental? Could the individual have been murdered? An individual dies in a single-car automobile accident. Did alcohol cause this person to misjudge speed and road conditions? Or did it simply give the person courage to go through with a suicidal act? Or did someone tamper with the car?

It is probable that thousands of suicides are attributed to accidental causes each year—whether intentionally or through error. There is no way of knowing how extensive such underreporting is or whether it is systematically skewed in a particular direction. (For example, are the wealthy more prone to hide the fact of suicide, or more likely to gain the cooperation of authorities in doing so, than the poor?) With such cautions in mind, we will briefly examine the statistical picture.[5]

General Population. As we mentioned earlier, almost 31,000 Americans killed themselves in 1986. This is a rate of 12.8 suicides per 100,000 people. In 1986, suicide was the eighth leading cause of death.[6] The suicide rate has been rising slightly over the years. (Of course, there is no way of knowing whether the actual suicide rate—as opposed to the official rate—has been simply rising slightly. Recently, there have been indications of an increase among young people. There are no reliable statistics regarding the proportion of suicide attempts, but a rough ratio of ten attempts to each completed suicide is thought to exist. This would mean that over 300,000 persons attempt to kill themselves each year.

Age. In general, the probability that persons will commit suicide increases with advancing age (Table 15.2). The relationship between aging and suicide is most marked for white men; the suicide rate among white males increases fairly steadily for all age groups up through those in their eighties. The pattern for white women is slightly different; their suicide rate tends to drop off in their sixties, after reaching a peak in the fifties.[7] Suicide and age correlate differently for minorities. Among blacks, for example, suicide is at its peak among the relatively young—persons aged twenty-five to thirty-four. With regard to attempted suicides, the rate is believed to be higher among the young than among the elderly. Older people are also more likely to use more lethal methods.

In recent years an increase in suicide rates among young people has generated attention and deep concern. Between 1970 and 1986 suicides among persons aged ten to fourteen have gone up 150 percent; among those fifteen to nineteen the rate has increased 137 percent. Even higher rates of increase are present if we confine our statistics to young white males.[8] A growing literature on child suicide exists.[9]

Sex. Men complete suicide far more frequently than do women, at a ratio of roughly 3 to 1.[10] On the other hand, suicide attempts are thought to be twice as common among women. For reasons not fully understood, methods of suicide differ between the sexes, just as they do between the old and the young. Men are most likely to choose such violent techniques as shooting and

[5] For a more detailed discussion, see Sanford Labovitz, "Variation in Suicide Rates," in Jack P. Gibbs, ed., *Suicide* (New York: Harper & Row Publishers, 1968), pp. 57–73.

[6] U.S. Department of Commerce, *Statistical Abstract of the United States, 1989*, p. 81.

[7] See Marv Miller, *Suicide After Sixty* (New York: Springer Publishing Company, 1979).

[8] U.S. Department of Commerce, *Statistical Abstract of the United States, 1989*, p. 84.

[9] See Israel Orbach, *Children Who Don't Want to Live* (San Francisco: Jossey-Bass Publishers, 1988).

[10] Some argue the real (as opposed to the official) rates may be closer. See Howard I. Kushner, *Self-Destruction in the Promised Land* (New Brunswick, N.J.: Rutgers University Press, 1989), pp. 95–111.

TABLE 15.2 Suicide Rates, by Sex, Race, and Age Group, 1970–86*

				Male						Female					
	Total†			White			Black			White			Black		
Age	1970	1980	1986	1970	1980	1986	1970	1980	1986	1970	1980	1986	1970	1980	1986
All ages‡	**11.6**	**11.9**	**12.8**	**18.0**	**19.9**	**22.3**	**8.0**	**10.3**	**11.1**	**7.1**	**5.9**	**5.9**	**2.6**	**2.2**	**2.3**
10–14 years	0.6	0.8	1.5	1.1	1.4	2.4	0.3	0.5	1.5	0.3	0.3	0.7	0.4	0.1	0.4
15–19 years	5.9	8.5	10.2	9.4	15.0	18.2	4.7	5.6	7.1	2.9	3.3	4.1	2.9	1.6	2.1
20–24 years	12.2	16.1	15.8	19.3	27.8	28.4	18.7	20.0	16.0	5.7	5.9	5.3	4.9	3.1	2.4
25–34 years	14.1	16.0	15.7	19.9	25.6	26.4	19.2	21.8	21.3	9.0	7.5	6.2	5.7	4.1	3.8
35–44 years	16.9	15.4	15.2	23.3	23.5	23.9	12.6	15.6	17.5	13.0	9.1	8.3	3.7	4.6	2.8
45–54 years	20.0	15.9	16.4	29.5	24.2	26.3	13.8	12.0	12.8	13.5	10.2	9.6	3.7	2.8	3.2
55–64 years	21.4	15.9	17.0	35.0	25.8	28.7	10.6	11.7	9.9	12.3	9.1	9.0	2.0	2.3	4.2
65 years and over	20.8	17.8	21.5	41.1	37.5	45.6	8.7	11.4	16.2	8.5	6.5	7.5	2.6	1.4	2.4
65–74 years	20.8	16.9	19.7	38.7	32.5	37.6	8.7	11.1	16.1	9.6	7.0	7.7	2.9	1.7	2.8
75–84 years	21.2	19.1	25.2	45.5	45.5	58.9	8.9	10.5	16.0	7.2	5.7	8.0	1.7	1.4	2.6
85 years and over	19.0	19.2	20.8	45.8	52.8	66.3	8.7	18.9	17.9	5.8	5.8	5.0	2.8	—	—

*Rates per 100,000 population.
†Includes other races not shown separately.
‡Includes other age groups not shown separately.
Source: U.S. Department of Commerce, Bureau of the Census, *Statistical Abstract of the United States, 1989* (Washington, D.C.: U.S. Government Printing Office, 1989), p. 84.

hanging, whereas women are more prone to use drugs, poisons, and gas. Women's use of firearms has been on the increase, however (Table 15.3). It is possible that the difference in the methods chosen partially accounts for the different rates of completed suicide by sex.

Race. According to official statistics, the suicide rate among whites is normally twice as high as that among minorities. But there are some important variations. For example, while the suicide rate is lower for blacks than for whites in the southern United States, the opposite is true in the northern states. One investigation of black suicide in New York City found that the suicide rate among young black men exceeded that of whites in the same age group.[11] It has also been noted that the suicide rate is inordinately high among Native American youth in comparison to white adolescents.

Religion. Overall, suicide is more frequent among Protestants than among either Jews or Roman Catholics. However, it is suspected that there are variations among particular Protestant denominations. It is possible that some Protestant denominations have lower rates than Jews and Roman Catholics.

Marital Status. A correlation between suicide rates and marital status has long been noted in official statistics. Single persons are twice as likely as married persons to complete the act of suicide. The widowed and divorced also kill themselves more frequently than the married. These generalizations must be qualified by noting variations. For example, the rate of suicide among young married persons is higher than that among young people who are single. Among the elderly, suicide is more frequent among those who are married than among those who are widowed.

Place of Residence. In the past decades, official statistics generally showed higher rates for cities than for rural areas. But suicide is not an urban phenomenon. Today the urban–rural differences are very small. There are also differences in the rates prevailing in particular cities and even in different regions of the country. For example, San Francisco has a higher suicide rate than virtually any other American city. The western states in general tend to have higher suicide rates than other regions.

Occupation. Even when they are available, official statistics relating suicide rates to occupation are not easy to interpret. Standard occupational categories are not used on death certificates, thus making comparisons between occupations difficult. In some cases, the occupation of the deceased may be unknown. Or those charged with filling out death certificates may simply put down the last known occupation. This could be misleading, for a person could be unemployed or employed in a different job than usual at the time of death. Thus, it is not surprising that the findings of studies attempting to correlate suicide rates with occupation have been contradictory. Nevertheless, there is evidence that suicide is more frequent among the unemployed than among jobholders—at least for men.[12] In addition, certain professions (such as psychiatry) appear to have unusually high rates.

Statistical Trends

As mentioned earlier, suicide rates have risen slightly over the years and recent trends up-

[11] Herbert Henden, *Black Suicide* (New York: Basic Books, 1969). See also Carlton Blake, "Suicide Among Black Americans," in Dorothy B. Anderson and Lenora J. McLean, eds., *Identifying Suicide Potential* (New York: Behavioral Publications, 1971), pp. 25–28.

[12] Stephen Platt, "Unemployment and Suicidal Behavior," *Social Science and Medicine,* 19, No. 2 (1984): 93–115.

TABLE 15.3 Suicides, by Sex and Method Used, 1960–86

	Male								Female							
Method	**1960**	**1970**	**1975**	**1980**	**1983**	**1984**	**1985**	**1986**	**1960**	**1970**	**1975**	**1980**	**1983**	**1984**	**1985**	**1986**
Total	**14,539**	**16,629**	**19,622**	**20,505**	**21,786**	**22,689**	**23,145**	**24,226**	**4,502**	**6,851**	**7,441**	**6,364**	**6,509**	**6,597**	**6,308**	**6,678**
Firearms*	7,879	9,704	12,185	12,937	13,959	14,504	14,809	15,518	1,138	2,068	2,688	2,459	2,641	2,609	2,554	2,635
Percent of total	54.2	58.4	62.1	63.1	64.1	63.9	64.0	64.1	25.3	30.2	36.1	38.6	40.6	39.5	40.5	39.5
Poisoning†	2,631	3,299	3,297	2,997	3,148	3,203	3,319	3,516	1,699	3,285	3,129	2,456	2,469	2,406	2,385	2,520
Hanging and strangulation‡	2,576	2,422	2,815	2,997	3,222	3,478	3,532	3,761	790	831	846	694	709	863	732	845
Other§	1,453	1,204	1,325	1,574	1,457	1,504	1,485	1,431	875	667	778	755	690	719	637	678

*Includes explosives through 1975.
†Includes solids, liquids, and gases.
‡Includes suffocation.
§Beginning 1980 includes explosives.
Source: U.S. Department of Commerce, Bureau of the Census, *Statistical Abstract of the United States, 1985* (Washington, D.C.: U.S. Government Printing Office, 1984), p. 79, and *Statistical Abstract of the United States, 1989* (Washington, D.C.: U.S. Government Printing Office, 1989), p. 84.

ward seem largely due to increased rates among young people. There seems, however, to be a relationship between the size of the fifteen- to twenty-four-year-old cohort in the population and their suicide rate. As the size of this group in the population increases, its suicide rate tends to rise. The reverse is also true. Since the size of this cohort is expected to decrease in the 1990s, it is possible that its suicide rate will begin to go down.[13]

We have also seen that the suicide rate advances with age, such that older Americans (particularly males) are far more likely to take their lives than younger persons. The average age of members of the American population has been increasing as the proportion of the population that is approaching old age (or has achieved it) has been going up. Members of the post–World War II "baby boom" are now into or nearing their forties. As a consequence, many more older Americans may be expected to take their lives simply in conjunction with demographic change.[14]

EXPLANATIONS FOR SUICIDE

There are many types of explanations of why people kill themselves. Such explanations can be categorized as physiological, psychological, and sociological. Most of them focus on completed suicides, rather than on other forms of suicidal behavior.[15]

Physiological Explanations

There has been an ongoing controversy about whether the act of suicide is confined to the human species.[16] Those who argue that other species engage in suicide usually point to the lemming—a mouselike rodent native to Sweden and Norway. It is believed that, during their semiannual migrations, lemmings pursue a straight path to their destinations, sometimes falling off cliffs or drowning. Those who dispute the idea that animals commit suicide usually point out that only human beings show evidence of intent. We have no wish to enter this debate, but we must point out that it exists.

Researchers have attempted to determine if people who kill themselves differ physiologically from those who show no sign of suicidal behavior.[17] For example, researchers have asked if those who kill themselves are less likely to be physically healthy than nonsuicidal individuals. Some studies have found this to be the case, while others have uncovered no relationship between health and suicidal behavior. This question thus remains open.

Other investigators have tried to determine if there are differences in physical traits, such as weight, between those who commit suicide and those who do not. It has been found that individuals who are disposed toward suicide are often overweight or underweight. However, such individuals could have lost or gained weight on the way toward completing the suicide act.

Hormonal and chemical imbalances have also been investigated. Researchers have theorized that such imbalances are more likely to be present in those who kill themselves than in nonsuicidal persons. The findings of such research have been mixed, and no hard conclusions may be drawn from them.

Research has focused on the possibility that individuals inherit the potential to commit suicide. Though suicide has been unusually frequent in certain families, investigators have no way of determining whether this is a result of environmental experiences or genetic factors. Thus, research in this area remains inconclusive.

---

[13] Herbert Henden, *Suicide in America* (New York: W. W. Norton & Company, 1982), pp. 52–54.

[14] Ibid., p. 60.

[15] For overviews, see David Lester, *Why People Kill Themselves* (Springfield, Ill.: Charles C Thomas, Publisher, 1972), and his second edition (1983). See also Steven Stack, "Suicide: A Decade Review of the Sociological Literature," *Deviant Behavior*, 4 (1982):41–66.

[16] Lester, *Why People Kill Themselves*, pp. 18–20.

[17] Ibid., pp. 25–35.

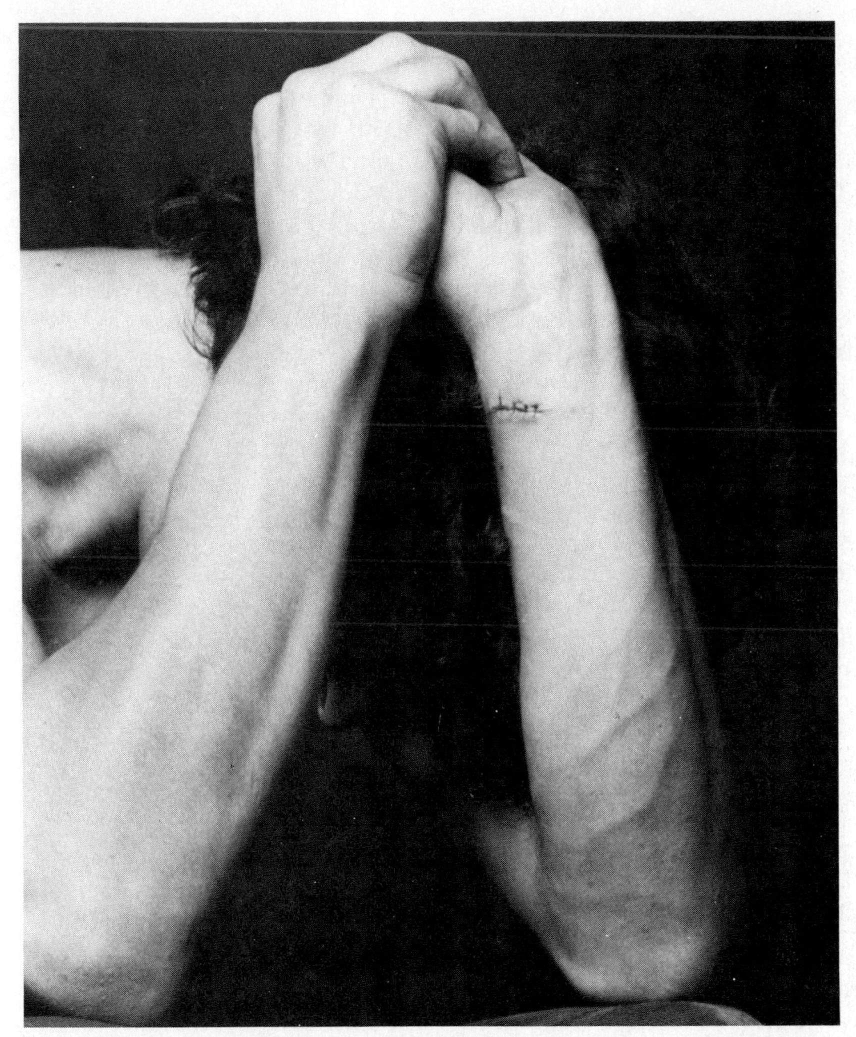

The suicide rate for young people in general, and for young white males in particular, has been on the increase. In this sad photograph, a young man buries his head in his arms, revealing the telltale stitches necessary to close a slashed wrist. His was an unsuccessful suicide attempt. *(Jock Pottle/Design Conceptions)*

Recently, the claim has been made that the majority of persons who commit suicide are, in part due to biological deficiencies, incapable of coping with stresses associated with their environment. Such persons, whose life-threatening behaviors are alleged to be a form of "gene expression," are said to carry little potential for making contributions to society. One proponent of this view has stated that suicide "may benefit the larger society because it extracts from the population individuals consuming resources but without productive and reproductive potential."[18]

[18] Denys de Catanzaro, *Suicide and Self-damaging Behavior: A Sociobiological Perspective* (New York: Academic Press, 1981), p. 143.

These and other efforts to explain suicide in terms of physiological traits all have one thing in common: they focus almost entirely on the constitution of individuals, and they tend to ignore the world in which suicidal individuals live. If most suicides are intentional acts, then explanations must take into account the fact that people have minds. Psychologists have tried to provide alternatives to physiological explanations by speculating on the personality traits of those who take their own lives.

Psychological Explanations

The mental makeup of persons who kill themselves is often difficult to ascertain. Frequently, researchers must rely on suicide notes or on people who knew the individuals. Occasionally, information on their state of mind is available from the records of medical and mental health practitioners. The reliability of all such information is open to question, but it has formed the basis for a number of theories on the psychological traits of those who commit suicide.[19]

For example, some psychologists have suggested that suicide-prone individuals are likely to have suffered from parental deprivation when young. Various forms of deprivation are said to be related to suicide, including the death or absence of parents and parental indifference to childhood needs. Deprivation, it is thought, disrupts the normal psychological development of children and provokes suicidal tendencies.

Others have claimed that suicide indicates—and is a result of—aggression that is directed inward. Children presumably learn to internalize aggressive impulses, rather than express them outwardly, as a result of parental disciplinary practices. In particular, parents who punish their children psychologically rather than physically are thought to foster inwardly directed aggression.

Some theorists believe that all people have both an instinct for self-preservation and an instinct for self-destruction (the so-called death instinct). Suicide is said to represent a breakthrough of the death instinct, a process most likely to occur among individuals who are suffering from mental problems.

It has also been postulated that persons who kill themselves are excessively rigid in their thinking and/or illogical in their reasoning and thought processes. These are considered mental disabilities that interfere with relations with other people and that deny the individual the flexibility needed to deal with everyday life. Suicide is the result.

Suicide has also been portrayed as stemming from a desire to manipulate others—perhaps to invoke love and attention. According to this theory, suicide is a cry for help from persons powerless to proceed in any other way. Alternatively, it has been suggested that suicide is an effort to hurt other people—a means of communicating deep-felt hostility or of exercising revenge.

Finally, mental illness is frequently invoked as a psychological explanation for suicide. In particular, it is thought that depressive psychoses are closely linked with suicidal behavior.[20]

Explanations for suicide that are limited to the mental state of individuals, while provocative, ignore the social context within which people kill themselves. The trend in "suicidology" (the study of suicide) is away from purely psychological interpretations of the act. Researchers are now more likely to see suicide as the outcome of an individual's biography or "suicide career"[21] and to ask "how psychic, social, and cultural factors are interwoven to pro-

[19] Lester, *Why People Kill Themselves*, pp. 57–71 and 193–218. See also Earl Grollman, *Suicide* (Boston: Beacon Press, 1971), pp. 33–39.

[20] See Eli Robins, *The Final Months* (New York: Oxford University Press, 1981).

[21] Ronald W. Maris, *Pathways to Suicide* (Baltimore: Johns Hopkins University Press, 1981), p. 9.

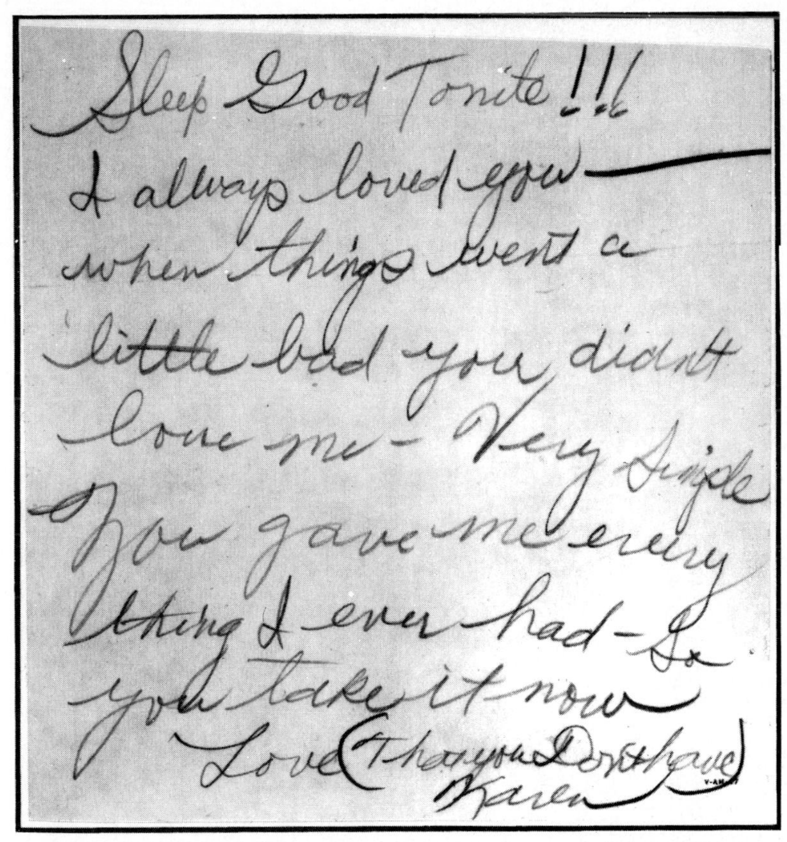

Sleep Good Tonite!!!
I allways loved you—
when things went a
little bad you didnt
love me— Very Simple
You gave me every
thing I ever had— So
you take it now
Love (Thankyou I Dont have)
Karen

There is very little reliable information on the personal or psychological motivations of persons who take their own lives. Even when suicide victims leave suicide notes, it is often difficult to determine their real reasons for killing themselves. *(Courtesy of Dr. Daryl Bem)*

duce suicidal behavior in Americans from very different backgrounds."[22] The importance of societal context and group membership in helping to produce and determine motivations for suicide has recently begun to be underscored by research on suicidal behavior in other societies.[23] (See Table 15.4.)

[22] Henden, *Suicide in America*, p. 18.
[23] See Norman L. Farberow, ed., *Suicide in Different Cultures* (Baltimore: University Park Press, 1975).

Sociological Explanations

Sociological explanations for suicide attempt to remedy the psychologists' omissions, but, unfortunately, often at the cost of ignoring the individual. Sociologists are much more concerned with explaining variations in suicide rates, such as those that appear in official statistics.

Durkheim's Theory. The starting point for virtually all sociological explanations for suicide is a theory put forth by French sociologist Emile

TABLE 15.4 Suicide Rates for Selected Countries, by Sex and Age Group

Age	United States, 1984	Australia, 1985	Austria, 1986	Canada, 1985	Denmark, 1985	France, 1985	Italy, 1983	Japan, 1986	Netherlands, 1985	Poland, 1986	Sweden, 1985	United Kingdom* 1985	West Germany, 1986
Male													
Total†	**19.7**	**18.2**	**42.1**	**20.5**	**35.1**	**33.1**	**11.0**	**27.8**	**14.6**	**22.0**	**25.0**	**12.1**	**26.6**
15–24 years	20.5	24.0	31.0	25.2	17.0	17.0	5.2	14.1	10.6	17.5	14.3	8.2	17.7
25–34 years	24.9	26.6	48.6	27.0	38.7	35.2	8.4	25.1	17.6	29.3	32.0	15.3	25.3
35–44 years	22.6	22.5	53.3	24.7	38.5	36.5	9.1	31.6	16.1	33.5	29.0	16.3	28.5
45–54 years	23.7	21.5	54.2	26.4	56.6	45.4	14.8	51.0	20.0	36.7	39.3	17.1	35.6
55–64 years	27.2	22.0	52.5	26.5	55.3	48.0	18.4	44.8	21.0	35.9	32.7	18.1	36.7
65–74 years	33.5	24.8	72.8	28.5	57.7	61.4	29.7	43.9	26.1	30.6	36.2	16.9	44.7
75 years and over	49.1	27.4	106.5	28.4	83.4	120.5	47.9	78.8	41.0	29.3	45.3	22.3	72.8
Female													
Total†	**5.4**	**5.1**	**15.8**	**5.4**	**20.6**	**12.7**	**4.3**	**14.9**	**8.1**	**4.4**	**11.5**	**5.7**	**12.0**
15–24 years	4.4	4.9	9.7	4.0	8.1	4.7	1.3	8.0	3.1	2.7	7.6	1.8	5.3
25–34 years	6.1	4.7	14.3	6.6	14.3	10.6	3.3	11.6	9.3	5.3	13.2	4.4	9.1
35–44 years	7.7	6.1	18.5	8.0	28.6	14.6	3.7	12.8	9.9	5.8	15.5	5.4	10.5
45–54 years	9.2	8.7	20.2	9.0	34.0	17.7	5.6	18.4	12.5	8.4	14.8	9.2	14.8
55–64 years	8.5	8.3	18.9	8.0	41.5	20.8	8.3	20.2	14.6	7.6	13.8	10.5	16.5
65–74 years	7.3	7.6	29.0	7.8	34.1	26.8	10.1	33.0	15.5	6.6	20.1	11.9	23.6
75 years and over	6.0	9.7	31.5	5.3	24.6	27.5	11.0	59.1	10.8	5.5	14.0	10.1	24.8

[Rate per 100,000 population. Includes deaths resulting indirectly from self-inflicted injuries.]
*England and Wales only.
†Includes other age groups not shown separately.
Source: U.S. Department of Commerce, Bureau of the Census, *Statistical Abstract of the United States, 1989* (Washington, D.C.: U.S. Government Printing Office, 1989), p. 820.

Durkheim.[24] Writing in 1897, Durkheim tried to demonstrate that the character of a society determined the probability that people would be pushed toward committing suicide. According to Durkheim, suicide could not be explained by physiological traits or psychological variables. Instead, one must look at the social forces impinging on and shaping the lives of the members of any given society. In Durkheim's view, the presence or absence of these forces accounted for variations in suicide rates.

According to Durkheim, suicide is related to the degree to which a society is *integrated*—in other words, the degree to which members of a society share common ideas and goals and sense their ties with one another. Where integration is low, *egoistic* suicides—due to the absence of meaningful social relationships or a sense of belonging—will be frequent. Conversely, where integration is high, individuals will be likely to willingly give up their lives for the group, committing *altruistic* suicides. Such self-sacrifices might take place in times of war or as part of religious rituals.

Durkheim also argued that *social regulation* plays a role in generating suicidal behavior. In a society with a high degree of control over its members' emotions and motivations, *fatalistic* suicide will occur. That is, people kill themselves out of a sense of overmanipulation or of hopelessness about altering their life conditions. Conversely, in a society that provides few guidelines for its members' feelings and inclinations—thereby leaving people unregulated or uncontrolled—*anomic* suicide will take place.

Because Durkheim did not provide measures of integration and social regulation, it has proven difficult to test his arguments. Nonetheless, many sociologists have been influenced by his theory in developing their own explanations. For example, French sociologist Maurice Halbwachs has theorized that suicide is a function of social isolation.[25] According to Halbwachs, suicide occurs most frequently among individuals who lack stable and enduring relationships with others. Since such social isolation is presumably more common among city-dwellers than among rural people, said Halbwachs, suicide rates should be higher in cities. Writing in 1930, Halbwachs found that the data on suicide rates available to him supported his hypothesis. Today, however, there is no significant difference between urban and rural suicide rates—at least in the United States—so the social isolation thesis does not appear helpful.

Class and Status. Borrowing some of Durkheim's ideas, Elwin H. Powell proposed an explanation that relates suicide to the status of different groups in American society.[26] Powell hypothesized that suicide rates would be highest in the lower and upper classes. He reasoned that individuals at the bottom of the class structure would be prone to suicide because they were dissociated from the larger society and had little hope of achieving cultural goals. The upper class, in his view, was so "enveloped" in these goals that many individuals could not find personal reasons for living. Using occupational data from suicide records in Tulsa, Oklahoma, Powell found support for his hypothesis. However, other studies have not found such correlations between occupational status and suicide rates,[27] and Powell's explanation is open to question.

Sociologists Andrew Henry and James Short have also investigated the relationship between

[24] Emile Durkheim, *Suicide*, trans. John A. Spaulding and George Simpson (New York: The Free Press, 1951).

[25] Maurice Halbwachs, *Les Causes du Suicide* (Paris: Alcan, 1930). Halbwachs' work is discussed in Douglas, *The Social Meanings of Suicide*, pp. 124–31.

[26] Elwin H. Powell, "Occupation, Status, and Suicide," *American Sociological Review*, 23 (April 1958): 131–40.

[27] See, for example, Ronald W. Maris, *Social Forces in Urban Suicide* (Homewood, Ill.: Dorsey Press, 1969).

status and suicide.[28] These researchers suggested that higher-status groups were least likely to be characterized by strong "relational systems" among their members. In other words, their emotional ties were weak. Society, they felt, places few "external constraints"—pressures toward conformity—on the behavior of high-status people. Henry and Short hypothesized that suicide rates would vary directly with social status. Thus, groups to which they assigned high status (men, whites, the affluent, the unmarried) could be expected to have the highest rates of suicide. In general, the statistics they mobilized supported their hypothesis. But there have been criticisms of Henry and Short's work. For example, how does one explain the high suicide rates that seem to prevail among northern blacks in comparison to whites? Such variations in the overall statistics on suicide rates are not easily handled within the framework of Henry and Short's explanation. Also, do unmarried people really have higher status than married people in this society? Although this assumption fits with Henry and Short's statistical findings on suicide rates, it does not make much sense.

More recent data seem to suggest an indirect relationship between class membership and suicide. That is, the higher the class position, the lower the suicide rate. The rate of suicide appears to be highest among the poor.[29] Stress, depression, and feelings of hopelessness associated with economic deprivation may account for this; however, such a conclusion requires quite a bit more empirical research.

Role Incompatibility. Other sociologists have hypothesized that suicide rates are related to people's ability to carry out the roles society assigns them.[30] Jack Gibbs and Walter Martin have pointed out that people must sometimes fill several roles simultaneously—that is, often they have to meet the demands and expectations of a variety of groups. If all these roles are compatible with one another, *status integration* is said to exist, and suicide is unlikely. On the other hand, if the roles are incompatible—if individuals are confronted with conflicting demands and expectations—suicide will be more frequent. In this case, individuals become more suicide-prone because they are unable to satisfy others, and their social relationships with other people weaken. The problem with this explanation is that there is no objective way of measuring the role incompatibility of those who have committed suicide. Instead, we can only assume that role conflict is highest among those who kill themselves. Thus, a crucial aspect of Gibbs and Martin's explanation remains difficult to demonstrate.

Societal Reaction. Another sociological explanation for variations in suicide rates holds that societal reaction to suicide is of key importance.[31] According to this explanation, where members of a society accept or condone acts of suicide, rates will be high; and where suicide is condemned, rates will be low. In other words, the cultural values of a group can either deter or facilitate self-destruction. Proponents of this explanation point to the fact that suicide rates among Roman Catholics, who explicitly condemn suicide, are much lower than suicide rates among Protestants, who do not condemn it as strongly. But the societal reaction theory is not helpful in shedding light on other variations in suicide rates. For example, there is no reason to believe that Americans are more accepting of

[28] Andrew F. Henry and James F. Short, Jr., *Suicide and Homicide* (New York: The Free Press, 1954).

[29] See Stack, "Suicide: A Decade Review of the Sociological Literature," and Dominique Lampert et al., "Occupation and Suicide," *Suicide and Life-Threatening Behavior*, 14, No. 4 (Winter 1984): 254–69.

[30] Jack P. Gibbs and Walter T. Martin, *Status Integration and Suicide* (Eugene: University of Oregon Press, 1964).

[31] Maurice L. Farber, *Theory of Suicide* (New York: Funk & Wagnalls Book Publishing, 1968).

suicide among men than among women, among the old as opposed to the young, or among the poor as opposed to the affluent.

The Meaning of Suicide. The failure of sociologists to explain variations in suicide rates should be evident. Despite the hints provided by Durkheim and the efforts by many sociologists to reformulate and test his ideas, existing explanations are inadequate. Recognizing this, and concerned by sociologists' willingness to use questionable official statistics to test their hypotheses about suicide, Jack Douglas proposed an entirely different approach, based on the "meaning" of suicide to persons who take their lives.[32]

In effect, Douglas has called for investigation of the motives or intentions that underlie individual acts of suicide. In calling for sociologists to study the meaning of suicide, he has suggested that research should focus on the goals and objectives that suicidal persons are trying to fulfill through their behavior. In other words, we should view those who die by suicide as actors, rather than as those who have been acted upon by society.

In Douglas' view, the meaning of suicide can best be ascertained by examining a sample of individual cases. Researchers can document patterns of verbal and nonverbal communication of the suicide victim and of any others involved in the death situation. Douglas attempted to illustrate how this might be done. However, he was forced to rely on published case reports, thereby opening up the question of the reliability of such reports and of those who wrote them. Nevertheless, Douglas is one of the few sociologists who have examined the social determinants of individual suicides, rather than searching for explanations for variations in suicide rates.

Suicide and Imitation. In recent years some sociologists have theorized that news stories about suicidal acts foster imitative behaviors. Several studies have examined the effects of newspaper accounts and found that suicides do increase in the aftermath of such reporting. For example, Steven Stack demonstrated that highly publicized suicide stories involving celebrities with whom many people identify seem to foster suicide deaths. In particular, deaths of political heroes and entertainers have such an effect.[33] The reasons remain speculative, and no one knows whether such imitative suicides represent any more than a tiny minority of the total suicides that occur.

In response to so-called epidemics of suicide among clusters of adolescents in different communities around the country (from Westchester County, New York, to Plano, Texas), some have asked if suicide can be considered "contagious."[34] Suicide, it is thought, may contain an imitative component for some adolescents. However, a great deal more research is needed to determine whether this is the case and the conditions under which it occurs.

Other Explanations

Investigators have studied several other factors that seem to bear on suicide rates.[35] For example, suicide rates tend to vary in accordance with changes in the seasons. In terms of the overall U.S. suicide rate, most suicides are completed in the spring (April or May), whereas the fewest take place in the winter (December). How-

[32] Douglas, *The Social Meaning of Suicide.* See also Jack D. Douglas, "The Sociological Analysis of Social Meanings of Suicide," in Anthony Giddens, ed., *The Sociology of Suicide* (London: Frank Cass & Co., 1971, pp. 121–51.

[33] Steven Stack, "Celebrities and Suicide," *American Sociological Review,* 52 (June 1987): 401–12.

[34] See David K. Curran, *Adolescent Suicidal Behavior* (New York: Hemisphere Publishing Corporation, 1987), Chapter 7.

[35] Lester, *Why People Kill Themselves,* pp. 149–58.

ever, when particular geographical regions or cities have been examined, the results have been far less uniform. To date, no one has come up with an explanation for such overall seasonal variations. Nor have researchers found a reliable correlation between suicide and particular days of the week. While the results are somewhat mixed, it does appear that most persons who kill themselves do so during the day rather than at night. Again, there is no explanation for this.

At times researchers have investigated some unusual factors, hoping that they will shed some additional light on suicide rates. For example, research has been conducted to determine the relationship between suicide rates and the appearance of sunspots. No relationship has been found. Less unusual have been efforts to probe the possibility that weather influences suicide rates in some way. A popular idea is that people are most likely to kill themselves on rainy days. But the weather seems to have little to do with suicide.

The Unanswerable Question: Why?

Despite the accumulation of statistical data and other evidence bearing on completed suicides, social scientists continue to debate the causes of this phenomenon. In the words of one expert in suicidology, Louis Wekstein, "Research to date has neither unearthed nor revealed what possesses some individuals to effectuate their own demise and why such a desperate course of action is dictated."[36]

A major problem that continues to plague researchers is the quantity and quality of the data with which they have to work. Only recently have sociologists begun to mobilize studies that allow sufficient data to be generated to begin shedding more light on suicide.[37] Nonetheless, the basic question of "Why?" may continue to elude social scientists for some time to come.

The Question of Attempted Suicide

As we noted earlier, most of the efforts to explain suicide have been limited to completed suicides, ignoring the question of attempted suicide. Yet an estimated ten times as many persons are thought to make unsuccessful suicide attempts. Between 2 million and 5 million Americans are presently living after having made one or more attempts to die.

Unfortunately, there are no official statistics on attempted suicides; available information generally comes from hospitals and/or from physicians. These people probably never hear of a significant number of cases. For example, an act of attempted suicide may result in only minor injury. Many such attempts may be intentionally concealed. Finally, it may be difficult to judge whether an attempted suicide has indeed taken place (as opposed, for example, to an accident). Thus our knowledge of attempted suicide remains very limited, as do explanations for it.[38]

Women are more likely to attempt suicide than men, and women who attempt suicide are likely to be younger than men who do so. Women are also more likely to make repeated attempts than are men and to use less lethal methods.[39] Attempts are thought to be most frequent among housewives, in comparison to other groups of women.

Researchers have not been able to explain these differences between the sexes. Some have suggested that women use less lethal methods

---

[36] Wekstein, *Handbook of Suicidology*, p. 13.

[37] For an excellent review of theoretical literature, matched against evidence from a recent large-scale empirical inquiry, see Maris, *Pathways to Suicide*.

[38] See James Wilkins, "Suicidal Behavior," in Giddens, *The Sociology of Suicide*, pp. 398–418.

[39] Lester, *Why People Kill Themselves*, pp. 36–46.

because they are less aggressive or more concerned with their appearance after death than are men. It has been hypothesized that women often survive suicide attempts because they are the biologically "stronger sex" (which probably means that women generally live longer than men). But none of these observations gets at the question of why so many women attempt suicide in the first place.

One of the few other things we know is that attempted suicide is apparently correlated with age. The average age of persons who attempt suicide is much younger than the average age of those who complete suicide. It is believed that for every completed suicide among adolescents there are a hundred attempted suicides.[40] By contrast, adults have a rate of eight attempts to every completed suicide. Again, there is a difference in lethality of methods, with adolescents tending to use the least lethal of methods. Moreover, it is thought that suicidal behavior among the young is more likely to be impulsive and less likely to be premeditated. As with women, there is no real consensus about why the young attempt suicide so frequently.

The lack of reliable statistical information hampers our knowledge of attempted suicides. Also, there is disagreement over whether completed and attempted suicides involve the same types of people. Do people who attempt suicide and those who complete it make up two distinct groups possessing quite different characteristics? Since most persons who complete suicide have made one or more previous attempts, but relatively few who attempt suicide ultimately kill themselves, researchers have taken a middle position. It is thought that two distinct groups do exist, but that their membership overlaps to some degree. Thus, one can learn little about one of these groups by studying the other. But other researchers believe that this position is erroneous, arguing that more information about both attempted and completed suicides is crucial to an understanding of each.[41]

SUICIDE PREVENTION

At the start of this chapter, we noted that most Americans view suicide as an unnatural and abnormal act, possibly linked with mental illness. This view, which draws attention away from the societal context within which people move toward suicide, underlies suicide prevention programs. Such programs view the individual as the problem, not the society. In this section we look at suicide prevention programs and consider whether people have the right to choose death over life.

Suicide Prevention Centers

Approaches to preventing suicide range from counseling by clergy and mental health practitioners to pleas by police officers called to the scene of suicide attempts. In the last two decades, communities around the country have instituted organized efforts to prevent suicide, setting up suicide prevention centers and other crisis projects that try to assist troubled people.

Suicide prevention centers vary greatly in size, resources, and services, and their effectiveness is very difficult to assess. Even as more centers have opened, many with the help of governmental financing, the overall number of suicides is thought to have been increasing. It is possible that the presence of such centers—particularly the research involvement of a few—has promoted more careful investigations and record-keeping on causes of deaths. Thus, instead of an increase in suicides, we could sim-

[40] See Stuart M. Finch and Elva O. Poznanski, *Adolescent Suicide* (Springfield, Ill.: Charles C Thomas, Publisher, 1971).

[41] Lester, *Why People Kill Themselves*, pp. 314–16.

ply be seeing better detection and recording by medical officials.

In general, however, it is believed that suicide prevention centers have not really had their intended effect at the local level. "The evidence ... is fairly conclusive that suicide prevention centers have had no demonstrable effect on the suicide rates of their local communities,"[42] even though their services are no doubt of assistance to those with whom they interact.

Suicide prevention centers seek to keep people from taking their lives by being ready to assist anyone who voluntarily contacts them. Thus, such centers probably come into contact with or learn of only a small percentage of those who attempt and/or complete suicide. Their effectiveness therefore depends largely on how well they handle this minority.

Often workers at suicide prevention centers have very limited contact with potentially suicidal individuals, perhaps just a telephone conversation with the individual or concerned family members or friends. Workers thus must rely on guidelines to help them determine the seriousness of cases at hand. For example, some centers use the guidelines developed by psychologist Edwin S. Shneidman, one of the founders of the well-known Los Angeles Suicide Prevention Center:

1. Persons who are contemplating suicide wish to be stopped or rescued before death. They are mentally torn between wanting to live and wanting to die, and can be pushed toward living.
2. Contemplation of suicide occurs during a period of extreme crisis that may be relatively brief in duration. If the suicidal individual can be gotten through the crisis, the probability of suicide is minimized.
3. Persons who are about to kill themselves are almost always fully conscious of their intentions, although they may not communicate these intentions directly. Few people are unconscious of their intentions.
4. Suicidal behavior usually stems from a sense of isolation and is an act to stop an intolerable existence. Since people define "intolerable" differently, prevention efforts must take into account the perspective of the potential suicide.[43]

Shneidman has pointed out that almost all those who kill themselves drop *prodromal clues* before doing so.[44] That is, they signal their suicidal thoughts to others, often days or weeks before taking steps to die. Such clues may be verbal, involving direct or indirect statements of suicidal intentions. Or they may be behavioral, as when an individual makes a will and sets affairs in order, or actually makes a "practice run" in planning death. Prodromal clues may also be situational—for example, an individual is obviously caught up in conditions involving a great deal of stress-produced anxiety. Finally, the clues may be "prodromatic"—that is, a person appears to be deeply depressed, disoriented, or defiant. Though some persons kill themselves on impulse, Shneidman suggests that even in such cases some kind of warning is given beforehand. The problem is that such clues may go unrecognized or even ignored.

After suicide prevention center workers have used these or other guidelines and have decided that an individual who phones is suicidal, they ordinarily try to talk the person through the crisis period. They may attempt to convince the individual to seek out counseling or therapy. If they know the identity of the individual, they may contact family, friends, or others who can

---

[42] Henden, *Suicide in America,* p. 183.

[43] Edwin S. Shneidman, "Preventing Suicide," in Gibbs, *Suicide,* pp. 255–66. See also Edwin S. Shneidman and Philip Mandelkorn, "How to Prevent Suicide," in Shneidman et al., *The Psychology of Suicide* (Northvale, N.J.: Aronson, Jason, Inc., 1983), pp. 125–43.

[44] Ibid. See also Edwin Shneidman, "At the Point of No Return," *Psychology Today,* 21 (March 1987): 55–58.

All suicide threats should be treated seriously. Sometimes it is possible to stop people in the act. In this photograph an emergency medical technician talks to a man who is suicidal and has climbed onto a bridge. The man was persuaded to climb down. *(Jim Mahoney/The Image Works)*

intervene and secure assistance for the suicide-prone person. Therapy typically involves psychiatric treatment and/or drugs. In extreme cases, the suicidal individual may be involuntarily confined in an institution for observation and treatment.[45]

The ultimate goal of suicide prevention centers and other treatment services is to enable people to function in the prevailing social order. Thus, suicide prevention and therapy do not touch on the question of social changes that might reduce the frequency of self-initiated deaths. Speaking from a sociological perspective, Jack P. Gibbs has stated:

> If any theory on the suicide rate is valid, then conceivably the volume of suicide could be reduced substantially by deliberate social change. However, most theories deal with such basic structural components of society that few policymakers would contemplate making changes, let alone succeed. Further, neither policymakers nor the pub-

[45] See Ellen L. Bassuk et al., eds., *Lifelines: Clinical Perspectives on Suicide* (New York: Plenum, 1982.)

> lic is likely to view the "cost" of suicide as sufficiently great to justify undertaking any major remedial action. So in the final analysis, there appears to be only one way to reduce the incidence of suicide, and that is by instituting prevention programs that focus on individual cases.[46]

We cannot share Gibbs' pessimism about the possibility of social changes that will reduce suicide. To write this possibility off, as Gibbs does, is to ensure that such changes will never take place.

Is There a Right to Die?

As mentioned, the goal of suicide prevention programs is the preservation of individual lives, no matter what the circumstances. Workers in such programs believe that they know what is best for the suicide-prone. The basic precept of suicide prevention is that life is preferable to death and that suicide is a form of deviant behavior that must be fought.

Contrasted to these beliefs is the fact that many members of our society seem to find good reason to kill themselves. Psychologist David Lester put it this way: "Suicide is a way of living, a way of coping with problems that arise from living, and for many people it is a way of achieving a better life or avoiding a worse life."[47] Though we can all appreciate the pro-life thrust of suicide prevention efforts, it seems valid to consider whether people also have a right to die. A related question is whether there are circumstances under which suicide is rational behavior and efforts to prevent it irrational. Though we cannot provide definitive answers to these questions, we believe them worthy of consideration.

Despite the voluminous literature on suicide, most authors believe that suicide must be prevented—if only to keep from losing people who might otherwise make a contribution to society. One exception is Jacques Choron, who suggests that there is a phenomenon called *rational suicide*. Choron defines rational suicide as suicidal behavior on the part of those who are mentally normal (so far as can be judged), whose reasoning powers are not impaired, and whose motives can be considered justified. To Choron, justification refers to "approval by contemporaries, in the sense of their agreeing that in similar circumstances they might have done the same thing."[48] With regard to such persons, it could be argued that suicide prevention efforts are misdirected or inappropriate. Perhaps a counselor or therapist should tell them to go ahead, admitting that they are making the best decision.

Choron does not provide many examples of rational suicide, and he admits that we have no way of knowing how many suicides would fit his definition. But the following two cases are illustrative:

> A woman learns she is afflicted with a terminal illness for which there is no known cure. The process of dying promises to be long and tremendously uncomfortable. Her physical suffering is likely to have an adverse effect on the emotions of her family and friends. Well before the woman's illness reaches its terminal stage, she takes her life.
>
> A husband and wife, who are extraordinarily active and share a variety of interests in common, sit down and decide to die together twenty years hence. They anticipate a full and enjoyable life for these twenty years, and do not wish to endure old age (wherein they will have to slow down, and possibly cope with illness or death of the other). As planned, they initiate their own deaths when the twenty years are up.

---

[46] Jack P. Gibbs, "Suicide," in Robert K. Merton and Robert Nisbet, eds., *Contemporary Social Problems*, 3rd ed. (New York: Harcourt Brace Jovanovich, 1971), pp. 311–12.

[47] Lester, *Why People Kill Themselves*, pp. 325–26.

[48] Jacques Choron, *Suicide* (New York: Charles Scribner's Sons, 1972), p. 97.

PUBLIC PROBLEM, PRIVATE PAIN

At the Point of No Return

Rarely do we get to know what goes through the minds of those who are in the process of taking their lives. The following excerpts are from two people who survived serious suicide attempts. In one case, a woman jumped from a building; in the other, a man shot himself. The emotions of despair and anguish cry out for relief.

The Jumper

"I was so desperate. I felt, my God, I couldn't face this thing. Everything was like a terrible whirlpool of confusion. And I thought to myself: There's only one thing to do. I just have to lose consciousness. That's the only way to get away from it. The only way to lose consciousness, I thought, was to jump off something good and high.

"I just figured I had to get outside. ... I got to the other building by walking across a catwalk, sure that someone would see me, you know, out of all those windows. The whole building is made of glass.

"I just walked until I found this open staircase. As soon as I saw it, I made a beeline right up to it. And then I got to the fifth floor and everything just got very dark all of a sudden, and all I could see was this balcony. Everything around it just blacked out. It was just like a circle.

"I climbed over it and then I just let go. I was so desperate. Just desperation, and the horribleness and the quietness of it. There was no sound. And I sort of went into slow motion as I climbed over the balcony. I let go and it was like I was floating. I blacked out. I don't remember any part of the fall."

The Shooter

"I had done all I could and I was still sinking. I sat many hours seeking answers, and all there was was a silent wind. The answer was in my head. It was all clear now: Die....

"The next day a friend offered to sell me a gun, a .357 Magnum pistol. I bought it. My first thought was: What a mess this is going to make. That day I began to say goodbye to people: not actually saying it but expressing it silently.

"Friends were around, but I didn't let them see what was wrong with me. I could not let them know lest they prevent it. My mind became locked on my target. My thoughts were: Soon it will all be over. I would obtain the peace I had so long sought. The will to survive and succeed had been crushed and defeated. I was like a general on a battlefield being encroached on by my enemy and its hordes: fear, hate, self-depreciation, desolation. I felt I had to have the upper hand, to control my environment, so I sought to die rather than surrender....

"I was only aware of myself and my plight. Death swallowed me long before I pulled the trigger. The world through my eyes seemed to die with me. It was like I was to push the final button to end this world. I committed myself to the arms of death. There comes a time when all things cease to shine, when the rays of hope are lost.

"I placed the gun to my head. Then, I remember a tremendous explosion of lights like fireworks. Thus did the pain become glorious, an army rallied to the side of death to help destroy my life, which I could feel leaving my body with each rushing surge of blood. I was engulfed in total darkness."

Source: From Edwin Shneidman, "At the point of no return," *Psychology Today*, 21, March 1987, p. 56.

Though cases like these probably would not come to the attention of suicide prevention agencies, that is not the point. The philosophy or ideology of suicide prevention leaves no room for rational suicides of any type. If their intentions were to become known, the woman with the terminal illness and the couple who planned their deaths would be the focus of attempts to preserve their lives.

Suicide prevention workers are sometimes faced with elderly and/or severely ill persons who indicate intentions to undertake *euthanatic suicide*—in Choron's terms, "easy dying." In such cases, asks Choron: "Should not the multitudes who die painfully and miserably each year be allowed to decide for themselves what is best for them?"[49] In our society, this question is rarely answered affirmatively. The idea that the right to die should be legally protected and that the means for a quick and painless death should be provided to people on request is likely to be greeted with outrage. Meanwhile, many persons do undertake "easy dying" without legal sanction—often unsuccessfully or by violent means:

> It would be too much to expect that resistance to the idea of euthanatic suicide will be easily overcome. The most important step in that direction is the realization that considering suicide the wrong cure for the ills of the living does not necessarily exclude the possibility that it may be the right cure for the ills of the dying.[50]

In recent years a great deal of debate has developed over the "right to die" issue.[51] Some would argue that this right belongs to any who are terminally ill, while others would extend it to those who are aging. Still others would extend this right to any who prefer death over life. There are those who go so far as to advocate support, encouragement, and even technical help to potential suicides. Handbooks have been published to educate people about the various methods available to kill themselves, thus intensifying the controversy.

We have not presented this discussion because we are against suicide prevention or for the right to die. But in the absence of societal changes that might reduce the volume of suicide, much suicide might profitably be viewed as rational. Only when we begin to search for the rational components of self-initiated death—its "meaning" in sociologist Jack Douglas' terms—will more people begin to ask: What is it about the organization and operation of American society that leads so many to suicidal behavior? We must begin to ask this question if, at some future time, thousands of people are to avoid concluding:

> In this life it's not difficult to die.
> To make life is more difficult by far.[52]

SUMMARY

Each year thousands of people take their own lives. Official statistics no doubt underreport the actual number of suicides. Often it is difficult to determine the actual cause of a person's death. Moreover, the fact of suicide may be concealed and death attributed to other causes. There is no way to know how extensive underreporting is.

Official statistics indicate that the suicide rate has been relatively constant over the years, although increases have occurred recently (especially among young people). Older adults are more likely to take their lives than the young, men more than women, whites more than minority group members, and Protestants more than Catholics or Jews. Single, widowed, and divorced persons commit suicide at a higher rate than those who are married and living with their mates. City-dwellers take their lives at about the same rate as rural residents. Data on occupations and suicide are mixed, but it is thought the unemployed have higher rates than the employed.

A variety of explanations have been offered for why people kill themselves. Some researchers have sought to find indications that those who commit suicide differ physically from others and have suggested that genetic factors are involved. Others have offered explanations based on the presumed mental states of suicide

---

[49] Ibid., pp. 104–5.
[50] Ibid., p. 106.
[51] See M. P. Battin and D. Mayo, eds., *Suicide: The Philosophical Issues* (New York: St. Martin's Press, 1980). An antipermissiveness position is expressed in Henden, *Suicide in America*, pp. 209–28.

[52] Vladimir Vladimirovich Mayakovsky, "To Sergei Yessenin," in trans. and ed., Herbert Marshall, *Mayakovsky* (New York: Hill & Wang, 1965), p. 350.

victims, suggesting that such persons are mentally abnormal. Finally, it has been suggested both that societal forces are involved in pushing people toward suicide and that suicide may have a special social and cultural meaning to its victims.

Attempted suicide is thought to be ten times more frequent than completed suicide. Unfortunately, there are no official statistics on suicide attempts. It is known that women and the young make the most attempts and that they tend to use less lethal methods than men and older adults. There is controversy over whether completed and attempted suicides involve the same types of people.

In the last two decades, communities across the country have instituted organized efforts to prevent suicide. Suicide prevention centers have been established, but their effectiveness in lowering suicide rates has been questioned. Such centers probably come into contact with or learn of only a small percentage of those who attempt and/or complete suicide. While efforts to prevent suicides go on, some have suggested that people might have a right to choose death over life. Are there not circumstances under which suicide is rational behavior and efforts to prevent it irrational?

DISCUSSION QUESTIONS

1. What are the attitudes of people you know toward those who would attempt or complete the act of suicide? To what degree do you share these attitudes?
2. Do you think people should have the right to take their own lives if they wish? If so, should this be an absolute right or are there certain conditions you would attach?
3. If you assist a person in committing a suicidal act, you may be accused of a crime. Can you think of any circumstances under which you would violate the law in this way?
4. Your doctor tells you that by quitting smoking and losing excess weight you may add years to your life. You fail to heed your doctor's advice. Is this the same as committing suicide? Why?
5. According to official statistics, the suicide rate among young white males has been increasing. Speculate on why this is the case.
6. Visit a local suicide or crisis prevention center that often handles calls from persons who are potentially suicidal. On the basis of what the staff is able to tell you about the content of such calls, develop your own explanation for why people kill themselves. (Remember, however, that the center may have contact with only a small percentage of potential suicides.)

SUGGESTED READINGS

Farberow, Norman L., ed. *The Many Faces of Suicide* (New York: McGraw-Hill Book Company, 1980).
Consideration of a variety of self-destructive behaviors not commonly classified as "suicide."

Henden, Herbert. *Suicide in America* (New York: W. W. Norton & Company, 1982).
General discussion of the correlates of suicide among all age groups and policies aimed at its prevention.

Lester, David. *Why People Kill Themselves,* 2nd ed. (Springfield, Ill.: Charles C Thomas, Publisher, 1983).
Summary of research findings on suicidal behavior (updates the highly comprehensive 1972 first edition).

Orbach, Israel. *Children Who Don't Want to Live* (San Francisco: Jossey-Bass Publishers, 1988).
Part of a growing literature on child and adolescent suicide, warning signs of suicidal behavior, and underlying causes.

Roy, Alec, ed. *Suicide* (Baltimore: Williams & Wilkins, 1986).
Literature reviews by experts on suicide, with topics ranging from alleged biological and genetic influences to the role of mental illness and substance abuse.

Stack, Steven. "Suicide: A Decade Review of the Sociological Literature," *Deviant Behavior,* 4 (October–December 1982): 41–66.
Summarizes key sociological contributions to understanding a problem too often approached in psychological terms.

CARLYLE

CHAPTER 16

Alcoholism

Members of American society should be at peace with themselves and with one another. The vicarious rewards associated with alcoholism should have no attraction.

It is a common sight in the low-income, Skid Row districts of American cities. A middle-aged man is sprawled on the sidewalk. His clothing is stained and disheveled, and he looks like he needs a shower and a good meal. He is hugging a bottle wrapped in a brown paper bag. He is drunk—blind drunk. The drugged stupor in which he lies separates him from all surrounding realities. For reasons best known to him, he would rather escape to mental oblivion than stay sober.[1]

An estimated 124 million Americans aged eighteen and older drink alcoholic beverages.[2] Approximately 18 million adults are problem

[1] Life on Skid Row is detailed in Howard M. Bahr, *Skid Row* (New York: Oxford University Press, 1973).

[2] U.S. Department of Health and Human Services, *National Household Survey on Drug Abuse: 1988* (Washington, D.C.: U.S. Government Printing Office, 1989), p. 117.

drinkers and alcoholics—people whose use of alcohol has gotten out of control.[3] Skid Row residents comprise a very small percentage of the alcoholic population. Nevertheless, until quite recently the Skid Row drunk was the popular symbol of alcoholism. Today this stereotype is breaking down with the accumulation of new knowledge about this society's drinking habits.

Heavy use of alcohol—sometimes to the point of mental oblivion—occurs among both men and women, young and old, at all stations in life. Occasionally, we learn of important public figures (e.g., in politics, sports, or the entertainment world) whose lives have come to revolve around drinking. Such persons have a much different economic standing and more prestige than the Skid Row drunk. But they are alike insofar as they pursue the altered states of consciousness that alcohol can provide.

Between the Skid Row resident and the nationally known celebrity are the rest of the 18 million Americans for whom heavy alcohol use brings both pleasure and problems. Our focus in this chapter is primarily on this group. We begin by describing the general drinking population and considering the distinction between alcohol use and abuse. Then we turn to the phenomenon of alcoholism. We examine definitions of an alcoholic, alternative explanations for alcoholism, the costs of alcoholism and problem drinking, and the various modes of treating alcoholic individuals.

DRINKING IN AMERICA

Alcohol is a drug; pharmaceutically, it is a depressant or tranquilizer. Per capita consumption of this drug (consumption per person) increased steadily after World War II, primarily because an ever higher percentage of Americans became drinkers. Since 1980 consumption has gone down slightly, but it remains high. In 1987 per capita consumption of alcoholic beverages was 34.4 gallons of beer, 2.3 gallons of distilled spirits, and 3.4 gallons of wine.[4] That same year, consumers spent $75 billion on such products. In this section we look at the private and public interests that benefit from the use of alcohol. We then discuss American drinking practices and patterns of alcohol use and abuse.

Private Profit and Public Income

The term *drug pusher* is usually used to describe persons who loiter around street corners and attempt to lure the innocent into experimentation with heroin or cocaine. Alcohol is pushed quite openly by the alcoholic beverage industry. In its role as a drug pusher, this industry actively seeks to cut down on the percentage of abstainers in the adult population and to increase annual per capita consumption among those who drink. It has been active in past efforts to lower the legal drinking age in locations where people must be twenty-one in order to buy alcohol. It has also worked to turn the remaining "dry" communities (where the sale of alcoholic beverages is illegal) into "wet" ones.[5]

Though industry advertisements sometimes advise consumers to engage in "responsible drinking," such ads are a recent phenomenon that emerged only after the full dimensions of problem drinking and alcoholism became a matter of public concern. The alcoholic beverage industry still does not publicly acknowledge the fact that it is merchandising a drug. Nor does it advertise the fact that abuse of its product—alcoholism—is the nation's number one health problem.

---

[3] U.S. Department of Health and Human Services, *Alcohol and Health: Sixth Special Report to the U.S. Congress* (Washington, D.C.: U.S. Government Printing Office, 1987), p. 12.

[4] U.S. Department of Commerce, Bureau of the Census, *Statistical Abstract of the United States, 1989* (Washington, D.C.: U.S. Government Printing Office, 1989), p. 121.

[5] Michael Jacobson et al., *The Booze Merchants* (Washington, D.C.: Center for Science in the Public Interest, 1983).

The industry has a powerful incentive to push alcohol on the public—profit. While some 18 million problem drinkers and alcoholics drug themselves, many to the point of mental deterioration or death, the pushers flourish and seek to increase consumption and production levels.

The alcoholic beverage industry claims to provide employment for over 784,000 people with payrolls of $18 billion.[6] Its expenditures on newspaper, magazine, and television advertising—advertising that typically links drinking to youth, sexual pleasure, and relaxation—have risen to hundreds of millions of dollars a year.

While the industry counts its profits, government capitalizes on the tax revenues that flow from America's drinking practices. In 1986 federal, state, and local governments took in an estimated total of $12.2 billion in alcohol-related taxes. The federal government alone received $5.6 billion that year.[7] No other tax source—with the exception of income, gift, and estate taxes—provides so much income to the federal treasury. Yet, the economic costs of alcohol abuse and alcoholism are ten times the tax revenues taken in.[8]

American Drinking Practices

Over the last twenty-five years, sociologists and other social scientists have become increasingly interested in American drinking practices and patterns of alcohol use. As a result of their research, we have gained some knowledge about who the drinkers are. Most of this knowledge is based on surveys of the American population.

A landmark nationwide survey of drinking practices was conducted in 1964–65.[9] This survey studied adults aged twenty-one and over. (More recent investigations often include teenagers.) The researchers found that 68 percent of American adults drank at least once a year, or enough to be classified as "drinkers," while 32 percent claimed to be abstainers. A third of the abstainers had previously used alcohol. Among the drinkers, 52 percent drank once a month or more; the remaining 48 percent drank less frequently. Of those surveyed, 12 percent were heavy drinkers. Since this survey was released, many other studies have been conducted with similar results.[10]

Such surveys, surprisingly consistent over time, do mask one fact that has long gone unemphasized. That is, while two-thirds of the population drink, most of the alcohol is consumed by a few. According to the National Institute on Alcohol and Alcoholism, "The 10 percent of drinkers (6.5 percent of the total adult population) who drink the most heavily account for fully half of all alcohol consumed."[11]

National surveys of consumption provide statistics that are, at best, rough indicators of the characteristics of the drinking population. As such, they clearly are useful. One difficulty is that the definitions of light, moderate, and heavy drinking have often differed among surveys. As the definitions shift, so may the statistical findings.

Furthermore, survey findings are believed to understate the volume of alcohol consumed, since there is a clear gap between the amount of alcoholic beverages produced and sold and the amount survey respondents claim to drink.

---

[6] Don Cahalan, *Understanding America's Drinking Problem* (San Francisco: Jossey-Bass Publishers, 1987).

[7] U.S. Department of Commerce, *Statistical Abstract of the United States, 1989,* p. 268.

[8] "Economic Costs of Alcohol Abuse and Alcoholism," *Alcohol Health and Research World,* 9 (Winter 1984/85): 34–35.

[9] Don Cahalan, Ira H. Cisin, and Helen M. Crossley, *American Drinking Practices* (New Brunswick, N.J.: Rutgers Center of Alcohol Studies, 1969).

[10] U.S. Department of Health and Human Services, *Alcohol and Health: Sixth Special Report,* p. 3.

[11] Ibid.

Heavy users in particular are unlikely to be completely open about their true consumption.

Patterns of Alcohol Use

Patterns of alcohol use in the United States are believed to be associated with a number of variables.[12] Sex, age, race and ethnicity, and class-related factors all seem to be related to who drinks and how much one drinks.

Sex. Drinking has been considered a predominantly male activity. But since World War II, the gap between men and women has been narrowing, and more women than ever are drinking. Today, an estimated 73 percent of all adult men and 63 percent of all adult women drink at least once a year. Men are more likely than women to be moderate or heavy users of alcohol. According to federally sponsored surveys, 14 percent of adult men drink heavily, while only 3 percent of adult women do so.

There has been speculation that women have been closing this gap.[13] In particular, observers have pointed to the increasing numbers of women who are coming into contact with alcoholism treatment agencies as an indication that more women are drinking heavily. However, increased contact with treatment agencies could instead simply mean that individuals who had kept their heavy drinking secret are now seeking help. The fact that well-known women have sought aid for problems with alcoholism and drug abuse may encourage others to seek treatment.

Age. The use of alcohol is not confined to any one age category. But surveys reveal that a higher percentage of young people use alcohol than those over fifty years of age. The highest percentage of drinkers among males is found in the thirty to thirty-nine age group, and among females it is those aged eighteen to twenty-nine. Heavy drinking is also correlated with age. Males aged eighteen to twenty-nine drink most heavily. Among women, the ages are thirty to thirty-nine.

Older persons are more likely to be abstainers than the young, and it is believed that most persons taper off or stop drinking with advancing age. (See Table 16.1.) However, this does not mean that heavy drinking does not occur among the elderly. Recent analyses have begun to indicate that it may be undiagnosed and underreported to a significant degree.[14]

In the last few years attention has been drawn to the drinking practices of school-age youth, particularly in conjunction with automobile accidents and deaths involving alcohol. Most of today's junior and senior high school students have tried alcohol. Among seventh graders, approximately two-thirds of all boys and half of all girls have used alcohol. These percentages shoot up by the twelfth grade to 93 percent for boys and 87 percent for girls. Frequency of drinking and increases in the amounts consumed per occasion also rise steadily by school grade level.

The National Institute on Alcohol Abuse and Alcoholism has reported that while 25 percent of students in the tenth through twelfth grades view themselves as abstainers, at the other extreme 15 percent are self-professed "heavier drinkers." The latter drink at least once a week and drink large amounts (five or more drinks) on each occasion. One out of five males in grades 10–12 is a heavier drinker, while one out of eleven females falls into this category. As indicated, rates escalate with grade level.

---

[12] Many of the data in this section are summarized in U.S. Department of Health and Human Services, *Alcohol and Health: Sixth Special Report,* and earlier special reports.

[13] See Paul M. Roman, *Women and Alcohol Use* (Rockville, Md.: U.S. Department of Health and Human Services, 1988).

[14] "Alcohol and Aging," *Alcohol Alert,* 1 (October 1988): 1–4. This is a publication of the National Institute on Alcohol Abuse and Alcoholism.

TABLE 16.1 Frequency of Use of Alcohol Within Past Year (1988), by Sex and Age Groups for Total Population

Age and Sex	At least once	12 or more times	Once a week or more
	Rate		
12–17 years	44.6%	18.6%	5.7%
Male	47.7	19.9	7.7
Female	41.3	17.3	3.7
18–25 years	81.7	56.6	26.2
Male	85.5	65.1	37.5
Female	78.1	48.5	15.5
26–34 years	80.5	53.1	28.1
Male	83.4	65.5	41.2
Female	77.7	41.1	15.5
35 years or more	64.4	42.7	25.1
Male	71.4	53.4	36.7
Female	58.4	33.3	15.0
Total	68.1	44.3	23.9
Male	73.3	54.0	34.5
Female	63.3	35.5	14.1
	Population (in thousands)		
12–17 years	9,021	3,773	1,156
Male	4,933	2,058	793
Female	4,088	1,715	364
18–25 years	24,262	16,793	7,781
Male	12,386	9,427	5,427
Female	11,876	7,366	2,354
26–34 years	31,051	20,478	10,854
Male	15,823	12,425	7,812
Female	15,228	8,053	3,042
35 years or more	70,736	46,854	27,538
Male	36,426	27,276	18,716
Female	34,310	19,578	8,822
Total	135,071	87,898	47,328
Male	69,569	51,187	32,747
Female	65,502	36,712	14,581

Source: U.S. Department of Health and Human Services, *National Household Survey on Drug Abuse: 1988* (Washington, D.C.: U.S. Government Printing Office, 1989), p. 117.

Race and Ethnicity. Ethnicity has also been found to be correlated with patterns of alcohol use. For some groups, drinking is a part of cultural traditions associated with meals, rituals, or festivities. For other groups, it is not.

Persons whose fathers were born outside the United States are more likely to be drinkers than those with native-born fathers. Among the various American ethnic groups, the Irish, Italians, Poles, and Russians have a high proportion of drinkers. Persons of English and Scottish origins, on the other hand, are much more likely to be abstainers.

There does not appear to be much difference between blacks and whites in terms of alcohol use. Slightly more blacks are abstainers. But blacks have a similar proportion of heavy drinkers in comparison to whites.

Research on racial and ethnic differences in drinking practices is still quite limited. However, it is believed that ethnic groups maintaining cultural norms that limit the use of alcohol have fewer problem drinkers and fewer alcoholics than groups whose attitudes toward drinking are ambivalent or loose. Nevertheless, though group norms may impede or facilitate drinking, alcohol abuse is found among virtually all ethnic groups.[15]

Class, Occupation, and Education. As one moves up the class hierarchy, the use of alcohol becomes increasingly common. Members of the lower classes are more likely to be abstainers than are more affluent people. Moreover, moderate and heavy drinking also increases as class level rises.

In terms of educational level, the highest percentage of abstainers is found among persons with only an elementary school background. Most college graduates are drinkers, and the proportion of those who are heavy drinkers tends to go up as educational level increases.

The findings regarding class membership and educational level are consistent with those on occupational differences. Business executives

[15] Drinking practices among various groups are explored in *Alcohol Health and Research World*, 11 (Winter 1986/87), a special issue devoted to minorities.

As more research has accumulated concerning the harmful effects of alcohol abuse, alarm has risen over the popularity of drinking among teenage youth. Young people often proceed as if they can handle virtually any dangers associated with drinking; meanwhile, avoidable tragedies accumulate. *(Mike Rizzo/The Picture Cube)*

and professionals, who stand at the top of the occupational structure, are more likely to be drinkers than almost any other occupational group.

Alcohol Abuse

In most of the investigations of alcohol use, an individual who uses alcohol once or more per year is classified as a "drinker." Knowing how many drinkers there are, along with the correlates of drinking behavior (such as sex and age), gives us a sense of the dimensions of use. But most users of alcohol seem to be able to take it or leave it. Their occasional drinking does not pose serious difficulties for themselves or for others.

Correlates of Problem Drinking. At what point can we say that an individual is abusing alcohol to the point where he or she might be called a *problem drinker?* Most experts believe that people who exhibit any one of the following symptoms are problem drinkers:

1. Frequent bouts of intoxication, involving heavy alcohol consumption on each occasion.
2. Binge drinking—periodic episodes of intoxication that last for days at a time.
3. Physical dependence on and loss of control over the use of alcohol.
4. Psychological dependence on drinking in order to relieve depression or escape problems in living.
5. Ruptured relations with family members, friends, and/or neighbors due to drinking behavior.
6. Employment difficulties associated with alcohol use on or off the job.
7. Involvement in accidents and/or contact with law enforcement agencies in connection with alcohol use.
8. Health and/or financial problems due to drinking.[16]

Obviously, the more symptoms that are exhibited, the more serious the consequences are for the individual.

For both men and women, *psychological dependence* on drinking to relieve depression or escape problems in living is a most common symptom. Despite the fact that proportionately more of the poor are abstainers than the affluent, problem symptoms are most frequently found among those at the lowest class level. The proportion of drinkers with no problem symptoms is twice as high at the top of the class hierarchy than at the bottom.

The National Institute on Alcohol Abuse and Alcoholism has measured drinking behaviors that reflect dependence and loss of control. Symptoms include skipping meals when drinking; sneaking drinks; morning drinking; drinking before a party; blackouts; gulping drinks; drinking to get rid of a hangover; being afraid that one is an alcoholic; attempting to cut down or stop drinking but failing to do so; and finding it difficult not to drink to intoxication.[17] In a 1979 survey sponsored by the Institute, 15 percent of drinkers reported having experienced such symptoms. The rate for male drinkers was twice as high (20 percent) as that for females (10 percent).[18]

Correlates of Alcoholism. If we view problem drinking as a continuum, then *alcoholics* are persons who exhibit numerous symptoms of problem drinking. The line between problem drinking and alcoholism is not clear-cut. Consequently, experts disagree about what characteristics denote alcoholism.

Attempts to define alcoholism have been numerous. The following definitions are typical:

> We define alcoholism as a chronic behavioral disorder which is manifested by undue preoccupation with alcohol to the detriment of physical and mental health, by a loss of control when drinking has begun (although it may not be carried to the point of intoxication) and by a self-destructive attitude in dealing with personal relationships and life situations.[19]

> Alcoholism involves excessive use of the drug to an extent that measurably impairs the person's health, social functioning, or vocational adjustment.[20]

---

[16] See Don Cahalan, *Problem Drinkers* (San Francisco: Jossey-Bass Publishers, 1970); and Don Cahalan and Robin Room, *Problem Drinking Among American Men* (New Brunswick, N.J.: Rutgers Center of Alcohol Studies, 1974).

[17] U.S. Department of Health and Human Services, *Alcohol and Health: Fourth Special Report to the U.S. Congress* (Washington, D.C.: U.S. Government Printing Office, 1981), pp. 29–30.

[18] Ibid., p. 31.

[19] National Institute of Mental Health, *Alcohol and Alcoholism*, rev. ed. (Washington, D.C.: U.S. Government Printing Office, 1972), p. 9.

[20] Joel Fort, *Alcohol: Our Biggest Drug Problem* (New York: McGraw-Hill Book Company, 1973), p. 7.

> Alcoholism is a chronic disease, or disorder of behavior, characterized by the repeated drinking of alcoholic beverages to an extent that exceeds customary dietary use or ordinary compliance with the social drinking customs of the community, and which interferes with the drinker's health, interpersonal relations, or economic functioning.[21]

Despite the lack of consensus on how to define alcoholism, it is estimated that 10 million Americans are alcoholics.[22] Fully half are employed, and many more are employable. Most live in families. Between 75 and 80 percent of alcoholics are men. The average alcoholic drinks eleven times as much as the average nonalcoholic during the course of a year.[23]

EXPLANATIONS FOR ALCOHOLISM

How does one explain the presence of 10 million alcoholics in American society? A number of explanations have been offered, most of which focus on the alcoholic individual.[24] As with the phenomenon of mental illness, the victim is often blamed for his or her own plight.

Physiological Explanations

A great deal of research has been conducted to test the hypothesis that alcoholism is linked to the biological makeup of particular individuals. In conjunction with this idea, researchers have also explored the possibility that the chemical properties of alcohol itself or of other ingredients in alcoholic beverages produce alcoholism in certain people.

Some researchers have hypothesized, for example, that alcoholism is a hereditary condition, related to genetic makeup.[25] Other studies have tried to determine whether nutritional deficiencies or hormone imbalances cause alcoholism to develop. It has been suggested that alcoholism is a result of allergic reactions to alcohol and/or to the nonalcoholic components of alcoholic beverages. And researchers have tested the idea that alcoholics cannot metabolize (biologically process and eliminate) alcohol as easily as other people. To date, *none* of these hypotheses has been fully validated, and research (particularly on genetic factors influencing alcoholism) continues. While the use of alcohol has physiological effects on people—particularly on alcoholics—physiological causes have not been definitively linked to alcoholism per se.

The failure to find support for physiological explanations raises questions about the usefulness of viewing alcoholism as a "disease" in medical terms. As with mental illness (see Chapter 14), the medical model is often applied to alcoholism. The alcoholic may incur health problems in connection with drinking, but so far there is no reason to believe that people drink because they are "sick."

Psychological Explanations

Some psychological explanations attribute alcoholism to particular personality traits that only alcoholics presumably possess. Psychological explanations are also frequently framed in terms

---

[21] Mark Keller, "Alcoholism: Nature and Extent of the Problem," *Annals of the American Academy of Political and Social Science,* 315 (January 1958): 1.

[22] Gerald D. Williams et al., "Demographic Trends, Alcohol Abuse and Alcoholism," *Alcohol Health and Research World,* 11 (Spring 1987): 81.

[23] U.S. Department of Health, Education, and Welfare, *Facts About Alcohol and Alcoholism* (Washington, D.C.: U.S. Government Printing Office, 1974), pp. 15–16.

[24] These and other explanations are discussed in detail in U.S. Department of Health, Education, and Welfare, *Alcohol and Health: A Special Report to U.S. Congress* (Washington, D.C.: U.S. Government Printing Office, 1971), pp. 61–70. See also Ralph E. Tarter and Dorothea U. Schneider, "Models and Theories of Alcoholism," in Ralph E. Tarter and A. Arthur Sugarman, eds., *Alcoholism: Interdisciplinary Approaches to an Enduring Problem* (Reading, Mass.: Addison-Wesley Publishing Co., 1976), pp. 75–106.

[25] See the discussion of research in U.S. Department of Health and Human Services, *Alcohol and Health: Sixth Annual Report,* pp. 28–43.

of the medical model, on the assumption that the alcoholic's mind is "sick" or "disordered."

One influential theory, which incorporates both physiological and psychological causes, was developed by E. M. Jellinek.[26] In his analysis of questionnaires filled out by a group of alcoholics, Jellinek concluded that alcoholism is a disease that proceeds in cycles. An individual first becomes psychologically dependent on the use of alcohol. As the user begins to lose control over drinking, biological dependency occurs. In other words, according to Jellinek, a personality disorder leads to physical addiction to alcohol. While this explanation certainly sounds logical, no one has been able to demonstrate that alcoholism occurs for such reasons. In particular, there is no evidence that all alcoholics are biologically dependent on or addicted to the drug.

Other explanations have proceeded on the psychological level alone. It has been argued that individuals who received insufficient mothering engage in heavy drinking in order to make up for the oral gratifications they were denied in infancy. Another theory holds that alcoholics are actually latent homosexuals who drink in order to repress feelings they know to be socially unacceptable. Still another explanation suggests that alcoholics are suicide-prone individuals who drink in order to satisfy the urge for self-destruction. In each case, alcoholism is explained in terms of a personality or character disorder traceable to defective parent–child relations. None of these explanations has the support of sufficient evidence.

Another explanation focuses on the idea of an "alcoholic personality." Alcoholics are presumably maladjusted, immature, dependent on others, negative in their views of themselves, suffering from guilt feelings, and incapable of tolerating tension and frustration. However, experts cannot agree on the precise traits characterizing the alcoholic. Nor have researchers been able to develop a list of personality traits that distinguish those who become alcoholics from those who do not.

Finally, it has been suggested that alcoholism is the outcome of a learning process. Certain individuals who are afflicted with deep-seated fears and anxieties learn that drinking can help reduce or eliminate such feelings. It is theorized that alcoholism springs from a basic human instinct to avoid pain and seek pleasure. According to this view, alcohol provides pleasure. However, learning theory does not explain why individuals continue to drink when they begin to suffer from the unpleasant physical, mental, and social effects of alcoholism.

Sociological Explanations

Earlier we mentioned the discovery of a relationship between cultural traditions associated with ethnic group membership and drinking practices. The prevalence of alcoholism is believed to vary among different ethnic populations within the United States, just as it varies among different societies. (For example, rates are high in the Soviet Union and low in Israel.)

Researchers who believe that cultural factors are responsible for alcoholism hypothesize that the alcoholism rate will be low among groups with well-established, well-known, and generally accepted drinking customs. In groups with ambivalence about drinking and the absence of group norms and controls pertaining to the use of alcohol, rates of alcoholism are expected to be high.[27] This hypothesis, which has not been fully tested, addresses overall differences between groups. But it does not address the question of why particular individuals may come to focus their lives on drinking. Even among

[26] See E. M. Jellinek, *The Disease Concept of Alcoholism* (New Haven, Conn.: Hillhouse Press, 1960).

[27] See National Institute of Mental Health, *Alcohol and Alcoholism*, pp. 15–16.

groups with well-established drinking customs, alcoholism occurs.

A second major sociological explanation involves the concept of labeling. (See Chapter 14 for discussion of the labeling perspective.) In this view alcoholism is no more than a label attached to persons whose drinking habits are defined as deviant.[28] A number of variables may be involved in determining whether someone will be labeled an alcoholic. These include the quantity, rate, and frequency of drinking; the effects of alcohol consumption on the individual; the reactions of others to the observed effects; the visibility of the drinker to labeling agents (such as police, medical personnel, and employers); the social class position of the drinker; and the effectiveness of formal and informal controls over the individual's drinking behavior.

The labeling approach thus implies that there is no identifiable alcoholic individual whose characteristics may be taken as representative of alcoholics in general. Indeed, we have already noted that experts cannot agree on a definition of alcoholism and that it is difficult to draw the line between problem drinking and alcoholism. But the labeling approach sidesteps the question of why an individual adopts the drinking behavior that is at issue. What is it that leads people toward patterns of alcohol use that may, under certain conditions, be labeled alcoholism?

Alcoholism and Problems in Living

Most experts seem to agree that heavy users of alcohol are engaged in a retreat from reality. According to the Cooperative Commission on the Study of Alcoholism:

> Much American drinking is of an "escapist" nature. That is, alcohol is used as a means of relieving boredom or emptiness, of getting away from authority and restrictions that are considered intolerable, or of overcoming feelings of inadequacy or inferiority.[29]

Thus, the abuse of consciousness-altering drugs—in this case, alcohol—may be viewed as a method by which unhappy people attempt to deal with problems in living.

Unfortunately, the use of alcohol for escape is a false haven. The negative effects often associated with heavy drinking may simply exacerbate the problems in living confronting troubled individuals. With nowhere else to turn, and having no other ways to retreat from unendurable realities, the drug becomes everything, and individuals are destroyed.

In recent years, the idea that alcoholism is a disease has become increasingly popular. For example, the federal government contends that "alcoholism is a treatable disease, not a failure of character."[30] This application of the medical model to alcoholism is in some ways progressive. In the past, alcoholics were likely to be treated as moral degenerates, and it is still common for Skid Row alcoholics to be jailed, rather than sympathetically doctored. Since alcoholism is often accompanied by real health problems, some drinkers need medical help to survive.

The problem with conceptualizing alcoholism as a disease is that the medical model implicitly suggests that only the alcoholic needs to be changed. The medical model thereby draws attention away from consideration of societal conditions that may generate problems in

[28] Sidney Cahn, *The Treatment of Alcoholics* (New York: Oxford University Press, 1970), pp. 36–37.

[29] Cooperative Commission on the Study of Alcoholism, *Alcohol Problems* (New York: Oxford University Press, 1967), p. 130.

[30] U.S. Department of Health and Human Services, *Alcohol and Health: Fourth Special Report*, p. ix. A recent Supreme Court ruling, however, seems to question this contention. See David G. Savage, "Alcoholics May Be Denied Some Veterans Administration Aid," *Los Angeles Times* (April 21, 1988): p. 1.

living and thus escape through alcohol abuse.[31] It is these conditions that must ultimately be changed if the phenomenon of alcoholism is to be eliminated—or at least seriously reduced.

EFFECTS OF ALCOHOL ABUSE

There are many costs associated with problem drinking and alcoholism, costs that both drinkers and nondrinkers are forced to bear. In this section we examine the effects of alcoholism on the alcoholic's family and health, on highway safety, and on crime and look at some of the monetary costs associated with alcohol abuse.[32]

Personal and Family Relationships

The impact of alcoholism often dramatically affects the alcoholic's relationships with other people, especially family members. Disruptions of family life due to alcohol abuse often end up costing the taxpayer money. Though actual figures are not available, and though many of the costs are nonmonetary, the National Institute on Alcohol Abuse and Alcoholism has observed:

> Unhappy marriages, broken homes, desertion, divorce, impoverished families, and deprived or displaced children are all parts of the toll. The cost to public and private helping agencies for support of families disabled by alcohol problems amounts to many millions of dollars a year.[33]

When we count family members, it has been estimated that tens of millions of Americans are caught in "alcohol's web."[34] This does not take the impact on friends, neighbors, and acquaintances into account. The personal anguish of many of these millions of people is surely no less tragic than the self-harm alcoholics and problem drinkers impose on themselves.

Robert J. Ackerman has drawn attention to the "unseen casualties"—children of alcoholics, most of whom are adolescents and preadolescents. In his words,

> Alcoholic behavior in the family can prohibit intimate involvement and clearly impede the development of essential family bonds. When children's emotional needs have been stunted by neglect or destroyed by cruelty, the traditional image of parents as mentors and guides for their offspring becomes a farce.[35]

Since it is estimated that 40–60 percent of the children of alcoholics are likely to develop drinking problems themselves, the impact of living in a family setting plagued by alcohol abuse may persist well beyond childhood and young adulthood.

Personal Health

Problem drinkers and alcoholics pay severe penalties for their drinking. It has been estimated that alcoholics are likely to die ten to twelve years sooner than nonalcoholics. Half die before the age of fifty, which is one reason there are so few elderly alcoholics. The mortality rate (that is, the number of persons per 100,000 who die each year) among alcoholics is more than two and a half times higher than that of the general population.

Alcoholics often die under violent circumstances; serious accidents, homicide, and suicide are not uncommon. This, together with the physical deterioration accompanying alcoholism, helps explain the limits on life expectancy. No one really knows how many deaths are directly attributable to drinking, and all such sta-

---

[31] See Richard S. Shore and John M. Luce, *To Your Health* (New York: Seabury Press, 1976), pp. 146–79, for a discussion of alcoholism as a disease.

[32] Most data in this section are from special reports to the U.S. Congress entitled *Alcohol and Health*.

[33] U.S. Department of Health, Education, and Welfare, *Facts About Alcohol and Alcoholism*, p. 16.

[34] National Institute of Mental Health, *Alcohol and Alcoholism*, p. 10.

[35] Robert J. Ackerman, *Children of Alcoholics* (Holmes Beach, Fla.: Learning Publications, 1978), p. 13.

PUBLIC PROBLEM, PRIVATE PAIN

Getting Hooked

Drinking problems often start with innocent behaviors that escalate into patterns which an individual cannot seem to find a way out of. In this selection a young woman tells how her alcoholism began and relates some of its aftermath.

I didn't know what an alcoholic was until I was already well on my way. I didn't know drinking could do bad things to you. I didn't know it could be addictive. I didn't see any of that. Nobody ever talked about it.

My father was in the stock market, the manager of a mutual fund. He did regularly have a couple of bourbons with his *Wall Street Journal* when he came home from his daily trip to New York City. But I don't believe he drank alcoholically. So, unlike so many alcoholics I've met who are themselves children of alcoholics, I am not.

There's sort of a feeling that alcoholism is something that wouldn't happen in the Connecticut town I grew up in. People in that town do not go to bars. In fact, I can't think of any bars offhand. They call their liquor stores "package stores" so they don't have to even use the word liquor.

Most people have their package store deliver by the case, so they're all drinking in the privacy of their homes and a lot of them probably dying in the privacy of their homes, from alcoholism.

My first run in with alcohol was when I was fifteen. My parents went somewhere for the evening and I decided to experiment, so I went into their liquor cabinet and poured myself a whole lot of booze, not knowing that you were supposed to mix it and put ice in it. I just poured everything into a glass and drank it and ended up throwing up and blacking out. From my very first drink I could never handle it. I never knew when to stop.

When my parents came home a few hours later, they found their darling daughter passed out in the bathroom. I was very sick and vowed the next day I would never touch it again. And I never did, for about another two years.

My parents made me go to an all-girls private high school, much against my will. I hated it and built up four years of resentment about all the fun and parties I was missing. What kept me going was my vow that I would make up for those four years as soon as I got to college.

In my senior year, when I was seventeen, I started dating seriously. The guy was a year older than I and had already started college. The two of us went to parties and drank *a lot.* For instance, we'd go to the drive-in with another couple. They'd take a six-pack of beer *between* them to last through two movies. We would take a six-pack of beer for *each* one of us. There was a difference in tolerance and we would make little jokes about drinking more than the other people and say that they couldn't hold it and weren't we terrific, not knowing that this is one of the very first signs of alcoholism—to be able to hold a lot of booze and not show it.

I kept dating the same guy when I went away to Cedar College, the very good, well-respected Ivy League school that gives you lots of social status. Nice girls went there, and even if people noticed that I came back from the dorm drunk—which I'm sure they did—or that I stayed out after curfew—which I'm sure they did—it was considered general college fun and not an alcohol problem, because nice girls who go to Cedar College don't become alcoholics.

It went without saying that drinking would go on throughout the weekend. We went to dances and drank. We structured our events around alcohol. If you want to have fun, you want to be where alcohol is. We hardly ever did anything that did not involve alcohol.

So when it came time to graduate, my best idea was to go on and get some more school and a master's degree. Of course, that's a very socially acceptable thing to do. It looked real good. My parents were certainly willing to pay for it. But the real reason I was doing it was because I was too scared to do anything else.

I was scared to death going to a brand new school where I didn't know anybody. I didn't have a lot of social skills. I really didn't know how to relate to people—I was very shy. But I knew that if I had a couple of drinks in me, I would be fine.

PUBLIC PROBLEM, PRIVATE PAIN (continued)

On the very first day at the university, when class was over, I started talking to one of the guys in my class, and he casually said, "How would you like to go out for a beer?" And I said I thought that would be a fine idea. I was looking for a socially accepted way to get back into drinking again. We ended up going to a bar.

If you're not an alcoholic, I don't know how to tell you this other than to say, I think there is some kind of invisible antenna whereby alcoholics can find each other. We sat there and drank for three hours and I knew in my heart this man drank like I did.

And that's how it works with alcoholic women. We seek out other people, particularly men, who drink like we do because then we don't have to feel guilty about our alcohol consumption. We don't have to worry about someone looking at us funny and saying, "Boy, you're certainly drinking a lot." Because someone else who's doing the same is not going to say that to me. In fact, he's not going to say anything at all. And that's how we get ourselves into crazy relationships that we have a hell of a time getting out of and which cause us to drink even more.

Source: From Emanuel Peluso and Lucy Silvay Peluso, eds., *Women & Drugs: Getting Hooked, Getting Clean*, pp. 19–21.

tistics are estimates. One reason for our limited knowledge is that many physicians do not report alcoholism as the main cause of death out of concern for the feelings of the family of the deceased.

Research on the physiological effects of alcoholism has increased in the last few years. Heavy drinking is known to be associated with various types of cancer, particularly among persons who also use tobacco. Alcohol abuse also increases the probability of hypertension, stroke, and coronary heart disease. Alcoholics frequently suffer illness and death from cirrhosis of the liver, a disease in which the liver becomes fatty, scarred, and incapable of functioning normally. In large urban areas, cirrhosis is the fourth most common cause of death among men aged twenty-five to forty-five.

Alcohol affects the brain, often permanently damaging the mental functioning of alcoholics. Drinking may reduce the number of living cells in the brain. Since brain cells do not grow back, alcoholics may suffer from organic psychosis (a mental illness traceable to brain damage), loss of memory, and poor physical and mental coordination. One out of four persons who are admitted to mental hospitals are diagnosed as alcoholics, and 40 percent of all admissions are alcohol related. Many of the alcoholic inmates are unlikely to recover.

The unborn children of female alcoholics are subject to harm from drinking in what is called *fetal alcohol syndrome*. Because alcohol tends to be a substitute for a balanced diet, alcoholics are often malnourished. Consequently, the infants of alcoholic women are likely to be less healthy and less well developed than other babies. Moreover, when a pregnant woman drinks, so, in effect, does her fetus. The newborn children of alcoholic women may die shortly after birth unless they are medically treated for the shock to their systems from suddenly being cut off from alcohol. Furthermore, the impact of alcohol on the woman and her fetus is a major cause of birth defects and organically based mental deficiency among the newborn. The effects of fetal alcohol syndrome on the children of female alcoholics are usually chronic and may be permanently disabling.

Clearly, it is not too much of an exaggeration

TABLE 16.2 Licensed Drivers, Fatal Motor Vehicle Accidents, and Alcohol Involvement, by Age of Driver, 1987

		Age of Driver							
Variable	Total	16–17 years	18–21 years	22–24 years	25–34 years	35–44 years	45–54 years	55–64 years	65 years and over
Licensed drivers (estimated, in thousands)	161,975	4,202	12,400	11,583	40,738	32,369	21,367	19,339	19,880
Percent distribution	100.0	2.6	7.7	7.2	25.2	20.0	13.2	11.9	12.3
Licensed drivers involved in fatal accidents	61,434*	3,326	8,874	6,513	16,554	9,774	5,472	4,221	5,078
Percent distribution	100.0*	5.4	14.4	10.6	26.9	15.9	8.9	6.9	8.3
Drinking drivers involved in fatal accidents	20,384*	798	3,534	2,966	6,889	3,067	1,225	767	511
Percent distribution	100.0*	3.9	17.3	14.6	33.8	15.0	6.0	3.8	2.5

*Includes ages unknown and less than 16 years old.

Source: U.S. Department of Commerce, Bureau of the Census, *Statistical Abstract of the United States, 1989* (Washington, D.C.: U.S. Government Printing Office, 1989), p. 600.

to say that alcohol kills and maims people. When abused, alcohol is a highly dangerous drug.

Highway and Other Accidents

Each year, street and highway accidents take the lives of about as many Americans as died in the ten years of direct U.S. military involvement in Vietnam. Of the 50,000 to 60,000 deaths due to highway accidents that occur annually, many are estimated to be alcohol related. (See Table 16.2.) Some of those killed, it is suspected, are the victims or the perpetrators of alcohol-related suicides, in which the suicidal individual uses the automobile as the death weapon.

In addition to this annual slaughter, roughly 35 percent of crashes producing serious injuries involve drinking drivers. Approximately a third of the pedestrians who die in traffic accidents each year are heavily under the influence of alcohol. (Presumably, some of these pedestrians may also be committing suicide.)

No other drug has been found to play such a key role in accidental deaths. Despite warnings by government and public affairs groups not to mix drinking and driving, the deaths continue. The situation is no doubt exacerbated by the fact that arrests for drunk driving remain so infrequent in comparison with the amount of drunk driving. By one estimate, the probability of being arrested for drunk driving is 1 in 2,000.[36]

In addition to motor vehicle-related accidents, drinking is a major cause of death and injuries in many other settings. Of the 18,000 deaths and 10 million injuries incurred through industrial accidents annually, 40–50 percent are alcohol related. Many noncommercial aviation accidents involve pilots who have been drinking. Alcohol use is said to be associated with well over half of all drowning deaths and an even higher percentage of deaths and injuries from falls. Most fatalities and nonfatal burns stemming from fire accidents involve alcohol use.

[36] Mark H. Moore and Dean R. Gerstein, eds., *Alcohol and Public Policy* (Washington, D.C.: National Academy Press, 1981), p. 84.

Consciousness of the dangers of alcohol use by drivers has begun to increase among teenagers. Deaths and injuries involving drivers, passengers, occupants of other vehicles, and pedestrians are often underscored in school alcohol education programs. In this photograph, high school students are cautioned about where drinking and driving may lead. *(Chris Brown/Stock, Boston)*

Crime

The use of alcohol is closely tied to certain types of criminal activity and is substantially responsible for the enormous number of arrests made in the United States. Not all alcoholics commit crimes. Not all problem drinkers commit crimes. Of those who do, not all are identified and arrested. Hence, alcohol-related crime statistics—like most other statistics on alcohol—are rough estimates.

Half of all murders and a third of all suicides involve drinking, and many thousands of people die annually as a result. Physical assaults, child abuse, rape, and other sex crimes are thought to be associated with alcohol use. So are acts of vandalism, arson, and other property crimes. (See Table 16.3.)

In 1988, some 13.8 million arrests were made in this country. About a third of these arrests were for law violations related to alcohol use: public drunkenness, disorderly conduct, vagrancy, violation of liquor laws, and drunken driving. To this we may add many other arrests for crimes against people and property in which alcohol use was involved.

All these arrests do not involve different individuals. Public drunkenness, for example, accounts for about half of all arrests in urban areas. Most public drunkenness arrests involve persons (e.g., in or near Skid Row districts) who are being repeatedly arrested and released. For such individuals, jail is a "revolving door." In general, a relatively small proportion of the drinking population accounts for the majority of alcohol-related arrests.

The popular television show, "Cheers," uses barroom relationships as a medium through which to probe humorously the human condition. Rarely does television probe the serious side of alcohol use, and the enormous costs it exacts, including those attributable to crime, accidents, lost work productivity, and family stress. *(AP/Wide World)*

Economic Effects

While the alcoholic beverage industry is prospering from the sales of its products and government is benefiting from alcohol-related tax revenues, alcohol abuse is costly to business, government, and, of course, individuals. One study suggested that the cost of alcohol abuse came to $117 billion in 1983 alone.[37]

Reduced job productivity among members of the labor force due to drinking costs the American economy $71 billion. Most of this is due to absenteeism, accidents, and inefficiency. This figure covers only male workers and is thus undoubtedly an understatement.

An estimated $15 billion goes to pay for medical problems attributable to drinking. The largest share of the money goes to cover the costs of hospitalization for alcohol-related health problems.

Premature deaths involving drinking (e.g., from accidents or disease) cost Americans another $18 billion.

We have already noted that criminal activity is often alcohol related. Crimes accounted for costs of $3 billion in 1983.

Finally, there are costs associated with the responses that segments of society make to alcohol abuse and its consequences. These costs include income maintenance payments (e.g., unemployment, welfare, workmen's compensation) and social services; public and private programs directly aimed at alcoholics and alcohol abusers; and highway safety and fire pro-

---

[37] See Henrick J. Harwood et al., *Economic Costs to Society of Alcohol and Drug Abuse and Mental Illness: 1980* (Research Triangle Park, N.C.: Research Triangle Institute, 1984).

TABLE 16.3 Alcohol Use Among Convicted Offenders Just Before Committing Current Offense, by Crime Type, United States, 1983

Current offense	Number convicted	Percentage of convicted persons who used alcohol
Total	**132,620**	**48**
Violent	32,112	54
Murder/attempted murder	3,345	49
Manslaughter	1,188	68
Rape/sexual assault	4,017	52
Robbery	11,945	48
Assault	9,609	62
Other violent*	2,008	49
Property	51,660	40
Burglary	17,335	44
Auto theft	2,960	51
Fraud/forgery/embezzlement	5,976	22
Larceny	18,001	37
Stolen property	3,676	45
Other property†	3,712	51
Drugs	13,181	29
Traffic	5,469	26
Possession	6,830	30
Other drugs	882	44
Public order	34,036	64
Weapons	2,769	32
Obstructing justice	6,856	43
Traffic	3,734	36
Driving while intoxicated‡	13,406	93
Drunkenness/morals offenses§	4,894	70
Other public order‖	2,377	28
Other#	1,008	40
Information unavailable	623	—

*Includes kidnaping, purse-snatching, hit-and-run driving, and child abuse.

†Includes arson, destruction of property, property damage from hit-and-run driving, and trespass.

‡Includes driving while intoxicated and driving under the influence of drugs.

§Also includes vagrancy and commercialized vice.

‖ Includes rioting, habitual offender, family-related offenses such as nonsupport or abandonment, invasion of privacy, and contributing to the delinquency of a minor.

#Includes juvenile offenses and unspecified offenses.

Source: U.S. Department of Health and Human Services, *Alcohol and Health: Sixth Special Report to the U.S. Congress* (Washington, D.C.: U.S. Government Printing Office, 1987), p. 13.

tection expenditures. All told, these add another $10 billion to the cost of alcohol abuse.

The conservative estimate of total costs for 1983—just one year—was, again, $117 billion. Adjusting for inflation, the costs annually now would be many billions higher. One recent estimate put the costs in 1990 at $130 billion and projected them to rise to $150 billion by 1995.[38] These are financial resources lost to society that could have been used for other purposes. The overall economic costs of alcoholism and alcohol abuse in general clearly dwarf the amounts being spent to study and combat this micro problem.

TYPES OF TREATMENT

Several different kinds of treatment are used in cases of alcoholism. These treatment procedures are directed at altering the physical and/or mental state of the alcoholic. Most of them fall within the context of the medical model, in which the alcoholic is considered ill and in need of being cured. Instead of attacking the societal conditions that may help produce and sustain alcoholism, efforts are made to help the drinker function within the prevailing order.[39]

The "cure rate" for alcoholism is not very high. When we use abstinence for more than three or five years as the criterion for cure, fewer than 20 percent of those treated are cured. If, on the other hand, the criterion is the ability of the alcoholic to maintain control over drinking *most* of the time, the cure rate approaches two-thirds of those treated. Moreover, treatment outcomes appear to be highly correlated with such factors as social class. Among socially stable middle-class alcoholics, treatment outcomes are relatively successful. Among the lower socio-

[38] Thomas R. Burke, "The Economic Impact of Alcohol Abuse and Alcoholism," *Public Health Reports*, 103 (November–December 1988): 564–68.

[39] U.S. Department of Health and Human Services, *Alcohol and Health: Fourth Special Report*, pp. 137–67.

economic strata, the rate of success tends to be quite low.

The chances for cure depend on the severity of the impact of alcohol on the individual. People who have not been severely affected are much more likely to control their drinking. Persons placed in mental hospitals to be treated for alcoholic psychoses, on the other hand, have only one chance in ten of being cured.

These statistics come from agencies and institutions involved in treatment. It is difficult to know if their claims of successful treatment are real or are instead somewhat inflated. Moreover, an estimated 85 percent of the millions of alcoholics and problem drinkers never come into contact with treatment facilities. So it is possible that those who are treated are either more—or less—amenable to "cure" than the untreated. (See Table 16.4 for some characteristics of those being treated.)

Physiological Treatment

Alcoholics who suddenly stop drinking often suffer from withdrawal symptoms, in which the body, having adjusted to large amounts of alcohol, reacts to the shock of abstinence. Common withdrawal symptoms include trembling, nausea, nervousness, and inability to sleep. Some alcoholics suffer from the DTs, delirium tremens, when they stop drinking. The DTs are often characterized by nightmarish hallucinations, serious convulsions, and feverishness. The individual may be terror-stricken, convinced that snakes or insects are crawling all over his or her body.

The most common method of dealing with withdrawal symptoms is to provide the alcoholic with tranquilizers, a balanced intake of liquids and solids, and bed rest. Once the individual's bodily system has undergone detoxification (i.e., is cleansed of alcohol), further medical treatments may be undertaken to handle physical and mental problems that remain.

Detoxification, or the drying out of an alcoholic, is not the same as eliminating the desire to drink. Thus, further treatment often consists of drugging alcoholics with more tranquilizers in the hope of relieving this desire. The difficulty here is that the tranquilizing drugs may themselves be no more than alcohol substitutes. The alcoholic simply seeks escape from reality through drug treatment.

Attempts have been made to cure alcoholism by using a drug (disulfiram, or Antabuse) that induces a deep, reflexive aversion to drinking. The deterrent drug causes headaches, violent nausea, and other physical discomforts whenever alcohol is ingested. The idea is to condition the alcoholic to associate drinking with physical agony and thus to promote abstinence. Deterrent drugs can only be used if the alcoholic is willing to be subjected to such unpleasant treatment. Also, some alcoholics manage to drink themselves beyond the deterrent effects. While deterrent drugs may create an aversion to alcohol, they do not necessarily remove the desire to escape reality.

In general, the physiological approach to treatment does not guarantee abstention from alcohol or the production of "cured" alcoholics. For such reasons, psychologically oriented treatments have also been developed to deal with this "illness."

Psychological Treatment

Psychological treatments for alcoholism are based on the premise that underlying character disorders or weaknesses cause the individual to drink. A variety of approaches are in use. At one extreme, therapists have experimented with LSD, a chemical agent that causes unusual hallucinations and other mental experiences, in the hope that alcoholics will gain insights while under the influence of the drug. The results of such experiments have been minimal.

At the other extreme is psychotherapy, in which alcoholics receive individual counseling

TABLE 16.4 Number and Percent Distribution of Alcoholism Clients, by Age, Sex, and Race/Ethnicity According to Inpatient–Outpatient Setting, October 30, 1987

	Inpatients		Outpatients		Total	
Demographic characteristics	Number	Percent	Number	Percent	Number	Percent
Age*						
Under 18 years	3,535	7.2	17,474	6.3	21,009	6.4
18–20 years	2,562	5.2	18,287	6.6	20,849	6.4
21–24 years	6,166	12.5	38,755	13.9	44,921	13.7
25–34 years	15,113	30.7	86,433	31.0	101,546	31.0
35–44 years	11,858	24.1	66,849	24.0	78,707	24.0
45–54 years	6,036	12.3	32,316	11.6	38,352	11.7
55–64 years	2,919	5.9	13,986	5.0	16,905	5.2
65 years and over	1,046	2.1	4,363	1.6	5,409	1.7
Subtotal	49,235	100.0	278,463	100.0	327,698	100.0
Unknown	2,444		20,097		22,541	
Total	51,679		298,560		350,239	
Units reporting	2,715		3,781		5,674	
Sex†						
Male	38,916	78.5	218,088	75.9	257,004	76.3
Female	10,641	21.5	69,232	24.1	79,873	23.7
Subtotal	49,557	100.0	287,320	100.0	336,877	100.0
Unknown	1,262		12,065		13,327	
Total	50,819		299,385		350,204	
Units reporting	2,714		3,782		5,674	
Race/ethnicity‡						
White	34,566	71.6	201,347	71.5	235,913	71.5
Black	8,379	17.4	42,584	15.1	50,963	15.4
Hispanic	3,195	6.6	29,422	10.4	32,617	9.9
Asian or Pacific Islander	188	0.4	1,503	0.5	1,691	0.5
American Indian or Alaskan native	1,837	3.8	5,746	2.0	7,583	2.3
Other	88	0.2	1,137	0.4	1,225	0.4
Subtotal	48,253	100.0	281,739	100.0	329,992	100.0
Unknown	2,532		17,247		19,779	
Total	50,785		298,986		349,771	
Units reporting	2,712		3,778		5,671	

[Sum of units reporting inpatients and outpatients does not equal total units reporting because units may offer both types of services. Column percentages are based on subtotal, excluding unknowns for age, race and sex. Percentages may not sum to 100 because of rounding.]

*Excludes data from units that did not report clients by age.

†Excludes data from units that did not report clients by sex.

‡Excludes data from units that did not report clients by race/ethnicity.

Source: U.S. Department of Health and Human Services, National Institute on Drug Abuse, *National Drug and Alcoholism Treatment Unit Survey* (Rockville, Md.: DHHS, 1989), p. 53.

and are encouraged to contemplate the deep-seated reasons why they drink. Efforts are made to urge the alcoholic to overcome the psychological problems for which drinking is thought to provide an escape. Psychotherapy is very expensive. And many persons who face problems in living find such attempts to suggest that they are to blame for their own troubles less than helpful.

Group therapy often takes place in hospitals, churches, and mental institutions. One organization that claims a high level of success in fostering abstention is Alcoholics Anonymous.[40] In group therapy, the alcoholic is encouraged to talk honestly with other persons who are trying to or have managed to abstain. The alcoholic thus finds others who have been "saved" from the harmful effects of drinking and enjoys the fellowship of a sympathetic group. Alcoholics Anonymous encourages alcoholics to put themselves in the hands of a higher power and to take encouragement from the experiences and expectations of other AA participants. While several hundred thousand people are presently involved with AA, the spiritual orientation is not attractive to many other alcoholics. Though it claims great success with those who seek out its services, AA—like alcoholism treatment programs generally—touches only a small percentage of those thought to be alcoholics or problem drinkers.

What Treatment Works Best?

As is evident from our discussion of treatment statistics and practices, no one really knows how to "cure" alcoholism. According to the National Institute on Alcohol Abuse and Alcoholism:

> There is no evidence that any particular type of therapist—physician, clergyman, Alcoholics Anonymous member, psychiatrist, psychologist, or social worker—will have better results than another. The chances of a successful outcome apparently depend more on the combination of right patient and right treatment.[41]

Existing approaches to treatment fail to take into account the possibility that alcoholism may be a response to societal conditions that do harm to people. Unless these conditions are dealt with, it can be very difficult for alcoholics and problem drinkers to confront life in a sober state.

According to Joel Fort and Christopher T. Cory:

> Drug use may be a way for society to keep people with dissatisfactions and frustrations doped up so that they cannot challenge society to eliminate injustice, oppression, political corruption, boring jobs, and unfair economic conditions.[42]

In other words, these experts believe that alcohol facilitates users' escapism, diverting people from struggling against the kinds of problems analyzed in the first part of this book. Presumably, the more people who seek escape from reality and from societal conditions that are intolerable, the more likely it is that such conditions will continue.

SUMMARY

The use of alcohol is a popular and acceptable activity in American society, even among the very young. Because alcohol is a drug, many heavy drinkers look to it to relieve depression and to escape problems in living that are intolerable when faced in a state of sobriety. One out of ten drinkers uses this drug so heavily that he or she may be labeled a problem drinker or alcoholic.

Experts disagree about what alcoholism is and why it exists, but most, using the medical model, blame the drinker for his or her own plight. Treatment approaches, both physiological and psychological, generally operate within the context of the medical model and attempt to alter the drinking behavior that is in question. Such approaches to alcoholism and problem drinking tend to bypass processes by which people are labeled alcoholics and do not take

---

[40] See Barry Leach, "Does Alcoholics Anonymous Really Work?," in Peter G. Bourne and Ruth Fox, eds., *Alcoholism: Progress in Research and Treatment* (New York: Academic Press, 1973), pp. 245–84. See also Ernest Katz, *Not-God: A History of Alcoholics Anonymous* (Center City, Minn.: Hazeldon Educational Services, 1979).

[41] U.S. Department of Health, Education, and Welfare, *Facts About Alcohol and Alcoholism*, p. 24.

[42] Joel Fort and Christopher T. Cory, *American Drugstore* (Boston: Educational Associates, 1975), p. 61.

into consideration the societal conditions that may drive people to drink.

Meanwhile, massive costs are generated as a consequence of such drinking behavior—both for the individual drinker and for American society as a whole. But despite these costs, the alcoholic beverage industry continues to promote and profit from the drug it markets, and the government amasses huge tax revenues from alcohol production and use. Resources devoted to combating the costs associated with America's drinking practices are negligible in comparison with the profits and tax revenues collected. And alcoholism remains this society's number one health problem and a self-harmful means of escapism from the status quo.

DISCUSSION QUESTIONS

1. Are you a user of alcoholic beverages? Why?
2. Does anyone you know appear to meet the criteria for being an alcoholic or problem drinker? How would you explain this person's drinking behavior?
3. What arguments could be made for and against making alcoholic beverages available for purchase by persons of any age?
4. Examine a sample of advertisements for alcoholic beverages. What do these advertisements suggest, directly or indirectly, about the types of people who drink and the benefits of alcohol use?
5. If you normally drink at parties, bars, discos, etc., arrive at one of these settings late in the evening completely sober. How does the behavior of others appear to you when you stand back and view it as an uninvolved observer?
6. Visit a meeting of a local chapter of Alcoholics Anonymous. Summarize the impact of alcoholism on those persons who speak out at the meeting. Compare your impressions with the impressions of your classmates.

SUGGESTED READINGS

Cahalan, Don. *Understanding America's Drinking Problem* (San Francisco: Jossey-Bass Publishers, 1987).
The scope of alcohol abuse, failure of efforts to control it, and suggestions for what else might be done.

Greeley, Andrew M., et al. *Ethnic Drinking Subcultures* (New York: Praeger Publishers, 1980).
Drinking practices among different ethnic groups, showing how group norms may affect alcohol use and abuse.

Jacobson, Michael, et al. *The Booze Merchants* (Washington, D.C.: Center for Science in the Public Interest, 1983).
The contributions made by the alcoholic beverage industry in promoting the desirability of alcohol use.

Lender, Mark Edward, and James Kirby Martin. *Drinking in America: A History* (New York: The Free Press, 1982).
Americans' love affair with this mind-altering drug is traced back through time, indicating the issue of alcohol abuse is by no means new.

McConville, Brigid. *Women Under the Influence* (New York: Schocken Books, 1985).
The growing problem of alcohol abuse among women, as the number of female drinkers has grown.

Orford, Jim, and Judith Harwin, eds. *Alcohol and the Family* (New York: St. Martin's Press, 1982).
Alcoholism's "hidden victims"—implications for family members of the presence of a problem drinker in the household.

CHAPTER 17

Drug Abuse

Members of American society should be at peace with themselves and with one another. The vicarious rewards associated with drug abuse should have no attraction.

The use and abuse of drugs have become matters of particular public concern during the last twenty-five years. As people—particularly young adults and adolescents—use drugs for nonmedical purposes, moral, medical, legal, and political issues have emerged. Most of these issues revolve around the so-called problem drugs that are readily available through illicit channels. These include marijuana, heroin, cocaine, LSD and other hallucinogens, and "speed" (methamphetamine).

Paradoxically, far less controversy and attention surround the abuse of prescription drugs and over-the-counter preparations. Stimulants, barbiturates, and tranquilizers are used often for nonmedical reasons. Sociologist Charlotte Muller has characterized the United States as an "overmedicated society" in recognition of the degree to which drugs have become an important sought after adjunct to the daily lives of millions of people.[1] Although there has been some decrease in the abuse of legal drugs in recent years, it still remains an important problem.

A discussion of drug use would be incomplete without mention of the use of drugs for social control. In schools, mental institutions, nursing homes, and a variety of other settings, drugs are viewed as an appropriate means of controlling potentially disruptive people. They have been used as a tool in covert intelligence operations, and there are even drugs that can be used as weapons in warfare.

Our emphasis in this chapter is on self-administered drugs. We begin with a discussion of the difficulties involved in defining the term *drug*. Then we examine the nature and extent of abuse of some illegal and legal drugs. Finally, we look at explanations for drug use and abuse, briefly addressing the problem of the administration of drugs for social control.

WHAT IS A DRUG?

The term *drug* is subject to a wide variety of meanings and uses, each of which includes or excludes certain substances. From a strictly scientific perspective, a drug is typically defined as "any substance other than food which by its chemical nature affects the structure or function of the living organism."[2] This definition is overwhelmingly broad—under it, even air and water could qualify as drugs. By contrast, medical practitioners ordinarily use the term to mean substances appropriate for use in treating physical and mental illness or disease. In other words, to doctors drugs are medicines. Finally, from a legal point of view, a drug is any substance that is so defined under the law. Thus, law enforcement personnel may use the term quite differently from scientists and physicians.

Sociologist Erich Goode, an expert on drug use, has asked whether it is possible to arrive at an objective definition that would spell out just what a drug is and is not. In other words, is there any basis on which one could easily distinguish drugs from nondrugs, so that everyone will agree on the meaning of the term? According to Goode, there is not: "There is no effect that is common to all 'drugs' that at the same time is not shared by 'nondrugs.' "[3] Instead, any and all substances that are designated as drugs are *socially defined* as such. Society, or some segment of society, labels a substance as a drug, and the "social definition shapes attitudes toward the class of substances so described."[4]

What, then, distinguishes the so-called problem drugs from other drugs and from substances that have not been labeled as drugs? The answer is nothing—nothing, that is, except a different and more negative social definition. This social definition does not necessarily have anything to do with hazards or dangers potentially associated with the use and abuse of a substance. For example, there is one drug that

> has been massively used for decades; its mechanism of action on the brain and other organs is unknown; it accounts for thousands of deaths and illnesses each year, and it produces not only chromosomal breakage, but actual birth defects in lower animals.[5]

This sounds like a description of a problem drug, but actually the substance is aspirin—which most people probably do not consider a drug at all. Aspirin is associated with far more known health difficulties than, for example, marijuana.

The importance of social definition is indicated by the results of a poll conducted for the National Commission on Marihuana and Drug

[1] Charlotte Muller, "The Overmedicated Society," *Science*, 176 (May 5, 1972): 488–92.

[2] National Commission on Marihuana and Drug Abuse, *Drug Use in America* (Washington, D.C.: U.S. Government Printing Office, 1973), p. 9.

[3] Erich Goode, *Drugs in American Society*, 3rd ed. (New York: Alfred A. Knopf, 1989), p. 22.

[4] Ibid., p. 23.

[5] Joel Fort, *The Pleasure Seekers* (Indianapolis: The Bobbs-Merrill Co., 1969), p. 5.

Abuse. In a national sampling of adults, 95 percent regarded heroin as a drug, and 80 percent labeled marijuana a drug. Only 39 percent regarded alcohol as a drug, and even fewer adults—27 percent—thought that tobacco products deserved this label.[6] While there is no objective and meaningful basis for making such distinctions, the social definitions prevailing in the United States place alcohol and tobacco outside the realm of drug status, and thus not a part of the drug problem.

Social definitions of problem drugs frequently change over time. Within American society, different groups commonly disagree over such definitions. This has been the case with such addictive drugs as morphine and heroin.[7] Morphine first began to be used in the United States in the 1850s. As its pain-relieving qualities became known, its use increased—particularly during and after the Civil War. Physicians enthusiastically endorsed the drug, and medicine companies included morphine in a variety of home remedies. An estimated 2 to 4 percent of the population was addicted by the end of the nineteenth century. While a number of doctors had grown concerned about morphine addiction by that time, neither the press nor the public saw morphine or addiction to it as a problem.

At the beginning of the twentieth century, heroin was introduced into the United States. Physicians found it to be a stronger pain-reliever than morphine, and they believed heroin to be nonaddictive. Use of heroin quickly spread. Like morphine, it could be purchased without a prescription. Before the addictive qualities of heroin became known, the number of drug addicts in the United States further increased. Still, addiction was not viewed in a negative manner by the public.

[6] National Commission on Marihuana and Drug Abuse, *Drug Use in America*, p. 10.

[7] See David F. Musto, "The American Disease: Narcotics in Nineteenth Century America," in Maureen E. Kelleher et al., eds., *Drugs and Society: A Critical Reader*, 2nd ed. (Dubuque, Iowa: Kendall/Hunt Publishing Company, 1988), pp. 2–14.

In the early 1900s, a small group of concerned doctors began pressing for government regulation of addictive drugs. New York passed the first major piece of state legislation in 1904, and other states followed. In 1914 Congress approved the Harrison Narcotic Act. This act regulated the production and distribution of addictive drugs and required users to obtain them by prescription from physicians. Doctors were flooded with prescription-seekers and were soon refusing to supply addicts.

As subsequent drug laws further restricted or eliminated legal sources for addictive drugs, a flourishing black market emerged in which organized crime came to play an important role. When morphine and heroin became associated with crime and the underworld, public sentiment shifted against the addict and the drugs that were once available in respectable drugstores. Additional changes in the social definition of heroin are currently under way. The federal government has approved experimentation with heroin in the treatment of people who are in terrible pain, such as terminal cancer patients.

Because so many different types of substances can be defined as drugs, it is necessary to limit any discussion of drug use to particular types of drugs. In this chapter, we focus on *psychoactive substances*, drugs that may affect the minds of those who consume them.

ILLEGAL SUBSTANCES

In a survey commissioned by the U.S. Department of Health and Human Services in 1988, some 72.5 million Americans admitted to having engaged in illegal drug use at one or another point in their lives. Twenty-eight million had done so in the preceding year. Of those, half had used illegal drugs in the last month.[8]

On the surface it would appear that America was in the midst of an unprecedented drug-use

[8] U.S. Department of Health and Human Services, *National Household Survey on Drug Abuse: 1988* (Washington, D.C.: U.S. Government Printing Office, 1989), p. 17.

epidemic. The figures are indeed very high, indicating millions of members of U.S. society may be drug dependent, but the 1988 data represent a substantial *decrease* in illegal drug use.[9] These data, based on a survey of households, are substantiated by trends in drug use found among high school seniors. In 1988, high school seniors' use of illegal drugs was found to be at the lowest level since these surveys began in 1975.[10]

The overall downward trend no doubt reflects a number of factors. Americans have become much more concerned with health and fitness in recent years, and thus more attuned to the risks associated with certain types of drug use. The mass media have exploited the human suffering and criminal activity with which illegal drugs have become popularly associated. Celebrities have contributed to public discourse as they admit to drug problems and seek treatment, appear in anti–drug-use commercials, or even tragically die. And our politicians have adopted drug abuse as a major focal concern, both appealing to public fears and promising to take steps to alleviate them.

As we shall see here, however, not all trends are downward. There are indications of increased use of "crack," a highly addictive form of cocaine. Heroin use appears to be remaining stable. Use of methamphetamine ("speed") may be increasing, after a period of slowdown. It is clear that despite the overall downward trend, huge problems remain.

In this section we focus on select problem drugs—that is, illegal substances that are self-administered (knowingly and purposely used). Among the substances around which a great deal of fear and concern have arisen are marijuana, heroin, cocaine, LSD, PCP, and amphetamines.

[9] Michael Isikoff, "'Casual' Use of Drugs Found to Drop Sharply," *Washington Post* (August 1, 1989): 1.

[10] "High School Seniors' Drug Use Hits Record Low," *National Institute on Drug Abuse Notes*, 4 (Spring/Summer 1989): 34.

Marijuana

Marijuana is the most widely used illegal substance in the United States. The source of marijuana is the *Cannabis sativa* plant, and its potency, in terms of its potential effects on users, stems largely from tetrahydracannabinol, or THC, a chemical ingredient found in a resin exuded from the plant. Because marijuana can have differing amounts of THC, it is difficult to generalize about the effects of the drug on any particular user. Obviously, the smaller the THC content, the milder the effects of the drug.

Effects of Marijuana Use. Most marijuana users smoke the leaves, stems, and other parts of the *Cannabis sativa* plant. Some users ingest the drug orally—for example, by mixing it with food. Marijuana often causes

> mild euphoria; stimulation of the central nervous system and increased conviviality. The user experiences a pleasant heightening of the senses and relaxed passivity. In moderate doses the substance can cause short lapses of attention and slightly impaired memory and motor functioning. Heavy users have been known to become socially withdrawn and depersonalized and have experienced distortions of the senses.[11]

Despite the claims often made in the popular media, major scientific reviews of the impact of marijuana on health remain inconclusive. This is largely due to the fact that widespread use of the drug in the United States is relatively recent, and carefully controlled scientific studies using human subjects are few. Nonetheless, concern has been expressed by scientists over suspected or potential effects in the following areas: impairment of thinking, learning, and performance of complex tasks; deterioration in lung functioning, leading to cancer or lung disease; reductions in male fertility; de-

[11] National Commission on Marihuana and Drug Abuse, *Drug Use in America*, p. 158.

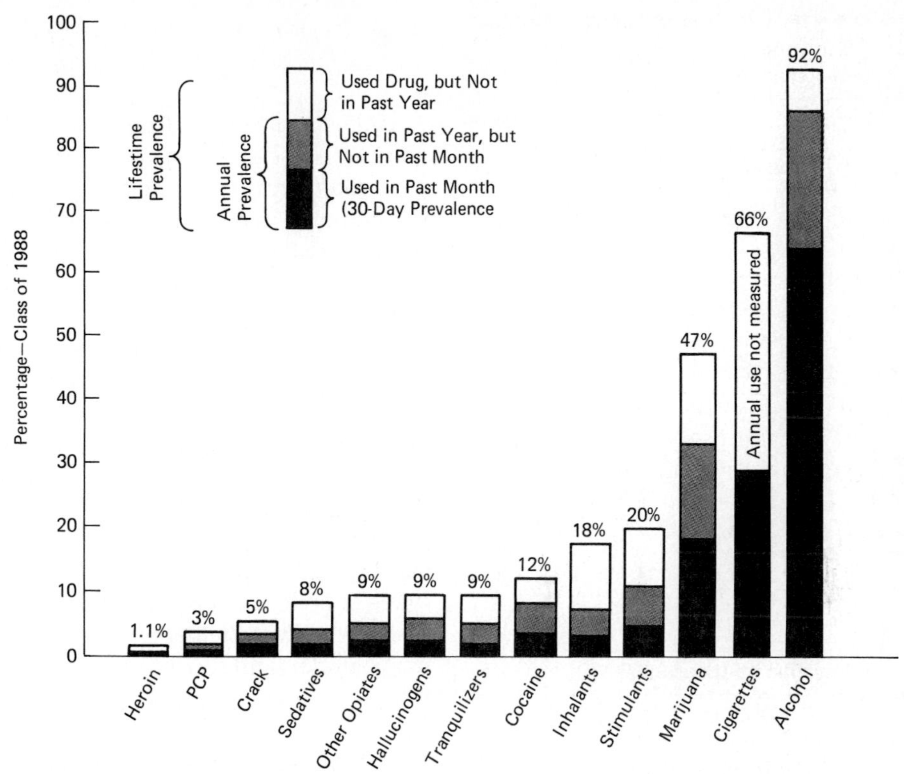

FIGURE 17.1 Prevalence and Recency of Use of Thirteen Types of Drugs, High School Class of 1988
Source: Lloyd D. Johnston et al., U.S. Department of Health and Human Services, *Drug Use, Drinking, and Smoking: National Survey Results from High School, College, and Young Adult Populations, 1975–1988* (Washington, D.C.: U.S. Government Printing Office, 1989), p. 33.

terioration in heart functioning; and decreases in the body's immune response to illness and disease. Evidence to date in these areas has led the U.S. Department of Health and Human Services to conclude "the use of marijuana is a serious public health concern."[12]

Unlike many other substances, including a large number of legal drugs, marijuana is not a lethal drug. There are no documented cases of deaths directly attributable to unadulterated marijuana, which suggests that lethal overdoses are highly unlikely even among the heaviest users. Nor is marijuana physically addictive. Users do not suffer compulsive cravings, and most individuals may at any time cease to employ the drug without suffering physical discomfort. Extremely heavy users may suffer temporary, mild withdrawal symptoms.

The question of whether marijuana is psychologically addictive—or whether users can become psychologically dependent on marijuana use—has been the subject of much debate. In the absence of firm evidence, particularly on the effects of long-term use, the answer seems to

[12] National Institute on Drug Abuse, *Marijuana and Health: Ninth Report to the U.S. Congress* (Washington, D.C.: U.S. Government Printing Office, 1982).

TABLE 17.1 Illicit Drug Use,* by Sex and Age Groups for Total Population

Age and sex	Ever used	Used past year (1988)	Used past month
	Rate		
12–17 years	24.7%	16.8%	9.2%
Male	23.7	15.8	9.5
Female	25.7	17.9	8.9
18–25 years	58.9	32.0	17.8
Male	58.8	36.8	21.8
Female	59.1	27.3	14.1
26–34 years	64.2	22.6	13.0
Male	69.9	27.9	16.4
Female	58.8	17.6	9.6
35 years and over	23.0	5.8	2.1
Male	26.8	6.4	2.5
Female	19.7	5.2	1.8
Total	36.6	14.1	7.3
Male	40.0	16.4	9.0
Female	33.4	12.0	5.8
	Population (in thousands)		
12–17 years	5,005	3,404	1,866
Male	2,458	1,635	983
Female	2,547	1,769	883
18–25 years	17,491	9,485	5,290
Male	8,513	5,332	3,151
Female	8,978	4,153	2,138
26–34 years	24,768	8,730	5,008
Male	13,257	5,292	3,119
Female	11,510	3,439	1,888
35 years and over	25,232	6,351	2,316
Male	13,681	3,275	1,272
Female	11,551	3,076	1,044
Total	72,496	27,971	14,479
Male	37,909	15,534	8,525
Female	34,587	12,436	5,954

*Illicit drugs include marijuana, nonmedical use of psychotherapeutics, inhalants, cocaine, hallucinogens, and heroin.

Source: U.S. Department of Health and Human Services, *National Household Survey on Drug Abuse: 1988* (Washington, D.C.: U.S. Government Printing Office, 1989), p. 17.

be that it is nonaddictive. Those who use the drug regularly do so because they find it to be pleasurable, just as people enjoy regular exercise or reading. Though a minority of marijuana users employ the drug repeatedly, this is no more a sign of addiction than is the fact that men seem "addicted" to wearing pants every day.

Unlike some other drugs, including alcohol, marijuana use does not cause people to engage in serious forms of antisocial behavior, including crime. It is not associated with aggressive or violent activity. The only criminality associated with marijuana is a matter of its illegality—the fact that possession, distribution, and sale of marijuana are against the law.

In recent years efforts have been made to explore possible uses of marijuana or THC, its key chemical ingredient, in the treatment of medical problems. Research has been under way in treatment of glaucoma (an eye disease that can lead to blindness), nausea accompanying cancer chemotherapy, asthma, as well as certain types of epileptic seizures and nervous system disorders. The federal government grows marijuana under tight security to ensure quality control for research purposes.

Extent of Marijuana Use. Over 65 million Americans are estimated to have used marijuana at least once. The greatest amount of experimentation with this drug has taken place in the last twenty-five years or so. During the past several years, national surveys have shown a sharp decrease in marijuana use. For the most part, those who experiment with or regularly use marijuana are under thirty-five years of age.

According to a 1988 survey commissioned by the U.S. Department of Health and Human Services, 17.4 percent of all youth and about 60 percent of young adults have used marijuana. All such figures are estimates. Many Americans prefer to conceal their participation in what remains illicit activity, even when anonymity is virtually guaranteed. Conversely, others may think that it is "in" to say that they have used the drug even if they haven't, since marijuana use is so widespread.

As was mentioned earlier, marijuana is the most commonly used illegal drug. Arrest rates remain high and criminal justice agencies have at times become choked with those caught participating in the victimless crime of marijuana possession. Efforts to identify and restrict domestic and foreign sources of marijuana have not been notably successful. About 60 percent of the marijuana reaching the U.S. market comes from Colombia and Mexico, with much smaller amounts filtering in from Jamaica and Southeast Asia. The federal government has been stepping up efforts to interdict incoming shipments and encouraging eradication programs in exporting nations. While little has resulted from such efforts, neither has the federal government been able to halt domestic production. Almost half of all marijuana consumed in the United States is domestically grown. Indeed, the U.S. Drug Enforcement Agency estimates production of marijuana by U.S. growers increased in the 1980s. Ironically, marijuana may be the most valuable crop cultivated in the United States.[13]

Eleven states (containing about a third of America's population) have taken steps toward the decriminalization of marijuana possession, establishing minimal penalties on a level with a traffic offense. However, it has not been legalized in any community. The prevailing social definition still holds that marijuana is a problem drug.

Heroin

Heroin is a derivative of morphine, which itself is derived from opium, a substance found in the *Papaver somniferum* poppy plant. There are several other opiate (opium-derived) drugs. Most heroin used in the United States originates in Southwest and Southeast Asia and in Mexico. Once imported, the substance is distributed and sold to users under the auspices of organized crime. The distribution network today includes organized crime groups of a variety of ethnic origins, many of whom retain personal and business ties with foreign producers and exporters in their nations of origin.

Effects of Heroin Use. Much like marijuana, the heroin available to users often varies in potential potency. Before it is sold to individual consumers, heroin is ordinarily "cut" or adulterated with other substances, such as milk sugar, at a number of stages during distribution. The drug is most commonly injected into the bloodstream with a needle and syringe (although it may also be sniffed, smoked, or ingested orally), and the variable potency can be a cause of fatal overdoses. Users who unknowingly purchase a unit of heroin that is relatively pure or unadulterated may die immediately upon injecting it because their bodies cannot tolerate the drug's strength. So it is not surprising that the death rate among heroin users is substantially higher than that of nonusers in the same age groups.

The effects of heroin are thought to vary. Nevertheless, most regular users report pleasurable experiences with the drug. Upon injecting it, many users experience a "rush" or wave of sensations somewhat like an intense sexual orgasm. The rush does not last long and is followed by a mild sense of euphoria, the relaxation of tensions, and the disappearance of any physical pains.

Users who take heroin repeatedly develop *tolerance* to it. This means that they must use larger and larger doses in order to achieve pleasurable effects. Tolerance also means that users must take a greater volume of the drug (or stronger dosages) to ward off discomfort similar to that which occurs when heroin use is suddenly discontinued. Increasing the frequency of use and the amounts used exposes individuals to greater risks of overdose.

Heroin and the other opiates are physically addictive. Heroin addicts who stop using the

[13] See Mary H. Cooper, "The Business of Illicit Drugs," *Editorial Research Reports*, 1 (May 20, 1988): 266–67.

drug suffer from serious withdrawal symptoms, including cramps, nausea, muscle tremors, diarrhea, chills, and extreme nervousness. Withdrawal symptoms typically begin abating after two or three days and are generally gone within a week. But many addicts make the withdrawal symptoms disappear almost instantaneously by taking more heroin—or even other opiates. Thus some heroin users are literally driven toward continued use of heroin to avoid the pain of withdrawal.[14] Besides being physically addicted, regular heroin users may also be psychologically "hooked" in the sense that every waking hour may be spent planning for and ensuring a dependable drug supply.

In recent years a number of long-held myths concerning heroin and its users have begun to be dispelled. For example, the drug apparently does not cause physiological damage (apart from the tragedy of accidental overdose). Though many heroin users are malnourished, this seems to be due to their lack of interest in any pleasures (including eating) other than those associated with the drug itself. Common diseases among heroin users, such as hepatitis and tetanus, are a result of the use of unsanitary paraphernalia—as when several persons share the same needles. As will be discussed later, shared needles are also a means by which AIDS virus is transmitted. Other common illnesses, like pneumonia, are thought to be related to the frenetic life-styles of addicts, who concentrate on the search for a "fix" and lack concern for health and well-being. This is not to say that heroin use is safe. But taken correctly, heroin does not—so far as we know now—damage the human organism. One need only think of the numerous doctors and nurses who have been addicted to one or another opiate drug for years and who continue to function into old age.

[14] Nonetheless, the top priority of all users is to get high. See William E. McAuliffe and Roberta A. Gordon, "A Test of Lindesmith's Theory of Addiction," *American Journal of Sociology*, 79 (January 1974): 795–840.

Heroin and Crime. It has long been believed that heroin causes users to engage in criminal acts. This is not the case. Most heroin addicts—at least those known to law enforcement agencies—had embarked on criminal activity well before becoming hooked. Nevertheless, though heroin itself does not cause crime, the drive to maintain a constant supply of the drug may require breaking the law. Heroin is expensive, primarily because those who market it take advantage of their monopoly position. Users often cannot afford to maintain their drug habits on the wages they could earn on a job. Thus, property crimes such as robbery and burglary may become a way of life. Property crimes committed by heroin users are thought to cost victims hundreds of millions of dollars annually.

Heroin does not, in and of itself, make users aggressive or prone to violence. Involvement in, for example, rapes, murders, and assaults is far more common among users of alcohol. But addicts who are desperate to get money to feed their habit may resort to violence if the victim of, say, a robbery attempt fights back.

Extent of Heroin Use. There are probably between 500,000 and 1,000,000 heroin addicts in the entire United States. This is a rough estimate. In addition to those who are addicted, there may be two to three times as many occasional users—so-called heroin chippers, whose existence belies the stereotype that all users are "hooked" and unable to control their use of the drug. Regular and persistent initial use must precede addiction.

Heroin addicts are likely to be young, male, and residents of large metropolitan areas.[15] A federally sponsored survey in 1988 found that 1.9 million Americans have used heroin. Un-

[15] John A. O'Donnell et al., *Young Men and Drugs* (Rockville, Md.: National Institute on Drug Abuse, 1976), pp. vii–viii. See also Richard R. Clayton and Harwin L. Voss, *Young Men and Drugs in Manhattan* (Rockville, Md.: National Institute on Drug Abuse, 1981).

like marijuana, whose use has recently gone down, heroin has continued to hold relatively steady appeal.

Law enforcement efforts have had limited impact on the marketing and consumption of heroin. Police have generally concentrated on finding easily identified users and small dealers. They have not been effective in attacking foreign producers' hold over the heroin market. The people who control the import, distribution, and sale of heroin make so much money that it is well worth it to bribe and corrupt customs inspectors and police. Periodic federal efforts to stem the international traffic in heroin have not yielded significant restrictions in domestic supplies. The poppies that supply opiates are a cash crop in some economically underdeveloped societies, and governments in these societies are generally reluctant to outlaw poppies—and thus contribute to their own demise—in the interest of limiting America's heroin usage.

Cocaine

Cocaine is a drug derived from the leaves of the coca plant, *Erythroxylon coca.* The plant grows in remote areas around the Andes Mountains in South America. Peru, Bolivia, Colombia, and Equador are the principal nations in which coca plants are cultivated. Most of the initial processing of the leaves takes place in these nations; however, the task of shipping and smuggling cocaine into the United States is largely carried out by a small number of criminal cartels in Colombia. These organizations have now expanded their activities to include direct involvement in the distribution of cocaine across the United States.

The whole cycle begins with the harvesting and initial processing of the coca leaves. From this processing comes coca paste, a product that may be smoked in marijuana or tobacco cigarettes. Typically, however, the paste is processed further to produce cocaine, which is usually in the form of a white crystalline powder. Light in weight and odorless, it is easily concealed and transported. While some of the smuggling entails shipment by boat, much comes in the form of delivery by air. Large shipments are broken down and delivered by car and truck across the U.S.–Mexican border.

Effects of Cocaine. Cocaine is a stimulant (as are nicotine, caffeine, and amphetamines).[16] It quickly acts on the central nervous system to produce a sense of euphoria, feelings of power and mastery, replacement of fatigue with limitless energy, and heightened sexual drive. This "high" is experienced as extremely pleasurable, although short-lived (from minutes to an hour or so, depending on how the drug is introduced, the dosage, and other factors). It is followed by an equally steep drop in feelings of psychological and physical well-being. Regular users develop, in many cases, tolerance to the drug. They require larger, more frequent, or more purified dosages to obtain the desirable results and to escape the anxiety and agitation that follow the cocaine high.

Most people who use cocaine inhale the crystalline powder. Other users, seeking more rapid and intense effects, inject themselves intravenously with a cocaine solution. The quickest and most dramatic results are obtained through smoking. By treating cocaine with volatile chemicals such as ether, users create cocaine "freebase." When heated, freebase gives off vapors that can be "smoked" (typically in a water pipe). Cocaine can also be processed with baking soda and water to form a solid known as "crack," which is easily smoked. Crack is less expensive for cocaine users to purchase than the powder, and its sharply increased use in recent years has drawn particular outcries of alarm from those who work in the fields of health and criminal justice.

---

[16] This section draws heavily on publications of the National Institute on Drug Abuse.

TABLE 17.2 Frequency of Use of Cocaine* Within Past Year (1988), by Sex and Age Groups for Total Population

Age and sex	At least once	12 or more times	Once a week or more
	Rate		
12–17 years	2.9%	1.1%	0.5%
Male	3.0	0.9	0.6
Female	2.9	1.4	—†
18–25 years	12.1	4.2	1.0
Male	15.1	5.8	1.5
Female	9.2	2.7	0.6
26–34 years	8.0	2.1	1.0
Male	11.2	2.7	1.7
Female	4.9	1.5	0.3
35 years or more	0.9	—†	—†
Male	1.3	—†	—†
Female	0.5	—†	—†
Total	4.1	1.2	0.4
Male	5.6	1.6	0.7
Female	2.8	0.8	0.2
	Population (in thousands)		
12–17 years	591	222	95
Male	308	88	60
Female	283	135	—†
18–25 years	3,584	1,246	304
Male	2,181	837	210
Female	1,403	408	94
26–34 years	3,089	813	367
Male	2,123	512	319
Female	967	302	49
35 years or more	945	—†	—†
Male	665	—†	—†
Female	280	—†	—†
Total	8,208	2,405	862
Male	5,276	1,542	666
Female	2,932	863	196

*Cocaine includes crack.

†Low precision; no estimates reported.

Source: U.S. Department of Health and Human Services, *National Household Survey on Drug Abuse: 1988* (Washington, D.C.: U.S. Government Printing Office, 1989), p. 111.

Cocaine use poses a variety of serious physical and psychological dangers. Regular users have been found to suffer from damage to the nasal membranes and lungs, possible neural damage, seizures and previously undiagnosed epilepsy, angina and irregular heartbeat, ruptured blood vessels and strokes, liver damage, and other problems. Overdoses can cause a shutdown of the user's respiratory system, convulsions, and seriously disturbed heart rhythms—all leading to instant death. Some users have died after using less of the drug than was their routine on previous occasions. "Crack babies," with severe health problems and disabilities, are born to pregnant female users. AIDS has emerged among cocaine users who share needles for intravenous injection and/or engage in sexual activity with multiple partners in exchange for money and cocaine.

Psychological dependence at a level tantamount to addiction is common among heavy users: people's lives come to revolve obsessively around the acquisition and use of cocaine much as is the case with those "hooked" on heroin. But there are other negative psychological effects, including depression, anxiety, short-temperedness, irrational suspicion of others, impaired concentration, and loss of interest in work and home responsibilities. Among heavy users, even food and sex ultimately come to be ignored in favor of pursuit of the cocaine high. For some, a "cocaine psychosis" occurs. Delusions and hallucinations, accompanied by violent behavior directed at imagined persecutors, are among the symptoms. Cocaine's effects can be such that people lose their jobs, rupture relationships with friends and family, sacrifice their homes and other assets—all to gain the transitory pleasure associated with drug taking.

Extent of Cocaine Use. According to a 1988 survey commissioned by the U.S. Department of Health and Human Services, nearly 25 percent of young adults and 3.4 percent of young-

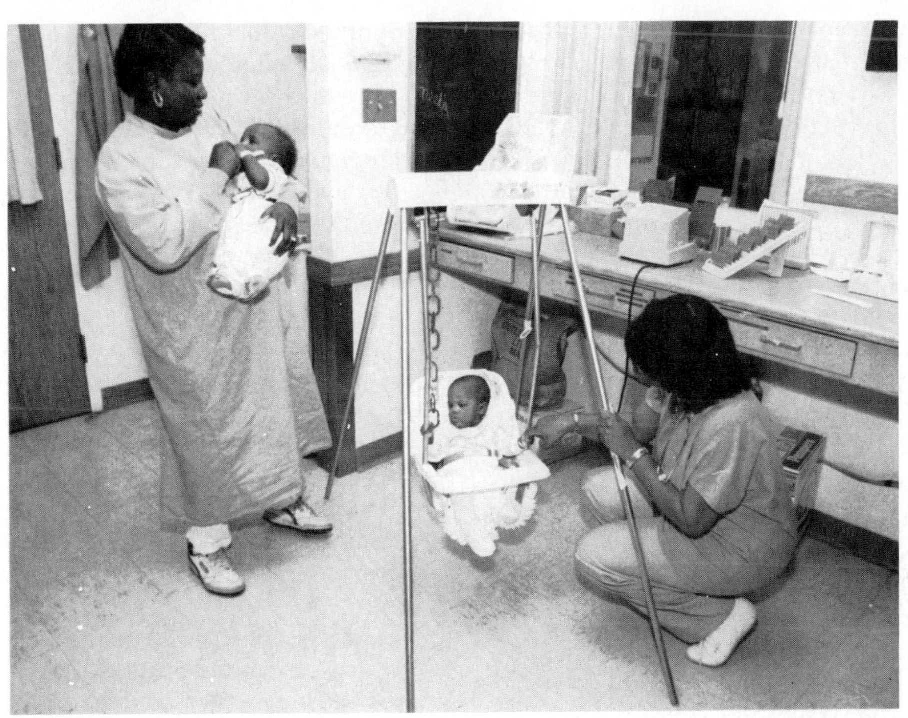

Drugs such as "crack" cocaine in many cases have tragic effects on users and their families. Due to the addictive features of crack, some mothers have become unable to maintain their responsibilities and have abandoned their children. Here, hospital staff nurture so-called "crack babies," infants born to crack addicts who themselves require extensive medical care. *(AP/Wide World)*

sters have tried the drug.[17] However, this same survey revealed that the number of current cocaine users actually dropped between 1985 and 1988, from 5.8 million users to 2.9 million. Still, although the numbers overall went down, many continue to use the drug intensively. In 1985 some 647,000 persons used cocaine once a week or more; by 1988 this number was up to 862,000. Daily users went from 246,000 in 1985 to 292,000 in 1988.[18]

The 1988 survey was the first in which research focused on the extent of use of crack cocaine, considered highly threatening as a public health problem. Its low cost, ready availability, potent effects, and addiction potential have been widely reported upon. It was found that among the 2.9 million current users of cocaine, almost half a million were using crack.

In contrast to the "business practices" associated with other drugs, those used in the cocaine trade have proved extraordinarily violent.[19] The criminal cartels based in Colombia have not hesitated to use murder and assassination to protect their interests, both at home and in the United States. From distribu-

[17] U.S. Department of Health and Human Services, *National Household Survey on Drug Abuse: 1988,* p. 29.

[18] "Americans' Current Illicit Drug Use Drops 37 Percent," *National Institute on Drug Abuse Notes,* 4 (Spring/Summer 1989): 42.

[19] "Where the War Is Being Lost," *Time* (March 14, 1988): 21, and "Cocaine's Dirty 300," *Newsweek* (November 13, 1989): 41.

tors to street-level hawkers of the drug, the use of firearms to capture market areas, enforce deals, or exact revenge has become commonplace. Children and youth enticed into the local drug trade in major central cities go about armed, and they have been losing their lives. Gun battles in cities such as Washington, D.C., leave innocent bystanders wounded or dead. Increasingly, the murder rate in many cities reflects the impact of drug-related warfare. It remains to be seen if the federal "War on Drugs" declared by President George Bush at the end of the 1980s will make inroads into this situation.

LSD

LSD, or lysergic acid diethylamide, is derived synthetically from the ergot fungus (a contaminator of rye). It is often referred to as a *hallucinogen* or psychedelic drug in recognition of its special psychoactive qualities, which include its ability to produce experiences akin to hallucinations. Other hallucinogens are mescaline, peyote, and various synthetic substances.

LSD is normally taken orally, for example, in tablet or capsule form. Because it is very potent, extremely small dosages are administered. Like many other drugs that are available only from illegal sources, the quality and purity of the LSD obtained by users often vary. It is not unusual for hallucinogens to be adulterated with other substances, unbeknownst to users.

Effects of LSD Use. LSD works slowly, and users may have to wait for half an hour before they begin to feel the drug. The resulting "trip," which lasts from six to twelve hours, involves altered consciousness and radical transformations of perceptions, emotions, and thoughts. Interviews with a number of LSD users have indicated that ingestion of the drug often produces:

1. Eidetic imagery. Physical objects are seen to be in motion, often in the form of colorful abstract patterns, when one's eyes are closed.
2. Synthesia. All senses are sharpened and occasionally altered so that music is "seen" and colors are "heard."
3. Perception of a multilevel reality. Objects and ideas may be viewed from a variety of perspectives, often simultaneously.
4. Fluidity. The surrounding environment appears to be in a state of constant flux, with shapes ebbing and flowing.
5. Subjective exaggeration. Unusual and detailed visions may occur wherein objects, events, and moods seem extraordinary and monumental.
6. Emotional lability. Sudden and extreme shifts in emotional states may occur, ranging from ecstasy to despair.
7. Feeling of timelessness. A sense of time, and even the meaning of time, may cease to exist.
8. Irrationalism. The forms of logic through which the world is ordinarily interpreted are replaced by new ways to perceive interrelationships and totalities.
9. Ambivalence. Overwhelming perceptions, thoughts, and emotions may be simultaneously experienced as pleasurable and unsettling.[20]

Effects like these have led some observers to label LSD "psychotomimetic"—a drug that causes users to mimic madness or states of psychosis. The only real parallel between LSD trips and psychosis is the loss of touch with reality that characterizes both.

Despite claims that LSD use can cause physical damage, no physiological harm has been found among LSD users that could be traced directly to the drug. Stories of brain damage and genetic harm have not been substantiated by responsible researchers. Nor is the drug physically or psychologically addictive. In fact, those

[20] See Goode, *Drugs in American Society*, pp. 166–71.

who use LSD frequently often find it difficult to obtain results such as those outlined above.

Users tend to be able to take LSD or leave it, and most limit their use to a few trials. But there are dangers associated with LSD use. One fairly common experience is the "bad trip," in which users experience intense fear and anxiety and may actually panic. Ordinarily, bad trips are of short duration, and they often can be handled through the calming influence of individuals who are familiar with such drug effects. In more extreme cases, persons have had to be hospitalized in a state of psychosis. Less frequently, users may experience "flashbacks"—that is, they begin to "trip" again long after the drug has been taken. Finally, because LSD alters perceptions of reality, users have sometimes exposed themselves to physical dangers, and a few have suffered accidental deaths.

Extent of LSD Use. According to the National Commission on Marihuana and Drug Abuse, LSD and other hallucinogens "are generally utilized only for 'spree' circumstantial or recreational use."[21] In 1988 the U.S. Department of Health and Human Services found that 3.5 percent of youth and 16 percent of young adults have used hallucinogens.[22] It is thought that the use of LSD declined somewhat in the 1980s, largely because of the dangers associated with use and fears about the purity of available LSD.

As is the case with marijuana, LSD is not associated with serious antisocial behavior or criminal acts. The only criminality involved with LSD use is a matter of the illicit status of the drug. Since LSD is relatively easy to manufacture and to conceal, efforts to dismantle the market within which the drug is distributed and sold have met with limited success.

[21] National Commission on Marihuana and Drug Abuse, *Drug Use in America,* p. 146.

[22] U.S. Department of Health and Human Services, *National Household Survey of Drug Abuse: 1988,* p. 47.

PCP ("Angel Dust")

PCP (phencyclidine hydrochloride) is another hallucinogen that has decreased in popularity over the last decade. This synthetic drug was originally developed for potential use as an anesthetic during surgery. On testing, its anesthetic qualities were found to be satisfactory, but adverse side effects offset this. These side effects included psychological disorientation, agitation and excitation, delirium, and hallucinations.

While rejected for medical purposes (aside from uses by veterinarians), PCP emerged on the illicit drug market in the early 1960s. Users then and since have reported largely unpleasant experiences, while concern over PCP's negative effects has grown among medical practitioners.[23]

PCP (known by many names, including "angel dust") may be taken orally, snorted, or smoked in a cigarette. Peak effects commence in thirty minutes to an hour. The "high" lasts four to six hours and complete cessation of effects can take twenty-four hours. Users report a change in the sense of their image of their bodies that is discomforting and often feelings of loneliness and isolation. Thought may be disorganized and users may engage in repetitive motor behavior. Individuals who take large doses may exhibit a loss of control over their emotions, expressing extreme rage. Others may have convulsions.

Poisoning cases have become more frequent because of overdoses, and some deaths have occurred, due both to PCP's pharmacological and its behavioral effects. Concern has been expressed about problems that seem to plague many chronic PCP users, such as prolonged psychotic-like symptoms and speech and memory difficulties.

In the past, much PCP use was due to decep-

[23] Addiction Research Foundation, *Drugs and Drug Abuse,* 2nd ed. (Toronto: Alcoholism and Drug Addiction Research Foundation, 1987), pp. 433–41.

tion; drugs that were offered as LSD or other hallucinogens were sometimes PCP or PCP adulterated. But in more recent years PCP appears to have come into the marketplace under its own identity. As with LSD, the use of PCP remains quite limited; it is hard to see why it would ever be a drug of choice, given the negative effects that have been documented. Nonetheless, over 6 million Americans have tried PCP.

Amphetamines

Amphetamines are synthetically derived stimulants that act on the central nervous system. While stimulants are available legally by means of physicians' prescriptions, an estimated 20 percent of those manufactured are annually diverted into the illicit drug market. Their nonmedical uses are subject to negative social definition.

Such stimulants as methamphetamine or "speed" are said to "activate organs and functions of the body, heighten arousal, increase overall behavioral activity, and suppress fatigue."[24] "Speed freaks" often inject large doses for the purpose of experiencing the drug's psychoactive effects. An immediate rush of euphoria is ordinarily followed by a period of dramatic hyperactivity. Users feel compelled to be constantly on the go, often walking and talking incessantly. After repeatedly taking the drug and experiencing its effects for several days, users are likely to reach a state of physical and mental exhaustion. When administration of the drug is halted, they are likely to "crash" or pass out and sleep for twenty-four hours. Speed freaks take the drug and crash over and over again, often using other drugs to make sleep possible when the effects of the stimulant become too debilitating.

Experts generally agree that this use of stimulants results in both mental and physical harm. Though overdoses are rare, stimulants may be physically addictive if used over a long period. Heavy users may experience withdrawal symptoms, such as fatigue and depression. Health problems—often stemming primarily from the frenetic life-styles of users and the tendency of stimulants to depress appetites—are not uncommon. Users often become physically weakened and susceptible to disease and illness.

Users of stimulants have been known to become mentally disturbed and to be troubled by psychotic-like states. Among the effects noted have been paranoia, loss of memory, inability to concentrate, extreme emotional surges, fixations and hallucinations, and a tendency toward violent behavior. Such psychological conditions stem directly from the action of the drugs themselves, not simply from the sleepless and hectic life-styles of heavy users.

The illegal use of speed and other stimulants seems to be largely limited to young adults. The popular phrase "speed kills" reflects the fact that the pleasures associated with the use of such drugs may not outweigh the dangers.[25] The U.S. Department of Health and Human Services found that 4.2 percent of youth and 14 percent of young adults have used stimulants for nonmedical purposes.[26]

LEGAL SUBSTANCES

As we mentioned at the beginning of the chapter, Americans have expressed less concern over the consumption of prescription and over-the-counter drugs than over illegal substances. Periodically, attention is turned to the abuse of legal drugs—as when Kitty Dukakis, wife of presidential candidate and governor Michael Dukakis, sought treatment for overmedication and problem drinking in the late 1980s. But in general, public concern fades as quickly as it forms.

---

[24] Goode, *Drugs in American Society*, p. 188.

[25] See U.S. Department of Health and Human Services, *Methamphetamine Abuse in the United States* (Washington, D.C.: U.S. Government Printing Office, 1989).

[26] U.S. Department of Health and Human Services, *National Household Survey of Drug Abuse: 1988*, p. 59.

TABLE 17.3 Drug Use, by Type of Drugs and Grade (Class of 1988)

Grade in which drug was first used	Type of Drug																
	Marijuana	Inhalants	Amyl/Butyl Nitrites	Hallucinogens	LSD	PCP	Cocaine	Heroin	Other opiates	Stimulants (adjusted)	Sedatives	Barbiturates	Methaqualone	Tranquilizers	Alcohol	Getting drunk	Cigarettes	Cigarettes (daily)
6	2.3%	2.4%	0.2%	0.1%	0.1%	0.1%	0.2%	0.1%	0.2%	0.2%	0.2%	0.2%	0.2%	0.2%	8.6%	3.3%	19.4%	1.5%
7–8	8.8	3.0	0.3	0.7	0.6	0.3	0.7	0.2	1.1	3.2	1.3	1.2	0.7	1.1	21.9	13.5	19.5	4.2
9	13.2	3.4	0.7	1.8	1.5	0.7	1.6	0.3	1.8	5.2	2.4	2.1	1.2	2.2	25.7	20.6	11.7	5.3
10	10.1	2.8	0.6	2.3	2.0	0.8	3.0	0.2	2.6	5.0	1.7	1.4	0.5	1.8	18.2	16.2	7.3	4.2
11	8.5	2.8	0.8	2.4	2.2	0.6	4.1	0.2	1.8	4.1	1.3	1.2	0.5	2.7	12.0	12.1	5.8	3.5
12	4.3	2.2	0.6	1.5	1.3	0.3	2.5	0.2	1.1	2.0	0.9	0.7	0.3	1.3	5.6	5.6	2.6	2.1
Never used	52.8	83.3	96.8	91.1	92.3	97.1	87.9	98.9	91.4	80.2	92.2	93.3	96.7	90.6	8.0	28.8	33.6	79.3

Source: Lloyd D. Johnston et al., *Drug Use, Drinking, and Smoking: National Survey Results from High School, College, and Young Adult Populations, 1975–1988,* U.S. Department of Health and Human Services (Washington, D.C.: U.S. Government Printing Office, 1989), p. 94.

PUBLIC PROBLEM, PRIVATE PAIN

A World of Crack

This is the story of Dooney Waters, a little boy whose family life in a low-income community was shattered by the intrusion of crack cocaine. Dooney's story, although far from unique, attracted national attention in 1989. President George Bush, declaring a "war on drugs," used this story to illustrate the devastating impact of drugs on people's lives. The story of Dooney Waters reminds us that the user is not a lone victim of drug abuse.

Dooney Waters, a thickset 6-year-old missing two front teeth, sat hunched over a notebook, drawing a family portrait.

First he sketched a stick-figure woman smoking a pipe twice her size. A coil of smoke rose from the pipe, which held a white square he called a "rock." Above that, he drew a picture of himself, another stick figure with tears falling from its face.

"Drugs have wrecked my mother," Dooney said as he doodled. "Drugs have wrecked a lot of mothers and fathers and children and babies. If I don't be careful, drugs are going to wreck me too."

His was a graphic rendering of the life of a child growing up in what police and social workers have identified as a crack house, an apartment in Washington Heights, a federally subsidized complex in Landover, Md., where people congregated to buy and use drugs. Dooney's life was punctuated by days when he hid behind his bed to eat sandwiches sent by teachers who knew he would get nothing else. Nights when Dooney wet his bed because people were "yelling and doing drugs and stuff." And weeks in which he barely saw his 32-year-old mother, who spent most of her time searching for drugs.

Addie Lorraine Waters, who described herself as a "slave to cocaine," said she let drug dealers use her apartment in exchange for the steady support of her habit. The arrangement turned Dooney's home into a modern-day opium den where pipes, spoons and needles were in supply like ketchup and mustard at a fast-food restaurant.

Addie's apartment was on Capital View Drive, site of more than a dozen slayings last year. Yet, the locks were removed from the front door to allow an unyielding tide of addicts and dealers to flow in and out. Children, particularly toddlers, often peered inside to ask: "Is my mommy here?"

While he was living in the crack house, Dooney was burned when a woman tossed boiling water at his mother's face in a drug dispute, and his right palm was singed when his 13-year-old half brother handed him a soft drink can that had been used to heat crack cocaine on the stove.

Teachers say that Dooney often begged to be taken to their homes, once asking if he could stay overnight in his classroom. "I'll sleep on the floor," Dooney told an instructor in Greenbelt Center Elementary School's after-school counseling and tutorial program. "Please don't make me go home. I don't want to go back there."

Dooney was painfully shy or exhaustively outgoing, depending largely on whether he was at home or in school—the one place where he could relax. In class, he played practical jokes on friends and passed out kisses and hugs to teachers. But his mood darkened when he boarded a bus for home.

The door that led to Waters's apartment was riddled with holes that once held locks, gaps that were usually stuffed with wads of paper or balled-up socks. The walls in the living room were painted bright blue. Holes ranging from the size of quarters to frying pans pockmarked nearly every wall.

No books or clocks were in evidence. People told time by watching the sun or the television sets that came and went as barter for drugs. The kitchen was littered with bottles and fast-food wrappers, and the refrigerator was a storehouse for half-eaten fried chicken, cupcakes and other molding items. Dead cockroaches occupied refrigerator egg holders, and mold grew along the sides of the sink.

Dooney's mother and others who congregated in her apartment were bound by a common desperation for drugs. The majority, in their late twenties or early thirties, described themselves as "recreational" drug users until they tried the highly addictive crack. Many said they had swapped welfare checks, food stamps, furniture and sexual favors to support their craving for crack. They had

PUBLIC PROBLEM, PRIVATE PAIN (Continued)

lost jobs, spouses, homes and self-respect. Nearly all were in danger of losing children, too.

Other children at Dooney's school knew that he lived in a crack house. Some were not allowed to visit his apartment. Others teased him by calling his mother "Crack Addie." Older children taunted him with a new version of an old children's rhyme: "I saw Addie sitting in a tree, smo-king a P-I-P-E."

Dooney staunchly defended his mother in front of his peers, sometimes attacking the pupils who called his mother names. "At least I know who my daddy is," Dooney sassed back.

But in private, particularly in conversations with his teachers and counselors, Dooney would bemoan his mother's drug use. "I hate drugs. I hate people who do drugs. I hate where I live," Dooney said.

Last spring Dooney said he hated drugs and what they have done to his life. Yet he seemed to view the drug trade as an inevitable calling in the way that some children look at the steel mills and coal mines in which their forebears worked.

Asked if he would sell or use drugs when he grows up, Dooney shook his head violently and wrinkled his nose in disgust. But the expression faded, and Dooney looked at the floor: "I don't want to sell drugs, but I will probably have to."

Source: Michele L. Norris, "Growing up in a world of crack," *The Washington Post National Weekly Edition* (September 11–17, 1989): 6 and 9.

Nature and Extent of Abuse of Legal Drugs

Of those Americans surveyed in 1988, some 23.5 million reported they had at some point in their lives engaged in nonmedical use of legal drugs. A surprisingly high number, 11.4 million, had done so in the last year.[27] Such nonmedical use is a form of drug abuse that is clearly widespread. Although the trend for such abuse was downward in the 1980s,[28] it is high enough to generate continued alarm. Among the legal drugs being abused by Americans are stimulants, barbiturates, and tranquilizers. Stimulants, as we saw, act on the central nervous system, producing arousal and intense hyperactivity. Amphetamines are legal stimulants. Barbiturates and tranquilizers, on the other hand, are *depressants* that act to relax the central nervous system.

Medical practitioners often prescribe depressants for medical reasons—both physical and mental. Such substances generally have a quieting and calming effect on users, dispelling anxiety and facilitating rest and sleep. In small or moderate doses, barbiturates and tranquilizers relax users; in larger doses, they may produce loss of consciousness. Large doses of some depressants—particularly barbiturates—may cause death. A significant number of accidental deaths and suicides are linked to overdoses of depressant drugs. Moreover, barbiturates and many types of tranquilizers are physically addictive for regular users. Withdrawal symptoms are often extremely severe. In some cases, withdrawal can bring about a coma or even result in death.

Certain key segments of American society are directly responsible for the increased use of legal psychoactive drugs. These segments are the pharmaceutical industry and the medical profession.[29] As they pursue their own inter-

[27] U.S. Department of Health and Human Services, *National Household Survey on Drug Abuse: 1988*, p. 53.

[28] Ibid. See also "High Prevalence of Prescription Drug Abuse and Misuse Seen," *National Institute on Drug Abuse Notes*, 4 (Spring/Summer 1989): 40.

[29] Richard Hewes and Robert Brewin, *The Tranquilizing of America* (New York: Harcourt Brace Jovanovich, 1979),

ests, they have helped foster an "overmedicated society" whose members are unaware of or confused about the dangers of the drugs to which they are exposed.

Drug Producers, Dispensers, and Users

America's pharmaceutical industry has been undergoing sustained growth since the 1950s. It is presently one of the largest and most profitable sectors of the American corporate economy. To remain profitable and to keep growing, drug firms constantly seek out new markets for their products and encourage increased use of existing drugs.

Drug firms aim their advertising at the general public and at medical practitioners. Advertising directed at the public is the major means of pushing over-the-counter psychoactive substances, such as nonprescription sleeping aids like Sominex and Nytol. Prescription drugs are advertised in medical journals for America's 275,000 office-based physicians. Drug firms also send traveling sales representatives, who are known as "detail men," to physicians' offices. The detail men press for the adoption of new drugs and sing the praises of older ones, leaving behind free samples and advertising brochures. Furthermore, the pharmaceutical industry sponsors displays and programs at medical conventions, where they try to woo physicians and point out or create the need for psychoactive drugs.

The point of the advertising and sales promotion directed at physicians and the general public is to spread the belief that all problems can and should be viewed in medical terms. If people are anxious, depressed, or lacking in vitality, the solution is medication. Since many Americans find it difficult to understand the sources of their discomfort or discontent, people are eager to try such a simple solution.

pp. 190–227. See also Henry L. Lennard et al., *Mystification and Drug Use* (San Francisco: Jossey-Bass, Publishers, 1971).

Medical practitioners are confronted with endless streams of patients, and they want to handle these patients quickly. After all, the more patients a physician sees each day, the higher the physician's annual income. But doctors also want to handle their patients effectively; they want to help people feel better, and they don't want to admit that they cannot. Over half of all persons who seek out physicians' services, it is estimated, have no easily diagnosable physical ailment. Physicians find that prescribing psychoactive drugs is a handy way of dealing with these cases. Not only is the patient usually satisfied, but the credibility of the "healing profession" and the doctor's own sense of mastery over his or her craft are sustained.

One outcome is that patients become mystified or confused about their own problems and potential solutions. They are encouraged to feel that psychoactive drugs are the solution to a lack of sense of well-being. But though the emotional pain may be blocked by drugs, as Henry L. Lennard and his associates note:

> Drugs do not remedy the unfavorable social and interpersonal arrangements and personal circumstances which generate anxiety or unhappiness. Through the creation of chemical barriers and through the diminishment of gross social deviance, drugs may in fact perpetuate malignant patterns and social arrangements. Were drugs not so readily available, pressure for other solutions and the pursuit of alternative options might be encouraged.[30]

Nonetheless, patients gladly accept drugs, just as the medical profession is pleased to be able to "help" patients with unknown ills. Unfortunately, the prescribed psychoactive substances may not only be inappropriate for whatever is causing patients' distress. There may also be hazardous side effects, including chronic de-

[30] Lennard et al., *Mystification and Drug Use*, pp. 24–25.

pendence on and physical addiction to certain routinely prescribed drugs.

A subtle side effect of reliance on psychoactive drugs is its effect on the nature of the role of the medical profession. To some extent, doctors downplay their role as healers in favor of the role of drug pusher, promoting the view that drugs are an acceptable and effective way of dealing with problems in living. Their assumption of this role is what helps keep the pharmaceutical industry and the medical profession in a state of affluence:

> It is in the interest of both of these groups to maintain large numbers of persons on drugs.... It is, moreover, in the interest of both groups to define more and more problems as medical in order to justify both the medical model and the intervention with drugs.[31]

Figures on the use of legal drugs indicate that these economic interests are being effectively served. For example, one national survey found that 20 percent of American women had used prescribed tranquilizers or other depressant drugs in the previous year, while almost 10 percent had used prescribed stimulants. Due to criticism, physicians' prescriptions of such drugs to women have decreased. Still, women are more likely than men to turn to physicians when they are troubled, and men are only half as likely as women to be users of prescribed psychoactive drugs. (Men are, however, heavy users of alcohol.) It is notable that the most frequent reason given by users for turning to their physicians for aid was psychological stress.[32]

Despite the hazards they pose, prescribed and over-the-counter psychoactive substances do not carry negative social definitions in American society. Thus, they are rarely considered part of the drug problem. As a consequence, millions of Americans decry the proliferation of "problem drugs" even while seeking to alter their own states of consciousness.

EXPLANATIONS FOR DRUG USE AND ABUSE

Theories about why people turn to psychoactive substances have generally focused on the use of illegal drugs, implying that the abuse of legal drugs is not a matter of concern or is, at least, an entirely different phenomenon. In this section, we look at some of the theories that have been put forth to explain the use of illegal substances.[33] We then present an explanation that covers both legal and illegal drug use. Finally, we analyze a third type of drug use—the involuntary ingestion of psychoactive substances administered for purposes of social control.

Use of Illegal Drugs

One explanation of why Americans use illegal drugs focuses on the ready availability of drugs and the interests of those who are in a position to benefit financially from their sale. This so-called peddler or seller theory suggests that drug use is a result of the inability of law enforcement agencies to exercise control over supplies of illegal substances and of the ability of sellers to exert wily promotional and sales tactics on innocent nonusers. According to this perspective, users are manipulated and seduced into illegal drug use. But though availability no doubt has something to do with use, and though some persons may be susceptible to "dope peddlers," this explanation is not very persuasive. Research has shown that most individuals do not embark on the use of illegal drugs as a consequence of contact with sellers.

[31] Ibid., p. 38.

[32] See Muriel Nellis, *The Female Fix* (Boston: Houghton Mifflin Company, 1980).

[33] See Joel Fort and Christopher T. Cory, *American Drugstore* (Boston: Little, Brown & Company, 1975), pp. 10–27. See also Dan J. Lettieri et al., eds., *Theories on Drug Abuse* (Washington, D.C.: National Institute on Drug Abuse, 1980).

Another explanation—which has been discredited, at least among sociologists—holds that individuals use illegal drugs because there is something mentally or morally wrong with them. According to this theory, "normal" people are not attracted to such drugs even when they are available. Nor do normal people succumb to the alleged influences exerted by sellers. They simply do not need to alter their minds with psychoactive substances. Thus, say proponents of the theory, those who use illegal drugs must have psychological deficiencies, character disorders, or personal maladjustments. There is no credible evidence to support this theory. Illegal drug use is not reducible to the underlying psychological characteristics of a minority of the population. Research has not discovered psychological characteristics that distinguish users from nonusers. (Of course, the *effects* of some illegal drugs may include undesirable mental reactions.) In sum, an explanation that blames the victim is even more untenable than one that places the blame on the seller.

A more far-reaching explanation for illegal drug use focuses on the place of drugs in American culture. According to Joel Fort:

> We live in a drug-ridden, drug-saturated society, in which from infancy we have been taught to accept and live the industrial slogan of "Better Living Through Chemistry." We are taught that there is a pill, a drink, or a cigarette for every real or imagined pain, trouble, or problem, and that the more of these substances we use, the better off we will be.[34]

In such a society, according to proponents of this theory, people will use illegal drugs when they have the opportunity to do so.

This explanation has a nice ring to it, but it is overly deterministic. People are not automatons who react to pains, troubles, or problems by taking drugs. Drug use involves a decision—there are, after all, other ways to react to problems. Moreover, this explanation does not address the question of why most Americans continue to shun illegal substances, even while using many that are legal. On the other hand, there is evidence that the ready availability and widespread use of legal drugs (including alcohol and tobacco products) make it more likely that individuals will use illegal substances:

> Users of illegal drugs tend to become recruited out of segments of society that use legal drugs.... Abstainers from alcohol, cigarettes, and prescription drugs stand a relatively low likelihood of experimenting with illegal drugs.[35]

This is not to say that the use of legal substances *causes* illegal drug use. Instead, it merely means that there is a correlation between the two. For example, aspirin users are more likely to smoke marijuana than nonaspirin users. But most aspirin users do not do so.

Most recent sociological explanations emphasize that illegal drug use is learned behavior. Specifically, people learn appropriate attitudes and modes of behavior favorable to drug use through social intercourse. For example, there is evidence that parents exert some influence over their children's attitudes toward drug use.[36] The main finding to date is that the children of parents who are themselves users of legal or illegal psychoactive substances are more likely to use illegal drugs than the children of drug abstainers. It is believed that friends and peers play a far more important role than parents. Rarely will parents actually introduce their chil-

[34] Fort, *The Pleasure Seekers,* p. 194.

[35] Erich Goode, *The Drug Phenomenon* (Indianapolis: The Bobbs-Merrill Co., 1973), p. 22.

[36] See Richard H. Blum et al., *Horatio Algers's Children* (San Francisco: Jossey-Bass Publishers, 1972).

dren into the use of illegal drugs; peer associations and influence perform this function.[37]

The importance of being inducted into the use of illegal drugs was underscored almost forty years ago by sociologist Howard Becker. According to Becker, marijuana users (who, at that time, comprised a comparatively small number of persons) provided assurances to potential users that the drug was safe and worthwhile. In other words, those who already smoked the drug helped convert the neophytes to their view of the drug. Moreover, neophyte users had to be taught exactly how to smoke marijuana, what effects they should expect, and how they should perceive and react to these effects.[38] Obviously, people are most likely to embark into such activity with those they know and trust—their friends and peers.

Sociologists generally agree that becoming a user of illegal drugs involves being a member of and identifying with a group of people who are already users. Participation with others in an illegal and, hence, secret activity may also help cement interpersonal relationships. Group members have something in common with one another, and those who do not use illegal drugs may be viewed as "outsiders." Though Becker's work deals primarily with marijuana use, more recent investigations suggest that the influence of friends and peers is of importance in explaining the use of illegal drugs in general.[39]

But this explanation does not completely get at the heart of the matter. Though it tells us how people learn to become drug users, it does not explain what users of psychoactive substances—both illegal and legal—are really seeking to accomplish. Only by changing our focus from drug users to society in general can we get at an answer to that question.

[37] See Bruce D. Johnson, *Marihuana Users and Drug Subcultures* (New York: John Wiley & Sons, 1973).

[38] Howard S. Becker, "Becoming a Marihuana User," *American Journal of Sociology*, 59 (November 1953): 235–42.

[39] See Johnson, *Marihuana Users and Drug Subcultures.*

Drug Abuse and Social Conditions

In the view of sociologist John Clausen, both the legal and illegal use of psychoactive drugs may be interpreted as

> an aspect or manifestation of a much more general social problem. If substantial numbers of persons find it necessary to use drugs in order to feel comfortable, or if their lives are lacking in meaning and they therefore turn to drugs to provide it, the problem is less in the drugs than in the way of life that has been afforded them.[40]

Clausen's comments suggest that America's recent concern with drug abuse and the drug problem is misplaced in terms of its focus on the illegal substances of the moment and on users. The important questions are rarely brought up in public debate. What is it about American society that makes so many people seek out and accept the effects of psychoactive substances? What is it about this society and "the way of life that has been afforded" its members that renders the pursuit of altered states of consciousness preferable to nondrugged participation in the prevailing order?

As with mental illness, alcoholism, and suicide, widespread drug use may occur because many people are subjected to harmful social conditions. Drug use may be one of a variety of responses troubled people use to cope with problems in living. Psychoactive drugs must be available before they can be used. They must be introduced to nonusers—be it by peers, physicians, or peddlers (a category that includes the pharmaceutical industry). But once such substances are available and introduced, many people grasp onto them as palliatives for ills that may really be societal, although experienced as personal.

The tragedy is that drugs are false palliatives,

[40] John A. Clausen, "Drug Use," in Robert K. Merton and Robert Nisbet, eds., *Contemporary Social Problems*, 4th ed. (New York: Harcourt Brace Jovanovich, 1976), p. 145.

for their use leaves the ultimate sources of peoples' troubles untouched. In the words of Theodore Roszak, drug use "is simply another safety valve. If anything, it allows one to bear up under any grim business-as-usual with a bit less anxiety."[41] Psychoactive substances, Roszak observes, function much like the "soma" described in Aldous Huxley's science fiction novel, *Brave New World*, which helped make otherwise unbearable existences bearable.[42]

Drugs and Social Control

The Brave New World Huxley described was a politically repressive society of social unequals. Drugs were made available to the populace so that rulers could wield their power without the danger of rebellious disruption. The Brave New World was a fictional society, but its use of drugs for social control reflects real-life developments.

In the last twenty years the American public has become aware of the uses of psychoactive substances for social control. Controversy has surrounded physicians' diagnoses of upwards of 1 million children said to be suffering from "MBD," or minimal brain dysfunction. Symptoms are said to include hyperactivity, learning disability, and short attention spans. Most of those so diagnosed have been boys. The medical response to MBD frequently has involved prescribing amphetamines (stimulants), which seem to allow many children to calm down and focus on the tasks at hand. An estimated 3 million to 4 million children may have been so treated since MBD was first diagnosed in the late 1960s.

Often parents and teachers were the initiators of medical attention in a search for ways to make children's behavior more manageable and acquiescent to authority. Controversy surrounds the vagueness of the catchall label *minimal brain dysfunction* and the abuse of this diagnosis. It is seen as being used to medically harness children whose behavior simply does not measure up to adult expectations.[43] Indiscriminate diagnosis and medicating of schoolchildren resulted in public outrage during the 1970s, leading to sharp decreases in drug prescription for behaviors associated with MBD.

Similar practices are routine in mental hospitals, prisons, and nursing homes. In their report to the Ford Foundation, Patricia M. Wald and Peter Barton Hutt noted the "emerging problem" of the "overprescription of drugs to control the behavior of captive populations" in such settings.[44] For example, Wald and Hutt documented the extensive use of drugs "on elderly patients in nursing homes to keep them from clamoring for the attention of overworked attendants."[45] These researchers predicted that "as the range of behavior-controlling drugs becomes wider, we can anticipate even greater problems in their use in unwarranted situations."[46]

Most studies of drug use in the United States barely mention the ways in which drugs are used for political purposes. The powerless are being subjected to chemical manipulation—students, not teachers; inmates, not guards or caretakers; old people, not those who administer the institutions in which the dying eke out their final days. As Howard Becker observed:

> When the one administering the drug has sufficient control over the user, he can safely ignore the other's interests altogether, and his actions can be designed solely to serve his own interests, personal or (more likely) organizational.[47]

---

[41] Theodore Roszak, *The Making of a Counter Culture* (Garden City, N.Y.: Anchor Books, 1969), pp. 176–77.

[42] Aldous Huxley, *Brave New World* (London: Chatto & Windus, 1970).

[43] Hewes and Brewin, *The Tranquilizing of America*, pp. 112–41.

[44] Patricia M. Wald and Peter Barton Hutt, "The Drug Abuse Survey Project," in Patricia M. Wald et al., eds., *Dealing with Drug Abuse* (New York: Praeger Publishers, 1972), p. 11.

[45] Ibid.

[46] Ibid., p. 12.

[47] Howard S. Becker, "Consciousness, Power, and Drug Effects," *Society*, 10 (May–June 1973): 31.

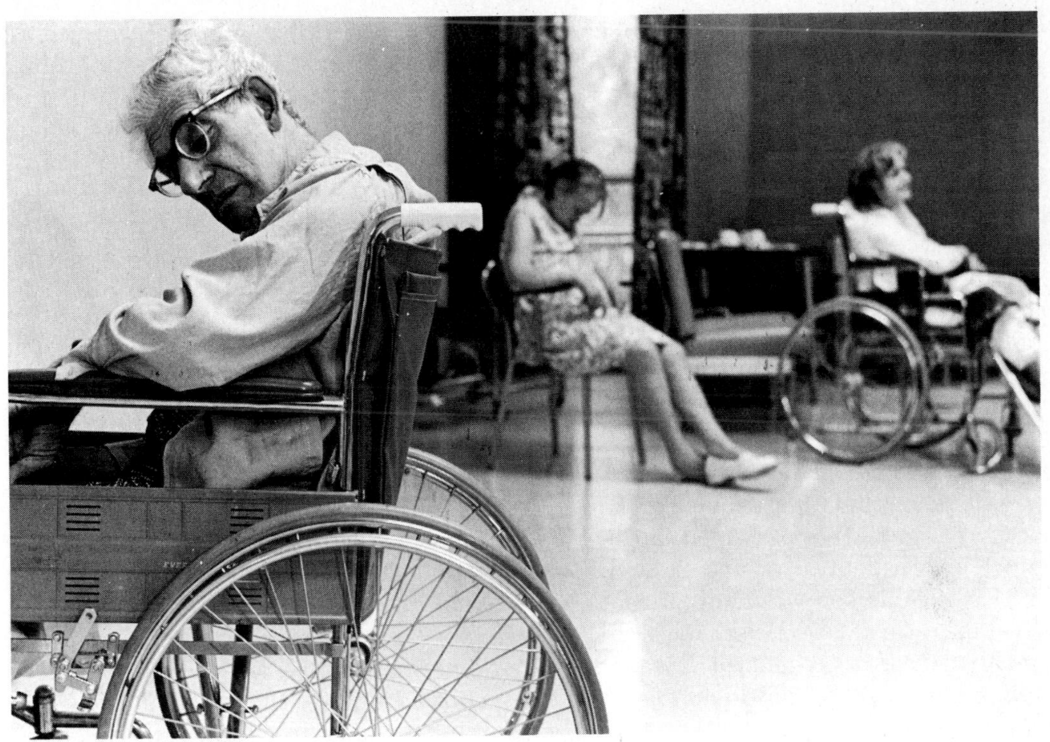

Many nursing homes and other institutions feed drugs to patients in order to keep them from making demands on staff members' time and attention. Practices like this not only infringe upon the rights of individuals but may also have serious medical consequences. *(Alex Webb/Magnum Photos)*

Administrators in charge of schools, hospitals, prisons, and nursing homes find drugs to be a useful tool for the efficient processing of large numbers of people. They are the ones who claim that the best interests of those subject to such chemical pollution are simultaneously being served. The interests of the powerless are being defined from above.

The use of drugs by such American intelligence forces as the Central Intelligence Agency borders on the bizarre. To take but one instructive example, investigations by the news media and Congressional hearings in 1977 revealed that the CIA had set up a secret drug experimentation program in 1953.[48] The purpose of this program, code named MK-Ultra, was to learn how to control the human mind. Presumably this knowledge would be used against foreign enemies. For over twenty years, using $25 million in tax funds, the CIA paid for projects conducted by researchers in eighty-six institutions—including colleges and universities, hospitals, prisons, and pharmaceutical companies.

The CIA-sponsored projects included LSD experiments with federal prison inmates and college students, experimentation with tranquilizers and alcohol on inmates and staff of mental hospitals, and the use of a "knockout" drug on unwitting terminally ill cancer patients. The CIA set up special apartments where researchers

[48] See "Mind-Bending Disclosures: CIA Testing," *Time* (August 15, 1977): 9, and Tad Szulc, "CIA's Electric Kool-Aid Acid Test," *Psychology Today*, 11 (November 1977): 92–94 ff.

could observe the effects of LSD and marijuana on unsuspecting men who had been lured to the apartments from bars. A professional magician was employed to write a manual on the use of sleight of hand and how to secretly slip drugs into drinks. No efforts were made to contact the subjects of experiments later to see whether or how their well-being was affected. The American military is known to have conducted similar experiments on members of the armed forces.

This kind of activity has not been limited to research conducted out of concern with foreign enemies. In 1976 the news media discovered that conspirators involved in the Nixon administration's Watergate scandal had planned to slip a psychoactive drug to Jack Anderson, a columnist critical of President Nixon and his staff. They hoped that Anderson would experience the effects of the drug at a public speaking engagement and make a fool of himself. The plot fell through only because the conspirators failed to get hold of a drug.

Clearly, not all the substances we call drugs are harmful. Many drugs, moreover, are known to have extremely beneficial effects. One need only consider the many substances that have helped wipe out serious illness and disease and that have helped prolong people's lives. Drugs are tools that may either be used to enhance human well-being or to harm it. As we begin to learn more about the harmful uses to which drugs are being put—and about the *social* implications of such uses—Americans may begin to react against those forces that have led us to become the "overmedicated society."

DRUGS AND PUBLIC HEALTH: THE CASE OF AIDS

AIDS is, of course, an acronym for acquired immune deficiency syndrome. People with AIDS find that their bodies lose natural immunity against infection and disease. They grow vulnerable to serious illnesses that cannot be overcome. Although there is no known cure for AIDS, some drug treatments have shown promise in slowing the final and inevitable outcome, death.

The source of AIDS is a virus, now carried by perhaps 1 million to 1.5 million Americans. (No one knows just how many for sure.) Those infected with the virus—called human immunodeficiency virus, or HIV—may have no AIDS symptoms and be unaware they are infected. Scientists believe that all persons carrying HIV will eventually be stricken with AIDS.

The first AIDS cases appeared in the United States in 1981. By 1989 over 112,000 cases had been diagnosed and more than half of those diagnosed had died. By the mid-1990s known cases may be up to a half million. The data and projections keep changing as new developments affecting the spread of HIV are identified.

The most common way the virus is and has been spread involves sexual contact, but almost 30 percent of diagnosed cases are attributed to intravenous drug use. Out of an estimated 1.3 million intravenous drug users, some 20 percent already are infected with HIV and the numbers continue to grow.[49]

The spread of the virus is rooted in users' habits of sharing needles.[50] Small amounts of HIV-contaminated blood may remain on the needle after use by an infected individual, and this blood is then injected along with the drug by the next needle user. Today the injected drug is most likely to be cocaine, followed by heroin and methamphetamine.

Needle sharing is thought to be simply a matter of convenience, friendship, or ritual among drug users. In a ten-city study of 3,724 intravenous users, none of whom were undergoing any treatment, some 85 percent admitted to needle sharing. Most admitted sharing with two or more persons, and the practice of borrowing

[49] "Methadone Maintenance," *National Institute on Drug Abuse Notes*, 4 (Spring/Summer 1989): 3.

[50] Robert J. Battjee and Roy W. Pickens, eds., *Needle Sharing Among Intravenous Drug Abusers* (Washington, D.C.: U.S. Government Printing Office, 1988).

others' injection equipment was common. The use of new needles or the cleaning of needles between uses (e.g., with bleach, which kills HIV) was uncommon.[51]

The growing number of AIDS cases is further enhanced by the sexual practices of intravenous drug users. Since HIV can be spread by sexual contact, it is noteworthy that the previously cited study found that most of the users were sexually active, many had multiple sexual partners, and few took precautions to minimize the risk of HIV infections (e.g., condom use). Consequently, the virus is being transmitted not only to other drug users but to sex partners who do not participate in intravenous drug use at all.

The spread of the virus is most acute among specific segments of the intravenous user population. For example, it is higher among cocaine users than heroin users, in part because the former "shoot up" or inject more frequently. Those drug users who patronize "shooting galleries," back rooms or apartments where drugs and needles are shared (and where money and drugs may be traded for sex acts), are heavily exposed to HIV infection. And since intravenous drug use is high among blacks and Hispanics, they are disproportionately represented among drug-related AIDS cases.

In the 1980s the rate at which AIDS spread was most rapid in the homosexual male population. This is no longer the case. AIDS is now spreading at the same rate among heterosexuals. This development is directly linked to drug abuse. According to a study by the National Institute on Drug Abuse, 61 percent of U.S.-born heterosexual AIDS patients reported sexual activity with someone who used drugs intravenously.[52]

Solutions to date include outreach programs to encourage those at risk to avoid sharing injection equipment, use new or cleaned needles, cease sexual contact with those whose behaviors raise the possibility of infection, and practice "safe sex," which would include protective measures. Some advocate the wide-scale dispensing of free or low-cost needles and syringes to discourage sharing and borrowing. Opponents of this practice feel it would communicate tolerance or even encouragement of drug abuse. In the meantime, America's pursuit of the alteration of consciousness continues to make a contribution to an incredibly deadly epidemic.

A POSTSCRIPT: DRUG ABUSE WARNING NETWORK

As we have suggested, the abuse of drugs can cause people to need emergency medical treatment and may result in untimely death. In recent years the federal government's National Institute on Drug Abuse has been trying to monitor the incidence of drug abuse emergencies and fatalities. In 1988 the Drug Abuse Warning Network (DAWN) drew data from 738 hospital emergency rooms in 21 metropolitan areas, as well as from 87 medical examiners in 27 areas. While not a scientifically representative sample, the cases that pass through these facilities do give us some idea as to problem trends.[53]

According to DAWN, in 1988 hospital emergency rooms handled 160,170 drug abuse episodes. (An episode is an emergency room admission. Over the course of the year some individuals were admitted more than once.) In 56 percent of the cases the patients were male. White patients were 41 percent of the cases, blacks 39 percent, and Hispanics 11 percent. Most of those brought to the emergency room were young: 38 percent were 20–29 years of age, while another 32 percent were 30–39. The most

[51] "NIDA Outreach Demonstration," *National Institute on Drug Abuse Notes*, 4 (Spring/Summer 1989): 1.

[52] "AIDS Is Spreading at Same Rate in Heterosexuals," *National Institute on Drug Abuse Notes*, 3 (Winter 1988/1989): 14.

[53] For the data that follow see National Institute on Drug Abuse, *Data from the Drug Abuse Warning Network (DAWN), Annual Data 1988* (Washington, D.C.: U.S. Government Printing Office, 1989).

One way to combat AIDS is to educate prostitutes and intravenous drug users about ways they can protect themselves and others from the epidemic. Outreach workers have advocated use of condoms and clean needles. Promotion of the latter has been controversial, since law enforcement agencies are constantly under pressure to combat drug use in local communities. *(R. Maiman/Sygma)*

frequently abused drug for patients was cocaine, followed by alcohol in combination with other drugs. Drug dependence was the most common motive for use mentioned by those brought in for treatment.

In 1988 DAWN's participating medical examiners reported 6,756 drug abuse-related deaths (the data exclude cases involving AIDS and those where the drugs involved were unknown). Whites made up 46 percent of those who died, blacks 30 percent, and Hispanics 13 percent. While most of the deaths involved persons over 30, 26 percent of those who died were between 18 and 29 years of age! Seventy-three percent of the deaths were males. Cocaine was reported to be involved in half of the deaths, followed by alcohol in combination with other drugs. In 68 percent of the cases of death, drug overdoses were involved; in the remaining cases, drugs were a contributing factor to loss of life.

These treatment episodes and deaths are all the more disturbing and tragic because they are preventable. They represent the presence of a great deal of alienation in our midst, the elimination of which will require change in many of the macro problems discussed earlier in this book.

SUMMARY

The term *drug* is subject to a wide variety of meanings and uses—scientific, medical, and legal. In actuality, there is no single quality that would distinguish substances designated as drugs from nondrugs. Any and all substances that are designated as drugs are socially defined as such. So-called problem drugs (e.g., marijuana and heroin) differ from other drug and nondrug substances in that they have a different and more negative social definition. Social definitions frequently change with time, and different groups commonly disagree over such definitions.

Among the most used problem drugs are marijuana, heroin, cocaine, LSD, PCP, and amphetamines. Marijuana is the most widely used illegal substance in the United States. Less public concern has been expressed over the high consumption of legal prescription and over-the-counter psychoactive drugs than over illegal substances. The forces underlying this high consumption include the pharmaceutical industry, which constantly seeks out new markets and encourages increased use of existing drugs, and medical practitioners, who often prescribe psychoactive drugs to patients who have no easily diagnosable physical ailment. Many people have come to believe that drug taking is an acceptable and effective way of dealing with problems in living. Despite the hazards they pose, prescribed and over-the-counter drugs are rarely considered part of America's drug problem.

There are a number of explanations for why people use psychoactive drugs. Illegal drug use has been said to stem from manipulation of people by drug pushers, moral or mental weaknesses of users, and a cultural environment that extols drug use in general. Each of these explanations is open to criticism. Most recent sociological explanations emphasize that illegal drug use is learned behavior. Peers, and to a lesser extent parents, are important influences and sources of knowledge about drug use. Widespread use of both illegal and legal psychoactive substances may be a response to harmful societal conditions, a false palliative but nonetheless one that helps make an otherwise unbearable existence bearable.

Recently, concern has been expressed over the use of drugs for social control purposes. Drugs have been administered to schoolchildren, inmates of mental hospitals and prisons, and elderly persons in nursing homes. Drugs have been used to make such persons more "manageable." Political use of drugs extends to American military and intelligence forces.

Not all drugs are harmful, and many are known to have extremely beneficial effects. Drugs may be used to heighten human well-being or to thwart it.

DISCUSSION QUESTIONS

1. What arguments could be made for and against legalizing all so-called problem drugs and leaving the choice of use up to individuals?
2. In certain settings, such as mental hospitals, persons may be made to take drugs even if they do not want to. Imagine that you are in such a situation, and present reasons why you should not be made to take drugs involuntarily.
3. During the Prohibition Era, alcoholic beverages were produced, distributed, and consumed widely even though this was illegal. Prohibition laws were repealed largely because they could not be enforced. Speculate on the likelihood and the desirability of similar law changes relating to marijuana.
4. Obtain copies of several medical journals, and read the advertisements for psychoactive drugs. What might be said about the content of these advertisements? Are the sources of the problems to which they are directed necessarily medical?
5. Go to your local drugstore, and conduct an inventory of all over-the-counter products that allegedly will pep you up or calm you down. Record their advertising claims. Develop arguments for and against the passage of a law that would bar such substances from purchase without a prescription.
6. Visit a drug rehabilitation center or other agency that deals with victims of drug abuse. On the basis of discussions with clients, assess the role of drugs in their lives and the reasons

they became drug abusers. Compare your findings with those of other class members.

SUGGESTED READINGS

Adler, Patricia. *Wheeling and Dealing: An Ethnography of an Upper-Level Drug Dealing and Smuggling Community* (New York: Columbia University Press, 1985).
A unique look at the supply side of the drug abuse problem.

Goode, Erich. *Drugs in American Society*, 3rd ed. (New York: McGraw-Hill Book Company, 1989).
Review of research and theory on America's patterns of drug use and abuse.

Kelleher, Maureen E., et al., eds. *Drugs and Society: A Critical Reader*, 2nd ed. (Dubuque, Iowa: Kendall/Hunt Publishing Company, 1988).
The role played by drugs in our society, and the political and ideological forces affecting drug policies and use.

Musto, David F. *The American Disease: Origins of Narcotics Control*, rev. ed. (New York: Oxford University Press, 1988).
The origins of America's drug laws, their application, and their effectiveness.

Peluso, Emanuel, and Lucy Silvay Peluso, eds. *Women & Drugs: Getting Hooked, Getting Clean* (Minneapolis: CompCare Publications, 1988).
Firsthand accounts of drug problems as experienced by students, housewives, mothers, and career women.

Szasz, Thomas S. *Ceremonial Chemistry: The Ritual Persecution of Drugs, Addicts, and Pushers*, rev. ed. (Kalamazoo, Mich.: Learning Publications, 1985).
Views of a critic of state intervention into private individuals' use of mind-altering substances.

Name Index

Subject Index